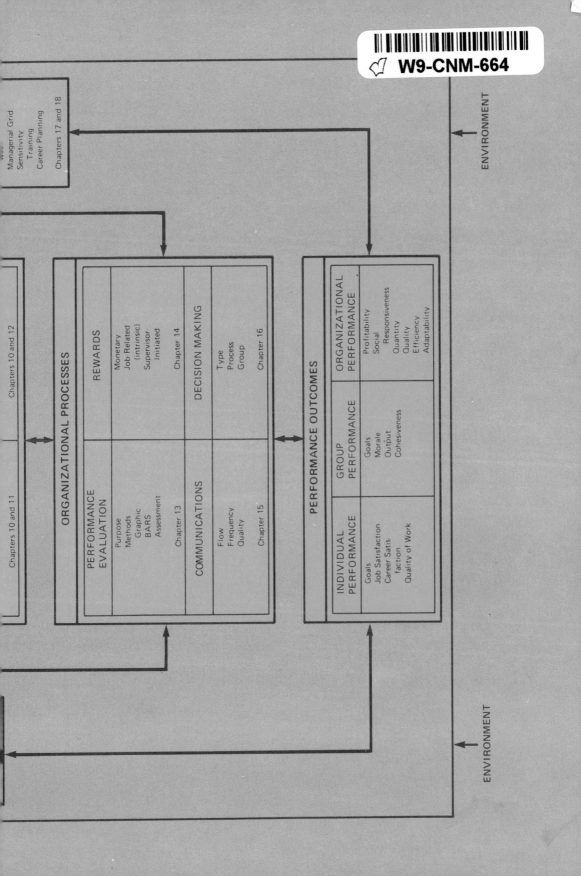

ORGANIZATIONS
Behavior, Structure, Processes

ORGANIZATIONS
Behavior, Structure, Processes

JAMES L. GIBSON
*Professor of Business Administration
University of Kentucky*

JOHN M. IVANCEVICH
*Professor of Organizational Behavior
and Management
University of Houston*

JAMES H. DONNELLY, JR.
*Professor of Business Administration
University of Kentucky*

1979 Third Edition

BUSINESS PUBLICATIONS, INC.   Dallas, Texas   75243
Irwin-Dorsey Limited   Georgetown, Ontario   L7G 4B3

ISBN 0-256-02210-0
Library of Congress Catalog Card No. 78–70017

Printed in the United States of America

4 5 6 7 8 9 0 K 6 5 4 3 2 1 0

Preface

The objective of this third edition remains the same as previous editions: *the achievement of individual, group, and organizational performance through enlightened, effective management.* It accomplishes this objective by providing the bases for applying the relevant contributions of behavioral science to the management of organizations.

Thus, the continuous thread throughout the book is *the effective management of organizational behavior.* Given this thread our task was to *interpret* behavioral science theory and research so that students of administration can comprehend the three characteristics common to all organizations—behavior, structure, processes—as affected by actions of managers. It is our intention to provide readers with a book which will illustrate how behavioral science theory leads to research and how theory and research provide the basic foundation for practical applications in business firms, hospitals, educational institutions, and governmental agencies. Based on the comments and suggestions of both adopters and nonadopters of previous editions, several important changes have been made in this edition that we believe will enable us to better achieve our objectives.

Although the page length is longer in this edition, the actual number of text pages is about the same. The difference in length is because additional cases and experiential exercises have been added to give instructors greater choice and to allow them greater freedom in constructing their own course format.

This edition includes important new subject matter as well as new learning approaches. *Intergroup behavior and conflict, job design, reward processes, performance evaluation processes,* and *organizational climate* are subjects of five new chapters written for this edition. These topics have become especially important in recent years and deserve more intensive treatment than given in previous editions. Each of the five new chapters is based upon the most recent theory, research, and application available in the literature. To make room for these new chapters, several chapters were combined into single chapters and one chapter was omitted.

In addition to new chapters, material in existing chapters was updated. New material on *personal stress, behavior modification, goal-setting, the Vroom-Yetton leadership theory, flexi-time, career pathing,* and *team building* was added to appropriate chapters. This new material complements existing material. Updated additional references provide sources for readers who desire more in-depth discussions of these and other topics presented in the text.

The new learning approaches in this edition are experiential exercises. We have included 10 exercises at the ends of those chapters which are most conducive to this type of learning. We have retained 18 of the short cases first introduced in the revised edition; we have also added 4 longer cases. These longer cases are in Appendix B. The exercises and cases provide opportunities to apply the text material in the analysis of practical managerial situations. Many of the cases are based upon the authors consulting and managing experiences. They cover a variety of different types and sizes of organizations and include problems of all levels of management. Every case has been written to emphasize a particular issue or managerial technique.

In addition to the practical relevance that the exercises and cases contribute, the text discussion carries out our intention to interpret the practical significance of theory and research. Of course, many issues in management and organizational behavior are unresolved and alternative theories compete. These issues are presented and readers are encouraged to consider the relative strengths of each treatment of those issues. Whenever possible, we have acknowledged the tenuousness of contemporary theory and practice.

To heighten student interest and to highlight the contingency nature of the subject matter, most chapters begin by introducing an "Organizational Issues of Debate." These short discussions of arguments for and arguments against a particular principle, theory, practice, or model set the tone for the chapter. Managing people in organizations requires the use of many different approaches. In most circumstances there is no "one best way" to improve individual or group performance or to motivate people. Therefore, an approach that is considered sound by one person is often viewed differently by someone else. The "issues" illustrate the point that most of what is known about managing people in organizations is controversial and tenuous.

The framework in which the content of the book is organized is based on the three characteristics cited above as common to all organizations: *behavior, structure,* and *processes.* This order of presentation is in response to numerous adopters who found it easier to discuss the behavioral material first, followed by structure and processes. It should be mentioned, however, that in the present edition each of the parts on these three subjects is written as a self-contained unit and can be presented in whichever order the instructor prefers.

The text is presented in six parts:

Part One consists of three chapters which together introduce the subject matter. Chapter 1 presents the significance of organizations as means by which societies produce and distribute goods and services. Chapter 2 introduces the reader to ways of acquiring knowledge and understanding about management and organizational behavior. Chapter 3 develops important ideas concerning the roles of management in achieving effective individual, group, and organizational performance. A framework which integrates the material presented in the remainder of the text is presented and briefly described.

Part Two includes six chapters which focus on *organizational behavior.* Separate chapters are devoted to individual characteristics, motivation, group behavior, group conflict, trait and behavioral theories of leadership, and contingency theories of leadership. A significant change in this edition is the inclusion of a new chapter on group conflict as well as updating of all material.

Part Three, on *organizational structure,* is considerably different from previous editions. A new chapter on *job design,* Chapter 11, has been written specifically for this edition. The theoretical and research literature on job design provides a rich source of practical ideas, and we have attempted to distill as many of them as space allows for inclusion in this edition. To make room for this material, two chapters from previous editions were combined into one, Chapter 12.

Part Four includes four chapters dealing with *organizational processes.* In addition to communications and decision-making two new chapters are included in this edition. *Performance evaluation* is the topic of Chapter 13 and *rewards* is the topic of Chapter 14. The inclusion of these two chapters reflects the increasing importance of performance, performance evaluation, and rewards for performance in modern organizations.

Part Five consists of two chapters concerned with *organizational development.* New material has been added to these chapters but more important the material has been rearranged. Chapter 17, in this edition, presents the theory of organizational development in the context of an integrated model. The model describes the OD process as logically linked phases which begins with forces for change and ends with evaluation. Issues such as employee participation, the use of change agents, diagnostic procedures, and selection of appropriate OD techniques are integrated through the model. Chapter 18 describes and evaluates the more widely used OD techniques, including flexi-time, team building, and career pathing.

Part Six is one chapter on *organizational climate.* Our purpose for adding this material to this edition is to integrate the text material. Organizational climate, as used in this context, is a summary concept. It reflects the interaction of behavior, structure, and processes of organizations and summarizes the effects of that interaction.

Special thanks are due to those colleagues who made specific suggestions for improving this third edition. Particularly helpful were Sara Freedman, Bob Keller, Mike Matteson, Tim McMahon, Dick Montanari, and John Zuckerman, all of the University of Houston, and Phil Berger and Sam White, University of Kentucky. Other reviewers were William P. Anthony, Florida State University; David E. Blevins, University of Mississippi; Jean-Marc Cote, University of Ottawa; David Gray, University of Texas, Arlington; Troy H. Jones, Florida Technological University; Jack N. Kondrasuk, University of Portland; Richard Leifer, University of Massachusetts; B. J. Linder, California State University, Chico; Richard C. Martin, Wilfred Laurier University; Larry K. Michaelsen, University of Oklahoma; and John Miller, Yale University.

A special thank you is also due Margaret Fenn of the University of Washington and the Fellows of Harvard Business School who permitted us to use cases. We want to acknowledge and thank Vic Vroom of Yale University and Art Jago of the University of Houston for permitting us to use their creative ideas and cases to develop a part of our leadership material.

We also received positive support and insightful suggestions from Lillian Nawalanic. Her help made our material more relevant and easier to read. In addition, Carla Krenek, Darlas Palmer, and Judy Holladay are due a special thank you for their assistance throughout the completion of the book.

January 1979

James L. Gibson
John M. Ivancevich
James H. Donnelly, Jr.

Contents

Performance Evaluation Connection. Administering Rewards: *Positive Reinforcement. Modeling and Social Imitation. Expectancy Theory.* Rewards and Organizational Membership. Rewards and Turnover and Absenteeism. Rewards and Organizational Commitment. Different Managerially Initiated Reward Systems: *Cafeteria-Style Fringe Benefits. Banking Time Off. The All-Salaried Team.*

Case for Analysis

Experiential Exercise

An Organizational Issue for Debate: *The Value of Upward Communication, 407*

Introduction: *The Importance of Communication.* The Communication Process: *How Communication Works. The Elements of Communication.* Communicating within Organizations. Barriers to Effective Organizational Communication: *Frame of Reference. Selective Listening. Value Judgments. Source Credibility. Semantic Problems. Filtering. In-Group Language. Status Differences. Time Pressures. Communication Overload.* Improving Communication in Organizations: *Following Up. Regulating Information Flow. Utilizing Feedback. Empathy. Repetition. Encouraging Mutual Trust. Effective Timing. Simplifying Language. Effective Listening. Using the Grapevine.*

Case for Analysis

Experiential Exercise

An Organizational Issue for Debate: *The Decision Participation Controversy, 431*

Introduction. Types of Decisions. The Decision-Making Process: *Establishing Specific Goals and Objectives and Measuring Results. Identifying Problems. Developing Alternatives. Evaluating Alternatives. Choosing an Alternative. Implementing the Decision. Control and Evaluation.* Behavioral Influences on Individual Decision Making: *Values. Personality. Propensity for Risk. Potential for Dissonance.* Group Decision Making: *Individual versus Group Decision Making. Managing Group Decisions. Improving Group Decisions.*

Case for Analysis

PART FIVE
DEVELOPING ORGANIZATIONAL EFFECTIVENESS

An Organizational Issue for Debate: *External Change Agents Are Necessary for Successful OD, 457*

Introduction. Learning Principles in the Context of OD Programs: *Expectations and Motivations. Reinforcement and Feedback. Transfer of Learning.* A Model for Managing Organizational Development. Forces for Change: *Environmental Forces. Internal Forces.* Diagnosis of a Problem: *The Degree of Subordinate Participation. The Role of Change Agents.* Alternative Development Techniques. Recognition of Limiting Conditions. Implementing the Method. Evaluating the Program.

Case for Analysis
Evaluation of an MBO Program, 482

Part One
Introduction

Chapter 1

Organizations in Society

INTRODUCTION

If we were to examine our lives, most of us would conclude that organizations pervade both society and our lives. We come into contact with organizations daily. In fact, most people probably spend the majority of their lives in organizations. If they do not spend a sizable amount of their time as members (work, school, social, civic, church, and so forth), they are affected as clients, patients, customers, or citizens. Our experiences in or with these organizations may be good or bad. Sometimes they may appear to be efficiently run and responsive to human needs and at other times our experiences with them may be extremely frustrating and irritating. At other times they may actually harass us.

These personal experiences in or with organizations provide each of us with a commonsense understanding of what it means to be "organized." While our attitudes about organizations may be positive or negative, this commonsense understanding can at least provide us with a good foundation for examining organizations in a more systematic manner. This is one primary objective of this book.

Organizations in Society

The idea of individual achievement is very strong in American folklore, and undoubtedly is strong and popular today. The truth is, however, that the vast majority of accomplishments which occur in our modern society happen because "groups of people" get involved in "joint efforts." In fact, our society has developed through the creation of specialized organizations which provide the goods and services it requires. It is doubtful that a great deal could be accomplished in our society through the efforts of one person. We are, indeed, an "organizational society" in which organizations, especially large ones, are the prime "doers."[1]

The primary rationale for the existence of organizations is that certain goals can be achieved only through the concerted action of groups of people. Thus, whether the goal is profit, providing education, religion, or health care, getting a candidate elected, or having a new football stadium constructed,

---

[1] Robert Presthus, *The Organizational Society* (New York: Alfred A. Knopf, Inc., 1962).

organizations are characterized by their *goal directed behavior.* That is, *they pursue goals and objectives that can be more efficiently and effectively achieved by the concerted action of individuals.* Organizations are vital instruments in our society. Their accomplishments in industry, education, health care, and defense have resulted in impressive gains in our standard of living and international power. They have become models for other nations. The very magnitude of the organizations with which we deal every day of our lives should illustrate to each of us the vast political, economic, and social power that they separately possess.[2]

Organizations are, however, far more than mere instruments for providing goods and services. They also create the settings in which the majority of us spend our lives, and in this respect have a profound influence on our behavior. However, because of the relative recency of the development of large organizations, we are just now beginning to become aware of some of the psychological effects of this type of involvement and the necessity for studying it. We are just beginning the process of developing procedures to study the behavior of people in organizational settings. Understanding the behavior of people in organizations is another objective of this book.

The Need for Managers in Organizations

We have stated that our society has developed through the creation of specialized organizations which provide the goods and services it desires. All of these organizations are guided by the decisions of one or more persons who are designated managers. Managers allocate scarce resources to alternative and often competing ends. It is they who determine the means-end relationship. They have the authority (as granted by society) and the responsibility (as accepted by them) to build or destroy cities, to wage peace or war, to purify or pollute the environment. They establish the conditions for the provision of jobs, incomes, products, services, protection, health care, and knowledge. Managers, like organizations, pervade our society. It would be extremely difficult to find anyone in our society who is neither a manager nor subject to the decisions of a manager.[3]

If well-managed organizations are critical to our society, then managers are an important social resource. As with organizations, each of us knows something about management because of our daily contacts with various organizations and with the managers in these organizations. Here again our experiences may be both good and bad and our attitudes about managers either positive or negative. Unfortunately, while management is a field that everyone knows a little about, it is something which most of us practice ineffectively. This becomes very apparent if we compare our optimistic plans for yesterday with our actual accomplishments.

---

[2] For additional discussion see L. F. Urwick, "That Word 'Organization,'" *Academy of Management Review* (January 1976), pp. 89–91.

[3] Ibid.

Important as effective managerial performance may be for the individual, its real payoff is for the organizations which are so critical in our society. The simple fact is that *organizations need managers.* Effective organizational performance in our society is more important today than ever before. Because of the increased complexity of our society and the increasing size of organizations, individual management decisions can have far reaching impacts on society. Consider the impact of Penn Central's bankruptcy in the early 1970s, and the monumental problems faced by the Lockheed Aircraft Corporation, Rolls Royce Corporation, Chrysler Corporation, and many of the nation's major airlines and financial institutions throughout the decade.

Consider also, the managerial problems our society faces in effectively providing health care and energy; and the continuing problems of huge cost overruns and other inefficiencies in state and federal government contracts. Finally, the results of many years of ineffective managerial performance in several of the nation's largest cities are now, unfortunately, beginning to show.[4]

Each of these should serve to remind us of our society's critical need for effective managers. Contributing to the achievement of more effective managerial performance is the ultimate goal of this book.

A FRAMEWORK FOR THE STUDY OF ORGANIZATIONS

The framework in which the content of this book is presented is based on three characteristics common to *all* organizations: *behavior, structure,* and *processes.* It has evolved from the authors' concept of what all organizations are. Our chain of logic is presented in Figure 1–1.[5]

Accordingly, the middle three sections of the book contain chapters related to the three characteristics of all organizations: behavior, structure, and processes. These are shown in Figure 1–1 in the middle column. For example, Part Two contains several chapters on human *behavior* and is concerned with such topics as those in the right-hand column in Figure 1–1. Chapters are included on individual characteristics, motivation, groups, and leadership. Part Three contains chapters concerned with various concepts related to the *structure* of organizations (that is, the design of the fixed relationships that exist among the jobs in the organization). Part Four contains chapters on the *processes* which make organizations "tick." Thus, our logic is as follows: people bring with them certain *behavior* (for example, needs, personality, attitudes) when they become part of an organization *structure,* and within this organization structure they engage in the *processes* of communication, decision making, rewarding, and evaluating.

One might argue, however, that the design of an organization structure

---

[4] For additional discussion see J. L. Bower, "Effective Public Management," *Harvard Business Review* (March–April 1977), pp. 131–40.

[5] The idea for this figure was stimulated by the discussion of Geoffrey Hutton, *Thinking about Organizations* (London: Tavistock Publications, 1972).

Figure 1–1
A Framework for the Study of Organizations

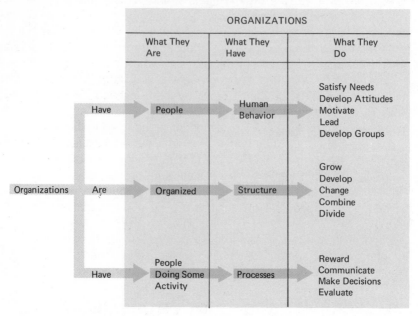

should be discussed before human behavior. Admittedly, it is possible to think about an organization in terms of structure and shape without having people in mind. In fact, the "ideal" organization of early management writers was designed without specific people in mind. They believed it was important to design an organization that was best for achieving the stated goals. People were fit into the design after it was developed. A major belief of the present authors is the importance of human behavior in determining the effectiveness of any organization. People are one resource common to all organizations. There is no such thing as a "peopleless" organization. For this reason we believe it makes good sense to discuss concepts of human behavior in organizations before discussing the design of an organization.

It is people who make organizations work and it is also people trying to influence other people in organizations that eventually results in either effective or ineffective organizational performance. One thing therefore is certain, a knowledge of organizational behavior requires the understanding of *people* and *organizations* one way or the other.

Purpose of the Book

Therefore, the specific purpose of this book is to review available theory and research on what we describe as the behavior, structure, and processes of organizations. While not the sole interest, a major interest of this book will be the behavioral sciences which have produced theory and research concerning human behavior in organizations. However, no attempt will be made here to write a book which will teach the reader "behavioral science." The continuous thread throughout the book will be the *management of organizational behavior*. Given this thread, our task is to *interpret* behavioral science materials so that students of administration can comprehend the behavior, structure, and process phenomena as affected by actions of managers. It is our intention to provide the reader the basis for applying the relevant contributions of behavioral science to the management of organizations.

Organizations and Their External Environment

Thus far, no specific mention has been made of the external environment in which organizations must exist. In fact, some readers, based on their experience with many organizations, may believe that most managers do not consider environmental forces in their day-to-day activities. It is true that many business and government organizations, schools, and hospitals seem to treat customers, citizens, students, and patients as if they existed for the organization, rather than the reverse. It is also probably true that many managers know less about the environment in which they must function than about any other aspect of their activities.

No organization exists in a vacuum. Each must deal with its environment every day. Each organization continually interacts with other organizations and individuals in that environment—client publics (customers, students, patients, citizens), suppliers, creditors, stockholders, government bodies, and many, many more. Each has some claim on the organization, a set of expectations, and each is affected by different issues in different ways. For example, the alumni of a university have different expectations than students and may not be affected by the same issues (for example, co-ed dormitories) that affect students.

Managers can no longer ignore what is "outside" of their organizations. It is no coincidence that during the last 5–10 years demands for more social awareness among the managers of large business organizations, student unrest, minority group protests, the consumer movement, the women's rights movement, discontent on the nation's assembly lines, concern about ecology, and problems in the nation's prisons, have all shown an upsurge. The last few years have been characterized by such phrases as "the meaning of work," "the quality of life," "the environment," "power to the people," and numerous others. Each of these so-called movements will continue to profoundly influence every type of organization in the future. They are part of the overall attempt on the part of people to make all organizations serve the people, not use the people.

The message to the future manager should be clear: The values and needs of society must be reflected in the alternatives considered and the priorities assigned by managers. It is our intention in this book to develop a better appreciation and understanding regarding environmental forces. To understand environmental forces requires an appreciation of some of the key environmental components which underlie the management of every organization. We shall see later that environmental considerations must be integrated into management planning (establishing goals and objectives), and that identifying relevant environmental components is critical in the process of decision making.

LEARNING ABOUT ORGANIZATIONS

This is a book about organizations written for future managers, but we do not intend to imply that this is the only or best way to learn about organizations. In fact, no book can make one a manager. The only way to become a manager is to "manage." What this book seeks to do is to provide future managers with frameworks and intellectual skills to apply to their experience. So while this book will certainly not make you an effective manager, it will help you accomplish this goal.

In studying the physical and biological sciences, one is fortunate because the real world can be brought into the laboratory. If you wish to test the theory of gravity or observe a chemical process all you need do is perform the required experiments in a laboratory. In this way you can acquire the needed knowledge and skills of the field.

Unfortunately, learning how to manage organizational behavior is much more difficult. It is highly unlikely that a business organization, government agency, or hospital will allow you access to its members so that you may study their behavior and experiment with them and the organization. People must, however, gain knowledge about how organizations work, and acquire the knowledge and develop the skills that are essential to become effective managers. The task of writing a book on organizational behavior is, therefore, not an easy one.

This raises the overworked question of "theory versus practice." Our experience has shown that most practicing managers are very uncomfortable with the word theory. When they refer to something as being "theoretical," they usually mean that it is unrelated to the everyday problems they face. What these managers do not realize, however, is that they themselves are theorists. For example, every manager has a theory on how best to motivate subordinates, or which type of leadership technique (for example, "easy going" or "whip") is most effective. They may not formally recognize (or wish to admit) it as a theory; they may instead look upon it as their own "concept" or "approach," developed through years of experience.

If you will be taking managerial action at some time, you will be influenced by assumptions (for example, people like to work or don't like to work; money is the best motivator). These assumptions will either be good ones or bad ones, valid or invalid. Our intent is to introduce you to several viewpoints and the support for these viewpoints so that, hopefully, when the time comes, you will be able to "make sense" of your experience and develop your own theories in the light of alternatives. We shall not try to convince you that one management technique or approach is more effective than another.

Unfortunately, managing organizations has not yet become that easy. Our assumption is a very simple one: since you are going to have theories one way or another, our mission is to help you to be more intelligent about them.

SUMMARY AND INTRODUCTION

The chances are very good that educated persons will sooner or later find themselves in managerial positions whether or not they ever took formal courses or had specific training in the field. Every type of organization needs managers, so the material discussed in this book will, for the most part, apply wherever a group of people is attempting to achieve a goal.

We hope that the reader appreciates the significance of knowing about organizations. Our society tends to organize its resources through specialized institutions. As a result, managers are a critical resource in our society. The potential impact of individual managerial decisions and actions (or inactions) has never been more pervasive than it is today. The cost of effective management is very high, but the cost of ineffective management (as well as the potential for error) is even greater. Large organizations have great power and it is the managers of these organizations who determine how this power will be wielded.

As you read this book you will find that there are no neat solutions to most organizational problems. In fact, there are probably very few neat organizational problems. Defining what the problem is may in itself be a monumental task. However, the difficulty of achieving organizational effectiveness is not sufficient reason to avoid it. Our theme throughout this book will be the achievement of organizational effectiveness through enlightened managers. Good management is vital to the success of each and every organization and there is a tremendous demand for managerial talent. Managing organizations effectively is a challenge. We hope that this book will help you meet the challenge.

DISCUSSION AND REVIEW QUESTIONS

1. Do you believe that organizations pervade your life? List each organization to which you belong. Do they have any consequences as far as you are concerned?

2. The word bureaucracy is often used as a synonym for red tape, inefficiency, and a generally unresponsive organization. The truth is that these are exactly opposite of what a bureaucracy is supposed to be: an efficient and effective organization. What's happened?

3. What are your attitudes and feelings about organizations? What has influenced your attitudes?

4. Think of a particularly frustrating experience you've had recently with an organization. It may have been at school or at work; or it may have been an organization with which you dealt as a customer, patient, or citizen. Describe the experience and try to outline what may have been some of the causes.

5. Should managers be considered a resource in society? Why?

6. Many individuals believe that most organizations are unresponsive to their external environments and are "out of control," pursuing their own interests at the expense of society. Do you agree? Why?

7. "The kind of problems faced by America today are such that they will only be solved by large organizations." Comment.

ADDITIONAL REFERENCES

Ackerman, R. W. "How Companies Respond to Social Demands." *Harvard Business Review* (1973), pp. 88–98.

"America the Inefficient." *Time,* March 23, 1970, pp. 72–78, 80.

Cass, E. L., and Zimmer, F. G. *Man and Work in Society.* New York: Van Nostrand Reinhold Co., 1975.

Cyert, R. *The Management of Nonprofit Organizations with Emphasis on Universities.* Lexington, Mass.: Lexington Books, 1975.

Donnelly, J. H.; Gibson, J. L.; and Ivancevich, J. M. *Fundamentals of Management: Functions, Behavior, Models.* 3d ed. Dallas: Business Publications, Inc., 1978.

Drucker, P. *Management: Tasks, Responsibilities, Practices.* New York: Harper & Row, 1974.

Eels, P., and Walton, C. *Conceptual Foundations of Business.* Homewood, Ill.: Richard D. Irwin, Inc., 1974.

Fielden, J. S. "Today the Campuses, Tomorrow the Corporation," *Business Horizons* (1970), pp. 13–20.

Fretz, C. F., and Hayman, J. "Progress for Women—Men Are Still More Equal." *Harvard Business Review* (1973), pp. 133–42.

Hackman, J. R., and Suttle, J. L., eds. *Improving Life at Work.* Santa Monica: Goodyear Publishing Co., 1977.

Hellriegal, D., and Slocum, J. W. *Organizational Behavior: Contingency Views.* St. Paul: West Publishing Co., 1976.

Henderson, H. "Ecologists versus Economists." *Harvard Business Review* (1973), pp. 28–36, 152–59.

Luthans, F., and Hodgetts, R. *Social Issues in Business.* New York: The Macmillan Company, 1972.

Mayhew, B. H. "System Size and Ruling Elites." *American Sociological Review* (1973), pp. 468–75.

Mintzberg, H. *The Nature of Managerial Work.* New York: Harper & Row, 1973.

Schulz, R., and Johnson, A. C. *Management of Hospitals.* New York: McGraw-Hill Book Co., 1976.

Tosi, H., and Hamner, W. C., eds. *Organizational Behavior and Management: A Contingency Approach.* rev. ed. Chicago: St. Clair Press, 1978.

Chapter 2

The Study of Organizations

INTRODUCTION

In order for us to learn about organizations and their functioning, someone has to study them and report about them. Otherwise, the only way we could learn about the functioning of organizations would be to become associated with one for many years and, hopefully, learn from experience. The study of organizations must involve someone using some method, and reporting the results in some fashion, whether it is a successful executive discussing 25 years of experience or a professor reporting the results of interviews with a group of employees. Otherwise a book such as this would not be possible. This chapter is concerned with how we go about studying organizations. Its purpose is to answer three questions: *who* studies organizations, *how* they study them, and *where* they report the results of what they studied.

THE STUDY OF ORGANIZATIONS

How do we know what we know about organizations? In other words, aside from personal experience, how can one learn about the functioning of organizations? Numerous sources of knowledge exist and each has provided important insights. While some are used more today than others, each has been an important source and together they form the basis for the knowledge presented in this book. Let us examine each source of knowledge in more or less chronological order. In doing so, we shall answer the first two questions of *who* studies organizations and *how* they study them.

History as a Way of Knowing about Organizations

The oldest approach to the study of organizations is through the history of organizations, societies, and institutions. Organizations are as old as man's history. Throughout time, people have joined with others to accomplish their goals, first in families, later in tribes and other more sophisticated political units. Ancient people constructed pyramids, temples, and ships; they created systems of government, farming, commerce, and warfare. For example, Greek historians tell us that it took 100,000 men to build the great pyramid of Khufu in Egypt. The project took over 20 years to complete, and was almost as high as the Washington Monument with a base that would cover eight modern football fields. Remember, these people had no construction equipment or computers. One thing they did have though, was *organization*. While these "joint efforts" did not have formal names such as "XYZ Corporation," the idea of "getting organized" was quite widespread throughout early civilizations. The literature of the times refers to such managerial concepts as planning, staff assistance, division of labor, control, and leadership.[1]

The administration of the vast Roman Empire required the application of organization and management concepts. In fact, it has been said that "the real secret of the greatness of the Romans was their genius for organization."[2] This is because the Romans used certain principles of organization to coordinate the diverse activities of the Empire.

If judged by age alone, the Roman Catholic Church would have to be considered the most effective organization of all time. While its success is the result of many factors, one of these factors is certainly the effectiveness of its organization and management. For example, the development of the hierarchy of authority with a territorial organization, specialization of activities by function, and use of the staff principle were integral parts of early church organization.

Finally, it is not surprising that some important concepts and practices in modern organizations can be traced to military organizations. This is because, like the Church, they were faced with problems of managing large, geographically dispersed groups. As did the Church, military organizations early adopted the concept of staff as an advisory function for line personnel.

There is no doubt that knowledge of the history of organizations in earlier societies can be useful for the future manager in the 20th century. In fact, many of these early concepts and practices are being utilized successfully today. However, one may ask whether heavy reliance on the past is a good guide to the present and future. We shall see that time and organizational setting have much to do with what works in management. For now let us simply note that the organization structure of the Church or the leadership style of Napoleon may not be effective in a present-day business organization in a highly competitive, volatile, and unionized industry, or in a large hospital with numerous professional staffs.

Experience as a Way of Knowing about Organizations

Some of the earliest books on management and organizations were written by successful practitioners. Most of these individuals were business executives, and their writings focused on "how it was" for them during their time

---

[1] For an excellent discussion of organizations in ancient societies, see Claude S. George, Jr., *The History of Management Thought* (Englewood Cliffs, N.J.: Prentice-Hall, Inc., 1968), pp. 3–26.

[2] James D. Mooney, *The Principles of Organization* (New York: Harper and Brothers, 1939), p. 63.

with one or more companies. They usually put forward certain "general principles" or "practices" which had worked well for them. For example:

1. In 1929, Henri Fayol, a managing director of a large coal mining company in France during the early part of the century, described the managerial process by identifying five functions in which managers must engage: planning, organizing, commanding, coordinating, and controlling. He also proposed 14 principles which should guide the thinking of managers in resolving concrete problems.[3]

2. In 1938, Chester I. Barnard, president of New Jersey Bell Telephone, wrote that the basic function of a manager is to provide the basis for cooperative effort, and defined organization as a system of goal-directed cooperative activities. He believed that a manager's functions include the formulation of objectives and the acquisition of resources and efforts required to meet the stated objectives. He emphasized *communication* as the means for acquiring cooperation.[4]

3. In 1964, Alfred P. Sloan, former chief executive of the General Motors Corporation, wrote on the need for top management not to rely totally on what subordinates tell them (upward communication). He believed management should have independent communication concerning the activities of widely dispersed organizational units.[5]

A great deal of what we know about organizations and their managing has been learned from the experiences of such practitioners, and examples can be found throughout this book. As "practical" as this approach sounds, it does have its drawbacks. Successful managers are susceptible to the same perceptual phenomena as each of us. What we read from them are their own accounts, based on their own preconceptions and biases. No matter how objective the approach, their accounts may not be entirely complete or accurate. In addition, their accounts may also be superficial since they are often after-the-fact reflections of situations in which, when they were occurring, the managers had little time to think about how or why they were doing something. As a result, their suggestions are often oversimplified. Finally, as with history, what worked yesterday may not work today or tomorrow.[6]

Science as a Way of Knowing about Organizations

In the first chapter we noted that a major interest in this book will be the behavioral sciences which have produced theory, research, and generalizations concerning the behavior, structure, and processes of organizations.

---

[3] See Henry Fayol, *General and Industrial Management,* translated by J. A. Conbrough (Geneva: International Management Institute, 1929), and the more widely available translation by Constance Storrs (London: Pitman Publishing Corp., 1949).

[4] Chester I. Barnard, *The Functions of the Executive* (Cambridge: Harvard University Press, 1938).

[5] Alfred P. Sloan, *My Years with General Motors* (Garden City, N.Y.: Doubleday Inc., 1964).

[6] An excellent article on this subject is W. H. Gruber and J. S. Niles, "Research and Experience in Management," *Business Horizons* (1973), pp. 15–24.

The interest of behavioral scientists in the problems of organizations is relatively new, becoming popular in the early 1950s. It was at that time that an organization known as the Foundation for Research on Human Behavior was established. The goals and objectives of this organization were to promote and support behavioral science research in business, government, and other types of organizations. Today this approach receives much attention in the literature on organizations. It can be defined as *the study of human behavior in organizations using scientific procedures.* It is interdisciplinary in that it draws heavily on work in psychology, sociology, and anthropology.

Many advocates of this approach believe that practicing managers and teachers have accepted many of the practices and "principles" that preceded them without the benefit of scientific validation. They believe that scientific procedures should be used whenever possible to validate practice. Because of their work, many earlier "principles" have been discounted or modified, while in other instances they have been validated.

In this section we have examined three important approaches which have been used to gain knowledge about organizations: the history of societies and other institutions, the experience of practitioners, and behavioral science. All three are very important, and each has provided knowledge which appears in this book. For the specific purpose of this book, however, behavioral science is by far the most important. Since the majority of the knowledge in this book draws from the behavioral sciences or has been derived from behavioral science research in organizations, the remainder of the chapter will examine this approach in detail.

THE BEHAVIORAL SCIENCES

To answer the question of *who* studies organizations from the behavioral science viewpoint, one must become familiar with various disciplines. The term "behavioral sciences" refers to the disciplines of psychology, sociology, and anthropology.[7]

Psychology is the study of human behavior. There are many branches of general psychology which have provided concepts useful to the study of organizations. For example, *social psychology* deals with human behavior as it relates to other individuals. It examines how groups and individuals influence and modify each other's behavior. *Organizational psychology* is a relatively new branch which is appearing in many schools of business and public administration. It deals specifically with human behavior in organizational settings and examines the effect of organizations upon the individual and the individual's effect upon organizations. Psychologists have also been concerned with such topics as personnel selection, training, job satisfaction, employee morale, and job performance, which are of interest to students of management. In addition, their concern with more general topics such

---

[7] The term "social sciences" usually refers to six disciplines: anthropology, economics, history, political science, psychology, and sociology.

as human motivation, personality, attitudes, and perception has also provided knowledge useful for the purposes of this book.

Sociology seeks to isolate, define, and describe the behavior of groups. It strives to develop generalizations about human nature, social interaction, and culture. One of the major contributions sociologists have made to our knowledge of organizations has been their focus on small groups. Much has been learned about the behavior of small groups in organizations, the influence groups have had on members, and their impact on the organization. Sociologists have also studied leadership and organization structure as related to organizational effectiveness. They approach the study of organizations as the study of bureaucracy, focusing on bureaucratic behavior as well as the structural relationships in bureaucratic organizations. Finally, sociologists have provided knowledge for this book related to leader and follower roles and the patterns of power and authority in organizations.

Anthropology studies all of the behaviors of man which have been learned, including all of the social, technical, and family behaviors which are a part of the broad concept of "culture." This is the major theme of cultural anthropology, the behavioral science devoted to the study of different peoples and cultures of the world, and is a key concept in all of the behavioral sciences. In fact, the ways in which individuals behave, the priority of needs they seek to satisfy, and the means they choose to satisfy them are functions of their culture. Anthropologists have also provided knowledge for this book with respect to the impact of culture on organizations, individual personality, and perception.

Research in the Behavioral Sciences

Present research in the behavioral sciences is extremely varied with respect to the scope and methods used. However, the common thread found among the various disciplines is that members in each attempt to study human behavior by using scientific procedures. Thus, it is necessary to examine the nature of science as it is applied to human behavior. There are those who believe that a science of human behavior is unattainable and that the same scientific procedures used to gain knowledge in the physical sciences cannot be adapted to the study of humans, especially humans in an organization.

The authors do not intend to become involved in these arguments. This is for scholars in the behavioral sciences to decide. However, we believe that the scientific approach is applicable to management and organizational studies.[8] Furthermore, as we have already seen in this chapter, there are means other than scientific procedures which have provided important knowledge concerning people in organizations.

The manager of the future will draw from the behavioral sciences just as

---

[8] A similar debate has taken place for years over the issue of whether management is a science. The interested reader should consult R. E. Gribbins and S. D. Hunt, "Is Management a Science?" *Academy of Management Review* (January 1978), pp. 139–43, for a recent article on this issue.

the physician draws from the biological sciences. The manager must know what to expect from the behavioral sciences, their strengths and weaknesses, just as the physician must know what to expect of bacteriology and how it can serve as a diagnostic tool. However, the manager, like the physician, is a practitioner who must make decisions in the present whether or not science has all the answers, and certainly cannot wait until it finds them before acting.

The Scientific Approach

Most current philosophers of science define "science" in terms of what they consider to be its one universal and unique feature: *method.* The greatest advantage of the scientific approach is that it has one characteristic that no other method of attaining knowledge has: *self-correction.*[9] It is an objective, systematic, and controlled process with built-in checks all along the way to knowledge. These checks control and verify the scientist's activities and conclusions to enable the attainment of knowledge independent of the scientist's own biases and preconceptions.

Table 2–1
Characteristics of the Scientific Approach

1. *The procedures are public.* A scientific report contains a complete description of what was done, to enable other researchers in the field to follow each step of the investigation as if they were actually present.

2. *The definitions are precise.* The procedures used, the variables measured, and how they were measured must be clearly stated. For example, if examining motivation among employees in a given plant, it would be necessary to define what is meant by motivation and how it was measured (for example, number of units produced, number of absences).

3. *The data-collecting is objective.* Objectivity is a key feature of the scientific approach. Bias in collecting and interpreting data has no place in science.

4. *The findings must be replicable.* This enables another interested researcher to test the results of a study by attempting to reproduce them.

5. *The approach is systematic and cumulative.* This relates to one of the underlying purposes of science, to develop a unified body of knowledge.

6. *The purposes are explanation, understanding, and prediction.* All scientists want to know "why" and "how." If they determine "why" and "how" and are able to provide proof, they can then predict the particular conditions under which specific events (human behavior in the case of behavioral sciences) will occur. Prediction is the ultimate objective of behavioral science, as it is of all science.

Source: Bernard Berelson and Gary A. Steiner, *Human Behavior: An Inventory of Scientific Findings* (New York: Harcourt, Brace and World, 1964), pp. 16–18.

---

[9] See Fred N. Kerlinger, *Foundations of Behavioral Research* (New York: Holt, Rinehart, and Winston, 1973), p. 6.

Most scientists agree that there is no single scientific method, but rather several methods that scientists can and do use. Thus it probably makes more sense to say that there is a scientific "approach." Table 2–1 summarizes the major characteristics of this approach. While only an "ideal" science would exhibit each of them, they nevertheless are the hallmarks of the scientific approach. They exhibit the basic nature—objective, systematic, controlled— of the scientific approach, which enables others to have confidence in research results. What is important is the overall fundamental idea that the scientific approach is a controlled rational process.

Methods of Inquiry Used by Behavioral Scientists

How do behavioral scientists gain knowledge about the functioning of organizations? Just as physical scientists have certain tools and methods for obtaining information, so do behavioral scientists. These are usually referred to as *research designs.* In broad terms, there are three basic designs used by behavioral scientists: the case study, the field study, and the experiment.

Case Study.   A case study attempts to examine numerous characteristics of one or more people usually over an extended time period. For years, anthropologists have studied the customs and behavior of various groups by actually living among them. Some organizational researchers have done the same thing. They have actually worked and socialized with the groups of employees they were studying.[10] Such reports are usually in the form of a case study. For example, a sociologist might report the key factors and incidents which led to a strike by a group of blue-collar workers.

The chief limitations of the case study approach for gaining knowledge about the functioning of organizations are:

1. Rarely can you find two cases that can be meaningfully compared in terms of essential characteristics. In other words, in another firm of another size the same factors may not have resulted in a strike.

2. Rarely can case studies be repeated or their findings verified.

3. The significance of the findings is left to the subjective interpretation of the researcher. This is similar to the problem discussed earlier concerning practitioners' reports of their experiences. Like the practitioner, the researcher attempts to describe reality but it is reality as perceived by one person (or a very small group). The researcher has training, biases, and preconceptions which can inadvertently distort the report. A psychologist may give an entirely different view of a group of blue-collar workers than a sociologist.

4. Since the results of a case study are based on a sample of one, the ability to generalize from them may be limited.[11]

---

[10] See E. Chinoy, *The Automobile Worker and the American Dream* (Garden City, N.Y.: Doubleday Inc., 1955); and D. Roy, "Banana Time—Job Satisfaction and Informal Interaction," *Human Organization* (1960), pp. 158–69.

[11] Based in part on Robert J. House, "Scientific Investigation in Management," *Management International Review* (1970), pp. 141–42.

Despite these limitations, the case study is widely used as a method of studying organizations. It is extremely valuable in answering exploratory questions.

Field Study. In attempts to add more reality and rigor to the study of organizations, behavioral scientists have developed several systematic field research techniques such as personal interviews, observation, and question-naire surveys which are used individually or in combination. They are used to investigate current practices or events and, unlike some other methods, the researcher does not rely entirely on what the subjects say. The researcher may personally interview other people in the organization—fellow workers, subordinates, and superiors—to gain a more balanced view before drawing conclusions.

A very popular field study technique involves the use of expertly prepared questionnaires. Not only are they less subject to unintentional distortion than personal interviews, but also enable the researcher to greatly increase the number of individuals participating. For example, Figure 2–1 presents part of a questionnaire used in the Department of Business Administration at the University of Kentucky to measure students' perceptions of their instructor. It enables the collection of data on particular characteristics which are of interest (for example, enthusiasm, originality, and so on). The seven-point scales are used to measure students' perceptions of the degree to which their instructor possesses a given characteristic.

There are certain questions, such as student perceptions of teaching, that can only be answered by a survey. In most cases, surveys are limited to simply a description of the current state of the situation. However, if research-ers are aware of factors that may account for survey findings, they can make conjectural statements (known as hypotheses) about the relationship between two or more factors and relate the survey data to those factors. Thus, instead of just describing student perceptions of teaching, finer distinctions could be made among groups of students (for example, year in school, major area, grade-point average). Comparisons and statistical tests could then be applied to determine differences, similarities, or relationships. Finally, there are also *longitudinal* studies involving observations made over time which are used to describe changes that have taken place. Thus, in the situation described here, we can become aware of changes in overall student percep-tions over time as well as those relating to individual instructors.[12]

Despite their advantages over many of the other methods of gaining knowl-edge about organizations, field studies are not without problems. Here again, researchers have training, interests, and expectations which they bring with them.[13] Thus, a psychologist may inadvertently ignore a vital technological

---

[12] The designing surveys and the development and administering of questionnaires is a skill better left to trained individuals if valid results are to be obtained. The reader interested in an introductory discussion might consult R. H. Helmstadter, *Research Concepts in Human Behavior* (New York: Appleton-Century-Crofts, 1970).

[13] For an excellent article on the relationship between what researchers want to see and what they do see, consult G. Nettler, "Wanting and Knowing," *American Behavioral Scientist* (1973), pp. 5–26.

Figure 2–1
Student Perceptions of Instructor

PART II: DESCRIPTIVE ITEMS

A. Listed below are 15 sets of items. Place in the box at the right
the number on the scale which best describes your feeling about
the instructor for each of the 15 sets. Please indicate only one
number for each set.

Fair 1 2 3 4 5 6 7 Unfair	☐
Muddled Thinking 1 2 3 4 5 6 7 Clear Thinking	☐
Irresponsible 1 2 3 4 5 6 7 Responsible	☐
Sincere 1 2 3 4 5 6 7 Insincere	☐
Confident 1 2 3 4 5 6 7 Lacks Confidence	☐
Helpful 1 2 3 4 5 6 7 Not Helpful	☐
Unoriginal 1 2 3 4 5 6 7 Original	☐
Enthusiastic 1 2 3 4 5 6 7 Unenthusiastic	☐
Likes Teaching 1 2 3 4 5 6 7 Does Not Like Teaching	☐
Idealistic 1 2 3 4 5 6 7 Realistic	☐
Poor Listener 1 2 3 4 5 6 7 Good Listener	☐
Patient 1 2 3 4 5 6 7 Impatient	☐
Prejudiced 1 2 3 4 5 6 7 Tolerant	☐
Deep 1 2 3 4 5 6 7 Shallow	☐
Humorless 1 2 3 4 5 6 7 Humorous	☐

B. In comparison to faculty members outside of the Department of
Business Administration, how would you rate your instructor?
Place the number in the box at right.

(1)	(2)	(3)	(4)	(5)	(6)	(7)	☐
One of the Worst	Very Poor	Below Average	Average	Above Average	Very Good	One of the Best	

factor when conducting a study of employee morale while concentrating on the psychological factors. Also, the fact that a researcher is present may often influence how the individual responds. This weakness of field studies has long been recognized and is noted in some of the earliest field research in organizations.

Experiment. Like the physical scientist, the behavioral scientist also wants to experiment. The experiment is the most rigorous of scientific techniques. For an investigation to be considered an experiment it must contain two elements—manipulation of some variable (independent variable) by the researcher and observation or measurement of the results (dependent variable) while maintaining all other factors unchanged. Thus, in an organization a behavioral scientist could change one organizational factor and observe the results while attempting to keep everything else unchanged.[14] There are two general types of experiments.

In a *laboratory experiment* the environment is created by the researcher. For example, a management researcher may work with a small voluntary group in a classroom. The group may be students or managers. They may be asked to communicate, perform tasks, or make decisions under different sets of conditions designated by the researcher. The laboratory setting permits the researcher to control closely the conditions under which observations are made. The intention is to isolate the relevant variables and to measure the response of dependent variables when the independent variable is manipulated. Laboratory experiments are useful when the conditions required to test a hypothesis are not practically or readily obtained in natural situations, and when the situation to be studied can be replicated under laboratory conditions. For these situations, many schools of business have behavioral science laboratories where such experimentation is done.

In a *field experiment* the investigator attempts to manipulate and control variables in the natural setting rather than in a laboratory. Early experiments in organizations included manipulating physical working conditions such as rest periods, refreshments, and lighting, while today behavioral scientists attempt to manipulate a host of additional factors.[15] For example, a training program might be introduced for one group of managers but not for another. Comparisons of performance, attitudes, and so on could be obtained later at one point or at several different points (a longitudinal study) to determine what effect, if any, the training program had on the managers' performance and attitudes.

The experiment is especially appealing to many researchers because it is the prototype of the scientific approach. It is the ideal toward which every

[14] For a volume devoted entirely to experiments in organizations see W. M. Evan, ed., *Organizational Experiments: Laboratory and Field Research* (New York: Harper & Row, 1971).

[15] See an account of the classic Hawthorne Studies in Fritz J. Roethlisberger and W. J. Dickson, *Management and the Worker* (Boston: Division of Research, Harvard Business School, 1939). The studies, which were conducted at the Chicago Hawthorne Plant of Western Electric, had as their original purpose to study the relationship between productivity and physical working conditions.

science strives. However, while its potential still is great, it has not produced a great breadth of knowledge about the functioning of organizations. Laboratory experiments suffer the risk of "artificiality." The results of such experiments often do not extend to real organizations. Teams of business administration or psychology students working on decision problems may provide a great deal of information for researchers. Unfortunately, whether this knowledge can be extended to a group of executives making decisions under severe time constraints is questionable.[16]

Field experiments also have drawbacks. First, researchers cannot "control" every possible influencing factor (even if they knew them all) as they can in a laboratory. Also, here again the fact that a researcher is present may make people behave differently, especially if they are aware that they are participating in an experiment. Experimentation in the behavioral sciences and more specifically in organizations is a complex matter. The interested reader may consult Appendix A of this book for an introductory discussion of the topic.

Finally, with each of the methods of inquiry utilized by behavioral scientists, some type of *measurement* is usually necessary. For knowledge to be meaningful, it often must be compared to, or related to, something else. As a result, research questions (hypotheses) are usually stated in terms of how differences in the magnitude of some variable is related to differences in the magnitude of some other variable. For example, earlier in our discussion of Figure 2–1 we mentioned that student perceptions of teaching could be compared to grade point averages. This may be meaningful to the instructor.

The variables studied are measured by research instruments. These instruments may be psychological tests such as personality or intelligence tests, questionnaires designed to obtain attitudes or other information such as Figure 2–1, or in some cases electronic devices to measure eye movement or blood pressure.

It is very important that a research instrument be both *reliable* and *valid*. Reliability is the consistency of the measure. In other words, repeated measures with the same instrument should produce the same result or score. Validity is concerned with whether the research instrument actually measures what it is supposed to be measuring. Thus, it is possible for a research instrument to be reliable but not valid. For example, a test designed to measure intelligence could yield consistent scores over a large number of people; but not be measuring intelligence. Behavioral science researchers have ways to ensure that as much as possible their research instruments are both reliable and valid.[17]

This concludes our discussion of the study of organizations. We have answered the questions of *who* studies organizations and *how* they study

---

[16] See K. E. Weick, "Laboratory Experimentation With Organizations: A Reappraisal," *Academy of Management Review* (January 1977), pp. 123–27, for a complete discussion of this problem.

[17] See Kerlinger, *Foundations of Behavioral Research.*

them. We have seen that management practitioners and management researchers are the two primary groups who study organizations and that the history of other societies and institutions, experience of practitioners, and behavioral science research are the primary ways to learn about the functioning of organizations. The knowledge presented in this book will draw from both groups and all methods. However, the primary focus of the book is to interpret behavioral science knowledge in such a way that students of management can comprehend human *behavior* in organizations. Throughout the discussions we will draw upon material from each of the behavioral sciences. While the disciplines may differ, the knowledge drawn upon will, for the most part, have a common base. It will have been arrived at using the methods we have described for gaining knowledge in the behavioral sciences. The only question which remains to be answered in this chapter is, *"Where* do we learn about organizations?"

SOURCES OF KNOWLEDGE ABOUT ORGANIZATIONS

The vast majority of reports and writing on organizations are contained in technical papers known as journals. Some of these such as the *Academy of Management Review* are devoted entirely to topics of management and organization while *Organizational Behavior and Human Performance* is devoted largely to the results of laboratory studies. Others such as the *Harvard Business Review* are general business journals while the *American Sociological Review* and the *Journal of Applied Psychology* are general behavioral science journals. These general business and general behavioral science journals often contain articles of interest to students of management. Table 2–2 presents a list of selected journals.

Table 2–2
Selected Sources of Writing and Research on Organizations

1. *Academy of Management Journal*	18. *Journal of Applied Behavioral Science*
2. *Academy of Management Review*	19. *Journal of Applied Psychology*
3. *Administrative Management*	20. *Journal of Business*
4. *Administrative Science Quarterly*	21. *Journal of Management Studies*
5. *Advanced Management Journal*	22. *Management of Personnel Quarterly*
6. *American Sociological Review*	23. *Management International Review*
7. *Business Horizons*	24. *Management Review*
8. *Business Management*	25. *Management Science*
9. *Business Topics*	26. *Organizational Behavior and Human Performance*
10. *California Management Review*	
11. *Fortune*	27. *Organizational Dynamics*
12. *Harvard Business Review*	28. *Personnel*
13. *Hospital and Health Services Administration*	29. *Personnel Journal*
	30. *Personnel Psychology*
14. *Human Organization*	31. *Public Administration Review*
15. *Industrial and Labor Relations Review*	32. *Public Personnel Review*
16. *Industrial Engineering*	33. *Training and Development Journal*
17. *Industrial Management Review*	

SUMMARY AND EXPECTATIONS

In this chapter we have examined the various ways of learning about organizations. It is clear that no one of the approaches is perfect. Each has strengths and weaknesses, but together they have produced a large body of useful knowledge. As a future manager you will draw (knowingly or unknowingly) on all of the approaches for knowledge that will be helpful in your situation. Hopefully, you will be aware of the strengths and weaknesses of the knowledge you are using.

We have stated that actually managing is the only way to become a manager; that no book can guarantee your success. What then should you expect of this book? Our goal is to communicate knowledge to you. Specifically, knowledge of the behavior, structure, and processes of organizations. Our fundamental belief is that the knowledge you acquire about organizations will increase your probability of becoming an effective manager in a shorter period of time by making your experience more meaningful. Managing organizations is and will remain a mixture of science and art, of knowledge and skill. The material presented in this book will provide you the science and knowledge foundation. Hopefully, your experiences will provide the art and the skill.

Your behavior as a manager will always reflect a theory. It may be a theory about what an organization is, what people are, or human rights and values. If your behavior as a manager is going to implicitly or explicitly reflect a theory, at least you should make an attempt to insure that the theory is a good one *for you*. Being exposed to what others say will enable you to evaluate and select what appears most useful. This book will help you do this.

Since our goal is to help you become a more effective manager, the next chapter of the book deals with this topic: managing organizations effectively. It serves as the foundation for studying the remainder of the book.

DISCUSSION AND REVIEW QUESTIONS

1. Discuss briefly each of the methods outlined in the chapter for gaining knowledge about organizations. Why is behavioral science research considered the most effective method?

2. Think of something you have had "experience" in. It might be a particular job, sport, etc. If you were to tell a group of people about your experience or attempt to teach them what you know, can you see any possible problems? What might be some considerations?

3. A noted baseball player authors a book about "My Ten Years as a Major League Pitcher." How useful is a book such as this to an aspiring major league pitcher? How might it compare to a similar book written by a successful executive?

4. Think of something you believed was true for quite some time only to find out at some later point through experience or some other method that it was not

true. Describe it and discuss what happened. Did you learn anything from this experience? What does it point out?

5. Discuss the three basic research designs used by behavioral scientists. Give an example of each type, other than those provided in the chapter. Develop your own if necessary.

6. A popular magazine features an article entitled, "Study and Social Habits of College Males." Upon reading the article you find that it is based on a case study where the reporter lived for two months as a member of a fraternity at a private school in the northeastern part of the country. Evaluate this article based upon your knowledge of the characteristics of the scientific approach.

7. Select and read an article in one of the journals listed in Table 2–2. Which one of the approaches for gaining knowledge about organizations did the author use? Evaluate the article as to its usefulness. What criteria did you use to make your judgment?

ADDITIONAL REFERENCES

Argyris, C. *The Applicability of Organizational Sociology.* New York: Cambridge University Press, 1972.

Conner, P. E. "Research in the Behavioral Sciences: A Review Essay." *Academy of Management Journal* (1972), pp. 219–28.

Emshoff, J. R. *Analysis of Behavioral Systems.* New York: Macmillan, 1971.

Ford, C. H. "A Manager's View of Business Journals." *Business Horizons* (1978), pp. 219–28.

Heald, K. "Using the Case Survey Method to Analyze Policy Studies." *Administrative Science Quarterly* (1975), pp. 371–81.

Kaplan, A. *The Conduct of Inquiry.* San Francisco: Chandler Publishing Co., 1964.

Lachenmeyer, C. "Experimentation—A Misunderstood Methodology in Psychological Research." *American Psychologist* (1970), pp. 617–24.

Massarik, F., and Krueger, B. E. "Through the Labyrinth: An Approach to Reading in Behavioral Science." *California Management Review* (1970), pp. 70–75.

Meltzer, H., and Nord, W. "The Present Status of Industrial and Organizational Psychology." *Personnel Psychology* (1973), pp. 11–29.

Schein, E. H. "Behavioral Sciences for Management." In McGuire, J. W., ed. *Contemporary Management.* Englewood Cliffs, N.J.: Prentice-Hall, Inc., 1974.

Seashore, S. E. "Field Experiments within Formal Organizations." *Human Organization* (1964), pp. 164–70.

Webber, R. A. "Behavioral Science and Management: Why the Troubled Marriage?" *Proceedings of the Academy of Management 1970,* pp. 377–95.

Weiland, G. F. "The Contributions of Organizational Sociology to the Practice of Management." *Academy of Management Journal* (1975), pp. 318–33.

Chapter 3

Managing Organizational Performance

AN ORGANIZATIONAL ISSUE FOR DEBATE

Employee Satisfaction Leads to Organizational Performance

ARGUMENT FOR

The argument for the idea that satisfied people produce more is firmly established in the human relations literature. "Improve the morale of a company and you improve production," is the oft-stated claim. Or as George Allen, former coach of the Los Angeles Rams, put it: Happy football players win games. The view that satisfaction leads to production was established by the Hawthorne studies and subsequently rooted in the motivation theories of Herzberg and the leadership theories of Likert.

These views are the bases for humanistic leadership training. The training exercises attempt to instill in managers the understanding that they must provide the necessary motivators which satisfy people. Managers must provide the "right" motivators to tap employee productivity through increased satisfaction.

An important part of this argument is that employee satisfaction is important only as it leads to productivity. That is, the sole criterion of organizational performance is efficient production. If there were no relationship between satisfaction and production, there would be no compelling reason to be concerned with the satisfaction and morale of employees.

ARGUMENT AGAINST

The argument against the idea that satisfaction leads to performance cites numerous studies showing no, or negative, relationship between the two. Thus employee satisfaction and performance may be subject to more complex relationships than posed by the supportive argument. For example, employee satisfaction may itself be based upon rewards other than those obtained through production. But if rewards are related to production, then satisfaction may be the *result* of performance not the cause of it. As Dallas Cowboy coach Tom Landry no doubt has said: If the players win football games (and championships) then they are happy.

The implications of this argument is that employees must be selected and trained to perform their assigned tasks; managers must provide positive paths to task completion and assure that rewards are related to performance. Salary structures must clearly reflect differential levels of production.

The counter-argument also includes the idea that both satisfaction and production are criteria of organizational effectiveness. The interactive relationship between satisfaction and production indicates that managers must balance and reconcile the two, rather than assume that one leads to the other. This consideration suggests that organizational effectiveness is measured by more than production alone; it is at best a two-dimensional concept, and perhaps multidimensional.

INTRODUCTION

Societies create organizations to provide goods and services and evaluate those same organizations by how well they carry out their tasks. That is, societies expect effective performances of their organizations. But what do we mean by effective performance? From a society's point of view *effectiveness* is the extent to which organizations produce goods and services with limited resources. Effectiveness is measured in terms of (1) achieving ends with (2) limited resources. The concept of *efficiency* must be added to that of effectiveness. Efficiency refers to the extent to which the organization maximizes its ends with minimum use of resources. These two concepts, effectiveness and efficiency, are related but there are some important differences.

We can cite instances which exemplify effective, yet inefficient, performance. For example, society is becoming aware that it can produce some economic goods effectively, yet inefficiently. If the social costs of polluted air and water were included in the profit and loss statements of organizations contributing to that pollution, prices could be so high that society would decide to stop using their products. Another example of the effective yet inefficient organization is the monopoly which effectively achieves its objective of maximum profits, but which, from society's point of view, does so through the inefficient use of resources. The meaning of organizational performance emphasizes two points:

1. Achieving desirable ends is necessary for effective performance.
2. Efficient use of resources is necessary but insufficient for effectiveness.

These two points represent society's interest in an organization's performance and managers of organizations must be responsive to that interest.

Managers are accountable for the performance of organizations. This accountability and the authority that goes with it are derived from those who provide resources. For example, property owners supply the resources for business organizations and taxpayers supply the resources for governmental organizations. Of course, both groups can have interests in the same organization or can share their interests with other groups, such as students, patients, and clients. Communications Satellites Consortium (COMSAT) is an example of an organization which is supported by both stockholders and taxpayers; a public university is supported by taxpayers and tuition-paying students. Thus the managers of organizations are intimately linked to the society in which they operate because they are ultimately accountable to those groups which contribute resources to the organizations.

Organizational performance depends upon individual and group performance. Organizations consist of people performing jobs alone and with others. In order to achieve high levels of organizational performance, managers must achieve high levels of performance from the people within the organization. Society evaluates organizational performance, but managers evaluate individual performance. Organizational, group, and individual performance are separate, but interrelated, concepts; the primary thrust of this textbook is to discuss and evaluate means by which managers can achieve effective performance at all three levels.

The actual process of evaluating performance is considerably more difficult than one might suspect. It is easy to say that managers should direct organizations in such ways as to maximize ends with efficient use of resources. It is much more difficult to know how to do this. Our approach to this managerial problem is to acquaint managers with the basic concepts of systems theory. Through systems theory, the concept of effectiveness can be defined in terms that are meaningful to the managers of organizations, whether business firms, hospitals, governmental agencies, or universities.

Systems theory enables us to describe the behavior of organizations both internally and externally. Internally we can see how and why people inside organizations perform their individual and collective tasks. Externally, we can relate the transactions of organizations with other organizations and institutions. It is a fundamental principle that all organizations acquire resources from the larger environment of which they are a part and, in turn, provide the goods and services which are demanded by the larger environment. Managers must deal simultaneously with the internal and external aspects of organizational behavior. This essentially complex process can be simplified, for analytical purposes, by employing the basic concepts of systems theory.

SYSTEMS THEORY

In the context of systems theory the organization is viewed as one element of a number of elements which interact interdependently.[1] The flow of inputs and outputs is the basic starting point in the description of the organization. In the simplest terms, the organization takes resources (inputs) from the larger system (environment), processes these resources, and returns them in changed form (output). Figure 3–1 displays the fundamental elements of the organization as a system.

We have alluded to this flow in our earlier discussion of the societal perspective. There we noted that society expects the organization to use its resources in an efficient manner to provide certain needed outputs. Implicit in this statement is the assumption that the survival of the organization depends upon how well it satisfies society. An organization will cease to exist when it no longer contributes to the larger system of which it is one part; it will no longer contribute when it is ineffective.[2]

---

[1] An alternative framework for the analysis of organizational effectiveness is termed the "goal" model. This approach emphasizes that organizational effectiveness should be evaluated solely in terms of goals, or outputs. The goal model is deficient as a conceptual framework for a number of reasons, the most important of which is that it does not account for the fact that managers must allocate resources to activities which have little to do with goals, or outputs. For example, resources must be allocated to recruitment of personnel. For a complete discussion of the limitations of the goal model see Amitai Etzioni, "Two Approaches to Organizational Analysis: A Critique and a Suggestion," *Administrative Science Quarterly* (September 1960), pp. 257–78.

[2] This discussion of the organization as a system is based upon E. J. Miller and A. K. Rice, *Systems of Organizations* (London: Tavistock Publications, 1967).

Figure 3–1
The Basic Elements of a System

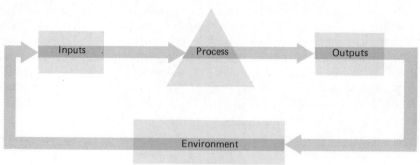

Systems Theory and Feedback

The concept of the organization as a system which is related to a larger system introduces the importance of feedback. As noted above, the organization is dependent upon the environment not only for its inputs, but also for the acceptance of its outputs. It is imperative, therefore, that the organization develop means for adjusting to environmental demands. The means for adjustment are information channels which enable the organization to recognize these demands. In business organizations, market research is an important feedback mechanism.

In a more general sense, feedback is the dynamic process by which any organism learns from its experiences with its environment. Throughout this text, we will see how important feedback is for reinforcing learning, and developing personality, group behavior, and leadership. In simplest terms, feedback refers to information which reflects the outcomes of an act or a series of acts by an individual, group, or organization. Systems theory emphasizes the importance of responding to the content of the feedback information.

Examples of the Input-Process-Output Cycle

The business firm has two major categories of inputs: human and natural resources. Human inputs consist of the people who work in the firm—operating, staff, and managerial personnel. They contribute their time and energy to the organization in exchange for wages and other rewards, tangible and intangible. Natural resources consist of the nonhuman inputs which will be processed, or which will be used in combination with the human element to provide other resources. A steel mill uses people and blast furnaces (along with other tools and machinery) to process iron ore into steel and steel products. An auto manufacturer takes steel, rubber, plastics, fabrics, and—in combination with people, tools, and equipment—makes automobiles. A business firm survives as long as its output is purchased in the market in quantities at prices that enable it to replenish its depleted stock of inputs.

Similarly, a university uses resources to teach students, to do research, and to provide technical information to society. The survival of a university depends upon its ability to attract students' tuitions and taxpayers' dollars in sufficient amounts to pay the salaries of its faculty and staff and the other costs of resources. If a university's output is rejected by the larger environment so that students enroll elsewhere and taxpayers support other public endeavors, or if a university is guilty of expending too great an amount of resources in relation to its output, it will cease to exist. Like a business firm, a university must provide the right output at the right price if it is to survive.[3]

As a final example, we will describe a hospital in terms of systems theory. The inputs of a hospital are its professional and administrative staff, equipment, supplies, and patients. The patients are processed through the application of medical knowledge and treatment. To the extent that its patients are restored to the level of health consistent with the severity of disease or injury which they suffered, the hospital is effective. Yet the criterion of efficiency must also be met. The rising cost of medical care has initiated considerable search for alternative forms of medical care delivery. This activity is in direct response to society's discontent with the seeming inefficiencies of the present medical-care delivery system.

The systems concept emphasizes two important considerations: (1) The ultimate survival of the organization depends upon its ability to *adapt to the demands of its environment,* and (2) in meeting these demands, *the total cycle of input-process-output must be the focus of managerial attention.* Criteria of performance must reflect these two considerations and we must define effectiveness accordingly. As Etzioni has observed, the systems framework assumes that "some means have to be devoted to such nongoal functions as service and custodial activities, including means employed for the maintenance of the unit (organization) itself."[4] In other words, *adapting to the environment and maintaining the input-process-output flow* require that resources be allocated to activities that are only indirectly related to the organization's social mission.

CRITERIA OF ORGANIZATIONAL EFFECTIVENESS

The concept of organizational effectiveness in this book relies upon our previous discussion of systems theory, but we must develop one additional point, the dimension of time. Recall that two main conclusions of systems theory are that (1) effectiveness criteria must reflect the entire input-process-output cycle, not simply output; and (2) effectiveness criteria must reflect the interrelationships between the organization and the larger environment in which it exists. From these two points, we can derive two corollaries:

---

[3] For a treatment of university organization in terms of systems theory, see A. K. Rice, *The Modern University* (London: Tavistock Publications, 1970).

[4] Amitai Etzioni, "Two Approaches to Organizational Analysis: A Critique and a Suggestion" in Jaisingh Ghorpade," *Assessment of Organizational Effectiveness* (Pacific Palisades, Calif.: Goodyear Publishing Co., 1971), p. 36.

1. Organizational effectiveness is an all-encompassing concept which includes a number of component concepts.
2. The managerial task is to maintain the optimal balance among these components.

Presently, we are proposing a tentative set of ideas. Much additional research is needed to develop knowledge about the components of effectiveness. There is little consensus not only about these relevant components, but also the interrelationships *among them* and the effects of managerial action *on them*.[5] We are attempting to provide the basis for asking the right questions about what constitutes effectiveness and how those qualities which characterize effectiveness interact.

The dimension of time enters into the model when an organization is conceptualized as an element of a larger system (the environment) which *through time* takes, processes, and returns resources to the environment. Accordingly, the final test of organizational effectiveness is whether it is able to sustain itself in the environment. *Survival* of the organization, then, is the ultimate, or long-run, measure of organizational effectiveness. Yet, management and others who have interests in the organization must have indicators which assess the probability that it will survive. These indicators are of short-run nature and include *production, efficiency,* and *satisfaction* measures. Two other criteria which are termed intermediate, are *adaptiveness* and *development*. The relationship between these effectiveness criteria and the time dimension are shown in Figure 3–2. As is true of all classification schemes, the list of short, intermediate, and long-run criteria is somewhat arbitrary and dependent upon definitions. Accordingly let us define our meanings.

Figure 3–2
Criteria of Organizational Effectiveness

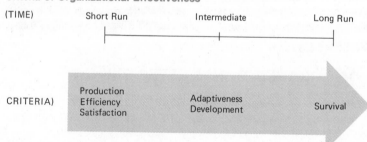

(TIME)	Short Run	Intermediate	Long Run

| CRITERIA) | Production
Efficiency
Satisfaction | Adaptiveness
Development | Survival |

Production

As used here, production reflects the ability of the organization to produce the quantity and quality of output which the environment demands. The con-

[5] J. Barton Cunningham, "Approaches to the Evaluation of Organizational Effectiveness," *Academy of Management Review* (July 1977), pp. 463–74, and Richard M. Steers, "Problems in Measurement of Organizational Effectiveness," *Administrative Science Quarterly* (December 1975), pp. 546–58.

cept excludes any consideration of efficiency as will be defined below. The measures of production include profit, sales, market share, students graduated, patients released, documents processed, clients served, and the like. These measures relate directly to the output that is consumed by the organization's customers and clients.

Efficiency

This concept is defined as the ratio of outputs to inputs. This short-run criterion focuses attention on the entire input-process-output cycle, yet it emphasizes the input and process elements. The measures of efficiency include rate of return on capital or assets, unit cost, scrappage and waste, downtime, cost per patient, per student, or per client, occupancy rates, and the like. Measures of efficiency must inevitably be in ratio terms; the ratios of benefit to cost or to output or to time are the general forms of these measures.

Satisfaction

The conceptualization of the organization as a social system requires that some consideration be given to the benefits received by its participants as well as its customers and clients. Satisfaction and morale are similar terms which refer to the extent to which the organization satisfies the needs of employees. We will use the term satisfaction to refer to this criterion. Measures of satisfaction include employee attitudes, turnover, absenteeism, tardiness, and grievances.

Adaptiveness

Adaptiveness is the extent to which the organization *can and does* respond to internal and external changes. However, contrary to its use elsewhere, adaptiveness is viewed here as an intermediate criterion; it is more abstract than production, efficiency, or satisfaction. This criterion refers to management's ability to sense changes in the environment as well as within the organization itself. Ineffectiveness in achieving production, efficiency, and satisfaction can signal the need to adapt managerial practices and policies; or the environment may demand different outputs or provide different inputs, thus necessitating change. To the extent that the organization cannot or does not adapt, its survival is in jeopardy. The usual measures of adaptiveness for research purposes are provided by responses to questionnaires. But how can one really know whether the organization is effectively adaptive? Unlike the short-run measures of effectiveness, there are no specific and concrete measures of adaptiveness. The management can implement policies which encourage a sense of readiness for change; and there are certain managerial practices which, if implemented, facilitate adaptiveness. Yet when the time comes for an adaptive response, the organization either adapts or does not—and that is the ultimate measure.

Development

An organization must invest in itself to enhance its capability to survive in the long run. The usual development endeavors are training programs for managerial and nonmanagerial personnel, but more recently the range of organizational development has enlarged to include a number of psychological and sociological approaches.

Time considerations enable us to speak of effectiveness in the short, intermediate, and long run. For example, we could evaluate a particular organization as effective in terms of production, satisfaction, and efficiency criteria, but ineffective in terms of adaptiveness and development. A manufacturer of buggywhips may be optimally effective in the short run, but with little chance of survival. *Thus when we speak of optimal balance, we are speaking, in part, of balancing the organization's performance over time.*

Another aspect of optimal balance is *that of achieving the proper relationships among the criteria within a given time period.* There are no fixed relationships among production, satisfaction, and efficiency. Neither research nor actual practice provides the basis for saying that production and satisfaction are positively related. These two measures can move in the same or opposite direction depending upon the circumstances. Therefore it is necessary for managers to recognize what potential relationships they want to affect, prior to implementing policies designed to affect them.

We know that the more distant the future, the more uncertain are our predictions. A forecast of tomorrow's events is, by definition, more certain than a forecast of next year's events. The case of effectiveness criteria is similar. We would expect, for example, measures of production, satisfaction, and efficiency to be relatively more *concrete, specific, verifiable,* and *objective* than measures of adaptiveness and development. Furthermore we know that relative effectiveness is much easier to determine if short-run rather than long-run criteria are used.

THE MANAGERIAL PERSPECTIVE ON EFFECTIVENESS

The question of effectiveness is concerned with *performance,* by which is meant the *execution of an act.* We think of performance in casual terms when discussing our reaction to a sports event, a concert, a play, or an automobile. And in these contexts we make judgments about those performances. Specifically, we grade, or evaluate, them in terms of whether they meet our expectations. If a basketball team is expected to have a winning season, and does, then it has performed well; if it is not expected to have a winning season but does, then it has performed even better. Thus in a general sense the concept of performance is used whenever there is some previously established expectation.

Managers, by the nature of their jobs, are accountable for the performance of the organization (the entity) itself, a group within the organization, or an individual within the group. A university president is concerned with the performance of the total organization—the university; whereas a dean is concerned with a college, i.e., a group. Finally, a department chair's perspective is that of the performance of individual faculty members. This is not to say that deans or chairpersons have no occasion to evaluate group performance. The existence of groups is pervasive as subsequent chapters will acknowledge. The point is simply that the perspective must be identified whenever managers evaluate performance, and that the distinction between organization, group, and individual is useful for identifying the perspective.

Organizational effectiveness as developed in the previous section is derived from theories and research on effectiveness from the organizational perspective. As such it is a relatively broad and abstract model, but it should accomodate issues associated with group and individual performance. From a practical standpoint, the question is whether the concepts of production, efficiency, satisfaction, adaptiveness, and development are meaningful at the levels of groups and individuals. The authors believe they are and will apply them throughout the discussions that follow. At the outset, we can certainly appreciate the fact that individuals are more or less efficient, productive, and satisfied; they also are more or less developed and adaptive.

A MODEL FOR MANAGING ORGANIZATIONS: BEHAVIOR, STRUCTURE, PROCESSES

A model for understanding organizations is presented in Figure 3–3. The model will serve as the focal point for discussion and analysis of behavior, structure, processes, performance outcomes, change and development, environment, and organizational climate. At this point in the book, many of the dimensions, relationships, and issues presented may not be clearly defined or understood. By presenting the model at the outset, it can serve as the focal point for each section and chapter. It will also serve as the framework for analyzing the cases and experiential exercises used throughout the book. The model is not presented as being predictive or exhaustive. Instead it is designed to:

a. Identify crucial behavioral, structural, and process variables.
b. Suggest how the external environment influences organizational decision makers.
c. Provide a framework for charting the course of the book.
d. Emphasize the importance of viewing the manager's responsibilities concerning individuals, groups, and the overall organization.
e. Stress the importance of performance outcomes at three levels—individual, group, and organizational.

Society and Organizations

Organizations exist in societies; in fact, organizations are created by societies. Systems theory draws attention to the relationships between organiza-

Figure 3–3
A Model for Managing: Behavior, Structure, and Processes

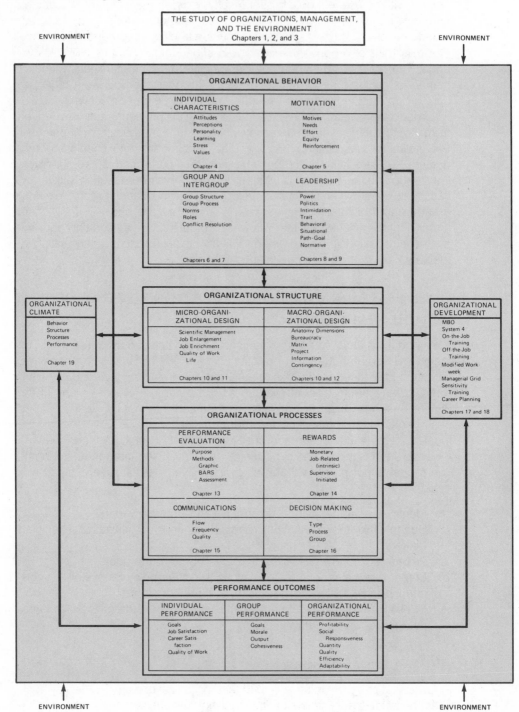

tions and the society which creates and sustains them. Within a society, many factors impinge upon an organization, and management must be responsive to them. Every organization must respond to legal and political constraints and to economic, and technological change and development. Figure 3–3 reflects environmental forces interacting with the organization and throughout the discussion of each aspect of the model, the relevant societal factors will be identified and discussed.

Individual Characteristics

Individual performance is the foundation of organizational performance. Consequently managers must have more than passing knowledge about the determinants of individual performance. Psychology and social psychology contribute a great deal of relevant knowledge about the relationship between attitudes, perceptions, personality, and values and individual performance. Managers must understand these relationships when planning and directing organizational and individual behavior. Individual capacity for learning and coping with stress has become, in recent years, more and more important. Managers cannot ignore the necessity for acquiring and acting on knowledge of individual characteristics of their subordinates and themselves.

Group and Intergroup Variables

Groups form in organizations because of managerial action, but also because of individual efforts. Managers create work groups to carry out assigned jobs and tasks. Command and task groups include departments, task forces, committees, and boards. These groups are created by managerial decision and they are termed formal groups. As these groups function and interact with other groups they develop characteristics, including structure, processes, norms, roles, and cohesiveness. In addition, they may cooperate or compete with other groups; the intergroup competition can lead to conflict.

Groups also form as a consequence of employees actions. Such groups, termed informal groups, develop around common interests and friendship. Even though not sanctioned by management these groups can affect organizational and individual performance. The affect can be positive or negative depending upon the intention of the group's members. Effective managers recognize the consequences of the individual's need for social affiliation.

Leadership

Leaders exist within all organizations. They may be found in formal and informal groups, they may be managers or nonmanagers. The importance of effective leadership for obtaining organizational, group, and individual performance is so important as to have stimulated a great deal of effort to determine its causes. Theories and research have been advanced which suggest that effective leadership depends upon leaders' traits and behaviors—separately, and in combination. Some managers and researchers believe that one leadership style is effective in all situations; others believe that each situation requires a specific leadership style. The state of knowledge about leadership is still too tentative to permit firm conclusion about the validity of any one leadership theory. The contemporary approach reflects a *contingency* perspective. This perspective suggests that variables such as the manager's delegated authority, the routineness of subordinate's work, needs of subordinates, and the degree of trust between the manager and subordinates determine the relative effectiveness of a particular leadership style.

Motivation

Motivation to work and ability to do the work interact to determine performance. This statement is, however, a tautology and not an explanation. Motivation theory attempts to explain and predict how behavior of individuals is aroused, started, sustained, and stopped. Not all managers and researchers agree on the "best" theory of motivation. The topic is so complex that it may be impossible to have one, simple, all-encompassing theory. It is more likely that various theories will always compete for acceptance. Yet the complexity of the issue should not deter attempts to understand it. Managers must be concerned with motivation because they are concerned with performance. Concepts such as needs, expectancies, valences, and equity are components of modern motivation theory and in a subsequent chapter these concepts are fully developed from a managerial perspective.

Macro-Organizational Design

An important determinant of effective performance at all levels is the macro-organization design. The design of an organization involves the application of principles of division of labor, departmental bases, span of control, and delegation of authority. The result of applying these principles is a *structure* of tasks and authority relationships intended to channel the behavior of individuals and groups toward high levels of performance. Organization structures can take different forms and can be characterized as simple or complex, centralized or decentralized. Contemporary approaches to macro-organization stress the importance of a contingency rather than a universalistic point of view. The contingency perspective suggests that managers must consider the nature of technological and environmental demands when designing the macro-organization structure.

Micro-Organizational Design

Micro-organizational design refers to the process by which managers specify the contents, methods, and relationships of jobs to satisfy organizational as well as individual requirements. This managerial concern has perhaps the longest history since the earliest attempts to develop systematic ways to design jobs can be traced to the scientific management era. Those early efforts relied almost exclusively on engineering and physiological studies and resulted in jobs which met organizational demands to the exclusion of individual requirements. More recent theory and practice of job design emphasize the necessity to achieve a balance. Through methods such as job enlargement and job enrichment, managers are now able to make significant improvements in the quality of work life for some employees.

Reward Process

One of the most powerful processes influencing individual performance is the organization's reward system. Not only can management use rewards to increase performance of its present employees, it can also use rewards to attract skilled employees to join the organization. Monetary rewards are important aspects of the reward system, but not the only aspect. Performance of the work itself can provide employees with *intrinsic* satisfaction particularly if performance of the job leads to a sense of personal responsibility, autonomy, and meaningfulness. To the extent that managers can design work to include these potentialities, the reward system is considerably more powerful than one which relies exclusively on *extrinsic* rewards. Pay, promotion, fringe benefits, bonuses, and commissions are important sources of extrinsic rewards. If they are tied to performance they can be powerful influencers of effective individual and group performance.

Decision-Making Process

The quality of decision making depends upon selecting proper goals and identifying appropriate means for achieving them. Through optimal integration of *behavioral* and *structural* factors, management can increase the probability that high-quality decisions are made. For example the proper placement of individuals in compatible jobs involves matching the motivations and abilities of the individual with the skill requirements of the job. If properly matched, the decisions of the job holder should result in proper goal selection. Organizations rely upon the quality of group decisions as well as individual decisions. Executive committees, steering committees, and task forces are only a few of the kinds of groups which managers form to make decisions. Effective management requires knowledge about the process of group decision making.

Communication Process

Organizational survival is related to the ability of management to receive, transmit, and act on information. Communication processes link the organization to its environment as well as to its constituent parts. Information flows across the boundaries of the organization from the environment. It flows within the organization from individual to individual, from group to group. Thus information serves to integrate the activities of the organization to the demands of the environment, but it also integrates the internal activities of the organization.

Performance Evaluation Process

Managers must evaluate the performance of individuals and groups within their organizations. Figure 3–3 indicates that individual, group, and organization performance are the outcomes, or dependent variables, of organizational behavior, structure, and processes. The system which management installs to evaluate performance serves many purposes, including reward decisions (pay, promotion, transfer), identification of training needs, and provision of feedback to employees. An effective system is one which includes evaluation criteria that are related to the purposes of the system and information which measures the criteria. Many different methods exist to evaluate performance and the challenge to management is to select the method which most closely approximates the purposes of the system.

Performance Outcomes: Individual, Group, and Organizational

Performance is the bottom-line consideration, and, as we have noted throughout the discussion it consists of three levels of analysis: individual, group, and organizational. No one measure, or criterion, adequately reflects performance at any level. Systems theory conclusions caution against the use of a single criterion. Rather managers are encouraged to consider multiple measures within a time framework. From the manager's perspective, ineffective performances at any level is a signal to take corrective action. The focus of corrective action are elements of organizational behavior, structure, and process.

Organizational Change and Development

Concerted, planned, and evaluated efforts to improve performance have great potential for success. The requirements for success include accurate diagnosis of the causes of poor performance. Management often will engage the services of an outside consultant, a change-agent, to facilitate the change and development program. The diagnostic efforts will trace the causes of performance problems to structural or behavioral causes. A method such as job restructuring, leadership training, sensitivity training, career planning, or team building will be implemented. If the diagnosis is accurate and if the method is correctly implemented, the target of the program (individuals and groups) should change toward more effective performance.

Organizational Climate

The final concept of the model shown in Figure 3–3 is organizational climate. This concept refers to the *properties* of the work environment which employees perceive as characterizing the *nature* of their work environment. Climate is a summary concept in that it consists of perceptions of those behavioral, structural, and process variables in combination. That is, what employees believe an organization to be is based upon their perceptions of all its parts. Whether they view it as personal or impersonal, aggressive or passive, depends upon their reactions to peer and leadership behavior, their jobs, and organizational decision making and communication. Organizational climate is, in this context, an employee's "shorthand" description of the organization from his or her vantage point. The model for managing organizational behavior, structure, and process reflects the complexity of managers' tasks. They are better able to deal with that complexity by acquiring knowledge from organizational behavior theory and research. Knowledge alone and by itself does not eliminate the difficulties, it does not change complexity to simplicity. But when combined with experience and common sense, the realization of performance is enhanced.

The following section will describe the manner in which managers attempt to achieve effective performances of organizations, groups, and individuals. As we will see, managers engage in activities which plan, organize, and control performance.

THE NATURE OF MANAGERIAL WORK

Theories which describe managerial work are many and varied.[6] These theories, produced by academicians and practitioners alike, are intended to provide the bases for research as well as for selecting, training, and developing managers. The academic purpose of theory is to suggest research questions which, in turn, are the bases for refining existing theory and developing new theory. The practical purpose of theory is to guide decisions. Managers must be identified, selected, trained, evaluated, developed, rewarded, and disciplined. But without a theoretical framework for *describing what managers do* and for *prescribing what they should do,* no basis exists for making those decisions.

The first attempts to describe managerial work were undertaken in the early 1900s by writers of the Classical School of Management.[7] The writers of the Classical School proposed that managerial work consists of distinct, yet interrelated, *functions* which taken together comprise the *managerial process.* The view that management should be defined, described, and analyzed in terms of what managers do has prevailed, but whether the functions as

---

[6] Surveys of the history of management thought can be found in Daniel A. Wren, *The Evolution of Management Thought* (New York: The Ronald Press Company, 1972); and Claude S. George, Jr., *The History of Management Thought* (Englewood Cliffs, N.J.: Prentice-Hall, Inc., 1968).

[7] The term Classical School of Management refers to the ideas developed by a group of practitioners who wrote of their experiences in management. Notable contributors to these ideas include Frederick W. Taylor, *Principles of Management* (New York: Harper and Brothers, 1911); Henri Fayol, *General and Industrial Management,* translated by J. A. Conbrough (Geneva: International Management Institute, 1929); James D. Mooney, *The Principles of Organization* (New York: Harper and Brothers, 1947); and Lyndall Urwick, *The Elements of Administration* (New York: Harper and Brothers, 1944).

identified by the Classical School are appropriate is a matter of continuing debate.

No doubt management can be defined as a *process,* that is, as a series of actions, activities, or operations which lead to some end. The definition of management should also recognize that the process is undertaken by more than one person in most organizations. This definition should be broad enough to describe management wherever it is practiced, yet specific enough to identify differences in the relative importance of the functions associated with a particular manager's job. A definition which meets these tests has not been fully developed.

The definition of management developed here is based upon the assumption that the necessity for managing arises whenever work is specialized and undertaken by two or more persons.[8] Under such circumstances, the specialized work must be *coordinated* and it is this imperative that creates the necessity for performing managerial work. Managerial work, i.e., the managerial process, can be subdivided into three major *functions:* planning, organizing, controlling. It is certainly possible to expand the list to include other functions, but these three can be defined with sufficient precision to differentiate them and, at the same time, to include all others which management writers have proposed.

The final elements of the management concept are *activities,* that is, the specific acts, behaviors, and interactions comprising each managerial function. Thus management is viewed as a set of activities which can be classified as concerned with planning, organizing, or controlling. For example, hiring a new employee to fill an existing position would be a *controlling activity;* defining the skill requirements of a new position would be an *organizing activity;* and forecasting the number of potentially qualified people in the labor market would be a *planning activity.*

Managerial Functions

The managerial functions discussed here are found in some degree in every instance where the work of others needs to be coordinated. The logic is fairly simple: If work is to be coordinated there must be some understanding of what is to be done (planning), how it is to be done (organizing), and whether it was done (controlling).

Planning Effective Performance.   The planning function includes defining the ends to be achieved and determining *appropriate means to achieve the defined ends.* The necessity of this function follows from the nature of organizations as purposive, i.e., end-seeking, entities. Planning activities can be complex or simple, implicit or explicit, impersonal or personal. For example, the sales manager who is forecasting the demand for the firm's major product may rely upon complex econometric models or upon casual conversations with salespersons in the field. The intended outcomes of planning

---

[8] This idea is essentially that of James D. Mooney as developed in *Principles of Organization.*

activities are mutual understandings about what the members of the organization should be attempting to achieve. These understandings may be reflected in the form of complicated plans which specify the intended results or they may be reflected in a general consensus of the members.

Discussions of planning in practical and academic writings tend to be confused by the absence of definitions of such terms as mission, goal, and objective. In some instances the terms are used interchangeably, particularly the terms goal and objective. In other instances the terms are specifically defined, but there is no general agreement as to these definitions. Depending upon their backgrounds and purposes, managers and authors will use the terms differently. However, the pivotal position of planning as a management function requires us to make very explicit the meanings of these key concepts. Accordingly, mission, goal, and objective will be defined as follows:

1. *Mission* refers to the broad purpose that society expects the organization to serve. Missions are the linkages between the environment and the organization. Thus mission statements can be viewed as consisting of criteria for assessing the long-run effectiveness of an organization. Effective managers will state the mission of their organization in terms of those conditions which, if realized, will assure the organization's survival. Statements of mission are to be found in laws, articles of incorporation, and other extraorganizational sources. Mission statements are broad, abstract, and value-laden, and as such they are subject to various interpretations. For example, the mission of a state public health department as expressed in the law that created it mandates the agency to "protect and promote the health and welfare of the citizens of the Commonwealth." It is from this source that the organization will create its specific programs.

An example of the stated mission of a large corporate entity, American Telephone and Telegraph, can be found in the words of a former board chairman:

> When I ask people in our business what they think the goals of the telephone company ought to be, they make practical, down-to-earth answers.
>
> Give us good service, they say, at reasonable prices. Be human and considerate in your dealings. Play fair with employees and share-owners and bondholders. Look ahead—be progressive. Don't ever be complacent or self-satisfied.[9]

Kappel went on to state that these expectations of "outsiders" were the mission of AT&T. They were, as he admits, "plain, uncomplicated ideas"; yet ". . . the success of the Bell Telephone System will mostly depend on how well we live by such ideas . . ."[10]

2. *Goal* refers to a future state or condition which when realized contributes to the fulfillment of the mission. A goal is relatively more concrete and specific than a mission, yet not as concrete or specific as an objective. Goals can also be thought of as expressions of relatively intermediate criteria of effective-

---

[9] Frederick R. Kappel, *Business Purpose and Performance* (New York: Duell, Sloan, and Pearce, 1964), p. 31.

[10] Ibid., p. 3.

ness. But they can also be stated in terms of production, efficiency, and satisfaction. For example, one goal of the public health agency could be stated as "the eradication of tuberculosis as a health hazard by the end of 1980." In a business setting, a goal might be "to have viable sales outlets established in every major population center of the country by the end of 1985." It is entirely possible for an organization to have multiple goals which contribute to its mission. For example, a hospital may pursue patient care, research, and training. Universities typically state three significant goals: teaching, research, and community service. The existence of multiple goals places great pressure on managers to coordinate not only the routine operations of the units which strive for these goals, but also to plan and allocate scarce resources to those goals.

3. *Objectives* are derived from goals and are ordinarily short-run, specific, and measurable. The public health agency's objective can be stated as "to reduce the incidence of tuberculosis from 6 per 10,000 to 4 per 10,000 by the end of the current year." The firm seeking to have sales outlets in all major population centers could state its current year's objective as "to have opened and begun operations in Chicago, Los Angeles, Louisville, and New York." Thus even as goals are derived from the organization's mission, so are its objectives derived from the goals.

Thus, mission statements reflect managements' attempts to state the long-term criteria for assessing organizational performance. Consequently, goals derive from the organization's mission and provide criteria for assessing organizational performance in the intermediate, one- to five-year period. Finally each goal can be the basis for specific objectives which are the bases for determining the effectiveness of the organization in the short run.

The development of a coherent set of missions, goals, and objectives defines the scope and direction of the organization's activities. In fact, the development of a set of activities (or means) follows from the prior determination of ends. Planning involves not only the specification of where the organization is going, but how it is to get there. In specific terms, alternatives must be analyzed and evaluated in terms of criteria that follow from the mission, goals, and objectives. And once the determination of appropriate means is completed, the next managerial function must be undertaken, organizing.

Organizing Effective Performance. The organizing function includes *all managerial activities which are taken to translate the required planned activities into a structure of tasks and authority.* In a practical sense, the organizing function involves four subfunctions:

1. *Defining the nature and content of each job in the organization.* The tangible results of this subfunction are job specifications, position descriptions, or task definitions. These documents indicate what is expected of persons holding the job in the way of responsibilities, outcomes, and objectives. In turn, the skills, abilities, and training required to meet the defined expectations are also specified.

2. *Determining the bases for grouping the jobs together.* The essence

of defining jobs is specialization, that is, dividing the work. But once the overall task is subdivided into jobs, they must be put back together in groups, or departments. The managerial decision involves the selection of appropriate bases. For example, all the jobs which require similar machinery may be grouped together, or the manager may decide to group all the jobs according to the product or service they produce.

3. *Deciding the size of the group.* The purpose of grouping jobs is to enable a person to supervise the group's activities. Obviously there is a limit on the number of jobs that one person can supervise, but the precise number will necessarily vary depending upon the situation. For example, one can see that it would be possible to supervise a greater number of similar, simple jobs than dissimilar, complex jobs. But there are other factors which underlie the appropriate *span of control,* such as the competence of the supervisor, the routineness of the group's overall task, the extent of geographic dispersion, and the availability of standardized procedures.

4. *Delegating authority to the assigned manager.* The preceding subfunctions create groups of jobs with defined tasks. It then becomes necessary to determine the extent to which managers of the groups should be able to make decisions and use the resources of the group without higher approval. This right is termed *authority.*

The interrelationships between planning and organizing are apparent. The planning function results in the determination of organizational ends and means; that is, it defines the "whats" and "hows." The organizing function results in the determination of the "whos," that is, *who will do what with whom to achieve the desired end results.* The structure of tasks and authority should facilitate the fulfillment of planned results, but it is apparent that there can be a bad fit between the two. Yet even with the most appropriate fit, the fact that the organization operates in an environment which may change and with people who are unique means that variances between expected and actual outcomes may occur.

Controlling Effective Performance.   The controlling function includes *activities which managers undertake to assure that actual outcomes are consistent with planned outcomes.* Three basic conditions must exist to undertake control.

1. *Standards,* or norms of acceptable outcomes, must be articulated. These standards come from the planning and organizing functions and are reflected in accounting, production, marketing, financial, and budgeting documents. In more specific ways they are reflected in procedures, rules of conduct, professional ethics, and work rules. Standards, therefore, reflect desirable levels of achievement spelled out by criteria of organizational effectiveness.

2. *Information* which compares actual and planned outcomes must be available. Many organizations have developed sophisticated information systems which provide managers with control data. Prime examples are standard cost accounting and quality control systems which modern manufacturing

firms use extensively. In other instances the sources of information may consist of nothing more than supervisors' observations of the behavior of people assigned to their departments.

3. *Corrective action* must be possible. Without the ability to take corrective action, the controlling function has no point or purpose. It becomes an exercise without substance. Corrective action is made possible through the organizing function if managers have been assigned the authority to take action.

Simply stated, managers undertake control to determine *whether* intended results are achieved and if not *why* not. The conclusions managers reach because of their controlling activities are that the planning function was (and is) faulty or that the organizing function was (and is) not faulty, or both. Controlling is, then, the completion of a logical sequence. The activities which comprise controlling include employee selection and placement, materials inspection, performance evaluation, financial statement analysis, and other well-recognized managerial techniques.

The concept of management in terms of the three functions of planning, organizing, and controlling is certainly not complete. There is nothing in this conceptualization which indicates the specific behaviors or activities associated with each function. Nor is there any recognition of the relative importance of these functions for overall organizational effectiveness. The point has been made that these three functions conveniently and adequately define management.

Managerial Work and the Behavior, Structure, and Processes of Organizations

The concept of managerial work which has been developed in the preceding pages can now be brought into perspective. The focus of this text is the *behavior of individuals and groups in organizations.* The purpose of managers in organizations is to achieve coordinated behavior so that an organization is judged effective by those who evaluate its record. To achieve coordinated behavior, managers engage in activities, which are intended to *plan, organize,* and *control* behavior. Major factors in determining individual and group behavior are task and authority relationships; therefore managers must design organizational *structures* and *processes* to facilitate communication among employees.

The intended effect of structure and processes is to predetermine what people will do, with whom they will do it, what decisions they will make, what information they will receive, and when, how, and how often they perform certain actions and make certain decisions. The development of formal structures and processes requires the application of technical-administrative activities primarily, but not exclusively. Certainly it is possible to interact with other managers and nonmanagers in individual and group settings to establish plans, policies, procedures, rules, job descriptions, reporting channels, and lines of authority and communication. Yet the bulk of interpersonal activities occurs in the day-to-day routine as managers relate to others. It is not possible to predetermine completely the behavior of people. Environmental demands change, people change, and managers themselves change.

No matter how formal and circumscribed the manager's job, much leeway exists. Managers must make judgments and these judgments often reflect the manager's own sense of what is right and wrong in the particular situation. This sense of rightness and wrongness reflects values. We believe that a discussion of managing organizational performance is incomplete without a recognition of the important place of values.

MANAGER'S VALUES

Many personal forces will interact to determine the behavior of a person in a managerial role.[11] Perceptions, attitudes, motivations, personality, learning, skills, and abilities are a few of the psychological variables which are important for understanding the behavior of people. They are no less relevant for understanding the behavior of people at work, whether they are managers or nonmanagers. However, here we are interested in examining what may well be the crucial and underlying determinant of behavior—values.

According to an early and influential writer, values are defined "as the constellation of likes, dislikes, viewpoints, shoulds, inner inclinations, rational and irrational judgments, prejudices, and association patterns that determine a person's view of the world."[12] Certainly the work that one does is an important aspect of one's world. Moreover the importance of a value constellation is that once internalized it becomes, consciously or subconsciously, a standard or criterion for guiding one's actions. Thus the study of manager's values is fundamental to the study of managing. Some evidence exists that values are also extremely important for understanding effective managerial behavior.[13]

In recent years a number of studies have been undertaken to discover the values that managers actually espouse. The most influential theory is

[11] The origins, backgrounds, and careers of managers have been the focus of much analysis and study. A sample of the literature would include Roy Lewis and Rosemary Stewart, *The Managers: A New Examination of the English, German and American Executive* (New York: Mentor Books, 1961); William R. Dill, Thomas L. Hilton, and Walter R. Reitman, *The New Managers: Patterns of Behavior and Development* (Englewood Cliffs, N.J.: Prentice-Hall, Inc., 1962); Walter Guzzardi, Jr., *The Young Executives* (New York: Mentor Books, 1966); and Jay W. Lorsch and Louis B. Barnes, *Managers and Their Careers* (Homewood, Ill.: Richard D. Irwin, Inc. and The Dorsey Press, 1972).

[12] Edward Spranger, *Types of Men* (Halle, German: Max Niemeyer Verlag, 1928) as quoted in Vincent S. Flowers et al., *Managerial Values for Working* (New York: American Management Association, 1975), p. 11.

[13] Flowers et al., *Managerial Values,* undertook a questionnaire study of members of the American Management Association. Questionnaires were mailed to 4,998 members and the researchers were able to use 1,707 replies. Based upon these results and other studies, these researchers state that the impact of values on managerial and nonmanagerial behavior is sufficiently important to account for some variation in the relative effectiveness of managers. Also see Andrew F. Sikula, "Values, Value Systems, and Their Relationship to Organizational Effectiveness," *Proceedings of the Thirty-First Annual Meeting of the Academy of Management* 1971, pp. 271–72.

based upon the thinking of Spranger who defined six types of value orientations as shown in Table 3–1. Using a questionnaire which measured the relative importance of each value, Guth and Tagiuri studied the expressed values of 653 executives. The results are shown in Table 3–2 and it is obvious that these managers place a higher value on economic, theoretical, and political ends than religious, aesthetic, and social ones. It should be kept in mind that the scores in Table 3–2 reflect the relative importance of each value; that is, one can increase one value only at the expense of another.

Table 3–1
Six Types of Value Orientation

1. The *theoretical man* is primarily interested in the discovery of truth, in the systematic ordering of his knowledge. In pursuing this goal he typically takes a "cognitive" approach, looking for identities and differences, with relative disregard for the beauty or utility of objects, seeking only to observe and to reason. His interests are empirical, critical, and rational. He is an intellectual. Scientists or philosophers are often of this type.

2. The *economic man* is primarily oriented toward what is useful. He is interested in the practical affairs of the business world; in the production, marketing, and consumption of goods; in the use of economic resources; and in the accumulation of tangible wealth. He is thoroughly "practical" and fits well the stereotype of the American businessman.

3. The *aesthetic man* finds his chief interest in the artistic aspects of life, although he need not be a creative artist. He values form and harmony. He views experience in terms of grace, symmetry, or harmony. Each single event is savored for its own sake.

4. The essential value for the *social man* is love of people—the altruistic or philanthropic aspect of love. The social man values people as ends, and tends to be kind, sympathetic, unselfish. He finds those who have strong theoretical, economic, and aesthetic orientations rather cold. Unlike the political type, the social man regards love as the most important component of human relationships. In its purest form the social orientation is selfless and approaches the religious attitude.

5. The *political man* is characteristically oriented toward power, not necessarily in politics, but in whatever area he functions. Most leaders have a high power orientation. Competition plays a large role in all life, and many writers have regarded power as the most universal motive. For some men, this motive is uppermost, driving them to seek personal power, influence, and recognition.

6. The *religious man* is one "whose mental structure is permanently directed to the creation of the highest and absolutely satisfying value experience." The dominant value for him is unity. He seeks to relate himself to the universe in a meaningful way and has a mystical orientation.

Source: William D. Guth and Renato Tagiuri, "Personal Values and Corporate Strategies," *Harvard Business Review* (September–October 1965), pp. 125–26.

Table 3–2
Value Orientations of a Sample of
American Managers

Value	Score
Economic	45
Theoretical	44
Political	44
Religious	39
Aesthetic	35
Social	33

Source: William T. Guth and Renato Tagiuri, "Personal Values and Corporate Strategies," *Harvard Business Review* (September–October 1965), p. 126.

Whether such choices are, in fact, mutually exclusive is a debatable point. Second, the results are in terms of group averages; individual managers may have responded differently from the group.[14]

The idea that managers as a group tend to emphasize the importance of economic, or practical, ends is intuitively appealing, particularly if it is business management that is the focus of attention. After all, the theory and research of the managerial process suggests that persons with such values would be compatible with it. Additional support is available in the studies of George W. England.[15] Consistent with the findings of others, his results bore out the relative importance of pragmatic values as descriptive of business managers. A follow-up study of England's results some seven years later found that managers' values had not shifted.[16] The researchers stated that the stability of this value orientation among managers could be accounted for by the fact that managers self-select their jobs or are selected by others having similar values, that the job of managing reinforces the pragmatic orientation, and that values are inherently stable over time.

The Importance of Values

The value orientations of managers underlie managerial behavior. How managers go about planning, organizing, and controlling the behavior of individuals, groups, and organizations necessarily reflects and must be compatible with their values. From the selection of missions, goals, and objectives to the evaluation of progress toward those ends, values will be pervasive.

---

[14] For a complete discussion see William T. Guth and Renato Tagiuri, "Personal Values and Corporate Strategies," *Harvard Business Review* (September–October 1965), pp. 123–32.

[15] George W. England, "Personal Value Systems of American Managers," *Academy of Management Journal* (March 1967), pp. 53–68.

[16] Edward J. Lick and Bruce L. Oliver, "American Managers' Personal Value Systems—Revisited," *Academy of Management Journal* (September 1974), pp. 549–54.

American managers view the goals of profit, efficiency, and productivity to be of primary importance, followed by goals which reflect growth and stability. Ranked in third and fourth positions are goals which reflect employee welfare and social and community interests.[17] These goals were found to prevail among managers included in a survey of subscribers to the *Harvard Business Review,* an important periodical in the field of management.[18] The responsibility for interpreting society's expectations for its organizations is largely that of managers. The relative importance they attach to the competing interests of various groups who make their expectations known will be based in part upon what managers think is the right thing to do, and that is a matter of values.

Values will affect not only the perceptions of appropriate ends, but also the perceptions of appropriate means to those ends. From the design and development of organization structures and processes, to the utilization of particular leadership styles and the evaluation of subordinate performance, value systems will be pervasive. An influential theory of leadership is based upon the argument that managers cannot be expected to adopt a particular leadership style if it is contrary to their "need-structures," or value orientations.[19] Moreover, when managers evaluate the performance of subordinates, the effects of their values will be noticeable. For example, one researcher reports that managers can be expected to evaluate the performance of subordinates with similar values as more effective than those with values dissimilar from their own.[20] The impact of values will be more pronounced in those decisions involving little objective information and, consequently, a greater degree of subjectivity.

Another aspect of the importance of values occurs when the interpersonal activities of managers bring them into a confrontation with different, and potentially contradictory, values. Studies have shown that assembly-line workers, scientists, and various professional occupations are characterized by particular, if not unique, value orientations.[21] Day-to-day activities will create numerous situations in which managers must relate to others having different views of what is right and wrong. Conflicts between managers and workers, administrators and teachers, line and staff personnel have been documented and

---

[17] George W. England, "Organizational Goals and Expected Behavior of American Managers," *Academy of Management Journal* (June 1967), pp. 658–69.

[18] Rama Krishman, "Business Philosophy and Executive Responsibility," *Academy of Management Journal* (December 1973), pp. 658–69.

[19] Fred E. Fiedler, *A Theory of Leadership Effectiveness* (New York: McGraw-Hill Book Co., 1967).

[20] John Senger, "Managers' Perceptions of Subordinates' Competence as a Function of Personal Value Orientations," *Academy of Management Journal* (December 1971), pp. 415–24.

[21] For example, see Flowers et al., *Managerial Values,* and also Renato Tagiuri, "Value Orientations and Relationships of Managers and Scientists," *Administrative Science Quarterly* (June 1965), pp. 39–51.

discussed in the literature of management. The manner in which these conflicts are resolved is particularly crucial to the effectiveness of the organization.[22]

Values and the Managers of Tomorrow

Many readers of this book are not now managers. No doubt many have had experience in managing clubs, sororities, fraternities, and other school-oriented organizations. Others may have had part- or full-time employment in jobs requiring some degree of managerial work. But the purpose for which many are reading this book is to acquire a basis for a career in management. The question that this raises is the extent to which the values of today's young people are compatible with those of today's managers. If young people have values which conflict with the demands of managerial work, will they change their values to conform with their work, or will they change their work to conform with their values?

Some recent studies of the values of college students indicate the potential for conflict.[23] There is the suggestion that today's students, similar to today's managers, stress pragmatic and practical values; but unlike managers they would prefer to achieve their ends through their own efforts, not the efforts of others. That is, they would prefer to do it themselves, rather than have others do it. This orientation conflicts with the very essence of management—coordinating the work of others. Perhaps the students who hold such values most strongly will not seek careers in organizations, but rather become the entrepreneurs of tomorrow.

Other basic differences have been noted. Many students espouse social and humanistic values. They appear to be more concerned with what is good for society rather than what is good for self, or the organization that employs them. They believe that organizations, whether in business, education, government, or health care, should take on more socially-oriented goals than they have pursued historically. Business organizations are expected to deal with the social costs of production—pollution and unemployment. Educational institutions are expected to provide remedial programs for culturally-deprived groups. Government is expected to become even more involved with social welfare; hospitals are expected to provide care for all, even those

---

[22] In recent years the increasing tendency of American firms to use foreign nationals to manage overseas offices has created a concern for understanding the impact of culture on managers' values. See William T. Whitely and George W. England, "A Comparison of Value Systems of Managers in the U.S.A., Japan, Korea, India, and Australia," *Proceedings of the Thirty-Fourth Annual Meeting of the Academy of Management* 1974, p. 11; and Richard B. Peterson, "A Cross-Cultural Perspective of Supervisory Values," *Academy of Management Journal* (March 1972), pp. 105–17.

[23] D. A. Ondrack, "Emerging Occupational Values: A Review and Some Findings," *Academy of Management Journal* (September 1973), pp. 423–32; Donald N. Deslava and Gary R. Gemmill, "An Exploratory Study of the Personal Value Systems of College Students and Managers," *Academy of Management Journal* (June 1971), pp. 227–38; and John S. Fielden, "Today the Campuses, Tomorrow the Corporations," *Business Horizons* (June 1970), pp. 13–29.

who cannot pay. These values were expressed in quite vocal ways during the 60s, and even though the campuses are quieter and more subdued today, there is no reason to believe that the basic values have changed.

How then will the managerial process be affected by the values of the younger generation? The basic functions will no doubt remain unchanged, but the form of the activities undertaken to accomplish them may in fact change. The theory and research of the behavioral sciences emphasize the importance of interpersonal activities and the significance of enlightened understanding of individual, group, and leadership behavior; the prevailing values reinforce that importance and add to it. There will no doubt be considerable diversity in managerial behavior, differences which take into account the values of managers and those of nonmanagers. One recent study indicates the coexistence of a number of different value orientations among contemporary managers; and for each value system there are different ways to go about such traditional managerial activities as reviewing performance, communicating, and counseling.[24] Contemporary organizations appear to be able to accommodate different values among managers. There is no reason to believe that they will be less able to do so in the future.

SUMMARY

Concepts of organizational effectiveness and managerial process have been developed in this chapter. The concepts depicted in Figure 3–3 emphasize the need for balanced perspectives, yet they allow for the identification of differences from manager to manager and from organization to organization. An overriding consideration that is documented in many studies of managerial work is that the managerial process is inherently a human process—people relating to people. The recognition of this fact does not deemphasize the importance of technical-administrative activities, but it does establish the importance of understanding human behavior in the workplace. The behavior of individuals and groups is principally important for achieving effective organizational performance, but there is also the behavior of managers themselves to be understood.

Only one, but potentially the most important, determinant of managerial behavior has been discussed—values. The value orientations of managers and the demands of managers' jobs interact and affect the manner in which the managerial process is carried out. The demands are, in turn, the consequences of intra- and extraorganizational factors. Differences in the way managers undertake the managerial process result from differences in values and environmental demands.

This chapter also provides the basis for evaluating managerial practice. Managerial techniques such as motion and time study, work standards, network communications, participative leadership, job enlargement, management by objectives, and sensitivity training are all directed toward improving

---

[24] Flowers et al., *Managerial Values*, p. 41.

effectiveness. But to understand the impact of these techniques, one must evaluate the effectiveness criteria used to judge those techniques. Some techniques affect the short-run criteria of production, satisfaction, and efficiency; others affect the longer-run criteria of adaptiveness and development. Furthermore, as the impact of a managerial technique becomes more distant in the future, the measures of its effectiveness become more subjective, general, and qualitative. It is simply easier to know, and to know concretely the effect of a piece-rate program on production than it is to know the effect of leadership training on adaptiveness or development.

DISCUSSION AND REVIEW QUESTIONS

1. Can the evaluation of the effectiveness of an organization ever be made in absolute terms? Or is it always necessary to state effectiveness criteria in relative terms? Explain and give examples to support your argument.

2. Is the distinction between short-run, intermediate, and long-run criteria meaningful for evaluating the effectiveness of a college course? Explain.

3. "An organization is effective if its employees believe that it is." Discuss.

4. If you were a training director responsible for instructing first-line supervisors in the techniques of supervision, how would you evaluate the effectiveness of your training program?

5. "Effectiveness criteria are relevant only in terms of the evaluator. For example, the state legislators look for some things, the federal people look for other things. I give each group whatever it wants." Comment on this statement which was made by the administrator of a state governmental agency.

6. Explain why effectiveness criteria of subunits tend to emphasize the short run rather than the long run.

7. How would you evaluate the effectiveness of contemporary American society in terms of production, efficiency, satisfaction, adaptiveness, and development? Rate each criterion on a five-point scale and compare your evaluation with that of other classmates.

8. One writer on management theory states that management is aptly defined as "getting work done through other people." Compare this concept of management with the one proposed in this chapter.

9. Based upon your own experiences with college students of today, discuss whether you believe that a gap exists between their and business managers' value orientations.

10. Describe the process by which society makes known its expectations for the missions of universities. Based upon your knowledge of the university or college you attend, how satisfactorily is it achieving its mission?

11. A public official with a talent for simplifying matters stated: "Planning is concerned with doing the right things, organizing is concerned with doing things right." Comment.

12. Can an organization go out of business even if its management is proficient in the performance of the managerial process?

13. Explain the important differences between managing an investment fund and managing an organization.

ADDITIONAL REFERENCES

Barnard, C. I. *The Functions of the Executive.* Cambridge, Mass.: Harvard University Press, 1938.

Burns, T. "Management in Action." *Operations Research Quarterly* (1957), pp. 45–60.

Connors, E. J., and Hutts, J. C. "How Administrators Spend Their Time." *Hospitals* (1967), pp. 45–50.

Deniston, O. L., and Rosenstock, I. M. "Evaluating Health Programs." *Public Health Reports* (1970), pp. 835–40.

Drucker, P. *Management: Tasks, Responsibilities, Practices.* New York: Harper & Row, 1974.

Dubin, R., and Spray, S. L. "Executive Behavior and Interaction." *Industrial Relations* (1964), pp. 99–108.

England, G. W.; Dhingra, O. P.; and Agarwal, N. C. *The Manager and the Man: A Cross-Cultural Study of Personal Values.* Kent, Ohio: Kent State University Press, 1974.

Flanagan, J. C. "Defining the Requirements of the Executive's Job." *Personnel* (1951), pp. 28–35.

Georgopoulos, B. S., and Mann, F. C. *The Community General Hospital.* New York: Macmillan, 1967.

Greenburg, L. *A Practical Guide to Productivity Management.* Washington, D.C.: The Bureau of National Affairs, Inc., 1973.

Grusky, O. "Managerial Succession and Organizational Effectiveness." *American Journal of Sociology* (1963), pp. 21–30.

Hemphill, J. K. "Job Descriptions for Executives." *Harvard Business Review* (1959), pp. 55–67.

Jones, H. R. "A Study of Organizational Performance for Experimental Structures of Two, Three, and Four Levels." *Academy of Management Journal* (1969), pp. 351–66.

Katz, D., and Kahn, R. L. *The Social Psychology of Organizations.* New York: John Wiley & Sons, 1966.

Kay, B. R. "Key Factors in Effective Foreman Behavior." *Personnel* (1959), pp. 25–31.

Kay, E., and Meyer, H. H. "The Development of a Job Activity Questionnaire for Production Foremen." *Personnel Psychology* (1962), pp. 411–18.

Koontz, H. *Toward a Unified Theory of Management.* New York: McGraw-Hill Book Company, Inc., 1964.

McGregor, D. *The Human Side of Enterprise.* New York: McGraw-Hill Book Company, Inc., 1960.

McGuire, J. W., ed. *Contemporary Management: Issues and Viewpoints.* Englewood Cliffs, N.J.: Prentice-Hall, Inc., 1974.

Mahoney, T. A. "Managerial Perceptions of Organizational Effectiveness." *Management Science* (1967), pp. 76–91.

Mahoney, T. A., and Weitzel, W. "Managerial Models of Organizational Effectiveness." *Administrative Science Quarterly* (1969), pp. 357–65.

Miner, J. B. *Management Theory.* New York: The Macmillan Co., 1971.

Neuhauser, D. *The Relationship Between Administrative Activities and Hospital Performance.* Chicago: University of Chicago Center for Health Administrative Studies, 1971.

O'Neill, H. E., and Kubany, A. J. "Observation Methodology and Supervisory Behavior." *Personnel Psychology* (1959), pp. 85–96.

Ponder, Q. "Supervisory Practices of Effective and Ineffective Foremen." Unpublished Ph.D. Dissertation, Columbia University, 1958.

Price, J. L. "The Study of Organizational Effectiveness." *The Sociological Quarterly* (1972), pp. 3–15.

"Report of the Committee on Non-Financial Measures of Effectiveness." *The Accounting Review* (1971), pp. 165–211.

Rice, A. K. *The Enterprise and Its Environment: A System Theory of Management Organization.* London: Tavistock Publications, 1963.

Urwick, L. F. *The Pattern of Management.* Minneapolis: University of Minnesota Press, 1956.

Weaver, J. L. *Conflict and Control in Health-Care Administration.* Beverly Hills, Calif.: Sage Publications, 1975.

Webb, R. J. "Organizational Effectiveness and the Voluntary Organization." *Academy of Management Journal* (1974), 663–77.

Yuchtman, E., and Seashore, S. E. "A Systems Resource Approach to Organizational Effectiveness." *American Sociological Review* (1967), pp. 891–903.

CASES FOR ANALYSIS

EFFECTIVENESS OF A FAMILY PLANNING PROGRAM

The Director of the State-Wide Coordinating Unit for Family Planning Services had recently requested a private management consulting firm to evaluate the state's programs in family planning. The director reported to the governor and recommended funding levels for the various state agencies engaged in family planning. In anticipation of difficulties to be faced in the upcoming legislature during a period of economic decline, falling tax revenues, and general skepticism of all social programs, the director had engaged the consulting firm to provide him with information which he could use in making his case to the governor and the legislature.

The family planning programs of the state were carried on by many private and public agencies. Because the problems addressed by family planning programs had social, economic, and health-related consequences, many different agencies had legitimate interests in solving them. But, at the same time, the multiagency approach led to administrative and operational problems which had created the necessity for the coordinating unit.

The report of the consulting firm was lengthy; its highlights were as follows:

1. The central fact emerging from this review of family planning programs is that no statewide policy exists to explicitly set forth the objectives of the program. The executive and legislative branches have not provided a positive guide to those responsible for administering family planning programs. In fact, an important part of the written policy that exists is essentially a negative guide, such as: (1) local school districts may *not* teach information with regard to birth control devices, and (2) abortions may *not* be performed unless the life of the mother is threatened.

2. The Departments of Social Services and Public Health share responsibility for administering family planning funds. The Department of Social Services (DSS) has thus far not produced a rationale for its involvement in the program. By contrast, the Department of Public Health (DPH) has recently taken steps toward the development of such a plan. Tardy initiation of a plan is preferable to the abdication of responsibility implicit in the DSS citation of federal requirements as the major reason for providing family planning services to its clients.

3. Local health departments are almost totally free to set their own priorities in deciding not only *if* they want to participate in a family planning program, but *how* they shall participate. The program content of one local family planning program may consist of leaflets on a table, contrasting with a neighboring local health department that may have a nurse-social worker family planning team that virtually greets a new mother outside the delivery room.

4. The social, economic, and medical bases for the programs have been largely ignored by the state agencies. It is virtually impossible to find any analytical statement of family planning-related problems prepared by a state department. Problem statements prepared by the Department of Public Health center around management problems, as opposed to health or social problems. Without this kind of analysis of the problem, objectives also tend to be unanalyzed. As a result, many of the objectives stated in connection with family planning

programs turn out, upon closer inspection, to be nearly meaningless, and certainly unmeasurable. This is especially true of "objectives" regarding "unwanted children" and "freedom of choice." These kinds of objectives may, in fact, be valid. But unless they are translated into more precise terms, they remain only unanalyzed abstractions, which are useless for determinations of effectiveness or as guides to program management.

5. Thus, elected state officials have not supplied a clear policy to guide the administration of publicly supported family planning programs. Further, state agencies have not set forth clear family planning program objectives. Finally, adequate measures do not exist for judging attainment of the objectives which do exist for family planning programs. Therefore, citizens have little opportunity to hold their elected and appointed officials accountable for the resources expended.

The director was disheartened by the report. It certainly did not provide the bases for making a strong plea for additional funding; in fact he became even more concerned that the funding would be reduced. He acknowledged the accurateness of the report's basic findings; he had known for some time that the programs suffered from the defects noted in the report. But at the same time he believed that the programs had made some impact on the problems which they sought to remove. Yet the consultants remained adamant in their position that "you cannot determine effectiveness if you don't have objectives."

Questions for Consideration

1. Do you agree with the point of view expressed in this report? How would you have evaluated the family planning programs?
2. What criteria would you use to measure the effectiveness of a family planning program?
3. What other bases than the consultants' report will the director be able to offer in justification for the continuation of family planning?

COMPATIBLE VALUE ORIENTATIONS*

The Jason Manufacturing Company had for some time used a form of the "buddy system" in its management trainee program. The system involved assigning trainees, ordinarily young college graduates, to senior managers who would work closely with them over a period of six months. During that time the trainees would learn to practice management the way in which it was expected at Jason.

---

* This case is based upon the discussion and supporting exhibits in Vincent S. Flowers et al., *Managerial Values for Working* (New York: AMACOM, 1975), pp. 39–43.

The relationship between the trainees and their mentors was expected to be very informal and supportive, but at the same time the senior managers were required to evaluate the trainees' performance at the end of the third and six months. The initial assignments of trainees to managers was based upon the trainees expressed career orientations. Thus they could be assigned to any one of the several functions of the business—production, finance, marketing, engineering, personnel.

This approach did not always work out to the mutual satisfaction of everyone concerned. Some trainees requested transfers prior to the completion of their six months training; others quit the company. And on several occasions the senior managers requested the management development officer to reassign them to other trainees. The usual explanation for these requests by both the trainees and the managers was that they simply didn't get along with each other. Terms such as "personality clash" and "mismatch" were often used to describe the problem. The management development officer had for some time recognized that it was important to try to assign the trainees to managers with whom they would be compatible, but had never been able to develop a systematic way of doing it.

After experiencing a particularly unsuccessful training attempt, one that was marred by the resignation of over half the trainees and even two senior managers, the management development staff was instructed to devise a more systematic assignment process. After researching the literature, the staff settled on using an approach which attempted to match compatible value orientations. That is, they would obtain indications of both trainees' and managers' beliefs about the two critical aspects of the training experience—performance review and communications—and then try to match them in the assignment process.

Exhibit 1
Value Orientations of the Senior Management Group

Value Category	Orientation toward Performance Review	Orientation toward Communication
1	I should work with the trainees in setting goals and reviewing progress.	I should discuss things informally with them, and give them any information they want.
2	I should try to review their performance without hurting their feelings.	I should try to be on good terms with them so they will feel free to discuss anything with me.
3	I believe that the carrot and stick approach works the best.	I should give them the information I think they need to get their job done.
4	I should define the goals and standards that I expect them to follow.	I should give them the information they need and keep our relations businesslike.
5	I should make it clear what they have to do to retain their jobs.	I should tell them only what I feel like telling them.

Source: Based upon Vincent S. Flowers et al., *Managerial Values for Working* (New York: AMACON, 1975), p. 41, Exhibit 25.

Exhibit 2
Value Orientations of the Management Trainee Group

Value Category	Orientation toward Performance Review	Orientation toward Communication
1	I don't believe anyone should find fault with me or tell me how to act.	The less I hear from a boss, the better I like it.
2	I should be informed of the company's goals and how I can contribute to achieving them.	I should be told what I am supposed to know to do my job properly.
3	I believe that I should set my own goals and be recognized for achieving them.	I should know everything my boss knows if I am to do a good job.
4	The boss should use the performance-review to get better acquainted with me.	I believe a boss should be easy to talk to and interested in me personally.
5	I believe that I should have a major role in defining my goals and methods for achieving them.	I believe that I should be free to talk to anyone and to get any information I want.

Source: Based upon Vincent S. Flowers et al., *Managerial Values for Working* (New York: AMACON, 1975), p. 41, Exhibit 25.

The staff began collecting information from trainees and managers. The information was obtained primarily by using questionnaires which measured and differentiated value orientations. At the end of an extensive study, the staff proposed that the values of the two groups with respect to performance review and communications could be classified into five categories. Exhibit 1 describes the five categories for the senior management group in terms of statements regarding performance review and communications; Exhibit 2 shows the same information for the trainees.

The management development officer took the report of the staff to a meeting of top management. He proposed that the next group of trainees be assigned to managers whose values were compatible with the trainees.

Questions for Consideration

1. How would you match up the five value categories of managers with the five categories of trainees? Is, for example, category 4 of the managers compatible with category 1 of the trainees?

2. How would you evaluate the relative effectiveness of this approach to assigning trainees to managers?

3. If this approach proves successful for matching trainees and managers, couldn't it be used to assign employees generally to a manager? Explain.

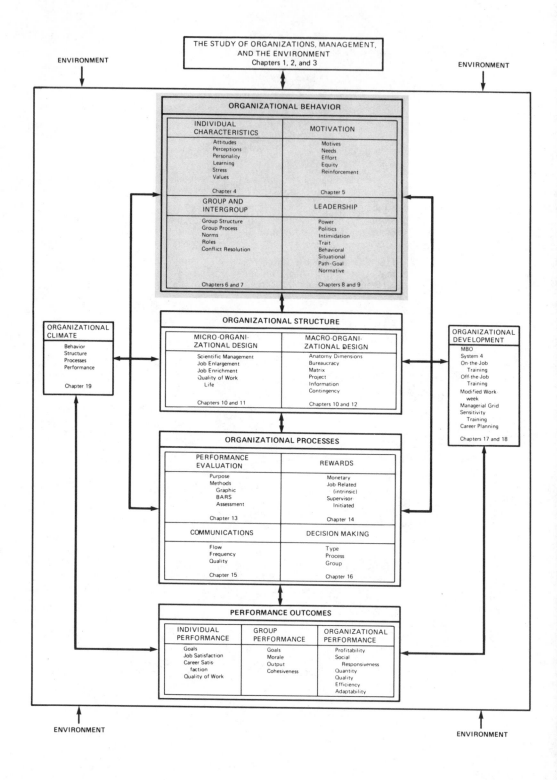

ENVIRONMENT

ENVIRONMENT

THE STUDY OF ORGANIZATIONS, MANAGEMENT,
AND THE ENVIRONMENT
Chapters 1, 2, and 3

ORGANIZATIONAL BEHAVIOR

INDIVIDUAL CHARACTERISTICS	MOTIVATION
Attitudes	Motives
Perceptions	Needs
Personality	Effort
Learning	Equity
Stress	Reinforcement
Values	
Chapter 4	Chapter 5

GROUP AND INTERGROUP	LEADERSHIP
Group Structure	Power
Group Process	Politics
Norms	Intimidation
Roles	Trait
Conflict Resolution	Behavioral
	Situational
	Path-Goal
	Normative
Chapters 6 and 7	Chapters 8 and 9

ORGANIZATIONAL
CLIMATE

Behavior
Structure
Processes
Performance

Chapter 19

ORGANIZATIONAL STRUCTURE

MICRO-ORGANI- ZATIONAL DESIGN	MACRO-ORGANI- ZATIONAL DESIGN
Scientific Management	Anatomy Dimensions
Job Enlargement	Bureaucracy
Job Enrichment	Matrix
Quality of Work	Project
Life	Information
	Contingency
Chapters 10 and 11	Chapters 10 and 12

ORGANIZATIONAL
DEVELOPMENT

MBO
System 4
On-the-Job
 Training
Off-the-Job
 Training
Modified Work
 week
Managerial Grid
Sensitivity
 Training
Career Planning

Chapters 17 and 18

ORGANIZATIONAL PROCESSES

PERFORMANCE EVALUATION	REWARDS
Purpose	Monetary
Methods	Job Related
Graphic	(intrinsic)
BARS	Supervisor-
Assessment	Initiated
Chapter 13	Chapter 14

COMMUNICATIONS	DECISION MAKING
Flow	Type
Frequency	Process
Quality	Group
Chapter 15	Chapter 16

PERFORMANCE OUTCOMES

INDIVIDUAL PERFORMANCE	GROUP PERFORMANCE	ORGANIZATIONAL PERFORMANCE
Goals	Goals	Profitability
Job Satisfaction	Morale	Social
Career Satis-	Output	Responsiveness
faction	Cohesiveness	Quantity
Quality of Work		Quality
		Efficiency
		Adaptability

ENVIRONMENT

ENVIRONMENT

Part Two

Behavior within Organizations

Chapter 4

Individual Characteristics, Behavior, and Stress

AN ORGANIZATIONAL ISSUE FOR DEBATE
Avoiding Stress and Remaining Healthy

ARGUMENT FOR

It has long been a common opinion that prolonged strain resulting from job stress can make individuals sick. Medical researchers have collected some evidence that job related stress can be and is a contributor to chronic illnesses such as heart disease and peptic ulcers. Managers being bombarded by stress producing job demands, and nonmanagers being prodded by restrictive managers, may eventually become statistics in reports on coronary heart disease or other illnesses. Thus, some advice being offered is that stressful jobs or hard-charging life styles should be avoided.

The hard-driving, competitive perfectionist who is valued by organizations is considered a prime candidate for an early coronary. If not a coronary, it may be migraines, ulcers, asthma, ulcerative colitis, or even adult acne. The hard charger has been called a Type A personality. He (usually a male) marches to a "drummer" who requires winning at all costs. Individuals differ in their style of working with others and performing on the job. The Type A style is to wade in, do the job, enjoy the taste of success, and move on to the next challenge. This "racehorse" style will mean that the Type A has a one in five chance of having a heart attack before reaching his sixtieth birthday. The message here is that avoiding stress means that life can be prolonged.

ARGUMENT AGAINST

Unfortunately, there is a great deal of confusion about what stress is and how individuals deal with it. We hear a great deal about the dangers of the Type A personality. However, others claim that the "racehorse" can't be a "turtle" without suffering anxiety and stress. Individual differences must be considered when discussing stress and how people react to it. It would be far more stressful for many Type A's to change their style than to continue being a hard-charger.

There is also some concern over the practice of classifying individuals as Type A, Type B, Type Z, or whatever. Can we be sure that the measurements or inventories being used are accurate? Hans Selye, a leading medical authority on stress, believes that all the stress inventories used to classify respondents are flawed because they fail to give enough weight to individual differences.* He states that each individual is really the best judge of his/her stress threshold. Instead of using an inventory to detect stress tolerance or conditions, each person should be the judge. Self-awareness is the best way to deal with stress conditions. The Type A may know without a doubt that he/she is a hardcharger, competitive, and a perfectionist. This person may also know how healthy he or she feels physically and psychologically. There are just some individuals who need stress, long hours, and a lot of work pressure. Instead of stating that Type A is bad, it is more accurate to state that some people are not suited to be Type A's.

* Hans Selye, "On The Benefits of Eustress," *Psychology Today* (March 1978), p. 63.

61

INTRODUCTION

Any attempt to learn why people behave as they do in organizations requires some understanding about individual characteristics and behavior. Managers planning and organizing work, or controlling and directing individuals must spend time making judgments about the fit between individuals, job tasks, and effectiveness. These judgments typically are influenced by the manager's, as well as the subordinate's, individualistic characteristics. Making decisions about who will perform what tasks in a particular manner without some understanding of people is dangerous and can lead to irreversible long run consequences.

This chapter focuses on four major individual characteristics that influence organizational effectiveness. These are perception, attitudes, personality, and learning. Each of these factors influences the behavioral patterns of managers and their subordinates. Managers as well as subordinates perceive people and objects, form attitudes about others or the organization, have a personality structure, and learn while working. In addition, employees at all levels of the organization experience some degree of job related stress. Thus, effective management includes understanding the four major individual characteristics as well as being familiar with the relationship between job stress and job performance.

Individuals join organizations at different ages, from varying cultural backgrounds, with various skills, and at different points in their careers. One person may become a member of the organization at age 19, while another joins at age 46. One person may be a black from Chicago's South Side, while another may be the son of a Kansas farmer. One person may be a skilled machinist, while another may want to *become* a skilled machinist. One person may join at the lowest skill-level job, while another joins the organization as a vice-president. One individual may find the job very stressful, while another may be motivated by the stresses of the job.

The differences among people require forms of adjustment for the individual and those with whom he or she will work. Managers who ignore individual differences often become involved in practices which hinder achieving organizational goals and personal goals.

A FRAMEWORK FOR ANALYZING
INDIVIDUAL DIFFERENCES

The ability to deal with and cope effectively with individuals in work organizations requires a framework for understanding behavior. A framework provides a basis for considering why individuals behave as they do. No framework can provide perfect answers and predictions. However, a systematic and logical framework can initiate thinking about what to look for when attempting to understand performance differences among individual employees.

The analysis of individual behavior requires a consideration of the types of variables shown in Figure 4–1. An examination of Figure 4–1 suggests that people enter organizations with these variables in various states of devel-

Figure 4–1
Some Variables That Influence Behavior

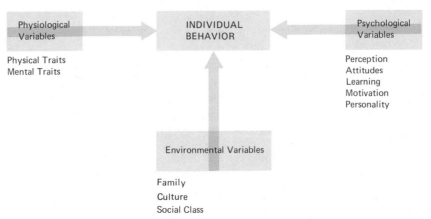

Physiological Variables → INDIVIDUAL BEHAVIOR ← Psychological Variables

Physical Traits
Mental Traits

Perception
Attitudes
Learning
Motivation
Personality

Environmental Variables

Family
Culture
Social Class

opment. Behavior is anything that an employee does. Talking, completing a job, daydreaming, reporting late to work, or anything that can be observed is considered behavior. Many behavior patterns of people have been developed before they join an organization. Whether managers can modify, mold, or reconstruct behaviors is a much debated issue among behavioral scientists and practitioners. It is usually agreed that changing any of the psychological variables requires time and a thorough program of diagnosis, implementation, evaluation, and modification. There is no universally agreed-upon method that can change personalities, attitudes, perceptions, or learning patterns. People are always changing, although slightly, their behavior patterns. It is the direction and kind of behavior change that managers want to influence. A manager who can or who has encouraged positive behaviors such as excellent job performance, promptness in reporting to work, and willingness to help train and develop new employees is usually considered to be successful in an organizational context.

Models of Behavior

Numerous models exist to help explain the various behaviors of individuals in home, work, and leisure situations. These models have been used to aid in the prediction of behavior. Most of the models present a dichotomy of views to explain differences in individuals.

Economic People and Self-Actualizing People. Classical management theorists such as Frederick W. Taylor conceptualized employees primarily in economic terms. They viewed the workers' primary goal as economic betterment. Workers would produce more and better output if they could increase their incomes through these actions. This model of the employee corresponded well with the principle of specialization. The creation of routine, limited jobs would raise efficiency and maximize economic benefits.

The antithesis of the concept of the economic person is that of the self-actualizing person. Psychologists such as McClelland, Herzberg, and Maslow assume that many people are motivated by the opportunity to self-actualize— that is, to grow and mature. Maslow summarizes the notion that a person strives for self-actualization in the following manner:

> Even if all these [lower-level] needs are satisfied we still may often (if not always) expect that a new discontent and restlessness will soon develop, unless the individual is doing what he is fitted for. A musician must make music, an artist must paint, a poet must write, if he is to be ultimately happy. What it is man can be, he must be. This need we call self-actualization. . . . [Self-actualization] refers to the desire for self-fulfillment, namely, to the tendency for one to become actualized in what one is potentially. This tendency might be phrased as the desire to become more and more what one is, to become everything that one is capable of becoming.[1]

A manager who accepts the economic view of people and attempts to enable workers to accomplish economic goals would probably act differently than one who attempts to aid them in self-actualizing. We are not assuming that either viewpoint is correct. We are only pointing to potential differences in managerial behavior which could follow from these two divergent views.

Behavioristic and Phenomenologic Views of People.   There are some theorists who assume that people can be understood solely in terms of *behavior.* In essence the view holds that all human behavior is environmentally controlled. This is the view advocated by B. F. Skinner.[2]

The *phenomenologic* view of people stresses that humans can be analyzed and described in terms of consciousness and uniqueness. Man is viewed as rational in terms of behavior, attitudes, and personality.[3] From a phenomenological perspective, management must somehow get "inside" the head of an employee to understand the behavior of that person. In an extreme sense the purely scientific understanding of employees cannot be observed by a manager because what a manager perceives is only a partial representation of the person.

Theory X and Theory Y.   One of the most influential models of people was developed by McGregor.[4] This model contrasts two views of man in work situations, termed Theory X and Theory Y. According to *Theory X:*

> The average person has an inherent dislike of work and will try to avoid it when possible.
>
> The average person lacks ambition, dislikes job responsibilities, and prefers to be closely directed.
>
> The average person is by nature self-centered and indifferent to overall organizational goal achievement.

---

[1] Abraham H. Maslow, "A Theory of Human Motivation," *Psychological Review* (July 1943), pp. 370–96.

[2] B. F. Skinner, *Beyond Freedom and Dignity* (New York: Alfred A. Knopf, 1971).

[3] W. D. Hitt, "Two Models of Man," *American Psychologist* (July 1969), pp. 651–58.

[4] Douglas McGregor, *The Human Side of Enterprise* (New York: McGraw-Hill Book Co., 1960).

The average person is resistant to change.

The average person desires job security and economic rewards above all else.

In contrast *Theory Y* assumes:

The average person is not by nature passive or resistant to the organization's needs.

Economic benefits and job security are only two of the possible rewards desired by the average person. In fact the average person is committed to goals that will enable him or her to self-actualize.

The average person learns, under rewarding conditions, to seek and accept job responsibilities.

The average person wants to exercise autonomy and creativity to aid in his or her own growth and the accomplishment of organizational goals.

These two opposing views of people can obviously result in diametrically different managerial practices.

It seems reasonable to say that each of these three dichotomous models has some validity. There certainly are some employees who want to work 40 hours a week or less, collect a pay check every Friday, and forget the "job grind" at 5:00 P.M. There are other people who want more from a job than a paycheck. They may want to create, interact with others socially, and utilize their skills to a maximum degree. Some people are lazy, while others are self-starters and high achievers.

Obviously human behavior is too complex to be explained by a generalization that applies to all people. Some of the relevant variables which influence human behavior are presented in Figure 4–1. Coverage of each of the variables presented in this figure is beyond the scope of the book. The psychological variables will be covered, however, because they form the foundation for our discussion of motivation, group behavior, and leadership.

INDIVIDUAL DIFFERENCES

In the field of industrial psychology there is little doubt that understanding individual differences is of major importance in understanding employee behavior and performance. Obviously each person is unique and responds to organizational policies, programs, requests, and commands in a particular manner. Some people like routine work, while others prefer challenging tasks; some like total autonomy and decision-making latitude, while others become frustrated when faced with making a decision; some prefer promotional opportunities, while others thrive on wage or salary increases. Effective managerial practice requires that individual differences be recognized and when feasible taken into consideration when designing jobs, conducting performance evaluation interviews, or developing reward strategies to encourage improved performance.

In addition to understanding individual differences, it is necessary to (1) measure the differences, (2) study relationships between variables, and (3) discover causal relationships.[5] Being able to predict behavior and performance is a goal of management in any type of organizational setting. However, prediction is possible without understanding. It is possible to predict accurately that an employee will resist the introduction of new equipment or a new performance evaluation program. These accurate predictions tell little about why the behavior occurred or how the behavior can be altered.

Some researchers believe that many issues concerning individual differences are not being addressed by managers. In a series of observational studies of different groups performing different tasks, the "typical" interpersonal relationships formed a pattern which was described as individuals tending to express their ideas in ways that supported the norm of conformity. There was almost no experimenting with ideas and feelings, and also no trust observed in the groups. Individual differences in creativity, understanding, influence, and problem solving ability tended to be smothered.[6] This finding underlines the relevance of studying individual differences to better understand how people interact within the work environment.

How an employee responds to stimuli such as work group norms, job design, leadership style, or technology in the organizational environment depends upon what we are referring to as individual characteristics. These characteristics can and often do differ. Such characteristics as knowledge, skill, needs, goals, past experiences, and attitudes will have some bearing on behavior and performance. The individual characteristics that are used in our model of behavior are categorized as physiological, environmental, and psychological.

Some specific key factors which account for individual differences in behavior include perception, attitudes, personality, and learning. In Figure 4–2 a model of behavior which includes these factors is presented. The model is assumed to be similar in many respects for all employees, both managerial and nonmanagerial. The particular behavior which develops is certainly

Figure 4–2
A Model of Behavior

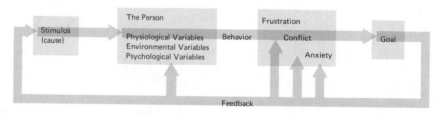

[5] C. Argyris, "Problems and New Directions for Industrial Psychology," in M. D. Dunnette, ed., *Handbook of Industrial and Organizational Psychology* (Chicago: Rand McNally, 1976), p. 153.

[6] C. Argyris, "The Incompleteness of Social-Psychological Theory," *American Psychologist* (December 1964), pp. 893–908.

unique for each person, but the underlying process is basic to all people. The model makes four important assumptions about individual behavior:[7]

1. *Behavior* is caused.
2. *Behavior* is goal directed.
3. *Behavior* toward goals can be disrupted by frustration, conflict, and anxiety.
4. *Behavior* is motivated.

Frustration, conflict, and anxiety are important factors in this model. Anything that interferes with goal-directed behavior causes *frustration.* Each of us knows from first-hand experience that frustration is often encountered in school, work, and family life. Frustration may result from a lack of time to study for an examination or from the lack of a technical skill which is needed for a desirable promotion or increase in salary. Frustrations can also be the result of obstacles such as a boss who is an extremely biased evaluator of performance.

An important form of frustration is *conflict.* A conflict consists of the simultaneous operation of mutually incompatible patterns of behavior. The person facing conflict must choose one pattern or the other (or reach some compromise). Until the choice is made the person remains in a state of conflict. For example, a head nurse who is being pressed by doctors to control the floor nurses more closely and is also asked to train new nurses and to give special attention to critically ill patients, is in a state of conflict because of the many demands made by her superiors.

Anxiety is a state of arousal caused by a threat to one's well-being. Arousal means a condition of tension, unrest, or uneasiness. Threat means anticipation of danger or interference with goal-directed behavior. Nervous tension, emotional tension, and stress are used to describe anxious conditions. Competition between two second-level supervisors for a vacant managerial job can be the arousal factor that results in anxiety. It should be noted that while this competitive situation may increase the anxiety of one person, it may not increase the anxiety of the other.

This model provides the manager with a starting point for understanding behavior. The important points to note are that (1) the behavior process is similar for all people, (2) actual behavior can differ because of physiological, environmental, and psychological variables, and such factors as frustration, conflict, and anxiety, and (3) many of the variables influencing behavior have been shaped before the person enters the work organization.

PERCEPTION

Perception is the process by which an individual gives meaning to the environment. The manner in which a person organizes, interprets, and pro-

---

[7] Items 1, 2, and 4 are proposed by Harold J. Leavitt, *Managerial Psychology* (The University of Chicago Press, 1978), p. 10.

cesses various stimuli are transmitted into a psychological experience. Because each person gives meaning to stimuli, different individuals will see the same thing in different ways.[8] The way an employee "sees" determines his or her behavior. Therefore, the way a person "sees" the situation often has much greater meaning for understanding behavior than does the situation itself.

Since perception refers to the acquisition of specific knowledge about objects or events at any particular moment, it occurs whenever stimuli activate the sense organs.[9] Perception also involves cognition (knowledge). Thus, perception involves the interpretation of objects, symbols, and people in the light of pertinent experiences. In other words, perception involves receiving stimuli (inputs), organizing the stimuli, and translating or interpreting the organized stimuli in such a manner to influence behavior. Some of the factors that influence perception are

1. A person may be influenced by considerations that cannot be identified. For example, a judgment as to the size of an object may be influenced by its color even though color is not an important consideration.
2. A person may accept perceptual evidence from a respected source more readily than information coming from other sources. A supervisor from the headquarters division may comment on the quality of output from a new machine and this information is valued more than the analysis of output offered by a mechanic who works with the machine.
3. A person may be influenced by emotional factors—what is liked is perceived as correct.
4. When required to form difficult perceptual judgments, a person may respond to irrelevant cues to arrive at a judgment. When hiring a new salesperson the recruitment coordinator may decide to hire the person who does not wear glasses. The coordinator may assume that wearing glasses detracts from a person's appearance in a salesperson-client relationship.[10]

These four illustrations indicate issues to consider when analyzing the behavioral patterns of employees. Each person selects various cues that influence his or her perceptions of people, objects, and symbols. Because of these factors and their potential imbalance, people often misperceive another person, group, or object. To a considerable extent, people interpret the behavior of others in the context of the setting in which they find themselves.[11]

---

[8] W. R. Nord, ed., *Concepts and Controversy in Organizational Behavior* (Santa Monica, Calif.: Goodyear Publishing Co., 1976), p. 22.

[9] Rudolf Pinter et al., *Educational Psychology* (New York: Harper & Row, 1970), p. 74.

[10] Sheldon S. Zalkind and Timothy W. Costello, "Perception: Some Recent Research and Implications for Administration," *Administrative Science Quarterly* (September 1962), pp. 218–35.

[11] See J. S. Brunner, "Personality Dynamics and The Process of Perceiving," in R. R. Blake and G. V. Ramsey, *Perception: An Approach to Personality* (New York: The Ronald Press Co., 1951), pp. 124–25.

Perceptual Organization

As previously stated perception occurs when stimuli activate the sense organs. An important aspect of what is perceived involves organization. One of the most elemental organizing principles of perception is the tendency to pattern stimuli in terms of *figure-ground* relationships. Not all stimuli reach one's awareness with equal clarity. The factor that is focused on is called the *figure*. That which is experienced and is out of focus is called the *ground*. As you read this page your perceptions are organized in terms of figure and ground. The printed words are the figure and the white spaces are the ground.[12] In every perceptual act the figure-ground principle is operating. The mountains stand out against the sky and the dangerous working area stands out in a particular work laboratory.

The organizing nature of perception is also apparent when similar stimuli are grouped together and stimuli in close proximity are grouped. Another grouping principle that shapes perceptual organization is called *closure*. This refers to the tendency to want to close something with missing parts. There is a strong need in some individuals to complete a configuration, a job, or a project. For example, if a person with a high need for closure is prevented from finishing a job or task, this could lead to frustration or a more drastic behavior such as quitting.

Stereotyping. The manner in which managers categorize others often is a reflection of a perceptual bias. The term stereotype has been used to describe judgments made about people on the basis of their ethnic group membership. Other stereotypes are also common.

For example, men stereotype women executives, managers stereotype union stewards, and women stereotype aggressive men. Most people engage in stereotyping. Stereotyping of employees can result in implementing improper programs for motivation, job design, or performance evaluation.

Selective Perception. The concept of selective perception is important to managers since they often receive large amounts of information and data. Consequently, they may tend to select information that supports their viewpoints. People tend to ignore information that may make them feel discomfort.

For example, after recommending a person for promotion a manager may pay closer attention to the person's positive contributions and tend to disregard some of the negative aspects of his or her performance. This tendency to ignore certain types of information is called selective perception.

The Manager's Characteristics. People tend to use themselves as benchmarks in perceiving others. Research suggests that (1) knowing oneself makes it easier to see others accurately,[13] (2) one's own characteristics

---

[12] B. V. H. Gilmer, *Applied Psychology* (New York: McGraw-Hill, 1975), p. 229.

[13] R. D. Norman, "The Interrelationships among Acceptance-Rejection, Self-Other Identity, Insight into Self, and Realistic Perception of Others," *Journal of Social Psychology* (1953), pp. 205–35.

affect the characteristics identified in others,[14] and (3) persons who accept themselves are more likely to see favorable aspects of other people.[15]

Basically, these conclusions suggest that managers perceiving the behavior and individual differences of employees are influenced by their own traits. If they understand that their own traits and values influence perception they can probably perform a more accurate evaluation of their subordinates.

The Situational Factor

The press of time, the attitudes of people a manager is working with, and other situational factors influence perceptual accuracy. If a manager believes that certain people in a group are different because of their particular skin color or speech habits, these differences can be magnified and also perceived in other areas. Such perceived differences are likely to lead to inaccurate perceptions of employee performance, loyalty, and commitment. The manager is searching for differences because of a predisposition to believe that they exist.

The manager of a project team may view people, objects, and directives differently than the other members of the team. The relevance of the work environment to one's needs is an important determinant of one's perception of it. Information, actions, and behavior that appear to satisfy needs will be perceived more readily than those that do not; when they are threatening to an individual they may also be perceived readily, but be screened out of conscious thought.[16] Managers who are striving to improve individual, group, and organizational performance need to understand the influence of perception on behavior.

Needs and Perceptions

Perceptions are significantly influenced by needs and desires. In other words, the employee, the manager, the vice president, the director see what they want to see. Like the mirrors at the amusement park, the world can be distorted; the distortion is related to needs and desires.

The influence of needs in shaping perceptions has been studied in laboratory settings. Subjects at various stages of hunger were asked to report what they saw in ambiguous drawings flashed before them. It was found that as hunger increased up to a certain point, the subjects saw more and more of the ambiguous figures as articles of food. The hungry subjects saw

---

[14] J. Bossom and A. H. Maslow, "Security of Judges as a Factor in Impressions of Warmth in Others," *Journal of Abnormal and Social Psychology* (1959), pp. 147–48.

[15] K. T. Omivake, "The Relation between Acceptance of Self and Acceptance of Others Shown by Three Personality Inventories," *Journal of Consulting Psychology* (1954), pp. 443–46.

[16] Leavitt, *Managerial Psychology,* p. 20.

steaks, salads, and sandwiches, while the subjects who had recently eaten saw nonfood images in the same figures.

Emotions and Perceptions

A person's emotional state has a lot to do with perceptions. A strong emotion, such as total distaste for an organizational rule, can make a person perceive negative characteristics in most company policies and rules. Determining a person's emotional state is difficult. Thus, managers need to be concerned about what issues or practices trigger strong emotions within subordinates. Strong emotions can and often do distort perceptions.

ATTITUDES

Attitudes are determinants of behavior, since they are linked with perception, personality, learning, and motivation. An *attitude* is a mental state of readiness, organized through experience, exerting a specific influence upon a person's response to people, objects, and situations with which it is related.

This definition of attitude has certain implications for the manager. First, attitudes define one's predispositions toward given aspects of the world. Employees formulate attitudes about their jobs, bosses, evaluation systems, pension plans, and other organizationally relevant factors. Second, attitudes provide the emotional basis of one's interpersonal relations and identification with others. Third, attitudes are organized and are close to the core of personality. Some attitudes are persistent and enduring. Yet like each of the psychological variables, attitudes are subject to change.

Attitudes: Cognition and Affect

It is generally accepted that attitudes are an intrinsic part of a person's personality. However, a number of theories attempt to account for the formation and change of attitudes. One such theory proposes that people "seek a congruence between their beliefs and feelings toward objects," and suggests that the modification of attitudes depends on changing either the feelings or beliefs.[17] It further assumes that people have structured attitudes that are composed of various affective and cognitive components. The interrelatedness of these components means that a change in one will set in motion a change in the other. When these components are inconsistent or exceed the person's "tolerance level," instability results. Rosenberg, the developer of the theory, believes that instability can be corrected by either (1) disavowal of a message which is designed to influence attitudes, (2) "fragmentation"

---

[17] M. J. Rosenberg, "A Structural Theory of Attitudes," *Public Opinion Quarterly* (Summer 1960), pp. 319–40.

of the attitudes, or (3) acceptance of the inconsistency so that a new attitude is formed.

The theme of Rosenberg's theory is that cognition, affect, and behavior are determinants of attitudes and attitudes in turn determine affect, cognition, and behavior. *Cognition* means a conscious process of acquiring knowledge. It refers to the thought processes of a person, with emphasis on rationality and logic. *Affect* refers to the feelings of liking and disliking. The interrelatedness of these factors is presented in Figure 4–3.

Figure 4–3
The Development of Employee Attitudes

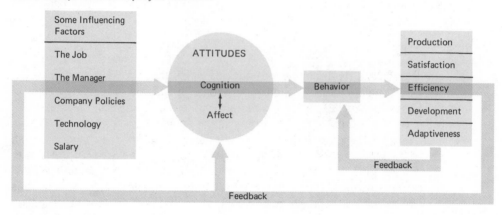

The Rosenberg theory of cognitive and affective components as determinants of attitudes and attitude change has significant implications for managers. The manager has to be able to demonstrate that the positive aspects of contributing to the organization in the form of good performance outweigh the negative aspects. It is through attempts to develop generally favorable attitudes toward the organization and the job that many managers hope to achieve effectiveness.

Attitude Formation

There are many sources of attitude formation. Attitudes are learned from family, peer groups, society, and previous job experiences. The early *family* experiences help shape the attitudes of individuals. The attitudes of young children usually correspond to those of their parents. As children reach their teen years, they begin to be more strongly influenced by *peers*. Peer groups are able to influence attitudes because individuals want to be accepted by others. Teen-agers seek approval by sharing similar attitudes or by modifying attitudes to comply with those of a group.

The culture, mores, and language of a society influence attitudes. The attitudes of French Canadians toward France, Americans toward the Chinese, and Russians toward capitalism are learned in society. Within the United States there are sub-cultures in the form of ethnic communities, ghetto communities, and religious groups that help shape attitudes of people. The person moving from one of these to a management job or operating employee job in an organization would bring these attitudes to the job.

Through job experiences, individuals learn attitudes. They develop attitudes about such factors as pay equity, performance review, managerial capabilities, job design, and work group affiliation. Previous experiences can account for some of the individual differences in performance, loyalty, and commitment that are occasionally discovered by managers over a period of time.

Changing Attitudes

Managers are often faced with the task of changing attitudes because previously structured attitudes are believed to be hindering the job performance of individuals. Although there are many variables that affect attitude change, they can all be described in terms of two general factors—trust in the sender and the message itself.[18] If employees do not trust the manager, they will not accept the message nor change an attitude. Similarly, if the message is not convincing, there will be no pressure to change.

One of the more reliable research findings is that the greater the prestige of the communicator, the more attitude change is produced.[19] A manager who has little prestige and is not shown respect by peers and superiors will be in a difficult position if the job requires changing the attitudes of subordinates in order to get them to work more effectively.

Liking the communicator produces attitude change because people try to identify with a liked communicator, and tend to adopt attitudes and behaviors of the liked person.[20] Not all managers, however, are fortunate to be liked by all of their subordinates. Therefore, it is important to recognize the concept of liking but to consider the issues of trust and strength of the message as being more controllable variables.

Even if a manager is trusted, presents a convincing message, and is liked, this does not mean that the problems of changing people's attitudes are over. An important factor is the strength of commitment to an attitude by the employee. A worker who has decided not to accept a promotion is more committed to the belief that it is best to remain in his or her present position than to accept a promotion. Attitudes that have been publicly expressed

---

[18] Jonathan L. Freedman, J. Merrill Carlsmith, and David O. Sears, *Social Psychology* (Englewood Cliffs, N.J.: Prentice Hall, Inc., 1974), p. 271. Also see D. Coon, *Introduction To Psychology* (St. Paul: West Publishing Co., 1977), pp. 626–29.

[19] Freedman, Carlsmith, and Sears, *Social Psychology*, p. 272.

[20] H. C. Kelman, "Process of Opinion Change," *Public Opinion Quarterly* (Spring 1961), pp. 57–78.

are more difficult to change because the person has shown commitment, and to change would be to admit a mistake.

These are some of the factors that affect attitude change. Astute managers who want to change attitudes will begin by examining their prestige, the strength of their messages, how much their employees like them, and the commitment of the employees to a particular attitude.

PERSONALITY

The relationship between behavior and personality is perhaps one of the most complex matters managers have to understand. Personality is significantly influenced by cultural and social factors. Regardless of how personality is defined, certain ideas are generally accepted among psychologists. These are:

1. Personality is an organized whole, otherwise the individual would have no meaning.
2. Personality appears to be organized into patterns. These are to some degree observable and measurable.
3. Although there is a biological basis to personality the specific development is a product of social and cultural environments.
4. Personality has superficial aspects, such as attitudes toward being a team leader, and a deeper core, such as sentiments about authority or the Protestant work ethic.
5. Personality involves both common and unique characteristics. Every person is different from every other person in some respects, while being similar in other respects.

These five ideas are included in the following definition of personality.

> An individual's personality is a relatively stable set of characteristics, tendencies, and temperaments that have been significantly formed by inheritance and by social, cultural, and environmental factors. This set of variables determines the commonalities and differences in the behavior of the individual.[21]

The third idea points out some of the forces that are major determinants of personality. These forces are presented in Figure 4–4. Studies of family history, of identical twins, and of early childhood behavior indicate the importance of *hereditary* factors in personality formation. The importance of heredity varies from one personality trait to another. For example, heredity is generally more important in determining a person's temperament than values and ideals.

The degree to which every person is molded by *culture* is enormous. We do not clearly recognize the impact of culture in shaping our personalities. It happens gradually, and usually there is no alternative but to accept the

---

[21] This definition is based upon Salvatore R. Maddi, *Personality Theories: A Comparative Analysis* (Homewood, Ill.: The Dorsey Press, 1976).

Figure 4–4
Some Major Forces Influencing Personality

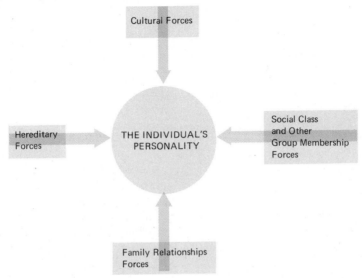

culture. The stable functioning of a society requires that there be shared patterns of behavior among its members and that there be some basis for knowing how to behave in certain situations. To insure this, the society institutionalizes various patterns of behavior. The institutionalization of some patterns of behavior means that most members of a culture will have certain common personality characteristics.

Social class is also important in shaping personality. The various neighborhoods of cities and towns tend to be populated by different social classes, each with its own mores. The neighborhood or community in which a child grows up is the setting in which he learns about life. Social class influences the person's self-perception, perception of others, and perceptions of work, authority, and money. In terms of such pressing organizational problems as adjustment, quality of work life, and dissatisfaction, the manager attempting to understand employees must give attention to social class factors.

The nature of a person's expectations of others, the ways a person attempts to derive satisfaction, the manner used to express feelings and resolve emotional conflicts are all formed in an interpersonal context. A key factor in this context is the family or parent-child relationships. They set a pattern of behavior which, like a mold, leaves a significant imprint on all later behavior in the work organization.[22]

A review of each determinant that shapes personality (Figure 4–4) should indicate that the manager has little control over these forces. This should

---

[22] Lawrence A. Pervin, *Personality* (New York: John Wiley & Sons, 1970), p. 36.

not lead the manager to conclude that personality is not an important factor in workplace behavior because it is formed outside the organization. The behavioral responses of an employee simply cannot be thoroughly understood without considering the concept of personality. In fact, personality is so interrelated with perception, attitudes, learning, and motivation that any analysis of behavior or attempt to predict behavior is grossly incomplete unless it is considered.

Assessing Personality

Although the term personality is used in a broad sense as indicated by the definition stated above, personality tests are instruments used to measure emotional, motivational, interpersonal, and attitudinal characteristics. There are hundreds of tests available to organizations. Especially numerous are the personality inventories and the projective techniques. One of the most widely used inventories is the Minnesota Multiphasic Personality Inventory (MMPI). To date over 3,500 references have been published about this test. It consists of affirmative statements, to which a person responds: "True," "False," or "Cannot Say." The MMPI items cover such areas as health, psychosomatic symptoms, neurological disorders, and social attitudes; and many well known neurotic or psychotic manifestations such as phobias, delusions, and sadistic trends.[23]

The proper interpretation of any personality test such as the MMPI requires considerable psychological sophistication. Managers do not normally have the sophistication needed to use and interpret such tests. It is important to use experts when any test is given, especially personality inventories such as the MMPI.

Projective techniques are also used to assess personality. These tests have an individual respond to a picture, an inkblot, or story. In order for the person to freely respond, only brief, general instructions are given. For the same reason, the test pictures or stories are vague. The underlying reason for this is that the individual perceives and interprets the test material in a manner that will display his or her psychological functioning. That is, the person will project his or her attitudes, needs, anxieties, and conflicts.

In general, projective testing requires expert interpretation. It is also less susceptible to faking than self-report inventories. The issue of validity and reliability also should be considered before using personality measurements. In short, any form of inventory or projective test to measure personality variables needs to be carefully examined. The evidence to date suggests that managers should be aware of how personality influences behavior, but to attempt to use inventories or projective tests is for experts and not nonqualified managers.

---

[23] A. Anastasi, *Psychological Testing* (New York: Macmillan, 1976), Chapters 17, 18, and 19.

Personality and Behavior

An issue of interest to behavioral scientists and researchers is whether personality factors such as those measured by inventories or projective tests can predict behavior or performance in organizations. Using a total inventory to examine whether personality is a factor in explaining behavior is rarely done in organizational behavior research. Typically, a few select personality factors such as locus of control, tolerance of ambiguity, or risk taking propensity are used to examine behavior and performance.

Locus of Control. Some people believe that they are autonomous— that is, they are masters of their own fates and hence bear personal responsibility for what happens to them. They see the control of their lives as coming from inside themselves. Rotter calls these people *internalizers*.[24]

On the other hand, Rotter proposes that many people believe that they are helpless pawns of fate, that they are controlled by outside forces over which they have little if any influence. Such people believe that their *locus of control* is external rather than internal. These people are called *externalizers*.

A study of 900 employees in a public utility found that internally controlled employees are more satisfied with their jobs, more likely to be in managerial positions, and are more satisfied with a participative management style than are employees who perceive external control.[25]

In an interesting study of 90 entrepreneurs, locus of control, perceived stress, coping behaviors, and performance were examined.[26] The study was done in a business district over a three-and-one-half year period following the flooding of Hurricane Agnes. Internals were found to perceive less stress, employ more task-centered coping behaviors, and fewer emotion-centered coping behaviors than externals. In addition, the task-oriented coping behaviors of internals were associated with better performance.

The concept of locus of control appears to be of some use in understanding behavior and performance. However, it appears to be too inflexible to categorize individuals as either an internalizer or externalizer. Rather, we all probably have mixed tendencies; even the most fatalistic of externalizers will, in some situations, probably meet challenges head-on rather than denying that they exist.

Tolerance of Ambiguity. The interest in tolerance-intolerance of ambiguity derives from attempts to establish the relationship of this personality factor to the authoritarian syndrome. *Intolerance of ambiguity* is defined as the tendency to perceive (i.e., interpret) ambiguous situations as sources

---

24 J. R. Rotter, "Generalized Expectancies for Internal versus External Control of Reinforcement," *Psychological Monographs* (1966), 80 (1, Whole No. 609).

25 T. R. Mitchell, C. M. Smyser, and S. E. Weed, "Locus of Control: Supervision and Work Satisfaction," *Academy of Management Journal* (September 1975), pp. 623–31.

26 C. R. Anderson, "Locus of Control, Coping Behaviors, and Performance in a Stress Setting: A Longitudinal Study," *Journal of Applied Psychology* (August 1977), pp. 446–51.

of threat; *tolerance of ambiguity* is the tendency to perceive ambiguous situations as desirable. An ambiguous work situation would exist when it cannot be adequately structured by the individual because of the lack of sufficient cues. A new situation (e.g., a new job) where there are few familiar cues; a complex situation (e.g., a middle manager receiving orders from six different sources) in which there are numerous cues to consider; and a contradictory situation (e.g., a project leader) in which difficult cues suggest different instructions are three potential ambiguous situations. In various work situations involving changes in technology, structure, or personnel the tolerance of ambiguity factor could be significant in understanding or predicting behavioral reactions.

Risk-Taking.   Propensity for taking risks is a personality attribute that influences behavior and performance. Research studies were made to examine an individual's tendency to take risks—individually or within a group setting. Results seem to indicate that there *are* individual differences that influence individual and group decision making.

A study of 79 managers in a manufacturing company examined risk-taking propensity, dogmatism, intelligence, and decision-making strategies. The managers worked on personnel decision simulations. The decision performance for each manager was evaluated. High risk-taking participants made more rapid decisions and used less information to make decisions than the low risk-taking managers. The high risk takers were about as accurate as the low risk takers, but they took more time to process information. The findings suggest that although high risk-taking managers reach rapid decisions, they give careful attention to the information they acquire to make decisions.[27]

Determining whether groups or individuals have greater risk-taking propensity may be helpful in selecting the best situations for using decision-making groups. A number of studies indicate that groups make riskier decisions than do individuals. Many of the studies used a choice dilemma problem in which individuals are first asked to provide a minimum probability for making a decision.[28] Then, groups are formed which discuss a problem until a consensus is reached. The groups usually recommend a probability higher than the average of the individual recommendations, implying a shift toward risk. Various explanations for the shift are offered, such as (1) responsibility is diffused through a group, (2) there is some social value in being viewed as a risk taker, and (3) leaders most influencing group discussions are likely to be more risk inclined.[29] Group decision making will be discussed in detail

[27] R. N. Taylor and M. D. Dunnette, "Influence of Dogmatism, Risk-Taking Propensity, and Intelligence on Decision-Making Strategies for a Sample of Industrial Managers," *Journal of Applied Psychology* (August 1974), pp. 420–23.

[28] N. Kogan and M. A. Wallach, "Risk-Taking as a Function of the Situation, The Person, and The Group," in G. Mandler, ed., *New Directions of Psychology, III* (New York: Holt, Rinehart, and Winston, 1967).

[29] A. Vinokur, "Review and Theoretical Analysis of the Effects of Group Processes upon Individual and Group Decisions Involving Risk," *Psychological Bulletin* (October 1971), pp. 231–50.

in Chapter 16 which is concerned solely with the process of decision making.

There are many other popularly studied personality variables including dogmatism, authoritarianism, higher order need strength, and cognitive complexity. These and the three factors discussed above seem to have some influence on behavior and performance in various work situations. The importance of personality variables appears to differ from job to job, person to person, and situation to situation. If they can be measured validly they can provide managers with improved accuracy in predicting behavior and job performance. Measuring personality variables validly requires careful attention before making any assumptions about how personality and behavior are related.

LEARNING

Learning is one of the fundamental processes underlying behavior. The majority of behavior within organizations is learned behavior. Goals and emotional reactions can be learned. Skills, such as programming a computer or counseling a troubled employee, can be learned. The meanings and uses of language are learned. Perceptions and attitudes can also be learned.

Learning can be defined as the process by which a relatively enduring change in behavior occurs as a result of practice. The words "relatively enduring" signify that the change in behavior must be more or less permanent. The term "practice" is intended to cover both formal training and uncontrolled experiences. The changes in behavior which characterize learning may be adaptive and promote effectiveness, or they may be nonadaptive and ineffective. The definition also indicates that learning is a process in which certain changes in behavior occur. The process cannot be directly observed. It must be inferred from changes in behavior.

Learning Process: Classical and Operant Conditioning

Learning can be viewed as the process of conditioning. The term conditioning refers to the modification of behavior. Two types of learning processes are classical and operant conditioning.

Classical. The study of classical conditioning had its beginnings with the work of a Russian physiologist Pavlov around the turn of the 20th century. While studying the automatic reflexes associated with digestion, he noticed that his laboratory dog salivated not only in the presence of food but also at the presentation of other stimuli before food was placed in its mouth. Pavlov reasoned that food automatically produced salivation. This phenomenon was an unlearned association; he therefore labeled "food" an *unconditioned stimulus* and salivation an *unconditioned response*. Since he believed that the response of salivating to other, seemingly unrelated, stimuli had to be learned, he labeled it a *conditioned response* initiated by a *conditioned stimulus.*

As part of his experiments, Pavlov rang a bell (conditioned stimulus) fol-

Figure 4–5
The Pavlov Procedure for Classical Conditioning

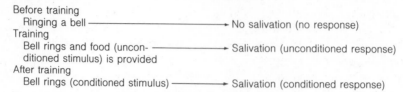

Before training
   Ringing a bell ————————————→ No salivation (no response)
Training
   Bell rings and food (uncon- ——————→ Salivation (unconditioned response)
   ditioned stimulus) is provided
After training
   Bell rings (conditioned stimulus) ————→ Salivation (conditioned response)

lowed by placing food in the dog's mouth (unconditioned stimulus). Soon the bell alone evoked salivation. Thus, salivation produced by food is an unconditioned response, whereas salivation produced by the bell alone is a conditioned (or learned) response. Figure 4–5 graphically presents the Pavlov work on classical conditioning.[30]

Operant. The name most associated with operant conditioning is B. F. Skinner. This form of conditioning is concerned with learning that occurs as a consequence of behavior. In classical conditioning, the sequence of events is independent of the subject's behavior. Behaviors which can be controlled by altering consequences (reinforcers and punishments) which follow them are referred to as *operants.* An operant is strengthened (increased) or weakened (decreased) as a function of the events which follow it. Most workplace behaviors are operants. Examples of operant behaviors are performing job-related tasks, reading a budget report, or coming to work on time. Operants are distinguished by virtue of being controlled by their consequences.

In classical conditioning, the response to be learned (salivating) is already present in the animal and may be triggered by the presentation of the appropriate unconditioned stimulus (food). In operant conditioning, however, the desired response may not be present in the subject. Teaching a subordinate to prepare an accurate weekly budget report is an example of operant conditioning. There is no identifiable stimulus that will automatically evoke the response of preparing the budget. The superior works with the subordinate

Figure 4–6
An Example of Operant Conditioning

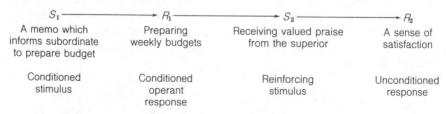

S_1 ————————→ R_1 ————————→ S_2 ————————→ R_2

A memo which | Preparing | Receiving valued praise | A sense of
informs subordinate | weekly budgets | from the superior | satisfaction
to prepare budget

Conditioned | Conditioned | Reinforcing | Unconditioned
stimulus | operant | stimulus | response
  | response

---

[30] An excellent and clear presentation of the conditioning process is given in Bernard M. Bass and James A. Vaughn, *Training in Industry: The Management of Learning* (Belmont, Calif.: Brooks/Cole Publishing Co., 1966). Also see Alan E. Kazdin, *Behavior Modification in Applied Settings* (Homewood Ill.: Richard D. Irwin, 1975).

and reinforces him or her for preparing an accurate budget. Figure 4–6 illustrates the operant conditioning process.

The interrelationships of $S_1 \rightarrow R_1 \rightarrow S_2 \rightarrow R_2$ are referred to as the contingencies of reinforcement.[31] Skinner believes that the consequences (reinforcers and punishments) determine the likelihood that a given behavior will be acted out in the future.[32] This notion lends itself particularly well to the study of various learning principles such as reinforcement and knowledge of results.

Principles of Learning

There are a number of important principles of learning that can aid the manager attempting to influence behavior. Some of these principles are being used in organizations.

Reinforcement. An extremely important principle of learning is the concept of reinforcement. It can be stated that without reinforcement no measurable modification of behavior takes place. Managers often use *positive reinforcers* to modify behavior. In some cases the reinforcers work as predicted, while in other instances they do not modify behavior in the desired direction because of competing reinforcement contingencies. When reinforcers are not made contingent on the behavior desired by the manager, desired behaviors do not occur. Also when reinforcers are given long after desired behaviors have occurred, the probability of the resulting behavior occurring again is decreased.

A positive reinforcer is a stimulus which, when added to a situation, strengthens the probability of a behavioral response.[33] The reason it strengthens the behavioral response is clarified by the law of effect.[34] This law proposes that behavior which appears to lead to a positive consequence tends to be repeated, while behavior which appears to lead to a negative consequence tends not to be repeated. If the reinforcer has value to a person, it can be used to improve performance. It should be remembered, however, that which has value to one person may not have value to another person.

Negative Reinforcement. Negative reinforcement refers to an increase in the frequency of a response following removal of a negative reinforcer immediately after the response. An event is a *negative reinforcer* only if it's removed after a response increases performance of a response. A familiar example of negative reinforcement in the summer months in Phoenix and Houston is turning on the automobile air conditioner on a stifling hot day. Turning on the air conditioner (the behavior) usually minimizes or terminates

---

[31] See W. Clay Hamner, "Reinforcement Theory and Contingency Management in Organizational Settings," in Henry L. Tosi and W. Clay Hamner, eds., *Organizational Behavior and Management: A Contingency Approach* (Chicago: St. Clair Press, 1974), pp. 86–112.

[32] Skinner, *Beyond Freedom and Dignity,* and B. F. Skinner, *Contingencies of Reinforcement* (New York: Appleton-Century-Crofts, 1969).

[33] B. F. Skinner, *Science and Human Behavior* (New York: The Macmillan Co., 1953), p. 73.

[34] E. L. Thorndike, *Animal Intelligence* (New York: The Macmillan Co., 1911).

an aversive condition, namely being hot (negative reinforcer). The probability of having an efficient operating air conditioning system in the summer months is increased. Similarly, exerting high degrees of effort to complete a job may be negatively reinforced by not having to listen to the nagging "boss." Completing the job through increased effort (behavior) usually minimizes the chance of listening to a nagging stream of advice (negative reinforcer) from a superior.

Punishment.   Punishment is defined as presenting an uncomfortable consequence for a particular behavioral response.[35] It is certainly a controversial method of behavioral modification. There are some people who believe that punishment is the opposite of reward and is just as effective in changing behavior. Zalkind and Costello disagree with this simplistic assumption.

> Reward tends to increase the probability of a response's future occurrence; the effect of punishment cannot be said, unequivocally, to decrease its probability. . . . If we are seeking a way to find punishment to be the opposite of reward, perhaps the answer can be found by saying the impact of reward on behavior is simple (it reinforces it); the impact of punishment on behavior is complex.[36]

Consequently, punishment may be a poor approach to learning because:

1.   The results of punishment are not as predictable as those of reward.
2.   The effects of punishment are less permanent than those of reward.
3.   Punishment frequently is accompained by negative attitudes toward the administrator of the punishment, as well as toward the activity that led to the punishment.

There are two types of punishment. First, an aversive stimulus can be applied after a response; this is *punishment by application.* Familiar organization examples include being reprimanded or publicly removed from a job after engaging in what is considered inadequate behavior. Second, a positive reinforcer can be removed after a response; this is called *punishment by removal.*[37] Organizational examples would be being removed from the promotion list for being continually late or having your paycheck decreased because of excessive absenteeism.

Punishment can suppress behavior if used effectively. Generally, the following enhances the effects of punishment:

Immediate application or removal of the contingent stimulus after the undesired employee responses.

Punishment of every occurrence of the response.

Training of an acceptable response, especially when the motivation for the undesired response is difficult to eliminate.

---

[35] W. E. Craighead, A. E. Kazdin, and M. J. Mahoney, *Behavior Modification* (Boston: Houghton Mifflin Co., 1976), pp. 112–20.

[36] Zalkind and Costello, "Perception," p. 214.

[37] Craighead et al, *Behavior Modification,* pp. 118–19.

Reinforcement of responses that are incompatible with the punishment response.

Some work related factors that can be considered punishments include a superior's criticism, being fired, being suspended, receiving an undesirable transfer or assignment, being demoted, being passed over for promotion, or not receiving desirable positive reinforcers which may include job recognition, a bonus, feedback, and praise.

Avoidance Learning.   When behavior can prevent an uncomfortable stimulus the procedure is called avoidance behavior. Complying with a group norm of low productivity is often maintained by avoidance learning. The uncomfortable stimulus could be the reactions of peers or fellow workers to the person producing "too much." In order to avoid the discomfort the employee could work at the group-sanctioned level of production.

Extinction.   While positive reinforcement and avoidance learning are available to managers for influencing behavior, the principle of extinction can be used to reduce undesired behavior. When positive reinforcement for a learned response is withheld, individuals will continue to practice that behavior for some period of time. If the behavior continues not to be reinforced, the behavior decreases and will eventually disappear. The decline in response rate because of nonreinforcement is defined as extinction.

Knowledge of Results.   Since human behavior is goal-directed there is a need to have some knowledge of goal accomplishment. Knowing why the behavior is not acceptable and how much modification is needed is important. New management trainees who have no idea of whether they are doing an acceptable job have little chance of improving their performances.

Accurate feedback from a manager furnishes information which can be used to correct mistakes and improve job performance. The knowledge of correct behavior is reinforcing and strengthens the preceding behavior, while knowledge of incorrect responses is not reinforcing and could extinguish the preceding behavior.

Locke in laboratory research studies has found that feedback affects performance only to the extent to which subjects set higher performance goals in response to such feedback.[38] In addition other investigators have concluded that providing employees with incomplete or erroneous feedback may actually result in poorer performance than providing no feedback at all.[39] The best job performance can be achieved when employees are provided with accurate feedback on performance based on clear and publicized criteria.

Schedules of Positive Reinforcement.   There are a number of ways in which a manager can schedule reinforcement. A continuous schedule is one that reinforces behavior every time the exhibited behavior is correct.

---

[38] Edwin A. Locke, "Toward a Theory of Task Performance and Incentives," *Organizational Behavior and Human Performance* (May 1968), pp. 157–89.

[39] L. L. Cummings, D. P. Schwab, and M. Rosen, "Performance and Knowledge of Results as Determinants of Goal Setting," *Journal of Applied Psychology* (December 1971), pp. 526–30.

This plan creates considerable dependency on the reinforcer, and when it is removed performance decreases rapidly. From a practical viewpoint it is difficult to reinforce continually every desirable behavior.

An intermittent schedule means that reinforcement does not occur after every acceptable behavior. The assumption is that learning is more permanent when correct behavior is rewarded only part of the time.[40] Ferster and Skinner have presented four types of intermittent reinforcement schedules for operant learning situations.[41] Briefly the four are:

1. *Fixed Interval Schedule.* A reinforcer is applied only when the desired behavior occurs after the passage of a certain period of time since the last reinforcer was applied. An example would be to only praise positive performance once a week and not at other times. The fixed interval is one week.

2. *Variable Interval Schedule.* A reinforcer is applied at some variable interval of time. The use of "pop quizzes" is an example of a variable interval schedule.

3. *Fixed Ratio Schedule.* A reinforcer is applied only if a fixed number of desired responses has occurred. An example would be paying a lathe operator a $5.00 bonus when the operator has produced 50 consecutive pieces which pass the quality control inspection.

4. *Variable Ratio Schedule.* A reinforcer is applied only after a number of desired responses, with the number of desired responses changing from situation to situation, around an average. Under this type of schedule the number of responses required for reinforcement changes unpredictably from occasion to occasion. A classic example would be slot machines.

Learning is at the core of motivating, leading, and changing others. Like the other topics covered in this chapter, learning is complex. The important considerations are not whether classical or operant conditioning is valid but (1) how people learn, (2) what managers need to know about learning, and (3) what principles of learning are generally applicable in management.

STRESS IN ORGANIZATIONS

The organization as a system exerts its own set of forces on each individual employee. One manifestation of the forces impinging on an employee is called job stress. Job stress occurs at every job level from the line-worker to the president; from the production manager to the fork lift operator. Each person has some capacity to deal with job-related stress. A person's physical health, experience, personality, and family life influence his or her capacity to deal with job stress.

---

[40] Bass and Vaughn, *Training in Industry,* p. 20. Also see Walter R. Nord, "Beyond the Teaching Machine: The Neglected Area of Operant Conditioning in the Theory and Practice of Management," *Organizational Behavior and Human Performance* (November 1969), pp. 375–401.

[41] C. B. Ferster and B. F. Skinner, *Schedules of Reinforcement* (New York: Appleton-Century-Crofts, 1957).

Although medical researchers have for years systematically studied physio-logical factors and stress, few organizational researchers have conducted studies of the relationship of organizational stressors and various outputs such as coronary heart disease, ulcers, and migraine headaches. This lack of organizational research interest is surprising since over 50 percent of the waking hours of over 85 million Americans and millions of other citizens in other industrialized nations such as Canada, Germany, and Japan are spent in organizations. In addition, in the United States each year more than 600,000 people die of heart attacks and over 29 million Americans have some form of heart and blood vessel diseases.[42] The role or impact of job-related stress on coronary disease, as well as other diseases, needs to be examined in much more depth and probably will be by teams of behavioral and medical scientists in the next decade.

Definition of Stress

In everyday use, the word "stress" contains two different and, in a sense, antithetical meanings stemming from its derivation. On the one hand, it is derived from the Latin word stringere, to draw tight, and on the other, as an apathetic form of stress.[43] In medicine, Selye equated stress with the second more general sense of hardship. He saw a variety of events or "stressors" as all producing a single specific pattern of bodily reaction.[44] There is an internal lowering of bodily resistance during which a variety of infectious diseases may develop, that under normal circumstances would be successfully resisted. An activation of bodily defense mechanisms then occurs increasing heart rate, blood pressure, muscle tone, and digestive secretion. If this defensive bodily state is prolonged, it can initiate what Selye terms "diseases of adaptation" (e.g., cardiovascular diseases). Therefore, stress is defined here as an experience that creates a physiological or psycho-logical imbalance within the person.

Most people think of stress as something to be avoided. Yet too little stress can be very harmful. In Figure 4–7 the relationship between job stress and performance is presented. Note that as stress increases, so does perform-ance, up to a particular point. This point may vary between individuals because of different personality patterns, levels of physical condition, or capacities to cope with ambiguity or risk. Any manager with a group of subordinates will have people placed somewhere along the curve. Each subordinate will generally require some special treatment so that job stress does not become harmful physiologically or psychologically.

---

[42] Michael T. Matteson and John M. Ivancevich, "Organizational Stressors and Coronary Heart Disease," Academy of Management Review (in press).

[43] H. Pearson and J. Joseph, "Stress and Occlusive Coronary-Artery Disuse," The Lancet (February 1963), pp. 415–18.

[44] Hans Selye, The Stresses of Life (New York: McGraw-Hill, 1956).

Figure 4–7
The Job Stress and Job Performance Inverted-U Relationship

Performance Level

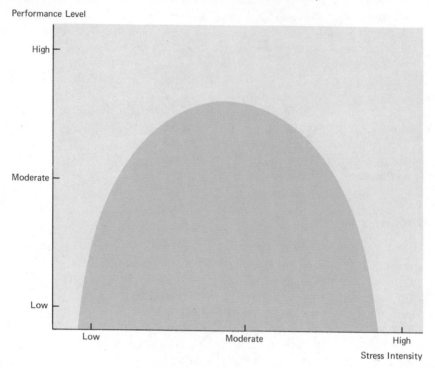

The Stress Personality: Type A and Type B Behavior Patterns

Although a major portion of the research on organizational stress emphasizes organizational factors such as role overload, role conflict, and role ambiguity, the personality differences in people should be given special recognition. Approximately 20 years ago, two cardiologists, Rosenman and Friedman, were involved in studying the traditional heart disease risk factors: cigarette smoking, blood pressure, diet, obesity, and exercise.[45] They decided to study accountants and how they responded to work. Accountants were chosen for study because their work requirements rise and fall in intensity before and after income tax time, April 15. All of the accountants kept diaries of what they ate, and were examined twice a month. Friedman and Rosenman found that there was an overall jump in fatty acids in the blood from March to mid-April. This jump was independent of individual variations in diet, weight, or amount of exercise.

At about the time of the accountant study, they also noticed individual

[45] R. Rosenman and M. Friedman, "The Possible Relationship of Occupational Stress to Clinical Coronary Heart Disease," *California Medicine* (1958), pp. 165–72.

differences in temperament that might influence people's reactions to stress. Thus, emerged the Type A and Type B classification system. A Type A person is characterized by:

1. Intense drive, aggressiveness, ambition, competitiveness, and pressure for getting things done.
2. Speaks in staccato and has tendency to end sentences in a rush.
3. Seldom is out on sick leave.
4. Rarely goes to a doctor and almost never to a psychiatrist.
5. Is often hard to get along with. This person values respect and is not overly concerned with affection from subordinates.
6. Has little time for exercise or social functions.

Rosenman and Friedman's largest study to date involves a total of 3,500 male subjects, aged 31 to 59 and with no known history of heart disease at the time they entered the study. A few years after the start of the study, 257 of these men developed coronary heart disease, 70 percent were Type A's. A's had more heart attacks than B's even if they didn't smoke, even if their blood pressure was normal, and even if their family background showed no coronary disease.[46]

Despite the large volume of data provided by the Friedman and Rosenman team, there are critics of their work. A noted cardiologist, Paul Dudley White, insisted that stress never hurt a healthy heart. Other critics complain that the methods for classifying people as A or B are rather subjective. Once again, the difficulty in measuring personality is a problem in scientifically studying the relationship of stress, behavior, and performance.

Methods of Reducing Stress

Because stress in industrialized societies is so widespread, many techniques are available to cope with it. Some techniques are individually controlled, while others can be used by managers to help subordinates reduce harmful stress. Once again, we are emphasizing that the reduction of potentially harmful stress is the focal point and not stress that serves a positive role in motivating people.

Individual. Friedman who admits to and is considered a Type A person suffered a heart attack in 1967. Since his almost fatal experience, he has attempted to change his lifestyle. He has attempted to slow his pace and change his regimen.[47] These changes require will power and an appreciation of the potential consequences of excessive stress. The self-management of a program to minimize the dangers of job stress is a personal activity. Discipline and perseverance are certainly needed to be successful.

Another popular individual method for reducing stress involves the use

---

[46] M. Friedman and R. H. Rosenman, *Type A: Behavior and Your Heart* (New York: Knopf, 1974).

[47] W. McQuade and A. Aikman, *Stress* (New York: E. P. Dutton & Co., 1974), p. 30.

of *biofeedback control.*[48] This method uses electronic machines that help monitor and improve awareness of bodily sensations. Through improved awareness it is assumed that a person can then control impulses. For example, by using biofeedback a person could slow down breathing rate. An increased breathing rate often indicates a certain degree of discomfort, panic, or uneasiness. Biofeedback equipment is used to monitor rapid breathing or other emotional arousal on a speedometer-like panel. The panel can be read by the person. In essence, biofeedback is a relaxation procedure that uses equipment to monitor bodily sensations.

Organizational.   Managers have the ability to reduce or minimize such organizational stressors as role conflict, role overload, role ambiguity, and intergroup conflict. They can structure jobs, provide clear job descriptions and expectations, and be responsive to subordinate needs. Each situation requires a slightly different and specific managerial approach. Thus, managerial flexibility and willingness to listen are important ingredients for reducing harmful stress.

Another method for reducing stress is to increase the resources available to subordinates. With additional resources, it is often easier to meet goals and deadlines. Of course, there is a limit on how many resources can be provided to employees.

In this chapter, we have examined the concepts of perception, attitudes, personality, and learning. Any manager attempting to help subordinates cope with harmful job stress must incorporate these behavioral factors into his or her approach. For example, determining what are considered positive reinforcers and applying them when possible could be very effective in reducing harmful job stress for some individuals. Understanding why attitudes are extremely difficult to change could also be important information when considering whether to introduce a major technological or personnel change quickly or over a period of time.

The manager has an endless stream of techniques available that can reduce harmful job stress. Being willing to work hard at determining what is too stressful and at applying various techniques is a personal decision that each manager must make. An exciting part of the manager's job in organizations is to become more involved with diagnosing and monitoring job stress and selecting the best program or approach to reduce potentially harmful stress factors. Each of these important managerial responsibilities is just beginning to be taken seriously by society and managers. The medical community has attacked the stress-disease relationship for many years. It appears that finally organizational researchers will begin to study the consequences of harmful job stress more earnestly during the next decade.

---

[48] A good discussion of methods of coping with stress is found in A. DuBrin, *Human Relations: A Job Oriented Approach* (Reston, Va.: Reston Publishing Co., Inc., 1978), Chapter 4, pp. 64–84.

MAJOR ISSUES FOR THE MANAGER TO CONSIDER

A. Employees joining an organization must adjust to a new environment, new people, and new tasks. The manner in which people adjust to situations and other people will depend largely on their psychological makeup and personal backgrounds.

B. The behavioral patterns of most people are established before joining an organization. To modify these patterns requires time, patience, and understanding. Simplistic assumptions about people are generally incomplete.

C. Individual perceptual processes help the person face realities of the world. People are influenced by other people and by situations, needs, and past experiences. While a manager is perceiving employees, they are also perceiving the manager.

D. Attitudes are linked with behavioral patterns in a complex manner. They are organized and they provide the emotional basis of most of a person's interpersonal relations. To change attitudes is extremely difficult and requires at least trust in the communicator and strength of message.

E. Personality is primarily developed long before a person joins an organization. It is influenced by hereditary, cultural, and social determinants. To assume that it can be easily modified can result in managerial frustration and ethical problems. The manager should try to cope with personality differences among people and not try to change personalities to fit his or her model of the ideal person.

F. A number of personality variables such as locus of control, tolerance of ambiguity, and risk-taking propensity have been related to behavior and performance. Although difficult to measure, these variables appear to be important in explaining and predicting organizational behavior.

G. Learning is a process by which a relatively enduring change in behavior occurs as a result of practice. It is an important cognitive process because it is at the very heart of motivation. Adequate motivation not only sets in motion the activity which results in learning, but also sustains and directs it.

H. The operant conditioning approach involves the use and understanding of positive and negative reinforcement and punishment.

I. Job stress is inevitable in organizations. Instead of viewing stress as harmful to everyone, it is better to consider the relationship between job stress and job performance as curvilinear.

J. The Type A personality is a charger; that is, task oriented, somewhat intolerant of others, and competitive. In addition, this type of person seems to have a higher rate of premature coronary heart disease.

DISCUSSION AND REVIEW QUESTIONS

1. What type of positive reinforcers could be used to reduce harmful stress in some employees?

2. If a manager were concerned about the job performance of his or her subordinates, would learning principles be important factors to consider? Explain.

3. Explain why managers who are not treated favorably by their superiors would have problems changing their subordinates' negative attitudes toward the organization.

4. Provide some examples of selective perception that would be used in purchasing a new automobile and accepting a new position with an organization.

5. Some critics of operant conditioning believe that it cannot be used in all situations. They believe that many of Skinner's conclusions would result in treating people like animals. Do you agree? Why?

6. Why would it be difficult for a manager to determine the personality, behavior, and performance relationships for his or her subordinates?

7. Suppose you heard a person state that, "Stress is a major factor in reducing the quality of job performance of employees." Would you agree with this assumption? Why?

8. What reinforcers motivate you to do a better job?

9. Some people state that being too concerned with individual differences can cause chaos in an organization. Do you agree? Why?

10. Why is it difficult to measure such factors as personality and other individual differences?

ADDITIONAL REFERENCES

Andrisani, P. J., and Miljus, R. C. "Individual Differences In Preferences For Intrinsic versus Extrinsic Aspects of Work," *Journal of Vocational Behavior* (August 1977), pp. 14–30.

Argyris, C. *Personality and Organization.* New York: Harper, 1957.

Argyris, C., and Schon, J. *Organizational Learning: A Theory of Action Perspective.* Reading, Mass.: Addison-Wesley Publishing Co., 1978.

Bandura, A. *Social Learning Theory.* New York: General Learning Press, 1971.

Berger, S. M., and Lambert, W. W. "Stimulus-Response Theory in Contemporary Social Psychology." In G. Lindzey and E. Aronson, eds. *The Handbook of Social Psychology.* Reading, Mass.: Addison-Wesley, 1971.

Blythe, P. *Stress Disease.* New York: St. Martin's Press, 1973.

Carruthers, M. *The Western Way of Death.* New York: Pantheon Books, 1974.

Domm, D. R.; Blakeney, R. N.; Matteson, M. T.; and Scofield, R. *The Individual and the Organization.* New York: Harper and Row, 1971.

Douglas, M. E. "Stress and Personal Performance," *Personnel Administrator* (August 1977), pp. 60–63.

"At Emery Air Freight: Positive Reinforcement Boosts Performance," *Organizational Dynamics* (Winter 1973), pp. 41–50.

Frost, P.; Mitchell, V.; and Nord, W. R., eds. *Organizational Reality: Observations From the Firing Line.* Santa Monica, Calif.: Goodyear Publishing Co., 1978.

Hall, D. T., and Mansfield, R. "Organizational and Individual Response to External Stress." *Administrative Science Quarterly* (1971), pp. 533–47.

Lundin, Robert W. *Personality.* New York: Macmillan Publishing Co., 1974.

Luthans, F., and Kreitner, R. *Organizational Behavior Modification.* Glenview, Ill.: Scott, Foresman and Co., 1975.

McGrath, J. E. "Stress and Behavior in Organizations." In M. D. Dunnette, ed. *Handbook of Industrial and Organizational Psychology.* Chicago: Rand McNally Publishing Co., 1976, pp. 1351–95.

Schein, E. H. "The Individual, the Organization, and the Career: A Conceptual Scheme." *Journal of Applied Behavioral Science* (1971), pp. 401–26.

Schneir, C. E. "Behavior Modification in Management: A Review and Critique." *Academy of Management Journal* (September 1974), pp. 528–48.

Scott, W. E., and Cummings, L. L. *Readings in Organizational Behavior and Human Performance.* Homewood, Ill.: Richard D. Irwin, 1973.

Watson, R. I. *The Great Psychologists.* Philadelphia: J. B. Lippincott Co., 1978.

Watson, D. L., and Tharp, R. G. *Self-Directed Behavior.* Monterey, Calif.: Brooks/Cole Publishing Co., 1977.

Whyte, W. F. "Pigeons, Persons, and Piece Rates." *Psychology Today* (1972), pp. 66–68.

Wiggins, J. S. *Personality and Prediction.* Reading, Mass.: Addison-Wesley Publishing Co., 1973.

Yukl, G. A.; Latham, G. P.; and Pursell, E. D. "The Effectiveness of Performance Incentives under Continuous and Variable Ratio Schedules of Reinforcement," *Personnel Psychology* (Summer 1976), pp. 221–31.

CASE FOR ANALYSIS

REFUSING A PROMOTION

Ron Riddell, 36 years old, is a project manager for the Dowling Products Corporation and has established a reputation as a conscientious, prompt, and creative manager. He presently is working on a new cleansing product that can be used to clean sink tops. The cleanser is expected to generate gross sales of $3 million the first year it is on the market.

Ron has a permanent team of eight men and three women and a temporary team of two women and two men assigned to him only for the important cleansing product. The team plans, organizes, and controls the various project phases from development to pilot marketing testing. The team must work closely with engineers, chemists, production managers, sales directors, and marketing research specialists before a quality product can be finally marketed.

Ron, in the past eight years, has directed four projects that have been considered outstanding market successes and one that has been considered a "superloser" financially. His supervisor is Norma Collins, Ph.D., a chemical engineer. Norma has direct responsibility for seven projects, three of which are considerably smaller than Ron's and three of which have about the same potential and size as Ron's.

Norma has recently been selected to be the overseas divisional coordinator of research and development. She and three top executives have met for the past two weeks and have decided to offer Norma's present position to Ron. They believe that the new job for Ron will mean more prestige and authority, and certainly an increase in salary.

Norma is given the task of offering the position to Ron. This is the discussion that occurs in Norma's office:

Norma: Ron, how is the cleansing project going?

Ron: As good as could be expected. I sometimes think that Joe Rambo is trying to slow down our progress. He is just a "bear" to get along with.

Norma: Well, everyone has been a little concerned because of the main competitor's progress on their cleansing product. I'm sure we can put everything together and effectively compete in the market.

Ron: I know we can.

Norma: I wanted to talk to you about a new job that is becoming vacant in 30 days. The executive selection committee unanimously believes that Ron Riddell is the right person for the job.

Ron: What new job are you talking about?

Norma: My job, Ron. I have been promoted to overseas divisional coordinator of research and development. We want to begin turning over my job to you as soon as possible. If we drag our feet, the cleansing project may not be the success that we need to bolster our financial picture.

Ron: I am flattered by this opportunity and really believe that professionally I can handle the challenge. My real concern is the personal problems I'm having.

Norma: Do you mean personal problems here at Dowling?

Ron: No, I mean problems in my family that have led to sleepless nights, arguments with my wife, and hostility between myself and my best neighbor. My brother Mark has been arrested two times recently, once for vagrancy and once for possession of narcotics. As you know, my Dad died four years ago and my mother just can't handle the kid. So I have pitched in and am trying to straighten the kid out. Connie, my wife, is fed up with the time I spend here at work and my meddling into my brother's problems. She has even threatened to leave me and take the kids with her to Denver. The new job is really interesting, but I'm afraid it would be the "straw that breaks the camel's back."

Norma: I'm sorry to hear about these problems Ron. I know that it is hard to separate outside problems and pressures from Dowling problems and pressures. If you are going to become a more important part of the management team it will mean that separation is mandatory. The new job is the challenge that we have trained you for and is a reward for your outstanding past performance. Please think over the job offer and let me know in three days. We need your talents, experience, and leadership.

Ron left Norma's office with a sick feeling in his stomach. He had worked hard for years and the goal he was striving for was within his reach. All he had to do was to say yes to Norma. He thought about the additional money, status, and authority attached to the new job. Then he thought about his wife who had become more depressed about his working on Saturdays and Sundays; his daughter whom he really had not talked to for six months; his mother who had helped pay for his college education; and his brother who always called and asked him to play golf or shoot pool only to be told, "I have to work Steve, sorry."

After thinking over the offer for three days Ron walks into Norma's office.

Norma: Come on in, Ron, and relax.

Ron: I can't relax, because I am extremely nervous. I really want the job, but my family must come first. My daughter, wife, and mother have helped me get to my present position. I just feel that taking on this new job will lead to so many problems that I must turn it down.

Norma: I sympathize with your dilemma and wish you the best of luck. I want you to understand, however, that this type of opportunity may never happen again. The company needs your talents now. Can't you get your wife and mother to understand the importance of this job in your career? I just can't believe that they would not understand.

Ron: Norma, we all have priorities and personal backgrounds that just can't be ignored.

Norma: Ron, you are sounding like a behavioral scientist. I know this just as well as you. What I'm saying is that you have worked this long and hard and now decide not to accept the challenge. This is what puzzles me.

Questions for Consideration

1. What organizational responsibilities does Norma believe that Ron is shirking by turning down the new job offer?

2. Why would the behavioral orientations of Ron and Norma differ?

3. Do you consider personal needs and problems as more important than organizational needs and problems? Why?

4. Should organizations force an employee like Ron to fit their plans for him? Why?

EXPERIENTIAL EXERCISE

ANALYSIS OF JOB-RELATED STRESS

Objectives

1. To illustrate that individuals view job-related stress factors differently.
2. To display how groups can reach different conclusions than individuals about job-related stress.
3. To emphasize how positive job-related factors can initiate some amount of stress within individuals.

Related Topics

Life event changes influence the behavior and performance of employees. They are important and vary in the amount of influence that they exert physiologically.

Starting the Exercise

Allow individuals to complete Phase I of the exercise without any consultation between each other. Then set up small groups to complete Phase II. In Phase III individuals will be involved in reviewing the work of the groups.

The Facts

Thomas Holmes and other researchers at the University of Washington School of Medicine have developed a stress scaling system that can be used to address the issue of life change stressors. Table A shows the relative impact of different life changes, with the most stressful life event—death of a spouse—given a scale value of 100 points. Some of the events listed are generally considered to be positive life events—outstanding personal achievement (28), gain of a new family member (44), and marital reconciliation (45). Even these positive events generate stress because of new roles, expectations, and activities that go along with the changes. Holmes has found through empirical analysis that the accumulation of more than 200 scale points in a year results in a better than 50 percent chance that the individual will sustain some type of major illness in the following year. The assumption offered is that when a person's endocrine system is overburdened with stress-

Table A
Scaling of Life-Change Units for Various Experiences

Life Event	Scale Value
Death of spouse	100
Divorce	73
Marital separation	65
Jail term	63
Death of a close family member	63
Major personal injury or illness	53
Marriage	50
Fired from work	47
Marital reconciliation	45
Retirement	45
Major change in health of family member	44
Pregnancy	40
Sex difficulties	39
Gain of a new family member	39
Business readjustment	39
Change in financial state	38
Death of a close friend	37
Change to a different line of work	36
Change in number of arguments with spouse	35
Mortgage over $10,000	31
Foreclosure of mortgage or loan	30
Change in responsibilities at work	29
Son or daughter leaving home	29
Trouble with in-laws	29
Outstanding personal achievement	28
Wife begins or stops work	26
Begin or end school	26
Change in living conditions	25
Revision of personal habits	24
Trouble with boss	23
Change in work hours or conditions	20
Change in residence	20
Change in schools	20
Change in recreation	19
Change in church activities	19
Change in social activities	18
Mortgage or loan less than $10,000	17
Change in sleeping habits	16
Change in number of family get-togethers	15
Change in eating habits	15
Vacation	13
Christmas	12
Minor violations of the law	11

Source: From L. O. Ruch and T. H. Holmes, "Scaling of Life Change: Comparison of Direct and Indirect Methods," *Journal of Psychosomatic Research*, 1971, *15*, 224.

ful events, the body cannot perform its normal function of fighting off diseases. Perhaps an accumulation of job related stresses could also result in overburdening the body's disease resistant mechanisms. Listed in Table B are some job factors that could cause stress. The three sets of factors are supervi-

Table B
A List of Job Factors

Supervisor Initiated	Individually Initiated	Peer Initiated
Demotion	Challenging production goals	Production norms
Criticism	Challenging career goals	Praise
Suspension	High effort	Acceptance
Probation	Poor attitudes	Cohesiveness
Praise	Personal development	Reprimand
Recognition	Self-assessment	Improved status
A bonus	Request for pay raise	
Promotion		
Positive performance evaluation session		
Negative performance evaluation session		

sor, individual, and peer initiated. Assume that these factors apply to an individual working in a typical organization. Also assume that the individual is relatively young and has about six years experience in the organization.

Exercise Procedures

Phase I: 20 minutes
1. Individually place scale values on each of the job factors listed in Table B. Place 100 points on the factors you consider to be the most potentially stressful.
2. Record your individual evaluations on a separate sheet of paper.

Phase II: 40 minutes
1. Set up groups of 5 to 6 people and discuss the individual assignments of scale points made by members.
2. Reach some type of group consensus on what is a reasonable value for each of the items.

Phase III: 30 minutes
1. Each group places the group consensus for the scale values on the board or a chart for each class member to review.
2. Discuss the different values developed by each of the groups.

Chapter 5

Motivation, Behavior, and Performance

AN ORGANIZATIONAL ISSUE FOR DEBATE
Skinner's Approach to Reinforcement

ARGUMENT FOR

Some researchers and managers believe that the behaviorism work of Skinner has been overlooked, misinterpreted, and misapplied. Some of the neglect has been pointed out as follows:

Since the major concern of managers of human resources is the prediction and control of behavior of organizational participants, it is curious to find that people with such a need are extremely conversant with McGregor and Maslow and totally ignorant of Skinner.*

The increasing attention in the applied organizational behavior literature to Skinnerian behaviorism should minimize some of the misinterpretation.

At the very heart of Skinnerian behaviorism is a major contention: Behavior is a function of its consequences. Skinner's approach is based on what is called an external approach; it emphasizes the effect of environmental consequences on objective, observable behavior. He believes that behavioral scientists should abandon their preoccupation with the inner thoughts of a person and concentrate more on the fit between the person and the environment.

According to Skinner's approach, work behavior is shaped and maintained by its consequences; these consequences (reinforcers) can be either positive or negative, but positive reinforcers are more effective. Through the use of reinforcers, be-

ARGUMENT AGAINST

The critics of Skinnerian behaviorism are numerous. One of the most respected and articulate critics is William F. Whyte. It is Whyte's contention that Skinner's operant conditioning theory tells us little about prediction and control of behavior. It also fails to deal with four crucial elements of real-life behavior in organizations. These are:

1. *The Cost-Benefit Ratio*—Skinner, in using pigeons to develop his principles would disregard the costs of the action to the actor. The costs were trifling compared to the benefits (food) the experimental pigeon received as a consequence of action. This is not generally true with people. Individuals weigh what they receive for their efforts in terms of personal investments. Thus, providing positive reinforcers for production is much more complex than giving pigeons food.

2. *Conflicting Stimuli*—Employees face conflicting stimuli of the reward system, requests from subordinates, meeting schedules, and other organizational sources. They do indeed respond, as Skinner argues, in terms of the consequences of past behavior. But many situations provide conflicting stimulus conditions and managers cannot easily predict any response simply by analyzing the relationship between the individual and the anticipated reinforcement.

98

ARGUMENT FOR *(continued)*

havior can be learned. A learned behavior is called an *operant* because it operates on the environment to produce a consequence. Skinner called unlearned behavior *respondent behavior.*

The supporters of Skinner's principles have recommended that behavior modification be applied to training and personal development, job design, compensation, organizational design, and performance. They believe that managers who take the time to study Skinner's principles of behavior control will see the potential managerial applications. The advocates state that even Skinner's critics admit that his behavior principles work in organizations.†

---

* Walter Nord, "Beyond the Teaching Machine: The Neglected Area of Operant Conditioning in the Theory and Practice of Management," *Organizational Behavior and Human Performance* (November 1969), p. 375.

† For support for applying behavior modification see Fred Luthans and Robert Kreitner, *Organizational Behavior Modification* (Glenview, Ill.: Scott, Foresman & Co., 1975); and Everett E. Adam, Jr., "Behavioral Modification in Quality Control," *Academy of Management Journal* (December 1975), pp. 662–79.

ARGUMENT AGAINST *(continued)*

3. *Time Lag and Trust*—Few of a person's acts bring immediate rewards. The time span between behavior and reinforcement in organizations can be quite long. There is also the issue of trust that an individual must have if a time lag must exist. The individual must trust the person applying reinforcers. These are not issues when experimental animals are used.

4. *One-Body Problem*—In the Skinner laboratory experiments, the researcher's attention is only on the environmental conditions that induce the pigeon to behave a certain way. When working with people, the contingencies to which an individual responds are provided by another person or persons. Thus, it is necessary to learn to deal with the contingencies affecting the behavior of the person initating the reinforcers and the worker.

Whyte does not want to discard Skinner's theory, but asks that it be treated cautiously. He would like Skinner and his supporters to not make grandiose claims since the claims do not serve to develop what is an important set of ideas regarding motivation.‡

---

‡ Whyte's position appears in William F. Whyte, "Skinnerian Theory in Organizations," *Psychology Today* (April 1972), pp. 67–68, 96–100, and "An Interview with William F. Whyte," *Organizational Dynamics* (Spring 1975), pp. 51–66.

INTRODUCTION

An important determinant of individual performance is motivation. It is not the only determinant; other variables such as effort expended, ability, and previous experience also influence performance. This chapter, however, concentrates on the motivation process, behavior, and individual performance. First, an integrated model depicting the motivation process and other variables influencing behavior and performance is developed. Second, distinctions between selected theories of motivation are described. Finally, some applications of motivation theory are presented. Specifically, behavior modification and the modified workweek are discussed. Later in the book other motivation practices such as the use of pay reward systems, job enrichment, and flexitime will be discussed.

The Motivation Dilemma

A continual and perplexing problem facing managers is why some employees perform better than others. A number of interesting and important variables have been used to explain performance differences among employees. For example, such variables as ability, instinct, intrinsic and extrinsic rewards, aspiration levels, and personal backgrounds explain why some employees perform well and others are poor performers.

Despite the obvious importance of motivation, it is difficult to define and to apply in organizations. One definition proposes that motivation has to do with (1) the direction of behavior; (2) the strength of the response (i.e., effort) once an employee chooses to follow a course of action; and (3) the persistence of the behavior, or how long the person continues to behave in a particular manner.[1]

Another viewpoint suggests that the analysis of motivation should concentrate on the factors which incite and direct a person's activities.[2] One theorist emphasizes the goal-directedness aspect of motivations.[3] Yet another states that motivation is "concerned with how behavior gets started, is energized, is sustained, is directed, is stopped and what kind of subjective reaction is present in the organism while all this is going on."[4]

A careful examination of each of these views leads to a number of conclusions about motivation:

1. Theorists present slightly different interpretations and place emphasis on different factors.
2. It is related to behavior and performance.

---

[1] John P. Campbell, Marvin D. Dunnette, Edward E. Lawler III, and Karl E. Weick, *Managerial Behavior, Performance, and Effectiveness* (New York: McGraw-Hill Book Company, 1970), p. 340.

[2] J. W. Atkinson, *An Introduction to Motivation* (Princeton, N.J.: Van Nostrand, 1964).

[3] D. Bindra, *Motivation: A Systematic Reinterpretation* (New York: Ronald Press, 1959).

[4] M. R. Jones, ed., *Nebraska Symposium on Motivation* (Lincoln: University of Nebraska Press, 1955), p. 14.

3. It involves goal directedness.
4. Physiological, psychological, and environmental differences of individual employees are important factors to consider.

The Starting Point: The Individual

Most managers must consider motivating a diverse, and in many respects unpredictable, group of people. The diversity results in different behavioral patterns that are in some manner related to needs and goals.

The needs of a person change with time, partly because of maturation and satisfaction. *Needs* refer to deficiencies that an individual experiences at a particular point in time. The deficiency may be physiological—a need for food; psychological—a need for self-esteem; or sociological—a need for social interaction. Needs are viewed as energizers or triggers of behavioral responses. The implication is that when need deficiencies are present, the individual is more susceptible to managers' motivational efforts.

The importance of goals in any discussion of motivation is apparent. The motivational process, as interpreted by most theorists, is goal directed. The goals, or outcomes, an employee seeks are viewed as forces that attract the person. The accomplishment of desirable goals can result in a significant reduction in need deficiencies. In organizational settings, goals can be *positive,* such as praise, recognition, pay increase, promotion; or *negative,* such as being passed over for promotion or reprimanded for poor performance. Negative goals for most employees are unattractive; therefore they will try to avoid them.

THE MOTIVATION PROCESS

Needs and goals are concepts which provide the bases for construction of an integrated model. The initial step in developing a model for clarifying the motivation process is to relate these variables in a sequential manner as shown in Figure 5–1.

As illustrated in Figure 5–1 people seek to reduce various need deficiencies. Need deficiencies trigger a search process for ways to reduce the tension caused by the discomfort. A course of action is selected and goal (outcome)-directed behavior occurs. After a period of time, managers assess that performance. The performance evaluation results in some type of reward or punishment. These are weighed by the person, and the need deficiencies are reassessed. This, in turn, triggers the process and the circular pattern is started again.

A more complete and integrative model can be developed using the circular model as a foundation. A number of factors such as effort and ability that are extremely important for understanding the motivational process are not represented in Figure 5–1. However, these factors should be included in a more complete motivation model. *Effort* involves the energy a person exerts while performing a job. *Ability* designates the capabilities of a person, such

Figure 5–1
The Motivational Process: An Initial Model

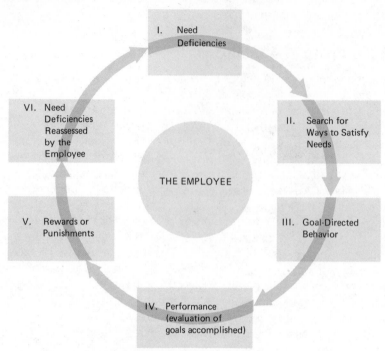

as intelligence and dexterity. The amount of effort expended is related to some extent to ability. An employee who does not have the ability to analyze a problem will probably not exert much effort to solve it.[5]

Organizational variables also influence the motivational process. The job design, span of control, leader's style, group affiliations of the person, and technology are some of the organizational variables influencing motivation. The individual's behavior and performance are significantly influenced by these factors.

Another variable that is part of the motivational process is satisfaction. *Satisfaction* generally means the fulfillment acquired by experiencing various job activities and rewards. The term satisfaction is used to analyze outcomes already experienced by an employee.[6] Thus, satisfaction is a consequence of rewards and punishments associated with past performance. The employee can be satisfied, or dissatisfied with the behavior, performance, and reward relationships that currently exist.

Motivation and satisfaction are related, but are not synonymous concepts.

---

[5] L. L. Cummings and Donald P. Schwab, *Performance in Organizations* (Glenview, Ill.: Scott, Foresman and Co., 1973), p. 8.

[6] John Wanous and Edward E. Lawler III, "Measurement and Meaning of Job Satisfaction," *Journal of Applied Psychology* (April 1972), pp. 95–105.

Figure 5–2
An Integrated Model of the Motivational Process

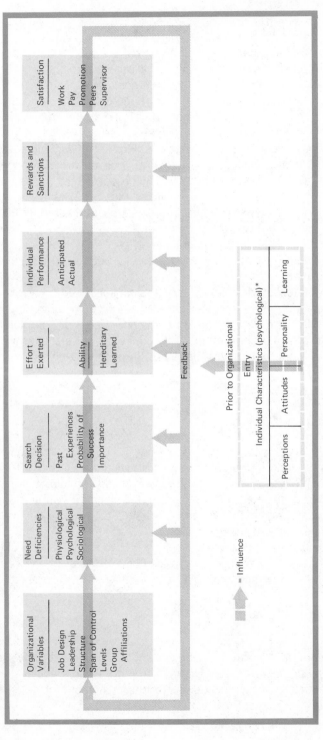

* Note that these variables are also influenced by the person's life in an organization.

Motivation is primarily concerned with goal-directed behavior. The manager who works extra hours to perfect the budget is displaying a high degree of motivation. A counterpart manager who boasts about "slapping together the important budget" in spare moments just to quiet the accountants is displaying low motivation from the organization's perspective. This manager may enjoy every aspect of the job, and this state represents high job satisfaction. On the other hand, the manager who works long hours to prepare a sound budget may be dissatisfied with the job.

Combining the concepts represented in Figure 5–1 with effort, ability, organizational variables, satisfaction, and various psychological concepts results in an integrated model of the motivation process. This model, Figure 5–2, shows how these various factors are linked together. The organizational variables influence needs which initiate the search process until ultimately the employee evaluates rewards and punishments associated with performance. Note that each of the factors is influenced by psychological variables (e.g., perception) that have been shaped primarily before the employee entered the organization.

The integrated model highlights the complexities involved in attempting to cope with the motivation process. This is exactly what the manager must do: cope with the process. Managers cannot control or completely alter the process. In order to cope, managers require an understanding of theories, research, and applications that have been proposed by theorists and practicing managers.

MOTIVATION THEORIES AND RESEARCH

Each person is attracted to some set of goals. If a manager is to predict an employee's behavior with any accuracy, it is necessary to know something about this set, and the actions the person will take to obtain it. There is no shortage of motivation theories and research findings that attempt to provide explanations of the behavior-outcome relationship. Two categories can be used to sort theories of motivation.[7] The *content* theories focus on the factors *within* the person that energize, direct, sustain, and stop behavior. They attempt to determine specific needs which motivate people. The second category includes what are called the *process* theories. They provide a description and analysis of the process of *how* behavior is energized, directed, sustained, and stopped.

CONTENT THEORIES

Three important content theories of motivation are Maslow's need hierarchy, Herzberg's two-factory theory, and McClelland's achievement theory. These theories have stimulated an extensive number of research studies

---

[7] Campbell et al., *Managerial Behavior,* pp. 340–56.

and numerous application endeavors by managers. This is the reason why we have chosen to discuss these three content motivation theories.

Maslow's Need Hierarchy

The crux of Maslow's theory is that needs are arranged in a hierarchy.[8] The lowest-level needs are the physiological and the highest level are the self-actualization needs. These needs are assumed to mean the following:

1. Physiological: The need for food, drink, shelter, and relief from pain.
2. Safety and security: The need for freedom from threat, i.e., the security from threatening events and/or surroundings.
3. Belongingness, social, and love: The need for friendship, affiliation, interaction, and love.
4. Esteem: The need for self-esteem, and esteem from others.
5. Self-actualization: The need to fulfill oneself by maximizing the use of abilities, skills, and potential.

Based on Maslow's opinions, it is assumed that a person attempts to satisfy the more basic needs (food, shelter) before directing behavior toward satisfying upper-level needs (self-actualization). The lower-order needs must be satisfied before a higher order need begins to control the conscious thoughts of a person. A crucial point in Maslow's thinking is that a satisfied need ceases to motivate. When a person decides that he or she is earning enough pay for contributing to the organization, money loses its power to motivate.

The Maslow theory is built on the premise that people have a need to grow and develop. This assumption may be true for some employees, but not be accurate for others. This is an inherent problem with the Maslow hierarchy: it was not scientifically tested by its founder. In a declarative manner, Maslow proposed that the typical adult has satisfied 85 percent of the physiological need, 70 percent of the safety and security need, 50 percent of the belongingness, social, and love need, 40 percent of the esteem need, and 10 percent of the self-actualization need. This assertion is highlighted in Figure 5–3.

The implication of the high degree of need deficiency in the self-actualization and esteem categories (Figure 5–3) is that managers should focus attention on strategies to correct these deficiencies. This logic assumes that attempts to satisfy these deficiencies have a higher probability of succeeding than directing attention to the already satisfactorily fulfilled lower order needs.

---

[8] A. H. Maslow, "A Theory of Human Motivation," *Psychological Review* (July 1943), pp. 370–96; and A. H. Maslow, *Motivation and Personality* (New York: Harper, 1954).

Figure 5–3
The Typical Person's Need Deficiency and Satisfaction

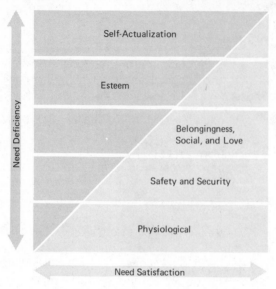

Furthermore, the highly deficient needs are a potential danger for managers. An unsatisfied need can cause frustration, conflict, and stress. The skilled technician in a research laboratory who is given paperwork assignments instead of more challenging project assignments is an example of a person being blocked from satisfying self-actualization needs. This type of blockage in the fulfillment of needs can lead to frustration and stress that may eventually result in undesirable performance.

People cope with frustration and stress in a number of ways. The reaction mechanisms differ from person to person because of environmental, situational, and personal factors. The inability to reduce a need deficiency can lead to a more concerted effort to perform even better, or to try harder to satisfy the need "the next time." It can, however, also result in various *defensive behaviors.*

Defensive behavior often occurs because of the need to protect one's self image. Absenteeism or *withdrawal* is a defensive behavior to avoid the unpleasant and dissatisfying work environment. This behavior can be physical or nonphysical absence or withdrawal. An example of a physical absence is simply not going to work. A nonphysical absence or withdrawal is not showing any concern about the job, peers, or the company. The person is on the job physically, but certainly not mentally.

Aggression is a reaction to nonsatisfaction of needs in the work organization. The aggression may be directed toward an object, a person, or the organization. It can be verbal or physical. The physical form can lead to equipment damage or personal injuries. The verbal form is directed at a person and can be very emotional.

Rationalization is a widely utilized form of defensive behavior. The objective of this behavior is to explain failure in a manner that is accepted, at least partially, by others. The ploy of blaming a poor examination grade on the professor is a form of rationalization in some cases. An employee may rationalize poor performance because of improper supervision, when in fact the person has not exerted the effort to perform well.

Regression is used by some people when they are frustrated. A worker may regress to childlike behavior to overcome frustration. An example would be an effervescent person who becomes sullen after being passed over for a promotion.

These and other defensive behaviors result from the inability of an employee to satisfy needs. Such behaviors are realities that managers face when working with subordinates, as well as when considering their own experiences.

Some Selected Need Satisfaction Research

A number of research studies have attempted to test the need hierarchy theory. The first reported field research that tested a modified version of Maslow's need hierarchy was performed by Porter.[9] At the time of the initial studies, he assumed that physiological needs were being adequately satisfied for managers and he substituted a higher-order need called autonomy. This was defined as the person's satisfaction with opportunities to make independent decisions, set goals, and work without close supervision.

Since the early Porter studies, other studies have reported

1. Managers higher in the organizational chain of command place greater emphasis on self-actualization and autonomy.[10]
2. Managers at lower organizational levels in small organizations (less than 500 employees) are more satisfied than their counterpart managers in large firms (more than 5,000 employees); however, the managers at upper levels in the large organizations are more satisfied than their counterparts in small companies.[11]
3. American managers overseas are more satisfied with autonomy opportunities than their counterparts working in the United States.[12]

Despite these findings there have been a number of issues raised about the need hierarchy theory. First, longitudinal data from managers in two differ-

[9] Lyman W. Porter, "A Study of Perceived Need Satisfaction in Bottom and Middle Management Jobs," Journal of Applied Psychology (February 1961), pp. 1–10.

[10] Lyman W. Porter, Organizational Patterns of Managerial Job Attitudes (New York: American Foundation for Management Research, 1964).

[11] Lyman W. Porter, "Job Attitudes in Management: Perceived Deficiencies in Need Fulfillment as a Function of Size of the Company," Journal of Applied Psychology (December 1963), pp. 386–97.

[12] John M. Ivancevich, "Perceived Need Satisfactions of Domestic versus Overseas Managers," Journal of Applied Psychology (August 1969), pp. 274–78.

ent companies provided little support that a hierarchy of needs exists.[13] The data suggested that only two levels of needs exist: one is the biological level and the other a global level which includes all other needs. Further evidence also disputes the hierarchy notion.[14] Researchers found that as managers advance in an organization, their needs for safety decrease, with a corresponding increase in their needs for social interaction, achievement, and self-actualization. These researchers suggest that career advancement rather than lower-order need fulfillment are the causes for changes in need deficiencies.

Alderfer condenses the Maslow hierarchy into existence, relatedness, and growth needs which he refers to as the ERG theory. The *existence* needs include Maslow's physiological needs, pay, fringe benefits, and working conditions. The *relatedness* needs include the Maslow social and esteem categories. The *growth* needs include the person's desire to be self-confident and productive. Thus, the growth need overlaps the Maslow esteem and self-actualization needs.[15]

Researchers have examined the ERG theory using nurses, bank employees, and life insurance personnel. The researchers concluded that need satisfaction is "perhaps most appropriately conceptualized as a global construct, in the Gestalt sense, a general state of the organism which may be greater than the sum of its parts."[16] They proposed that Maslow's theory is not specifically applicable to employees in organizational settings.

A review of research concludes that there is little support for the Maslow theory. There is some support for the notion that physiological needs take precedence over other needs, but there is no sound evidence that the other needs are activated as suggested by Maslow. Furthermore, the concepts of "esteem" and "self-actualization" are not well-defined.[17]

Although many of the recent research results fail to substantiate the five-level need hierarchy, it still has a "common sense" appeal for managers. It is simple and has some relevance because needs, no matter how they are categorized, are important for understanding behavior, as reflected in Figure 5–2. Since understanding the behavior of another person is such a complex task for managers, an approach that is intuitively appealing such as Maslow's model is popular.

---

[13] Edward L. Lawler III and J. L. Suttle, "A Causal Correlation Test of the Need Hierarchy Concept," *Organizational Behavior and Human Performance* (April 1972), pp. 265–87.

[14] Douglas T. Hall and K. E. Nougaim, "An Examination of Maslow's Need Hierarchy in an Organizational Setting," *Organizational Behavior and Human Performance* (February 1968), pp. 12–35.

[15] Clayton P. Alderfer, *Human Needs in Organizational Settings* (New York: The Free Press, 1972).

[16] Benjamin Schneider and Clayton P. Alderfer, "Three Studies of Need Satisfactions in Organizations," *Administrative Science Quarterly* (December 1973), pp. 489–505.

[17] M. A. Wahba and L. G. Birdwell, "Maslow Reconsidered: A Review of Research on the Need Hierarchy Theory," *Organizational Behavior and Human Performance* (April 1976), pp. 212–40.

Herzberg's Two-Factor Theory

Herzberg developed the two-factor theory of motivation.[18] The two factors are called the dissatisfiers-satisfiers or the hygiene-motivators or the extrinsic-intrinsic factors, depending on the discussant of the theory. The original research testing this theory included a group of 200 accountants and engineers. Herzberg used interview responses to questions like, "Can you describe, in detail, when you felt exceptionally good about your job?" and "Can you describe, in detail, when you felt exceptionally bad about your job?" It is reported that rarely were the same kind of factors categorized as both good and bad. This systematic procedure resulted in the development of two distinct kinds of factors—satisfiers and dissatisfiers.

The initial Herzberg study resulted in two specific conclusions about the theory:

First, there is a set of *extrinsic* job conditions which result in *dissatisfaction* among employees when they are not present. If these conditions are present, this does not necessarily motivate employees. These conditions are the *dissatisfiers* or *hygiene* factors since they are needed to maintain at least a level of "no dissatisfaction." These factors include:

a. Salary.
b. Job security.
c. Working conditions.
d. Status.
e. Company procedures.
f. Quality of technical supervision.
g. Quality of interpersonal relations among peers, with superiors, and with subordinates.

Second, a set of *intrinsic* job conditions exist and operate to build strong levels of motivation which can result in good job performance. If these conditions are not present, they do not prove highly dissatisfying. This set of factors is called the *satisfiers* or *motivators*. They include:

a. Achievement.
b. Recognition.
c. Responsibility.
d. Advancement.
e. The work itself.
f. The possibility of growth.

The Herzberg model basically assumes that job satisfaction is not a unidimensional concept. His research leads to the conclusion that two continua correctly interpret satisfaction. Figure 5–4 presents graphically two views of job satisfaction.

One appealing aspect of Herzberg's work to managers is that the terminology is work-oriented. There is no need to translate psychological terminology to everyday language. Despite this important feature, Herzberg's work has been criticized for a number of reasons. First, the theory was originally based

---

[18] Frederick Herzberg, B. Mausner, and B. Synderman, *The Motivation to Work* (New York: John Wiley and Sons, 1959).

Figure 5–4
Traditional versus Herzberg Satisfaction Continua

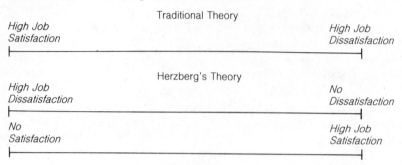

Traditional Theory

High Job
Satisfaction

High Job
Dissatisfaction

├───┤

Herzberg's Theory

High Job
Dissatisfaction

No
Dissatisfaction

├───┤

No
Satisfaction

High Job
Satisfaction

├───┤

on a sample of accountants and engineers. Critics ask whether this limited sample can justify generalizing to other occupational groups. The technology, environment, and backgrounds of the two occupational groups are distinctly different from such groups as nurses, medical technologists, salespeople, computer programmers, clerks, and police officers.[19]

Second, some researchers believe that Herzberg's work oversimplifies the nature of job satisfaction. Dunnette et al. state that:

> Results show that the Herzberg two-factor theory is a grossly oversimplified portrayal of the mechanism by which job satisfaction or dissatisfaction comes about. Satisfaction or dissatisfaction can reside in the job context, the job content, or both jointly. Moreover, certain dimensions—notably Achievement, Responsibility, and Recognition—are more important for both satisfaction and dissatisfaction than certain other job dimensions—notably Working Conditions, Company Policies and Practices, and Security.[20]

Other criticisms focus on Herzberg's methodology, which requires people to look at themselves retrospectively. Can people be aware of all that motivated or dissatisfied them? These critics believe that unconscious factors are not identified in Herzberg's analysis. The "recency of events" bias of being able to recall the most recent job conditions and feelings is embedded in the methodology.[21]

Another criticism of Herzberg's work is that little attention has been directed toward testing the motivational and performance implications of the theory.[22]

---

[19] For critiques of the Herzberg theory see Robert J. House and L. Wigdor, "Herzberg's Dual-Factor Theory of Job Satisfaction and Motivation: A Review of the Empirical Evidence and a Criticism," *Personnel Psychology* (Winter 1967), pp. 369–80, and Joseph Schneider and Edwin Locke, "A Critique of Herzberg's Classification System and a Suggested Revision," *Organizational Behavior and Human Performance* (July 1971), pp. 441–58.

[20] Marvin Dunnette, John Campbell, and M. Hakel, "Factors Contributing to Job Dissatisfaction in Six Occupational Groups," *Organizational Behavior and Human Performance* (May 1967), p. 147.

[21] Abraham K. Korman, *Industrial and Organizational Psychology* (Englewood Cliffs, N.J.: Prentice-Hall, 1971), pp. 148–50.

[22] Edward E. Lawler III, *Motivation in Work Organizations* (Monterey, Calif.: Brooks/Cole Publishing Co., 1973), p. 72.

In the original study of engineers and accountants, only self-reports of performance were used and, in most cases, the respondents were reporting on job activities that had happened over a long period of time. Herzberg has offered no explanation as to why various extrinsic and intrinsic job factors should affect performance. The two-factor theory also fails to explain why various job factors are important. In reality, the theory, because of its heavy emphasis on job factors, is basically a theory of determinants of job dissatisfaction and satisfaction.

Although the list of critics seems to grow annually, the impact of this theory on practicing managers should not be underestimated. Managers appear to feel comfortable about many of the things Herzberg includes in his two-factor discussion. From a scientific vantage point, this has some dangers because of misuse, but from a real-world perspective it is appealing to managers.

McClelland's Learned Needs Theory

McClelland has proposed a theory of motivation that is closely associated with learning concepts. He believes that many needs are acquired from the culture.[23] Three of these needs are: the need for achievement (n Ach), the need for affiliation (n Aff), and the need for power (n Pow).

McClelland proposes that when a need is strong in a person, its effect is to motivate the person to use behavior which leads to satisfaction of the need. For example, having a high n Ach encourages an individual to set challenging goals, work hard to achieve the goals, and use the skills and abilities needed to accomplish the goals.

Based on research results, McClelland developed a descriptive set of factors which reflect a high need for achievement. These are:

1. The person likes to take responsibility for solving problems.
2. The person tends to set moderate achievement goals and is inclined to take calculated risks.
3. The person desires feedback on performance.

The need for affiliation reflects a desire to interact socially with people. A person with a high need for affiliation is concerned about the quality of important personal relationships. Thus, social relationships take precedent over task accomplishment for such a person.

A person who has a high need for power concentrates on obtaining and exercising power and authority. The person is concerned with influencing others and winning arguments. Power has two possible orientations according to McClelland: it can be negative in that the person exercising it emphasizes dominance and submission, or power can be positive in that it reflects persuasive and inspirational behavior.

---

[23] David C. McClelland, "Business Drive and National Achievement," *Harvard Business Review* (July–August 1962), pp. 99–112.

The main theme of McClelland's theory is that these needs are learned through coping with one's environment. Since needs are learned, behavior which is rewarded tends to recur at a higher frequency. Managers who are rewarded for achievement behavior learn to take moderate risks and to achieve goals. Similarly, a high need for affiliation or power can be traced back to a history of receiving rewards for sociable, dominant, or inspirational behavior. As a result of the learning process, individuals develop unique configurations of needs that affect their behavior and performance.

Individuals may have a high need in one area, but this does not mean that they will have low needs in other areas. For example, a manager or operating employee with a high *n Pow* does not necessarily have a low *n Ach* or a low *n Aff.* The optimal mix of needs to be successful in performing a particular job can only be determined by analysis of the job tasks, the organizational system, and the individuals involved.

The implications to managers of the McClelland theory and research are significant. If the needs of employees can be accurately measured, organizations can improve the selection and placement processes. For example, an employee or recruit with a high need for achievement could be placed in a position that would enable the person to achieve. This could result in improved performance because of the fit of need intensities and job characteristics. Thus, it is important to identify the behaviors required to perform a set of tasks effectively, and then to determine what individual characteristics are most associated with these behaviors.[24]

A Synopsis of Three Content Theories

Each content theory attempts to explain behavior from a slightly different perspective. None of the theories has been accepted as the sole basis for explaining behavior. Although critics are skeptical, it appears that people have innate and learned needs and that various job factors result in a degree of satisfaction. Thus, each of these theories provides the manager with some understanding of behavior and performance.

The three theories are compared in Figure 5–5. McClelland proposed no lower order needs. However, his needs for achievement and power are not identical with Herzberg's motivators, or Maslow's higher order needs, but there are some similarities. A major difference between the content theories is McClelland's emphasis on socially acquired needs. The Maslow theory offers a need classification system and Herzberg discusses intrinsic and extrinsic job factors.

PROCESS THEORIES

The content theories we have examined focus mainly on the needs and incentives that cause behavior. The *process* theories of motivation are con-

---

[24] Paul R. Lawrence and Jay W. Lorsch, *Developing Organizations: Diagnosis and Action* (Reading, Mass.: Addison-Wesley, 1969).

Figure 5–5
Maslow's Need Hierarchy; McClelland's Achievement, Affiliation, and Power Needs;
and Herzberg's Two-Factor Theory

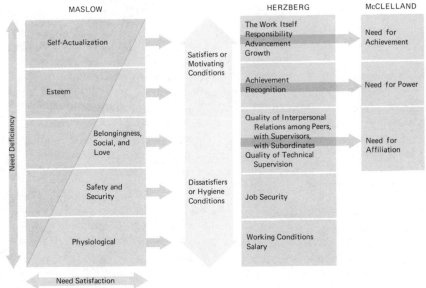

cerned with answering the question of *how* individual behavior is energized, directed, maintained, and stopped. In this section we shall examine three process theories: expectancy theory, equity theory, and goal setting theory.

Expectancy Theory

Several theories of motivation have been developed in recent years which have become known as expectancy, or instrumentality theories. One of the more popular versions was developed by Victor Vroom.[25] He bases his theory on three important concepts—expectancy, valence, and instrumentality. Over 50 studies have been done to test the accuracy of expectancy theory in predicting employee behavior.[26]

The term *expectancy* refers to the perceived probability that a given level of effort will result in a given outcome. For example, "How likely is it that high performance (effort) will result in a promotion (outcome)?" Before deciding however, the worker needs to know the value of the outcome. Vroom terms this value *valence*. It reflects the strength of the individual's desire

[25] Victor H. Vroom, *Work and Motivation* (New York: John Wiley and Sons, 1964). For earlier work see Kurt Lewin, *The Conceptual Representation and the Measurement of Psychological Forces* (Durham, N.C.: Duke University Press, 1938); and E. C. Tolman, *Purposive Behavior in Animals and Men* (New York: Appleton-Century, 1932).

[26] David A. Nadler and Edward E. Lawler III, "Motivation: A Diagnostic Approach," in J. R. Hackman, E. E. Lawler III, and L. W. Porter, eds., *Perspectives on Behavior in Organizations* (New York: McGraw-Hill, 1977), pp. 26–38.

for (or attraction toward) the outcomes of different courses of action. Vroom would describe performance as a *first-level outcome* and its valence (strength) is determined by the individual's probability estimate that it will lead to a series of *second-level outcomes* (e.g., promotion, salary increase) and the valences associated with these outcomes.

For example, an individual may believe that if he performs outstandingly he will get a promotion. The degree to which the employee believes that high performance leads to a promotion is a subjective probability estimate which Vroom labels as *instrumentality*. Finally, a promotion has some importance or valence attached to it. The combination of the valences of second-level outcomes and the instrumentality that the first-level outcome (performance) will result in the second-level outcome (promotion) determine the importance, or valence, associated with the first-level outcome.

Thus, according to Vroom what the individual does will depend on a three-step thought process. This thought process may be conscious or subconscious.

1. How important are the various second-level outcomes, e.g., promotion, salary increase? (valence)
2. Will the first-level outcome (high performance) lead to a promotion or salary increase? (instrumentality)
3. Will exerting effort in fact achieve high performance? (expectancy)

Figure 5–6 illustrates the process of motivation according to Vroom. The Vroom model provides the manager with a schema for explaining the behaviors of employees and for highlighting the desirable and undesirable outcomes associated with task performance. When more than one employee is considered and numerous means-ends alternatives are considered, the manager could become overwhelmed with conflicting employee outcome interests.

The manager in applying expectancy theory needs to consider the person and the environment. Specifically, managers should do the following:

a. *Determine* what outcomes are important to each employee. This can be done by asking, observing, and listening.

Figure 5–6
The Expectancy Theory of Motivation

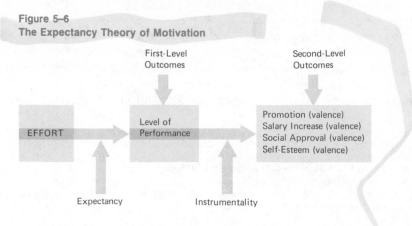

First-Level Outcomes

Second-Level Outcomes

EFFORT → Level of Performance → Promotion (valence) / Salary Increase (valence) / Social Approval (valence) / Self-Esteem (valence)

Expectancy   Instrumentality

b. *Clearly identify* what behavior and performance are desired. The subordinate should understand the manager's expectations.

c. Establish levels of performance that are *challenging,* yet attainable. If the levels of performance are too high, then motivation will be dampened.

d. *Link* important outcomes to desired performance levels. The reward system must be accurate, prompt, and visible. Any system that is inequitable will cause problems. Equity should not be interpreted as equality where everyone receives the same rewards.

e. Make *sure* that *changes* in outcomes are large enough. In examining the motivational program, a manager should attempt to make sure that changes in outcomes or rewards are large enough to motivate significant behavior. Small changes often result in small increases in effort.[27]

There are a number of difficulties associated with expectancy theory. Many of the problems are highlighted by critiques designed to review the model.[28] One of the major problems seems to be testing the entire model using representative work groups. This problem is stressed by Lawler and Suttle when they state that expectancy theory "has become so complex that it has exceeded the measures which exist to test it."[29] The measurements used are typically survey questionnaires that have not always been scientifically validated. Thus, expectancy theory is interesting but two crucial questions remain unanswered: (1) can behavioral scientists completely test it? and (2) can managers use their findings?

Equity Theory

The essence of equity theory is that employees make comparisons of their efforts and rewards with those of others in similar work situations. Equity exists when employees perceive that the ratios of their inputs (efforts) to outcomes (rewards) are equivalent to the ratios of other employees. Inequity exists when these ratios are not equivalent; an individual's own ratio of inputs to outcomes could be greater than or less than others.[30]

The existence of perceived inequity creates tension to restore equity; the greater the inequity, the greater the tension. Depending upon the source and intensity of the inequity, a number of courses of action can be followed. For example, individuals may attempt to increase or decrease their outcomes if they are lower than those of the comparison person. Or they may increase

---

[27] These and other suggestions for managers are derived from Nadler and Lawler, "Motivation," pp. 30–32.

[28] Robert J. House, H. Jack Shapiro, and Mahmoud A. Wahba, "Expectancy Theory as a Predictor of Work Behavior and Attitude: A Reevaluation of Empirical Evidence," *Decision Sciences* (July 1974), pp. 481–506.

[29] Edward E. Lawler III and J. Lloyd Suttle, "Expectancy Theory and Job Behavior," *Organizational Behavior and Human Performance* (June 1973), p. 502.

[30] J. Stacy Adams, "Toward an Understanding of Inequity," *Journal of Abnormal and Social Psychology* (November 1963), pp. 422–36.

Figure 5–7
The Equity Theory of Motivation

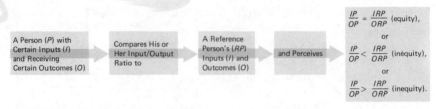

IP = inputs of the person.
OP = outputs of the person.
IRP = inputs of reference person.
ORP = outputs of reference person.

or decrease their inputs by increasing or decreasing their efforts. If these courses of actions are not possible, individuals may stay away from the work situation so that their perceptions are not continually reinforced. The extreme course of action is to quit the job. Figure 5–7 illustrates the equity theory of motivation.

An example can highlight equity theory concepts. Suppose Fred is working as a management trainee in an industrial section of Pittsburgh. Each day he eats lunch with a friend, Hal, who is also a management trainee in another firm. The salary for a trainee in Fred's organization is $1,000 per month, while Hal is receiving $1,240 per month. As Fred compares notes about his experiences with Hal it becomes obvious that the jobs of management trainee are almost identical in the two companies. Fred becomes a little irritated at what seems to be an inequity. An alternative available would be to ask for a raise (increase the outcome), or to reduce efforts to do a good job (decrease inputs). Of course, Fred can also stop seeing Hal or change reference persons. The important point in the example is that as long as a perceived inequity exists, Fred will continue to be uncomfortable.

Most of the research on equity theory has focused on pay as the basic outcome.[31] The failure to incorporate other relevant outcomes limits the impact of the theory in work situations. A review of the studies also reveals that the reference person is not always clarified. A typical research procedure is to ask a person to compare inputs and outcomes with a specific person. In most work situations, the comparison person is selected after working for some time in the organization. Two issues to consider are whether reference persons are within the organization and whether reference persons change during a person's work career.

Despite limitations, the equity theory provides a relatively simple model to help explain and predict employee attitudes about rewards. The theory has also emphasized the importance of comparisons in the work situation.

---

[31] Paul S. Goodman and Abraham Friedman, "An Examination of Adam's Theory of Inequity," *Administrative Science Quarterly* (December 1971), pp. 271–88.

The identification of comparison persons seems to have some potential value when attempting to restructure a reward program. The theory also raises the issue of methods for inequity resolution. The inequitable situation can cause morale, turnover, and absenteeism problems.

An important implication clarified by equity theory is that employees tend to see rewards received in a relative rather than an absolute fashion, the notion being that what a person receives will be compared to what others doing the same or a similar job are receiving. The tendency to make comparisons should not be underestimated by any manager.

Another managerial implication is that managers must attempt to determine reference persons, desired outcomes, and input capabilities of their subordinates. Each motivation theory requires the manager to attempt to diagnose individual needs, expectations, and goals. Equity theory is no different since diagnosis is one way to reduce unhappiness, poor performance, turnover, and absenteeism.

Goal Setting Theory

A significant and interesting contribution for understanding individual motivation has been presented by Locke. It is his contention that an individual's goals or intentions influence behavior. Furthermore, Locke states that challenging or stimulating task goals result in higher levels of performance than do easy or routine task goals. The more specific and clear the goal the better the level of performance. Generalized or "do your best" goals are not as powerful in motivating desirable performances.[32]

Some of the major concepts discussed by theorists, researchers, and managers interested in goal setting include:

Conscious Goal—The goal the person is striving toward and is aware of.

Task Goal—A performance benchmark that is job related.

Personal Development Goal—A goal that focuses on personal improvement or growth. It may or may not be specifically related to the job.

Goal Participation—The amount of involvement a person has in setting task and personal development goals.

Goal Challenge—The amount of challenge associated with a particular goal.

Goal Acceptance—The degree to which the task or personal development goal becomes the conscious goal.

Goal Commitment—The amount of effort used to accomplish a conscious goal.

---

[32] Edwin A. Locke, "Toward a Theory of Task Motivation and Incentives," *Organizational Behavior and Performance* (May 1968), pp. 157–89.

These concepts have been important in applying goal-setting programs for improving employee attitudes about the organization, supervision, and the job. A study of goal setting in Tenneco, Inc. a large, diversified, multi-industry company illustrates each of these goal concepts.[33] This longitudinal study in eight different Tenneco companies determined that a balanced focus on task and personal development goals can have a positive influence on organizational factors such as job satisfaction, job design, and climate. The problems and benefits of applying goal setting are spelled out in the Tenneco goal setting study. Some of the implications derived from the Tenneco study include:

a. The importance of top management involvement in the goal-setting program.
b. The importance of using a goal-setting task force to implement the program.
c. The importance of evaluating and monitoring the goal-setting participants.
d. The need to examine not only task goals, but also to include personal development goals so that goal acceptance and goal commitment become realities.

The philosophical rudiments of goal setting are presented in Figure 5–8. The key steps in most organizationally applied goal-setting programs are (1) diagnosis, (2) preparation, (3) goal setting, (4) intermediate reviews, and (5) final review. Each step needs to be systematically planned if goal setting is to result in such anticipated outcomes as better planning, more efficient control, personal development, and an increased state of motivation. In too many situations many of the factors shown in Figure 5–8 are not considered when implementing a goal-setting program.

The goal-setting approach to motivation is different than the expectancy or equity approaches. While incentives or rewards may influence goal acceptance and commitment, the most important factor is the *goal*.[34] Goals are what individuals are striving for and the major antecedent to job behavior is the intention of the person to reach conscious and meaningful goals. The goals serve as the major cause of behavior, not comparisons to reference persons or the potential reward associated with performing well.

Previous empirical research findings with a variety of managerial and student samples have provided support for the theory that conscious goals regulate behavior. Yet, a number of important issues concerning goal setting still need to be examined more thoroughly. One area of debate concerns the issue of how much subordinate participation in goal setting is optimal. A field experiment of skilled technicians compared three levels of subordinate participation: full (the subordinates were totally involved), limited (the subordinates made some suggestions about the goals that the superior set), and

---

[33] John M. Ivancevich, J. Timothy McMahon, J. William Streidl, and Andrew D. Szilagyi, Jr., "Goal Setting: The Tenneco Approach to Personnel Development and Management Effectiveness," *Organizational Dynamics* (Winter 1978), pp. 58–80.

[34] Terence R. Mitchell, *People in Organizations: Understanding Their Behavior* (New York: McGraw-Hill, 1978), p. 165.

Figure 5–8
Goal-Setting Model for Superior–Subordinate Objective Setting

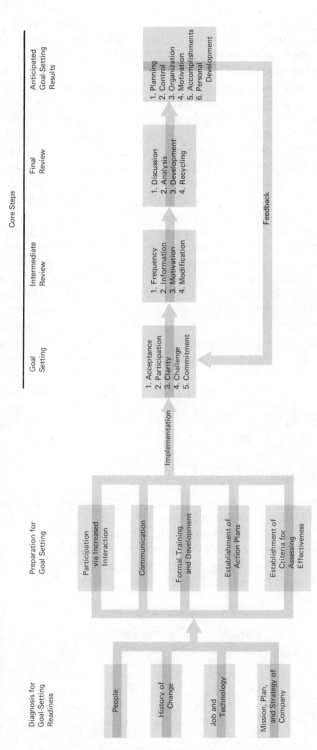

none.[35] Measures of performance and satisfaction were taken over a 12-month period. The full and limited participant involvement in goal-setting groups showed significantly more performance and satisfaction improvements than the group that did not participate in goal setting. Interestingly, these improvements began to dissipate 6 to 9 months after the program was started. This study suggests that there is no universally valid procedure for implementing goal setting. A contingency approach to goal setting seems to be more appropriate than prescribing a specific approach to fit all situations.

Another area of discussion which needs to be studied centers on individual differences and their impact on the success of goal-setting programs. Such factors as personality, career progression, training background, and personal health are important individual differences that need to be considered when implementing goal-setting programs.

Finally, there is a need to subject goal-setting programs to ongoing empirical examination to monitor attitudinal and performance consequences of such programs. Since some research has demonstrated that goal-setting programs tend to lose their potency over time, there is a need to discover why this phenomenon occurs in organizations. A sound evaluation program could assist management in identifying successes, problems, and needs.

Although literature reviews of goal-setting practices in organizations and a number of studies support the positive impact of setting goals on motivation, managers need to be cautious.[36] Managers need to seriously consider whether goal setting is feasible for their particular jobs, individual subordinates, particular situations, and individual style of management. Other decisions such as how to use goal setting as a part of performance evaluation and as an organizational change and development method will be discussed in Chapters 13 and 17.

A Synopsis of the Process Theories

Expectancy, equity, and goal-setting theories provide explanations of motivation. The Vroom theory is an attempt to explain individual motivation in an effort-outcome framework. The Adams equity approach focuses primarily on motives that are developed through a reference person comparison. Both theories are concerned with needs but do not discuss or analyze them in a similar manner. Goal-setting theory focuses on consciously recognized and pursued goals.

THE APPLICATION OF MOTIVATION THEORY IN ORGANIZATIONS

There is an increased interest among management, employees, unions, and the government to improve the quality of work life. To some the quality

---

[35] John M. Ivancevich, "Different Goal-Setting Treatments and Their Effects on Performance and Job Satisfaction," *Academy of Management Journal* (September 1977), pp. 406–19.

[36] Gary P. Latham and Gary A. Yukl, "A Review of Research on the Application of Goal Setting in Organizations," *Academy of Management Journal* (December 1975), pp. 824–45.

of work life refers to participation in organizational decision making and the integration of individual and organizational goals. To others, especially management, the term suggests any of a variety of efforts to increase performance through improvements in human inputs into the production process. Whether using the employee or the managerial perspective, one basis for improving the quality of a person's work life is to create an organizational climate that is motivational. Two specific organizational efforts that apply motivation theory to the work place are behavior modification and the modified workweek. Other applications such as job enrichment, flexi-time, monetary rewards, and goal setting are discussed later in the book.

Behavior Modification

An applied approach to motivation which is beginning to be used more widely in organizations is called *behavior modification.* This technique is built on the law of effect and the concept of operant conditioning. The law of effect states that if behavior is reinforced it will tend to be repeated. The operant conditioning approach calls for positive reinforcement of desired behavior. The administration of a reward is assumed to increase the probability that the behavior immediately preceding the reinforcement will reoccur.

The closer positive reinforcement follows desired behavior the more likely it will be repeated. This could be one of the reasons why pay has been found to be a hygiene factor by Herzberg. It is something an employee receives at some date that is often long after the occurrence of the desired behavior. Because of the lag between the desired behavior and a reinforcer such as pay, behavioral scientists recommend the use of such reinforcers as praise, public complements, recognition, and other verbal approaches. These are easier to apply and can be given soon after desired behaviors are recognized or assessed.

Reinforcements, of course, can be negative. Generally, research findings suggest that positive reinforcers are more effective than negative ones in achieving lasting changes in behavior. Negative reinforcement can be effective in causing the short-run termination of an undesirable behavior. In reality negative reinforcement is an avoidance strategy (if you do not punch in on time, your pay will be docked) in which the person's behavior is influenced by what are assumed to be negative or aversive consequences.

Emery Air Freight has used behavior modification in those jobs where optimal performance gains could potentially occur.[37] Each manager is provided with two workbooks which have been specifically prepared for Emery management team. One deals with *recognition* and *rewards,* the other with *feedback.* The recognition and reward workbook enumerates 150 kinds which can be used by a manager. These workbooks serve as instructional materials that managers are encouraged to consult and utilize.

According to a company vice president, the company has saved over

---

[37] "At Emery Air Freight: Positive Reinforcement Boosts Performance," *Organizational Dynamics* (Winter 1973).

$3 million in the first three years of the program. Before the positive reinforcement program, performance standards were met only 30 to 40 percent of the time; after the program was initiated, the figure was 90 to 95 percent.

At the early stages of the positive reinforcement program, the vice president urged managers to supply praise and recognition at least twice a week. He believed that it is impractical to require them to use positive reinforcement more frequently. The vice president advocated keeping the worker guessing as to when or whether he's going to be praised or recognized by the manager. This is an example of a variable ratio reinforcement schedule.

Emery does not use money as a positive reinforcer. They have no employees on incentive payments and there is no need to link dollar payments to performance improvements. It is also assumed that adequate performance is what management has a right to expect if the pay plans for various employees are equitable and competitive.

The Emery experience indicates that positive reinforcement can be successful where work can be measured and quantifiable standards set and where the levels of performance are significantly below company established standards. It also indicates that after almost four years of applying positive reinforcement, performance deteriorates rapidly when the program is stopped. Apparently, natural reinforcers, an internally generated sense of job satisfaction, have not yet replaced the contrived or management-induced reinforcers.

Positive reinforcement programs have also been used in such diverse settings as Michigan Bell, Connecticut General Insurance, Weyerhaeuser, and ACDC Electronics.[38] The scope, goals, reinforcers, and results of these applied programs are summarized in Table 5–1.

The programs highlighted in Table 5–1 and other behavior modification programs typically use a number of specific steps. These are

1. *Define* the behavioral aspects of performance and determine the behavioral and job related aspects of a work unit, such as the rate of absenteeism, the percentage of accidents, or the cost of completing a unit. Of course, for some jobs it may be difficult to define specific job-related factors. Attempting to define such factors as job stress, friendliness, or loyalty are more difficult than specifying the rate of absenteeism.

2. *Develop* a set of goals that are challenging for each employee. These goals may be task or personal development. The development aspect involves defining any goals in reasonably measurable terms.

3. The *employee* must be involved in keeping accurate records of his or her work. This self-feedback step allows the individual to maintain a continuous schedule of reinforcement.

---

[38] For specific discussions of behavior modification programs, see W. Clay Hamner and Ellen P. Hamner, "Behavior Modification on the Bottom Line," *Organizational Dynamics* (Spring 1976), pp. 2–21; and Edwin A. Locke, "The Myths of Behavior Mod in Organizations," *Academy of Management Review* (October 1977), pp. 543–53.

Table 5–1
Some Selected Examples of Positive Reinforcement Programs*

Company	Number of Employees Involved	Program Goals	Schedule of Reinforcement	Reinforcers Used	Results
Michigan Bell—Operating Services	2,000	1. Decrease turnover and absenteeism 2. Increase production 3. Improve union-management relations	1. Lower level—weekly and daily 2. Upper level—monthly and quarterly	Praise and recognition	Improved attendance and improved production
Connecticut General Insurance	3,000	1. Decrease absenteeism 2. Decrease lateness	1. Immediate	Self-feed-back, system feedback, and earned time off	Absenteeism and lateness drastically cut
Weyerhaeuser	500	1. Teach managers to minimize criticism and maximize praise 2. Teach managers to make rewards contingent on specified performance	1. Immediate	Pay, praise, and recognition	Increased production
ACDC Electronics	350	1. Increase productivity 2. Improve standards being met 3. Reduce costs	1. Daily and weekly	Positive feedback	Increased profit; and cost reduced by $550,000

* Data derived from W. C. Hamner and E. P. Hamner, "Behavior Modification on the Bottom Line," *Organizational Dynamics* (Spring 1976), pp. 12–14.

4. The fourth step focuses on *managerial* involvement in the reinforcement program. The supervisor should review the employee self-reports and other relevant information and then apply the appropriate reinforcer.

The manager's role in each step of any reinforcement or behavior modification program is essential. To help an employee learn a new behavior requires a manager to closely follow the progress of an individual. In addition, the manager must consider (1) how frequently to give positive reinforcement, and (2) how close in time rewards should follow the desirable behavior.

Research evidence indicates that employees should be rewarded often but not continuously. If you worked as an office manager, it might be rewarding if occasionally your immediate superior came around and told you, "The company is pleased with your results. Your group seems pleased with your style of leadership. I'm sure that with this type of performance your future is very bright." This same praise on a daily basis would probably lose its impact.

The best results in organizational behavior modification programs seem to occur when rewards (or punishments) follow close in time to the desired behavior. For a person selling cars, the motivation to work harder is greater

Figure 5–9
Graphic Illustration of Five Schedules of Reinforcement Used By Managers*

1. Continuous Reinforcement

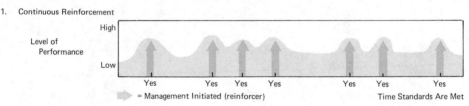

2. Fixed Interval Schedule

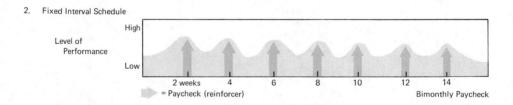

3. Variable Interval Schedule

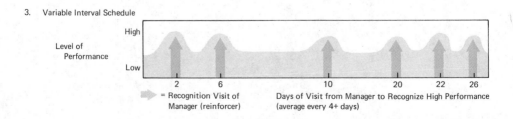

Figure 5–9 *(continued)*

4. Fixed-Ratio Schedule

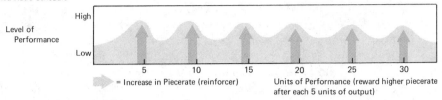

Level of
Performance

High

Low

5   10   15   20   25   30

 = Increase in Piecerate (reinforcer)

Units of Performance (reward higher piecerate after each 5 units of output)

5. Variable-Ratio Schedule

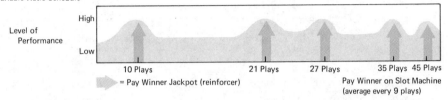

Level of
Performance

High

Low

10 Plays   21 Plays   27 Plays   35 Plays 45 Plays

= Pay Winner Jackpot (reinforcer)

Pay Winner on Slot Machine (average every 9 plays)

* Idea for generating graphical examples of schedules 2, 3, 4, and 5 based on W. C. Hamner and D. W. Organ, *Organizational Behavior* (Dallas: Business Publications, Inc., 1978), pp. 55 (Figure 3–2).

when commissions are received close to the time of the sale. Accumulating commissions over a six month period would not be recommended by advocates of behavior modification. The notion of developing a reinforcement schedule can help a manager apply reinforcers at the appropriate time.

As stated in Chapter 4, there are many possible schedules of positive reinforcement that are used by managers. A number of examples and a graphical illustration shown in Figure 5–9 highlights the schedules managers can use. A *continuous reinforcement* schedule means that each time a correct response is given by the person, it is followed by a positive reinforcer. If an employee is complimented every time production standards are met, the response of meeting the standard is being continuously reinforced. The continuous reinforcement can be effective as long as reinforcement follows every desirable act. For a manager to reward through a compliment the behavior of meeting standards every time is almost impossible since most managers must attend to other activities and people.

Another form of reinforcement is called *partial* or intermittent. Under this category reinforcement does not occur after every single correct response. There are a number of intermittent schedules used by managers. A *fixed interval* schedule designates reinforcement of acceptable responses after a specific period of time has passed. For example, paying employees bimonthly is a form of fixed interval reinforcement. Every two weeks the individual is paid (reinforced). A *variable interval* schedule is used on a random arrangement. An example would be for a manager to randomly drop by a group of employees without prior notice to recognize some of the outstanding performers.

A *fixed ratio* reinforcement schedule involves issuing a reward after a fixed number of desired responses have occurred. For example, paying workers a higher rate per unit of output after a certain level of production is reached is a fixed ratio reinforcement. Under a *variable ratio* schedule, rewards are granted after a number of desired responses occurs, but the number of responses is randomly selected. In order for any of the schedules to be effective, the manager must specify the contingency between the desired behavior and the reinforcer. In fact, managers will probably have to use each of these schedules to motivate subordinates to perform more effectively.

The organizational examples in Table 5–1 and the discussion have primarily addressed positive reinforcers. In fact, the most widely applied behavior modification strategy is positive reinforcement. However, there are three other behavior modification strategies that can be and are used by managers: negative reinforcement, punishment, and extinction. Each of these strategies was discussed in Chapter 4.

As with most applied managerial programs there are critics who are opposed to behavior modification. Some believe that behavior modification is a threat to individual freedom. The manipulation of reinforcers on the basis of managerially controlled schedules is considered unethical and threatening. The individual is not usually involved in manipulating the reinforcers.

The overemphasis of behavior modification on externally applied reinforcers is also criticized. For example, Deci states that, ''It follows that there are many important motivators of human behavior which are not under the direct control of managers and, therefore, cannot be contingently administered in a system. . . .''[39] The theme of Deci's recommendation is to develop reinforcement systems in which individuals can be motivated by the job itself. This suggestion is not disputed by Skinner who also recommends self-reinforcement programs and challenging jobs. However, like much of the work of Skinner, various interpretations by others result in occasional misunderstanding and controversy.

The Modified Workweek

Numerous organizational attempts have been made to improve the performance and satisfaction of employees by implementing a modified workweek. The term modified workweek applies to the reduction of the number of days a week an employee actually works. Typically, a worker puts in 8 hours a day five days a week. A modification of this would be to work four days a week for 10 hours a day. The total hours worked can be the same in both cases, but the modified arrangement allows the worker to remain away from the job for three days a week instead of the traditional two days.

A number of inherent problems are associated with the modified workweek.

---

[39] E. L. Deci, ''The Effects of Contingent and Noncontingent Rewards and Controls on Intrinsic Motivation,'' *Organizational Behavior and Performance* (October 1972), pp. 217–29.

Some of the problems include legal restrictions on the hours a female worker can work in a day, whether overtime should be paid for any work after the 8-hour period in one particular day, and the arrangement of schedules so that machines are used and serviced efficiently. Unions have resisted modifying the workweek because of legal and overtime issues.

A study of the impact of a modified workweek was performed in a nonunionized medium-sized pharmaceutical company. The researchers found that over a period of time employees adjusted to the modified workweek.[40] Absenteeism decreased after the introduction of the shortened workweek. They also found that some important factors which influenced attitudes toward the shorter workweek were age, plans for the use of nonwork time, and job pace.

Another investigation of a modified workweek used unionized operating employees in two separate divisions of the same company. Major differences in this study and the pharmaceutical study were (1) methodology (use of scaled questions), (2) the research design (experimental and control), (3) the technology (mass production manufacturing), and (4) the fact that the plant was unionized. There were some improvements in performance and reduced anxiety-stress in the experimental devision. There was no discernible improvement in autonomy or self-actualization need satisfaction in either group. The study found some areas in which the experimental group showed improvement after the introduction of the modified workweek.[41]

In a follow-up study of the research just mentioned, the effects of the 4-day, 40-hour workweek were examined in two experimental units and one comparison unit over a 25-month period.[42] The analysis indicated that at the end of 13 months, the workers in the 4-day, 40-hour plants were: *(a)* more satisfied with autonomy, personal worth, job security, and pay; *(b)* experienced less anxiety-stress; and *(c)* performed better than did the comparison plant. The short-run impact of the modified workweek is congruent with the claims of 4–40 workweek advocates. However, these improvements were totally eliminated when the 25-month data were analyzed. The rapid extinction of these gains suggests that long-run benefits of the modified workweek may be quite elusive.

Although there are currently only a few studies of the modified workweek, there are still numerous examples of firms applying this approach. It was estimated that at one time between 60 and 70 companies a month were converting to the four-day workweek.[43] There is no available evidence that

---

[40] W. R. Nord and R. Costigan, "Worker Adjustment to the Four-Day Week: A Longitudinal Study," *Journal of Applied Psychology* (August 1973), pp. 60–66.

[41] John M. Ivancevich, "Effects of the Shorter Workweek on Selected Satisfaction and Performance Measures," *Journal of Applied Psychology* (December 1974), pp. 717–21.

[42] John M. Ivancevich and Herbert L. Lyon, "The Shortened Workweek: A Field Experiment," *Journal of Applied Psychology* (February 1977), pp. 34–37.

[43] K. E. Wheeler, R. Gurman, and D. Tarnowieski, "The Four-Day Week," An AMA Research Report (New York: American Management Association, 1972).

this trend has or will decline in the foreseeable future. Although many organizations are using modified workweeks, the impact has not been studied on a longitudinal basis.

MAJOR ISSUES FOR THE MANAGER TO CONSIDER

A. Any attempt to improve job performance of individuals must invariably utilize motivational theories. This results from the fact that motivation is concerned with behavior or, more specifically, goal-directed behavior.

B. A major reason why behaviors of employees differ is that needs and goals of people vary. Social, cultural, hereditary, and job factors are forces that influence behaviors. In order to understand the circular nature of motivation, the manager must learn about the needs of subordinates.

C. An integrated perspective of the motivational process is important because it is necessary to bring together such factors as organizational dimensions, needs, search processes, effort expended, ability, performance, rewards and sanctions, satisfaction, and psychological variables like perception, attitudes, personality, and learning.

D. The theories of motivation can be classified as being either content or process. Each theory in both categories emphasizes a "particular" orientation. Some of course are more explicit but each illustrates that employees desire some goal(s) in performing their jobs. The manager should try to determine the various goals desired by subordinates.

E. The Maslow theory assumes that people have a need to grow and develop. The implication is that motivational programs will have a higher probability of success if the upper-level need deficiencies are reduced. Although Maslow's need hierarchy has not met most of the standards of scientific testing, it appears that an adequately fulfilled need does not provide a good target for managers in building motivators that can influence performance.

F. McClelland has proposed a theory of learned needs. The behavior associated with the needs for achievement, affiliation, and power is instrumental in the job performance of an individual. A manager should attempt to acquire an understanding of these needs.

G. Herzberg's two-factor theory of motivation identifies two types of factors in the workplace, satisfiers and dissatisfiers. One apparent weakness of the theory is that its findings have not been replicated by other researchers. Despite this and other shortcomings it focuses on job-related factors in managerial terminology. The manager should categorize what factors seem to motivate employees and which factors do not seem to be significant.

H. Expectancy theory of motivation is concerned with the expectations of a person and how they influence behavior. One value of this theory is that it can provide a manager with a means for pinpointing desirable and undesirable outcomes associated with task performance. Major weaknesses of the theory are the terminology used; the inability to research the full theory, and the complexity involved when introducing numerous first- and second-level outcomes, expectancies, and instrumentalities. The behavioral scientist has not made this theory practical for the manager to implement.

I. Equity theory focuses on comparisons, tension, and tension reduction. Most of the research work to date has involved pay. It is a more straightforward and understandable explanation of employee attitudes about pay than expectancy theory. The manager should be aware of the fact that people compare their rewards, punishments, job tasks, treatment from the manager, and other job-related dimensions to those of others.

J. Goal-setting theory assumes that establishing challenging goals influences individual performance. The more specific and clear the goal, the better the level of performance. Goals are the main antecedent to job behavior and performance.

K. Two specific examples of managerial applications of motivation principles are:

Behavior modification, an approach built on the law of effect and the concept of operant conditioning is being used by more organizations. The issues of positive reinforcement, negative reinforcement, punishment, extinction, contingencies, and reinforcement schedules are important in applying behavior modification. The main orientation of this approach is that individual behavior can be influenced by managers who understand these issues.

Modified workweeks are assumed to improve need deficiencies (Maslow), serve as a motivator of more positive behavior and performance (Herzberg), and allow for more achievement and affiliation (McClelland). These are classified as second-level outcomes in the Vroom theory.

DISCUSSION AND REVIEW QUESTIONS

1. Vroom's expectancy model includes the concepts of valence, expectancy, and instrumentality. What are the meanings of the concepts, and how could a manager determine these concepts as they apply to his or her subordinates?

2. Could a manager who understood the equity theory utilize this knowledge in developing pay programs? How?

3. What is the stigma associated with behavior modification? What do you think is necessary to reduce some of the managerial resistance to this approach?

4. Some people believe that pay satisfaction is a factor which reduces need deficiencies at upper- and lower-need levels. What is the logic of those who assume that pay satisfaction permeates the entire need hierarchy?

5. What is the relationship between performance and satisfaction? What are some of the variables which influence this relationship?

6. What type of schedules of reinforcement can be used by managers? Explain.

7. What is the difference between motivation and satisfaction? Can an employee be motivated and indicate low job satisfaction? Explain.

8. Would environmental conditions such as double-digit or runaway inflation influence the need deficiencies that an employee experiences on the job? How?

9. Why is goal setting so difficult to implement in organizational settings? Do you believe that goal setting should be implemented in the entire organization? Why?

10. How do learning principles and positive reinforcement influence needs such as those discussed by McClelland? How can a company utilize the McClelland theory of motivation in personnel selection and placement programs?

ADDITIONAL REFERENCES

Adams, J. S., and Freedman, S. "Equity Theory Revisited: Comments and Annotated Bibliography." In L. Berkowitz, ed., *Advances in Experimental Social Psychology.* New York: Academic Press, 1976, Vol. 8.

Behling, O.; Schriesheim, C.; and Tolliver, J. "Alternatives to Expectancy Theories of Work Motivation." *Decision Sciences* (1975), pp. 449–61.

Carrell, M. R. "A Longitudinal Field Assessment of Employee Perceptions of Equitable Treatment," *Organizational Behavior and Human Performance* (1978), pp. 108–18.

Dunnette, M. D.; Hough, L.; Rosett, H.; Mamford, E.; and Fine, S. A. "Work and Nonwork: Merging Human and Societal Needs." In M. D. Dunnette, ed., *Work and Nonwork in the Year 2001.* Monterey, Calif.: Brooks/Cole, 1973.

Fein, M. "Motivation for Work." In R. Dubin, ed. *Handbook of Work, Organization, and Society.* Chicago: Rand McNally, 1976.

Ivancevich, J. M., and McMahon, J. T. "Black-White Differences in a Goal Setting Program." *Organizational Behavior and Human Performance* (1977), pp. 287–300.

Komaki, J.; Wadell, W. M.; and Pearce, M. G. "The Applied Behavior Analysis Approach and Individual Employees: Improving Performance in Two Small Businesses," *Organizational Behavior and Human Performance* (August 1977), pp. 337–52.

Lazer, R. I. "Behavior Modification as a Managerial Technique." *The Conference Board Record* (1975), pp. 22–25.

Nord, W. R. "Job Satisfaction Reconsidered." *American Psychologist* (1977), pp. 1026–35.

Pedalino, E., and Gamboa, V. U. "Behavior Modification and Absenteeism: Intervention in One Industrial Setting." *Journal of Applied Psychology* (1974), pp. 694–98.

Staw, B. M. "Motivation in Organizations: Toward Synthesis and Redirection." In B. M. Staw and G. R. Salancik, *New Directions In Organizational Behavior.* Chicago: St. Clair, 1977, pp. 55–96.

Terkel, S. *Working.* New York: Avon Books, 1974.

White, S. E.; Mitchell, T. R.; and Bell, C. H., Jr. "Goal Setting, Evaluation Apprehension, and Social Cues as Determinants of Job Performance and Job Satisfaction in a Simulated Organization," *Journal of Applied Psychology* (1977), pp. 665–73.

Yukl, G. A.; Latham, G. P.; and Pursell, E. L. "The Effectiveness of Performance Incentives under Continuous and Variable Ratio Schedules of Reinforcement," *Personnel Psychology* (1976), pp. 221–31.

CASE FOR ANALYSIS

A MOTIVATOR OF MEN MUST BE REPLACED: THE AFTERMATH

The McLaughlin Engineering Corporation employs approximately 1,200 operating employees. The plant is old, but is kept reasonably clean and is known as one of the better production facilities in the area. The plant has a research and development department, an industrial relations department, an accounting and financial control department, a distribution department, and four operating departments that produce valves, metal brackets, metal shelves, and pistons. Exhibit 1 is an organizational chart of a typical operating department.

Exhibit 1

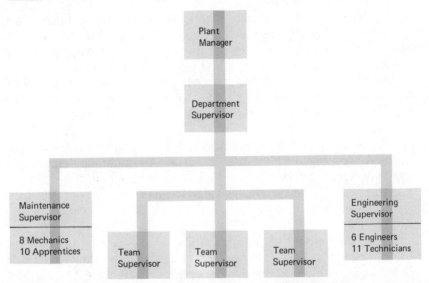

The plant manager, Joe Ruggio, was responsible for all production, maintenance, and engineering work performed in the departments. The department supervisor of the unit represented above was Clyde Campbell. He reported directly to Joe and had two support units—maintenance and engineering. Clyde also had three team supervisors reporting directly to him. These men were each responsible for one of the three shifts—days (8–4), afternoons (4–12), nights (12–8).

The maintenance team consisted of eight mechanics and ten apprentice mechanics who worked on maintaining the machinery. They worked closely with the engineering team who worked primarily on experimenting with new equipment, new plant layouts, and other problems of technological change.

Although the engineers were college graduates they worked extremely well with the mechanics and respected their technical knowledge.

The mechanics and engineers also respected the team supervisors who worked hard and were interested in task accomplishment and people problems. The smooth coordination and mutual respect among the managerial and operating employees were certainly trademarks of McLaughlin. At the annual supervisory conference, the founder Tommy McLaughlin, even at age 62, would mention the importance of respect, trust, and confidence. This message was continually presented in the company newspaper and at almost every annual award dinner.

Clyde had worked with McLaughlin for 18 years and had a reputation of being a technical expert in every phase of production. In fact, all of the four operating department supervisors were known throughout the organization for their technical and engineering skills.

The company has been one of the most popular within the community. In fact, the personnel department typically has an employment waiting list of at leat 50 engineers, 100 mechanics, and 300 operating employees. Generally, about 80 percent of these people are qualified, but turnover is so low that there has been little hiring in the past three years.

The engineering group had no desire to unionize, and the mechanics who were unionized did not become involved in union politics. The plant has never had a strike, although other plants in the area are continually striking for better wages, fringe benefits, and other related matters.

The performance of the plant had been improving in every area—in quality, quantity, and costs—for the past ten years. The operating employees said that they respected the company and the management team because the managers knew what the employees' problems were all about. The managers were viewed as possessing technical knowledge and not just "paper shuffling" expertise.

Clyde became seriously ill around Christmas. He tried to come back to work in March, but was too weak physically and eventually had to take a disability leave in June. The three team supervisors were all considered for promotion to Clyde's position, but it was felt that they lacked experience to handle the job. The selection committee felt that promoting an engineer to the department supervisory position might be interpreted as favoritism by the mechanics. Thus Nelson Morley, a 43-year-old engineer from Staley Engineering Corporation was hired to replace Clyde.

Nelson changed a few of Clyde's operating procedures concerning the reporting of productivity. The performance report procedure was one major change that many people disliked. Nelson would meet with the team supervisors once a month to go over reports on performance of the three shifts. Clyde had met with the managers only as a team and did not meet separately with supervisors, engineers, and mechanics. There had been no regularity in Clyde's arrangement; the teams might meet once a week, twice a month, or once every six months.

Even before Nelson joined the company a number of mechanics, engineers, and operating employees had said that they would leave if Clyde did not return. They believed that they performed well because of him. He was what they described as a "motivator of men."

Nelson was called an "outside renegade" behind his back. The quality of work and timeliness in filling orders suffered significantly after Nelson took over. The total team had been split because of his practice of only meeting with team supervisors. The engineers and mechanics began to quarrel with the supervisors about standards and procedures. These disagreements seemed to be most intense immediately after the monthly meetings between Nelson and the team supervisors.

One supervisor said, "Nelson is now the boss and we must get into step and follow his procedures." This feeling was not shared by a single mechanic or engineer. It appeared to them that the team supervisors were joining up with Nelson.

Joe was very concerned with the turn of events in the department and asked Nelson to visit with him. The objective of the meeting was to work out a plan so that performance and satisfaction would return to more acceptable levels.

Questions for Consideration

1. What type of plan could Joe and Nelson develop to correct the situation described?
2. Will Nelson be viewed as the "motivator of men" in this situation? Explain your answer in terms of a need satisfaction model.

EXPERIENTIAL EXERCISE

PRACTICING MANAGEMENT AND APPLYING MOTIVATION THEORY

Objectives

1. To evaluate the merits of different motivation theories.
2. To emphasize the decisions that must be made by managers in motivating people.
3. To apply motivation principles.

Related Topics

The manager must make decisions to succeed.
The difficulty of diagnosing situations.

Starting the Exercise

Set up groups of five to eight students to read the facts and the situation facing Margo Williams.

The Facts

In the chapter a number of popular content and process theories were discussed. Some of the major points raised were the following:

Maslow—Motivation involves satisfying needs in a hierarchical order.

Herzberg—Some job factors are intrinsically satisfying and motivate individuals.

McClelland—Motives are acquired from a person's culture.

Expectancy Theory—Motivation is a function of (*a*) expectancy; (*b*) valence; and (*c*) instrumentality.

Equity Theory—Individuals are motivated to achieve equity between their inputs/outputs in comparison to the inputs/outputs of a comparison person(s).

Goal Setting—Conscious and challenging goals can be powerful motivators of behavior.

With these six theories in mind, review the work situation that is currently facing Margo Williams.

Margo Williams is a project engineer director in a large construction company. She is responsible for scheduling projects, meeting customers, reporting progress on projects, costs, and subordinate development. A total of 20 men and 8 women report to Margo. All of them are college graduates and have at least eight years of job experience. Margo is a Ph.D. engineer, but only has four years of project engineering experience.

The biggest problems facing Margo involve the lack of respect and response she receives from her subordinates. These problems have been considered by Margo's supervisor and it is assumed that her moderate record of success could be improved if she could correct the situation. Margo is now considering a course of, or some combined, action that could motivate her subordinates to show more respect and respond more favorably to her requests.

Exercise Procedures

1. Set up small discussion groups of five to eight students to develop a motivation plan for Margo. The group should work on developing a plan that uses the motivation principles discussed in the chapter.
2. After working as a group for approximately 30 minutes, a group leader should present the plan to the class.
3. Discuss each group's plan for the remainder of the class period.

Chapter 6

Group Behavior

AN ORGANIZATIONAL ISSUE FOR DEBATE

*Does Allowing Work Groups More Freedom Improve Group Performance?**

ARGUMENT FOR

Supported in a Paper Mill

The belief here was that autonomous work groups are a better way to utilize human resources and increase member satisfaction. The idea was to break away from the one-man—one-machine organization and have a small group monitor several machines. The experiment began in the chemical pulp department, with division of thirty-five workers into four continuous shift groups of eight to nine workers. Foremen were eliminated, and the number of supervisors cut in half. Workers were trained in quality control and information handling.

The experiment worked. In six years it spread virtually throughout the plant, and reduced turnover from 25 to 6 percent a year while doubling productivity. Cross training gave management much more flexibility in scheduling work and enabled the plant to stay open through holiday periods.

ARGUMENT AGAINST

Not Supported in a Steel Fabricating Plant

Here the belief was also that autonomous work groups would improve performance. Attempts were made to break away from the one-man—one-machine organization. Workers were allowed to move among the various machines, and also be responsible for some equipment maintenance.

This experiment did not work. Both workers and middle managers were hostile to the idea. In one instance one of five workers was ill for two weeks. The remaining workers handled the five machines and, in addition, produced more than all five workers had previously done. Unfortunately, the experiment was halted because both workers and middle management were unwilling to alter the basic work patterns or wage structure.

* Source: *Behavioral Sciences Newsletter* (August 8, 1977), p. 1

INTRODUCTION

In this chapter we shall examine groups in organizations. While the existence of groups in organizations probably does not alter the individual's motivations or needs, the group does influence the behavior of individuals in an organizational setting. In other words, organizational behavior is more than the logical composite of individuals' behavior. It is not their sum or product but rather a much more complex phenomenon, a very important part of which is the group. This chapter will provide the reader with a model for understanding the nature of groups in organizations. It will include the various types of groups, reasons for the formation of groups, the characteristics of groups, and some end results of group membership.

No generally accepted definition of a group exists. Instead of immediately offering a definition, it seems more appropriate to present a range of definitions and then to synthesize these to develop a broad definition of a group. There is certainly much overlap in these definitions, and it is evident that the originators were looking at different aspects of groups.

A Group in Terms of Perception

One definition is based on the perceptions of group members. It is proposed that members must perceive their relationships to others to be considered a group. An example of this type of definition is as follows:

> A small group is defined as any number of persons engaged in interaction with one another in a single face-to-face meeting or series of such meetings, in which each member receives some impression or perception of each other member distinct enough so that he can, either at the time or in later questioning, give some reaction to each of the others as an individual person, even though it may be only to recall that the other was present.[1]

This definition points out that members of the group must perceive the existence of each member as well as the existence of a group.

A Group in Terms of Organization

Sociologists view the group primarily in terms of organizational characteristics. One such definition follows:

> . . . an organized system of two or more individuals who are interrelated so that the system performs some function, has a standard set of role relationships among its members, and has a set of norms that regulate the function of the group and each of its members.[2]

---

[1] R. F. Bales, *Interaction Process Analysis: A Method for the Study of Small Groups* (Cambridge, Mass.: Addison-Wesley, 1950), p. 33.

[2] J. W. McDavid and M. Harari, *Social Psychology: Individuals, Groups, Societies* (New York: Harper & Row, 1968), p. 237.

This definition emphasizes some of the important characteristics of groups, such as roles and norms, which will be discussed later in this chapter.

A Group in Terms of Motivation

A group that fails to aid its members in satisfying their needs will have a difficult time remaining a viable group. Employees who are not satisfying their needs in a particular group will search for other groups to aid in important need satisfactions. This motivational interpretation defines a group as:

> . . . a collection of individuals whose existence as a collection is rewarding to the individuals.[3]

As pointed out in the previous chapter, it is difficult to ascertain clearly what facets of the work organization are rewarding to individuals. The problems of identifying and verifying a need hierarchy point out the shortcomings of defining a group in terms of motivation.

A Group in Terms of Interaction

Some theorists assume that interaction in the form of interdependence is the core of "groupness." A definition which stresses interpersonal interactions is the following:

> We mean by a group a number of persons who communicate with one another often over a span of time, and who are few enough so that each person is able to communicate with all the others, not at secondhand, through other people, but face-to-face.[4]

In our view, each of these definitions is correct, since they point to important features of groups. Furthermore, we assume that if a group exists in an organization, then its members:

1. Are motivated to join.
2. Perceive the group as a unified unit of interacting people.
3. Contribute in various amounts to the group processes (i.e., some people contribute more time or energy to the group).
4. Reach agreements and have disagreements through various forms of interaction.

Therefore, for our purposes in this book, a group is defined as:

> Two or more employees who interact with each other in such a manner that the behavior and/or performance of a member is influenced by the behavior and/or performance of other members.[5]

---

[3] Bernard M. Bass, *Leadership, Psychology, and Organizational Behavior* (New York: Harper & Row, 1960), p. 39.

[4] G. C. Homans, *The Human Group* (New York: Harcourt, Brace, and World, 1950), p. 1.

[5] Marvin E. Shaw, *Group Dynamics* (New York: McGraw-Hill, 1971).

TYPES OF GROUPS

An organization has technical requirements which arise from its stated goals. The accomplishment of these goals requires certain tasks to be performed and employees are assigned to perform these tasks. Thus, as a result, most employees will be members of a group based on their position in the organization. These groups we shall label as *formal groups*. On the other hand whenever individuals associate on a fairly continuous basis there is a tendency for groups to form whose activities may be different from those required by the organization. These groups we shall label as *informal groups*. While this distinction is convenient for our discussion of the types of groups in organizations, both types of groups exhibit the same general characteristics.

Formal Groups

The demands and processes of the organization lead to the formation of different types of groups. Specifically, two types of formal groups exist.

Command Group.   The command group is specified by the organization chart. The group is comprised of the subordinates who report directly to a given supervisor. The authority relationship between a department manager and the foremen, or between a senior nurse and her subordinates, constitutes a command group.

Task Group.   A task group is comprised of the employees who work together to complete a particular task or project. For example, the activities of clerks in an insurance company when an accident claim is filed are required tasks. These activities create a situation in which several clerks must communicate and coordinate with each other if the claim is to be handled properly. These required tasks and interactions facilitate the formation of a task group. The nurses assigned to duty in the emergency room of a hospital usually constitute a task group, since certain activities are required when a patient is treated.

Informal Groups

Informal groups are natural groupings of people in the work situation in response to social needs. In other words, they do not arise as a result of deliberate design but rather evolve naturally. Two specific informal groups are identified.

Interest Group.   Individuals who may not be members of the same command or task group may affiliate to achieve some mutual objective. Employees grouping together to present a unified front to management for more benefits and waitresses "pooling" their tips are examples of interest groups. Also, note that the objectives of such groups are not related to those of the organization but are specific to each group.

Friendship Group.   Many groups form because the members have something in common such as age, political beliefs, or ethnic background.

These friendship groups often extend their interaction and communication to off-job activities.

If employees' affiliation patterns were documented, it would become readily apparent that they belong to numerous and often overlapping groups. A distinction has been made between two broad classifications of groups: formal and informal. The major difference between them is that formal groups (command and task) are designated by the formal organization and are a means to an end while informal groups (interest and friendship) are important for their own sake (that is, they satisfy a basic need for association).

WHY PEOPLE FORM GROUPS

Formal and informal groups form because of various reasons. Some of the reasons concern needs, proximity, attraction, and goals.

The Satisfaction of Needs

The desire for need satisfaction can be a strong motivating force leading to group formation.[6] Specifically, the security, social, esteem, and self-actualization needs of some employees can be satisfied to a degree by affiliating in groups.

Security.   Without the group to lean on when various management demands are made, certain employees may assume they are standing alone facing management and the entire organization system. This "aloneness" leads to a degree of insecurity. By being a member of a group, the employee can become involved in group activities and discuss management demands with other members who hold supportive views. The interactions and communications existing between members of the group serve as a buffer to management demands. This may be especially true in the case of a new employee. The new employee may depend heavily on the group for aid in correctly performing the job. This reliance can certainly be interpreted as providing the new employee with a form of security need satisfaction.

Social.   The gregarious nature of man often results in the need for affiliation. This desire to belong and to be a part of a group points up the intensity of the social needs of American people. This is true not only on the job but also away from the work place as evidenced by the numerous social, political, civic, and fraternal organizations that exist.

A very insightful discussion of the social needs of Americans has been offered by Schein. He discussed the concern which was voiced about the behavior of United States prisoners of war during the Korean conflict. At the time, many people in the United States were distressed by the fact that there were few escape attempts on the part of prisoners and numerous in-

---

[6] For a discussion of the group as an instrument for satisfaction of individual needs see C. Gratton Kemp, *Perspectives on Group Processes* (Boston: Houghton Mifflin Co., 1970), pp. 26–29.

stances of apparent collaboration. Schein suggested that one possible explanation was the manner in which the prisoners were treated.[7]

In the North Korean POW camps, officers (supervisors) were separated from enlisted men (subordinates). Groups were systematically broken up and prisoners were regularly transferred between barracks to forestall the development of groups. The fact that groups could not be formed on a continuing basis could explain the low escape rate: because the men could not get organized, they could not develop the type of plan that was needed to break free. Also, they could not develop the trust in each other that is so essential for escape. Without the required trust, the "belongingness" urge was reduced and so was the overall morale in the POW camps.

Schein's discussion would appear to have implications for managers in organizations. It indicates that groups can satisfy the social needs of individuals and that group affiliation enables the individual to self-identify and to deal with the immediate environment. Small-group research in organizations has found that employees who are isolated from other employees because of the physical layout of the plant report that their jobs are less satisfying than those employees who are group members and can interact on the job.[8] The isolated employee has been unable to fulfill the basic human need to associate with others.

Esteem.   In a particular work environment, a certain group may be viewed by employees as being a high-prestige group for a variety of reasons (for example, technical competence, outside activities, and so on). Consequently, membership in this group carries with it a certain prestige which is not enjoyed by nonmembers. For employees with high esteem needs, membership in such a group can provide much need satisfaction.

Proximity and Attraction

Interpersonal interaction can result in group formation. Two important facets of interpersonal interaction are proximity and attraction. By *proximity* we mean the physical distance between employees performing a job. The term *attraction* designates the attraction of people to each other because of perceptual, attitudinal, performance, or motivational similarity.

Individuals who work in close proximity have numerous opportunities to exchange ideas, thoughts, and attitudes about various on- and off-the-job activities. These exchanges often result in some type of group formation. This proximity makes it possible for individuals to learn about the characteristics of other people. To sustain the interaction and interest, a group often is formed.

---

[7] Edgar Schein, "The Chinese Indoctrination Program for Prisoners of War," *Psychiatry* (May 1956), pp. 149–72.

[8] Elton Mayo, *The Human Problems of an Industrial Civilization* (Boston: Graduate School of Business Administration, Harvard University, 1946), pp. 42–52.

Group Goals

The group's goals, if clearly understood, can be a reason why an individual is attracted to a group. For example, an individual may join a group that meets after work to become familiar with the metric measuring system. Assume that this system is to be implemented in the work organization over the next two years. The person who joins voluntarily the after-hours group believes that learning the new system is a necessary and important goal for employees.

It is not always possible to identify group goals. The assumption that formal organizational groups have clear goals must be tempered by the understanding that perception, attitudes, personality, and learning can distort goals. The same can be said about informal group goals.

Economic Reasons

In many cases groups form because individuals believe that they can derive greater economic benefits from their jobs if they form into groups. For example, individuals working at different points on an assembly line may be paid on a group incentive basis where the production of the group determines the wages of each member. By working and cooperating as a group, the individual may actually obtain higher economic benefits.

There are numerous other instances where economic motives result in group formation: workers in nonunion organizations form a group to exert pressure on top management for more benefits, waitresses in a restaurant "pool" their tips and share equally. Whatever the circumstances, the group members have a common interest—increased economic benefits—which leads to group affiliation.

These are only some of the numerous reasons why people join groups. It appears that people join groups because they are perceived as a means of satisfying needs. It is also obvious that the activities and goals of a group are factors in attracting members. Another important facet of group formation involves the proximity of people to each other, which is a reason for interaction and the discovery of similar characteristics.

STAGES OF GROUP DEVELOPMENT

Like individuals, groups learn. The performance of a group depends on both individual learning and how well the members learn to work with each other. In this section we will describe some general stages through which groups develop. It is impossible, of course, to present a general development model for all types of groups. We will, however, describe the process for two distinctly different types of groups: a problem-solving group and a training group. Our purpose here is to point out that some kind of sequential developmental process is involved. Basically, the models are similar in that they indicate that group members progress from concern about trusting each other to concern about communication and finally maintaining controls.[9]

Development of a Problem-Solving Group

A problem-solving group may be involved in scheduling equipment maintenance, recruiting and selecting a new vice president, or deciding whether to develop a new product line. Problem solving is a task that all formal and some informal groups are engaged in continually. One model of group development assumes that problem-solving groups proceed through four stages of development: (1) mutual acceptance; (2) communication and decision making; (3) motivation and productivity; and (4) control and organization.[10]

Mutual Acceptance.   In the early stages of group formation, members are generally reluctant to communicate with each other. Although the problem-solving group has a task to perform, the members typically are not willing to express opinions, attitudes, and beliefs. This is similar to the situation facing a faculty member at the start of a new semester. Assume that the class objective is to develop and offer to the city government a plan for traffic control. The class response to the instructor's questions of any form is disappointing and in many cases nonexistent.

Communication and Decision Making.   After a problem-solving group reaches the point of mutual acceptance, the members begin to communicate openly with each other. This communication results in increased confidence and even more interaction within the group. The discussions begin to focus more specifically on problem-solving tasks and the development of alternative strategies to accomplish the tasks.

Motivation and Productivity.   This is the stage of development in which effort is expended to accomplish the group's goals. In a problem-solving group, the task is to produce the best solution. The group is working as a cooperative unit and not a competitive unit.

Control and Organization.   This is the stage in which group affiliation is valued and members are regulated by group norms. The group goals take precedence over individual goals, and the norms are complied with or sanctions are exercised. The ultimate type of sanction is ostracism for not complying with the group goals or norms. Other forms of control are temporary isolation or harassment.

Development of a Training Group

A group distinctly different from a problem-solving group is one that is engaged in formal organizational training. Whereas problem-solving groups

---

[9] For a recent study of group development see J. M. Ivancevich and J. T. McMahon, "Group Development, Trainer Style and Carry-Over Job Satisfaction and Performance," *Academy of Management Journal* (September 1976), pp. 395–412.

[10] Bernard Bass, *Organizational Psychology* (Boston: Allyn and Bacon, 1965), pp. 197–98.

have the specific goal of reaching the best solution to a problem, formal training groups have, in some cases, vaguely defined goals. The trainers may have a clear understanding of the goals, but the training group members are often uncertain about them.

Tuckman has proposed a group development sequence which has been applied primarily to sensitivity training groups.[11] It is Tuckman's assumption that any group, regardless of type or setting, will eventually concern itself with the completion of a task. While attempting to accomplish this task, the group members will relate to one another and function as a whole unit. The total pattern of *interpersonal relationships* is referred to as the *group structure*. The interaction related directly to the task is referred to as the *task activity*. Tuckman specifies the following sequence of *group structure* development:

1. Testing and Dependence.   This is an attempt by group members to discover what interpersonal behaviors are acceptable in the group. The member is dependent on the group or a person for guidance.

2. Intragroup Conflict.   The members are hostile toward each other and there is a lack of unified group effort.

3. Development of Group Cohesion.   The members accept the group and the idiosyncracies of fellow members. Harmony is of maximum importance.

4. Functional Role-Relatedness.   Members begin to adopt roles that will enhance the task accomplishments of the group.

There are four phases of *task activity* development. They are:

1. Orientation to the Task.   The members attempt to identify the task and determine what is needed to accomplish the task.

2. Emotional Response to the Task Demands.   Group members react emotionally to the task as a form of resistance to the demands of the task on the individual.

3. Open Exchange of Relevant Interpretations.   This takes the form of exchanging opinions, beliefs, and attitudes.

4. Emergence of Solutions.   The emphasis is on constructive activities and interactions to complete the task.

Although this concept of group development applies primarily to sensitivity training groups and the previous model focuses on problem-solving groups, there are distinct similarities. In both types of groups, the members initially attempt to become oriented to each other. The emphasis in the early stages of development is on interpersonal understanding. As members in both types of groups become more trusting, there is a shift toward concentrating on task accomplishments. Thus, although the objectives of problem-solving groups and training groups may be different, the development that occurs within them is quite similar. The stage of development is an important factor

---

[11] Bruce W. Tuckman, "Developmental Sequence in Small Groups," *Psychological Bulletin* (June 1965), pp. 384–99.

for a manager to assess. For example, to expect a newly formed group of accountants, engineers, or machinists to be immediately task oriented is an unrealistic expectation. Any newly formed group is at the initial interpersonal understanding stage of development and not at the solution generation stage.

CHARACTERISTICS OF GROUPS

As groups evolve through their various stages of development they begin to exhibit certain characteristics. To understand group behavior it is necessary to be aware of these general characteristics.

Structure

Within any group, some type of structure evolves over a period of time. The group members are differentiated on the basis of such factors as expertise, aggressiveness, power, and status. Each member occupies a *position* in the group. The pattern of relationships among the positions constitutes a *group structure.*

Members of the group evaluate each position in terms of its prestige, status, and importance to the group. In most cases there is some type of status difference among positions such that the group structure is hierarchical. The occupant of each position is expected by the members to enact certain behaviors during group interaction. The set of expected behaviors associated with a position in the structure constitutes the role of the occupant of that position.

Status Hierarchy

Status and position are so similar that the terms are often used interchangeably. The status *assigned* to a particular position is typically a consequence of certain characteristics which differentiate one position from the other. In some cases, a person is *ascribed* status because of such factors as job seniority, age, or assignment. The oldest worker may be perceived as being more technically proficient and is ascribed status by a group of technicians.

Status differences exert a powerful influence upon the pattern and content of communications in a group. For example, more communications tend to be directed toward high-status group members and the content of such messages tends to be more positive than messages initiated from a high-status person to lower-status individuals.[12]

---

[12] For a recent relevant study see L. A. Nikolai and J. D. Bazley, "An Analysis of the Organizational Interaction of Accounting Departments," *Academy of Management Journal* (December 1977), pp. 608–21.

Roles

Each position in the group structure has an associated role which consists of the expected behaviors of the occupant of that position. The director of nursing services in a hospital is expected to organize and control the department of nursing. The director is also expected to assist in preparing and administering the budget for the department. A nursing supervisor, on the other hand, is expected to supervise the activities of nursing personnel engaged in specific nursing services, such as obstetrics, pediatrics, and surgery. These expected behaviors are generally agreed upon not only by the occupants, the director of nursing and the nursing supervisor, but also by other members of the nursing group and by other hospital personnel.[13]

The *expected role* is only one type of role. There are also a "perceived role" and an "enacted role." The *perceived role* is the set of behaviors which a person in a position believes he or she should enact. In some cases, the perceived role may correspond to the expected role. As discussed in Chapter 4, perception can, in some instances, be distorted or inaccurate. The *enacted role* is the behavior that a person actually carries out. Thus three possible behaviors can result. There is then a possibility of conflict and frustration resulting from differences in these three role types. In fairly stable or permanent groups, there is typically good agreement between expected and perceived roles. When the enacted role deviates too much from the expected role, the person can either become more like the expected role or leave the group.

Individuals, because of membership in different groups, perform multiple roles. These multiple roles result in a number of expected role behaviors. In many instances, the behaviors specified by the different roles are compatible. However, in many circumstances, they are not. When this occurs, the individual experiences role conflict. There are several types of role conflict and some important consequences. Role conflict will be discussed later in the chapter.

Norms

Norms are the standards that are shared by members of the group. Norms have certain characteristics that are important to group members. First, norms are only formed with respect to things that have significance for the group. If production is important, then a norm will evolve. If helping other group members complete a task is important, then a norm will develop.[14] Second,

---

[13] For example, see C. E. Schneier and P. W. Beatty, "The Influence of Role Prescriptions on the Performance Appraisal Process," *Academy of Management Journal* (March 1978), pp. 129–34.

[14] For an example see R. J. Burke, T. Weir, and G. Duncan, "Informal Helping Relationships in Work Organizations," *Academy of Management Journal* (September 1976), pp. 370–77.

norms are accepted in various degrees by group members. Some norms are accepted by all members completely, while other norms are only partially accepted. Third, norms may apply to every member, or they may apply to only some group members. Every member is expected to comply with the production norm, while only group leaders are expected to disagree verbally with a management directive.

Norm Conformity. An issue of concern to managers is why employees conform to group norms. This is especially important when a person with skill and capability is performing significantly below his or her capacity so that group norms are not violated. Four general classes of variables influence conformity to group norms.

1. Personality of group members.
2. The stimuli which evoke the response.
3. Situational factors.
4. Intragroup relationships.[15]

Personality is the relatively stable set of characteristics, tendencies, and temperaments that have been formed by inheritance and by social, cultural, and environmental factors. Research on personality characteristics suggests that the more intelligent are less likely to conform than the less intelligent,[16] and that authoritarians conform more than nonauthoritarians.[17]

Stimulus factors include all the stimuli that are related to the norm to which the group member is conforming. The more ambiguous the stimulus, the greater will be the conformity to group norms. For example, suppose that top management adopts a specific type of performance appraisal interview. The group of managers who are to conduct the interviews may be initially unsure of the process because of its newness and complexity. The lack of clarity generally results in the group performing closer to the old group performance appraisal procedures than to the new ones as outlined by top management. The managers conform to a group-imposed norm until the interview process is clarified and key group members begin to utilize the procedure.

The *situational factors* pertain to variables such as the size and structure of the group. Asch found that conformity to false answers about line sizes increased with group size up to size four and was constant thereafter.[18] He also found that conformity was greater when there is unanimity.

---

[15] H. T. Reitan and M. E. Shaw, "Group Membership, Sex-Composition of the Group, and Conformity Behavior," *Journal of Social Psychology* (October 1964), pp. 45–51.

[16] Bernard M. Bass, C. R. McGehee, W. C. Hawkins, P. C. Young, and A. S. Gebel, "Personality Variables Related to Leaderless Group Discussion," *Journal of Abnormal and Social Psychology* (January 1953), pp. 120–28.

[17] E. B. Nalder, "Yielding, Authoritarianism, and Authoritarian Ideology Regarding Groups," *Journal of Abnormal and Social Psychology* (May 1959), pp. 408–10.

[18] S. E. Asch, "Effects of Group Pressure upon the Modification and Distortion of Judgments," in H. Guetzkow, ed., *Groups, Leadership and Men* (Pittsburg: Carnegie Press, 1951), pp. 177–90.

The term *intragroup relationship* includes such variables as the kind of group pressure exerted, how successful the group has been in achieving desired goals, and the degree to which a member identifies with the group.

Potential Consequences of Conforming to Group Norms. The research on conformity distinctly implies that conformity is a requirement of sustained group membership. The member who does not conform to important norms is often punished by a group. One form of punishment is to isolate or ignore the presence of the deviant. There are some potential consequences, negative and positive, of conformity. Conformity can result in a loss of individuality and the establishment of only moderate levels of performance. This type of behavior can certainly be costly to an organization which needs above-average levels of performance to remain competitive.

There are, of course, potential positive consequences of conforming to group norms. If no conformity existed, a manager would have an extremely difficult, if not impossible, time in predicting the group's behavior patterns. This inability to estimate behavior could result in unsuccessful managerial attempts to channel the group's effort toward the accomplishment of organizational goals. This, of course, is a problem facing managers of formal groups. They have no systematic way to predict behavior, such as a group's response to a new computer system or a new performance appraisal system, because there is a lack of conformity to group norms.

Leadership

The leadership role in groups is an extremely crucial group characteristic. The leader of a group exerts some influence over the members of the group. In the formal group, the leader can exercise legitimately sanctioned power. That is, the leader can reward or punish members who do not comply with the directives, orders, or rules.

The leadership role is also a significant factor in an informal group. The person who becomes an informal group leader is generally viewed as a respected and prestigious member who:

1. Aids the group in accomplishing its goals.
2. Enables members to satisfy needs.
3. Embodies the values of the group. The leader in essence is a personification of the values, motives, and aspirations of the membership.
4. Is the choice of the group members to represent their viewpoint when interacting with other group leaders.
5. Is a facilitator of group conflict, an initiator of group actions, and is concerned with maintaining the group as a functioning unit.

The informal leader can, and often does, change because of the situation and various conditions which exist at a particular moment. A leader who is not able to maintain the respect and prestige as perceived by members can be replaced by another leader thought to be more prestigious and worthy of the respect of the membership. To remain a leader in any type of group a person must have the necessary knowledge and skills needed to aid and guide the group toward task accomplishment.

Cohesiveness

Formal and informal groups seem to possess a closeness or commonness of attitude, behavior, and performance. This closeness has been referred to as cohesiveness. It is generally regarded as a force acting on the members to remain in a group that is greater than the forces pulling the member away from the group.[19] A cohesive group, then, involves individuals who are attracted to each other. The group that is low in cohesiveness does not possess interpersonal attractiveness for the members.

There are, of course, numerous sources of attraction to a group. A group may be attractive because:

1. The goals of the group and the members are compatible and clearly specified.
2. The group has a charismatic leader.
3. The reputation of the group indicates that the group successfully accomplishes its tasks.
4. The group is small enough to permit members to have their opinions heard and evaluated by others.
5. The members are attractive in that they support each other and help each other overcome obstacles and barriers to personal growth and development.[20]

These five factors are related to need satisfaction. As discussed earlier, one of the reasons for group formation is to satisfy needs. If an individual is able to join a cohesive group then there should be an increase in the satisfaction of needs through this group affiliation.

Since highly cohesive groups are composed of individuals motivated to be together, there is a tendency to expect effective group performance. This logic is not conclusively supported by research evidence. In general, as the cohesiveness of a work group increases, the level of conformity to group norms also increases and these norms may be inconsistent with those of the organization. The group pressures to conform are more intense in the cohesive group. A member who attempts to defy the group jeopardizes his or her position and status in the cohesive unit.[21]

---

[19] James H. Davis, *Group Performance* (Reading, Mass.: Addison-Wesley Publishing Co., 1969), p. 78.

[20] D. Cartwright and A. Zander, *Group Dynamics: Research and Theory* (New York: Harper & Row, 1968).

[21] A. J. Lott and B. E. Lott, "Group Cohesiveness as Interpersonal Attraction: A Review of Relationships with Antecedent and Consequent Variables." *Psychological Bulletin* (October 1965), pp. 259–309.

The importance of group cohesiveness was indicated in a study conducted by the Tavistock Institute in Great Britain.[22] The coal mining industry in England following World War II introduced a number of changes in mining equipment and procedures. Prior to this new technology, miners worked together as teams. The group of miners dug out the coal, loaded it into cars, and moved it to a station where it was taken from the mine. The tasks, physical proximity, and dangers of mining were forces that resulted in the development of cohesive teams. The teams provided the members with opportunities to interact. Thus, highly cohesive groups had developed prior to the introduction of the new equipment.

The new technology disrupted the groups. The machinery did some of the tasks previously accomplished by the miners. It also destroyed many of the opportunities for miners to socialize. Without the support of the highly cohesive groups, and with an increase in physical distance between miners, the coal miners began to slow down their production. Other groups or teams formed, but they were not as attractive to the miners as the traditional teams that worked close to each other.

The concept of cohesiveness is an important one for the understanding of groups in organizations. The degree of cohesiveness in a group can have positive or negative effects depending upon how congruent group goals are with those of the formal organization. In fact, four distinct possibilities exist as illustrated in Figure 6–1.

Figure 6–1 indicates that if cohesiveness is high and the group accepts and agrees with formal organization goals then group behavior will likely

Figure 6–1
The Relationship between Group Cohesiveness and Agreement with Organizational Goals and Group Performance

		Agreement with Organizational goals	
		Low	High
Degree of Group Cohesiveness	Low	Performance oriented away from formal organizational goals.	Performance oriented toward achievement of formal organizational goals.
	High	Performance probably oriented away from formal organizational goals.	Performance probably oriented toward achievement of formal organizational goals.

[22] E. L. Trist and K. W. Bamforth, "Some Social and Psychological Consequences of the Longwall Method of Coal Getting," *Human Relations* (February 1951), pp. 3–38. For other important research on group cohesiveness see S. E. Seashore, *Group Cohesiveness in The Industrial Work Group* (Ann Arbor: University of Michigan, Institute for Social Research, 1954) and S. M. Klein, *Workers under Stress: The Impact of Work Pressure on Group Cohesion* (Lexington: The University of Kentucky Press, 1971).

be positive from the formal organization standpoint. However, if the group is highly cohesive but with goals which are not congruent with the formal organization, then group behavior will likely be negative from the formal organization standpoint.

Figure 6–1 also indicates that if a group is low in cohesiveness and the members have goals not in agreement with those of management, then the results will probably be negative from the standpoint of the formal organization although the behavior will be more on an individual basis than on a group basis because of the low cohesiveness. On the other hand it is possible to have a group low in cohesiveness where the members' goals agree with those of the formal organization. Here the results will probably be positive although again more on an individual basis than a group basis.[23]

When the goals of a cohesive group conflict with those of management, some form of managerial intervention is usually necessary. These intervention techniques will be discussed in detail in the next chapter.

Intergroup Conflict

We have discussed the ways and means utilized by groups in handling conflict between members of the group. However, an important characteristic of groups is that they also conflict with other groups in the organization. There are many reasons why groups often conflict with one another. Many times the consequences of this conflict may be good for the organization while at other times they may be extremely negative.

This chapter is concerned mainly with what happens *within* groups: the types, development, and characteristics. The subject of what happens *between* groups (intergroup behavior) is also important. So much, in fact, that the next chapter is devoted entirely to the subject of intergroup behavior and conflict. At this point it is sufficient to note that intergroup conflict is an important characteristic of group behavior.

THE CONCEPT OF ROLE

Throughout this chapter, as well as the remainder of the book, the concept of role is very important to the understanding of organizational behavior. We use the term *role* to refer to the expected behavior patterns attributed to a particular position.

To communicate the importance of the concept of role, let us leave the organizational setting for a moment. The role of wife and husband is familiar to everyone. The role of a wife or husband is the culturally defined expectations associated with that particular position. It may include attitudes and values

---

[23] The research upon which Figure 6–1 is based appears in footnotes 18–21 and in the additional references at the end of the chapter. The general idea for the figure came from F. E. Kast and J. E. Rosenzweig, *Organization and Management* (New York: McGraw-Hill Book Co., 1970), p. 284.

as well as specific kinds of behavior. It is what the individuals must do in order to validate their occupancy of the particular positions.[24] In other words, what kind of a husband or wife an individual is depends a great deal on how he or she performs the culturally defined roles associated with positions. For example, consider your own perceptions of the roles associated with physicians, law enforcement officers, military officers, politicians, college professors, or business executives.

Certain activities are expected of all positions in the formal organization. These activities constitute the role for that position from the standpoint of the formal organization. The formal organization develops job descriptions which define the activities of a particular position and how it relates to other positions in the organization. However, roles may not be set forth explicitly by the formal organization and yet be clearly understood by group members. This is true for both formal (task and command) groups as well as informal (interest and friendship) groups. Thus, whether they are formally or informally established, status hierarchies and accompanying roles are integral parts of every organization.

Multiple Roles and Role Sets

Most individuals play many roles simultaneously. This is because we occupy many different positions in a variety of organizations—home, work organization, church, civic organization, and so forth. Within each of these organizations we occupy and perform certain roles. Thus, most individuals perform *multiple roles*. Also, for each position there may be different role relationships. For example, the position of college professor not only involves the role of teacher in relation to students, but also numerous other roles relating the position to administrators, peers, the community, and alumni. Each group may expect different things. This we term the *role set*. It refers to those individuals who have expectations for the behavior of the individual in the particular role. The more expectations the more complex the role set. A college professor likely has a more complex role set than a forest ranger and less than a politician.

Thus, multiple roles refers to different roles while role sets refers to the different expectations associated with one role. Therefore, an individual involved in many different roles, each with a complex role set faces the ultimate in complexity of individual behavior. The concepts of multiple roles and role sets are important because there may be complications which often make it extremely difficult to define specific roles especially in organizational settings.[25] This can often result in *role conflict* for the individual.

[24] See two classic discussions of these concepts in Robert K. Merton, *Social Theory and Social Structure* (New York: The Free Press of Glencoe, 1957): and Ralph Linton, "Concepts of Role and Status," in Theodore E. Newcomb and Eugene L. Hartley, eds., *Readings in Social Psychology* (New York: Holt, Rinehart & Winston, 1947).

[25] An important work in this field is R. L. Kahn, D. M. Wolfe, R. P. Quinn, and J. D. Snoek, *Organizational Stress: Studies in Role Conflict and Ambiguity* (New York: John Wiley and Sons, 1964), pp. 12–26.

Role Perception

The reader can readily imagine that different individuals can have different perceptions of the behavior associated with a given role. In an organizational setting accuracy in role perception can have a definite impact on performance. This matter is further complicated in an organization because there may be three different perceptions of the same role: that of the formal organization, the group, and the individual. This increases even further the possibility of role conflict.

The Organization. The positions which individuals occupy in an organization are the sum total of their organizationally defined roles. This would include the position in the chain of command, the amount of authority associated with the position, and the functions and duties of the position. These roles are defined by the organization and relate to the position and not a particular individual.

The Group. Role relationships develop which relate individuals to the various groups to which they belong. These may be formal and informal groups and the expectations evolve over time and may or may not be congruent with the organization's perception of the role. In this respect they are similar to group norms.

The Individual. Every individual who occupies a position in an organization or group has a clearly defined perception of his or her role. This perception will be greatly influenced by background and social class, since they affect the individual's basic values and attitudes. These are brought to the organization and will affect the individuals' perception of their roles.

Role Conflict

With an understanding of the concept of role and its many complexities let us now consider the idea of *role conflict.* Because of the multiplicity of roles and role sets, it is possible for an individual to face a situation of the simultaneous occurrence of two or more role requirements for which the performance of one precludes the performance of the other. When this occurs, the individual faces a situation of role conflict. We shall examine several forms of role conflict which can occur in organizations.[26]

Person-Role Conflict. This conflict occurs when role requirements violate the basic values, attitudes, and needs of the individual occupying the position. A supervisor who finds it difficult to dismiss a subordinate with a family, or an executive who resigns rather than engage in some unethical activity are examples of this type of role conflict.[27]

---

[26] R. Tagiuri, P. R. Lawrence, R. Barnett, and D. C. Dumphy, *Behavioral Science Concepts in Case Analysis* (Boston: Division of Research, Graduate School of Business Administration, Harvard University, 1968), pp. 106–10.

[27] For example, see N. Keeley, "Subjective Performance Evaluation and Person-Role Conflict under Conditions of Uncertainty," *Academy of Management Journal* (June 1977), pp. 301–14.

Intrarole Conflict. This occurs when different individuals define a role according to different sets of expectations, making it impossible for the person occupying the role to satisfy all. This is more likely to occur when a given role has a complex role set (many different role relationships). The foreman in an industrial situation has a rather complex role set and thus may face this type of conflict. On one hand, top management has a set of expectations which stress the foreman's role in the management hierarchy. However, being a first-line supervisor the foreman may have close friendship ties with members of the command group who may possibly be former working peers. This is why foremen and first-line supervisors are often described as being "in the middle."[28]

Interrole Conflict. This type of conflict is the result of facing multiple roles. It occurs because individuals simultaneously perform many roles, some of which have conflicting expectations. A scientist in a chemical plant who is also a member of an administrative group might experience role conflict of this kind. In such a situation the scientist may be expected to behave in accordance with the expectations of management as well as the expectations of professional chemists. A physician placed in the role of hospital administrator might also experience this type of role conflict. In the next chapter we shall see that this type of role conflict is often the cause of conflict between groups in many organizations.

The Results of Role Conflict

Behavioral scientists agree that an individual confronted with role conflict will experience psychological stress which may result in emotional problems and indecision. While there are certain kinds of role conflict which managers can do little to avoid, there are certain types which can be minimized. For example, some types of role conflict (especially intrarole conflict) can be the result of violations in the classical principles of chain of command and unity of command. The rationale of the early management writers for these two principles was that violation would likely cause conflicting pressures on the individual. In other words, when individuals are faced with conflicting expectations or demands from two or more sources the likely end result will be a decline in performance.[29]

In addition, interrole conflict can result from conflicting expectations of formal or informal groups with the results being similar to those of intrarole conflict. Thus, a highly cohesive group with goals not congruent with those

---

[28] For excellent discussions of the conflict-laden position of foremen see F. J. Roethlisberger, "The Foreman: Master and Victim of Double Talk," *Harvard Business Review,* vol. 45 (September–October 1965), pp. 23 ff.; and F. C. Mann and J. K. Dent, "The Supervisor: Member of Two Organizational Families," *Harvard Business Review,* vol. 6 (November–December 1954), pp. 103–12.

[29] For the view of an early writer on the behavioral end-results of violations in the principles of chain of command and unity of command see Chester I. Barnard, *The Functions of the Executive* (Cambridge, Mass.: Harvard University Press, 1938), p. 277.

of the formal organization can cause a great deal of interrole conflict for its membership.

One final point must be made concerning role conflict. Research has shown that role conflict does occur frequently and with negative effects on performance over a wide spectrum of occupations.[30] For example, unskilled employees, salespersons, school administrators, teachers, scientists, military chaplins, nurses, and managers have all been studied under various role conflict conditions.

AN INTEGRATED MODEL OF GROUP FORMATION AND DEVELOPMENT

Figure 6–2 summarizes what has been discussed to this point. It indicates the potential end results from group behavior: individual performances, group performances and overall organizational effectiveness and performance. The model also includes feedback from the potential behavioral consequences and each of the other elements in the model. Each segment can influence each of the other segments.

MAJOR ISSUES FOR THE MANAGER TO CONSIDER

A. A group can be defined in terms of perception, organization, motivation, or interaction. We recommend thinking about a group as employees who interact in such a manner that the behavior and/or performance of a member is influenced by the behavior and/or performance of other members.

B. Managers, by being aware of group characteristics and behaviors, can be prepared for the potential positive and negative end results of group activities. In a proactive sense, the manager could intervene to modify the perceptions, attitudes, and motivations which precede the end results.

C. People are attracted to groups because of the potential for satisfying needs, physical proximity and attraction, and the appeal of group goals and activities. In essence, people are attracted to each other; this is a natural process. The manager can structure a work area to minimize interaction, but no manager can or should eliminate interaction. Consequently, since interaction is inevitable, informal group formation is also certain to occur. The manager who per-

---

[30] For representative examples see A. Etzioni, "Authority Structure and Organizational Effectiveness," *Administrative Science Quarterly* (June 1959), pp. 43–67; N. Kaplan, "The Role of the Research Administrator," *Administrative Science Quarterly* (June 1959), pp. 20–41; W. A. Evans, "Role Strain and the Norm of Reciprocity in Research Organizations," *American Journal of Sociology* (November 1964), pp. 346–54; R. G. Corwin, "The Professional Employee: A Study of Conflict in Nursing Roles," *American Journal of Sociology* (May 1961), pp. 604–15; J. M. Ivancevich and J. H. Donnelly, Jr., "A Study of Role Clarity and Need For Clarity for Three Occupational Groups," *Academy of Management Journal* (March 1974), pp. 28–36; and R. H. Miles, "A Comparison of the Relative Impacts of Role Perceptions of Ambiguity and Conflict by Role," *Academy of Management Journal* (March 1976), pp. 25–34.

Figure 6–2
A Model of Group Formation and Development

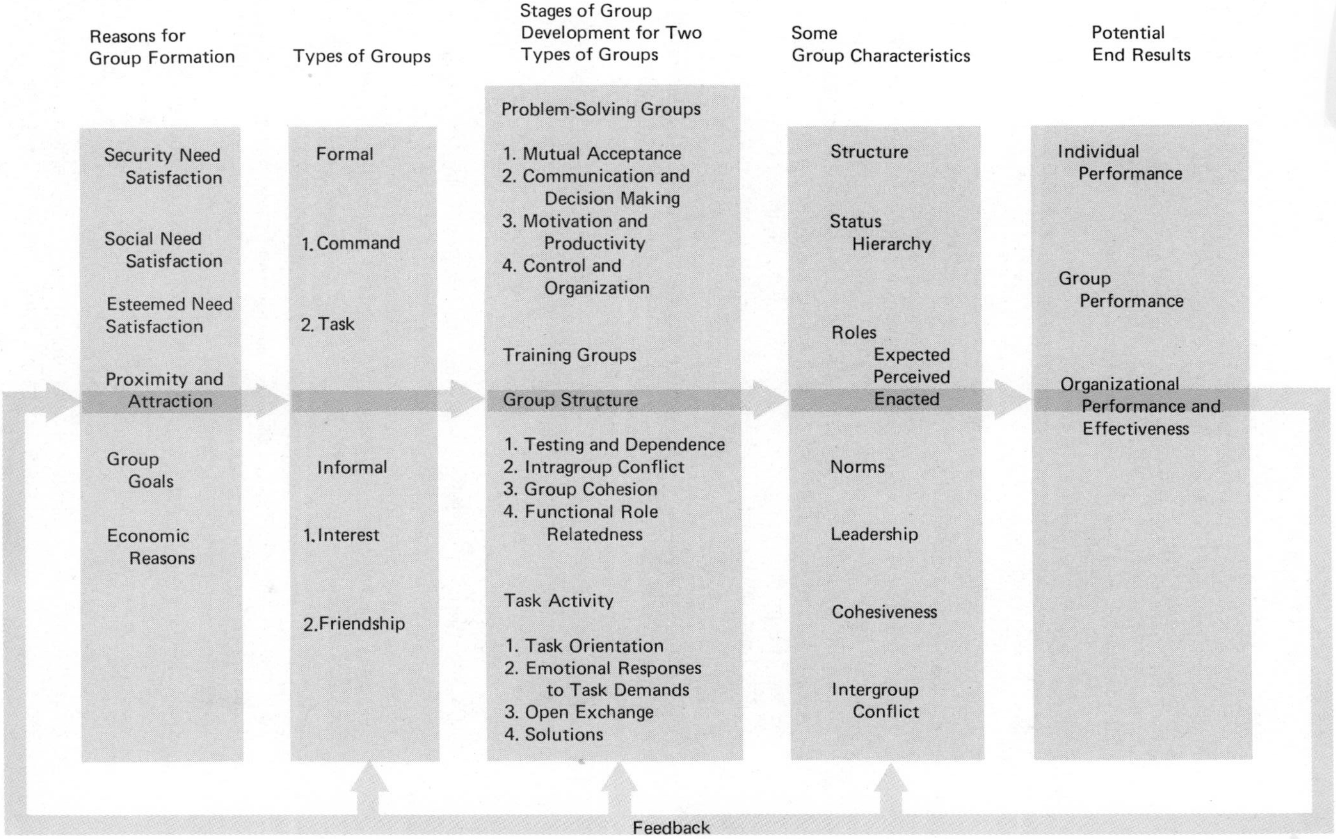

Reasons for Group Formation	Types of Groups	Stages of Group Development for Two Types of Groups	Some Group Characteristics	Potential End Results
Security Need Satisfaction	Formal	Problem-Solving Groups	Structure	Individual Performance
Social Need Satisfaction	1. Command	1. Mutual Acceptance	Status Hierarchy	Group Performance
Esteemed Need Satisfaction	2. Task	2. Communication and Decision Making		
Proximity and Attraction		3. Motivation and Productivity	Roles Expected Perceived Enacted	Organizational Performance and Effectiveness
Group Goals	Informal	4. Control and Organization		
Economic Reasons	1. Interest	Training Groups	Norms	
	2. Friendship	Group Structure	Leadership	
		1. Testing and Dependence	Cohesiveness	
		2. Intragroup Conflict	Intergroup Conflict	
		3. Group Cohesion		
		4. Functional Role Relatedness		
		Task Activity		
		1. Task Orientation		
		2. Emotional Responses to Task Demands		
		3. Open Exchange		
		4. Solutions		

Feedback

ceives the interactions as potential dangers will have difficulty reacting constructively to inevitable group formation.

D. Groups develop at different rates and with unique patterns depending on the task, the setting, the membership's individual characteristics and behavioral patterns, and the manager's style of managing.

E. Some characteristics of groups are:

1. Structure.
2. Status hierarchy.
3. Roles.
4. Norms.
5. Leadership.
6. Cohesiveness.
7. Intergroup conflict.

These characteristics pervade all groups and should be considered important. In an informal group, these characteristics emerge from within the unit, while in a formal group they are established by the managerial process. They provide a degree of predictability for the membership behavior patterns that is important to the group and to outsiders (e.g., management, other groups). A group that is unstable or unpredictable is a problem for members and others who interact with it.

F. Each group possesses some degree of cohesiveness. This attractiveness of the group can be a powerful force in influencing individual behavior and performance.

G. Research studies indicate that cohesive groups can formulate goals and norms which can be either congruent or incongruent with those of management. When these goals and norms are incongruent some form of managerial intervention is necessary.

H. The concept of role is important for an understanding of group behavior. These are the expected behavior patterns attributed to a particular position. Most individuals perform multiple roles each with its own role set (expectations of others for the role). An individual involved in many different roles, each with a complex role set, faces the ultimate in complexity of individual behavior.

I. In organizations there may be as many as three perceptions of the same role; the organization's, the group's, and the individual's. When an individual faces a situation of the simultaneous occurrence of two or more role requirements for which the performance of one precludes the performance of the other, the individual experiences role conflict. Three different types of role conflict: person-role conflict, intrarole conflict, and interrole conflict can occur in organizational settings. Each is important since research has shown that the consequences to the individual are increased psychological stress and other emotional reactions. Management can minimize certain types and should continually be aware that the consequences of role conflict to the organization is ineffective performance of individuals and groups.

DISCUSSION AND REVIEW QUESTIONS

1. Think of an informal group to which you belong. Does a status hierarchy exist in the group? What is it based upon?

2. For the group you have selected above, can you describe any evolution or developmental process such as described in the chapter? Discuss.

3. What are some of the attitudes, beliefs, etc., you held when you first joined the class in which you are using this book? Describe them and then indicate if you believe they have had any impact on your behavior and performance in the class.

4. Are there any cohesive subgroups in your class? How do you know? Do you think it has influenced their behavior or performance in the class?

5. Describe some sources of person-role conflict, intrarole conflict, and interrole conflict that you have either experienced personally or have watched others experience.

6. Why is it important for a manager to be familiar with concepts of group behavior?

7. Why is cohesiveness an important concept in managing group behavior?

ADDITIONAL REFERENCES

Alderfer, C. P. "Effect of Individual, Group, and Intergroup Relations on Attitudes toward a Management Development Program." *Journal of Applied Psychology* (1971), pp. 302–11.

Allen, V. L., and Levine, J. M. "Social Support and Conformity: The Role of Independent Assessment of Reality." *Journal of Experimental Social Psychology* (1971), pp. 48–58.

Bouchard, R. J., and Hare, M. "Size, Performance and Potential in Brainstorming Groups." *Journal of Applied Psychology* (1970), pp. 51–55.

Delbecq, A. L., and VandeVen, A. "A Group Process Model for Problem Identification and Program Planning." *Journal of Applied Behavioral Science* (1971), pp. 466–92.

Graham, G. H. "Interpersonal Attraction as a Basis of Informal Organization." *Academy of Management Journal* (1971), pp. 483–95.

Green, Thad B. "An Empirical Analysis of Nominal and Interacting Groups." *Academy of Management Journal* (1975), pp. 63–73.

Hackman, J. R. "Group Influences on Individuals." From M. D. Dunnette, ed., *Handbook of Industrial and Organizational Psychology*. Chicago: Rand McNally Publishing Co., 1976.

Lewis, G. H. "Role Differentiation." *American Sociological Review* (1972), p. 424–34.

Mazar, A. "A Cross-Species Comparison of Status in Small Established Groups." *American Sociological Review* (1973), pp. 513–30.

Reif, W. F.; Monczka, R. M.; and Newstrom, J. W. "Perceptions of Formal and Informal Organizations: Objective Management through the Semantic Differential Technique." *Academy of Management Journal* (1973), pp. 389–403.

Smith, P. B. *Groups within Organizations.* New York: Harper and Row Publishers, 1973.

Steiner, I. D. *Group Processes and Productivity.* New York: Academic Press, 1972.

Turner, A. N. "A Conceptual Scheme for Describing Work Group Behavior." From P. R. Lawrence et al., eds., *Organizational Behavior and Administration.* Homewood, Ill.: Richard D. Irwin, 1961, pp. 213–23.

CASE FOR ANALYSIS

THE "NO MARTINI" LUNCH

Jim Lyons had just completed his second month as manager of an important office of a nationwide sales organization. He believed that he had made the right choice in leaving his old company. This new position offered a great challenge, excellent pay and benefits, and tremendous opportunity for advancement. In addition, his family seemed to be adjusting well to the new community. However, in Jim's mind there was one very serious problem which he believed must be confronted immediately or it could threaten his satisfaction in the long run.

Since taking the job, Jim had found out that the man he replaced had made an institution of the hard-drinking business lunch. He and a group of other key executives had virtually a standing appointment at various local restaurants. Even when clients were not present, they would have several drinks before ordering their lunches. When they returned it was usually well into the afternoon and they were in no condition to make the decisions or take the actions that were often the pretext of the lunch in the first place. This practice had also spread to the subordinates of the various executives and it was not uncommon to see various groups of salespersons doing the same thing a few days each week. Jim decided that he wanted to end the practice, at least for himself and members of his group.

Jim knew this was not going to be an easy problem to solve. The drinking had become institutionalized with a great deal of psychological pressure from a central figure—in this case, the man he replaced. He decided to plan the approach he would take and then discuss the problem and his approach for solving it with his superior, Norm Landy.

The following week Jim made an appointment with Norm to discuss the situation. Norm listened intently as Jim explained the drinking problem but did not show any surprise at learning about it. Jim then explained what he planned to do.

"Norm, I'm making two assumptions on the front end. First, I don't believe it would do any good to state strong new policies about drinking at lunch, or lecturing my people about the evils of the liquid lunch. About all I'd accomplish there would be to raise a lot of latent guilt which would only result in resentment and resistance. Second, I am assuming that the boss is often a role model for his subordinates. Unfortunately, the man I replaced made a practice of the drinking lunch. The subordinates close to him then conform to his drinking habits and exert pressure on other members of the group. Before you know it everyone is a drinking buddy and the practice becomes institutionalized even when one member is no longer there.

Here is what I intend to do about it. First, when I go to lunch with the other managers, I will do no drinking. More importantly, however, for the members of my group I am going to establish a new role model. For example, at least once a week we have a legitimate reason to work through lunch.

In the past everyone has gone out anyway. I intend to hold a business lunch and have sandwiches and soft drinks sent in. In addition, I intend to make it a regular practice to take different groups of my people to lunch at a no-alcohol coffee shop.

My goal, Norm, is simply to let my subordinates know that alcohol is not a necessary part of the workday, and that drinking will not win my approval. By not drinking with the other managers, I figure that sooner or later they too will get the point. As you can see I intend to get the message across by my behavior. There will be no words of censure. What do you think Norm?"

Norm Landy pushed himself away from his desk and came around and seated himself beside Jim. He then looked at Jim and whispered, "Are you crazy? I guarantee you, Jim, that you are going to accomplish nothing but cause a lot of trouble. Trouble between your group and other groups if you succeed, trouble between you and your group, and trouble between you and the other managers. Believe me, Jim, I see the problem, and I agree with you that it is a problem. But the cure might kill the patient. Will all that conflict and trouble be worth it?"

Jim thought for a moment and said "I think it will be good for the organization in the long run."

Questions for Discussion

1. Do you agree with Norm Landy or Jim Lyons? Why?
2. Do you think anything can be done about this situation? Why? What is your opinion of Jim's plan?
3. What would you do in Jim's situation? Be specific.

Chapter 7

Intergroup Behavior and Managing Conflict

AN ORGANIZATIONAL ISSUE FOR DEBATE

*Should Management Seek To Eliminate Conflict?**

ARGUMENT FOR

Many practicing managers view group conflict negatively and thus seek to resolve or eliminate all types of conflict. These managers adhere to the beliefs of classical organization theorists that conflict disrupts the organization and prevents optimal performance. As such it is a clear indication that something is wrong with the organization and that sound management principles are not being applied in directing the activities of the organization.

Since their desire was to eliminate conflict, early writers based their approaches on principles of authority, delegation of authority, and unity of command. They believed that conflict could be eliminated or avoided by recruiting the right people, carefully specifying job descriptions, structuring the organization in such a way as to establish a clear chain of command, and establishing clear rules and procedures to meet various contingencies.

Many writers believe that this view is held today by the majority of practicing managers. They view all conflict as disruptive; their task is to eliminate it by more effective management and organizational structure.

ARGUMENT AGAINST

Many theorists and some managers believe that a more realistic view of conflict is that it cannot be avoided. They believe it is inevitable and can result from numerous factors including the structure of the organization itself, the performance evaluation system, and even something as seemingly unimportant as the physical design of an office and its furnishings.

In fact, these individuals believe that a certain amount of conflict is not only useful but that optimal organizational performance requires a moderate level. Without it, there will be no felt need to change and attention will not be called to problem areas.

Obviously, these individuals realize that too much conflict is undesirable. Thus, they believe that conflict may either "add to" or "detract from" organizational performance in varying degrees. In other words, conflict can be functional or dysfunctional for the organization depending on the amount and kind. Under this viewpoint, management's task becomes one of managing the level of conflict in order to achieve optimal performance.

---

* The first view is discussed in detail in C. B. Derr, *A Historical Review of Management Organization Conflict* (Boston: Harvard University, Graduate School of Education, 1972), pp. 1–22. The opposing view is discussed in detail in M. Olson, *The Logic of Collective Action* (Cambridge: Harvard University Press, 1965).

INTRODUCTION

For any organization to perform effectively, interdependent individuals and groups must work out their relations across organizational boundaries, between individuals, and among groups. Each individual or group depends on another. It may be for information, assistance, or coordinated action. But the fact is, they are interdependent. Such interdependence may foster cooperation or conflict.

For example, the entire faculty of a college may meet to discuss ways to convince the university administration that the annual budget for the college must be increased. Such a meeting may be reasonably free of conflict. Decisions get made, strategies are developed and faculty return to their duties. This is intergroup cooperation to achieve a common goal. However, this may not be the case if a budget increase is granted. Individual departments in the college have their own goals and conflict is likely to result at this point because of conflicting departmental goals and competition for resources (new faculty, secretarial assistance). This example illustrates that quite a range can exist between cooperation and conflict and that groups can cooperate on one point and at the same time conflict on another.

This chapter focuses on conflict that occurs between groups in organizations. This is certainly not the only type of conflict that can exist in organizations. Conflict between individuals, however, can usually be more easily resolved through existing mechanisms such as terminations, transfers, or changes in work schedules. As we saw in the last chapter, groups usually socialize individuals—or the individual leaves. Thus, conflict between an individual and a group is relatively short-lived. Conflict between groups is also likely to be the most disruptive to the organization.

We shall begin the chapter by examining attitudes toward conflict. Reasons for the existence of intergroup conflict and its consequences are then presented. Finally, we shall outline various techniques used to successfully manage conflict.

A REALISTIC VIEW OF INTERGROUP CONFLICT

Recognizing the reality that conflict is inevitable in organizations, the authors take the view that intergroup conflict can be both positive and negative. How positive or negative it is depends upon the impact the conflict has on the organization's goal achievement. Conflict may be beneficial if it is used as an instrument for change or innovation and results in better problem solving. However, too much conflict is likely to result in chaos. We saw in an earlier chapter that individuals and groups have differing abilities to withstand stress. Thus, it appears that the critical issue is not conflict itself but rather how it is managed. Using this approach we can define conflict in terms of the *effect it has on the organization*. In this respect we shall discuss both *functional* and *dysfunctional* conflict.[1]

---

[1] This view reflects current thinking among management theorists and a growing number of practitioners. It has been labeled the *interactionist* view. For a major work devoted entirely

Functional Conflict

Functional conflict represents a confrontation between groups that enhances and benefits the organization's performance. Two departments in a
hospital may be in conflict concerning the most efficient and adaptive method
of delivering health care to low-income rural families. The conflict supports
the organization's performance and each group agrees on the goal but not
on the means to achieve the goal. Whatever the outcome, low-income rural
families will likely end up with better medical care. Without this type of conflict
in organizations, there would be little commitment to change and most groups
would likely become stagnant.

Dysfunctional Conflict

Any confrontation or interaction between groups that hinders the achievement of organizational goals can be considered dysfunctional. Management
must seek to eliminate this type of conflict. The point at which functional
conflict becomes dysfunctional is, in most cases, impossible to identify precisely. Because of such factors as tolerance for stress and conflict, a level
that creates healthy and positive movement toward one group's goals, may,
in another group (or at a different time for the same group), be extremely
disruptive and dysfunctional.[2] Another contingency would be the type of organization. Routine manufacturing organizations, professional sports teams,
and crises organizations such as police and fire departments would have
different points where functional conflict becomes dysfunctional than would
organizations such as universities, research and development firms, and motion picture production firms.

Conflict and Organizational Performance

Thus far we have said that conflict may either have a positive or negative
impact on organizational performance depending on how it is managed. For
every organization there is an optimal level of conflict which can be considered
highly functional and which positively influences performance. If the conflict
level is too low, performance suffers. Innovation and change are difficult
and the organization has difficulty adapting to change in its environment. If
this low conflict level continues, the very survival of the organization can
be threatened.[3] On the other hand if the level of conflict is too high, the

---

to the subject of organizational conflict which discusses this and other views, see Stephen P.
Robbins, *Managing Organizational Conflict* (Englewood Cliffs, N.J.: Prentice-Hall, Inc., 1974).

[2] Ibid., p. 24.

[3] At this point it is interesting to speculate on the relationship (if any) between conflict and
organizational performance in organizations such as Xerox, McDonalds, and Sear's. These organizations were "high" performers during the last decade. Consider the same relationship in
such "low" performers as A&P, Hersheys, and Montgomery Ward. Such a study, if it were
possible to conduct, would certainly have been interesting.

Figure 7–1
Proposed Relationship between Intergroup Conflict and Organizational
Performance

Level of Organizational Performance

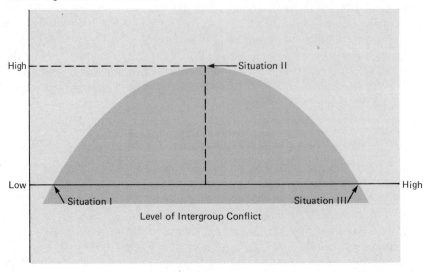

	Level of Intergroup Conflict	Probable Impact on Organization	Organization Characterized by	Level of Organizational Performance
Situation I	Low or none	Dysfunctional	Slow adaptation to environmental changes Few challenges Little stimulation of ideas Apathy Stagnation	Low
Situation II	Optimal	Functional	Positive movement toward goals Innovation and change Search for problem solutions Creativity and quick adaptation to environmental changes	High
Situation III	High	Dysfunctional	Disruption Interference with activities Coordination difficult Chaos	Low

resulting chaos can also threaten the organization's survival.[4] This proposed relationship is presented in Figure 7–1 and explained for three hypothetical situations.

The question we must ask at this point is, "Does research support this view of conflict?" Is evidence available which supports the relationship between level of conflict and performance? Such a relationship would be difficult to determine in a large-scale organization such as a business firm. There is, however, a growing body of research conducted in smaller field experiments using problem-solving groups, research teams, and work groups, and in laboratory experiments which do support this relationship.

One study found that performance definitely improved when there was conflict in the group than when little or no conflict was present. In fact, when each group reviewed decisions that had been reached by individual members, the average improvement for the conflict groups was significantly higher than the improvement of the groups with little or no conflict.[5] Related research has also found that the more diverse a group's membership is with respect to such factors as personality, backgrounds, and attitudes, the more likely the group will be superior in performance. In addition, high incompatibility *between* groups has been found to be related to high performance.[6]

Views toward Intergroup Conflict in Practice

Though evidence exists which supports the view that dysfunctional conflict should be eliminated and functional conflict encouraged, what actually happens in most organizations?[7] In practice, most managers attempt to eliminate all types of conflict, whether dysfunctional or functional. Why is this the case? Some reasons which have been advanced are:

1. Anticonflict values have historically been reinforced in the home, school, and church. Conflict between children and/or children and parents has for the most part been discouraged. In school systems conflict has tradition-

---

[4] An example familiar to the reader is the popular press coverage of the results of "dissension" on professional sports teams and its impact on performance. When performance suffers, the conflict is usually blamed on the coach or manager who is held responsible by the press.

[5] J. Hall and M. S. Williams, "A Comparison of Decision-Making Performance in Established and Ad Hoc Groups," *Journal of Personality and Social Psychology* (February 1966), pp. 217–22.

[6] See L. R. Hoffman and N. R. F. Maier, "Quality and Acceptance of Problem Solutions by Members of Homogeneous and Heterogeneous Groups," *Journal of Abnormal and Social Psychology* (April 1961), pp. 401–7; C. G. Smith, "Scientific Performance and the Composition of Research Teams," *Administrative Science Quarterly* (December 1971), pp. 486–95; W. J. Underwood and L. J. Krafft, "Interpersonal Compatibility and Managerial Work Effectiveness: A Test of the Fundamental Interpersonal Relations Orientation Theory," *Journal of Applied Psychology* (October 1973), pp. 89–94; and Raymond E. Hill, "Interpersonal Compatibility and Work Group Performance among Systems Analysts: An Empirical Study," *Proceedings of the 17th Annual Midwest Academy of Management Conference* (Kent, Ohio, April 1974), pp. 97–110.

[7] This section is based on Stephen P. Robbins, *Managing Organizational Conflict,* and Stephen P. Robbins, *The Administrative Process: Integrating Theory and Practice* (Englewood Cliffs, N.J.: Prentice-Hall, Inc., 1976), chapter 7.

ally been discouraged. Teachers had the answers and both teachers and children were rewarded for orderly classrooms. Finally, most religious doctrines stress peace and tranquility, and acceptance without questioning.

2. Managers are often evaluated and rewarded for the lack of conflict in their areas of responsibility. Anticonflict values, in fact, become part of the "culture" of the organization. Harmony and satisfaction are viewed positively while conflicts and dissatisfaction are viewed negatively. Under such conditions, the obvious result is that managers seek to avoid conflict which could disturb the status quo.[8]

WHY INTERGROUP CONFLICT OCCURS

It has been suggested that every group is in at least partial conflict with every other group it interacts with.[9] Whether or not this is an exaggeration is not important. The important point is that intergroup conflict is very common. In this section we shall examine why such conflicts are so common.

Interdependence

Work interdependence occurs when two or more groups must depend on each other to complete their tasks. The conflict potential in such situations is high. Three distinct types of interdependence among groups have been identified.[10]

Pooled Interdependence. Pooled interdependence occurs when it is not necessary for the groups to interact except through the total organization which supports them. For example, an IBM sales office in one region may have no interaction with their peers in another region. Similarly, two bank branches will have little or no interaction. However, in both cases the groups are interdependent because the performance of each must be adequate if the total organization is to thrive. The conflict potential in pooled interdependence is relatively low and management can rely more on standard rules and procedures developed at the main office for coordination.

Sequential Interdependence. Sequential interdependence occurs when one group must complete its task before another group can complete its task. For example, in a manufacturing plant the product must be assembled before it can be painted. Thus the assembling department must complete its task before the finishing department can begin theirs.

Under these circumstances, since the output of one group serves as the input for another, conflict between the groups is more likely to occur. Coordinating this type of interdependence involves effective use of the management function of planning.

---

[8] Ibid.

[9] This has been referred to as the "law of interorganizational conflict." See Anthony Downs, *Inside Bureaucracy* (Boston: Little, Brown and Co., 1968).

[10] J. Thompson, *Organizations in Action* (New York: McGraw-Hill, Inc., 1967).

Reciprocal Interdependence. In this situation the output of each group serves as input to other groups in the organization. Consider the relationship which exists between the anesthesiology staff, nursing staff, technician staff, and surgeons in a hospital operating room. This is reciprocal interdependence of a high degree. The same interdependence exists among groups involved in space launchings and between airport control towers, flight crews, ground operations, and maintenance crews. Clearly, the potential for conflict is greater in this situation and effective coordination involves management's effective use of the organizational processes of communication and decision making.

Thus, all organizations have pooled interdependence among groups. More complex organizations have sequential interdependence while the most complex organizations will have pooled, sequential, and reciprocal interdependence among groups. The more complex the organization the greater potential for conflict and the more difficult the task facing management.

Differences in Goals

Often, various groups in an organization have goals that cannot be achieved simultaneously. As the subunits of an organization become specialized, they often develop dissimilar goals. This differentiation among the various functions of the organization can lead to different expectations in many areas. For example, a group of assembly-line workers may expect close supervision while a group of research scientists may expect a great deal of participation in decision making. The more complex the organization, the greater the differentiation of functions is likely to be and, therefore, the greater potential for conflict. Examples of such conflict are the age-old conflicts between production departments and marketing departments, and marketing departments and credit departments. Production departments can best achieve their goal of low production costs with long production runs. This means fewer models, colors, and so forth, which conflicts with marketing's goal of broad product lines, many models, colors, etc., for greater customer satisfaction. Finally, marketing departments usually seek to maximize gross income, while the credit department seeks to minimize credit losses. Depending upon which goal is used, different customers might be selected. There are certain conditions which foster this type of conflict.

Limited Resources. If money, space, manpower, materials, and so forth, were unlimited, each group could pursue, at least to a relative degree, its own goals. Unfortunately, this is not the case and resources must be shared or allocated. When resources are limited and must be allocated, mutual dependence increases and any differences in group goals become more apparent. What often occurs is a win-lose competition which can easily result in dysfunctional conflict.

Reward Structures. Intergroup conflict is more likely to occur when the reward system is related to individual group performance rather than to overall organizational performance. Under such circumstances performance is, in fact, viewed as an independent variable although the performance of the group is in reality very interdependent. Suppose that in the example provided above, the marketing group is rewarded for sales produced and the credit group on the amount of credit losses. In such a situation, competition will be directly reinforced and dysfunctional conflict will be inadvertently rewarded.

Intergroup conflict arising from differences in goals can be dysfunctional to the organization as in the examples provided above. It is important to note, however, that depending on the type of organization, it can also be dysfunctional to third party groups—usually the clients the organization serves. The present controversy over the conflict between the goals of quality health care for patients and teaching needs of future physicians is an example.

Differences in Perceptions

The differences that groups may have in goals may also be accompanied by different perceptions of reality. Differing perceptions of what constitutes reality is likely to lead to conflict. A problem in a hospital may be viewed in one way by the administrative staff and in another way by the medical staff. Alumni and faculty may have different perceptions concerning the importance of a winning football program. Later in the book we shall see that differing perceptions are leading causes of breakdowns in communication. There are many factors which cause groups in organizations to form differing perceptions.

Different Goals.   Differences in group goals is an obvious contribution to differing perceptions. If marketing's goal is to maximize sales they will certainly view a major breakdown in production differently than the production department whose goal is to minimize production costs.

Different Time Horizons.   How a group perceives reality is influenced by the time perspective it has. This will influence the priorities and importance they assign to different activities. The research scientists working for a chemical manufacturer may have a time perspective of several years while the manufacturing engineers one of less than a year. A bank president might focus on five and ten year time spans while middle managers probably think in much shorter spans. With such differences in time horizons it is easy to see that problems and issues deemed critical by one group may be dismissed as not important by the other.

Status Incongruency.   Conflicts concerning the relative status of different groups are common and influence perceptions. Usually, many different standards are utilized (rather than an absolute one) the result being that there are many status hierarchies, depending upon which standard is used. For example, conflict often occurs because of work patterns—which group initiates work and which responds. One group may perceive a status difference because they must accept the salesman's initiation of work, a status difference the salesman may reinforce. Academic snobbery is popular in many colleges and universities where members of a particular academic discipline perceive themselves as having higher status than others for one reason or another.

Inaccurate Perceptions. Inaccurate perceptions often result in developing stereotypes of the other group. While differences between the groups may certainly exist, each group exaggerates them when the actual differences may be small. Thus we hear that "all women executives are a certain way" or "all bank trust officers behave in a certain manner." Since the differences between the groups are emphasized the stereotypes are reinforced, relations deteriorate, and conflict develops.

The Increased Demand For Specialists

Early in management history conflicts were recorded between staff specialists and line generalists. Today line/staff differences is probably the most common type of intergroup conflict.[11] With the growing necessity for technical expertise in all areas in organizations the role of staff can be expected to expand and with it, line and staff conflict. As a result we are including the expected increase in the use of specialists as an additional source of intergroup conflict.

The major cause of line/staff conflict has been mentioned above. Line and staff persons simply view each other and their role in the organization from different perspectives.[12] They have all the problems we have discussed: different goals, time horizons, and status perceptions. Table 7–1 summarizes some additional causes of conflict between staff specialists and line

Table 7–1
Common Causes of Line/Staff Conflict

Perceived Diminishing of Line Authority. Line managers perceive that the specialist will encroach on their job thereby diminishing their authority and power. As a result, often-heard complaints by specialists are that line executives do not make proper use of staff specialists and do not give staff members sufficient authority. This complaint is voiced by staff specialists in consumer products firms, banks, hospitals, and government agencies.

Social and Physical Differences. Often major differences exist between line managers and staff specialists with respect to age, education, dress, and attitudes. In many cases staff specialists are younger, with higher educational levels or training in a specialized field.

Line Dependence on Staff Knowledge. Since line generalists often do not have the technical knowledge necessary to manage their departments, they realize they are dependent on the specialist. This gap between knowledge and authority may be even greater when the staff specialist is lower in the organizational hierarchy than the manager, which is often the case. As a result staff members often complain that line managers resist new ideas.

Different Loyalties. Often, divided loyalties exist between line managers and staff specialists. The staff specialist may be loyal to a discipline while the line manager is loyal to the organization. The member of the product development group may be a chemist first and a member of the organization second. The production manager's first loyalty, however, may be to the organization.

---

[11] For some recent research see J. A. Belasco and J. A. Alutto, "Line and Staff Conflicts: Some Empirical Insights," *Academy of Management Journal* (March 1969), pp. 469–77.

[12] For a classic discussion see L. A. Allen, "The Line-Staff Relationship," *Management Record* (September 1955), pp. 346–49.

generalists.[13] With the growth of sophistication, specialization, and complexity in most organizations, line/staff conflict will continue to be a major concern in the management of organizational behavior.

THE CONSEQUENCES OF DYSFUNCTIONAL INTERGROUP CONFLICT

Behavioral scientists have spent a great deal of effort analyzing how dysfunctional intergroup conflict affects groups experiencing it.[14] Over two decades of research on this topic enable us to state that groups that have been placed in a conflict situation will react in fairly predictable ways. We shall examine changes which occur within the groups and then changes which occur between the groups.

Changes within Groups

The following are changes which are likely to occur *within* the groups involved in intergroup conflict.

Increased Group Cohesiveness. Competition, conflict, or external threat usually result in group members putting aside individual differences and closing ranks. Members become more loyal to the group and group membership becomes more attractive.

Rise in Autocratic Leadership. In extreme conflict situations where threats are perceived, democratic methods of leadership are likely to become less popular. Members want strong leadership. Thus, the leadership is likely to become more autocratic.

Focus on Activity. The emphasis is on doing what the group does and doing it very well. Tolerance for members who "goof off" is low and

---

[13] See M. Dalton, "Conflicts between Staff and Line Managerial Officers," *American Sociological Review* (June 1950), pp. 342–51; A. W. Gouldner, "Cosmopolitans and Locals: Toward an Analysis of Latent Social Roles," *Administrative Science Quarterly* (December 1957), pp. 281–306; A. Etzioni, ed., *Complex Organizations,* (New York: Holt, Rinehart and Winston, 1961); A. Etzioni, *Modern Organization* (Englewood Cliffs, N.J.: Prentice-Hall, Inc., 1964); R. W. Scott, "Professionals in Bureaucracies: Areas of Conflict," in H. M. Vollmer and D. L. Mills, eds., *Professionals* (Englewood Cliffs, N.J.: Prentice-Hall, Inc., 1966); P. R. Lawrence and J. W. Lorsch, *Organization and Environment: Managing Differentiation and Integration* (Boston: Graduate School of Business Administration, Harvard University, 1967); E. Rhenman, *Conflict and Cooperation in Business* (New York: John Wiley & Sons, 1970); P. K. Berger and A. J. Grimes, "Cosmopolitan-Local: A Factor Analysis of the Construct," *Administrative Science Quarterly* (June 1973), pp. 223–35; and J. E. Sorensen and T. L. Sorensen, "The Conflict of Professionals in Bureaucratic Organizations," *Administrative Science Quarterly* (March 1974), pp. 98–106.

[14] The classic work is M. Sherif and C. Sherif, *Groups in Harmony and Tension* (New York: Harper and Brothers, 1953). Their study was conducted among groups in a boys' camp. They stimulated conflict between the groups and observed the changes which occurred in group behavior. Also see their "Experiments in Group Conflict," *Scientific American* (March 1956), pp. 54–58.

there is less concern for individual member satisfaction. The emphasis is on accomplishing the group's task and defeating the "enemy."

Emphasis on Loyalty. Conformity to group norms becomes even more important in conflict situations. Group goals take precedence over individual satisfaction as members are expected to demonstrate their loyalty. In extreme conflict situations, interaction with members of the "other group" may be outlawed.

Changes between Groups

In conflict situations certain changes are likely to occur *between* the groups involved.

Distorted Perceptions. The perceptions of the group by its members becomes distorted as well as their perceptions of the other group. Obviously, the members' perception of the importance of their group becomes distorted. They are superior in performance to the other and more important to the survival of the organization. The other group, of course, is not as important. For example, nurses might conclude that they are more important to a patient than physicians, while the physicians might consider themselves more important than the hospital administrators in a conflict situation. The marketing group in a business organization might think "without us selling the product there would be no money to pay anyone else's salary." The production group might say, "If we don't make the product, there is nothing to sell." The point, of course, is that no one group is more important but that conflict can cause these gross misperceptions of reality.

Negative Stereotyping. As the conflict increases and perceptions become more distorted, all the negative stereotypes previously developed are reinforced. A management representative may say, "I've always said these union guys are just plain greedy. Now they've proved it." The head of a local teacher's union might say, "Now we know that all politicians are interested in is getting reelected, certainly not the quality of secondary education." As a result of the conflict, the members of the group see less differences *within* their group than actually exist and greater differences *between* the groups than actually exist.

Decreased Communication. In conflict situations, communication between the groups involved usually breaks down. This can be extremely dysfunctional especially in situations where a sequential interdependence or reciprocal interdependence relationship exists between the groups. The decision-making process can be adversely affected, and the groups the organization serves can be hurt. Consider the possible consequences to patients if a conflict between hospital technicians and nurses reached the point where the quality of health care provided was negatively influenced. While this is an extreme situation the point should be clear.

While these are not only dysfunctional consequences of intergroup conflict, they are the most common and have been well documented in the research literature. Others such as violence and aggression are certainly possible and have occurred. The dysfunctional consequences of intergroup conflict discussed here are, however, the most typical which occur within and between groups in conflict.[15]

MANAGING INTERGROUP CONFLICT THROUGH RESOLUTION

Since managers of organizational behavior must live with intergroup conflict, they must confront the problem of managing it. In this section we shall examine techniques which have been used successfully in resolving intergroup conflict when it has reached a level that is dysfunctional to the organization.[16]

Problem Solving

Problem solving is also referred to as the confrontation method since it seeks to reduce the conflict through face-to-face meetings of the conflicting groups. The purpose of the meeting is to identify and solve the problem. The conflicting groups openly debate the issue bringing together all relevant information until a decision is reached. For conflicts resulting from misunderstandings or language barriers this method has been effective. For solving more complex problems (e.g., where the groups have different value systems) this method will usually not work.

Superordinate Goals

Superordinate goals involves developing a common set of goals and objectives. These goals and objectives cannot be attained without the cooperation of the groups involved. In fact, they are unattainable by one group singly and supersede all other goals of any of the groups involved in the conflict.[17] For example, several unions in the airline industry have, in recent years, agreed to no pay increases and in some cases to pay reductions because the survival of the airline was threatened. When the crises is over, demands for higher wages will undoubtedly return.

---

[15] For additional discussion see J. Litterer, "Conflict in Organization: A Re-Examination," *Academy of Management Journal* (September 1966), pp. 178–86; J. W. Lorsch and J. J. Morse, *Organizations and Their Members: A Contingency Approach* (New York: Harper and Row, 1974); and E. Schein, "Intergroup Problems in Organizations," in W. French, C. Bell, and R. Zawacki, eds., *Organization Development: Theory, Practice, and Research* (Dallas: Business Publications, Inc., 1978), pp. 80–84.

[16] Based on Robbins, *Managing Organizational Conflict*, pp. 67–77.

[17] See M. Sherif and C. Sherif, *Social Psychology* (New York: Harper and Row, 1969), pp. 228–62, for a detailed discussion of this method. Also see J. D. Hunger and L. W. Stern, "An Assessment of the Functionality of the Superordinate Goal in Reducing Conflict," *Academy of Management Journal* (December 1976), pp. 591–605.

Expansion of Resources

As we have noted earlier, a major cause of intergroup conflict is limited resources. Whatever one group succeeds in obtaining is at the expense of the other. The scarce resource may be a particular position (e.g., president of the firm), money, space, and so forth. For example, one major publishing firm decided to expand by establishing a subsidiary firm. Most observers believed the major reason was to become involved in other segments of the market. While this is partially correct, one real reason was to enable the firm to keep valued personnel who previously had left the firm. By establishing the subsidiary they practically doubled their executive positions since each had a president, various vice presidents, and other executives. Obviously, this technique is very successful in most cases since everyone is satisfied. In reality, however, resources do not usually exist in such amounts that they can be so easily expanded.

Avoidance

Like most other unpleasant realities, some way can usually be found to avoid conflict. While it may not bring any long-run benefits, it certainly works in the short run. As a result the conflict is not effectively resolved, nor is it eliminated. The limitations of avoiding conflict are obvious but it is an alternative and in some circumstances may be the best short-run alternative.

Smoothing

Here the emphasis is on the common interests of the conflicting groups and a deemphasis of their differences. The basic belief is that by stressing the shared viewpoints on certain issues, movement toward a common goal is facilitated. If the differences between the groups are serious, smoothing—like avoidance—is at best a temporary short-run solution.

Compromise

Compromise is a traditional method used to resolve conflicts. Hopefully, there is no distinct winner or loser because the decision reached is probably not ideal for either group. Compromise can be used very effectively when the sought after goal (e.g., money) can be divided. If this is not possible, one group gives up something of value for a concession. Compromise may involve third-party interventions as well as total-group or representative negotiating and voting.

Authoritative Command

As we noted at the opening of the chapter, the use of the formal authority hierarchy may be the oldest and most frequently used method for resolving intergroup conflict. Subordinates will usually abide by a superior's decision whether or not they agree. Thus, it usually works in the short run. As with the previous three methods, however, it does not focus on the cause of the conflict but rather on the results of it.

Altering the Human Variable

Altering the human variable involves changing the behavior of the members of the groups involved. While certainly difficult, this method does center on the cause of the conflict. Part Five of this book focuses specifically on this topic with two chapters concerned solely with changing organizational behavior. At that time we shall see that while the method is slower and often costly, the results can be significant in the long run.

Altering the Structural Variables

Altering the structural variables involves changing the formal structure of the organization. Structure refers to the fixed relationships among the jobs of the organization and includes the design of jobs and departments. How organizations are structured is the subject of the next section of the book. At this point let us say that altering the structure of the organization as a means of resolving intergroup conflict would involve such things as transferring, exchanging, or rotating members of the groups, or creating a position to serve as a coordinator or "go-between."

Identifying a Common Enemy

In some respects identifying a common enemy is the negative side of superordinate goals. Groups in conflict may temporarily resolve their differences to combat a common enemy. The common enemy may be a competitor who has just introduced a clearly superior product. Conflicting groups in a bank may work in close harmony when the government bank examiners make a visit. This phenomenon is very evident in domestic conflicts. Most police officers prefer not to become involved in heated domestic conflicts because, in far too many cases, the combatants "close ranks" and turn on the police officer.

We have provided brief discussions of some of the most commonly used methods for managing intergroup conflict. Note that each has strengths and weaknesses and is successful under different conditions and in different situations. At this point it would be useful to summarize what we have said thus far about intergroup conflict. This summary is presented as Figure 7–2. It indicates the relationship between causes and types of intergroup conflict, the consequences of intergroup conflict, and techniques for resolving it.

Figure 7–2
An Overview of Intergroup Conflict

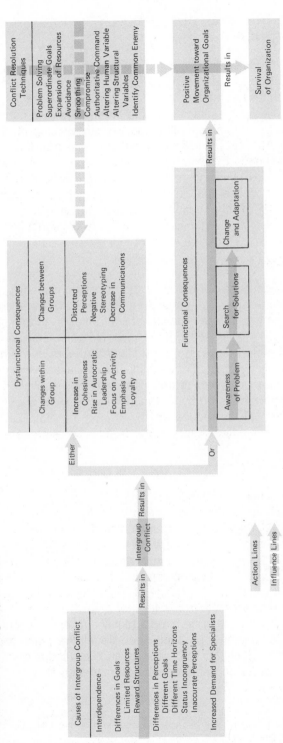

Causes of Intergroup Conflict

Interdependence

Differences in Goals
Limited Resources
Reward Structures

Differences in Perceptions
Different Goals
Different Time Horizons
Status Incongruency
Inaccurate Perceptions

Increased Demand for Specialists

Results in

Intergroup Conflict

Results in

Either

Or

Dysfunctional Consequences

Changes within Group

Increase in Cohesiveness
Rise in Autocratic Leadership
Focus on Activity
Emphasis on Loyalty

Changes between Groups

Distorted Perceptions
Negative Stereotyping
Decrease in Communications

Functional Consequences

Awareness of Problem

Search for Solutions

Change and Adaptation

Results in

Conflict Resolution Techniques

Problem Solving
Superordinate Goals
Expansion of Resources
Avoidance
Smoothing
Compromise
Authoritative Command
Altering Human Variable
Altering Structural Variables
Identify Common Enemy

Positive Movement toward Organizational Goals

Results in

Survival of Organization

Action Lines

Influence Lines

MANAGING INTERGROUP CONFLICT
THROUGH STIMULATION

The previous section centered entirely on conflict management techniques designed to *resolve* intergroup conflict. We have throughout the chapter, however, stressed the fact that some conflict is beneficial. This is even noted in Figure 7–2 which indicates some of the functional consequences of intergroup conflict. It indicates that change can develop out of conflict, from an awareness of problems, and from creative search for alternative solutions. We have already examined the situation where conflict is dysfunctional because it is too high and requires resolution. Following our logic, therefore, it is also possible that intergroup conflict may be too low and require stimulation.[18] In this section we shall examine techniques that have been used successfully to stimulate conflict to a functional level.[19]

Communication

By intelligent use of the organization's communication channels, a manager can stimulate conflict. Information can be carefully placed into formal channels to create ambiguity, reevaluation, or confrontation. Information which is threatening (e.g., a proposed budget cut) can stimulate functional conflict and improved performance. Carefully planted rumors in the grapevine can also serve a useful purpose. For example, a hospital administrator started a rumor concerning a proposed reorganization of the hospital. His purpose was to stimulate new ideas on how to more effectively carry out the mission of the hospital as well as reduce apathy among the staff. Later in the book we shall devote an entire chapter to the organizational process of communication.

Bringing Outside Individuals into the Group

A widely used technique to "bring back to life" a stagnant organization or subunit of an organization is to bring in (hire or transfer) individuals whose attitudes, values, and backgrounds differ from present members. Many college faculties consciously seek new members with different backgrounds and often discourage the hiring of graduates of their own programs. This is to insure a diversity of viewpoints on the faculty. This technique is also widely used in government and business. Recently a courageous bank president decided not to promote from within for a newly created position of Marketing Vice President. Instead he hired a highly successful executive from the very competitive consumer products field. He felt that while she knew little about marketing services, her approach to, and knowledge of, marketing was what the bank needed to become a strong marketer.

---

[18] This view is consistent with the *interactionist* view of conflict management.
[19] See Robbins, *Managing Organizational Conflict,* Chapter 9.

Altering the Organization Structure

In the last section we saw that changing the structure of the organization can be a useful technique for resolving intergroup conflict. It also is excellent for creating conflict. For example, a school of business has several departments. One department is entitled the Department of Business Administration and includes all the faculty which teach courses in management, marketing, finance, production management, and so forth. Accordingly, the department is rather large with 32 members under one department chair who reports to the Dean. When a new Dean was recently hired he was told of the great faculty apathy which seemed to be present in the department. Presently he is considering dividing the department into several separate departments (e.g., departments of marketing, finance, management), each with five or six members and a chairperson. The reasoning is that reorganizing in this manner will create competition among the groups for resources, students, faculty, and so forth, where none existed before because they were all in the same group. Whether this change will do away with faculty apathy as well as improve their performance remains to be seen.

Stimulating Competition

The use of various incentives such as awards and bonuses for outstanding performance is likely to stimulate competition. If property utilized such incentives may maintain a healthy atmosphere of competition which may result in a functional level of conflict. Incentives can be given for least defective parts, highest sales, best teacher, greatest number of new customers, or in any area where increased conflict will likely lead to more effective performance.

MAJOR ISSUES FOR THE MANAGER TO CONSIDER

A. Conflict between groups is inevitable in organizations. This conflict may be positive or negative depending upon its impact on the organization's goal achievement.

B. Functional conflict represents a confrontation between groups that enhances and benefits the organization's performance.

C. Dysfunctional conflict results from a confrontation or interaction between groups that hinders the achievement of organizational goals.

D. While most managers try to eliminate conflict, evidence exists which indicates that for most organizations an optimal level of conflict can positively influence organizational performance.

E. Intergroup conflict results from such factors as work interdependence, differences in goals, differences in perceptions, and the increasing demand for specialists.

F. Dysfunctional conflict results in changes taking place within and between the groups involved. Within the group there may be an increase in group cohesiveness, a rise in autocratic leadership, a focus on the task, and an emphasis on loyalty. Changes occurring between the groups include distorted perceptions, negative stereotyping, and a decrease in communication.

G. One of the difficult tasks a manager must confront is diagnosing and managing intergroup conflict. Some useful techniques for resolving intergroup conflict include problem solving, superordinate goals, expansion of resources, avoidance, smoothing, compromise, authority, and changing either the people or the organization's structure. Each is useful in specific situations and circumstances.

H. Conflict management techniques also exist for those situations where the manager diagnoses a level of conflict that is dysfunctional because it is too low. Conflict stimulation techniques include using the communication channels, hiring or transferring-in outside individuals, and changing the organization's structure. The important point is that effective conflict management involves both resolution and stimulation.

DISCUSSION AND REVIEW QUESTIONS

1. From your personal experiences, describe situations where conflict was functional and where it was dysfunctional.

2. Is the competition for grades among students functional or dysfunctional? Why?

3. Some individuals believe that conflict is necessary for change to take place. Comment.

4. Why is union-management conflict often so dysfunctional?

5. Identify an intergroup conflict situation at your school. Is it functional or dysfunctional? Why? If dysfunctional, what conflict management technique would you recommend to either resolve it or stimulate it?

6. Assume you were chosen by the president of your school to recommend strategies for eliminating student apathy. What would your recommendation be?

7. What is meant when it is said that a manager must be able to diagnose intergroup conflict situations? How can a manager obtain these diagnostic skills?

8. Discuss your personal view toward intergroup conflict in organizations.

ADDITIONAL REFERENCES

Aldrich, H. "Organizational Boundaries and Interorganizational Conflict." *Human Relations* (1971), pp. 279–93.

Campbell, D. R. "Stereotypes and the Perception of Group Differences." *American Psychologist* (1967), pp. 817–29.

Cherington, D. J. "Satisfaction in Competitive Behavior." *Organizational Behavior and Human Performance* (1973), pp. 47–71.

Coser, L. A. *The Functions of Social Conflict.* New York: The Free Press, 1956.

Doob, L. W., and Foltz, W. J. "The Belfast Workshop: An Application of Group Techniques to a Destructive Conflict." *Journal of Conflict Resolution* (1973), pp. 489–512.

Dutton, J. M., and Walton, R. E.   "Interdepartmental Conflict and Cooperation: Two Contrasting Studies." *Human Organization* (1966), pp. 207–20.

French, W. L.; Bell, C. H.; and Zawacki, R. A.   *Organization Development: Theory, Practice, Research.* Dallas: Business Publications, Inc., 1978.

Kelly, J.   "Make Conflict Work for You." *Harvard Business Review* (1970), pp. 103–13.

Kilmann, R. H., and Thomas, K.   "Four Perspectives on Conflict Management: An Attributional and Normative Theory." *Academy of Management Review* (1978), pp. 59–68.

Pondy, L.   "Organizational Conflict: Concepts and Models." *Administrative Science Quarterly* (1967), pp. 296–320.

Schmidt, S. M., and Kochan, T. A.   "Conflict: Toward Conceptual Understanding." *Administrative Science Quarterly* (1972), pp. 359–70.

Twomey, D. F.   "The Effects of Power Properties on Conflict Resolution." *Academy of Management Review* (1978), pp. 144–50.

Underwood, W. J., and Krafft, L. J.   "Interpersonal Compatibility and Managerial Work Effectiveness: A Test of the Fundamental Interpersonal Relations Orientation Theory." *Journal of Applied Psychology* (1973), pp. 89–94.

Zechmeister, K., and Druckman, D.   "Determinants of Resolving a Conflict of Interest." *Journal of Conflict Resolution* (1973), pp. 63–68.

CASE FOR ANALYSIS

WE'LL JUST LET THEM SHOW THEIR STUFF

Seven months ago Captain John Shea announced that he would retire as Police Chief of Bay Ridge in one year. This was to allow Mayor Foster Taff and the City Commissioners one year to initiate the search and selection process for his replacement. Captain Shea had come to Bay Ridge from a much larger city in Florida six years ago. He had served as assistant police chief in that city for five years.

During his term as Chief, Shea had initiated many changes in the Department. For the most part the changes had been accepted and nearly everyone agreed that Shea had done a fine job. The crime rate was presently below the national average, citizen/police relations appeared good and morale of the police officers also seemed very good. The Bay Ridge Police Association (BRPA), the organization which represented the police officers, occasionally had minor disagreements with the Chief and the city administration. However, these conflicts were small compared to the conflicts taking place in other cities. During the last five years, salaries for foot patrol officers had surpassed the national average for cities the size of Bay Ridge.

Many individuals were quite surprised at the relative success of Shea. He had been the "outside candidate" for the job and was selected over two veteran members of the force. The two inside candidates had engaged in a bitter in-fight which had divided the department at that time. One of the men has subsequently taken a chief's position elsewhere. One city commissioner had recently stated off the record, "I don't know how Shea did it. I didn't give him a snowball's chance six years ago. I thought he was crazy for taking the job and jumping in that hornet's nest. I guess being 1,000 miles away he may not have known what he was getting into. But he sure has done one helluva job."

During the last seven months an intensive search had been conducted. Applications had been received from all over the country. In addition to the search committee made up of city officials, three professors from the management department of a local university were hired as consultants to serve as an advisory committee to the search committee.

A total of twelve candidates were invited to personally interview for the job. Each candidate was interviewed intensively by both committees. Surprisingly, both committees agreed on the top three choices although not in the same order. They were:

Phillip Kinney—23 years on the Bay Ridge Police Force. Holds the rank of Captain and has been the head of the Robbery Division for 3 years. Excellent record in the Robbery Division. Holds every departmental commendation. He is 51 years old, married with 3 grown children. He is a graduate of Bay Ridge High School and was one of the final two inside candidates in the search seven years ago. According to inside sources he barely missed getting appointed.

Anthony Jackson—presently holds the rank of Lieutenant in the Narcotics Division. He has an outstanding record of accomplishment since becoming the first black person on the police force 15 years ago. He is extremely popular in the black community and has been credited by the press with being instrumental in improving relations between the department and the black community. In fact, many black civic leaders have encouraged him to take a leave of absence to run for political office. He is 39 years old, married with two young children, and holds a B.S. degree in law enforcement. He ran unsuccessfully for President of the BRPA in the last election.

Paul Stephens—20 years in the department. Presently holds the rank of Captain in the Homicide Division. He is considered to be one of the top homicide detectives in this region of the country, often serving as a consultant to police departments in other cities on difficult cases. Holds every department commendation. He is presently single and has one child by an earlier marriage. He holds a B.S. degree in law enforcement and is President of the BRPA.

The recommendations were presented to Mayor Taff by City Manager Bill Joslin with the recommendation that he select one of the three to replace Shea. His first comment to Taff was "Shea must have also developed some good people while he was here. None of the outside candidates made the cut."

"Who does Shea like?" the Mayor asked. "He's not saying," Joslin replied. He said since he won't have to work for the guy, he shouldn't influence the selection. That's also why he declined to serve on the search committee. He has also told that to the press this morning. Apparently, someone leaked the names of the three finalists to a TV station and they cornered Shea on the way out of his house this morning.

"Which one do you like?" asked Joslin adding "I think you should announce your choice as soon as you've made it."

"No" said the Mayor. "I think I'll wait. We've got about five months." "Why wait?" asked Joslin. There was a short silence and the Mayor replied, "We'll just let them show their stuff."

Questions for Discussion

1. What do you think of the Mayor's decision to wait? Why?
2. What are the advantages of waiting? The disadvantages?
3. Could the Mayor's decision have any positive or negative impact outside the Department? Discuss.

EXPERIENTIAL EXERCISE

LOST ON THE MOON: A GROUP DECISION EXERCISE*

Objective

After reading the "Situation" below, you will first individually, and then as a member of a team, rank in importance a number of items available for carrying out your mission. Your objective is to come as close as possible to the "best solution" as determined by experts of the National Aeronautics and Space Administration.

Instructions

PHASE I: Read the "Situation" below and the directions which follow it. Then, in Column 2 ("Your Ranks") of the worksheet, assign priorities to the fifteen items listed. Use a pencil since you may wish to change your rankings. Somewhere on the sheet it may be useful to note your logic for each ranking.
TIME: 15 minutes

PHASE II: Your instructor will assign you to a team. Your task is to arrive at a consensus on your rankings. Share your individual solutions and reach a consensus—one ranking for each of the fifteen items that best satisfies all the team members. Thus, by the end of Phase II, all members of the team should have the same set of rankings in Column 4 ("Group Rankings"). Do *not* change your individual rankings in Column 2.
TIME: 25 minutes

PHASE III: Your instructor will provide you with the "best solution" to the problem, i.e., the set of rankings determined by the NASA experts, along with their reasoning. Each person should note this set of rankings in Column 1 ("NASA's Ranks"). (Note: While it is fun to debate the experts' rankings and their reasoning, don't forget that the objective of the game is to learn more about decision making, not how to survive on the moon!)

Evaluation

It is time now to see how well you did, individually and as a team. First, find your individual score by taking the absolute difference between Your Rank (Column 2) and NASA's Rank (Column 1), and writing it in the first Error Points column (Column 3). (Thus, for "Box of Matches," if you ranked it 3 and NASA's rank were 8, you would put a 5 in Column 3 next to "Box of Matches." Then total the error points in Column 3, and write the total in the space at the bottom of the column.

Next score your group performance in the same way, this time taking the absolute differences between Group Ranks (Column 4) and NASA's ranks (Column 1), and writing them in the second Error Points column (Column 5). Total the group error points. (Note that all members of the team will have the same Group Error Points.)

Finally, prepare three pieces of information to be submitted to your instructor when he calls on your team:

1. Average Individual Error Points (the average of the points in the last space in Column 3. One team member should add these figures and divide by the number of team members to get the average).
2. Group Error Points (the figure at the bottom of Column 5).
3. Number of team members who had fewer Individual Error Points than the Group Error Points.

Using this information, your instructor will evaluate the results of the exercise and discuss your performance with you. Together, you will then explore the implications of this exercise for the group decision-making process.

"LOST ON THE MOON"
The Situation

Your spaceship has just crash-landed on the moon. You were scheduled to rendezvous with a mother ship 200 miles away on the lighted surface of the moon, but the rough landing has ruined your ship and destroyed all the equipment aboard, except for 15 items listed below.

Your crew's survival depends on reaching the mother ship, so you must choose the most critical items available for the 200-mile trip. Your task is to rank the 15 items in terms of their importance for survival. Place number one by the most important item, number two by the second most important, and so on through number 15, the least important.

WORKSHEET Items	1 NASA'S Ranks	2 Your Ranks	3 Error Points	4 Group Ranks	5 Error Points
Box of Matches					
Food Concentrate					
50 ft. of Nylon Rope					
Parachute Silk					
Solar-Powered Portable Heating Unit					
Two .45 Caliber Pistols					
One Case of Dehydrated Pet Milk					
Two 100-Pound Tanks of Oxygen					
Stellar Map (of the Moon's Constellation)					
Self-Inflating Life Raft					
Magnetic Compass					
Five Gallons of Water					
Signal Flares					
First-Aid Kit Containing Injection Needles					
Solar-Powered FM Receiver-Transmitter					

Total Error Points: Individual _____   Group _____

Chapter 8

Leadership: Trait and Personal-Behavioral Approaches

AN ORGANIZATIONAL ISSUE FOR DEBATE

A General Description of Leadership *

ARGUMENT FOR

There are writers who believe that a new type of person is taking over leadership of the most technically advanced companies in the United States. In contrast to the "jungle fighter" industrialists of the past, the new leader is driven not to build or to preside over a large empire, but to plan, organize, and control winning teams. Unlike the security-seeking organization man of William F. Whyte, the new kind of leader is excited by the chance to cut deals and to gamble. The new leader is called a *gamesman.*

The most dynamic companies with these innovative leaders are able to create their own markets. Companies like IBM, Xerox, Dow Chemical, and TRW Systems have many of these gamesmen types. These companies are able to face tough competition and develop new products and technology.

Some of the different types of leaders who manage in organizations are described using some catchy terminology.

1. *The Craftsman*—This is the type of individual

ARGUMENT AGAINST

Although books like *The Gamesman* become best-sellers, they really do not improve our understanding of what is effective leadership in organizations around the world. They are imaginative, but not very explanatory, scientifically based, or accurate. In fact, it is even dangerous to reach any conclusions on the basis of interviews conducted with only 250 managers. This is what the author of *The Gamesman,* Michael Maccoby did to develop his conclusions about the *Craftsman,* the *Jungle Fighter,* the *Company Man,* and the *Gamesman.*

It may be true that some effective executives in organizations are *gamesmen,* but to suggest that this or any similarly developed framework adds to our knowledge is disappointing because the study of organizational leadership has advanced past the practice of listing descriptions of types of individuals. It has become rather clear that effective leadership is contingent upon having the right person for the situation at hand and a particular group of subordinates. Leader behavior character-

ARGUMENT FOR (*continued*)

who is production oriented, concerned with quality, and interested in building a sound record.

2. *The Jungle Fighter*—This type individual is interested in gaining power. Life and work are viewed as a jungle. Peers are viewed as accomplices or enemies. Two types of jungle fighters are the *lions,* who conquer and build, and *foxes,* who move ahead by politicking.

3. *The Company Man*—This individual is interested in cooperation, commitment, and security.

4. *Gamesman*—This is the new type of leader. This person thrives on challenge, competitive activity, and new and fresh approaches. The main goal of this type of person is to be a winner. This person is interested in developing the tactics and strategies needed to be a winner.

ARGUMENT AGAINST (*continued*)

istics, subordinate characteristics, organizational climate, and goals must be considered. These situational variables are not investigated scientifically by Maccoby.

The failure to scientifically study situational variables results in just another list of descriptions of types of leaders. What is needed and is more appropriate is a careful analysis of what leaders do and what the results of this behavior is in terms of performance.

---

* Based on Michael Maccoby, *The Gamesman* (New York: Simon and Schuster, 1976).

INTRODUCTION

Leadership has long been a focus of theorists, researchers, and practitioners. Nevertheless, it appears that despite numerous theories and research studies of leadership, there is no universally accepted approach. Some of the highlights of leadership research will be covered in this and the next chapter.[1] The reader is asked to give special attention to the common themes which pervade the work of different theorists and practitioners. It will also become apparent that effective leadership is necessary for organizational effectiveness and that the performance of employees is typically poorer when it is absent.

LEADERSHIP IN THE ORGANIZATION

The idea that leadership is a synonym for management is not completely valid. A manager in a formal organization is responsible and entrusted to perform such functions as planning, organizing, and controlling. However, leaders also exist in informal groups. Informal leaders are not always formal managers performing managerial functions which are required by the organization. Consequently, leaders are only in some instances actually managers.

The concept of role was clarified in the chapter dealing with group behavior. In the formal organization, roles often have specific responsibilities associated with them. For example, the first-line supervisory role may be one in which the role occupant is responsible for the level and quality of production generated by a particular group of employees. Exactly how the supervisor fulfills the responsibility involves the occupant's style. Some first-line supervisors rely on the *authority* of the position to secure compliance with performance standards, while others use a more *participative* approach which involves joint decision making on the part of the leader (manager) and followers (subordinates).

A hierarchy of roles also exists in informal groups. The informal leader is accepted as the person to carry out the duties of the position. Once again, how the leader brings about compliance from followers will largely depend on the leadership style used. What is effective for one leader may not be for another. This, in essence, is the crux of the leadership issue: what makes for effective leadership? As indicated earlier, there is no simple or single answer to this important question. Two important considerations involve power and acceptance by followers.

THE BASES OF POWER

Generally, power includes the personal and positional attributes that are the basis for a leader's ability to influence others. Note that power includes personal and positional attributes, while the concept of *authority* involves

---

[1] For a thorough compilation of leadership theory and research see Ralph M. Stogdill, *Handbook of Leadership* (New York: The Free Press, 1974).

the use primarily of position-related power. For example, a first-line supervisory position has authority because of hierarchy rank—not because of personal characteristics, such as the charisma of the supervisor.

The ability to influence, persuade, and motivate followers is based largely upon the perceived power of the leader. French and Raven identify forms of power a leader may possess as follows:

Coercive—power based upon fear. A follower perceives that failing to comply with the request initiated by a leader could result in some form of punishment: a reprimand or social ostracism from a group.

Reward—power based upon the expectation of receiving praise, recognition, or income for compliance with a leader's request.

Legitimate—power derived from an individual's position in the group or organizational hierarchy. In a formal organization, the first-line supervisor is perceived to have more power than operating employees. In the informal group, the leader is recognized by the members as having legitimate power.

Expert—power based upon a special skill, expertise, or knowledge. The followers perceive the person as having relevant expertise and believe that it exceeds their own.

Referent—power based on attractiveness and appeal. A leader who is admired because of certain traits possesses referent power. This form of power is popularly referred to as charisma. The person is said to have charisma to inspire and attract followers.[2]

The Two-Way Power Flow

Power in organizations is a two-way phenomenon, flowing from one individual (leader) to other people (subordinates) and back. A supervisor may control the amount of salary increment a subordinate receives, but subordinates have some say in what the supervisor will receive as a raise. If subordinates perform well, the evaluation of their outputs and effort can help the supervisor receive a high rating. However, if subordinates create production problems, restrict and disrupt output, and are generally not cooperative, they can negatively influence the performance evaluation of the supervisor. In fact, it is very likely the negative subordinate behavior will be the main contributor to a poor performance rating for the supervisor. Therefore, it is best to consider power as a two-way flow between the leader and subordinates.

Power and Politics

Political maneuvering involves acquiring power within the organization. People try to achieve goals that are important to them. One means of achieving

---

[2] This typology was developed by John R. P. French and Bertram Raven, "The Bases of Social Power," in Darwin Cartwright and A. F. Zander, eds., *Group Dynamics,* 2d ed. (Evanston, Ill.: Row, Peterson, and Co., 1960), pp. 607–23.

these goals is to gain as much power as possible. Only so much position power is available within any organization. As we move down the management hierarchy, each successive level of people has less position power than the one above.[3] The nonskilled machinist compared to the plant manager has very little power. A salesperson would have less position power than a district sales manager.

Zaleznik, a consultant and organizational researcher, assumes that power is inevitable in organizations. He states:

> Whatever else organizations may be . . . they are political structures. This means that organizations operate by distributing authority and setting a stage for the exercise of power. It is no wonder, therefore, that individuals who are highly motivated to secure and use power find a familiar and hospitable environment in business.[4]

Since power and politics are used in organizations, it is important for managers to understand the manner in which both are applied. Individuals do not like to have power used on them. The French and Raven model does not address the issue of potential behavioral reactions to the application of power. The use of expert and referent power is not usually resisted by subordinates or followers. However, when coercive power is used, there tends to be some resistance. Furthermore, it is important to understand that people seek power through such political maneuverings as joining ranks with individuals with power, developing expertise in an important field or area, controlling crucial information, displaying loyalty and commitment, and making the immediate superior look good. These political actions are not being recommended, but they are identified here as methods that are used to acquire power.

LEADERSHIP DEFINED

The five bases of power suggest that power can be defined as the ability to influence another person's behavior. Where one individual attempts to affect the behavior of a group, we describe the effort as leadership. More specifically:

> Leadership is an attempt at interpersonal influence, directed through the communication process, toward the attainment of some goal or goals.[5]

This definition implies that leadership involves the use of influence and that all interpersonal relationships can involve leadership. Relationships in committees, between line and staff personnel, supervisors and subordinates, patients

---

[3] Andrew J. DuBrin, *Human Relations: A Job Oriented Approach* (Reston, Va.: Reston Publishing Co., 1978), p. 110.

[4] Abraham Zaleznik, "Power and Politics in Organizational Life," *Harvard Business Review* (May–June 1970), p. 47.

[5] Edwin A. Fleishman, "Twenty Years of Consideration and Structure," in Edwin A. Fleishman and James G. Hunt, eds., *Current Developments in the Study of Leadership* (Carbondale: Southern Illinois University, 1973), p. 3.

and doctors, and friends on a bowling team can include leadership and followership.

A second element in the definition involves the importance of communication. The clarity and accuracy of communication affect the behavior and performance of followers. The inability to communicate is a serious deficiency when improvement in effectiveness is being sought.

Another element of the definition focuses on the accomplishment of goals. The effective leader may have to deal with individual, group, and organizational goals. Leader effectiveness is typically considered in terms of the degree of accomplishment of one or a combination of these goals. Individuals may view the leader as effective or ineffective in terms of their satisfactions derived from the total work experience. In fact, acceptance of a leader's directives or requests rests largely on the followers' expectations that a favorable response will lead to an attractive outcome.

Coercive, reward, and legitimate power are primarily specified by an individual's role in a hierarchy. This role can, of course, be in a formal or an informal group. The degree and scope of a leader's expert and referent power are dictated primarily by personal attributes. Some leaders, because of personality or communication difficulties, cannot influence others through expert or referent power. Figure 8–1 summarizes the key power and leadership factors.

Figure 8–1
Power Bases: Organizational and Individual

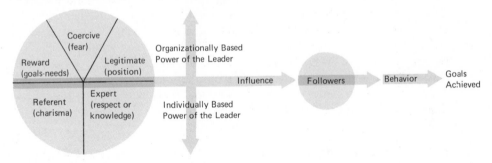

TRAIT THEORIES

Much of the early work on leadership focused on identifying the traits of effective leaders. This approach was based on the assumption that a finite number of individual traits of effective leaders could be found. Thus, most research was designed to identify intellectual, emotional, physical, and other personal characteristics of successful leaders. The personnel testing component of scientific management supported to a significant extent the trait theory of leadership.[6] Besides personnel testing, the traits of leaders have been

───────────
[6] Ralph M. Stogdill, "Historical Trends in Leadership Theory and Research," *Journal of Contemporary Business* (Autumn 1974), p. 4.

studied by observing behavior in group situations, choice of associates (voting), by nomination or rating by observers, and by analysis of biographical data.

Intelligence

In a review of 33 studies, Stogdill found that there is a general trend which indicates that leaders are more intelligent than followers.[7] One of the most significant findings is that extreme intelligence differences between leaders and followers may be dysfunctional. For example, a leader with a relatively high IQ who is attempting to influence a group with members with average IQ's may be unable to understand why the members do not comprehend the problem. In addition such a leader may have difficulty communicating ideas and policies. Being too intelligent would be a problem in some situations.

Personality

Some research results suggest that such personality traits as alertness, originality, personal integrity, and self-confidence are associated with effective leadership.[8] Ghiselli reported several personality traits which tend to be associated with leader effectiveness.[9] For example, he found that initiative, and the ability to act and initiate action independently, were related to the level in the organization of the respondent. The higher the person went in the organization the more important this trait became. He also found that self-assurance was related to hierarchical position in the organization. Finally, he found that individuals who exhibited individuality were the most effective leaders. Some writers argue that personality is unrelated to leadership. This view is too harsh if we consider how personality has been found to be related to perception, attitudes, learning, and motivation. The problem is finding valid ways to measure personality traits. This goal has been difficult to achieve, but some progress, although slow, is being made.[10]

Physical Characteristics

Studies of the relationship between effective leadership and physical characteristics such as age, height, weight, and appearance provide contradictory results. Being taller and heavier than the average of a group is certainly

---

[7] Stogdill, *Handbook of Leadership,* pp. 43–44.

[8] For example, see Chris Argyris, "Some Characteristics of Successful Executives," *Personnel Journal* (June 1955), pp. 50–63; and J. A. Hornaday and C. J. Bunker, "The Nature of the Entrepreneur," *Personnel Psychology* (Spring 1970), pp. 47–54.

[9] Edwin E. Ghiselli, "The Validity of Management Traits in Relation to Occupational Level," *Personnel Psychology* (Summer 1963), pp. 109–13.

[10] For example, see Robert W. Lundin, *Personality* (New York: Macmillan Publishing Co., 1974); and Leonard Krasner and Leonard P. Ullman, *Behavior Influence and Personality* (New York: Holt, Rinehart and Winston, 1973).

not advantageous for achieving a leader position.[11] However, many organizations believe that it requires a physically large person to secure compliance from followers. This notion relies heavily on the coercive or fear basis of power. On the other hand, Truman, Gandhi, Napoleon, and Stalin are examples of individuals of small stature who rose to positions of leadership.

Supervisory Ability

Using the leaders' performance ratings, Ghiselli found a positive relationship between a person's supervisory ability and level in the organizational hierarchy. The supervisor's ability is defined as the "effective utilization of whatever supervisory practices are indicated by the particular requirements of the situation."[12] Once again, a measurement of the concept is needed and this is a difficult problem to resolve.

Although some traits appear to differentiate effective and ineffective leaders, there still exist many contradictory research findings. There are a number of possible reasons for the disappointing results. First, the list of potentially important traits is endless. Every year new traits, such as the sign under which a person is born, handwriting style, and order of birth are added to personality, physical characteristics, and intelligence. This continual "adding on" results in more confusion among those interested in identifying leadership traits. Second, trait test scores are not consistently predictive of leader effectiveness. Traits do not operate singly, but in combination, to influence followers. This interaction influences the leader-follower relationship. Third, the patterns of effective behavior depend largely on the situation. Third, the patterns of effective behavior depend largely on the situation. The leadership behavior which is effective in a bank may be ineffective in a laboratory. Finally, the trait approach does not provide insight into what the effective leader does on the job. Observations are needed that describe the behavior of effective and ineffective leaders.

PERSONAL-BEHAVIORAL THEORIES

A number of theorists argue for the use of a particular style to bring about high performance levels in areas such as production and satisfaction. The style, or personal-behavioral leadership approaches that have been the most widely used in practice appear to be the University of Michigan work, the Ohio State work, the Blake and Mouton managerial grid, and the four-factor approach of Bowers and Seashore. These approaches have been widely publicized, researched, and applied in organizational settings. Each of the approaches attempt to identify what leaders do when leading.[13]

---

[11] Ralph M. Stogdill, "Personal Factors Associated with Leadership," *Journal of Applied Psychology* (January 1948), pp. 35–71.

[12] Edwin E. Ghiselli, *Exploration in Managerial Talent* (Pacific Palisades: Goodyear Publishing Co., 1971).

[13] Jeffrey C. Barrow, "The Variables of Leadership: A Review and Conceptual Framework," *Academy of Management Review* (April 1977), pp. 231–51.

The University of Michigan Studies: Job-Centered and Employee-Centered

Since 1947, Likert has been studying how best to manage the efforts of individuals to achieve desired performance and satisfaction objectives.[14] The purpose of most of the leadership research from the University of Michigan Institute for Social Research has been to discover the principles and methods of effective leadership. The effectiveness criteria used in many of the studies include:

Productivity per man-hour or other similar measures of the organization's success in achieving its production goals.

Job satisfaction of members of the organization.

Turnover, absenteeism, and grievance rates.

Costs.

Scrap loss.

Employee and managerial motivation.

Studies have been conducted in a wide variety of industries: chemical, electronics, food, heavy machinery, insurance, petroleum, public utilities, hospitals, banks, and government agencies. Data have been obtained from thousands of employees doing different job tasks, ranging from unskilled work to highly skilled research and development work.

Through interviewing leaders and followers, the researchers identified two distinct styles of leadership which are referred to as *job-centered* and *employee-centered*. The job-centered leader practices close supervision so that subordinates perform their tasks using specified procedures. This type of leader relies on coercion, reward, and legitimate power to influence the behavior and performance of followers. The concern for people is viewed as important, but is a luxury that cannot always be practiced by a leader.

The *employee-centered* leader believes in delegating decision making and aiding followers in satisfying their needs by creating a supportive work environment. The employee-centered leader is concerned with followers' personal advancement, growth, and achievement. These actions are assumed to be conducive for the support of group formation and development.

The potential effect of these two personal-behavioral styles was tested in an experimental study conducted by the Institute for Social Research.[15] This study included 500 clerical employees in four divisions which were organized in the same way, used the same technology, did the same kind of work, and employed individuals of comparable aptitudes.

The work load of the divisions varied and peaked from time to time. At any one time a given amount of work had to be processed. The volume

---

[14] For a review of this work see Rensis Likert, *New Patterns of Management* (New York: McGraw-Hill, 1961); and Rensis Likert, *The Human Organization* (New York: McGraw-Hill, 1967).

[15] Nancy C. Morse and E. Reimer, "The Experimental Change of a Major Organizational Variable," *Journal of Abnormal and Social Psychology* (January 1956), pp. 120–29.

was impossible to change and the only way to increase production was to increase the size of the group.

The experiment with these four divisions lasted for one year. There was a training period for supervisory and managerial staffs lasting approximately six months. Production was measured continuously and computed weekly. Employee and supervisory attitudes, perceptions, motivations, and related variables were measured just before and just after the experimental year.

In two of the four divisions, an attempt was made to make the decision-making process more participative. More general supervision was introduced. In addition, the formal leaders were given training in participative leadership. In the other two divisions which were called the "hierarchically controlled divisions," there was an effort to increase the closeness of supervision and to centralize decision making. The formal leaders in these divisions were trained for the same length of time as their counterparts in the participative divisions, but the training focused on company policies, rules, and procedures.

Production increased under both systems, with the increase being 25 percent in the hierarchically controlled and 20 percent in the participative. These increases were achieved by different procedures in the two systems. In the hierarchically controlled divisions, direct pressure and the job-centered behavior of the leaders were assumed to be the reasons for the increase. However, in the participative divisions the clerks themselves reduced the size of the work force and developed a number of procedural changes. It was also believed that production in the participative divisions increased because of the more cohesive effort of the groups and less absenteeism. The indicators of employee satisfaction included absenteeism, turnover, and attitudes. The findings revealed that these indicators improved in the participative divisions and deteriorated in the hierarchically controlled divisions.

The researchers believe that these results suggest that similar organizations typically focus on short-run effectiveness measures. The reward and promotion systems are integrated with production results. In addition, managers are transferred often and are forced to generate short-run results. Thus, if we only look at production the hierarchically controlled divisions are more effective. However, if the satisfaction indicators are considered, the acceptance of the superiority of the job-centered style becomes tenuous and questionable. Likert believes that the short-run increases are gained at a cost of negative attitudes and increased absenteeism and turnover. The conclusions reached by Likert and other supporters of this leadership approach suggest that employee-centered leadership behaviors are more effective.

The Ohio State Studies: Initiating Structure and Consideration

Among the several large research programs on leadership that developed after World War II, one of the most significant was Ohio State's, which resulted in a two-factor theory of leadership.[16] These studies isolated two independent leadership factors referred to as *initiating structure* and *consideration.* The definitions of these factors are as follows: *Initiating structure* involves behavior in which the leader organizes and defines the relationships in the group, tends to establish well-defined patterns and channels of communication, and spells out ways of getting the job done. *Consideration* involves behavior indicating friendship, mutual trust, respect, warmth, and rapport between the leader and followers.

These dimensions are measured by two separate questionnaires. The Leadership Opinion Questionnaire (LOQ) attempts to assess how leaders think they behave in leadership roles. The Leader Behavior Description Questionnaire (LBDQ) measures the perceptions of subordinates, peers, or superiors.

The initiating structure and consideration scores derived from the responses to the questionnaires provide a way to measure leadership style. Figure 8–2 provides a hypothetical view of the behaviors of five different leaders. These hypothetical points indicate that leaders have scores on both of these dimensions. Individual 1 is high on both initiating structure and considerations; individual 4 is low on both dimensions.

Figure 8–2
The Scores of Five Leaders: Initiating Structure and Consideration

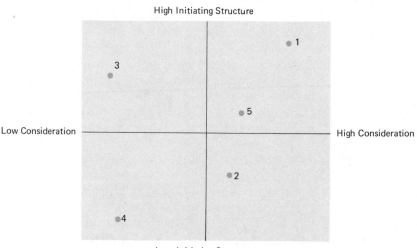

High Initiating Structure

Low Consideration

High Consideration

Low Initiating Structure

[16] For a review of the studies see Stogdill, *Handbook of Leadership,* chapter 11. Also see Edwin A. Fleishman, "The Measurement of Leadership Attitudes in Industry," *Journal of Applied Psychology* (June 1953), pp. 153–58; C. L. Shartle, *Executive Performance and Leadership* (Englewood Cliffs, N.J.: Prentice-Hall, 1956); Edwin A. Fleishman, E. F. Harris, and H. E. Burtt, *Leadership and Supervision in Industry* (Columbus: Ohio State University, Bureau of Educational Research, 1955); and Edwin A. Fleishman, "Twenty Years of Consideration and Structure," in *Current Developments in the Study of Leadership,* Edwin A. Fleishman and James G. Hunt, eds. pp. 1–37.

Since the original research undertaken to develop the questionnaire, there have been numerous studies of the relationship of these two leadership dimensions and various effectiveness criteria. Many of the early results stimulated the generalization that leaders above average in both consideration and initiating structure were more effective. In a study at International Harvester, however, the researchers began to find some more complicated interpretations of the two dimensions. In a study of supervisors, it was found that those scoring higher on structure had higher proficiency ratings (ratings received from superiors), but also had more employee grievances. The higher consideration score was related to lower proficiency ratings and lower absences.[17]

A study of research and development departments introduced the issue of organizational climate to the leadership-effectiveness question.[18] The focus of this study was research, development, and engineering personnel in three large organizations: a petroleum refinery, a business machine manufacturer, and an air frame manufacturer. The results indicated that leadership behavior had differential effects on employee satisfaction depending upon different organizational climates. For example, the climate of the air frame company was rigidly structured and formalized. In this type of climate, the opportunity for a leader to be instrumental in aiding the followers in satisfying pay, security, social, and advancement needs may be limited. Thus, organizational climate appears to affect the relationship between the leader's consideration behavior and the follower's satisfaction.

This study also found positive relationships between initiating structure and satisfaction. These relationships were weakest in the highly structured air frame company. Perhaps these results are explained by the fact that the air frame company is already highly structured and the leader initiating more structure is engaging in an effort which is not required.

The Ohio State personal-behavioral theory has been criticized because of simplicity, lack of generalizability, and reliance on questionnaire responses to predict leadership effectiveness. The critique of Korman is perhaps the most publicized.[19] He has criticized the Ohio State research on leadership in the following manner:

1. The researchers have made little attempt to conceptualize situational variables and their influence on leadership behavior.
2. Most of the research studies yield generally insignificant correlations between leader behavior measures and effectiveness criteria.
3. The theory has not provided any answer to the question of causality.

---

[17] Fleishman, Harris, and Burtt, *Leadership and Supervision.*

[18] Robert J. House, Alan C. Filley, and Steven Kerr, "Relation of Leader Consideration and Initiating Structure to R and D Subordinates' Satisfaction," *Administrative Science Quarterly* (March 1971), pp. 19–30.

[19] Abraham K. Korman, "Consideration, Initiating Structure, and Organizational Criteria—A Review," *Personnel Psychology* (Winter 1966), pp. 349–61.

Some of the problems have been partially corrected.[20] For example, it has been pointed out in more recent research that many variables affect the relationship between leadership behavior and organizational effectiveness. Some of these include employee experience, competence, job knowledge, expectations for leader behavior, the upward influence of leaders, the degree of autonomy, role clarity, and urgency of time.[21]

Managerial Grid®: Concern for People and Concern for Production

The conceptual framework for the managerial grid assumes that there is an unnecessary dichotomy in the minds of most leaders about the concern for people and concern for production. It is Blake and Mouton's assumption that people and production concerns are complementary, rather than mutually exclusive.[22] They further believe that leaders must integrate these concerns to achieve effective performance results.

The thoughts of Blake and Mouton resulted in development of the grid chart. An example of the managerial grid is provided in Figure 8–3. Theoretically, there are 81 possible positions on the grid, representing as many leadership styles, but the focus usually centers around five styles: 1, 1; 1, 9; 9, 1; 5, 5; and 9, 9.

The 9, 1 leader is primarily concerned with production task accomplishment and has little, if any, concern for people. This person wants to meet schedules and get the job done at all costs. The 1, 9 style reflects a minimal concern for production coupled with a maximal concern for people; the 1, 1 style reflects minimal concern for both people and production; and the 5, 5 style reflects a moderate concern for both. The 9, 9 style is viewed as the ideal approach for integrating a maximum concern for production with a maximum concern for people. This leader regards the managerial job as that of coach, advisor, and consultant.

According to Blake and Mouton, the grid enables leaders to identify their own leadership styles. Furthermore, it serves as a framework for leaders to use in assessing their styles before undertaking a training program that is designed to move them to the 9, 9 style.

Although the managerial grid has not been thoroughly supported by research, it is still a popular theory of leadership among managers. The available

---

[20] Steven Kerr and Chester Schrieshem, "Consideration, Initiating Structure, and Organizational Criteria—An Update of Korman's 1966 Review," *Personnel Psychology* (Winter 1974), pp. 555–68.

[21] R. C. Cummins, "Leader-Member Relations as a Moderator of the Effects of Leader Behavior and Attitude," *Personnel Psychology* (Winter 1972), pp. 655–60 and James G. Hunt and V. K. C. Liebscher, "Leadership Preference, Leadership Behavior, and Employee Satisfaction," *Organizational Behavior and Human Performance* (February 1973), pp. 59–77.

[22] Robert R. Blake and Jane S. Mouton, *The Managerial Grid* (Houston, Tex.: Gulf Publishing Co., 1964); and Robert R. Blake and Jane S. Mouton, "Managerial Facades," *Advanced Management Journal* (July 1966), pp. 29–36.

Figure 8–3
Managerial Grid®

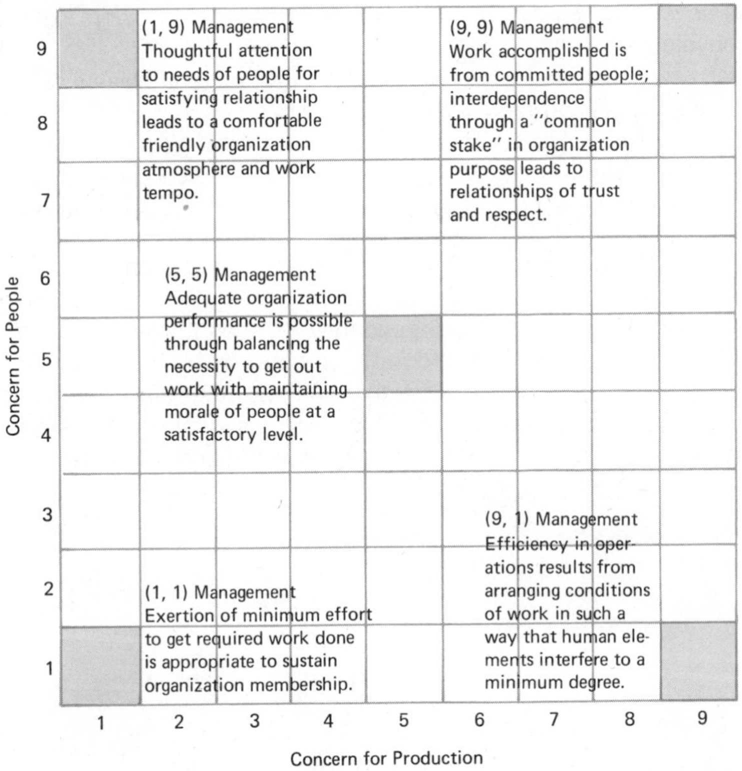

9	(1, 9) Management Thoughtful attention to needs of people for			(9, 9) Management Work accomplished is from committed people;			
8	satisfying relationship leads to a comfortable friendly organization			interdependence through a "common stake" in organization			
7	atmosphere and work tempo.			purpose leads to relationships of trust and respect.			
6	(5, 5) Management Adequate organization						
5	performance is possible through balancing the necessity to get out						
4	work with maintaining morale of people at a satisfactory level.						
3					(9, 1) Management Efficiency in oper-		
2	(1, 1) Management Exertion of minimum effort			ations results from arranging conditions of work in such a			
1	to get required work done is appropriate to sustain organization membership.			way that human ele- ments interfere to a minimum degree.			

Concern for People (vertical axis)

1   2   3   4   5   6   7   8   9

Concern for Production

Source: Robert R. Blake and Jane S. Mouton, *The Managerial Grid* (Houston: Gulf Publishing Company, 1964), p. 10.

research is in the form of case analysis. Thus, the grid is popular among practitioners and is controversial among theorists and researchers because of its lack of empirical support.

Four-Factor Leadership Approach

The theories and research studies presented thus far each employ two factors: employee-centered and job-centered, initiating structure and consideration, and concern for production and concern for people. There are those who believe that leadership is too complex to be adequately explained by two dimensions or factors. Bowers and Seashore, who are also from the Institute of Social Research at the University of Michigan, believe that the Likert work and the early Ohio State work provide evidence that four factors more adequately define leadership.[23] They propose that leadership behavior involves the following:

---

[23] David G. Bowers and Stanley E. Seashore, "Predicting Organizational Effectiveness with a Four-Factor Theory of Leadership," *Administrative Science Quarterly* (September 1966), pp. 238–63.

1. *Support*—behavior which enhances the followers' feelings of personal worth and esteem.
2. *Interaction Facilitation*—behavior which encourages followers in the group to develop close, mutually satisfying relationships.
3. *Goal Emphasis*—behavior which motivates an enthusiasm within the group for achieving high levels of performance.
4. *Work Facilitation*—behavior which helps achieve goal accomplishment by such activities as scheduling, coordinating, and planning, and by providing resources such as tools, materials, and technical knowledge.

A study of 40 agencies of a leading life insurance company tested the relationship between the four leadership factors and various performance criteria. These agencies are independently owned businesses performing identical functions in their separate parts of the country. This study was concerned with relating leadership styles to measures of satisfaction and agency performance. The satisfaction indices focused on the sales agent satisfaction with the company, with fellow agents, with the regional manager, and with

Figure 8–4
A Brief Presentation of the Insurance Company Study: Four-Factor Theory of Leadership*

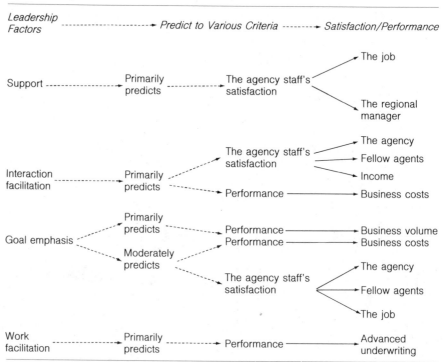

* Based on David G. Bowers and Stanley E. Seashore, "Predicting Organizational Effectiveness with a Four-Factor Theory of Leadership," *Administrative Science Quarterly* (September 1966), pp. 238–63. The idea for presenting this data in the figure was stimulated by Ross A. Webber, *Management: Basic Elements of Managing Organizations,* rev. ed. (Homewood, Ill.: Richard D. Irwin, 1979), p. 179.

income, office costs, and the job. The performance factors which showed the most significant relationships to the leadership dimensions were the following:

Staff Client Maturity—the difference in the kind of business produced by the agency attributable to the age and experience of the agency staff, and the clientele they reach.

Business Growth—the growth of business volume over preceding years.

Business Costs—the costs per unit of business.

Business Volume—the dollar volume of new business obtained by the agency.

Advanced Underwriting—the extent to which there is emphasis by the agency staff upon advanced underwriting.

There were, therefore, several measures of satisfaction and of performance closely monitored in the study. Figure 8–4 illustrates some of the major findings. The four leadership behaviors apparently are associated with different combinations of satisfaction and performance. The four-factor leadership approach to date has only been evaluated in a limited number of studies and much more work is needed.[24]

A Synopsis of the Personal-Behavioral Theories

A careful review of the various personal-behavioral theories and research indicates a number of common threads. First, each of the theories attempts to isolate broad dimensions of leadership behavior. The logic of this appears to be that multidimensions confound the interpretation of leadership behavior and complicate the research designs developed to test the particular theory.

Second, each of these theories has proponents who believe their approach to describing and predicting leadership effectiveness is the best. The followers of the Likert, Ohio State, and four-factor approaches are primarily researchers from the behavioral sciences. The managerial grid advocates are predominately consultants and practicing managers who have used it in their organizations.

Third, the measurement of leadership style for each of the theories is accomplished through paper-and-pencil questionnaire responses. This method of measurement is, of course, limited and controversial. Fourth, the Likert, Bowers and Seashore, and Ohio State work has primarily focused on group satisfaction and performance. The common bases of these theories are presented in Table 8–1.

The numerous personal-behavioral approaches are impressive, but practicing managers are interested in guidelines, results, and procedures to improve their styles. Each of the approaches is associated with highly respected theo-

---

[24] James C. Taylor, "Technology and Supervision in the Post Industrial Era" (invited paper for the Second Leadership Symposium, Southern Illinois University, 1973), pp. 1–29.

Table 8–1
A Review of the Predominant Personal-Behavioral Approaches

Leadership Factors	Prime Initiator(s) of the Theory	How Behavior Is Measured	Subjects Researched	Principal Conclusions
Employee-centered and job-centered	Likert	Through interview and questionnaire responses of groups of followers.	Formal leaders and followers in public utilities, banks, hospitals, manufacturing, food, government agencies.	Employee-centered and job-centered styles result in production improvements. However, after a brief period of time the job-centered style creates pressure that is resisted through absenteeism, turnover, grievance, and poor attitudes. The best style is *employee-centered*.
Initiating structure and consideration	Fleishman, Stogdill, and Shartle	Through questionnaire responses of groups of followers, peers, the immediate superior, and the leader.	Formal leaders and followers in military, education, public utilities, manufacturing, and government agencies.	The combination of initiating structure and consideration behavior which achieves individual, group, and organizational effectiveness depends largely on the situation.
Concern for production and concern for people	Blake and Mouton	Through interviews and questionnaire responses of groups of followers and the leader.	Formal leaders in electronics and petroleum companies.	The 9, 9 style is related to improvements in productivity, cost, and timeliness of output. Organizations should attempt to stimulate leaders to adopt the 9, 9 style.
Support, interaction facilitation, goal emphasis, and work facilitation	Bowers and Seashore	Through questionnaire responses of groups of followers.	Formal leaders in insurance, petroleum, glass products, plastics, cellophane, and aluminum casting.	Effective leadership behavior is significantly moderated by the technology of the organization. The various dimensions also predict different outcomes in various situations.

rists, researchers, or consultants, and each has been studied in different organizational settings. Yet, the linkage between leadership and such important performance indicators as production, efficiency, and satisfaction is not conclusively resolved by any of the four personal-behavioral theories.

The theme evolving from contemporary leadership theory and research is referred to as the situational or contingency approach. This approach will be discussed in the next chapter.

MAJOR ISSUES FOR THE MANAGER TO CONSIDER

A. Leadership is the ability to influence followers which involves the use of power and the acceptance of the leader by followers. The ability to influence is related to the followers' need satisfaction.

B. Power flows from the leader to subordinates and from subordinates to the leader. This mutual influence can affect the rewards and punishments received by both parties.

C. The trait approach has resulted in attempts to predict leadership effectiveness from physical, sociological, and psychological traits. The search for traits has led to studies involving effectiveness and such factors as height, weight, intelligence, and personality.

D. There continues to be a great deal of semantic confusion and overlap regarding the definition of leadership behavior. Such terms as employee-centered, job-centered, initiating structure, consideration, concern for production, concern for people, support, interaction facilitation, goal emphasis, and work facilitation are classified as personal-behavioral descriptions of what the leader does.

E. Research studies have resulted in generally inconclusive insights about the relation of leader behavior to follower effectiveness. The evidence to date is in some cases suggestive. For example, most studies indicate that leaders who are considerate (employee-centered, concerned for people, supportive) will have generally more satisfied followers.

F. The personal-behavioral approaches suggest that situational variables such as the followers' expectations, skills, role clarity, and previous experiences should be seriously considered by leaders. Leaders can do little to improve effectiveness unless they can properly modify these variables or change their style of leadership.

DISCUSSION AND REVIEW QUESTIONS

1. Some view organizations as very political systems. Do you believe that politics within an organization can be used to achieve goals? Explain.

2. Is there a one best style of leadership? Why?

3. Why is the Blake and Mouton managerial grid approach attractive to many practicing managers?

4. What could be the consequences of leaders assuming that subordinates have no power to exert on them?

5. Is it possible to educate, in management or organizational behavior courses, leaders in the way to lead followers? Explain.

6. Does the informal leader posses legitimate power? Explain.

7. What are the similarities between the employee-centered, consideration, and concern for people concepts?

8. Why would a leader be replaced in a formal organizational group and in an informal group?

ADDITIONAL REFERENCES

Bennis, W. "Leadership: A Beleaguered Species." *Organizational Dynamics* (1976), pp. 3–16.

Greiner, L. E. "What Managers Think of Participative Leadership." *Harvard Business Review* (1973), pp. 111–18.

Jacobs, T. O. *Leadership and Exchange in Formal Organizations.* Alexandria: Human Resources Research Organization, 1971.

Kotler, J. P. "Power, Success, and Organizational Effectiveness." *Organizational Dynamics* (1978), pp. 26–40.

McClelland, D. C., and Burnham, D. H. "Power is the Great Motivator." *Harvard Business Review* (1976), pp. 100–110.

Schriesheim, C. A.; House, R. J.; and Kerr, S. "Leader Initiating Structure: A Reconciliation of Discrepant Research Results and Some Empirical Tests." *Organizational Behavior and Human Performance* (1976), pp. 297–321.

Sheridan, J. E., and Vredenburgh, D. J. "Usefulness of Leadership Behavior and Social Power Variables in Predicting Tension, Performance, and Turnover of Nursing Employees." *Journal of Applied Psychology* (1978), pp. 89–95.

Vroom, V. H. "Decision Making and Leadership." *Journal of Contemporary Business* (1974), pp. 47–64.

CASE FOR ANALYSIS

THE DISMISSAL OF AN INFORMAL LEADER

The Houston Engineering Corporation was feeling the crunch of inflation and the cutback in orders from customers in the Houston, Dallas and New Orleans regional areas. The sales personnel were primarily college educated with approximately 70 percent having B.S. degrees in engineering.

Recently, the sales people in the Houston region have complained about such factors as pay inequities, the performance appraisal system, and restrictions placed on expense accounts. The following memo from an area manager, Tom Murphy, especially irritated a number of senior sales persons. It read as follows:

Ladies and Gentlemen:

As you know, we are currently in an extreme period of low order intake and we must cut our expense budgets lower than ever before. I must ask you to do things in line with expense account reduction that I have not requested in my ten years as area manager. Eliminate all potentially nonproductive lunches with clients and submit an accurate account for your weekly mileage. Unless we have more orders and better control of expenses, there will be a further cut in your budgets. I need your help to accomplish the corporate objective of cutting expense accounts by 18 percent.

If you require clarification, please contact me immediately.

Houston Area Manager,

Tom Murphy

Tom Murphy

Each Friday morning the Houston-area group met with Tom to map out the strategy and market coverage for the forthcoming week. These meetings also provided the sales people with an opportunity to exchange ideas and interact informally with each other.

This memo was discussed by the sales people after the regular meeting with Tom. The senior sales people were upset about the content of the memo and wanted John Nester to present their complaints to Tom. There were six senior sales people in the group, nine sales representatives, and nine sales trainees. The large number of trainees was due to the increased growth in the Houston sales area in the past 18 months. Houston was now the fifth largest city in the United States, and more corporations were moving their headquarters into the city than into any other in the country. This growth rate had resulted in hiring 11 new sales trainees, 2 of whom quit because of offers received from other organizations.

The senior sales personnel were recognized as the most prestigious and best paid of the 24 in the area. John was viewed as the informal leader who always represented the group's attitudes clearly to the area manager. He was also the best sales person in terms of sales achieved and operating within expense account allocations. John was 38 years old, an electrical engineer and a prime candidate for taking over the slumping New Orleans sales area by the end of the year.

Before the expense account memo was circulated, the sales personnel had complained about the company's performance appraisal system. They wanted the company to grant merit increases based on specific sales objectives achieved during the year. John and two other senior sales people, Sam Wilson and Mike Hansen, had worked up a recommendation for changing the present system. It was rejected summarily by Tom, who told them to pay more attention to selling the company's products. It was his contention that unless more orders were received there might be some cutbacks in personnel.

John visited with Tom this past Friday after the regularly scheduled meeting and discussed the memo. He explained that the sales personnel were doing the best they could, but potential clients must be cultivated carefully and this required money for lunches and dinners. Tom listened attentively and explained that this was a company policy and not his idea. The two men talked for another two hours about the direction of the company and the bright future of the Houston sales area.

On Monday at 10:30 A.M., John was called into Tom's office and informed that his services were no longer needed by the company. He was given an envelope with the current month's pay and a dismissal notification. This turn of events completely shocked him since he had believed that his future with the company was especially promising. The news of John's dismissal spread through the sales group and angered everyone.

Questions for Consideration

1. Why was John the informal leader in the sales group?
2. What type of impact do you believe John's dismissal will have on the sales group's immediate sales and level of satisfaction?
3. Why has the expense account memo caused such a problem within the sales group?
4. Do you believe that the area sales manager could have improved the procedures which expressed the organization's concern about expenses? How?

Chapter 9

Leadership: Situational Approaches

AN ORGANIZATIONAL ISSUE FOR DEBATE

Can Leaders Learn to Lead?

ARGUMENT FOR

The Vroom-Yetton model of leadership and Fiedler's contingency model are similar in that both assume that effective leadership "depends on the situation." However, one major point of departure between the two approaches to leadership involves leadership training. Fiedler is pessimistic that training managers to improve their leadership skills will ever be effective. However, Vroom's position is that managers can be trained to be flexible leaders. The Vroom leadership training method involves providing managers with a picture of their styles of leading. This picture includes a comparison of the leader's style with that of others, the situational factors that influence the leader's willingness to share power with others, and an analysis of how the leader's style compares to a normative or *how it should be* style.

As part of the leadership training program, each participant works with a set of cases describing a leader facing a realistic organizational problem. In addition, the leaders are given a lecture describing the five processes of leadership outlined in

ARGUMENT AGAINST

Fiedler is a little more skeptical then Vroom about using training to improve the effectiveness of a leader. He believes that some people are helped by training, but just as many go through one program after another and perform just as badly as ever. He also suggests that many outstanding leaders have had little or no leadership training. On the average, people with much training perform about as well as people with little or no training. In fact, Fiedler cites his own research of military personnel and post office managers which found no relationship between amount of training and performance to support his negative impressions of leadership training.

It is Fiedler's contention that a number of questionable assumptions guide the development of leadership training programs. First, program developers often assume that a few training sessions telling or showing leaders how to behave and stressing that a certain style is best will result in the appropriate behavior changes. This assumption ignores the fact that leadership situations are the Vroom-Yetton model and view and discuss films exhibiting different processes used by leaders to make decisions. The participant's task is to select the decision process that comes closest to depicting what he or she would actually do in a situation. Small groups are formed in which the cases are discussed and the participants try to reach agreement on the best leadership style for each situation. The groups then analyze videotapes of group problem-solving and provide each other with feedback about one another's leadership style.

Admittedly research on the effectiveness of training in the use of the Vroom-Yetton model is limited. However, the evidence available clearly indicates that trained leaders showed greater agreement with the model's prescriptions than untrained leaders and are rated by co-workers (subordinates and superiors) as more effective leaders. Perhaps training does make a difference and leaders can learn to be more effective.

highly emotion-charged, interpersonal relationships. It is difficult to significantly alter emotional relationships through training. Second, it is assumed that the more powerful and influential leaders will be more effective because their groups will work harder. Thus, many training programs attempt to improve a leader's control and influence. Third, many training programs attempt to promote participative decision making. These programs claim that a leader who shares decision making with subordinates will be more effective.

Fiedler is opposed to devoting all of the resources and time of training efforts to change personalities. Instead he believes that organizations need to train leaders to change situations to match their needs and values. This match is easier than one that attempts to change a leader's style. Perhaps training is needed but it should focus on altering situations, not people.

INTRODUCTION

The search for the "best" leadership style never discovered an effective approach for all situations. What has evolved are situation-leadership theories which suggest that leadership effectiveness depends upon the fit between personality, task, power, attitudes, and perceptions.[1] This chapter will concentrate on four situational oriented leadership approaches: the life-cycle approach, the contingency model, the Vroom and Yetton normative model, and the path-goal theory. Each of these approaches relies on a diagnosis of the situation.

THE SITUATION VARIABLE

The importance of the situation was studied more closely by those interested in leadership only when inconclusive and contradictory results evolved from much of the early trait and personal–behavioral research. Eventually it became known that the type of leadership behavior needed to enhance individual and group performance depends largely on the situation. What is effective leadership in one situation may be disorganized incompetence in another situation. For example, using a strong, autocratic style with educated, self-motivated, confident, and high energy level employees may be a disaster. However, the autocratic style may be what is needed for unskilled, young, insecure employees working on unstructured tasks. The situational theme of leadership is appealing, but is certainly a challenging orientation to implement. Its basic foundation suggests that an effective leader must be flexible enough to adapt to the differences among subordinates and situations.

Deciding how to lead other individuals is difficult and requires an analysis of the leader, the group, and the situation. This theme is analyzed by Tannenbaum and Schmidt in their model of leadership.[2] Managers aware of the forces they face are able to more readily modify their styles to cope with changes in the work environment. Three factors of particular importance are the forces on the managers, forces in the subordinates, and forces in the situation. Tannenbaum and Schmidt state the situational theme:

> Thus, the successful manager of men can be primarily characterized neither as a strong leader nor as a permissive one. Rather, he is one who maintains a high batting average in accurately assessing the forces that determine what his most appropriate behavior at any given time should be and in actually being able to behave accordingly.[3]

As the importance of situational factors and leader assessment of forces became more recognized, leadership research became more systematic,

---

[1] Edwin A. Fleishman, "Twenty Years of Consideration and Structure," in Edwin A. Fleishman and James G. Hunt, eds., *Current Development in the Study of Leadership* (Carbondale: Southern Illinois University Press, 1973), pp. 1–37.

[2] The following discussion is based upon Robert Tannenbaum and Warren H. Schmidt, "How to Choose a Leadership Pattern," *Harvard Business Review* (May–June 1973), pp. 162–80.

[3] Tannenbaum and Schmidt, "How to Choose a Leadership Pattern," p.180.

and contingency models of leadership began to appear in the organizational behavior and management literature. Each model has its advocates and each attempts to identify the leader behaviors most appropriate for a series of leadership situations. Each contingency model attempts to identify the leader-situation patterns that are important for effective leadership.

THE LIFE CYCLE THEORY

According to this theory, as the level of maturity of one's followers increases, appropriate leadership behavior requires less structure (task) and less socioemotional support (relationships).[4] This cycle is illustrated in the four quadrants of Figure 9–1. By dividing the maturity continuum of the life

Figure 9–1
The Life Cycle Theory

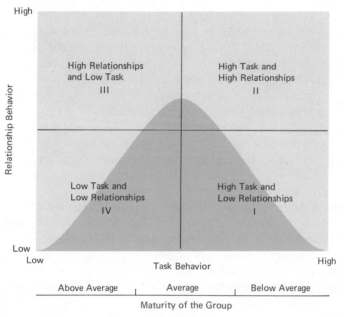

cycle into three levels (below average, average, and above average) some benchmarks of group maturity and leadership style can be provided. The theory proposes that if a leader has followers who are below average in maturity, a high task style (quadrant I) has the best possibility of being effective; whereas in dealing with followers of average maturity, the quadrant II and III styles seem most appropriate; and the quadrant IV style appears best for the above-average maturity group.

---

[4] Paul Hersey and Kenneth H. Blanchard, *Management of Organization Behavior* (Englewood Cliffs, N.J.: Prentice-Hall, 1977).

Maturity is defined in life cycle theory in terms of achievement motivation,[5] the willingness and ability to take responsibility, task-relevant education, and experience. It basically involves psychological maturity. The notion of maturity is similar to the Argyris immaturity-maturity continuum.[6] He proposes that as a person matures he or she moves from a passive state to a state of increasing activity, from dependency on others to relative independence. The concept emphasizes psychological maturity in the form of personal growth and development.

The maturity factor is considered in relation to a specific task to perform. That is, an individual or a group is not mature or immature in a total sense. All persons exhibit maturity in relation to a task, function, or objective a leader is attempting to accomplish through their efforts. Thus, an accountant may be very responsible in finishing an audit for a client and somewhat irresponsible when dealing with internal office reports. This may require the managing partner of the firm to closely supervise the accountant's report preparation and to supervise less closely the auditing work of the accountant.

The life cycle theory suggests that leader behavior, to be effective, must change as followers mature. The sequence of change should be from: (1) high task–low relationships behavior to (2) high task–high relationships behavior to (3) high relationships–low task behavior to (4) low task–low relationships behavior. For example, in working with highly trained and educated Research and Development personnel, it may be assumed that the most effective leadership style would be low task–low relationships (quadrant IV).[7] However, during the early stages of a costly and ill-defined project, the leader should impose some direction and structure so that the team understands the limitations and goals. Once these are understood, the leader would move through the life cycle to the quadrant IV style of low task–low relationships.

The high task–low relationship leader behavior is referred to as *telling* because the style is characterized by one-way communication. The high task–high relationship style is designated *selling.* The leader attempts through two-way communication and supportive behaviors to influence the follower(s) to agree to decisions that must be made.

The high relationship–low task behavior is called *participating* because the leader and follower(s) share in decision making through two-way communication and facilitative behavior from the leader. Low relationship–low task behavior is referred to as *delegating.* This means that follower(s) can work without close supervision because of high psychological maturity.

Advocates of the life cycle theory assume that many more employees today are educated, motivated, and technically competent than ever before. As a result these workers have higher potential for self-direction and self-control. These changes in maturity correspond to the assumption that lower

---

[5] This concept was identified in Chapter 5 when discussing McClelland's learned needs theory of motivation.

[6] Chris Argyris, *Integrating the Individual and the Organization* (New York: John Wiley & Sons, Inc., 1964).

[7] Hersey and Blanchard, *Management of Organization Behavior,* pp. 169–70.

order needs have been satisfactorily fulfilled for a majority of employees. The potential to motivate is greater when focusing on upper-level needs like self-actualization, autonomy, and esteem.

Thus, even though the research support of the life cycle theory is limited, a number of important conceptual issues has been clarified by the approach. First, the maturity level of a group, or the stage of group development, appears to be an important consideration in deciding how to lead. The mature group has developed structure, processes, and cohesiveness to cope with many internal and external problems. Second, as the situation changes, a leader may have to adopt a different style to be effective. Finally, any change in style should be based on the most accurate possible assessment of the situation, the group, and the leader. These are the same important forces isolated for attention by Tannenbaum and Schmidt and other situational theorists.

THE CONTINGENCY LEADERSHIP MODEL

The contingency model of leadership effectiveness was developed by Fiedler.[8] The model postulates that performance of groups is dependent on the interaction of leadership style and situational favorableness. Leadership is viewed as a relationship based on power and influence. Thus, two important questions are considered: (1) to what degree does the situation provide the leader with the power and influence needed to be effective, or how favorable are the situational factors? and (2) to what extent can the leader predict the effects of his or her style on the behavior and performance of followers?

The Situational Factors

Fiedler proposes three situational factors which influence a leader's effectiveness: leader-member relations, task structure, and position power. From a theoretical as well as an intuitive point of view, interpersonal relationships between leader and followers are likely to be the most important variable which determines power and influence. The leader's influence depends in part upon acceptance by the followers. If others are willing to follow because of charisma, expertise, or mutual respect, the leader has little need to rely on task structure or position power. If, however, the leader is not trusted and is viewed negatively by followers the situation is considered less favorable in Fiedler's theory.

The *leader-member* relations factor refers to the degree of confidence, trust, and respect followers have in the leader. This situational variable reflects the acceptance of the leader. It is measured in two ways. One method involves asking the followers to indicate on a sociometric preference scale whether they accept or endorse a leader. An alternative method of measurement is

---

[8] Fred E. Fiedler, *A Theory of Leadership Effectiveness* (New York: McGraw-Hill, 1967).

the "Group Atmosphere" scale. This measure consists of ten eight-point items, answered by the followers, one of which is:

Friendly ____: ____: ____: ____: ____: ____: ____: ____ Unfriendly
         8   7   6   5   4   3   2   1

The second most important measure of situational favorableness is referred to as *task-structure.* This dimension includes a number of components as follows:

Goal clarity—the degree to which the tasks and duties of the job are clearly stated and known to the people performing the job.

Goal-path multiplicity—the degree to which the problems encountered in the job can be solved by a variety of procedures. The assembly line worker solves problems within a systematic framework, while a scientist has a number of different ways to solve a problem.

Decision verifiability—the degree to which the "correctness" of the solutions or decisions typically encountered in a job can be demonstrated by appeal to authority, by logical procedures, or by feedback. A quality control inspector can show defective parts and clearly indicate why a part is sent back for reworking.

Decision-specificity—the degree to which there is generally more than one correct solution. An accountant working on preparing a balance sheet has few choices, while a research scientist may have numerous potentially correct alternatives to choose from.

The most obvious way in which the leader secures power is by accepting and performing the leadership role. The leader is recognized as having the right to direct, evaluate, reward, and punish followers, though this right must be exercised within defined boundaries. *Position power* in the contingency model refers to the power inherent in the leadership position. To determine leader position power questions such as the following are asked:

Can the supervisor recommend subordinate rewards and punishments to his boss?

Can the supervisor punish or reward subordinates on his own?

Can the supervisor recommend promotion or demotion of subordinates?[9]

Fiedler contends that such questions provide a profile of high or low position power. He further assumes that practically all managers, directors, supervisors, and superintendents have high position power. Likewise, Fiedler believes that committee chairpersons and leaders of groups of colleagues tend to have low position power; this assumption also applies to informal group leaders.

---

[9] Fred E. Fiedler and M. M. Chemers, *Leadership and Effective Management* (Glenview, Ill.: Scott, Foresman, 1974).

Favorableness of the Situation

The three situational factors which seem to be the most important in determining the leader's power and influence are: (1) whether leader-member relations are good or poor; (2) whether the task is relatively structured or unstructured; and (3) whether the position power is relatively strong or weak. A group can be classified as to each of these situational factors. The resulting classification is shown in Figure 9-2. It suggests that it is easier to be a leader in groups which fall into situation I in which you are liked, have a structured task, and position power. The situation is more favorable for the situation I leader than the situation VIII leader.

Figure 9-2
Fiedler's Classification of Situational Favorableness

Leader-Member Relations	Good				Poor			
Task Structure	High		Low		High		Low	
Position Power	Strong	Weak	Strong	Weak	Strong	Weak	Strong	Weak
Situations	I	II	III	IV	V	VI	VII	VIII

Very Favorable ◄————————————————————————————————————► Very Unfavorable

Fiedler contends that a permissive, more lenient (relationship-oriented) style is best when the situation is moderately favorable or moderately unfavorable. Thus, if a leader were moderately liked and possessed some power, and the job tasks for subordinates were somewhat vague, the leadership style needed to achieve the best results would be relationship oriented.

In contrast, when the situation is highly favorable or highly unfavorable, a task-oriented approach generally produces the desired performance. A well-liked office manager, who has power and has clearly identified the performance goals is operating in a highly favorable situation. A project engineer, who is faced with a group of suspicious and hostile subordinates, has little power, and has vague task responsibilities, needs to be task-oriented in this highly unfavorable situation.

The Least Preferred Co-Worker (LPC)

As we have seen in this and the previous chapter, no single style of leader behavior assures optimal individual or group performance in all situations. A person may be effective in one situation but very ineffective in another. a key variable in investigating leader effectiveness in the contingency model is the Least Preferred Co-Worker (LPC) score.[10] This is assumed to be an indicator of the leader's personality. The LPC score is obtained by asking the leader to think of everybody with whom he or she has ever worked and to describe the person with whom the leader could work least well, the "least preferred co-worker." A scale consisting of 16 items is used to develop the LPC score. Two of these items appear as follows:

Frustrating ___: ___: ___: ___: ___: ___: ___: ___ Helpful
　　　　　　　1　　2　　3　　4　　5　　6　　7　　8

Tense ___: ___: ___: ___: ___: ___: ___: ___ Relaxed
　　　　1　　2　　3　　4　　5　　6　　7　　8

The contingency model advocates believe that the LPC is an index of behavioral preferences of the leader. A leader with a high-LPC sees good points in the least preferred co-worker and has as his or her preference the desire to be "related." The leader seeks to have strong emotional and affective ties with others. The low-LPC person, however, has different preferences and derives satisfaction from achievement.[11]

Some Relevant Research

Over the past 20 years, Fiedler and advocates of the contingency model have studied military, educational, and industrial leaders. In a summary of 63 studies based on 454 separate groups, Fiedler suggests the kind of leadership which is the most appropriate for the situational conditions.[12] Figure 9–3 presents his analysis.

The situational characteristics are shown at the bottom of Figure 9–3. The vertical axis indicates the correlation between a leader's preference (style), as measured by the LPC score, and the group's performance. A median correlation above the midline shows that the relationship-oriented leaders tend to perform better than the task-oriented leaders. A median correlation below the midline indicates that the task-oriented leaders perform better than the relationship-oriented leaders.

The data presented in Figure 9–3 imply a number of things about effective leaders. First, task-oriented leaders tend to perform better than relationship-oriented leaders in situations that are very favorable (I, II, III) and in those that are unfavorable (VIII). Relationship-oriented leaders tend to perform better than task-oriented leaders in situations that are intermediate in favorableness (IV, V, and VII). These findings support the notion that both types of leaders are effective in certain situations.

Second, the findings indicate that the performance of a leader depends as much on the situational favorableness as it does on the individual in the

---

[10] Fiedler, *A Theory of Leadership Effectiveness*, p.41.

[11] Ibid.

[12] Fred E. Fiedler, "How Do You Make Leaders More Effective? New Answers to an Old Puzzle," *Organizational Dynamics* (Autumn 1972), pp. 3–18.

Figure 9–3
A Summary of Contingency Model Research

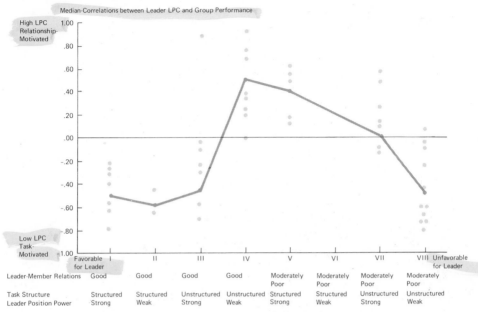

Median-Correlations between Leader LPC and Group Performance

	Favorable I for Leader	II	III	IV	V	VI	VII	VIII Unfavorable for Leader
Leader-Member Relations	Good	Good	Good	Good	Moderately Poor	Moderately Poor	Moderately Poor	Moderately Poor
Task Structure	Structured	Structured	Unstructured	Unstructured	Structured	Structured	Unstructured	Unstructured
Leader Position Power	Strong	Weak	Strong	Weak	Strong	Weak	Strong	Weak

Source: Fred E. Fiedler, *A Theory of Leadership Effectiveness* (New York: McGraw-Hill, 1967), p. 146.

leadership position. Hence, an organization can change leadership effectiveness by attempting to change the leader's personality and motivational preferences or by changing the leader's situation.

Can Leaders Be Trained?

Common sense suggests that it is difficult to change a leader's personality and motivational preferences to fit a particular situation. Fiedler states:

> Fitting the man to the leadership job by selection and training has not been spectacularly successful. It is surely easier to change almost anything in the job situation than a man's personality and his leadership style.[13]

It is assumed that changing a leader's style through training is an extremely difficult task.

Contingency theory and research reveal that a leader's performance depends on personality and situational favorableness. Fiedler contends that training programs and experience can improve a leader's power and influence

---

[13] Fred E. Fiedler, "Engineering the Job to Fit the Manager," *Harvard Business Review* (September–October 1965), p. 115. Also see Fred E. Fiedler, "The Effects of Leadership Training and Experience: A Contingency Model Interpretation," *Administrative Science Quarterly* (December 1972), pp. 453–70, and Walter Hill, "Leadership Style: Rigid or Flexible?" *Organizational Behavior and Human Performance* (February 1973), pp. 35–47.

if the situational favorableness is high. This means that a training program which improves a leader's power and influence may benefit the relationship-oriented person, but it could be detrimental to the task-oriented person.

Since training program stimulated changes are so elusive, the better alternative is to change the favorableness of the situation. A first step recommended by Fiedler is to determine whether leaders are task- or relationship-oriented. Next, the organization needs to diagnose and classify the situational favorableness of its leadership positions. Finally, the organization must select the best strategy to bring about improved effectiveness. If leadership training is selected as an option, then it should devote special attention to teaching participants how to modify their environments and their jobs to fit their styles of leadership. That is, leaders should be trained to change their leadership situations. Fiedler's recent work indicates that when leaders can recognize the situations in which they are most successful, they can then begin to modify their own situations.[14]

The work of Fiedler should be recognized as extremely important. Of course his work is still continuing, and the original model is being refined. The model is and will probably remain a rich source of new ideas, propositions, and hypotheses about leadership style and effectiveness.[15] The current thrust of contingency model research appears to be toward the introduction of more situational dimensions in testing the predictions.

THE VROOM AND YETTON MODEL OF LEADERSHIP

Many early attempts at explaining optimal leadership behavior had an autocratic orientation. The leader made decisions, issued orders to subordinates, monitored their performance, and made necessary adjustments. However, behavioral scientists have suggested that subordinates should participate more in the decision-making process.

The research evidence provides some but not overwhelming support for participative decision making (PDM). In fact, it appears that PDM, like all of the leader's behaviors and traits has consequences which vary from one situation to another. Vroom and Yetton have developed a leadership decision making model which indicates the kinds of situations in which various degrees of PDM would be appropriate.[16]

Vroom and Yetton in developing their model made a number of assumptions. These were:

a. The model should be of value to leaders or managers in determining which leadership styles they should use in various situations.

---

[14] Fred E. Fiedler, "The Leadership Game: Matching the Man to the Situation," *Organizational Dynamics* (Winter 1976), pp. 6–16.

[15] Fred E. Fiedler, "The Contingency Model: New Directions for Leadership Utilization," *Journal of Contemporary Business* (Autumn 1974), pp. 65–80.

[16] Victor H. Vroom and Philip Yetton, *Leadership and Decision Making* (Pittsburgh, Pa.: University of Pittsburgh Press, 1973). © 1973 by the University of Pittsburgh Press.

b. No single leadership style is applicable to all situations.

c. The main focus should be the problem to be solved and the situation in which the problem occurs.

d. The leadership style used in one situation should not constrain the method used in other situations.

e. There are a number of social processes that will influence the amount of participation by subordinates in problem solving. The leader must select the best processes to reach the best solution.

f. The leadership styles used vary with the number of the leader's subordinates who are affected by the decision.

Applying these assumptions resulted in a model that is concerned with the leadership decision making.

Decision Effectiveness: Quality and Acceptance

The Vroom and Yetton model emphasizes two criteria of decision effectiveness: quality and acceptance. *Decision quality* refers to the objective aspects of a decision that influence subordinates' performance aside from any direct impact on motivation. Some job related decisions are linked to performance, while other kinds of decisions are relatively unimportant. For example, determining work flow patterns and layout, performance goals and deadlines, or work assignments usually has an important influence on group performance. On the other hand, selecting work area location for water coolers or the type of cafeteria furniture to buy has no consequence on group performance. When decision quality is important for performance and subordinates possess the ability and information that the leader does not possess, the Vroom-Yetton model would indicate that the leader use a decision procedure that allows subordinate participation.

Decision acceptance is the degree of subordinate commitment to the decision. There are many situations in which a course of action, even if it is technically correct, can fail, because it is resisted by those who have to execute it. In judging whether a problem requires subordinate commitment, the leader needs to look for two things: (1) are subordinates going to have to execute the decision under conditions in which initiative and judgment will be required? and (2) are subordinates likely to "feel strongly" about the decision? If the answer to either or both of these questions is "yes," then the problem possesses an acceptance requirement. When subordinates can accept a decision as theirs, they will be more inclined to implement it effectively.

Five Decision-Making Styles of Leaders

The Vroom and Yetton model designates five decision-making styles that are appropriate for decisions involving none or all of the leader's subordinates.

Table 9–1
Five Decision Styles

Group Problems

AI. You solve the problem or make the decision yourself, using information available to you at the time.

AII. You obtain the necessary information from your subordinates, then decide the solution to the problem yourself. You may or may not tell your subordinates what the problem is in getting the information from them. The role played by your subordinates in making the decision is clearly one of providing the necessary information to you, rather than generating or evaluating alternative solutions.

CI. You share the problem with the relevant subordinates individually, getting their ideas and suggestions without bringing them together as a group. Then *you* make the decision, which may or may not reflect your subordinates' influence.

CII. You share the problem with your subordinates as a group, obtaining their collective ideas and suggestions. Then you make the decision, which may or may not reflect your subordinates' influence.

GII. You share the problem with your subordinates as a group. Together you generate and evaluate alternatives and attempt to reach agreement (consensus) on a solution. Your role is much like that of chairman. You do not try to influence the group to adopt "your" solution, and you are willing to accept and implement any solution which has the support of the entire group.

Source: Reprinted from *Leadership and Decision-Making*, p. 13, by Victor H. Vroom and Philip W. Yetton, by permission of the University of Pittsburgh Press. © 1973 by the University of Pittsburgh Press.

These styles include two types of autocratic style (AI and AII), two types of consultative style (CI and CII), and a joint or group style (GII). The five styles are defined in Table 9–1.

The Diagnosis Procedure for Leaders

Vroom and Yetton suggest that leaders perform a diagnosis of the situation and problem by applying a number of decision rules. These rules will help determine which decision-making style of leadership is appropriate for the particular situation. By using a careful diagnosis, the leader would minimize the chances of reducing decision quality and acceptance. The diagnosis decision rules are:

1. *The Leader Information Rule.* If the quality of the decision is important, and the leader does not possess enough information or expertise to solve the problem alone, then AI is eliminated as a possible style.
2. *The Goal Congruence Rule.* If the quality of the decision is important

and subordinates are not likely to pursue the organizational goals in their efforts to solve the problem, then GII is eliminated as a possible style.

3. *Unstructured Problem Rule.*   In decisions in which the quality of the decision is important, if the leader lacks the necessary information or expertise to solve the problem alone, and if the problem is unstructured, the method of solving the problem should provide for interaction among subordinates likely to possess relevant information. Thus, AI, AII, and CI are eliminated as possible styles.

4. *The Acceptance Rule.*   If the acceptance of the decision by subordinates is critical to effective implementation and if it is not certain that an autocratic decision will be accepted, AI and AII are eliminated as possible styles.

5. *The Conflict Rule.*   If the acceptance of the decision is critical, an autocratic decision is not certain to be accepted, and disagreement among subordinates in methods of attaining the organizational goal is likely, the methods used in solving the problem should enable those in disagreement to resolve their differences with full knowledge of the problem. Accordingly, under these conditions, AI, AII, and CI, which permit no interaction among subordinates and therefore provide no opportunity for those in conflict to resolve their differences, are eliminated as feasible styles. Their use runs the risk of leaving some of the subordinates with less than the needed commitment to the final decision.

6. *The Fairness Rule.*   If the quality of the decision is unimportant but acceptance is critical and not certain to result from an autocratic decision, it is important that the decision process generate acceptance. The decision process should permit the subordinates to interact with one another and negotiate over the fair method of resolving any differences with full responsibility on them for determining what is fair and equitable. Accordingly, under these circumstances, AI, AII, CI, and CII are eliminated from the feasible alternatives.

7. *The Acceptance Priority Rule.*   If acceptance is critical and not certain to result from an autocratic decision, and if subordinates are motivated to pursue the organizational goals represented in the problem, then methods that provide equal partnership in the decision-making process can provide greater acceptance without risking decision quality. Accordingly, AI, AII, CI, and CII are eliminated from the feasible set of styles.

These seven decision rules are used for determining what procedures should not be used by a leader in a given situation. The first three rules are designed to protect decision quality. The remaining four rules are designed to protect decision acceptance. The application of the seven decision rules is illustrated by use of a decision tree chart. One such chart is shown in Figure 9–4. The chart is read from left to right. Begin by considering the situation and asking question A. If the answer is no, question D is then asked, but if the answer to A is yes, ask question B. The leader would proceed

Figure 9-4
Decision Process Flowchart (feasible set)

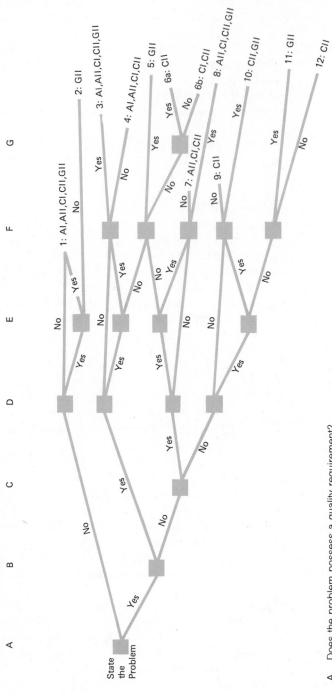

A. Does the problem possess a quality requirement?
B. Do I have sufficient information to make a high-quality decision?
C. Is the problem structured?
D. Is acceptance of the decision by subordinates important for effective implementation?
E. If I were to make the decision by myself, am I reasonably certain that it would be accepted by my subordinates?
F. Do subordinates share the organizational goals to be attained in solving this problem?
G. Is conflict among subordinates likely in preferred solutions?

from left to right until a terminal or end point is reached. For example, the feasible solutions at point 1 are AI, AII, CI, CII, and GII. On the other hand, the feasible solution suggested at point 11 is GII. Each of the styles suggested is likely to lead to a high quality decision acceptable to subordinates. Since this is the case, most leaders and managers believe it is wisest to choose the most autocratic of the styles. The leader can save time by doing so without risking decision quality or acceptance. The specific style of leadership attempted would be based on the time needed to make a decision, the leader's preference, and the ability, knowledge, and experience of subordinates. Vroom and Yetton have developed a time-efficient Model A version of the decision tree,[17] which would lead to the selection of the least time consuming leadership style. The decision tree used here is the Model B or group development version. It maximizes the development of subordinates through increased participation in decision making when possible.

Application of the Vroom/Yetton Approach

Vroom and Yetton have developed actual decision making scenarios that portray how the model shown in Figure 9–4 can be applied. A person reading

Figure 9–5
Application of the Vroom and Yetton Model to a Decision Scenario

---

Decision Situation

You are supervising the work of 12 engineers. Their formal training and work experience are very similar, permitting you to use them interchangeably on projects. Yesterday, your manager informed you that a request had been received from an overseas affiliate for four engineers to go abroad on extended loan for a period of six to eight months. For a number of reasons, he argued, and you agreed, that this request should be met from your group. All of your engineers are capable of handling this assignment, and from the standpoint of present and future projects, there is no particular reason why any one should be retained over any other. The problem is somewhat complicated by the fact that the overseas assignment is in what is generally regarded in the company as an undesirable location.

Analysis (based on Figure 9–4)

Question A (Quality requirement?): NO
Question D (Subordinate acceptance critical?): YES
Question E (Is acceptance likely without participation?): NO

Feasible set of decision procedures: GII
Minimum time solution: GII

Source: Adapted from *Leadership and Decision-Making,* pp. 41–42, by Victor H. Vroom and Philip W. Yetton by permission of the University of Pittsburgh Press. © 1973 by the University of Pittsburgh Press.

---

[17] Victor H. Vroom, "Can Leaders Learn to Lead?" *Organizational Dynamics* (Winter 1976), pp. 17–28.

the scenarios is asked to assume the role of a leader or manager and to describe the behavior or style (e.g., AI, AII, CI, CII, or GII) that he or she would apply to the situation described. An example of a decision situation scenario is presented in Figure 9–5.

Research on the Vroom-Yetton Model

The Vroom-Yetton model is still relatively new and many research questions raised by it need to be tested. However, the research to date can be divided into two types: (1) *verification*—which is aimed at verifying the model's prescriptions, and (2) *descriptive*—which attempts to identify the determinants of actual leader or managerial behavior and the degree to which such behavior conforms to the model's prescriptions.

Verification Research. One study examined 181 actual decision-making situations and behavior in these situations.[18] The model was then used to predict those decisions which would be effective (i.e., those in which the manager's behavior was one of the acceptable styles) and those decisions which would be ineffective (i.e., those in which the manager's behavior violated one of the seven decision rules pertaining to quality and acceptance). These predictions were then compared to the actual ratings of decision effectiveness. The results showed substantial support for the model. Of those decisions where the manager's behavior agreed with the feasible suggested style of leadership, 68 percent were judged to have successful results. Of those decisions where the manager's behavior disagreed with the feasible style of leadership, only 22 percent had successful results.

Another test of the model was conducted in 45 retail franchises in the cleaning industry.[19] Store managers who exhibited conformity to the Vroom-Yetton leadership style prescriptions had more productive operations and more satisfied subordinates than managers exhibiting less conformity to the model.

Descriptive Research. Descriptive research has attempted to better understand how leaders or managers *do* behave rather than how managers *should* behave. The research suggests that most managers permit a greater overall level of PDM than seems to be required.[20] Although the model suggests that the AI (autocratic) leadership style is appropriate for various situations, managers tend to avoid its use. On the other hand, managers seem to overuse the CI and CII styles.

Other research using the decision situation scenarios reveals that female

---

[18] Victor H. Vroom and Arthur G. Jago, "On the Validity of the Vroom-Yetton Model," *Journal of Applied Psychology* (April 1978), pp. 151–62.

[19] C. Margerison and R. Glube, "Leadership Decision Making: An Empirical Test of the Vroom and Yetton Model" (Unpublished manuscript, 1978).

[20] Victor H. Vroom and Arthur G. Jago, "Decision Making as a Social Process: Normative and Descriptive Models of Leader Behavior," *Decision Sciences* (October 1974), pp. 743–69.

managers are more participative than male managers,[21] and that business school students are more participative than actual managers.[22] In addition, it was found that managers higher in the managerial hierarchy are more participative than managers lower in the same hierarchy.[23]

The Vroom and Yetton model appears to be a promising approach for understanding leadership behavior. Additional research with different types of leaders in various settings is needed to more thoroughly examine the model. It appears that the research available shows that effective leaders are neither universally autocratic nor universally participative. They utilize various approaches in response to the demands of a situation. Above all, the Vroom-Yetton leader is portrayed as flexible enough to apply the skills needed to execute effective decision processes.

PATH-GOAL MODEL

Like the other situational or contingency leadership approaches, the path-goal model attempts to predict leadership effectiveness in different situations. According to this model, leaders are effective because of their positive impact on followers' motivation, ability to perform, and satisfaction. The theory is designated path-goal because it focuses on how the leader influences the followers' perceptions of work goals, self-development goals, and paths to goal attainment.[24]

The foundation of path-goal theory is the expectancy motivation theory, discussed in Chapter 5. Briefly, expectancy theory states that an individual's attitudes, job satisfaction, behavior, and job effort can be predicted from: (1) the degree to which the job or behavior is seen as leading to various outcomes (expectancy) and (2) the preferences for these outcomes (valences). Thus, it is proposed that individuals are satisfied with their jobs if they believe it leads to desirable outcomes, and they work hard if they believe that this effort will result in desirable outcomes. The implication of these assumptions for leadership is that subordinates are motivated by leader style or behavior to the extent it influences expectancies (goal paths) and valences (goal attractiveness).

Some early work on the path-goal theory asserts that leaders will be effec-

---

[21] Rick Steers, "Individual Differences in Participative Decision Making," *Human Relations* (September 1977), pp. 837–47.

[22] Arthur G. Jago and Victor H. Vroom, "Predicting Leader Behavior from a Measure of Behavioral Intent," *Academy of Management Journal* (in press).

[23] Arthur G. Jago, "Hierarchical Level Determinants of Participative Leader Behavior" (Doctoral dissertation, Yale University, 1977).

[24] Robert J. House, "A Path-Goal Theory of Leadership Effectiveness," *Administrative Science Quarterly* (September 1971), pp. 321–39. Also see Robert J. House and Terence R. Mitchell, "Path-Goal Theory of Leadership, *Journal of Contemporary Business* (Autumn 1974), pp. 81–98, which is the basis for the following discussion.

tive by making rewards available to subordinates and by making these rewards contingent on the subordinates' accomplishment of specific goals.[25]
It is argued that an important part of the leader's job is to clarify for subordinates the kind of behavior that will most likely result in goal accomplishment.
This activity is referred to as *path clarification.*

This early path-goal work led to the development of a complex theory
involving four specific kinds of leader behavior: directive, supportive, participative, and achievement; and three types of subordinate attitudes: job satisfaction, acceptance of the leader, and expectations about effort-performance-
reward relationships.[26] The *directive leader* tends to let subordinates know
what is expected of them. The *supportive leader* treats subordinates as
equals. A *participative leader* consults with subordinates and uses their suggestions and ideas before reaching a decision. The *achievement oriented*
leader sets challenging goals, expects subordinates to perform at the highest
level, and continually seeks improvement in performance.

Research studies suggest that these four styles can be practiced by the
same leader in various situations.[27] These findings are contrary to the Fiedler
notion concerning the difficulty of altering style. The path-goal approach suggests more flexibility than the Fiedler contingency model.

The Main Path-Goal Propositions

The path-goal theory has led to the development of two important
propositions:

1. Leader behavior is acceptable and satisfying to the extent that the subordinates perceive such behavior as an immediate source of satisfaction or
   as instrumental to future satisfaction.
2. Leader behavior will be motivational to the extent that it makes satisfaction
   of subordinates' needs contingent on effective performance and it complements the environment of subordinates by providing the guidance, clarity
   of direction, and rewards necessary for effective performance.[28]

According to the path-goal theory leaders should increase the number
and kinds of rewards available to subordinates. In addition, the leader should
provide guidance and counsel to clarify the manner in which these rewards
can be obtained. This means the leader should help subordinates clarify
realistic expectancies and reduce the barriers to the accomplishment of val-

---

[25] Martin G. Evans, "The Effects of Supervisory Behavior on the Path-Goal Relationship,"
Organizational Behavior and Human Performance (May 1970), pp. 277–98. Also see Martin
G. Evans, "Effects of Supervisory Behavior: Extensions of Path-Goal Theory of Motivation,"
Journal of Applied Psychology (April 1974), pp. 172–78.

[26] Robert J. House and Gary Dessler, "The Path-Goal Theory of Leadership: Some Post
Hoc and A Priori Tests," James G. Hunt, ed., *Contingency Approaches to Leadership* (Carbondale: Southern Illinois University, 1974).

[27] House, "A Path-Goal Theory," and House and Dessler, "Path-Goal Theory."

[28] These propositions are presented by House and Mitchell, "Path-Goal Theory," p. 84.

ued goals. For example, counseling employees on their chances of receiving a promotion and helping them eliminate skill deficiencies so that a promotion becomes more of a reality are appropriate leadership behaviors.

The Situational Factors

Two types of situational variables are considered in the path-goal theory. The two are the *personal characteristics of subordinates* and the *environmental pressures and demands* with which subordinates must cope in order to accomplish work goals and derive satisfaction.

A personal characteristic which is important is subordinates' perception of their own ability. The higher the degree of perceived ability relative to the task demands, the less the subordinate will accept a directive leader style. This directive style of leadership would be viewed as unnecessarily close.

The environmental variables include factors which are not within the control of the subordinate but which are important to satisfaction or to the ability to perform effectively.[29] These include the tasks, the formal authority system of the organization, and the work group. Any of these environmental factors can motivate or constrain the subordinate. The environmental forces may also serve as a reward for acceptable levels of performance. For example, the subordinate could be motivated by the work group and receive satisfaction from co-workers' acceptance for doing a job according to group norms.

The path-goal theory proposes that leader behavior will be motivational to the extent that it helps subordinates cope with environmental uncertainties. A leader who is able to reduce the uncertainties of the job is considered to be a motivator because he or she increases the subordinates' expectations that their efforts will lead to desirable rewards.

The testing of the variables in this theory is currently in the state of infancy. Whether the path-goal theory will create the degree of research interest that Fiedler's contingency model did is presently unknown. The theory is an attempt to extend the valuable contingency model of leadership. It not only attempts to suggest what type of leader may be effective in a given situation, it also attempts to explain why the leader is effective.

AN INTEGRATIVE MODEL OF LEADERSHIP

Based upon the leadership theories and research covered thus far, it becomes evident that there is certainly no "one best" style or model of leadership. In practice, leaders are seldom totally participative or supportive or directive. Many situational, personal, and group variables influence leadership effectiveness.

A number of important variables and considerations are important for accomplishment of acceptable levels of leadership effectiveness. It seems that

---

[29] House and Mitchell, "Path-Goal Theory," p. 87.

Figure 9–6
A Proposed Integrative Model of Leadership

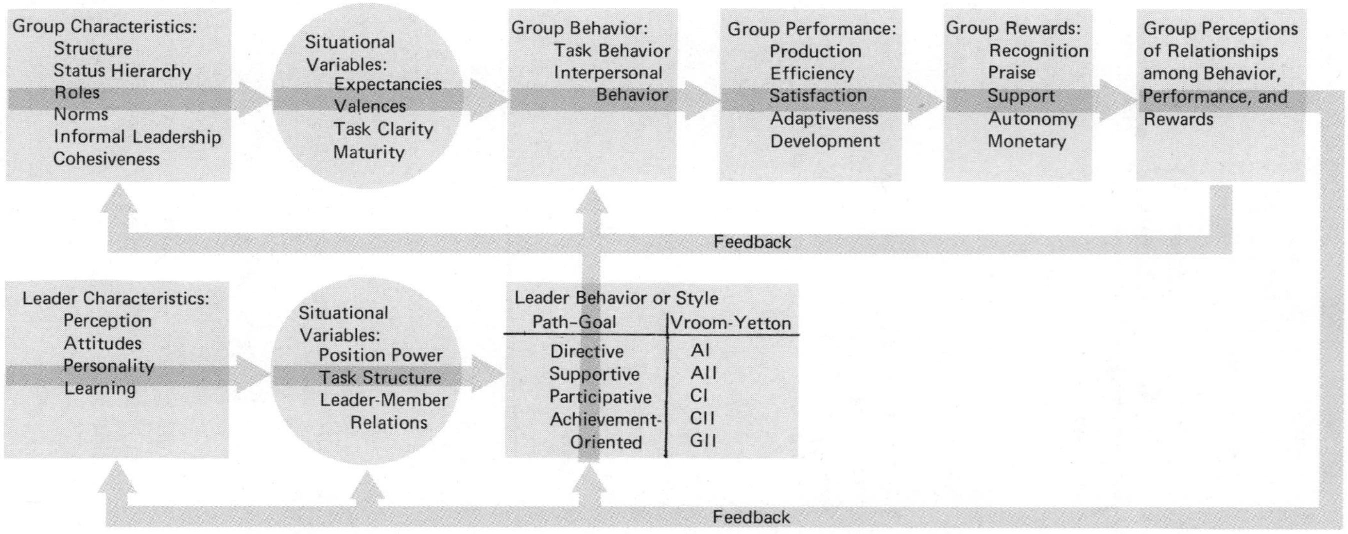

Group Characteristics:
Structure
Status Hierarchy
Roles
Norms
Informal Leadership
Cohesiveness

Situational
Variables:
Expectancies
Valences
Task Clarity
Maturity

Group Behavior:
Task Behavior
Interpersonal
Behavior

Group Performance:
Production
Efficiency
Satisfaction
Adaptiveness
Development

Group Rewards:
Recognition
Praise
Support
Autonomy
Monetary

Group Perceptions
of Relationships
among Behavior,
Performance, and
Rewards

Leader Characteristics:
Perception
Attitudes
Personality
Learning

Situational
Variables:
Position Power
Task Structure
Leader-Member
Relations

Leader Behavior or Style	
Path-Goal	Vroom-Yetton
Directive	AI
Supportive	AII
Participative	CI
Achievement-	CII
Oriented	GII

Feedback

Feedback

some form of integrative model would be a reasonable starting point in attempting to understand more thoroughly the role of a leader. The integrative model should include these variables:

Leader's Awareness of Self. A leader who is not aware of the impact his or her style has on others operates under difficult conditions. For example, a leader may perceive the style being used as conducive to trust and rapport, while subordinates view it as a practice of manipulation to be resisted. In order to minimize discrepancies, the leader must diagnose his or her style. The diagnosis must take into consideration the individual characteristics discussed in Chapter 4—the leader's psychological, sociological, and physiological makeup. An introspective analysis of one's style of leading, although revealing faults, is assumed to be healthy for the leader interested in achieving effectiveness.

Group's Characteristics. The leader must perform a diagnosis of such group characteristics as skills, maturity, expectation, norms, size, and cohesiveness. The effective leader will help the group determine path-goals and problems which are blocking the accomplishment of goals. The leader must also carefully assess the group's present feelings and future expectations about rewards, tasks, and style.

Understanding Individual Characteristics. The leader must be familiar with the complexity of personality, attitudes, perception, and motivation. In addition, knowing how these behavioral factors are shaped before a person enters an organization and are modified while in the organization should be considered a part of the leader's job duties. The effective leader must integrate the diverse mix of people in the group and provide positive leadership for as many subordinates as possible. Only through an understanding of individual differences will a leader be prepared for the demands, frustrations, and conflict involved in working with people.

Understanding Motivation. Motivation is related to behavior, performance, satisfaction, and rewards. Leaders must develop their understanding of motivation and recognize that it is complex and is related to individual differences. Money can motivate some workers to perform better, while it is not an effective motivator of other employees.[30] Who responds to what rewards and how they respond are questions the leader must search out when working with various motivational strategies.

An integrative model is presented in Figure 9–6. The model attempts to integrate the most reliable knowledge regarding leadership. It does not include every crucial variable, but some of the more important are isolated and represented. We should also note that while the leader influences group behavior, the group influences the leader in return. In essence, leadership should be viewed as a reciprocal process—leaders and groups influence each other.

---

[30] Herbert H. Meyer, "The Pay-for-Performance Dilemma," *Organizational Dynamics* (Winter 1975), pp. 39–50.

MAJOR ISSUES FOR THE MANAGER TO CONSIDER

A. The *situational approach* emphasizes the importance of forces within the leader, the subordinates, and the organization. These forces interact and must be properly diagnosed if effectiveness is to be achieved.

B. The *life cycle theory* of leadership introduces the concept of group maturity. This reflects the achievement-motivation and the willingness to take responsibility to complete a job task. As groups mature, the type of leadership to which they best respond generally changes.

C. Although the *life cycle theory* is intuitively insightful, it has not been refined or properly tested through scientifically based analysis. Thus, its assumptions and recommendations must be treated with caution.

D. The *contingency model* proposes that the performance of groups is dependent on the interaction of leadership style and situational favorableness. The three crucial situational factors are leader-member relations, task structure, and position power.

E. The *contingency model* is not without its critics. Although weaknesses are apparent in the model, there is refinement work being done by numerous researchers. This work is not, however, providing meaningful behavioral explanations to practicing managers who are interested in how they should lead others.

F. Vroom and Yetton have developed a leadership model that can be used to select the amount of group decision-making participation needed in a variety of problem situations. The model suggests that the amount of subordinate participation depends on the leader's skill and knowledge, whether a quality decision is needed, the extent the problem is structured, and whether acceptance by subordinates is needed to implement the decision.

G. Research gathered to date on the Vroom-Yetton model has been supportive of the prescriptions offered by applying the various decision rules. In general, it appears that leaders permit a greater level of subordinate participation than seems to be required. The research also points out the need for leaders to be flexible so that high quality decisions, that are accepted by subordinates, can be made in a reasonable amount of time.

H. The leader's role in the *path-goal theory* is to (1) increase the number and kinds of personal payoffs to subordinates, and (2) provide guidance and counsel for clarifying paths and reducing problems when seeking various outcomes.

I. Leaders should diagnose:
   1. Group characteristics.
   2. Situational variables (group related).
   3. Group behavior.
   4. Their own characteristics.
   5. Situational variables (leader related).
   6. Their own behavior.
   7. Group effectiveness.

   Only through attempts to diagnose these factors can adjustments in style, though slight in many cases, be properly initiated. The diagnostic skills of a leader are certainly as important, if not more crucial, as the technical and administrative skills.

DISCUSSION AND REVIEW QUESTIONS

1. A number of the models presented in the chapter emphasize the need for leaders to be flexible. Are there any potential problems associated with what would be classified as flexible leaders?

2. Diagnosis is mentioned as an important function of leadership. Is self-diagnosis of leadership traits, attributes, and styles difficult? Why?

3. What type of research is needed to further develop and modify the Vroom-Yetton model?

4. Select one of the situational models and develop a presentation which would clearly show why this one particular model is valuable to leaders who are actually working with subordinates.

5. According to the contingency theory, an alternative to modifying the style of leadership through training is changing the favorableness of the situation. What is meant by changing the favorableness of the situation?

6. What are the similarities in the contingency model and the path-goal leadership approach?

7. Why do some theorists believe that it is extremely difficult to change a leader's style?

8. What would be some indicators of a group's maturity?

9. Why is the life cycle theory intuitively appealing to practitioners?

10. Is personality an important factor in the life cycle, contingency, and path-goal theories of leadership? Explain.

ADDITIONAL REFERENCES

Argyris, C. "Leadership, Learning, and Changing the Status Quo." *Organizational Dynamics* (1976), pp. 29–43.

Bartol, K. M. "Male versus Female Leaders: The Effect of Leader Need for Dominance on Follower Satisfaction." *Academy of Management Journal* (1974), pp. 225–33.

Fox, W. M. "Limits to the Use of Consultative-Participative Management." *California Management Review* (1977), pp. 17–22.

Heller, F. A. "Leadership, Decision Making and Contingency Theory." *Industrial Relations* (1973), pp. 183–99.

Jago, A. G. "A Test of Spuriousness in Descriptive Models of Participative Leader Behavior." *Journal of Applied Psychology* (1978), pp. 383–87.

Janis, I., and Mann, L. *Decision Making: A Psychological Analysis of Conflict, Choice, and Commitment.* New York: Free Press, 1977.

Kavanaugh, M. J. "Expected Supervisory Behavior, Interpersonal Trust and Environmental Preferences: Some Relationships Based on a Dyadic Model of Leadership." *Organizational Behavior and Human Performance* (1975), pp. 17–30.

Keller, R. T., and Szilagyi, A. D. "A Longitudinal Study of Leader Reward Behavior, Subordinate Expectancies, and Satisfaction." *Personnel Psychology* (1978), pp. 119–29.

Lee, J. A.   "Leader Power for Managing Change." *Academy of Management Review* (1977), pp. 73–80.

Sims, H. P. Jr., and Szilagyi, A. D.   "Leader Reward Behavior and Subordinate Satisfaction and Performance." *Organizational Behavior and Human Performance* (1975), pp. 426–38.

Yukl, G.   "Toward a Behavioral Theory of Leadership." *Organizational Behavior and Human Performance* (1971), pp. 414–40.

CASE FOR ANALYSIS

A NEW LEADERSHIP POSITION

The Dancey Electronics Company is located in a suburb of Dallas. Management forecasts indicated that the company would enjoy moderate growth during the next ten years. This growth rate would require the promotion of a number of individuals to newly created positions of general manager which would, in turn, require them to spend most of their time working with departmental managers, and less time on production, output, and cost issues.

The majority of present candidates for the three new general manager positions had been with the company for at least 15 years. They were all skilled in the production aspects of operations. Don Kelly, the vice president, felt, however, that none of the candidates had the training or overall insight into company problems to move smoothly into the general manager positions. The board of directors had decided that the three new general managers would be recruited from within Dancey despite these anticipated problems.

Dancey, in attempting to find the best candidates for the new position, hired a consulting firm, Management Analysis Corporation (MAC), to perform an internal search for qualified individuals. Through interviews, testing, and a review of company records, the consulting firm generated a list of six candidates.

One of the candidates found by MAC was Joe Morris. The analysis used to assess Joe involved the study of environmental variables and his current style of leadership. Exhibit 1 presents a profile of Joe's leadership style and various environmental factors which have some impact on this style.

Joe's present style, which is reflected as being high in task orientation

Exhibit 1
Morris Profile of Leadership

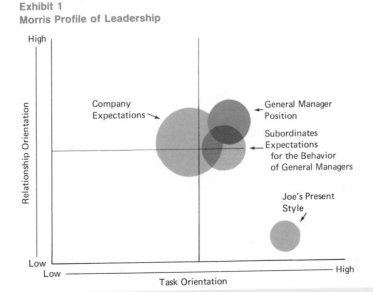

and low in relationship orientation, is similar to the style of the other five general manager candidates. The expectations of the company, the potential subordinates of the general manager, and the new position of general manager are not consistent with Joe's or any of the other candidates' present leadership styles. The shaded, intersecting area indicates where the expectations of the company, the new position, and subordinates would be consistent. This is assumed by MAC to be the ideal leadership style for candidates to use once they are promoted to the general manager position.

If Joe or any of the other candidates accepted the general manager jobs, they would have to significantly increase their relationships orientation. If they did not change their orientation there would be, according to the consulting firm, a high probability of failure.

Don Kelly was extremely adamant about not going outside of Dancey to find three potentially successful new general managers. He and the entire board of directors wanted to utilize a recruitment-from-within policy to secure the three best general managers. It was Don's belief that a leader could modify the style of leadership he or she has used to meet new situational demands. This belief, and the internal recruitment plan, led Don to call a meeting to discuss a program to improve the compatibility between the three general managers finally selected—Joe Morris, Randy Cooper, and Gregg Shumate—and the environmental factors: the company, the subordinates, and the requirements of the new position.

Questions for Consideration

1. Do you believe the diagnosis and resulting profile prepared by the Management Analysis Corporation was a necessary step in the process of finding a potentially successful group of general managers? Explain.
2. What alternatives are available to modify the potential effectiveness of Joe Morris in the new general manager position?
3. Why will it be difficult for Joe Morris to modify his style of leadership?

EXPERIENTIAL EXERCISE

LEADERSHIP STYLE ANALYSIS

Objectives

1. To learn how to diagnose different leadership situations.
2. To learn how to apply a systematic procedure for analyzing situations.
3. To improve understanding of how to reach a decision.

Related Topics

Decision making and problem solving when given a number of facts about a situation.

Starting the Exercise

Review the "Decision Process Flowchart" in Figure 9–4. Also examine the Decision Scenario presented in Figure 9–5. The instructor will then form groups of four to five people to analyze each of the following three cases. Try to reach a group consensus on which decision style is best for the particular case. You are to select the best style based on use of the Vroom-Yetton model, available styles, and decision rules. Each case should take between 30 and 45 minutes to analyze as a group.

Case I

Setting: Corporate Headquarters
Your Position: Vice President

As marketing vice president, nonroutine requests from customers are frequently sent to your office. One such request, from a relatively new customer, was for extended terms on a large purchase ($2,500,000) involving several of your product lines. The request is for extremely favorable terms which you would not normally consider except for the high inventory level of most product lines at the present time due to the unanticipated slack period which the company has experienced over the last six months.

You realize that the request is probably a starting point for negotiations and you have proven your abilities to negotiate the most favorable arrangements in the past. As preparation for this negotiation, you have familiarized yourself with the financial situation of the customer using various investment reports you regularly receive.

Reporting to you are four sales managers, each of whom has responsibility for a single product line. They know of the order and, like you, believe that it is important to negotiate terms with minimum risks and maximum return to the company. They are likely to differ on what constitutes an acceptable level of risk. The two younger managers have developed a reputation of being "risk takers" whereas the two more senior managers are substantially more conservative.

Case II

Setting: Toy Manufacturer
Your Position: Vice President, Engineering & Design

You are a vice president in a large toy manufacturing company with responsibilities that include the design of new products that will meet the changing demand in this uncertain and very competitive industry. Your design teams, each under the supervision of a department head, are therefore under constant pressure to produce novel, marketable ideas.

At the opposite end of the manufacturing process is the Quality Control Department which is under the authority of the Vice President, Production. When Quality Control has encountered a serious problem that may be due to design features, their staff has consulted with one or more of your department heads to obtain their recommendations for any changes in the production process. In the wake of consumer concern over the safety of children's toys, however, Quality Control responsibilities have recently been expanded to insure not only the quality but the safety of your products. The first major problem in this area has arisen. A preliminary consumer report has "black listed" one of your new products without giving any specific reason or justification. This has upset you and others in the organization since it was believed that this product would be one of the most profitable items in the coming Christmas season.

The consumer group has provided your company the opportunity to respond to the report before it is made public. The head of Quality Control has therefore consulted with your design people, but you are told that they became somewhat defensive and dismissed the report as "overreactive fanatic nonsense." Your people told Quality Control that, while freak accidents are always possible, the product is certainly safe as designed. They argued that the report should simply be ignored.

Since the issue is far from routine, you have decided to give it your personal attention. Because your design teams have been intimately involved in all aspects of the development of the item, you suspect that their response is itself extreme and perhaps governed more by their emotional reaction to the report than by the facts. You are not convinced that the consumer group is totally irresponsible, and you are anxious to explore the problem in detail and recommend to Quality Control any changes that may be required from a design standpoint. The firm's image as a producer of high quality toys could suffer a serious blow if the report is made public and public confidence is lost as a result.

You will have to depend heavily on the background and experience of your design departments to help you in analyzing the problem. Even though Quality Control will be responsible for the decision to implement any changes you may ultimately recommend, your own subordinates have the background of design experience that could help set standards for what is "safe" and to suggest any design modifications that would meet these criteria.

Case III

Setting: Corporate Headquarters
Your Position: Vice President

The sales executives in your home office spend a great deal of the time visiting regional sales offices. As marketing vice president, you are concerned that the expenses incurred on these trips are excessive—especially now when the economic outlook seems bleak and general belt tightening measures are being carried out in every department.

Having recently been promoted from the ranks of your subordinates, you are keenly aware of some cost saving measures that could be introduced. You have, in fact, asked the accounting department to review a sample of past expense reports, and they have agreed with your conclusion that several highly favored travel "luxuries" could be curtailed. Your executives, for example, could restrict first-class air travel to only those occasions when economy class is unavailable, airport limousine service to hotels could be used instead of taxis where possible, etc. Even more savings could be made if your personnel carefully planned trips such that multiple purposes could be achieved where possible.

The success of any cost saving measures, however, depends on the commitment of your subordinates. You do not have the time (nor the desire) to closely review the expense reports of these executives. You suspect, though, that they do not share your concerns over the matter. Having once been in their position, you know they feel themselves deserving of travel amenities.

The problem is to determine which changes, if any, are to be made in current travel and expense account practices in the light of the new economic conditions.

Exercise Procedures

Phase I: 10–15 minutes
Individually read case and select proper decision style using Vroom-Yetton model.

Phase II: 30–45 minutes
Join group appointed by instructor and reach group consensus.

Phase III: 20 minutes
Each group spokesperson presents group's response and rationale to other groups.

These phases should be used for each of the cases.

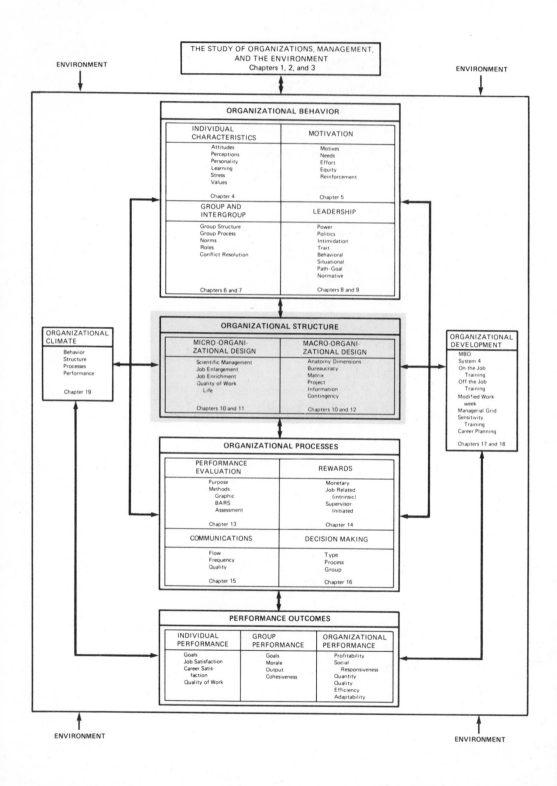

ENVIRONMENT   ENVIRONMENT

THE STUDY OF ORGANIZATIONS, MANAGEMENT,
AND THE ENVIRONMENT
Chapters 1, 2, and 3

ORGANIZATIONAL BEHAVIOR

INDIVIDUAL CHARACTERISTICS	MOTIVATION
Attitudes	Motives
Perceptions	Needs
Personality	Effort
Learning	Equity
Stress	Reinforcement
Values	
Chapter 4	Chapter 5

GROUP AND INTERGROUP	LEADERSHIP
Group Structure	Power
Group Process	Politics
Norms	Intimidation
Roles	Trait
Conflict Resolution	Behavioral
	Situational
	Path-Goal
	Normative
Chapters 6 and 7	Chapters 8 and 9

ORGANIZATIONAL CLIMATE

Behavior
Structure
Processes
Performance

Chapter 19

ORGANIZATIONAL STRUCTURE

MICRO-ORGANI-ZATIONAL DESIGN	MACRO-ORGANI-ZATIONAL DESIGN
Scientific Management	Anatomy Dimensions
Job Enlargement	Bureaucracy
Job Enrichment	Matrix
Quality of Work	Project
Life	Information
	Contingency
Chapters 10 and 11	Chapters 10 and 12

ORGANIZATIONAL DEVELOPMENT

MBO
System 4
On-the-Job
   Training
Off-the-Job
   Training
Modified Work
   week
Managerial Grid
Sensitivity
   Training
Career Planning

Chapters 17 and 18

ORGANIZATIONAL PROCESSES

PERFORMANCE EVALUATION	REWARDS
Purpose	Monetary
Methods	Job-Related
Graphic	(intrinsic)
BARS	Supervisor-
Assessment	Initiated
Chapter 13	Chapter 14

COMMUNICATIONS	DECISION MAKING
Flow	Type
Frequency	Process
Quality	Group
Chapter 15	Chapter 16

PERFORMANCE OUTCOMES

INDIVIDUAL PERFORMANCE	GROUP PERFORMANCE	ORGANIZATIONAL PERFORMANCE
Goals	Goals	Profitability
Job Satisfaction	Morale	Social
Career Satis-faction	Output	Responsiveness
Quality of Work	Cohesiveness	Quantity
		Quality
		Efficiency
		Adaptability

ENVIRONMENT   ENVIRONMENT

Part Three
Structure of Organizations

Chapter 10

The Anatomy of Organizations

AN ORGANIZATIONAL ISSUE FOR DEBATE: *The Fixed Optimal Span of Control**

ARGUMENT FOR

The argument regarding the optimal span of control has gone on for many years. The importance of the issue warrants the attention given it. The determination of the managers' spans of control, that is, how many people will report to them, has implications for the behavior of the managers, people reporting to them, and the organization itself. Some of the most influential writers on management and organizational behavior have argued that the optimal span of control is a fixed number— 5, 6, or 10 depending upon the writer.

The basis for these writers views is that the ability of managers to supervise is finite. As more and more people are added to their units, the proportionate amount of time that managers can spend on each individual decreases. Moreover the number of possible interpersonal relationships is 50 times greater for a span of 10 than for a span of 5. Thus it was apparent to writers such as Graicunas, Urwick, Gulick, and Davis that "No superior can supervise directly the work of more than five or, at the most, six subordinates whose work interlocks."

The organizational design implications of the idea that the optimal span of control is a fixed number are several. Most important is that the organization would tend to have many layers of management through which information and directives would pass. Consequently the organization would be unable to respond to environmental changes as quickly as might be appropriate. Nevertheless, the disadvantages of tall, layered organizations are outweighed, according to proponents of narrow spans, by the advantages of greater supervisory control.

ARGUMENT AGAINST

Those writers and practitioners who argue against the fixed optimal span of control take exception to two points. First they argue that wide spans of control and the resultant flat organizations foster greater employee participation and self-control. Managers having relatively wide spans of control are unable to direct closely the work of their subordinates; subordinates will therefore develop greater independence and learn to direct themselves. Moreover the flatter organization structure with fewer managerial levels will respond more quickly to environment changes because information and directives will pass through fewer levels. These outcomes—greater employee initiatives and more responsive organizations—are advantages in their own right.

A second point of debate has to do with the view of contingency organization behavior theory. According to this view, the optimal span of control varies depending upon the state of numerous other variables (contingencies). Managerial ability is one such contingency, but there are others. For example, wider spans of control are possible if subordinates' jobs are highly routine, similar, formalized, and performed in one location. In such instances the amount of supervision required tends to decline because the work, in effect, supervises itself. Thus for any given situation an optimal span of control may exist, but it cannot be represented by a specific number without examining the state of those variables which determine it.

---

* Based upon David D. VanFleet and Arthur G. Bedeian, "A History of the Span of Management" *Academy of Management Review* (July 1977) pp. 356–72.

INTRODUCTION

The behavior of individuals and groups in organizations is affected in significant ways by the *jobs* they perform. The job itself provides powerful stimuli for individual behavior. The demands on, and expectations of, individuals can result in high levels of personal satisfaction or stress, anxiety, and physiological dysfunctions.[1] People's jobs require them to perform activities in combination with other people in the organization. The activities can be routine or nonroutine; they can require high or low levels of skill; they can be perceived as challenging or as trivial. The required relationships can be with other co-workers, managers, clients, suppliers, or buyers. These relationships can result in feelings of friendship, competition, cooperativeness, and satisfaction or they can be causes of stress and anxiety. The determination of required job activities and relationships is a key managerial function and is covered in the following chapter.

The structure of an organization can be described by a number of characteristics. These characteristics not only describe the organization, but they also have implications for the behavior of individuals and groups as well as the organization itself. When the organization is the focus of attention, we are concerned with its adaptiveness, flexibility, growth, and development.[2] Managers must design jobs to achieve desirable work behavior and individual motivation and satisfaction and also design a larger structure which can respond to environmental pressures. The appropriate organization design must contain characteristics which enable it to meet and respond to economic, political, and social pressures for change and development. The design of macro-organization elements is the focus of Chapter 12.

ORGANIZATION DESIGN: CONCEPTUALIZATION OF THE PROBLEM

Organization design refers to the process by which managers create a structure of tasks and authority. The *process* is decision making through which managers evaluate the relative benefits of alternative tasks and authority structures. This process may be explicit or implicit, it may be "one-shot" or developmental, it may be done by a single manager or by a team of managers. *Structure* refers to relatively fixed relationships that exist among the jobs in the organization. The fixed relationships result from the following decision processes:

---

[1] See, for example, Lyman W. Porter and Edward E. Lawler III, "Properties of Organization Structure in Relation to Job Attitudes and Job Behavior," *Psychological Bulletin* (July 1965), pp. 23–51; John M. Ivancevich and James H. Donnelly, Jr., "Relation of Organizational Structure to Job Satisfaction, Anxiety-Stress, and Performance," *Administrative Science Quarterly* (June 1975), pp. 272–80; and Larry L. Cummings and Chris J. Berger, "Organization Structure: How Does It Influence Attitudes and Performance?" *Organizational Dynamics* (Autumn 1976) pp. 34–49.

[2] Geoffrey Hutton, *Thinking about Organizations* (London: Tavistock Publications, 1972).

1. The total task of the unit is broken down into successively smaller jobs. That is, the task is divided or specialized among the persons in the unit. This is the issue of *division of labor.*
2. The individual jobs are recombined and grouped together. A common basis for the combined job is defined to rationalize the grouping; this is the issue of *departmentalization.*
3. The appropriate size of the group reporting to one superior must be determined; this is the issue of *span of control.*
4. Authority is distributed among the jobs or groups of jobs. This is the issue of *delegation.*

The result of the process by which managers resolve these four subproblems is the structure of the organization and it can vary depending upon how each is resolved.

An organization in which there are loosely defined job descriptions, heterogeneous departments, wide spans of control, and decentralized authority differs markedly from one in which there are strictly defined jobs, homogeneous departments, narrow spans of control, and centralized authority. Consider for example only the impact of span of control. In Figure 10–1 we have a graphic comparison of two structures; each has the same total number of people to be managed, 24. In one case the maximum span of control is 12 and there are two levels of management and three managers (a president

Figure 10–1
Wide and Narrow Spans of Control

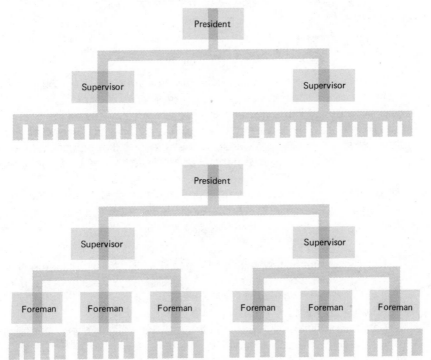

and two supervisors); in the second case, the maximum span of control is 4 and there are three levels of management and nine managers (a president, two supervisors, and six foremen).

The form and characteristics of an organizational structure vary depending upon the attributes of each of the four subproblems. Conceptually, each of the four can vary along a continuum as shown:

Division of Labor:

	Specialization	
High		Low

Departmentalization:

	Basis	
Homogeneous		Heterogeneous

Span of Control:

	Number	
Few		Many

Authority:

	Delegation	
Centralized		Decentralized

Generally speaking, organizational structures will tend toward one extreme or the other along each continuum. Structures tending to the left are characterized by a number of terms including formalistic, structured, bureaucratic, System 1, and mechanistic. Structures tending to the right are termed informalistic, unstructured, nonbureaucratic, System 4, and organic. These terms are in no way precise or universally understood; this imprecision provides evidence of the relative immaturity of the state of knowledge about organization design.

DIVISION OF LABOR

The issues associated with division of labor are concerned with the extent to which jobs are specialized. All jobs are specialized to a degree and the ability to divide work among many job holders is a key advantage of organizations. Rather than having a bookkeeper in a hospital performing emergency room tasks, the work is divided so that the bookkeeper concentrates on preparing bills and the emergency room clerk concentrates on admitting patients.

A major decision in developing an organizational structure is determining how much division of labor should exist. Advocates of dividing work into a small number of tasks often cite the advantages of specialization. Two of the major advantages are:

1. If a job contains few tasks it is possible to train replacements easily for personnel who are terminated, transferred, or absent. The minimum training effort results in a lower training cost.
2. When a job entails only a limited number of tasks the employee can become proficient in performing these tasks. This high level of proficiency is reflected in a better quality of output.

The benefits cited above are largely economic and technical and are usually applied to nonmanagerial jobs. However, similar economic and technical benefits are applicable to specialized managerial positions.

DEPARTMENTALIZATION

The process of defining the range and depth of individual jobs is analytical; that is, the total task of the organization is broken down into successively smaller tasks. But then it becomes necessary to combine the divided tasks into groups. The resultant groups are the command and task groups as discussed in an earlier chapter. The process of combining jobs into groups is termed *departmentalization,* and the managerial problem is to select a basis for combining these jobs. Numerous bases for departmentalization exist as will be demonstrated in the following discussion.

Functional Departmentalization

Jobs can be grouped according to the functions of the organization. The business firm includes functions such as production, marketing, finance, accounting, and personnel. The hospital includes such functions as surgery, psychiatry, housekeeping, pharmacy, and personnel.

The Oldsmobile Division of General Motors is structured on a functional basis. The functions are engineering, production, manufacturing, reliability, distribution, finance, and personnel as shown in Figure 10–2. The organizational structure of U.S. Ireland Army Hospital also illustrates a functional arrangement. Figure 10–3 presents the various departments and divisions in the hospital.

The functional basis is probably the most widely utilized scheme because of its commonsense appeal. That is, it seems logical to have a department which consists of experts in a particular field such as production or accounting. By having departments of specialists, management creates, theoretically, the most efficient unit possible. An accountant is generally more comfortable working with accountants and other individuals who have similar backgrounds and interests.

A major disadvantage of the departmental arrangement is that because specialists are working with and encouraging each other in their area of expertise and interest, the organizational goals may be sacrificed in favor of departmental goals. Accountants may see only their problems and not those of production or marketing or the total organization. In other words, the culture of, and identification with, the department are often stronger than identification with the organization and its culture.

Territorial Departmentalization

Another commonly adopted method for departmentalizing is to establish groups on the basis of geographical areas. The logic is that all activities in

Figure 10–2
General Motors Corporation (Oldsmobile Division, Car and Truck Group)

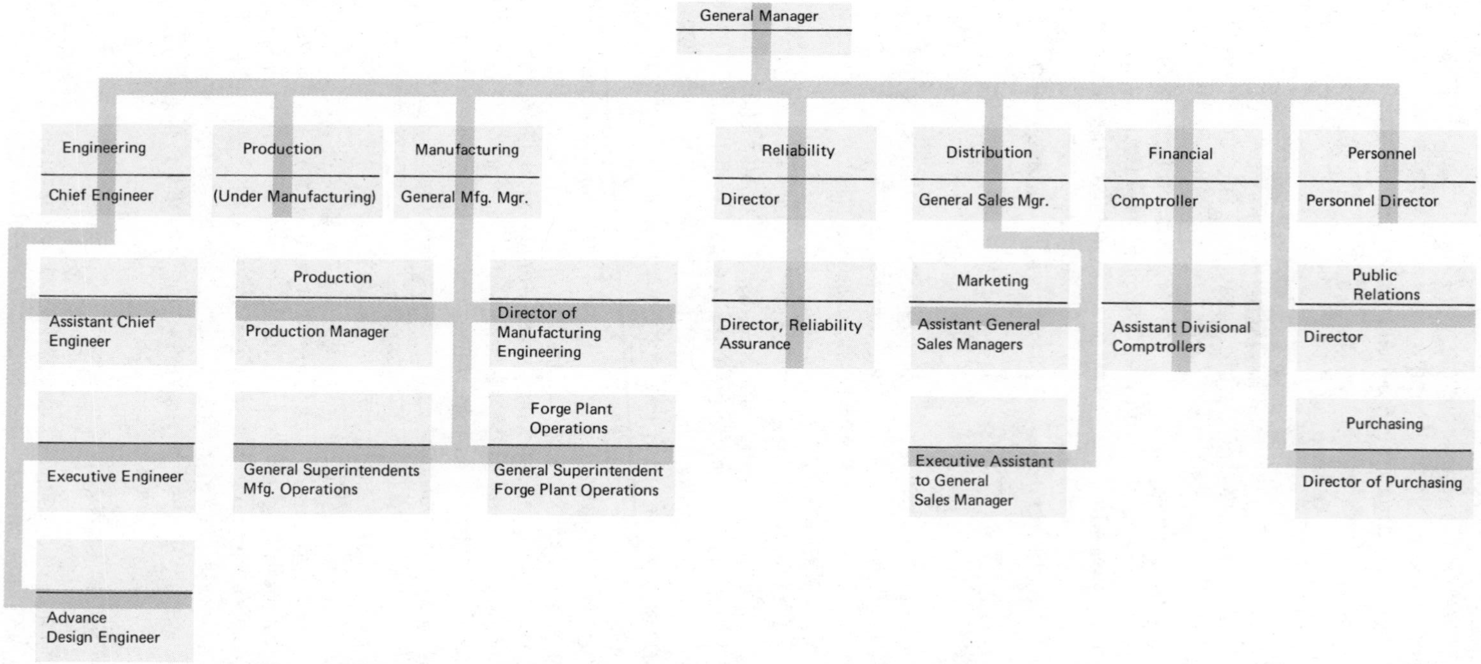

Source: Reproduced from *Corporate Organization Structures*, National Industrial Conference Board, Inc., no. 210 (1968), p. 67.

Figure 10–3
Organizational Structure for U.S. Ireland Army Hospital

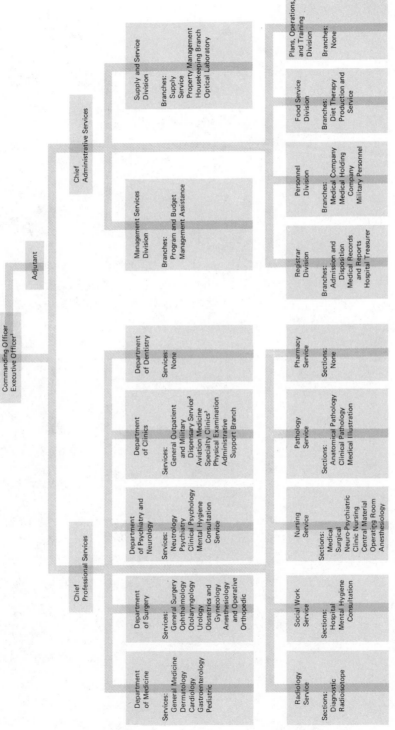

1. Also serves as Chief, Administrative Services.
2. Includes U.S. Army Dispensaries at DCSC and Lex-BG Depot.
3. Provides logistical and administrative support to Specialty Clinics.

Figure 10–4
R. H. Macy & Co., Inc.

Board of Directors

Vice Chairman

Executive Committee

President

Personnel and Industrial Relations	Operations and Expense Standards	Merchandise Research and Development	Corporate Buying	Corporate Control	Planning and Development	Engineering and Construction	Secretary and General Attorney
Vice President	Vice President	Vice President	Vice President	Vice President	Vice President	Vice President	

Treasurer

DEPARTMENT STORE DIVISIONS

Macy's New York	Bamberger's N.J.	Davison-Paxon Co.	LaSalle & Koch Co.	Macy's California	Macy's Missouri-Kansas
President	President	President	President	President	President
HERALD SQUARE, N.Y.	NEWARK, N.J.	ATLANTA, GA.	TOLEDO, OHIO	SAN FRANCISCO, CAL.	KANSAS CITY, MO.
Parkchester, N.Y.	Morristown, N.J.	Augusta, Ga.	Bowling Green, Ohio	Richmond, Cal.	Joplin, Mo.
Jamaica, N.Y.	Plainfield, N.J.	Macon, Ga.	Tiffin, Ohio	San Rafael, Cal.	Wichita, Kan.
Flatbush, N.Y.	Princeton, N.J.	Columbus, Ga.	Sandusky, Ohio	Hillsdale	Mission, Kan.
White Plains, N.Y.	Paramus, N.J.	Athens, Ga.	Findlay, Ohio	(San Mateo), Cal.	The Landing
Roosevelt Field, N.Y.	Menlo Park, N.J.	Sea Island, Ga.	Westgate	Valley Fair	(Kansas City), Mo.
Huntington, N.Y.	Monmouth, N.J.	Lenox Square	(Toledo), Ohio	(San Jose), Cal.	Red Bridge
Bay Shore, N.Y.	Cherry Hill, N.J.	(Atlanta), Ga.		Bay Fair	(Kansas City), Mo.
New Haven, Conn.	*Willowbrook, N.J.	Columbia, S.C.		(San Leandro), Cal.	Antioch
Queens, N.Y.		Cross Country		Stanford, Cal.	(Kansas City), Mo.
Colonie (Albany), N.Y.		(Columbus), Ga.		Sacramento, Cal.	Topeka, Kan.
*New Rochelle, N.Y.		Columbia Mall		Stockton, Cal.	
		(Atlanta), Ga.		*Concord, Cal.	

* Under construction.
Source: Reproduced from *Corporate Organization Structures*, National Industrial Conference Board, Inc., no. 210 (1968), p. 101.

a given area or region should be assigned to a manager. This individual would be in charge of all operations in that particular geographical area.

In large organizations territorial arrangements are attractive because physical dispersion of activities makes centralized coordination difficult. For example, it is extremely difficult for someone in New York to develop routes for salespersons in Kansas City. An example of a territorial structure is presented in Figure 10–4, which illustrates the organization chart of R. H. Macy & Co., Inc.

An advantage often associated with territorial departmentalization is that it provides a training ground for managerial personnel. The company is able to place managers in territories and then assess their programs and progress in that geographical region. The experience which managers acquire in a territory away from headquarters provides valuable insights about how products and/or services are accepted in the field.

Product Departmentalization

In many large diversified companies activities and personnel are grouped on the basis of product. As a firm grows it is difficult to coordinate the various functional departments and it becomes advantageous to establish product units. This form of organization allows personnel to develop total expertise in researching, manufacturing, and distributing a product line. Concentration of the authority, responsibility, and accountability in a specific product department allows top management to coordinate actions. The need for coordination of production, engineering, sales, and service cannot be overestimated.

The Consumer Products Division of Kimberly-Clark specifies a product arrangement. The specific product groups shown in Figure 10–5 include feminine hygiene, household, and commercial products. Within each of these units we find production and marketing personnel. Since product managers coordinate sales, manufacturing, and distribution of a product, they become the overseers of a profit center. This is the manner in which profit responsibility is exacted from product organizational arrangements. Managers are often asked to establish profit goals at the beginning of a time period and then to compare actual profit with planned profit. This is the approach used in the Buick, Cadillac, Chevrolet, Pontiac, and Oldsmobile divisions of General Motors.

Customer Departmentalization

Examples of customer-oriented departments are the organizational structures of educational institutions. Some institutions have regular (day and night) courses and extension courses. In some instances a professor will be affiliated solely with the regular students or extension students. In fact, the title of some faculty positions often specifically mentions the extension division.

Another form of customer departmentalization is the loan department in a commercial bank. Loan officers are often associated with industrial, com-

Figure 10–5
Kimberly-Clark Corporation (Consumer Products Division)

Vice President and General Manager Consumer Products Division

Director of Personnel
- Mgr., Management Dev.
- Mgr., Comp. & Pers. Serv.
- Personnel Mgr.

Director of Marketing Staff Services
- Mgr., Art & Design
- Mgr., Media Pl. & Coord.
- Mgr., Prod. & Distr.
- Education Director

Director of Marketing Research
- Mgr., Behavioral & Adv. Res.
- Mgr., Exp. Mktg. & Sales Res.

Director of Distribution and Planning
- Mgr., Prod. Pl.
- Mgr., Distr. Serv.
- Proj. Mgr., Distr. Analysis
- Mgr., Pkg. Spec.

Director of Quality Assurance
- Mgr., Qual. Serv. H.P.
- Mgr., Qual. Serv. F.H.P.
- Mgr., Qual. Serv. C.P.
- Consumer Repres.

Comptroller
- Mgr., Systems Dev.
- Mgr., Order & Stat. Serv.
- Mgr., Acctg. Serv.
- Mgr., Fin. Anal. & Cont.
- Credit Mgr.

Division Vice President and General Sales Manager
- Mgr., Inst. of Mktg.
- Mgr., Gov't Sales
- Mgr., Customer Serv.
- Mgr., Field Sales Serv.
- Regional Gen'l Sales Mgrs.
  - Division Sales Mgrs.
    - District Sales Mgrs.
      - Salespersons

Division Vice President and General Manager Feminine Hygiene Products
- Prod. Mgr., Fem. Hyg. Products
  - Asst. Prod. Mgr., Fem. Hyg. Prod.
- Mgr., New Prod. Dev.
- Dir., Fem. Hyg. Prod. Mfg.
- Mgr., Sales Promotion

Division Vice President and General Manager Household Products
- Prod. Mgr., Facial & Bath. Tissues
  - Project Mgr.
- Prod. Mgr., Towels & Napkins
  - Project Mgr.
- Mgr., New Product Dev.
- Dir., Household Prod. Mfg.
- Mktg. Res. Coord.
- Mgr., Sales Promotion
- Prod. Mgr., Housewares

Division Vice President and General Manager Commercial Products
- Marketing Mgr.
  - Mkt. Mgr., Mfg. & Process Mkts.
  - Mkt. Mgr., Indust. Mkts.
  - Mkt. Mgr., Comm. Mkts.
  - Mkt. Mgr., Prof. Mkts.
  - Project Mgr.
- Mgr., New Prod. Dev.
  - Project Mgr.
- Mgr., Comm. Mktg. Res.
  - Mktg. Res. Analyst
  - Mktg. Res. Analyst
- Dir., Comm. Prod. Mfg.
- National Sales Mgr.
  - Merchandising Mgr.
    - Supv. Adm. & Cust. Serv.
  - Mgr., Sales Dev.
  - Mgr., Comm. Dev.
  - Dir., Federal Serv.
  - Mgr., Hospital Sales
  - Regional Gen'l Sales Mgrs.

Vice President Manufacturing
- Neenah & Atlas Mills Gen'l Mgr.
  - Atlas Mill Mgr.
- Berkeley Mill Mgr.
- Fullerton Mill Mgr.
- Memphis Mill Mgr.
- New Milford Mill Mgr.
- Niagara Falls Mills Gen'l Mgr.
  - No. 2 Mill Mgr.
- Beech Island Plans Mgr.
- Project Specialist

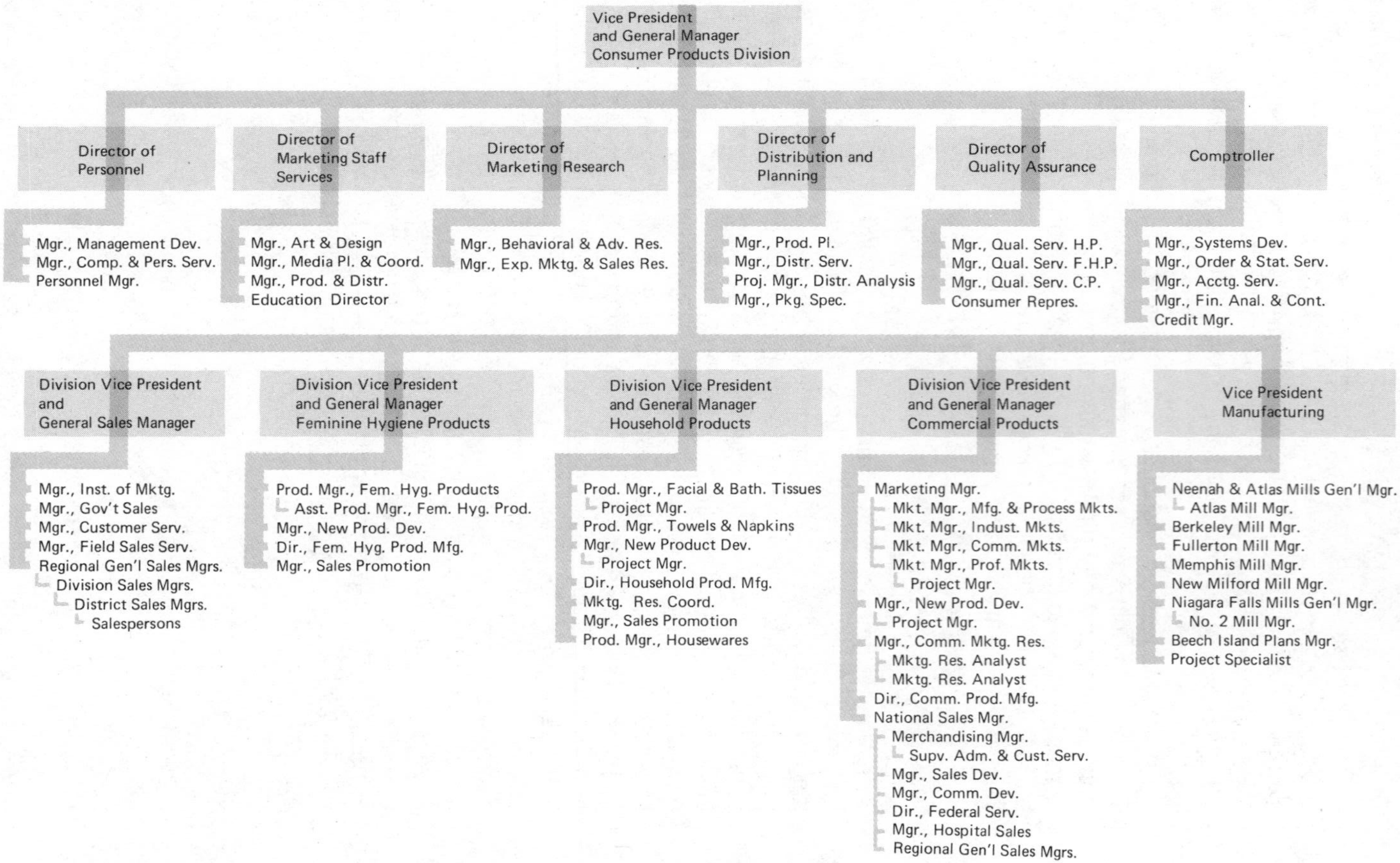

Source: Reproduced from *Corporate Organization Structures*, National Industrial Conference Board, Inc., no. 210 (1968), p. 90.

mercial, or agricultural loans. The customer will be served by one of these three broad categories.

Some department stores are departmentalized to some degree on a customer basis. They have groupings such as university shops, men's clothing, and boys' clothing. They have bargain floors that carry a lower quality of university, men's, and boys' clothing.

Mixed Departmentalization: Divisional Organization

An evaluation of the various forms of departmentalization suggests that each basis has its strengths and weaknesses. There is an increased desire to experiment with multiple or mixed bases within the same organization. The mixed strategies have emerged because managers are attempting to cope with growth, shifts in markets, proliferation of products and services, and government regulations. Organizations such as E. I. DuPont have struc-

Figure 10–6
Organization Chart of Textile Fibers Department

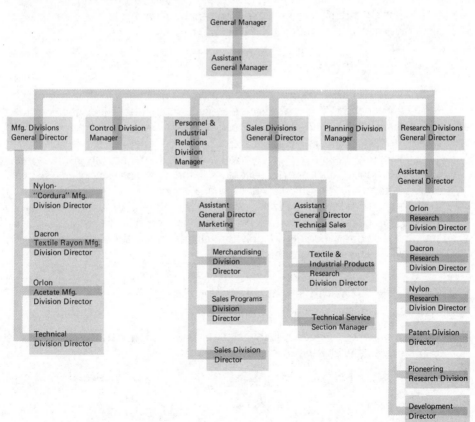

Source: Reproduced from E. Raymond Corey and Steven H. Star, *Organization Strategy: A Marketing Approach* (Boston: Division of Research, Harvard Business School, 1971), p. 194.

tured various divisions so that a number of departmental arrangements can be utilized.

At one time, the Textile Fibers Department of E. I. DuPont included five divisions, one for each of the five fibers the department made and sold. Each division, under a Division Manager, had a Sales Department and a Manufacturing Department. A centralized Research Division also existed.

Later, the five divisions were combined so that there was just one Sales Division, one Manufacturing Division, and one Research Division (functional grouping). Each of these departments was organized, however, along product lines. In the Sales Division there continued to be individual sales representatives for each fiber.

Eventually the structure was changed again and a Merchandising Division was added. There were six groups in the unit: men's wear, women's wear, home furnishings, industrial merchandising, advertising and promotion, and marketing research. The change reflects an interest in customer demands and is a form of customer departmentalization. Figure 10–6 shows the organization chart of the Textile Fibers Department after the changes.

The Sales Divisions of the Textile Fibers Department are shown in Figure 10–7. In this chart the various bases for departmentalization (functional, product, customer, and territorial) are illustrated.

SPAN OF CONTROL

The determination of appropriate bases for departmentalization establishes the *kinds* of jobs that will be grouped together. But that determination does not establish the *number* of jobs to be included in a specific group. That determination is the issue of *span of control*. Generally the issue comes down to the decision of how many people a manager can oversee; i.e., will the organization be more effective if the span of control is relatively wide or narrow? The question is basically concerned with determining the volume of interpersonal activities that the department's manager is able to handle. Moreover, as recent research has pointed out, the span of control must be defined to include not only formally assigned subordinates, but also those who have access to the manager.[3]

Potential Relationships between Manager and Subordinates

The number of *potential* relationships between a manager and subordinates can be calculated by the formula:

$$R = N\frac{2n}{2} + N - 1$$

---

[3] William G. Ouchi and John B. Dowling, "Defining the Span of Control," *Administrative Science Quarterly* (September 1974), pp. 357–65.

Figure 10–7
Organization Chart of Sales Divisions of Textile Fibers Department

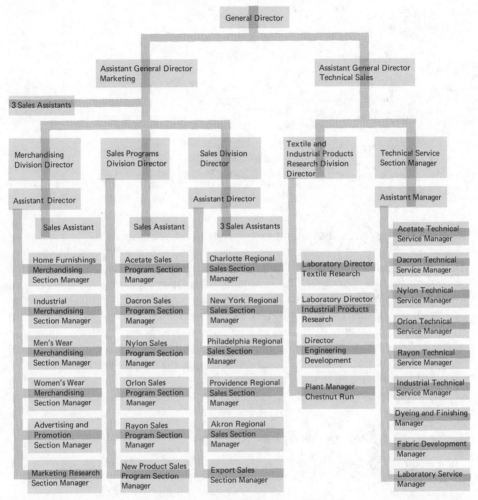

Source: Reproduced from E. Raymond Corey and Steven H. Star, *Organization Strategy: A Marketing Approach* (Boston: Division of Research, Harvard Business School, 1971), p. 196.

where R designates the number of relationships and N is the number of subordinates assigned to the manager's command group.[4] The relationship between R and N as calculated by the formula is shown in Table 10–1. Clearly the number of relationships, R, increases geometrically as the number of subordinates, N, increase arithmetically.

The calculation assumes that the managers must contend with three types of relationships: (1) direct single, (2) direct group, and (3) cross. Direct single

---

[4] A. V. Graicunas, "Relationships in Organization," in Luther Gulick and Lyndall F. Urwick, eds., *Papers on the Science of Administration* (New York: Columbia University, 1947), pp. 183–87.

Table 10–1
Potential Relationships

Number of Subordinates	Number of Relationships
1	1
2	6
3	18
4	44
5	100
6	222
7	490
8	1,080
9	2,376
10	5,210
11	11,374
12	24,708
18	2,359,602

relationships occur between the manager and each subordinate individually. Direct group relations occur between the manager and each possible permutation of subordinates. Finally, cross relationships occur when subordinates interact with one another. These potential relationships are illustrated in Figure 10–8 for a manager (M) and two subordinates (A and B) and three subordinates (A, B, and C). Direct group relationships differ depending upon which subordinate assumes the leadership role in interaction with the manager. And depending upon the issue to be discussed or the problem to be solved, we would expect different group members to emerge as leader.

At the same time that we note the number of *potential* interactions between a manager and subordinates, we must recognize that the crucial questions

Figure 10–8
Potential Relationships among a Manager and Two/Three Subordinates

Manager (M) and Two Subordinates (A and B)			Manager (M) and Three Subordinates (A, B, and C)		
Direct single	1.	M → A	Direct single	1.	M → A
	2.	M → B		2.	M → B
				3.	M → C
Direct group	3.	M → A with B	Direct group	4.	M → A with B
	4.	M → B with A		5.	M → A with C
				6.	M → B with A
				7.	M → B with C
				8.	M → C with A
				9.	M → C with B
				10.	M → A with B and C
				11.	M → B with A and C
				12.	M → C with A and B
Cross	5.	A → B	Cross	13.	A → B
	6.	B → A		14.	A → C
				15.	B → A
				16.	B → C
				17.	C → A
				18.	C → B

concern frequency and intensity. Not all interactions will occur, and those which do will vary in importance. At least three factors appear to be important in analyzing the span of control issue.

Required Contact. In research and development, medical, and production work there is a need for frequent contact and a high degree of coordination between a superior and subordinates. The use of conferences and other forms of consultation often aids in the attainment of goals within a constrained time period. For example, the research and development team leader may have to consult frequently with team members so that a project is completed within a time period that will allow the organization to place a product on the market. Thus, instead of relying upon memos and reports, it is in the best interest of the organization to have as many in-depth contacts with the team as possible. A large span of control would preclude contacting subordinates so frequently and this could have detrimental effects on completing the project.

Level of Subordinate Education and Training. The training of employees is a critical consideration in establishing the span of control at all levels of management. It is generally accepted that a manager at the lower organizational level can oversee more subordinates because work at the lower level is more specialized and less complicated than at higher levels of management.

Ability to Communicate. Instructions, guidelines, and policies must be communicated verbally to subordinates in most work situations. The need to discuss job-related factors influences the span of control. The individual who can clearly and concisely communicate with subordinates is able to manage more people than one who cannot do so.

One Approach to Determining the Optimal Span

The practical solution to the span of control problem is to identify the specific factors which are important in a particular situation. One such solution was undertaken at Lockheed Missiles and Space Company where a model for determining the optimal span was devised.[5] After carefully considering and observing the work flow and job requirements at Lockheed, the developers of the model concluded that the following variables must be considered in establishing spans of control:

1. Similarity of functions.
2. Geographic closeness of subordinates.
3. Complexity of functions.
4. Direction and control required by subordinates.
5. Coordination required.
6. Planning importance, complexity, and time required.
7. Organizational assistance received by supervisor.

Each of these variables was assigned weights. The weightings reflect the importance of each of the variables and are summarized in Table 10–2.

---

[5] Harold Stieglitz, "Optimizing Span of Control," *Management Record* (September 1962), pp. 25–29.

Table 10–2
Lockheed Weighting Scales

Span Factor

Similarity of functions	Identical	Essentially alike	Similar	Inherently different	Fundamentally distinct
	1	2	3	4	5
Geographic contiguity	All together	All in one building	Separate building, 1 plant location	Separate locations, 1 geographic area	Dispersed geographic areas
	1	2	3	4	5
Complexity of functions	Simple, repetitive	Routine	Some complexity	Complex, varied	Highly complex, varied
	2	4	6	8	10
Direction and control	Minimum supervision and training	Limited supervision	Moderate periodic supervision	Frequent continuing supervision	Constant close supervision
	3	6	9	12	15
Coordination	Minimum relation with others	Relationships limited to defined courses	Moderate relationships easily controlled	Considerable close relationships	Extensive mutual nonrecurring relationships
	2	4	6	8	10
Planning	Minimum scope and complexity	Limited scope and complexity	Moderate scope and complexity	Considerable effort required guided only by broad policies	Extensive effort required; areas and policies not chartered
	2	4	6	8	10

Source: Adapted from Harold Stieglitz, "Optimizing Span of Control," *Management Record* (September 1962), p. 27.

The most important variable is direction and control with a maximum weight of 15. This factor reflects the time necessary for directing and controlling the units within the organization. The weight values were based on common sense, experience, and experimentation with 150 different situations in Lockheed.

Every management position was evaluated, and point values for each of the variables were assigned. The point values were summed and the resultant figure was termed the "supervisory index." This index reflects the supervisor's burden arising from the type of work of the unit. The higher the index the greater the burden and consequently the narrower the appropriate span. Suggested spans of control were developed for middle-management positions and are shown in Table 10–3.

The Lockheed study revealed that when the span of control was increased, the number of supervisory levels was often reduced. For example, in one instance the average span of control was increased from 3.0 to 4.8 subordinates and the levels of management were reduced from 6 to 5.

Table 10–3
Middle-Management Indexes and Suggested
Spans of Control

Supervisory Index	Suggested Standard Span
40–42	4–5
37–39	4–6
34–36	4–7
31–33	5–8
28–30	6–9
25–27	7–10
22–24	8–11

Source: Adapted from Harold Stieglitz, "Optimizing Span of Control," *Management Record* (September 1962), p. 29.

The Lockheed model is a systematic device to use when studying span of control. It focuses attention upon important organization variables which significantly effect the span of control.

DELEGATION OF AUTHORITY

The final issue which managers must consider when designing an organizational structure is that of delegation of authority. In practical terms the issue concerns the relative benefits of decentralization, i.e., delegation of authority to the lowest possible level in the managerial hierarchy. The concept of decentralization does not refer to geographic dispersion of the organization's separate units; rather it refers to the delegated right of managers to make decisions without approval by higher management. In some respects the concept is related to the influence which an individual has by virtue of personal characteristics. In the context of Fiedler's theory of leadership, delegated authority is *position power*. Let us evaluate some of the arguments for decentralization and then describe it in one organization.

The Advantages of Decentralized Authority

There is no universal agreement in the management and organizational behavior literature about why it is better to decentralize authority. The following arguments are only partially agreed upon by many different scholars analyzing the decentralization approach. They may or may not be correct, depending upon such factors as the size of the firm, the desire for autonomy among employees, the availability of competent managers, government regulations, and other important factors.

First, some scholars assume that decentralization encourages the development of professional managers. The point is that as decision-making authority is pushed down in the organization, managers must adapt and prove themselves if they are to advance in the company. That is, they must become generalists who know something about the numerous job-related factors they must cope with in the decentralized arrangement.

Because managers in a decentralized structure often have to adapt and deal with difficult decisions, they are trained for promotion into positions of greater authority and responsibility. Managers can be readily compared with their peers on the basis of actual decision-making performance. In effect, the decentralized arrangement can lead to a more equitable performance appraisal program. This can lead to a more satisfied group of managers because they perceive themselves as being evaluated on the basis of results, not personalities. It should be remembered, however, that developing specific performance criteria for most managers is an extremely difficult task.

Second, the decentralized arrangement leads to a competitive climate within the organization. The managers are motivated to contribute in this competitive atmosphere since they are compared with their peers on various performance measures.

Finally, in the decentralized pattern managers are able to exercise more autonomy, and this satisfies the desire to participate in problem solving. This freedom is assumed to lead to managerial creativity and ingenuity which contribute to the adaptiveness and development of the organization and managers.

These are only three of the advantages associated with decentralization. These advantages are not free of costs. Certainly, most advocates of decentralization are aware that certain costs may have to be incurred if an organization shifts from a centralized to a decentralized design. Some of the costs are:

1. Managers must be trained to handle decision making and this may require expensive formal training programs.
2. Since many managers have worked in centralized organizations, it is very uncomfortable for them to delegate authority in a more decentralized arrangement. These old attitudes are difficult to alter and often lead to resistance.
3. To alter accounting and performance appraisal systems so they are compatible with the decentralized arrangement is costly. Administrative costs are incurred because new or altered accounting and performance systems must be tested, implemented, and evaluated.

These are, of course, only some of the costs of decentralizing. Like most issues there is definitely no clear-cut answer about whether decentralization is better for an organization. It would appear that considering each organizational factor (for example, manpower, size, and control mechanisms) thoroughly is a prerequisite for reaching decisions concerning decentralization.

Decentralization at General Electric

Most organizations are decentralized to some degree. One company which has decentralized on a large scale is General Electric (GE). Presently, GE

Figure 10-9
General Electric Company

CURRENT ASSIGNMENTS OF PRIMARY COGNIZANCE

President – Industrial Group; Corporate Planning; Management Manpower Development

Chairman – Power Transmission and Distribution Group; Accounting; Legal; Marketing and Public Relations; Treasury

Executive Vice President – Appliance and Television Group; Construction Industries Group; Power Generation Group; Personnel and Industrial Relations

Executive Vice President – Aircraft Engine Group; Information Systems Group; Engineering; Research

Executive Vice President – Aerospace Group; Components and Materials Group; Consumer Products Group; Manufacturing

VICE PRESIDENTS OF OVERALL CORPORATE FUNCTIONAL COMPONENTS

Comptroller
Corporate Planning
Engineering
Legal
Management Manpower Development
Manufacturing
Marketing and Public Relations
Personnel and Industrial Relations
Research and Development
Treasury

PRESIDENT'S OFFICE

President and Chief Executive Officer
Chairman of the Board

Executive Vice President
Executive Vice President
Executive Vice President

AEROSPACE GROUP	AIRCRAFT ENGINE GROUP	APPLIANCE AND TELEVISION GROUP	COMPONENTS AND MATERIALS GROUP	CONSTRUCTION INDUSTRIES GROUP	CONSUMER PRODUCTS GROUP	INDUSTRIAL GROUP	INFORMATION SYSTEMS GROUP	POWER GENERATION GROUP	POWER TRANSMISSION AND DISTRIBUTION GROUP
Vice President Group Executive	Vice President Group Executive	Vice President Group Executive	Vice President Group Executive	Vice President Group Executive	Vice President Group Executive	Vice President Group Executive	Vice President Group Executive	Vice President Group Executive	Vice President Group Executive
Aircraft Equipment Division	Aircraft Engine Operating Division	Appliance and Television Sales Division	Appliance Components Division	Community Development Division	Consumer Electronics Division	Industrial Drives Division	Advanced Development and Resources Planning Division	IGE Export Division	Power Distribution Division
Defense Programs Division	Aircraft Engine Support and Service Division	Distribution Finance and Service Division	Chemical and Medical Products Division	Construction Materials Division	Housewares Division	Industrial Process Control Division	Information Services Division	Industrial and Marine Power Generation Division	Power Protection and Conversion Division
Electronic Systems Division	Aircraft Engine Technical Division	Kitchen Appliance and Home Laundry Division	Electronic Components Division	Contractor Equipment Division	Lamp Division	Industrial Sales Division	Information Systems Equipment Division	Large Steam Turbine Generator Division	Power Transmission Division
Missile and Space Division	Commercial Engine Division	Overseas Appliance and Television Operations	Industry Components and Metallurgical Division	General Electric Supply Company Division	Area Division— Latin America	Transportation Systems Division	International Information Systems Division	Nuclear Energy Division	Power Transmission and Distribution Sales Division
	Military Engine Division	Refrigeration and Air Conditioning Division		Area Division— Far East	General Electric Credit Corporation	Area Division— Europe		Power Generation Sales Division	
		Television Division		Canadian General Electric Co., Ltd.					

Source: Reproduced from *Corporate Organization Structures*, National Industrial Conference Board, Inc., no. 210 (1968), p. 59.

is organized into more than 100 operating product departments. Ralph Cordiner, former president of GE, believed that because of the diversity of the company's product mix it would be necessary to decentralize operations. His plan required the fragmentation of the firm into separate operating departments, each with a high degree of decision-making autonomy that was free from close centralized control.

The operating department managers were given autonomy to make decisions on matters affecting the products of their departments. Thus, the managers had decision-making authority, and they were held accountable for the profit and/or loss of their operating units. The departments were in effect self-contained, relatively autonomous small companies within a major company framework.

An example of the decentralized nature of GE operations is illustrated in Figure 10–9. The manager of each of the product departments within a division has the authority to make decisions concerning the design, manufacturing, pricing, and marketing of the unit's products.

The nature and scope of General Electric's decentralization philosophy was stated by Mr. Cordiner in the following manner:

> . . . General Electric's products are engineered, manufactured, and marketed by nearly a hundred decentralized Operating Departments, each of them bearing full responsibility and authority for the Company's success and profitability in a particular product or service. . . . To demonstrate that the responsibility, authority, and accountability of these Operating Departments is real, not window dressing, consider their pricing authority. The price of a product can be raised or lowered by the managers of the Department producing it, with only voluntary responsibility on their part to give sensible consideration to the impact of such price changes on other company products.[6]

Mr. Cordiner's statement summarizes the issues and problems associated with delegation of authority. It notes that GE managers bear "full responsibility and authority" for the success of a product or service, but that they are expected to consider voluntarily the impact of their decisions on other company products. The dilemma between delegation of authority to subunit managers and overall organizational well-being is real; whenever top management delegates authority, it runs the risk of losing control. That risk is minimized to the extent that subordinate managers are committed to the organization's missions.

MATRIX ORGANIZATION DESIGN

An emerging organization design, termed *matrix organization,* attempts to maximize the strengths and minimize the weaknesses of both the functional and product structures.[7] Companies such as American Cyanamid, Avco, Car-

---

[6] Ralph J. Cordiner, *The New Frontiers for Professional Managers* (New York: McGraw-Hill Book Co. 1956), pp. 58–60.

[7] Robert Youker, "Organization Alternatives for Project Managers," *Management Review* (November 1977), p. 48.

borundum, Caterpillar Tractor, Hughes Aircraft, ITT, Monsanto Chemical, National Cash Register, Prudential Insurance, TRW, and Texas Instruments are only a few of the users of matrix organization. Public sector users include public health and social service agencies.[8] Although the exact meaning of matrix organization is not well established, the most typical meaning sees it as a balanced compromise between functional and product organization, between departmentalization by process and by purpose.[9]

The matrix organization form achieves the desired balance by superimposing, or overlaying, a horizontal structure of authority, influence, and communication. The arrangement can be described as in Figure 10–10; personnel

Figure 10–10
Matrix Organizations

Projects, Products	Functions			
	Manufacturing	Marketing	Engineering	Finance
Project or Product A				
Project or Product B				
Project or Product C				
Project or Product D				
Project or Product E				

assigned in each cell belong not only to the functional department, but also to a particular product or project. For example, manufacturing, marketing, engineering, and finance specialists will be assigned to work on one or more of projects or products A, B, C, D, and E. As a consequence, personnel will report to two managers, one in their functional department and one in the project or product unit. The existence of a *dual authority* system is a distinguishing characteristic of matrix organization. Traditional functional and product-based organizations maintain a strict chain-of-command wherein each employee reports to only one superior.

Matrix structures are found in organizations which require responses to rapid change in two sectors, such as technology and markets; which face uncertainties that generate high information processing requirements; and which must deal with financial and human resources constraints.[10] Managers confronting these circumstances must obtain certain advantages which are most likely to be realized with matrix organization.[11]

---

[8] Kenneth Knight, "Matrix Organization: A Review," *Journal of Management Studies* (May 1976), p. 111.

[9] Ibid. p. 114.

[10] Paul R. Lawrence, Harvey F. Kolodny, and Stanley M. Davis, "The Human Side of the Matrix," *Organizational Dynamics* (September 1977), p. 47.

[11] The following discussion is based upon Knight, *"Matrix Organization."*

Efficient Use of Resources.   Matrix organization facilitates the utilization of highly specialized staff and equipment. Each project, or product, unit can share the specialized resource with other units, rather than duplicating it to provide independent coverage for each. This advantage is particularly so when projects require less than the full-time efforts of the specialist. For example, a project may require only half a computer scientist's time. Rather than having several underutilized computer scientists assigned to each project, the organization can keep fewer of them fully utilized by shifting them from project to project.

Flexibility in Conditions of Change and Uncertainty.   Timely response to change requires information and communication channels which efficiently get the information to the right people at the right time. Matrix structures encourage constant interaction among project unit and functional department members. Information is channelled vertically and horizontally as people exchange technical knowledge. The result is quicker response to competitive conditions, technological breakthroughs, and other environmental conditions.

Technical Excellence.   Technical specialists interact with other specialists while assigned to a project. These interactions encourage cross-fertilization of ideas such as when a computer scientist must discuss the pros and cons of electronic data processing with a financial accounting expert. Each specialist must be able to listen, understand, and respond to the views of the other. At the same time specialists maintain ongoing contact with members of their own discipline because they are also members of a functional department.

Freeing Top Management for Long-Range Planning.   An initial stimulus for the development of matrix organizations is that top management increasingly becomes involved with day-to-day operations.[12] Environmental changes tend to create problems which cross functional and product departments and which cannot be resolved by the lower level managers. For example, when competitive conditions create the need to develop new products at faster than previous rates, the existing procedures become bogged down. Top management is then called upon to settle conflicts among the functional managers. Matrix organization makes it possible for top management to delegate ongoing decision making, thus providing more time for long-range planning.

Improving Motivation and Commitment.   Project and product groups are comprised of individuals with specialized knowledge. Mangement assigns to them, on the basis of their expertise, responsibility for specific aspects of the work. Consequently decision making within the group tends to be more participative and democratic than in more hierarchical settings. The opportunity to participate in key decisions fosters high levels of motivation and commitment, particularly for individuals with acknowledged professional orientations.

---

[12] Jay R. Galbraith "Matrix Organization Designs: How to Combine Functional and Project Forms," *Business Horizons* (February 1971), pp. 29–40.

Providing Opportunities for Personal Development. Members of matrix organizations are provided considerable opportunity to develop their skills and knowledge. They are placed in groups consisting of individuals representing diverse parts of the organization. They must, therefore, come to appreciate the different points of view expressed by these individuals; each group member becomes more aware of the total organization. Moreover they have opportunities to learn something of other specialties. Engineers develop knowledge of financial issues; accountants will learn about marketing. The experience broadens each specialist's knowledge not only of the organization, but of other scientific and technical disciplines.

At the present time the evidence to support the claims for these advantages is largely anecdotal. That is they rest on testimonials of participants in matrix organizations. One study of the experience with matrix organization structures concluded that they were relatively unsuccessful, but not because of defects in the structures. Rather it was due to faulty implementation resulting from managers' inability to adjust their traditional behavioral styles.[13] These managers were unable to cope with the stresses associated with dual authority and the natural conflict that arises out of such arrangements. Despite the absence of empirical studies to support the claims of matrix organization proponents, it will no doubt become more widely used in one form or another. In practice, management can select different variations on the basic theme of matrix organization.

Different Forms of Matrix Organization

Matrix organization forms can be depicted as existing in the middle of a continuum which has functional organizations at one extreme and product organizations at the other, Figure 10–11.[14] Organizations can move from

Figure 10–11
Alternative Matrix Organization Forms

| Functional | Matrix | Product |
| Organization | Organization | Organization |

functional to matrix forms or from product to matrix forms. Ordinarily the process of moving to matrix organization is evolutionary. That is, as the present structure proves incapable of dealing with rapid technological and market changes, management attempts to cope by establishing procedures and positions which are outside the normal routine.

[13] Chris Argyris, "Today's Problems with Tomorrow's Organizations," *Journal of Management Studies* (February 1967), pp. 31–55.

[14] This idea was first presented in Jay R. Galbraith, "Matrix Organization." A similar presentation is in Robert Youker, "Organization Alternatives for Project Managers."

Galbraith describes this evolutionary process as moving in successive steps from task forces to product management departments. The sequence is as follows.[15]

Task Force. When a competitor markets a new product that quickly captures the market, a rapid response is necessary. Yet in a functional organization new product development is often too time-consuming because of the necessity to coordinate the various units that must be involved. A convenient approach is to create a task force of individuals from each functional department and charge it with the responsibility to expedite the process. The task force achieves its objective and dissolves, as members return to their primary assignment.

Teams. If the product or technological breakthrough generates a family of products which move through successive stages of new and improved products, the temporary task force concept is ineffective. A typical next step is to create permanent teams which consist of representatives from each functional department. The teams meet regularly to resolve interdepartmental issues and to achieve coordination. When not involved with issues associated with new product development, the team members work on their regular assignments.

Product Managers. If the technological breakthrough persists such that new product development becomes a way of life, top management will create the roles of product managers. In a sense product managers chair the teams, but they now are permanent positions. Ordinarily they report to top management, but they have no formal authority over the team members. They must rely upon their expertise and interpersonal skill to influence the team members. Companies such as General Foods, Dupont, and IBM make considerable use of the product management concept.

Product Management Departments. The final step in the evolution to matrix organization is the creation of product management departments. Figure 10–12 depicts the organization which has a product manager reporting to top management and with subproduct managers for each product line. In some instances the subproduct managers are selected from specific functional departments and would continue to report directly to their functional managers. There is considerable diversity in the application of matrix organization, yet the essential feature is the creation of overlapping authority and the existence of dual authority.

Exactly where along the continuum an organization stops in the evolution depends upon factors in the situation. Specifically and primarily important are the rates of change in technological and product developments. The resultant uncertainty and information required to deal with the uncertainty varies. Chapter 12 reviews the important aspects of technology, environmental uncertainty, and information processing. At this point matrix organization is introduced in the discussion to illustrate an alternative organization design.

---

[15] Based on Jay R. Galbraith, "Matrix Organizations."

Figure 10–12
Fully Envolved Matrix Organization

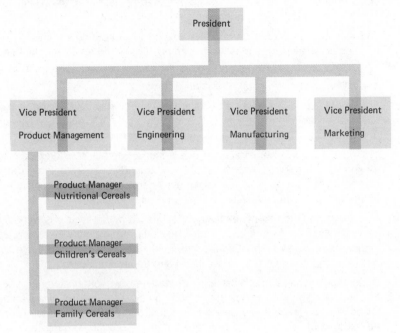

The anatomy of an organization structure results from managerial decisions. These decisions determine the degree of specialization of labor, bases for departmentalization, spans of control, delegated authority. As we have seen, the basis for each choice depends upon factors which vary from situation to situation, from organization to organization. Although many variations exist in practice, the two basic structures either departmentalize along functional and process bases or along product, customer, or territorial bases. Each design has advantages and disadvantages which managers must weigh. A design which tends to maximize the benefits of both general forms is matrix organizations. However not all organizations exist in environments which are conducive to the matrix design. In the subsequent two chapters, more specific guidelines will be developed to guide managers in making the organization design decision.

MAJOR ISSUES FOR THE MANAGER TO CONSIDER

A. The structure, or anatomy, of an organization consists of relatively fixed and stable relationships among jobs and groups of jobs. The primary purpose of organization structure is to channel the *behavior* of individuals and groups so as to achieve effective performance.

B. Four key managerial decisions determine organization structures. These decisions are defining specialization of labor, departmentalizing, determining spans of control, and delegating authority.

C. The four key decisions are interrelated and interdependent, although each has certain specific problems which can be considered apart from the others.

D. Defining the degree of specialization of labor depends initially on the technical and economic advantages of division of labor.

E. The grouping of jobs into departments requires the selection of common bases such as function, territory, product, or customer. Each basis has advantages and disadvantages which must be evaluated in terms of overall effectiveness.

F. The optimal span of control is no one specific number of subordinates. Although the number of *potential* relationships increases geometrically as the number of subordinates increases arithmetically, the important consideration is the frequency and intensity of the actual relationships.

G. The delegation of authority enables managers to make decisions without approval by higher management. Similar to other organizing issues, delegated authority is a relative, not absolute, concept. Managers by nature have some authority, the question is whether they have enough or too much.

H. In general, management must choose between two organizational types—functional or product designs. Each type has advantages and disadvantages which must be taken into account. Functional organizations tend to maximize efficiency and production performance criteria; product organizations tend to maximize adaptiveness and development criteria.

I. An emerging new design, matrix organization, tends to maximize the benefits of both functional and product organizations. Matrix organizations evolve as environmental uncertainty creates problems requiring rapid response. Through approaches such as task forces, teams, and product managers, the organization brings together resources and abilities to respond to the environmental pressure.

DISCUSSION AND REVIEW QUESTIONS

1. Describe the process of designing an organization by discussing how the manager of a retail store would analyze the four subproblems of the design decision.

2. Develop a model similar to the Lockheed Model which would enable you to analyze the spans of control of department chairpersons in the college you are attending. What would be the key variables? What would be the appropriate weights?

3. Compare functional and product departmentalization in terms of relative efficiency, production, satisfaction, adaptiveness, and development. Consider particularly the possibility that one basis may be superior in achieving one aspect of effectiveness, yet inferior in achieving another.

4. Describe and discuss the problems which matrix organization creates for subordinates who must report to both project and functional managers.

5. Discuss the statement that in order to manage effectively a person must have the authority to hire subordinates, assign them to specific jobs, and reward them on the basis of performance. Interview any chairperson of an academic department and determine whether he or she has this authority.

6. The terms "responsibility," "authority," and "accountability" appear in the management and organization literature. What is your understanding of these terms? Are they different? Do they refer to fundamental questions of organizational design?

7. How can a manager know that the organizational design is ineffective? Is there any difference between *designing* and *changing* organizational structure? Explain.

8. Explain the relationships between decentralization and divisional organizational structures. Is it possible to create divisional organizations without delegating considerable authority to divisional managers? Explain.

9. Explain the process by which a product-based organization would evolve to a matrix organization.

10. Describe managerial skills and behaviors which would be required to manage effectively in a matrix organization. Are these skills and behaviors different from those required in a traditional organization? Explain.

ADDITIONAL REFERENCES

Argyris, C. *Integrating the Individual and the Organization.* New York: John Wiley & Sons, 1964.

Blau, P. M. *On the Nature of Organizations.* New York: John Wiley & Sons, 1974.

Chandler, A. D., Jr. *Strategy and Structure.* Cambridge, Mass.: The M.I.T. Press, 1962.

Davis, L. E., and Taylor, J. C., eds. *Design of Jobs.* Middlesex, England: Penguin Books, 1972.

Etzioni, A. A. *Comparative Analysis of Complex Organizations.* Glencoe, Ill.: Free Press, 1961.

Evan, W. *Organization Theory: Structures, Systems and Environments.* New York: Wiley-Interscience, 1976.

Fisch, G. G. "Line-Staff Is Obsolete." *Harvard Business Review* (1961), pp. 67–79.

Galbraith, J. *Organization Design.* Reading, Mass.: Addison-Wesley, 1977.

Gross, E. "Universities as Organizations," in J. V. Baldridge, ed. *Academic Governance.* Berkeley, Calif.: McCutchan Publishing Corp., 1972, pp. 22–57.

Hall, R. H. *Organizations: Structure and Process.* Englewood Cliffs, N.J.: Prentice-Hall, Inc., 1977.

Hrebiniak, L. G. *Complex Organizations.* St. Paul, Minn.: West Publishing Co., 1978.

Jackson, J. H., and Morgan, C. *Organization Theory.* Englewood Cliffs, N.J.: Prentice-Hall, Inc., 1978.

Kilmann, R. H.; Pondy, L. R.; and Slevin, D. P., eds. *The Management of Organization Design: Strategies and Implementation, Volume I.* New York: Elsevier North-Holland, 1976.

Krupp, S.   *Pattern in Organization Analysis: A Critical Examination.* New York: Holt, Rinehart, & Winston, 1961.

Lawrence, P., and Lorsch, J.   *Organization and Environment.* Boston: Division of Research, Harvard Business School, 1967.

McGeer, R.   "The Organizational Structures of State and Local Correctional Services." *Public Administration Review* (November–December 1971), pp. 603–16.

Meyer, M. W.   *Theory of Organization Structure.* Indianapolis, Ind.: Bobbs-Merrill, 1977.

Urwick, L. F.   "V. A. Graicunas and the Span of Control." *Academy of Management Journal* (June 1974), pp. 349–54.

Vance, S. C.   *Managers in the Conglomerate Era.* New York: John Wiley & Sons, 1971.

CASES FOR ANALYSIS

SELECTING BETWEEN FUNCTION AND PRODUCT AS BASES FOR DEPARTMENTALIZATION

In the fall of 1978, the top management of a rapidly expanding consumer products company met to consider organizational issues. The present organization structure was departmentalized according to functions as shown in Exhibit 1.

The company's product line had expanded some 10 times during the previous 16 years, and although the current economic conditions caused some concern the management believed that its products were well established. Moreover it anticipated even greater expansion during the next 20 years.

Exhibit 1
Consumer Products Company Partial Organization Chart, September 1978

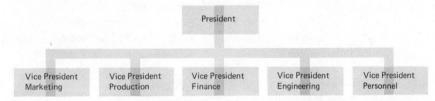

The present organization structure was the topic of discussion, because despite the growth and success of prior years management believed that in many instances the company had not been as responsive to opportunities as it might have been. Changes in consumer tastes, new manufacturing techniques, and engineering breakthroughs had not been exploited because of apparent isolation of these functions from the rest of the company. Each of the functional departments tended to emphasize its own goals and objectives; if new developments had not been included in the annually-prepared operating plan, they could not be acted upon. Top management believed that it should attempt to restructure the organization to emphasize the importance of its products.

The organizational planning staff, a part of the personnel function, was instructed to prepare an analysis of alternative structures. It returned six months later with the recommendation that the company adopt a product-based structure. The structure, often termed a "divisional" organization structure, would place under the authority of a single manager all the functions necessary to produce and sell a product or line of products. The recommended structure is shown in Exhibit 2.

Reporting to each vice president would be the heads of the marketing, production, finance, engineering, and personnel departments. These function heads would carry out the necessary work to produce and sell one or more complementary products. The organizational planning staff stated that its re-

Exhibit 2
Consumer Products Company Partial Organization Chart, Recommended

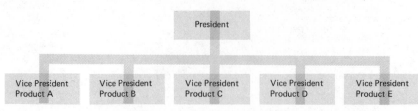

view of the literature on organizational structure indicated that product-based organizations were superior to function-based organizations in their ability to respond to external changes, but that they were somewhat less efficient. The impact on the profit and loss statement would be slightly higher unit costs because the size of the individual units would not be sufficient to take advantage of the economies of scale. It would also mean that the functional experts would have to be less specialized. For example, the marketing personnel would have to become involved in product development as well as selling. But the advantages of increased adaptability should offset the disadvantages of reduced efficiency.

The potential impact of the product-based organization on the satisfaction of employees was noted. According to the staff, the employees would suffer some decrease in satisfaction and increase of feelings of stress because they would have to orient their thinking toward the products and away from their specialties. The specialists would have to interact more often with other specialists in the integration of their functions. Consequently some of the bases for positive job satisfaction would be undermined. The staff could not predict how the reduction in satisfaction would affect turnover, absenteeism, or tardiness. They did state that employees should experience a greater sense of involvement in the total operations of the product departments.

Questions for Consideration

1. Has the organizational planning staff moved in the right direction in its analysis? Is its recommended structure appropriate given the nature of the company's environment?
2. How can management determine the relative advantages of the proposed organization if it cannot determine the relationship among the measures of effectiveness?
3. What differences in the two structures other than those identified by the staff would you expect?

PRINCIPLES OF ORGANIZATION IN AN OIL COMPANY*

A management consulting firm was engaged by the newly appointed president of an important petroleum company. The company was based in the United States with drilling and refining operations throughout the world. It had been under the direction of its founder during the 30 years of its existence, but he had retired and the new president had been appointed by the board of directors. As a first step, he had asked the consulting firm to evaluate the organization structure and management practices of the company.

The consultants spent six months gathering and analyzing facts about the company. They interviewed employees, reviewed company reports, and visited numerous offices and sites. They became aware of the former chief executive's influence on the company's management practices. His philosophy and beliefs had permeated the company and had been reflected in many different ways. And although the company had grown and prospered, the consultants were surprised to find that it had done so despite the fact that certain principles of organization were, in their opinion, flagrantly violated.

The consultants found, for example, that the company had never had an organization chart. Nowhere in the information collected by the consultants could they find documents which defined the duties and responsibilities of managers. Job descriptions were not used and there was no evidence of formal job titles. According to those who were interviewed, the former chief executive believed that formalizing the organization would result in loss of initiative because people would begin to think in jurisdictional terms. They would act on problems only if they were clearly in their bailiwick. He stressed that cooperation could achieve coordination.

Consistent with the absence of organization charts, there was also little use of other trappings of status. No names or titles appeared on doors or correspondence. Each executive was expected to know who did what in the company. There was no formal hierarchy of positions; each executive was considered equal although one or the other could assume prominence in dealing with a problem for which he had special competence. "The best man for the job at the time" was a phrase used throughout the company.

One consequence of the chief executive's philosophy was that his span of control consisted of 15 line executives. In addition, another 15 staff officers reported to him. The number of managerial levels, of course, was minimal in comparison to other companies. The consultants were particularly surprised to find such a wide span at the top of the organization. They also discovered that employees down the line received direction from numerous managers, including the chief executive himself, a clear violation of the unity of command principle. The tendency of this practice was to undermine the authority of intermediate managers, and to counteract that possibility subordinates were

---

* This case is based upon Joseph L. Massie, *Blazer and Ashland Oil: A Study in Management* (Lexington: University of Kentucky Press, 1960). The case does not reflect any actual historical event or person; it is a facsimile based upon fact.

instructed to communicate immediately with their superiors whenever they received orders from a higher level.

The consultants were convinced that the company should attempt to develop a more formal structure. The former chief executive may have been correct in thinking that undefined jobs, ambiguously delegated authority, wide spans of control and the like were appropriate during the early days of the company's growth, but that time had passed. Moreover, it was apparent that his personality and sense of commitment had been the most important forces in overcoming the "defects" of the structure. The consultants recommended that the new chief executive begin immediately to formalize the structure according to sound principles of organization.

Questions for Consideration

1. How would you account for the company's success in view of its organizational structure?

2. Do you agree with the consultants' recommendation? What additional information would you need to implement their recommendations?

3. Describe the circumstances which would be compatible with the former chief executive's philosophy of organization.

Chapter 11

Micro-Organization Design

AN ORGANIZATIONAL ISSUE FOR DEBATE

Job Redesign: Was It Successful?*

ARGUMENT FOR

General Foods Corporation opened a new pet-food plant in Topeka, Kansas in 1970. The plant was designed to minimize supervision by delegating authority to workers to make job assignments, schedule coffee breaks, interview prospective employees, and decide pay raises. The system, installed in the plant by a company task force with the assistance of Richard E. Walton, Harvard University, assigns three areas of responsibility—processing, packaging and shipping, and office duties—to self-managing teams of 7 to 14 workers.

The teams, directed by a "team leader," share responsibility for a variety of tasks including those typically performed by staff personnel, e.g., equipment maintenance and quality control. The team members rotate between dreary and meaningful jobs. Pay is related to the number of tasks each individual masters. The teams performed much of the work assigned to managerial and staff personnel. As stated by J. W. Bevans, Jr., manager of organizational development, the system attempted "to balance the needs of the people with the needs of the business."

The success of the program is unquestionable according to the former manager of pet-food operations, Layman D. Ketchum: "From the standpoint of humanistic working life and economic results, you can consider it a success." As evidence of the claim, the plants' unit costs are 5 percent less than other comparable sites, amounting to an annual saving of $1 million. Employee turnover is only 8 percent and the plant went almost 4 years before experiencing a lost-time accident.

* Based upon "Stonewalling Plant Democracy," *Business Week* (March 28, 1977), pp. 78, 81–82.

ARGUMENT AGAINST

Whether General Foods' experience with job redesign was successful depends upon who you talk to. Emphatically one employee states: "The system went to hell. It didn't work." According to the critics, problems arose because the system came up against the company's bureaucracy. Lawyers, fearing reactions from the National Labor Relations Board, opposed allowing workers to vote on pay raises. Personnel managers opposed the idea of workers making hiring decisions; engineers resented workers doing engineering work. These resentments resulted in power struggles among and between corporate level staff, plant managers, and workers. Several managers, including three from the pet-food plant itself, quit General Foods.

As a consequence of the pressures, the Topeka system began to change—workers participated less, job classifications were added, and supervisors supervised. These changes were perceived as weakening of management's commitment to the philosophy underlying the system. Quality has dipped, teams have fewer team meetings, and competition among shifts has increased. A major contribution to competition was jealousy, particularly as reflected in pay decisions. Workers found it particularly difficult to discard their subjective judgments of friends when considering their work performances. Workers at Topeka have also argued that they should share in the financial success of Topeka through the provision of bonuses tied to cost savings.

The critics observe that their negative evaluations of the Topeka system must have merit. They note as evidence, that General Foods no longer permits reporters inside the Topeka plant despite the fact that management once encouraged publicity. The critics also point out that the Topeka system has not been implemented in any other General Foods plant. One manager has predicted that "the future of that plant (Topeka) is to conform to the company norm."

271

INTRODUCTION

The building blocks of organizational structures are the jobs which people perform. Many factors determine the level of organizational performance; a major factor is the performance of its employees. Micro-organization design refers to the process by which managers create individual job tasks and responsibilities. Apart from the very practical issues associated with job design, that is, issues which relate to effectiveness in economic, political, and monetary terms, we can appreciate the importance of work in social and psychological terms. As noted in earlier chapters the jobs we hold can be sources of psychological stress and even mental and physical impairment. On a more positive note jobs provide income, meaningful life experiences, self-esteem, esteem from others, regulation of our lives, and association with others.[1] Thus, the well-being of organizations and people depend upon how well management is able to design jobs.

QUALITY OF WORK-LIFE

In recent years the issue of designing jobs has gone beyond the determination of the most efficient way to perform tasks. The concept of *quality of work-life* is now widely used to refer to "the degree to which members of work organizations are able to satisfy important personal needs through their experiences in organizations."[2] The emphasis on satisfaction of personal needs does not imply deemphasis of organizational needs. Instead contemporary managers are finding that when personal needs of employees are satisfied, the performance of the organization itself is enhanced. The concept, quality of work-life, embodies the theories and ideas of the human relations movement of the 1950s and the job enrichment efforts of the 60s and 70s.

Job design and redesign strategies, many of which are presented in this chapter, are based upon efforts (1) to identify the most important needs of employees and (2) to remove obstacles in the workplace which frustrate those needs. The hoped-for results are jobs which fulfill important needs and lead to performance outcomes such as job satisfaction, productivity, and organizational effectiveness. The remainder of this chapter reviews the important theories, research, and practices of job design. As will be seen, contemporary management has at its disposal a wide range of techniques which facilitate the achievement of personal and organizational performance.

A CONCEPTUAL MODEL OF JOB DESIGN

The conceptual model depicted in Figure 11–1 is based upon the extensive research literature which has appeared in the last 20 years. The model includes the various terms and concepts which appear in the current literature.

---

[1] David F. Smith, "The Functions of Work," Omega (1975), pp. 383–93.

[2] J. Richard Hackman and J. Lloyd Suttle, eds., *Improving Life at Work* (Santa Monica, Calif.: Goodyear Publishing Company, Inc., 1977), p. 4.

Figure 11-1
A Conceptual Framework of Job Design

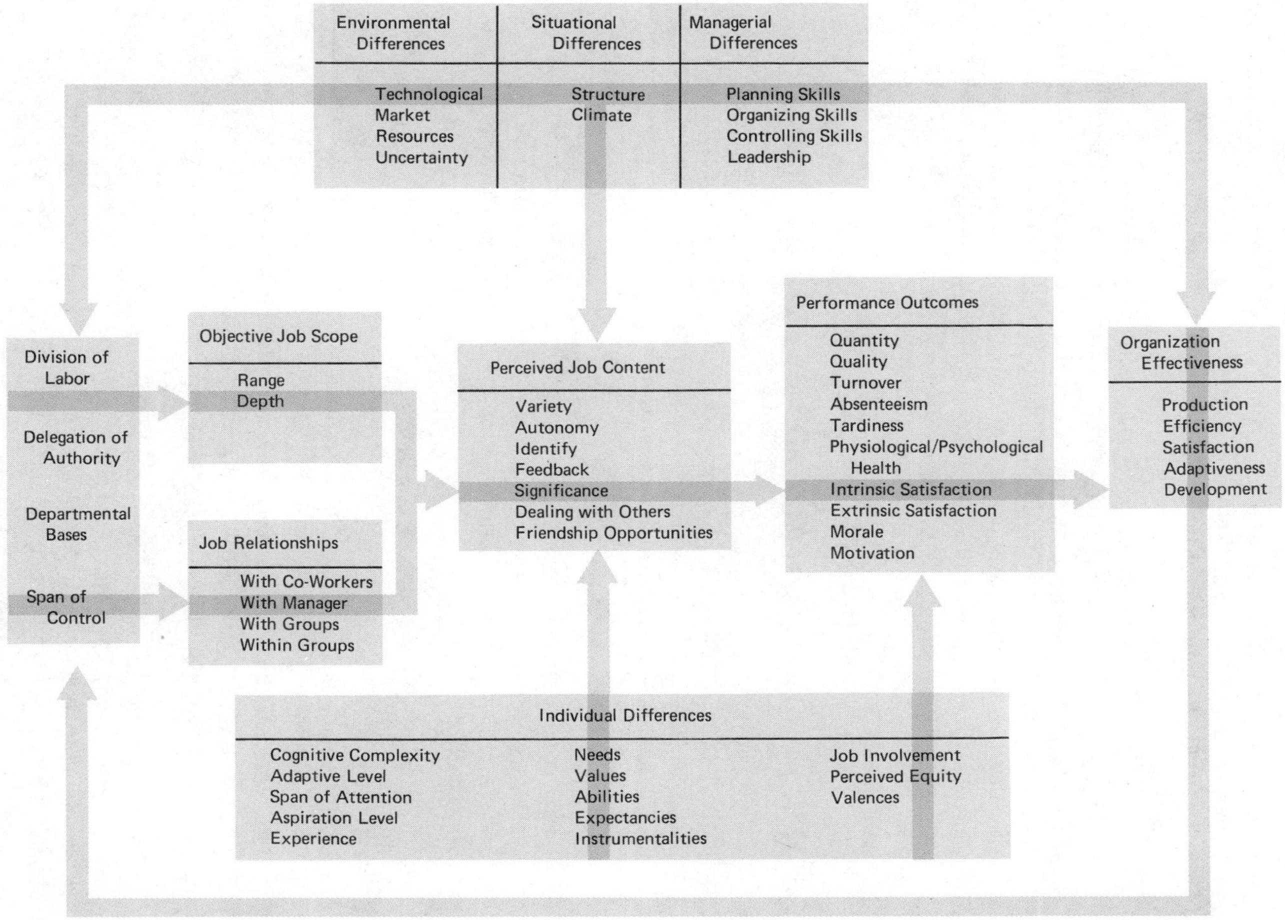

Environmental Differences	Situational Differences	Managerial Differences
Technological Market Resources Uncertainty	Structure Climate	Planning Skills Organizing Skills Controlling Skills Leadership

Organization Effectiveness

Production
Efficiency
Satisfaction
Adaptiveness
Development

Performance Outcomes

Quantity
Quality
Turnover
Absenteeism
Tardiness
Physiological/Psychological Health
Intrinsic Satisfaction
Extrinsic Satisfaction
Morale
Motivation

Perceived Job Content

Variety
Autonomy
Identify
Feedback
Significance
Dealing with Others
Friendship Opportunities

Individual Differences

Needs
Values
Abilities
Expectancies
Instrumentalities

Job Involvement
Perceived Equity
Valences

Cognitive Complexity
Adaptive Level
Span of Attention
Aspiration Level
Experience

Objective Job Scope

Range
Depth

Job Relationships

With Co-Workers
With Manager
With Groups
Within Groups

Division of Labor
Delegation of Authority
Departmental Bases
Span of Control

When linked together these concepts describe the important determinants of job performance and organizational effectiveness. The model is far from simple to understand, much less to apply in practice. Its complexity is due to the fact that individuals react differently to jobs. While one person may derive positive satisfaction from a job, another may not. A second difficulty is the trade-offs between organizational and individual needs. Thus, the technology of manufacturing may dictate that management adopt assembly-line mass production methods and low-skilled jobs to achieve optimal efficiency. Such jobs, however, may result in great unrest and worker discontent. For example, General Motors' Lordstown Vega plant represented a major application of industrial engineering and job specialization. The average time per job activity was reduced to 36 seconds and each worker completed work on an assigned component at the rate of almost 100 per hour. But the plant has suffered strikes, shutdowns, and sabotage.[3] Perhaps these costs could have been avoided by a more careful balancing of organizational and individual needs.

DESIGNING JOB SCOPE AND JOB RELATIONSHIPS

A significant managerial decision is the determination of job scope and job relationships. Through the application of the principles of division of labor and delegation of authority, job scope is created. Each of these principles contributes to the determination of what each job holder is expected to do and what activities, methods, and machinery will be used. The delegation of authority principle determines the degree of discretion, or choice, the job holder has in choosing methods, and in the case of managers, assigning other people to tasks. Job relationships are determined in part by the specific basis and size of the department, unit, or division within which the job is performed.

Job Scope

Two concepts which are useful for analyzing the problem of job scope are range and depth. The *range* of a job refers to the number of tasks a jobholder performs. The individual who performs eight tasks to complete a job has a wider job range than a person performing four distinct tasks. In most instances the greater the number of tasks performed the longer it takes to complete the job.

The second job dimension is *depth*. This dimension refers to the amount of discretion which an individual has to alter the job. Since the depth concept is related to individual factors such as personal influence, it should be recognized that an employee with the same job title and at the same organizational level as another employee may possess more, less, or the same amount of job depth.

---

[3] William F. Dowling, "Job Redesign on the Assembly Line: Farewell to Blue-Collar Blues?" *Organizational Dynamics* (Autumn 1973), p. 51.

Whether we are talking about educational institutions, business firms, hospitals, or government agencies it is essential to discuss job occupants' range and depth. The relation between job range and job depth is indicated in Figure 11–2 for selected employees of business firms, hospitals, and universities. The titles placed in each cell of Figure 11–2 reflect the relative range and depth of the positions cited. For example, the chief of surgery in a hospital would possess more range and depth than the bookkeeper in the same hospital.

As indicated in Figure 11–2, research scientists, chiefs of surgery, and university presidents generally have high job range and significant depth. Research scientists perform a large number of tasks and are not closely supervised by administrators. This is interpreted to mean that the scientists possess high job range and depth.

Figure 11–2
Job Depth and Range

High Depth

BUSINESS Packaging Machine Mechanics	HOSPITAL Anesthesiologists	UNIVERSITY College Professors		BUSINESS Research Scientists	HOSPITAL Chiefs of Surgery	UNIVERSITY Presidents

Low Range   High Range

BUSINESS Assembly-Line Workers	HOSPITAL Bookkeepers	UNIVERSITY Graduate Student Instructors		BUSINESS Maintenance Repairmen	HOSPITAL Nurses	UNIVERSITY Departmental Chairpersons

Low Depth

Range = the number of tasks a job occupant performs.
Depth = the amount of discretion to alter or influence the job.

Chiefs of surgery have significant job range in that they oversee and counsel on many diverse surgical matters. In addition they are not supervised closely and have the formal position to influence hospital surgery policies and procedures.

University presidents have a large number of tasks to perform. They must speak to alumni groups, politicians, community representatives, and students. They must develop, with the consultation of others, policies on admissions, fund raising, and adult education. They can alter the faculty recruitment philosophy and thus alter the course of the entire institution. For example, a university president may want to build an institution that is noted for high-quality classroom instruction and for providing excellent services to the community. This thrust may lead to recruiting and selecting professors who want to concentrate on these two specific goals. In contrast, another president may want to foster outstanding research and high-quality classroom instruction. Of course another president may attempt to develop an institution that is noted for instruction, research, and service. The critical point to recognize is that university presidents have sufficient depth to alter the course of a university's direction.

In the high-depth and low-range segment of Figure 11–2, we find packaging machine mechanics, anesthesiologists, and faculty members. Mechanics perform only the operations that pertain to the packaging machine. Thus, the number of tasks they perform is limited. But they can influence how breakdowns on the packaging machine are corrected—in other words, mechanics have relatively high job depth.

Anesthesiologists perform a limited number of tasks. They are concerned with administering anesthetics to patients, a job that has low range. However, they can control the type of anesthetic administered in a particular situation. This control is indicative of high job depth.

University professors specifically engaged in classroom instruction have relatively low job range. Teaching involves comparatively more tasks than the work of the anesthesiologist, yet fewer tasks than that of the business research scientist. However, professors' job depth is greater than that of graduate student instructors. This follows from the fact that they determine how they will conduct the class, what materials will be presented, and the standards to be used in evaluating students.

Job scope, then, involves the determination of activities (range) and authority (depth). A highly specialized job is one which has few tasks to accomplish by prescribed means. Such jobs are quite routine; they also tend to be controlled by specified rules and procedures. The managerial problem is simply put, but not simply answered. It is: given the economic and technical requirements of the organization's mission, goals, and objectives, what is the optimal point along the continuum of specialization?

Job Relationships

The application of the principles of departmentalization and span of control results in groupings of jobs. These groups become the responsibility of a manager to coordinate toward organization purposes. At the same time, these principles determine the nature and extent of job holders' interpersonal relationships, individually and within groups. As we already have seen in the discussion of groups in organizations, group performance is effected in part by group cohesiveness. And the degree of group cohesiveness depends upon the quality and kind of interpersonal relationships of job holders assigned to a task or command group.

The wider the span of control, the larger the group and consequently the more difficult it is to establish friendship and interest relationships. Simply, people in larger groups are less likely to communicate (and interact sufficiently to form interpersonal ties) than people in smaller groups. Without the opportunity to communicate, people will be unable to establish the bases for cohesive work groups.[4] Thus an important source of satisfaction may be lost for individuals who seek to fulfill social and esteem needs through relationships with co-workers.

---

[4] Stanley E. Seashore, *Group Cohesiveness in the Industrial Work Group* (Ann Arbor: University of Michigan, Institute for Social Research, 1954).

The basis for departmentalization which management selects also has important implications for job relationships. Functional and process bases tend to place jobs with similar depth and range in groups; while product and client bases tend to group jobs with dissimilar depth and range. Thus in functional and process departments people will be doing much the same specialty. Product and client departments, however, are comprised of jobs which are quite different and heterogeneous. Research has suggested that feeling of satisfaction, stress, and involvement are often related to the basis for departmentalization. One study suggests that job-holders in functional departments express greater satisfaction and less stress and involvement than their counterparts in production departments.[5] In part the interpretation of this finding is that people with homogeneous backgrounds, skills, and training have more common interests than those with heterogeneous attributes. Thus it is easier for them to establish social relationships which are satisfying.

Scientific Management and Objective Job Scope

The major theme of scientific management is that objective analyses of facts and data collected in the work place could provide the bases for determining the *one best way to design work*.[6] The essence of scientific management was stated as follows:

> First: Develop a science for each element of a man's work which replaces the old rule-of-thumb method.
>
> Second: Scientifically select and then train, teach, and develop the workman, whereas in the past he chose his own work and trained himself as best he could.
>
> Third: Heartily cooperate with the men so as to insure all of the work being done in accordance with the principles of the science which has been developed.
>
> Fourth: There is almost an equal division of the work and the responsibility between the management and the workmen. The management takes over all work for which they are better fitted than the workmen, while in the past, almost all of the work and the greater part of the responsibility were thrown upon the men.[7]

These four principles state and illustrate the thrust of scientific management methods: to determine a science for each job and then train people to execute

---

[5] Arthur H. Walker and Jay W. Lorsch, "Organizational Choice: Product versus Function," in Jay W. Lorsch and Paul R. Lawrence, eds., *Studies in Organization Design* (Homewood, Ill.: Richard D. Irwin, Inc., 1970), 48–49.

[6] The literature of scientific management is voluminous. The original works and the subsequent criticisms and interpretations would make a large volume. Of special significance are the works of the principal authors including: Frederick W. Taylor, *Principles of Scientific Management* (New York: Harper and Brothers, 1911); Harrington Emerson, *The Twelve Principles of Efficiency* (New York: The Engineering Magazine Co., 1913); Henry L. Gantt, *Industrial Leadership* (New Haven: Yale University Press, 1916); Frank B. Gilbreth, *Motion Study* (New York: D. Van Nostrand Co., 1911); Lillian M. Gilbreth, *The Psychology of Management* (New York: Sturgis and Walton Co., 1914).

[7] Taylor, *Principles of Scientific Management,* pp. 36–37.

the job according to the approved way (the role of management), and to remedy the difficulties created by the rule-of-thumb methods which evolved when the tasks of managers and workers were confused.

Taylor proposed that the way to improve work, that is, to make it more efficient, is to determine (1) the "best way" to do a task (motion study), and (2) the standard time for completion of the task (time study). The improvement of work involves an analysis of the entire context and environment within which the work is done. The objective of motion study is to determine a preferable work method with consideration to raw materials, product design, order of work, tools, equipment, work place layout, and the hand and body motions required by the workman.[8] In this context, motion and time studies are parts of the total process of work improvement.

The idea that job scope can be based solely on engineering approaches ignores the very large role played by the individual who performs the job. The conceptual framework in Figure 11–1 indicates that individual differences enter into the issue of job design at a number of points. In the following section, the issue of *job content* is examined. As we will see, the manner in which individuals react to job scope and relationships depends upon their psychological perceptions.

Job Content and Individual Differences

Job content refers to aspects of a job which define its general nature as *perceived by the job holder.* It is important to distinguish between the *objective* properties of a job as reflected in formal job descriptions and specifications and the *subjective* properties of a job as reflected in the perceptions of people who perform them. Scientific management techniques such as time and motion studies result in requisite activities (job range), authority (job depth), and interpersonal interactions (job relationships). However one cannot understand, much less predict, the relationship between these variables and job performance without consideration of individual differences such as cognitive complexity, adaptive level, and span of attention.[9]

If management is to understand the relationship between job content and performance, some method for measuring job content must exist. Moreover organization behavior researchers have attempted to measure job characteristics in a variety of work settings. These research efforts have accelerated in recent years as society's interest in the quality of work life has heightened. The methods which researchers use rely upon questionnaires which job holders complete and which measure their perceptions of certain job characteristics.

An early and pioneering effort to measure job content through employee

8 Marvin E. Mundel, "Motion and Time Study," in William G. Ireson and Eugene L. Grant, eds., *Handbook of Industrial Engineering and Management* (Englewood Cliffs, N.J.: Prentice-Hall, 1955), p. 285.

9 Donald P. Schwab and L. L. Cummings, "A Theoretical Analysis of the Impact of Task Scope on Employee Performance," *Academy of Management Review* (April 1976), p. 31–32.

responses to a questionnaire resulted in the identification of six characteristics: variety, autonomy, required interaction, optional interaction, knowledge and skill required, and responsibility.[10] These attributes reflect the job holder's opinion regarding necessary conditions for successful task completion. The consequent index of these six characteristics was termed the Requisite Task Attribute Index (RTAI). The original RTAI has been extensively reviewed and analyzed. One important development was the review by Hackman and Lawler who revised the index to include the six characteristics shown in Table 11–1.[11]

Table 11–1
Selected Job Characteristics

Variety—The degree to which a job requires employees to perform a wide range of operations in their work and/or the degree to which employees must use a variety of equipment and procedures in their work.

Autonomy—The extent to which employees have a major say in scheduling their work, selecting the equipment they will use, and deciding on procedures to be followed.

Task Identity—The extent to which employees do an entire or whole piece of work and can clearly identify with the results of their efforts.

Feedback—The degree to which employees receive information as they are working, which reveals how well they are performing on the job.

Dealing with Others—The degree to which a job requires employees to deal with other people to complete their work.

Friendship Opportunities—The degree to which a job allows employees to talk with one another on the job and to establish informal relationships with other employees at work.

Source: Henry P. Sims, Jr., Andrew D. Szilagyi, and Robert T. Keller, "The Measurement of Job Characteristics," *Academy of Management Journal* (June 1976), p. 197.

Variety, task identity, and *feedback* are perceptions of job range. *Autonomy* is the perception of job depth; and *dealing with others* and *friendship opportunities* reflect perceptions of job relationships. Thus employees sharing similar psychological perceptions *and* similar job scopes and relationships should report similar job characteristics.

Two approaches currently exist to measure perceived job content. The Job Characteristics Index (JCI) attempts to measure job holders' perceptions of the six characteristics shown in Table 11–1.[12] A more widely used approach is the Job Diagnostic Survey (JDS).[13] The JDS measures variety, autonomy, task identity, feedback, and significance. Unlike the JCI which includes job relationship dimensions, the JDS attempts to measure only the "core" dimen-

---

[10] Arthur N. Turner and Paul R. Lawrence, *Industrial Jobs and the Worker: An Investigation of Response to Task Attributes* (Boston: Harvard University Press, 1965).

[11] J. Richard Hackman and Edward E. Lawler III, "Employee Reactions to Job Characteristics," *Journal of Applied Psychology,* (1971), 259–86; and J. Richard Hackman and Greg R. Oldman, "Development of the Job Diagnostic Survey," *Journal of Applied Psychology* (1975), 159–70.

[12] Henry P. Sims, Jr., Andrew D. Szilagyi, and Robert T. Keller, "The Measurement of Job Characteristics," *Academy of Management Journal* (June 1976), pp. 195–212.

[13] J. R. Hackman and G. Oldham, "Development of the Job Diagnostic Survey."

sions of job content and in doing so, includes an additional dimension, significance, which reflects the perceived importance of the work to the organization or to others. The JDS has been widely used by researchers,[14] although some evidence exists that the JCI is an alternative measure.[15] Subsequent studies will no doubt improve the measurement of job content, but it is doubtful that any perceptual measurement will ever eliminate the effects of individual differences. The effect of individual differences is to "provide filters such that different persons perceive the same objective stimuli in different manners."[16] Yet even if individuals perceive job content similarly, we cannot expect similar job performance. The link between job content and job performance is complicated not only by individual differences but also by situational differences.

PERCEIVED JOB CONTENT AND PERFORMANCE OUTCOMES

The relationship between job content and job performance rests almost solely on factors which are unrelated to job scope and relationships. As shown in Figure 11–1, the relationship is moderated by individual and situational differences.

The case of individual differences in need strength, particularly the strength of growth needs, has been shown to influence the effect of feedback on job performance. That is employees with relatively weak higher order needs are less concerned about receiving feedback than are those with relatively strong growth needs.[17] Thus, managers expecting higher performance to result from increased feedback on goal attainment would be disappointed if the job holders did not demonstrate strong growth needs.

Situational differences also affect the relationship between job content and job performance. Examples of such differences include differences on organizational structure, climate, technology, product and market type.[18] We will return to this discussion when we turn our attention to job redesign strategies. But let us complete our discussion of the basic model by turning attention to the relationships between job performance, job outcomes, and job satisfaction.

---

[14] Jon L. Pierce and Randall B. Dunham, "Task Design: A Literature Review," *Academy of Management Review* (October 1976), pp. 83–97.

[15] Jon L. Pierce and Randall B. Dunham, "The Measurement of Perceived Job Characteristics: The Job Diagnostic Survey versus the Job Characteristics Inventory," *Academy of Management Journal* (March 1978), pp. 123–28.

[16] Randall B. Dunham, Ramon J. Aldag, and Arthur P. Brief, "Dimensionality of Task Design as Measured by the Job Diagnostic Survey," *Academy of Management Journal* (June 1977), p. 222.

[17] John M. Ivancevich and J. Timothy McMahon, "A Study of Task-Goal Attributes, Higher Order Need Strength and Performance," *Academy of Management Review* (December 1977), p. 561.

[18] Randall B. Dunham, "Reactions to Job Characteristics: Moderating Effects of the Organization," *Academy of Management Journal* (March 1977), p. 43.

Job Performance

Measures used to identify the performance of individuals include quantity and quality of output, absenteeism, tardiness and turnover. These measures take on different values and for each job some implicit or explicit standard exists. Industrial engineering studies establish standards for daily quantity, and quality control specialists establish tolerance limits for acceptable quality. These aspects of job performance account for characteristics of the product, client, or service for which the job holder is responsible. But job performance includes other aspects.

The jobholder reacts to the work itself, and reacts by either attending regularly or being absent, by staying with the job or by quitting. Moreover, physiological and health-related matters can ensue as a consequence of job performance. Stress related to job performance can contribute to physical and mental impairment; accidents and occupationally-related disease can also ensue. These obviously negative aspects of job stress are rightly considered undesirable and enlightened management would no doubt attempt to minimize its effects.

Job Outcomes

Job outcomes consist of intrinsic and extrinsic work outcomes. The distinction between intrinsic and extrinsic outcomes, while not always unambiguous, is important for understanding the reactions of people to their jobs.[19] In a general sense, intrinsic outcomes are objects or events which follow from the worker's own efforts, not requiring the involvement of any other person. More simply it is an outcome clearly related to action on the workers' part. Such outcomes typically are thought to be solely in the province of professional and technical jobs; yet all jobs potentially have opportunities for intrinsic outcomes. Such outcomes are considered to involve feelings of responsibility, challenge, and recognition; and result from such job characteristics as variety, autonomy, identity, and significance.

Extrinsic outcomes, however, are objects or events which follow from the workers' own efforts in conjuction with other factors or persons not directly involved in the job itself. Pay, working conditions, co-workers, and even supervision are objects in the workplace which are potentially job outcomes, but which are not a fundamental part of the work. Dealing with others and friendship interactions are sources of extrinsic outcomes.

Job Satisfaction

Job satisfaction depends on the levels of intrinsic and extrinsic outcomes and how the job holder views those outcomes. We have already noted that

---

[19] Arthur P. Brief and Ramon J. Aldag "The Intrinsic-Extrinsic Dichotomy: Toward Conceptual Clarity," *Academy of Management Review* (July 1977), pp. 496–500.

outcomes have different values (valences) for different people. For some people, responsible and challenging work may have neutral or even negative outcomes. For other people, such work outcomes may have high positive values. People differ in the valences they attach to job outcomes. Those differences alone would account for different levels of job satisfaction for essentially the same job tasks.

Another important individual difference is job involvement.[20] People differ in the extent (1) that work is a central life interest, (2) they actively participate in work, (3) they perceive work as central to self-esteem, and (4) they perceive work as consistent with self-concept. Persons who are uninvolved in their work cannot be expected to realize the same satisfaction as those who are. This variable accounts for the fact that two workers could report different levels of satisfaction for the same performance levels.

A final individual difference is the perceived equity of the outcome in terms of what the job-holder considers a fair reward.[21] If the outcomes are perceived to be unfair in relation to those of others in similar jobs requiring similar effort, the job holder will experience dissatisfaction and seek means to restore the equity, either by seeking greater rewards (primarily extrinsic) or by reducing effort.

MOTIVATIONAL PROPERTIES OF JOBS

The interest of organization behavior researchers and managers in the motivational properties of jobs is based upon the understanding that job performance depends upon more than the ability of the job holder. Specifically, job performance is determined by the interaction of ability and motivation as expressed by the equation:

$$\text{Job Performance} = \text{Ability} \times \text{Motivation}$$

The equation reflects the fact that job performance of a person can be greater than that of a second person because of greater ability, motivation, or both. It also reflects the possibility that job performance could be zero even if the job holder has ability; in such instances, motivation would have to be zero. Thus, it is imperative that management consider the potential impact of motivational properties of jobs.

We have in previous chapters discussed various motivation theories such as Maslow's need hierarchy, Herzberg's two-factor theory, and expectancy theory. These theories have significant implications for job design and redesign strategies, and it is in this context that we review them here. Specifically we will discuss the implications of three motivation theories for job design: Herzberg's two-factor theory, learned needs theory, and expectancy theory.[22]

---

[20] S. D. Saleh and James Hosek, "Job Involvement: Concepts and Measurements" *Academy of Management Journal* (June 1976), pp. 213–24.

[21] J. Stacy Adams, "Toward an Understanding of Inequity," *Journal of Abnormal and Social Psychology* (November 1963), pp. 422–36.

[22] This discussion is based on Richard M. Steers and Richard T. Mowday, "The Motivational Properties of Tasks," *Academy of Management Review* (October 1977), pp. 645–58.

Two-Factor Theory

According to Herzberg's theory, jobs consist of two distinct sets of factors, as perceived by job holders. One set of factors consists of opportunities to realize achievement, advancement, growth, and responsibility. Moreover the job itself when performed provides intrinsic satisfaction. Such factors are usually associated with challenging tasks which require a maximum utilization of the person's ability and skill. When such factors are present on the job, the job holder achieves a high state of motivation, satisfaction, and performance. Thus, these factors are termed *motivators,* and according to the theory, when they are present in a job the job holder will experience satisfaction—but not dissatisfaction if they are not present.

The second set of factors are termed *hygiene* factors. Included in this set are pay, supervision, company policies, working conditions, and status. These factors are not motivational properties when perceived in a job; rather when present the jobholder will report neutral motivation, satisfaction, and performance. Despite the widespread adoption of Herzberg's theory, it has some limitations as we noted in Chapter 5.

Learned Needs Theory

This content theory of motivation is based upon the early work of Murray, McClelland, and Atkinson.[23] This theory states that the needs for achievement, affiliation, and power are learned from a person's experiences with culture and they vary in strength from person to person. Need for achievement has been shown to be important in explaining the motivational characteristics of tasks. Persons with high need for achievement experience high motivation when their jobs contain opportunities for challenge, feedback, and responsibility. Persons with low achievement needs will experience low performance as well as anxiety and frustration in such jobs. Thus, this theory fills a partial void of the two-factor theory by taking into account the impact of individual differences in need strength.

Expectancy Theory

As noted in Chapter 5, expectancy theory states that behavior in organizations is related to (1) employees' beliefs that their efforts will lead to desired level of performance, (2) their beliefs that job performance will lead to desired outcomes and (3) the values that they place on the intrinsic and extrinsic outcomes. This process theory of motivation attempts to explain not only the sources of satisfaction but also the behavior of individuals seeking (or not seeking) and experiencing (or not experiencing) satisfaction. Thus Vroom and other proponents of the theory believe that motivation, performance, and satisfaction depend upon employees' *expectancies* that efforts lead to

---

[23] Henry A. Murray, *Explorations in Personality* (New York: Oxford University Press, 1938); David C. McClelland, *The Achieving Society* (Princeton, N.J.: Van Nostrand, 1961); and John W. Atkinson, *Introduction to Motivation* (Princeton, N.J.: Van Nostrand, 1964).

performance and performance leads to outcomes *and* the *valences* of those outcomes.[24]

The implications of this theory for the relationship between job design and performance are that

1. Individuals will react positively to task variety and interaction opportunities if they attach valences to task behavior.
2. Individuals will react positively to task identity, significance, and autonomy if they value highly these characteristics of task accomplishment.
3. Individuals will react positively to feedback if it improves their expectancies that performance leads to valued outcomes.

Thus, this theory places considerable emphasis on individual differences despite the fact that research studies have failed to take them into account.

In recent years organization behavior theorists have advanced a number of suggestions for improving the motivational properties of job design. These suggestions are based upon one or more of the foregoing theories of motivation. Invariably the suggestions, termed job redesign strategies, attempt to improve job performance and satisfaction through changes in job range and scope. In the next section the more significant of these strategies are reviewed.

REDESIGNING JOB RANGE: JOB ROTATION AND JOB ENLARGEMENT

The earliest attempts to redesign jobs date to the scientific management era. The efforts at that time emphasized efficiency criteria. In so doing, the individual tasks which comprise a job are limited, uniform, and repetitive.[25] This practice leads to narrow job range, and consequently, reported high levels of job discontent, turnover, absenteeism, and dissatisfaction.[26] Accordingly, strategies were devised which resulted in wider job range through increasing the requisite activities of jobs. Two of these approaches are *job rotation* and *job enlargement*.

Job Rotation

Managers of organizations such as Western Electric, Ford, Bethlehem Steel and TRW Systems have utilized different forms of the job rotation strategy. This practice involves rotating an individual from one job to another. In so doing the individual is expected to complete more job activities since each job includes different tasks. Job rotation involves increasing the range

---

[24] Victor H. Vroom, *Work and Motivation* (New York: John Wiley & Sons, 1964).

[25] Louis E. Davis, "Job Design and Productivity: A New Approach" in Gary A. Yukl and Kenneth N. Wexley, eds., *Readings in Organizational and Industrial Psychology* (New York: Oxford University Press, 1971), p. 172.

[26] An early and classic study of the dysfunctional consequences of narrow job range and scope is Charles R. Walker and Robert H. Guest, *The Man on the Assembly Line* (Cambridge, Mass.: Harvard University Press, 1952).

of jobs and the perception of variety in the job content. Increasing task variety should, according to expectancy theory, increase the intrinsic valence associated with job satisfaction. However, the practice of job rotation does not change the basic characteristics of the assigned jobs and critics state that this approach involves nothing more than having people perform several boring and monotonous jobs rather than one. An alternative strategy is job enlargement.

Job Enlargement

The Walker and Guest study[27] was concerned with the social and psychological problems associated with mass production jobs in an automobile assembly plant. The researchers found that many workers disliked numerous factors associated with their specialized jobs. It was determined that mechanical pacing, repetitiveness of operations, and a lack of a sense of accomplishment were job factors which employees disliked.

Walker and Guest also found a positive relationship between the number of operations performed and the overall interest an employee had in the job. These findings are summarized in Table 11–2. The findings of this research support those motivation theories which posit that permanent increases in job variety will produce gains in performance and satisfaction. Job enlargement strategies focus upon the opposite of dividing work—they are a form of despecialization or increasing the number of tasks which an employee performs. For example, a job is structured in such a manner that instead of performing three tasks the employee performs six tasks.

Although, in many instances, an enlarged job requires a longer training period, it is assumed that satisfaction of the worker increases because boredom is reduced. The implication, of course, is that the job enlargement will lead to more productivity and improved overall efficiency.

Several studies lend support to the applicability of job enlargement. One such study involved job redesign at an IBM plant.[28] A parts manufacturing

Table 11–2
Employee Interest and Job Variety

Number of Operations Performed	Number Reporting Work as Very or Fairly Interesting	Number Reporting Work as Not Very or Not at All Interesting	Total Employee
1	19	38	57
2–5	28	36	64
5 or more	41	18	59
Total	88	92	180

Source: Charles R. Walker and Robert H. Guest, *The Man on the Assembly Line* (Cambridge: Harvard University Press, 1952), p. 54.

---

[27] Walker and Guest, *The Man on the Assembly Line.*

[28] C. R. Walker, "The Problem of the Repetitive Job," *Harvard Business Review* (May 1950), pp. 54–58.

unit of the Endicott plant of IBM redesigned a number of jobs in an attempt to improve worker morale. The job of machine operator after the reorganization included setting up the job, sharpening tools, inspecting the work, and operating the equipment.

The findings of the IBM study suggest that the job enlargement strategy increased worker morale, lowered production costs, increased the interests of employees, and improved the quality of output. It was also possible to eliminate an entire level of management in the organizational structure because, under the new job enlargement program, employees had greater responsibilities and authority.

Another study which involves the effects of job enlargement is the Maytag Company study.[29] It was concerned with changing the job design on a mass-production assembly line. During different phases of the study, the job was changed. The different phases studied were as follows:

Phase I: Six operators assembled a washing machine pump on a conveyor line.
Phase II: The assembling of the pump was a four-man operation.
Phase III: The work previously done on the conveyor line was done at four individual *one-man work benches.*

Throughout each of these changes, the time required to assemble the pump decreased. The least time-consuming design for assembling involved the one-man work benches. This suggests that reducing assembly line delays and enlarging the job may increase productivity in some instances.

Since these early experiences with job enlargement, the concept has become considerably more sophisticated. In recent years effective job enlargement involves more than simply increasing task variety. In addition, it is necessary to redesign certain other aspects of job range, including providing the worker a meaningful work module, performance feedback, ability utilization, and worker-paced (rather than machine-paced) control.[30] Each of these changes involves balancing the gains and losses of varying degrees of division of labor. In terms of the conceptual framework presented in Figure 11–1, variety, work, modules, feedback, and worker-paced control involve questions of division of labor. Ability utilization recognizes that a greatly enlarged job which exceeds the abilities of employees will not result in improved performance.

The conceptual framework also indicates that psychological factors such as cognitive complexity, adaptive level, span of attention, and aspiration level intervene between job range and perceived job content. It is apparent that some employees simply cannot cope with enlarged jobs because they cannot

---

[29] M. D. Kilbridge, "Reduced Costs through Job Enlargement: A Case," *The Journal of Business* (October 1960), pp. 357–62.

[30] Kae H. Chung and Monica F. Ross, "Difference in Motivational Properties between Job Enlargement and Job Enrichment," *Academy of Management Review* (January 1977), pp. 114–15.

comprehend complexity; moreover they may not have an attention span sufficiently long to stay with and complete an enlarged set of tasks. However if employees are known to be amenable to job enlargement and if they have the requisite ability, then job enlargement should increase satisfaction and product quality and decrease absenteeism and turnover.[31] These gains are not without costs, including the likelihood that employees will demand larger salaries in exchange for their performance of enlarged jobs. Yet these costs must be borne if management desires to implement the redesign strategy which enlarges job depth, *job enrichment.* Job enlargement is a necessary precondition for job enrichment.

REDESIGNING JOB DEPTH: JOB ENRICHMENT

The impetus for redesigning job range was provided by Herzberg's two-factor theory of motivation.[32] The basis of his idea is that factors which meet man's need for psychological growth, especially responsibility, job challenge, and achievement must be combined with hygiene factors to accomplish effective performance.

Herzberg points out that to achieve good performance, people with proper abilities are needed. This means that a sound selection program is needed. He also stresses the fact that motivation through job enrichment requires reinforcement. The performance appraisal system must reinforce growth behavior and provide for continued opportunities for growth.

The implementation of job enrichment is realized through direct changes in the work itself. There are a number of important ingredients that Herzberg believes will encourage the motivator factors to emerge. Some of these are:

1. *Direct feedback:* The evaluation of performance should be timely and direct.
2. *New learning:* A good job enables people to feel that they are psychologically growing. All jobs should provide an opportunity to learn something.
3. *Scheduling:* People should be able to schedule some part of their own work.
4. *Uniqueness:* Each job should have some unique qualities or features.
5. *Control over resources:* If at all possible, the workers should have control over their job tasks.
6. *Personal accountability:* People should be provided with an opportunity to be accountable for the job.

A number of research studies support the assumption that job enrichment is a major determinant of better job performance and increased satisfaction. Ford states that 17 of 18 experiments at AT&T with clerical and other telephone company employees showed positive improvement after jobs were en-

---

[31] Ibid., p. 116.

[32] Frederick Herzberg, "The Wise Old Turk," *Harvard Business Review* (September–October 1974), pp. 70–80.

riched.[33] A study of technicians, engineers, and sales representatives indicated that job enrichment pays off in better performance and greater satisfaction.[34]

As defined by the executive in charge of the Texas Instruments program, job enrichment is a process for developing employees so that they think and behave like managers in managing their jobs, and a process for redefining the job and the role of the job incumbent to make such development feasible.[35] The process as implemented in TI is continuous and pervades the entire organization. Every one of the jobs in TI is viewed as subject to analysis to determine if it can be enriched to include managerial activities, and thereby made more meaningful. Moreover, as the jobs of nonmanagerial personnel are redesigned to include greater depth, the jobs of managers must be redesigned. The redesigned managerial jobs emphasize training and counseling of subordinates and deemphasize control and direction.

The job enrichment process at TI consists of learning and implementation cycles. Two approaches exist for implementing the cycles: the task force approach and the problem-solving—goal-setting approach.[36]

The Task Force Approach

This approach involves bringing together a group of managers to evaluate the potential for enriching a job. The group consists of the job incumbent's supervisor and other managers in the chain of command to the highest possible level. Prior to convening, all supervisors must have completed at least 16 hours of instruction in motivation theory, meaningful work, work simplification, and conference leadership. Much of the material covered in the instruction received by the supervisors has been discussed in this text. Critically important to the supervisors is the understanding that meaningful work is related to the extent to which responsibility, achievement, recognition, and growth are made possible for the job incumbent. The reader will recognize these four factors as "motivators" in the Herzberg theory of motivation.

Every member of the task force is prepared through this instructional program to participate with a common *frame of reference.* During the first day of the task force's deliberations, the participants are encouraged to think radically about the job that is to be enriched. The abstractions of responsibility, achievement, recognition, and growth must be translated into specific and concrete job factors. Through experience, TI has found that jobs can be analyzed in terms of three functions: planning, controlling, and implementing. The group members identify the ways in which the planning and controlling

---

[33] Robert Ford, "Job Enrichment Lessons for AT&T," *Harvard Business Review* (January–February 1973), pp. 96–106.

[34] William J. Paul, Jr., Keith B. Robertson, and Frederick Herzberg, "Job Enrichment Pays Off," *Harvard Business Review* (March–April 1969), pp. 61–78.

[35] M. Scott Myers, *Every Employee a Manager* (New York: McGraw-Hill Book Co., 1970), p. xii.

[36] Ibid., pp. 75–87.

functions of a job can be augmented by shifting supervisory activities to the worker level.

The brainstorming session ordinarily takes one full day. The second day is spent evaluating the soundness of ideas expressed during the first day's sessions. Each idea is rated as excellent, good, fair, or poor by group consensus. Toward the end of the second day the supervisors begin to select those ideas which they believe can be implemented to enrich the job. With the group's help, they list the anticipated problems to be met and plan tentative responses to the problems.

The supervisors then return to their workplaces and begin to implement the ideas which they and other members of the task force agreed upon. Implementation ordinarily takes from four to six weeks during which time the task force meets to discuss and review progress and to brainstorm other jobs. Thus, as practiced in TI, the task force concept is a permanent part of the organization structure since every job is continually evaluated and reevaluated for additional enrichment.

The Problem-Solving–Goal-Setting Approach

This approach differs from the task force approach in one significant way: it involves the job incumbent in the process. In every other respect the two approaches are similar. The initiative is provided by the supervisor who, when confronted with a customer problem, calls together the command or task group to consider ways to resolve the problem. The assumption is that the group has intimate knowledge of manufacturing processes because of its job experience and that it can make significant contributions to the decision. Technical experts, accountants, and engineers are invited to the discussion as the group recognizes the need for their expertise.

The discussion focuses on all aspects of the operation which contribute to producing the product for the customer. As problems emerge and are confronted, the group sets objectives which it commits itself to meeting and which contribute to the ultimate resolution of the problem as it was initially introduced by the supervisor. Through this exercise the group becomes full participating members of management, provided that the supervisor has learned well the lessons of Herzberg's two-factor theory.

One application of job enrichment led to significant increases in production and decreases in absenteeism.[37] A group of women who had been assembling radar equipment according to methods defined by the engineering department were given the responsibility for devising their own methods, manufacturing processes, and goals. The problem-solving–goal-setting approach was used as described above. After implementation of the group's own methods and goals, the assembly time per unit dropped from 138 hours to

---

[37] Charles L. Hughes, "Applying Behavioral Science in Manufacturing Supervision: Case Report," *Proceedings of the Ninth Annual Midwest Management Conference* (Carbondale: Bureau of Business Research, Southern Illinois University, 1966), pp. 85–89.

86 hours. At this point a second goal-setting session was held, and the women suggested that they did not need a supervisor; they could, in their own judgment, exercise self-control. The women did keep their supervisor informed, but they self-directed their activities. The assembly time for the unit was finally reduced to 36 hours.

In this instance of job enrichment, the employees were encouraged to evaluate their own task performance. They responded by not only enlarging the range of their jobs—by adding additional tasks—but also the depth, by assuming the responsibility for their own supervision. The applicability of job enrichment to other manufacturing situations is, of course, a matter of on-site determination; this illustration does suggest the positive gains which can be realized.

As the theory and practice of job enrichment has evolved, organization behavior theorists and managers have become aware that successful applications tap a number of motivational factors of jobs. These factors include employee participation, goal internalization, autonomy, and group management.[38] Realizing these changes involves delegating greater authority to workers to participate in decisions, set their own goals, and evaluate their (and their work groups') performance; it also involves changing the nature and style of leadership behavior. Given the ability of employees to carry out enriched jobs and the willingness of managers to share control, gains in performance can be expected. These positive outcomes are the result of increasing employees' expectancies that efforts lead to performance, that performance leads to intrinsic and extrinsic rewards, and that these rewards have power to satisfy needs.[39]

Like other approaches that have evolved from behavioral science theory, job enrichment has its critics. Fein believes that behavioralists tend to impose their own value systems when prescribing job enrichment. He believes that when job enrichment applications and research studies are examined closely, four things are found:

1. What actually occurred was quite different from what was reported.
2. Most of the studies were conducted with employees who do not represent a cross-section of the working population.
3. Only a handful of job enrichment cases have been reported in the past ten years, despite the impression that it is widespread.
4. In all instances, the experiments were initiated by management, never by workers or unions.[40]

---

[38] Chung and Ross, "Differences in Motivational Properties between Job Enlargement and Job Enrichment," pp. 116–17.

[39] Kae H. Chung, *Motivational Theories and Practices* (Columbus, Ohio: Grid Inc., 1977), p. 204.

[40] Mitchell Fein, "The Myth of Job Enrichment," in Roy P. Fairfield, ed., *Humanizing the Workplace* (Buffalo: Prometheus Books, 1974) pp. 71–78. For some excellent examples of job enrichment applications see J. Richard Hackman, Greg Oldham, Robert Janson, and Kenneth Purdy, "New Strategy for Job Enrichment," *California Management Review* (Summer 1975), pp. 57–71.

Whether job enrichment is a powerful motivator of positive behavior is still an unanswered question because of the points raised by Fein and others. Despite these problems job enrichment is a widespread application of Herzberg's two-factor theory. It may not be scientifically pure, but it continues to be adopted.

REDESIGNING JOB RANGE AND DEPTH: COMBINED APPROACH

Job enrichment and job enlargement are not competing strategies. Job enlargement but not job enrichment may be compatible with the needs, values, and abilities of some individuals. Yet job enrichment, when appropriate, necessarily involves job enlargement. A promising new approach to job redesign which attempts to integrate the two approaches is the job characteristic model. Hackman, Oldham, Janson, and Purdy devised the approach and based it upon the Job Diagnostic Survey cited in an earlier section.[41]

The model attempts to account for the interrelationships among (1) certain core dimensions of jobs, (2) psychological states associated with motivation, satisfaction, and performance, (3) job outcomes, and (4) growth need strength. Figure 11–3 describes the relationships among these variables. The core dimensions of the job consist of characteristics first described by Turner and Lawrence.[42] Although variety, identity, significance, autonomy, and feedback do not completely describe job content, they, according to this model, sufficiently describe those aspects which management can manipulate to bring about gains in productivity.

The steps which management can take to increase the core dimensions include combining task elements, assigning whole pieces of work (i.e., work modules), allowing discretion in selection of work methods, permitting self-paced control. These actions increase task variety, identity, and significance; consequently the "experienced meaningfulness of work" psychological state is increased. By permitting employee participation and self-evaluation and creating autonomous work groups, the feedback and autonomy dimensions are increased along with the psychological states "experienced responsibility" and "knowledge of actual results."

The positive benefits of these redesign efforts are conditioned by individual differences in the strength of employees' growth needs. That is, employees with strong need for accomplishment, learning, and challenge will respond more positively than those with relatively weak growth needs. In other, more familiar, terms employees who have high need for upper level needs such as self-esteem and self-actualization are the more likely candidates for job redesign. Employees forced to participate in job redesign programs but who

---

[41] J. Richard Hackman, Greg Oldham, Robert Janson, and Kenneth Purdy, "A New Strategy for Job Enrichment," *California Management Review* (Summer 1975), pp. 57–71; and J. Richard Hackman and Greg Oldham, "Development of the Job Diagnostic Survey," *Journal of Applied Psychology* (April 1975), pp. 159–70.

[42] Turner and Lawrence, *Industrial Jobs.*

Figure 11–3
The Job Characteristics Model

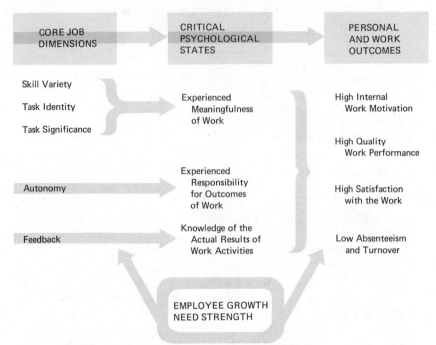

Source: J. Richard Hackman and Greg R. Oldham. "Development of the Job Diagnostic Survey,"
Journal of Applied Psychology, vol. 60 (1975), pp. 159–70.

lack either the need strength or the ability to perform redesigned jobs may experience stress, anxiety, adjustment problems, erratic performance, turnover, and absenteeism.

The available research on the interrelationships between individual differences, job design, and performance are meager. It is apparent, however, that managers must cope with significant problems in matching employee needs and differences and organizational needs. That difficulty is indicated by the finding of one study that of 125 firms included in the survey, only 5 had made any efforts to redesign jobs.[43] The problems associated with job redesign are several including:[44]

1. The program is time consuming and costly.
2. Unless lower level needs are satisfied, people will not respond to opportunities to satisfy upper level needs. And even though our society has been rather successful in providing food and shelter, these needs regain importance when the economy moves through periods of recession and inflation.

---

[43] Fred Luthans and W. E. Reif "Job Enrichment: Long on Theory, Short on Practice," *Organizational Dynamics* (Fall 1974), pp. 30–43.

[44] Chung, *Motivational Theories and Practices,* pp. 211–12.

3. Job redesign programs are intended to satisfy needs typically not satisfied in the work place. As workers are told to expect higher order need satisfaction, they may raise their expectations beyond that which is possible. Dissatisfaction with the program's unachievable aim may displace dissatisfaction with the jobs.
4. Finally job redesign may be resisted by labor unions who see the effort as an attempt to get more work with the same pay.

Despite these problems companies have turned to job redesign as a way to improve productivity and satisfaction.

SOME APPLICATIONS OF JOB REDESIGN

In this section we will review a number of actual attempts to implement job redesign. Terms such as job enrichment, job enlargement, and quality of work-life are often used interchangeably; yet in most instances the terms refer to efforts to change job range and depth. The most publicized efforts have occurred in the Volvo and General Motors automobile manufacturing plants.

The Volvo Experience

When Pehr Gyllenhammar joined Volvo in 1971 as its managing director, performance indicators such as productivity, absenteeism, and turnover were at an all-time low.[45] The company is the largest employer in Sweden with some 65,000 employees and in 1976 it ranked 61st on *Fortune's* international 500 list. Gyllenhammar took a keen interest in the experiments of Ingvar Barrby, head of the upholstery department, in job rotation (termed job alternation in Volvo). The reduction in turnover from 35 percent to 15 percent encouraged the new managing director to adopt other aspects of job redesign.[46] For example group management and work modules are used at the Torslanda car assembly plant. Employees, in groups, follow the same auto body for seven or eight work stations along the line for a total period of 20 minutes.

The concepts of group management and natural work modules is more highly developed at a truck assembly plant. Here groups of 5 to 12 men with common work assignments, elect their own supervisors, schedule their output, distribute work to their own members, and are responsible for their own quality control. Group piecerates, rather than individual piecerates, are the bases for wages and everyone earns the same amount except the elected supervisor. Subsequently absenteeism and turnover decreased and quality improved—due, in Gyllenhammar's opinion, to the effects of the job redesign program.

---

[45] John M. Roach, "Why Volvo Abolished the Assembly Line," *Management Review* (September 1977), p. 50.

[46] William F. Dowling, "Job Redesign on the Assembly Line: Farewell to Blue-Collar Blues?" *Organizational Dynamics* (Autumn 1973), pp. 51–67.

Job redesign at Volvo reached a major milestone in 1974 when the then new, Kalmar assembly plant opened. Gyllenhammar had been personally and visibly behind the design and construction phases of the new plant to assure that opportunities to provide job enrichment were parts of the physical and technological layout. The plant incorporates a technology of assembly in which overhead carriers move the auto body, chassis, and subassemblies to assembly team areas. There, work teams of 20 to 25 men complete major segments of auto assembly-electrical systems, instrumentation, finishing and so on. Each group is responsible for a whole piece of work. They function as autonomous units much as those at the truck assembly plant.[47]

The General Motors Experience

General Motors became involved with job redesign in 1971.[48] The company was formulating plans for building the GM mobile home, a new product in a rapidly growing market. GM management believed that the new product was amenable to new design concepts as well as innovative approaches to work organization. After analyzing several factors including the expected production rate, technological complexity, and size of the new operation, management determined that the work-team concept would be applicable.

The plan called for the eventual creation of 8 six-man teams to produce 32 vehicles per shift in the body-upfit area; 14 three-man teams would complete the same number of chassis; and 4 four-man teams would install air-conditioning. Implementing the plan began with the selection of a nucleus of 30 hourly employees who would build the pilot vehicles and later be the team leaders and trainers of the expanded work force. The pilot phase ended in December 1972, and additional employees were recruited to fill out the work teams.

Problems arose shortly thereafter. Efficiency and quality never reached acceptable levels. Teams were unable to maintain discipline and some team members did not carry their fair share of the load. Absenteeism, turnover, and job dissatisfaction increased. Some team members were unable to keep pace, due in large part to inadequate training and poor work layout. Management had underestimated the complexity of the assembly process and the training required to complete work cycles of up to 18 half-hour sequences.

The discouraging outcomes resulted in the team concept being phased out, beginning in 1973. Three years later only a few people continued to work in teams. In this instance the failure of job design was the consequence of flaws in implementing the concept rather than the concept itself. Here we see the importance of *management skill at coordinating work* to be a crucial moderator of the effects of job redesign on organizational effectiveness and job satisfaction.

---

[47] See Pehr Gyllenhammar, *People at Work* (New York: Addison-Wesley, 1977), for a full account of the Volvo experience.

[48] This discussion is based upon Noel M. Tichy and Jay N. Nisberg, "When Does Job Restructuring Work?" *Organizational Dynamics* (Summer 1976), pp. 63–80.

The General Foods Experience

In the early 1970s General Foods opened a plant in Topeka, Kansas which was designed to overcome problems in the company's other plants.[49] Specifically, management desired to find ways to combat product waste, absenteeism, shutdowns, and low morale. The new plant incorporated many of the features popularized in the Volvo experience including autonomous work groups, challenging jobs, job mobility, feedback, and group management.

Teams of 7 to 14 members were established that shared responsibility for doing the work. The teams worked for a coach rather than a supervisor. Members rotated from dreary to meaningful jobs in the hope that they would be motivated to perform more effectively. Pay was related to the number of tasks each team member mastered. Some status symbols such as parking privileges were removed so that managers and workers used the same parking area.

The initial results of this effort to motivate better performance resulted in lower production cost with savings estimated at $1 million annually. These savings resulted from lower overhead costs, fewer quality rejects, and lower absenteeism rates. Morale and job satisfaction also improved. However, recently there have been reports that some General Foods managers are openly hostile toward the program. Apparently some managers began to resist the program because it was perceived to be reducing their power, authority, and decision-making flexibility.

Other Experiences with Job Redesign

These three case histories are not the only instances of experiences, positive and negative, with job redesign. Early attempts were undertaken in IBM (1944) and Detroit Edison Company (1950s).[50] In both of these cases, job redesign, specifically job enlargement, resulted in lower costs, fewer absences, and increased productivity. AT&T, Arapahoe Chemical Company, the Internal Revenue Service, and Saab-Scandia of Norway have in some ways implemented job redesign. All these experiences have not been equally successful as we noted in the GM mobile home discussion. Another example of negative results ensuing from job enrichment was the Internal Revenue Service experience.[51]

In general the conclusions one reaches, when considering the experience of job redesign approaches, are that they are relatively successful in increasing quality of output, but not quantity. This conclusion pertains, however, only if the reward system already satisfies lower level needs. If it presently

---

[49] This discussion is based upon "Stonewalling Plant Democracy," *Business Week* (March 28, 1977), pp. 78, 81–82; and Richard E. Walton "How to Counter Alienation in the Plant," *Harvard Business Review* (November–December 1972), pp. 70–81.

[50] Peter Schoderbek and W. Rief, *Job Enlargement* (Ann Arbor: University of Michigan Press, 1969).

[51] Harold F. M. Rush, *Job Design for Motivation* (New York: The Conference Board, 1971), pp. 52–53.

does not satisfy lower level needs, employees cannot be expected to experience upper level need satisfaction (intrinsic rewards) through enriched job content.

Since a primary source of organizational effectiveness is job performance, managers should design jobs according to the best available knowledge. At present, the strategies for designing and redesigning jobs have evolved from scientific management approaches to work design with emphasis on quality of work life issues. Job enlargement and job enrichment are important, but often incomplete strategies. Strategies which take into account individual differences probably have the greatest probability of success, assuming compatible environmental, situational, and management conditions. Managers must diagnose their own people and organizations to determine the applicability of specific job design approaches.

MAJOR ISSUES FOR THE MANAGER TO CONSIDER

A. Micro-organization design involves managerial decisions and actions which specify objective job scopes and relationships to satisfy organizational requirements as well as the social and personal requirements of the job holders.

B. Contemporary managers must consider the issue of quality of work life when designing jobs. This issue reflects society's concern for work experiences which contribute to the personal growth and development of employees.

C. Strategies for increasing the potential of jobs to satisfy the social and personal requirements of job holders have gone through an evolutionary process. Initial efforts were directed toward job rotation and job enlargement. These strategies produced some gains in job satisfaction, but did not change primary motivators such as responsibility, achievement, and autonomy.

D. During the 1960s, job enrichment became a widely recognized strategy for improving quality of work-life factors. This strategy is based upon Herzberg's motivation theory and involves increasing the *depth* of jobs through greater delegation of authority to job holders. Despite some major successes, job enrichment is not universally applicable because it does not consider individual differences.

E. Individual differences are now recognized as crucial variables to consider when designing jobs. Experience, cognitive complexity, needs, values, valences, and perceptions of equity are some of the individual differences which influence the reactions of job holders to the scope and relationships of their jobs. When individual differences are combined with environmental, situational, and managerial differences, job design decisions become increasingly complex.

F. The most recently developed strategy of job design emphasizes the importance of core job characteristics as perceived by job holders. Although measurements of individual differences remain a problem, managers should be encouraged to examine ways to increase positive perceptions of variety, identity, significance, autonomy, and feedback. By doing so, the potential for high quality work performance and high job satisfaction is increased given that job holders possess relatively high growth need strength.

G. Many organizations including Volvo, Saab, General Motors, and General Foods have attempted job redesign with varying degrees of success. The current state of research knowledge is inadequate for making broad generalizations regarding the exact causes of success and failure in applications of job redesign. Managers must diagnose their own situations to determine the applicability of job redesign in their organizations.

DISCUSSION AND REVIEW QUESTIONS

1. Explain the difficulties that managment would encounter in attempting to redesign existing jobs as compared to designing new jobs.

2. Explain the relationships between job depth and perceived autonomy and significance.

3. It is possible to increase the depth of job without decreasing managers' authority? Explain.

4. What are the characteristics of individuals who would respond favorably to job enlargement, but not to job enrichment?

5. Explain why it is necessary to enlarge a job before it can be enriched.

6. Explain the relationships between feedback as a job content factor and personal goal setting. Is personal goal setting possible without feedback? Explain.

7. What specific core dimensions of jobs could be changed to increase employees' perceptions of instrumentalities and expectancies?

8. Which of the core dimensions do you now value most highly? Explain and list them in rank order of importance to you.

9. Compare the Volvo and General Motors experiences with job redesign and explain why Volvo's experience is relatively more successful.

10. In your opinion, was the General Foods experience with job redesign a success or a failure? Explain.

ADDITIONAL REFERENCES

Brief, A. P., and Aldag, R. J. "Employee Reactions to Job Characteristics: A Constructive Replication." *Journal of Applied Psychology* (1975), pp. 182–86.

Cummings, L. L; Schwab, D. P.; and Rosen, M. "Performance and Knowledge of Results as Determinants of Goal-Setting." *Journal of Applied Psychology* (1971), pp. 526–30.

Dubin, R. "Industrial Workers' Worlds: A Study of the Central Life Interests of Industrial Workers." *Social Problems* (1956), pp. 131–42.

Fein, M. "Job Enrichment: A Reevaluation." *Sloan Management Review* (1974), pp. 69–88.

Ford, R. N. "Job Enrichment Lessons from AT&T." *Harvard Business Review* (1973), pp. 96–106.

Foy, N., and Gadon, H. "Worker Participation: Contrasts in Three Countries." *Harvard Business Review* (1976), pp. 71–83.

Hackman, J. R., and Oldham, G. R. "Motivation through the Design of Work: Test of a Theory." *Organizational Behavior and Human Performance* (1976), pp. 250–79.

Hulin, C. L. "Individual Differences and Job Enrichment—The Case against General Treatments." In J. R. Maher, ed., *New Perspectives in Job Enrichment*. Princeton, N.J.: Van Nostrand Reinhold, 1971.

King, N. "Clarification and Evaluation of the Two-Factor Theory of Job Satisfaction." *Psychological Bulletin* (1970), pp. 18–31.

Lawler, E. E. "Job Design and Employee Motivation." *Personnel Psychology* (1969), pp. 415–44.

———; Hackman, J. R.; and Kaufman, S. "Effects of Job Design: A Field Experiment." *Journal of Applied Social Psychology* (1973), pp. 46–62.

Scott, W. E. "Activation Theory and Task Design." *Organizational Behavior and Human Performance* (1966), pp. 3–30.

Staw, B. M. *Intrinsic and Extrinsic Motivation*. Morristown, N.J.: General Learning Press, 1976.

Steers, R. M. "Effects of Need for Achievement on the Job Performance-Job Attitude Relationship." *Journal of Applied Psychology* (1975), pp. 678–82.

———. "Factors Affecting Job Attitudes in a Goal-Setting Environment." *Academy of Management Journal* (1976), pp. 6–16.

———, and Porter, L. W. "The Role of Task-Goal Attributes in Employee Performance." *Psychological Bulletin* (1974), pp. 434–52.

Umstot, D. D.; Bell, C. H.; and Mitchell, T. R. "Effects of Job Enrichment and Task Goals on Satisfaction and Productivity: Implications for Job Design." *Journal of Applied Psychology* (1976), pp. 379–94.

CASE FOR ANALYSIS

WORK REDESIGN IN AN INSURANCE COMPANY

The executive staff of a relatively small life insurance company was considering a proposal to install an electronic data processing system. The proposal to install the equipment was presented by the assistant to the president, John Skully. He had been charged with studying the feasibility of the equipment after a management consultant had recommended a complete overhaul of the jobs within the company.

The management consultant had been engaged by the company to diagnose the causes of high turnover and absenteeism. After reviewing the situation and speaking with groups of employees, the management consultant recommended that the organization structure be changed from functional to client basis. The change in departmental basis would enable management to redesign jobs to reduce the human costs associated with highly specialized tasks.

The present organization included separate departments to issue policies, collect premiums, change beneficiaries, and process loan applications. Employees in these departments complained that their jobs were boring, insignificant, and monotonous. They stated that the only reason they stayed with the company was because they liked the small company atmosphere. They believed the management had a genuine interest in their welfare, but felt that the trivial nature of their jobs contradicted that feeling. As one employee said, "This company is small enough to know almost everybody. But the job I do is so boring that I wonder why they even need me to do it." This and similar comments led the consultant to believe that the jobs must be altered to provide greater motivation. But he also recognized that work redesign opportunities were limited by the organization structure. He therefore recommended that the company change to a client basis. In such a structure each employee would handle every transaction related to a particular policyholder.

When the consultant presented his views to the executive staff, they were very much interested in his recommendations. And, in fact, the group agreed that his recommendation was well founded. They noted, however, that a small company must pay particular attention to efficiency in handling transactions. The functional basis enabled the organization to achieve the degree of specialization necessary for efficient operations. The manager of internal operations stated: "If we move away from specialization, the rate of efficiency must go down because we will lose the benefit of specialized effort. The only way we can justify redesigning the jobs as suggested by the consultant is to maintain our efficiency; otherwise there won't be any jobs to redesign because we will be out of business."

The internal operations manager explained to the executive staff that despite excessive absenteeism and turnover, he was able to maintain acceptable productivity. The narrow range and depth of the jobs reduced training time to a minimum. It was also possible to hire temporary help to meet peak loads and to fill in for absent employees. "Moreover," he said, "changing the jobs our people do means that we must change the jobs our managers do. They are experts in their own functional areas but we have never attempted to train them to oversee more than two operations."

The majority of the executive staff believed that the consultants' recommendations should be seriously considered. It was at that point that the group directed John Skully to evaluate the potential of electronic data processing (EDP) as a means to obtain efficient operations in combination with the redesigned jobs. He had completed the study and presented his report to the executive staff.

"The bottom-line," Skully said, "is that EDP will enable us to maintain our present efficiency, but with the redesigned jobs, we will not obtain any greater gains. If my analysis is correct, we will have to absorb the cost of the equipment out of earnings because there will be no cost savings. So it comes down to what price we are willing and able to pay for improving the satisfaction of our employees."

Questions for Analysis

1. What core characteristics of the employees' jobs will be changed if the consultants' recommendations are accepted? Explain.
2. What alternative redesign strategies should be considered? For example, job rotation and job enlargement are possible alternatives; what are the relevant considerations for these and other designs in the context of this company?
3. What would be your decision in this case? What should the management be willing to pay for employee satisfaction? Defend your answer.

EXPERIENTIAL EXERCISE

PERSONAL PREFERENCES

Objectives

1. To illustrate individual differences in preferences about various job design characteristics.
2. To illustrate how *your* preferences may differ from those of others.
3. To examine the most important and least important job design characteristics and how managers would cope with them.

Related Topics

This exercise will be related to intrinsic and extrinsic reward topics. The job design characteristics considered could be viewed as either intrinsic or extrinsic job issues.

Starting the Exercise

First you will respond to a questionnaire asking about your job design preferences and how you view the preferences of others. After working through the questionnaire *individually,* small groups will be formed. In the groups discussion will focus on the individual differences in preferences expressed by group members.

The Facts

Job design is concerned with a number of attributes of a job. Among these attributes are the job itself, the requirements of the job, the interpersonal interaction opportunities on the job, and performance outcomes. There are certain attributes that are preferred by individuals. Some prefer job autonomy, while others prefer to be challenged by different tasks. It is obvious that individual differences in preferences would be an important consideration for managers. An exciting job for one person may be a demeaning and boring job for another individual. Managers could use this type of information in attempting to create job design conditions that allow organizational goals and individual goals and preferences to be matched.

The Job Design Preference Form is presented below. Please read it carefully and complete it after considering each characteristic listed. Due to space limitations not all job design characteristics are included for your consideration. Use only those that are included on the form.

Job Design Preferences

A. Your Job Design Preferences

Decide which of the following is most important to you. Place a *1* in front of the most important characteristic. Then decide which is the second most important characteristic to you and place a *2* in front of it. Continue numbering the items in order of importance until the least important is ranked *10*. There are no right answers since individuals differ in their job design preferences. Do not discuss your individual rankings until the instructor forms groups.

_____ Variety in tasks
_____ Feedback on performance from doing the job
_____ Autonomy
_____ Working as a team
_____ Responsibility
_____ Developing friendships on the job
_____ Task identity
_____ Task significance
_____ Having the resources to perform well
_____ Feedback on performance from others (e.g.,
        the manager, co-workers)

B. Others Job Design Preferences

In the A. section you have provided your preferences, now number the items as you think others would rank them. Consider others who are in your course, class, or program. That is, those who are also completing this exercise. Rank the factors from 1 (most important) to 10 (least important).

_____ Variety in tasks
_____ Feedback on performance from doing the job
_____ Autonomy
_____ Working as a team
_____ Responsibility
_____ Developing friendships on the job
_____ Task identity
_____ Task significance
_____ Having the resources to perform well
_____ Feedback on performance from others (e.g.,
            the manager, co-workers)

Exercise Procedures

Phase I: 15 minutes
1. Individually complete the A and B portions of the Job Design Preference form.

Phase II: 45 minutes
1. The instructor will form groups of 4 to 6 students.
2. Discuss the differences in the rankings individuals made on the A and B parts of the form.
3. Present each of the *A* rank orders of group members on a flip chart or the blackboard. Analyze the areas of agreement and disagreement.
4. Discuss what implications the A and B rankings would have to a *manager* who would have to supervise a group such as the group you are in. That is, what could a manager do to cope with the individual differences displayed in steps 1, 2, and 3 above.

Chapter 12

Macro-Organization Design

AN ORGANIZATIONAL ISSUE FOR DEBATE: *The Technological Imperative**

ARGUMENT FOR

Since the pathbreaking studies of Joan Woodward the view that technology *determines* structure has been debated. According to the view, an optimal organization design exists for each technological type; managers, therefore, should match up the design with the technology. Woodward's studies indicated that the design strategy proposed by classical theorists is optimal only for mass-production-type technology; System 4 design strategy is appropriate for job order and process technologies. Her studies cast considerable doubt on the view that there is a universal one-best way to organize.

The evidence, that technology is the compelling force behind design decisions, accumulated as other researchers tested Woodward's findings in other settings. Although subsequent research studies differed in some respects, the conclusions were consistent. Studies of industrial organizations in the Minneapolis-St. Paul area, for example, confirmed that when management failed to match structure with technology, additional costs were incurred which resulted in lower than potentially attainable organizational performance.

The findings that technology determines structure prompted theorists to devise explanations for the relationship. Their theories attempt to provide general frameworks for thinking about the relationships between structure and technology. Thus in manufacturing as well as non-manufacturing business firms it is possible to argue that technology is the most important determinant, indeed the imperative.

ARGUMENT AGAINST

The argument against the technology imperative is based upon research which indicates that while technology is important, other considerations must be taken into account. The most compelling counterargument is that technology is the important variable for designing organization *units* which directly produce the product or service. Thus the production department or division should be designed to meet technological demands, but other units in the organization face different, nontechnological, demands. This view is based upon the theory that organizations must deal with various subenvironments each posing different constraints.

The view that technology is the primary influence on structure is not borne out by studies of very large organizations. Woodward's studies, and those of supportive researchers, included firms of relatively small size. The impact of technology is more noticeable in small firms than in larger ones since larger firms create staff units to deal with nonproduction environments—research, marketing, information, for example. Thus, the larger the organization, the less influential technology becomes. Size, then, according to the counter argument is the principal determinant of structure, not technology.

---

* Based upon John H. Jackson and Cyril P. Morgan, *Organization Theory* (Englewood Cliffs, N.J.: Prentice-Hall, Inc. 1978), pp. 175–98.

INTRODUCTION

Managers must choose among several design theories to guide their decisions. Some theories stress that there is "one best way" to design the organization, and these we term *universal* theories; others state that the optimal
structure can vary from situation to situation depending upon such factors
as technology and environmental differences, and these we term *contingency*
theories. The competing theories also differ in the manner in which they
have been devised. For example, some design theories result from logical
deduction, others from research investigations. Some theories seek solely
to provide the bases for describing organizations, while others seek to pre-
scribe the "best" organization. Finally, some theories focus on the task unit
as the important basis of analysis, while others attempt to analyze the total
organizational entity. These differences in approach, intent, and unit of analysis impair attempts to devise a general theory of macro-organization design.

UNIVERSAL DESIGN THEORIES

Organization design theories which suggest that there is "one best way"
to organization include classical organization theory, bureaucratic theory,
and System 4 theory. In this section these three important ideas are presented
as bases for understanding the modern approach, contingency design theory.
Figure 12–1 indicates the relationship among the important theories of macro-
organization design. Classical organization theory and bureaucratic theory

Figure 12–1
Development of Macro-Organization Design Theories

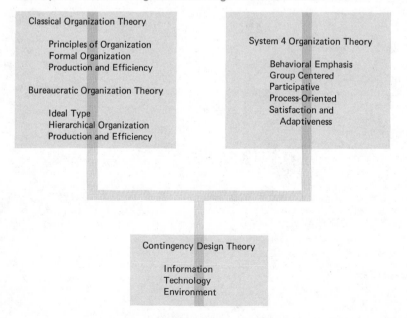

Classical Organization Theory

Principles of Organization
Formal Organization
Production and Efficiency

Bureaucratic Organization Theory

Ideal Type
Hierarchical Organization
Production and Efficiency

System 4 Organization Theory

Behavioral Emphasis
Group Centered
Participative
Process-Oriented
Satisfaction and
Adaptiveness

Contingency Design Theory

Information
Technology
Environment

are much alike. Each arrives at the same recommendations regarding the one-best way to organize. In contrast, System 4 organization theory proposes that the one-best way to organize is in the opposite direction from that of classical organization and bureaucratic theory. Contingency organization design theory, the more recent approach, rests on the idea that either classical or System 4-type organization can be optimal depending upon factors in the situation, i.e., contingencies.

Classical Organization Theory

A body of literature emerged during the early part of the 20th century which considered the problem of designing the structure of an organization as but one of a number of managerial tasks, including planning and controlling. The objective of these writers was to define *principles* which could guide managers in the performance of their tasks. To this end, an early writer, Henri Fayol, proposed a number of principles which he had found useful in the management of a large coal mining company in France.[1] Fayol believed that these principles had served him in good stead, yet he recognized their tentative nature. He viewed the art of management as consisting of selecting the appropriate principle for a given situation.

These principles provide guidelines for designing a system of interrelated tasks and authority. If we understand that the organizing function involves dividing a task into successively smaller subtasks, regrouping these tasks into related departments, appointing a manager of each department and delegating authority to that manager, and, finally, linking the departments through a chain of command, then we can understand the logic of Fayol's five structural principles.

The Principle of Division of Work. Through specialization, the number of objects to which attention and effort must be directed is reduced, and as Fayol stated, specialization "has been recognized as the best means of making use of individuals and groups of people." At the same time that Fayol stated the general case for specialization, he also recognized that there is an optimum point. As he stated, "division of work has its limits which experience and a sense of proportion teach us may not be exceeded." At the time of Fayol's writings, the limit of specialization, that is, the optimal point, had not been definitively determined. The work of industrial engineers, particularly Taylor and his followers, had resulted in the bases for work simplification methods. These methods, such as work standards and motion and time study, emphasized technical (not behavioral) dimensions of work.

The Principle of Unity of Direction. Activities which have the same objective should operate according to one plan and should be directed by one manager. The principle accounts for the necessity to appoint a manager to coordinate the related activities, but it says nothing about the scope of the manager's role.

---

[1] Henri Fayol, *General and Industrial Management,* translated by J. A. Conbrough (Geneva: International Management Institute, 1929). The more widely circulated translation is that of Constance Storrs (London: Pitman Publishing Corp., 1949).

The Principle of Centralization.   There exists for each situation an optimal balance between centralization and decentralization. That balance cannot be determined without reference to the capabilities of managers who are appointed to coordinate the departments. Contrary to some interpretations, this principle does not state that authority for all decisions should be centralized at the top of the organization. Rather, it states that managers' responsibilities should reflect their capacity to meet the responsibilities. Once responsibility is assigned, commensurate authority must also be assigned.

The Principle of Authority and Responsibility.   There must be some relationship between the responsibilities of managers and the authority that they exercise; the desired relationship is equality between the two. Yet there is no easy way to assess the relationship, particularly as one examines the tasks of upper level managers. Fayol understood that "as work grows more complex, as the number of workers involved increases, as the final result is more remote, it is increasingly difficult to isolate the share of the initial act of authority in the ultimate result and to establish the degree of responsibility of the manager." The principle states no formula by which one can equate authority and responsibility, and, in fact, no such formula may exist. Yet this recognition does not violate the basic premise of the principle, which is that if one is expected to direct the efforts of subordinates, one should also be delegated "the right to give orders and the power to exact obedience."

The Scalar Chain Principle.   The natural result of the implementation of the preceding four principles is a graded chain of superiors from the "ultimate authority to the lowest ranks." The scalar chain is the route for all vertical communications in an organization. Accordingly, all communications from the lowest level must pass through each superior in the chain of command. Correspondingly, communications from the top must pass through each subordinate until it reaches the appropriate level.

These five principles define the major issues to be resolved in creating the structure of tasks and authority. They do not specify fixed rules of conduct or precise answers. Instead they define the major considerations and propose guidelines for managerial action.

Fayol's writings became part of a literature which, although each contributor made unique contributions, had a common thrust. Writers such as Mooney and Reiley,[2] Follett,[3] and Urwick[4] all shared the common objective of defining the principles which should guide the design and management of organizations. A complete review of their individual contributions will not be attempted here; the reader can consult numerous sources for elaboration of classical organization theory. The major contribution of these writers *is to point out the importance of a rationally designed organization.*

---

[2] James D. Mooney and Allan C. Reiley, *Onward Industry* (New York: Harper and Bros., 1939). Subsequently revised under the authorship and title, James D. Mooney, *The Principles of Organization* (New York: Harper and Bros., 1947).

[3] Henry C. Metcalf and Lyndall Urwick, eds., *Dynamic Administration: The Collected Papers of Mary Parker Follett* (New York: Harper Bros., 1940).

[4] Lyndall Urwick, *The Elements of Administration* (New York: Harper and Bros., 1944).

Bureaucratic Organization Theory

Bureaucracy has various meanings. The traditional usage is the political science concept of government by bureaus but without participation by the governed. In laymen's terms, bureaucracy refers to the negative consequences of large organizations, such as excessive "red tape," procedural delays, and general frustration.[5] In Max Weber's analyses, bureaucracy refers to the sociological concept of rationalization of collective activities.[6] It describes a form, or design, of organization which assures predictability of the behavior of employees in the organization.

The inherent logic of the bureaucratic structure led Weber to believe that it is "superior to any other form in precision, in stability, in the stringency of its discipline and its reliability. It thus makes possible a high degree of calculability of results for the heads of the organization and for those acting in relation to it."[7] The bureaucracy compares to other organizations "as does the machine with nonmechanical modes of production."[8]

To achieve the maximum benefits of the bureaucratic form, Weber believed that the organization must adopt certain design strategies. Specifically:

1. All tasks necessary for the accomplishment of goals are divided into highly specialized jobs. This strategy is the familiar division-of-labor principle, and Weber argued its importance in the usual ways, namely, that jobholders could become expert in their jobs and could be held responsible for the effective performance of their duties.

2. Each task is performed according to a "consistent system of abstract rules"[9] to assure uniformity and coordination of different tasks. The rationale for this practice is that the manager can eliminate uncertainty in task performance due to individual differences.

3. Each member or office of the organization is accountable to a superior. The authority wielded by superiors is based upon expert knowledge and it is legitimized by the fact that it is delegated from the top of the hierarchy. A chain of command is thereby created.

4. Each official in the organization conducts business in an impersonal formalistic manner, maintaining a social distance with subordinates and clients. The purpose of this practice is to assure that personalities do not interfere with the efficient accomplishment of the office's objectives; there should be no favoritism resulting from personal friendships or acquaintances.

5. "Employment in the bureaucratic organization is based on technical quali-

---

[5] Michael Crozier, *The Bureaucratic Phenomenon* (Chicago: The University of Chicago Press, 1964), p. 3.

[6] Max Weber, *The Theory of Social and Economic Organization,* translated by A. M. Henderson and Talcott Parsons (New York: Oxford University Press, 1947).

[7] Ibid., p. 334.

[8] *From Max Weber: Essays in Sociology,* translated by H. H. Gerth and C. W. Mills (New York: Oxford University Press, 1946), p. 214.

[9] Weber, *The Theory of Social and Economic Organization,* p. 330.

fications and is protected against arbitrary dismissal.[10] Similarly, promotions are based on seniority and achievement. Employment in the organization is viewed as a lifelong career, and a high degree of loyalty is engendered.

To the extent that these characteristics are highly articulated in an organization, the organization approaches the "ideal type" of bureaucracy. Obviously few organizations exhibit all the characteristics of the ideal type, yet in some way, all organizations exhibit some degree of one or more of the characteristics. For example, all organizations practice some degree of division of labor, have superior-subordinate relationships, and some kinds of procedures, whether implicit or explicit.

System 4 Organization

The research which Likert has carried out at the University of Michigan has led him to argue that effective organizations differ markedly from ineffective organizations along a number of structural dimensions.[11] According to Likert an effective organization is one which encourages supervisors to "focus their primary attention on endeavoring to build effective work groups with high performance goals."[12] In contrast, less effective organizations encourage supervisors to:

1. Break the total operation into simple component parts or tasks.
2. Develop the best way to carry out each of the component parts.
3. Hire people with appropriate aptitudes and skills to perform each of these tasks.
4. Train these people to do their respective tasks in the specified best way.
5. Provide supervision to see that they perform their designated tasks, using the specified procedure and at an acceptable rate as determined by such procedures as timing the job.
6. Where feasible, use incentives in the form of individual or group piece-rates.[13]

The foregoing six points summarize the responsibilities of the manager in classical design theory. Yet Likert found through extensive research that these prescriptions did not result in effective organizations, thus substantiating the findings of other human relations researchers. He goes on to argue that organizations can be described in terms of eight dimensions, each of which is a continuum, with classical design organizations being at one extreme and "System 4" organizations at the opposite end. The eight dimensions and their extreme points are described in Table 12–1.

---

[10] Peter M. Blau, *Bureaucracy in Modern Society* (Chicago: The University of Chicago Press, 1956), p. 30.

[11] See Rensis Likert, *New Patterns of Management* (New York: McGraw-Hill Book Co., 1961); and Rensis Likert, *The Human Organization* (New York: McGraw-Hill Book Co., 1967).

[12] Likert, *New Patterns of Management*, p. 7.

[13] Ibid., p. 6.

Table 12–1
Classical Design and System 4 Organization

Classical Design Organization	*System 4 Organization*
1. *Leadership process* includes no perceived confidence and trust. Subordinates do not feel free to discuss job problems with their superiors, who in turn do not solicit their ideas and opinions.	1. *Leadership process* includes perceived confidence and trust between superiors and subordinates in all matters. Subordinates feel free to discuss job problems with their superiors, who in turn solicit their ideas and opinions.
2. *Motivational process* taps only physical, security, and economic motives through the use of fear and sanctions. Unfavorable attitudes toward the organization prevail among employees.	2. *Motivational process* taps a full range of motives through participatory methods. Attitudes are favorable toward the organization and its goals.
3. *Communication process* is such that information flows downward and tends to be distorted, inaccurate, and viewed with suspicion by subordinates.	3. *Communication process* is such that information flows freely throughout the organization—upward, downward, and laterally. The information is accurate and undistorted.
4. *Interaction process* is closed and restricted; subordinates have little effect on departmental goals, methods, and activities.	4. *Interaction process* is open and extensive; both superiors and subordinates are able to affect departmental goals, methods, and activities.
5. *Decision process* occurs only at the top of the organization; it is relatively centralized.	5. *Decision process* occurs at all levels through group process; it is relatively decentralized.
6. *Goal-setting process* is located at the top of the organization, discourages group participation.	6. *Goal-setting process* encourages group participation in setting high, realistic objectives.
7. *Control process* is centralized and emphasizes fixing of blame for mistakes.	7. *Control process* is dispersed throughout the organization and emphasizes self-control and problem solving.
8. *Performance goals* are low and passively sought by managers who make no commitment to developing the human resources of the organization.	8. *Performance goals* are high and actively sought by superiors, who recognize the necessity for making a full commitment to developing, through training, the human resources of the organization.

Source: Adapted from Rensis Likert, *The Human Organization* (New York: McGraw-Hill Book Co., 1967), pp. 197–211.

The organization described in the left-hand side of Table 12–1 is one which results from the implementation of classical design theory, although Likert does not identify it as such. He initially termed it "Exploitive-Authoritative," but later named it simply "System 1." He states that System 1 organizations are ineffective because they no longer reflect the changing character of the environments within which organizations must operate. System 1, that is, classical design organizations, tend toward status quoism and conservatism.

The major changes which Likert identifies as creating an environment that does not support classical design organizations include:

1. Increased competition from foreign countries with comparatively lower production costs, but with equal technology.

2. A trend in American society toward greater individual freedom and initiative and, concomitantly, less supervision from others.
3. A generally higher level of education resulting in persons more able and willing to accept responsible positions.
4. An increasing concern for mental health and the full development of the individual personality.
5. Increasingly complex technologies requiring expertness beyond the ability of any one person to comprehend. Consequently, the supervisor of specialists in these technologies often knows less about the unit's activities than subordinates.[14]

These environmental changes are creating pressures on managers to discover organizational designs which are able to adapt to these changes. And, according to Likert, System 4 is the direction toward which the more productive and profitable firms are moving.

As suggested in Table 12–1, the System 4 organization is more adaptable because its structural design encourages greater utilization of the human potential. Managers are encouraged to adopt practices which tap the full range of human motivations; decision making, control, and goalsetting processes are decentralized and shared at all levels of the organization. Communications flow throughout the organization, not simply down the chain of command as is the case in bureaucracies. These practices are intended to implement the basic assumption of System 4 which states that an organization will be optimally effective to the extent that its processes are "such as to ensure a maximum probability that in all interactions and in all relationships with the organization, each member, in the light of his background, values, desires, and expectations, will view the experience as supportive and one which builds and maintains his sense of personal worth and importance."[15]

To facilitate the realization of these processes, the organization design must implement three concepts: (1) the principle of supportive relationships, (2) group decisions making and group methods of supervision, and (3) high performance goals.[16] Structurally, the organization is viewed as a set of groups which are linked by managers. This view can be contrasted with the bureaucratic relationship. Figure 12–2 illustrates the System 4 organization design.

As shown in Figure 12–2 the groups consist of all persons reporting to a manager. Some managers are in the position of being members of two groups. In this dual capacity, these managers serve, in Likert's terms, as linking pins—they connect each group with its immediate superior's group. In this capacity they represent their groups to higher-ups and coordinate their groups with other dependent groups. The overlapping group structure, combined with the manager's use of group decision making, "represent an optimum integration of the needs and desires of the members of the organiza-

---

[14] Ibid, pp. 1–3.

[15] Ibid., p. 103.

[16] Likert, *Human Organization*, p. 47.

Figure 12–2
The System 4 Organization

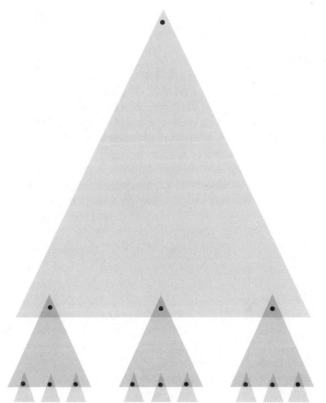

Source: Rensis Likert, *The Human Organization* (New York: McGraw-Hill
Book Co., 1967), p. 50.

tion, the shareholders, customers, suppliers, and others who have an interest
in the enterprise or are served by it."[17]

There is no question that Likert's views are widely shared by researchers
and practitioners. The literature is filled with reports of efforts to implement
System 4 in actual organizations.[18] Likert himself reports many of these
studies.[19] There is, likewise, no question that the proponents of the System
4 organization believe it is universally applicable; that is, the theory is proposed as the "one best way" to design an organization.

Thus, in retrospect, a result of the studies which tested the claims of classical design theory is System 4 theory. As we have seen, the two approaches

---

[17] Ibid., pp. 51–52.

[18] See particularly A. J. Marrow, D. G. Bowers, and S. E. Seashore, eds., *Strategies of
Organization Change* (New York: Harper and Row, 1967); and William F. Dowling, "At General
Motors: System 4 Builds Performance and Profits," *Organizational Dynamics* (Winter 1975),
pp. 23–38.

[19] Likert, *New Patterns of Management* and *The Human Organization*.

are diametrically opposed, yet each claims to be the most effective organization design.

CONTINGENCY DESIGN THEORIES

The current trend in management research and practice is to design organizations to fit the situation. Accordingly, neither classical theory nor System 4 is necessarily the more effective organization design; either can be the better approach depending upon the situation. The contingency point of view provides the opportunity to get away from the dilemma of choosing between classical theory and System 4. As such, it is an evolution of ideas, the bases for which can be found in the work of earlier writers.

The essence of the contingency design approach is expressed by the question: Under what circumstances and in what situations is either classical theory or System 4 organization more effective. The answer to this question requires the manager to specify the factors in a situation which influence the relative effectiveness of a particular design. Obviously, the contingency approach is considerably more complicated than the universalistic approach.

Two important lines of thought have attempted to determine the key situational factors. The first proposes that differences in *technology* determine the most effective organization design. The second suggests that differences in *environment and requisite information processing* are the crucial factors. As we will see, these two approaches are compatible and can be integrated into a general model of organization design.

TECHNOLOGY AND ORGANIZATION DESIGN

The organization theory literature includes a number of studies which show the relationship between technology and organization structure. We cannot possibly survey all these studies in this section; to do so would take considerable space and would go beyond the intent of our discussion. Rather, we will briefly review one study which stimulated a number of follow-up studies and has become quite important in the literature of organization design.

The Woodward Research Findings

The findings are based upon analyses of the organization structures of 100 manufacturing firms in southern England. The researchers collected information from each firm regarding:

1. History, background, and objectives.
2. Description of the manufacturing processes and methods.
3. Forms and routines through which the firm was organized and operated.
4. Facts and figures that could be used to make an assessment of the firm's commercial success.[20]

---

[20] Joan Woodward, *Industrial Organization: Theory and Practice* (London: Oxford University Press, 1965), p. 11.

The research team used this information to identify interfirm differences in organization structure, operating procedures, and relative profitability. At the outset, some obvious differences in structure were identified:

1. The number of managerial levels varied from 2 to 12 with a median of 4.
2. The spans of control of chief executives varied from 2 to 18 with a median of 6.
3. The spans of control of first-line supervisors varied from 10 to 90 with a median of 38.
4. The ratios of industrial workers to staff personnel varied from less than 1:1 to more than 10:1, and the ratios of direct to indirect labor varied from less than 1:1 to more than 10:1.[21]

These variations in structure stimulated the research team to seek out the causes. The team found that when the type of manufacturing was held constant, that is, "controlled," structural variations still appeared. Thus, type of manufacturing could not explain the variations. The team then examined the relationship between size, as measured by the number of employees, and structural variations. Again, the team was perplexed by the absence of a relationship—size of firm did not account for differences in organization structure.

The researchers sought to determine if there were structural differences between the more and less effective firms. The effectiveness of the firms was judged on the basis of their share of the market, the rate of change in market shares, profitability, capital expansion, and other less objective standards such as reputation of the firm and employee attitudes. The researchers classified the firms into three categories of effectiveness: above average, average, and below average. When the organization structures were compared within each category, no consistent pattern emerged. Thus, there was no relationship between effectiveness as defined by the researchers and organization structure.

It was then that the team began analyzing the information relating to technology—"the methods and processes of manufacture."[22] The team measured technology in terms of three related variables: "(1) stages in the historical development of production processes, (2) the interrelationship between the items of equipment used for these processes, and (3) the extent to which the operations performed in the processes were repetitive or comparable from one production cycle or sequence to the next."[23] The application of the measure to the information about the firm's manufacturing methods resulted in a continuum with job-order manufacturing and process manufacturing methods at the extremes, separated by mass production manufacturing.

[21] Ibid., pp. 25–34.

[22] Ibid., p. 35.

[23] J. J. Rackham, "Automation and Technical Change—The Implications for the Management Process," in Gene W. Dalton, Paul R. Lawrence, and Jay W. Lorsch, eds., *Organizational Structure and Design* (Homewood, Ill.: Richard D. Irwin, Inc., and The Dorsey Press, 1970), p. 299.

The measurement of technology can be understood through examination of the methods and processes of the three basic manufacturing methods. *Job-order* manufacturing is the oldest in terms of historical development, having emerged as the principal method in the preindustrial era. Since each unit of production is made to customer specifications, the operations which are performed on each unit of output are relatively nonrepetitive and noncomparable. The sequencing of material from one machine to the next depends upon the unique nature of the customer's specifications, not upon the inherent nature of the product. At the opposite extreme, *process,* or continuous-flow, manufacturing is the most recent historical development, having emerged during the present century. The product is standardized and moves in a predictable and repetitive sequence from one machine (or process) to the next. Between these two extremes is *mass production* of a more or less

Table 12–2
The Relationships between Certain Organizational Characteristics and Technology

	Job Order	Mass Production	Process Manufacturing
Median levels of management	3	4	6
Median executive span of control	4	7	10
Median supervisory span of control	23	48	15
Median direct to indirect labor ratio	9:1	4:1	1:1
Median industrial to staff worker ratio	8:1	5.5:1	2:1

Source: Joan Woodward, *Industrial Organization: Theory and Practice* (London: Oxford University Press, 1965), pp. 52–62.

standardized product; this manufacturing method was developed during the early stages of the industrial era and, in a historical sense, superseded job-order production. Mass-production technology introduces relatively more predictable sequences than those in job-order production, yet there remain sufficient product variations to create some unpredictability in production sequencing. The manufacture of printed matter, automobiles, and chemicals exemplify job-order, mass-production, and process manufacturing in respective order.

The three-way classification resulted in the identification of 24 job-order manufacturing firms, 31 mass production firms, and 25 process manufacturing firms. The researchers then analyzed the differences in organization structure *within* each of the three groups and among the three groups. These differences are shown in Table 12–2.

The number of managerial levels varied both within and among the three groups. Clearly the effect of advanced technology is to increase the number of managerial levels, that is, to lengthen the chain of command. Furthermore, the "above-average" firms in terms of success in each group tended to have the median number of managerial levels. The "below-average" and "average" firms had either more than, or less than, the median number of levels. Thus, though there are obvious differences among the three groups, the more effective firms within each group shared the common characteristic of having the median managerial levels.[24]

The spans of control of the chief executive varied in relation to technology. The effect of advanced technology was to increase the chief executive's span of control. The researchers also found that spans of control for the chief executive of the "above average" firms tended toward the median; whereas the executive spans of "below average" and "average" firms tended toward the extremes.

The spans of control of the first-line supervisor also varied with type of technology, but not linearly. In contrast with executive spans of control which increased with technological complexity, the supervisory spans of control were actually smaller in process manufacturing than in job-order production. The explanation lies partially in the different compositions of the work force, but also in the fact that machines are substituted for people at the production level in process manufacturing.

The ratio of direct to indirect workers varied with technology. The data showed the effect of technology on the composition of the work force and indicated clearly the increasing use of clerical and administrative personnel in more advanced technologies.

The ratio of industrial to staff workers decreased along the technology continuum. The data bear out the importance of technology for explaining variation in personnel composition and organization structure. The data indicated the shift of control away from the work force and toward machines and specialists in staff positions as the manufacturing process becomes more complex.

The differences in organization structures due to differences in technology are evident in Table 12–2. In addition to these differences, the research team noted other differences due to technology.[25]

1. The organizations at each end of the continuum were more flexible, that is, System 4, with "duties and responsibilities being less clearly defined." Organizations in the middle of the continuum were more rigid, that is, bureaucratic with detailed duties and responsibilities.

2. The organizations at each end of the continuum made greater use of verbal than written communications; organizations engaged in mass-production manufacturing made greater use of written communications. This pattern is consistent with distinctions between System 4 and bureaucratic theory.

3. The managerial positions were more highly specialized in mass production than in either job-order or process manufacturing. Consequently,

---

[24] Woodward, *Industrial Organization,* pp. 68–80, discusses the relationship between technology, organization, and success.

[25] Joan Woodward, *Management and Technology, Problems of Progress in Industry,* no. 3 (London: Her Majesty's Stationery Office, 1958), pp. 4–30; and in Gary A. Yukl and Kenneth N. Wexley, eds., *Readings in Organizational and Industrial Psychology* (New York: Oxford University Press, 1971), p. 19.

the mass production firms relied heavily on the traditional line-staff type of organization with the predictable conflict between the two groups. First-level supervisors engaged primarily in direct supervision, leaving the technical decisions to staff personnel. In contrast, managers in job-order firms were expected to have greater technical expertise and managers in process manufacturing were expected to have greater scientific expertise.

4. Consistent with the above point, the actual *control of production* in the form of schedule-making and routing was separated from *supervision of production* in mass production firms. The two functions were more highly integrated in the role of the first-level supervisor in organizations at the extremes of the continuum.

Thus the data indicated sharp organization and managerial differences due to technological differences. But how is it that technology affects organization? We offer our interpretation in the next section.

An Interpretation of Woodward's Findings

The relationship between technology and organizations can be understood with reference to the natural business functions—product development, production, and marketing. The job-order firm produces according to customer specifications; the firm must secure the order, develop the product, and manufacture it. The cycle begins with marketing and ends with production.

This sequence requires the firm to be especially adept at sensing market changes and being able to adjust to those changes. But more importantly, the product development function holds the key to the firm's success. This function must convert customer specifications into products which are acceptable to both the customer and the production personnel. The System 4 structure is most effective for promoting the kinds of interactions and communication patterns which are able to meet the market and product development problems associated with job-order or unit production.

At the other extreme of the technological continuum is the process manufacturer. In these firms the cycle begins with product development. The key to success is the ability to discover a new product through scientific research—a new chemical, gasoline additive, or fabric—which can be produced by already existing facilities or by new facilities once a market is established. The development, marketing, and production functions in process manufacturing all tend to demand scientific personnel and specialized competence at the highest levels in the organization. This concentration of staff expertise accounts for the higher ratios of staff and indirect to direct personnel in process manufacturing. Since the success of these firms depends upon adjustment to new scientific knowledge, the System 4 design is more effective than the bureaucratic design.

The bureaucratic design is effective for firms which use mass production technology. The market exists for a more or less standardized product— autos, foods, clothing—and the task is to manufacture the product through fairly routine means, efficiently and economically. The workers tend machines which are designed and paced by engineering standards. The actual control of the work flow is separated from the supervision of the work force. In such organizations the ideas of scientific management and classical organization theory are most applicable.

Subsequent research to test the effect of technology on structure has produced mixed results. The most complete replication was undertaken by Zwerman.[26] His findings were generally supportive of the "technological imperative" in that he found similar relationships between technology and executive spans of control and number of managerial levels. Another supportive study was completed by Harvey. He found that as technological diffuseness decreased, i.e., fewer product changes occurred over time, there was an *increase* in the number of specialized subunits, the number of managerial levels, the ratio of managerial to nonmanagerial personnel, and the extent of formalized rules and communication channels.[27]

More recent studies have indicated that at least two factors moderate the relationship between technology and structure, *size* and *managerial choice*. The effort of size is to reduce the impact of technology on the total organization structure. This relationship was noted in the Aston studies[28] and subsequently in those by Blau and his associates.[29] The structures of small organizations have not reached the stage of growth which permits the creation of support units such as engineering, research and development, product development, public relations, and the like. Consequently, the effect of technology on structure is more apparent than in firms which consist of a larger number of subunits whose goals and functions are unrelated to the production process.

The effect of *managerial choice* takes into account the range of choices that managers have in designing an organization.[30] The choices are constrained by factors such as technology and economies of scale, but managers have considerable discretion within those constraints. This point of view reconfirms the importance of management decision making for organizational performance. More important, it identifies technology as only one, albeit important, factor in the organization's *environment*.

---

[26] William L. Zwerman, *New Perspectives in Organization Theory* (Westport, Conn.: Greenwood Publishing Co., 1970).

[27] Edward Harvey, "Technology and the Structure of Organizations," *American Sociological Review* (1968), pp. 247–59.

[28] David J. Hickson, Derek S. Pugh, and Diana C. Pheysey "Operations Technology and Organizations Structure: An Empirical Reappraisal," *Administrative Science Quarterly* (September 1969), pp. 378–98.

[29] Peter M. Blau, Cecilia M. Falbe, William McKinley, and K. Tracy Phelps, "Technology and Organization in Manufacturing," *Administrative Science Quarterly* (March 1976), pp. 20–30.

[30] John R. Montanari, "An Expanded Theory of Structural Determination: An Empirical Investigation of the Impact of Managerial Discretion on Organization Structure," D.B.A. Dissertation, University of Colorado, Boulder, Colorado, 1976.

ENVIRONMENT AND ORGANIZATION DESIGN

The relationship between technology and effective organization design was firmly established in the Woodward study. Yet, as we saw, the interpretation of these relationships required that the *environment* of the organizations be taken into account. Thus the more basic explanation for differences in organization is differences in the environment. This line of reasoning has been pursued by a number of researchers, notably Lawrence and Lorsch. We shall review some of their theory and research findings in this section.

The Lawrence and Lorsch Findings

The data base of the Lawrence and Lorsch findings consisted of detailed case studies of firms in the plastics, food, and container industries.[31] The initial study consisted of case studies of six firms operating in the plastics industry. Lawrence and Lorsch analyzed these studies to answer the following questions.

1. How are the environmental demands facing various organizations different and how do environmental demands relate to the internal functioning of effective organizations?
2. Is it true that organizations in certain or stable environments make more exclusive use of the formal hierarchy to achieve integration, and, if so, why? Is it because less integration is required, or because in a certain environment these decisions can be made more effectively at higher organization levels or by fewer people?
3. Is the same degree of differentiation in orientation and in departmental structure found in organizations in different industrial environments?
4. If greater differentiations among functional departments is required in different industries, does this influence the problems of integrating the organizations' parts? Does it influence the organizations' means of achieving integration?[32]

These four questions not only summarize the thrust of the research, but also introduce three key concepts: *differentiation, integration,* and *environment.*

Differentiation. The "state of segmentation of the organizational system into subsystems, each of which tends to develop particular attributes in relation to the requirements posed by its relevant external environment" is termed differentiation.[33] This concept refers in part to the idea of specialization of labor, specifically to the degree of departmentalization. But it is broader and

---

[31] Paul R. Lawrence and Jay W. Lorsch, "Differentiation and Integration in Complex Organizations," *Administrative Science Quarterly* (June 1967) pp. 1–47; Jay W. Lorsch, *Product Innovation and Organization* (New York: Macmillan, 1965); Paul R. Lawrence and Jay W. Lorsch, *Organization and Environment* (Homewood, Ill.: Richard D. Irwin, Inc. 1969).

[32] Lawrence and Lorsch, *Organization and Environment,* p. 16.

[33] Lawrence and Lorsch, "Differentiation and Integration in Complex Organizations," pp. 3–4.

also includes the behavioral attributes of employees of these subsystems, or departments. The researchers were interested in three behavioral attributes:

1. They believed that the employees of some departments would be more or less task-or-person-oriented than employees in other departments.
2. They proposed that the employees of some departments would have longer or shorter time horizons than members of other departments. They hypothesized that these differences could be explained by different environmental attributes, specifically the length of time between action and the feedback of results.
3. They expected to find some employees more concerned with the goals of their department than with the goals of the total organization.

The organization of each department in the six firms was classified along a continuum from bureaucratic to System 4. They employees in bureaucratically organized departments were expected to be more oriented toward tasks and have shorter time horizons than employees in System 4-type departments.

Integration.   The "process of achieving unity of effort among the various subsystems in the accomplishment of the organization's task" is defined as integration, and it can be achieved in a variety of ways.[34] The classical theorists argued for integration through the creation of rules and procedures to govern the behavior of the subsystem members. As observed by Thompson, this means of integration can be effective only in relatively stable and predictable situations.[35] He observes that rules and procedures lose their appeal as the environment becomes more unstable and that integration by *plans* takes on greater significance. But as we approach the highly unstable environment, coordination is achieved by mutual adjustment.[36] Coordination by mutual adjustment requires a great deal of communication through open channels throughout the organization. In terms of the Lawrence and Lorsch research, the type of integrative devices which managers use should be related to the degree of differentiation. It would be expected that highly differentiated organizations would tend to use mutual adjustment as a means of achieving integration.

Environment.   The independent variable, environment, was conceptualized from the perspective of the organization members as they looked outward. Consequently, the researchers assumed that a basic reason for differentiating into subsystems is to deal more effectively with subenvironments. Following the lead of Brown, Lawrence and Lorsch identified three main subenvironments: the *market* subenvironment, the *technical-economic* subenvironment, and the *scientific* subenvironment.[37] These three subenvironments

---

[34] Ibid., p. 4.

[35] James D. Thompson, *Organizations in Action* (New York: McGraw-Hill Book Co., 1967), p. 56.

[36] Ibid.

[37] Wilfred B. D. Brown, *Exploration in Management* (Middlesex, England: Penguin Books, 1965), pp. 143–45.

correspond to the sales, production, and research and development functions within organizations.

The researchers hypothesized that the degree of differentiation within each subsystem would vary depending upon certain attributes of the relevant subenvironment. Specifically, the subenvironment could vary along three dimensions: (1) the rate of change of conditions over time, (2) the certainty of information about conditions at any particular time, and (3) the time span of feedback on the results of employee decisions.[38] Thus, in terms of this conceptualization, we can state the principal hypothesis as follows:

> The greater the rate of change, the less certain the information; and the longer the time span of feedback within the relevant subenvironment, the greater the differentiation among the subsystems. Furthermore, the greater the differentiation among the subsystems, the greater the need for, and the difficulty of, achieving integration.

The three concepts and the principal hypotheses are depicted in Figure 12–3. There we see that the Lawrence and Lorsch model recognizes that

Figure 12–3
A Conceptualization of the Lawrence and Lorsch Model

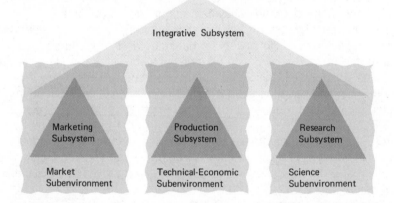

parts of the organization must deal with parts of the environment. The organizational parts, or subsystems, are identified as marketing, production, and research. The environmental parts, or subenvironments, are identified as market, technical-economic, and science. The subsystems must be organized in such a way as to deal effectively with their relevant subenvironments. The greater the differences among the three subenvironments in terms of rate of change, certainty of information, and time span of feedback, the greater will be the differences among the three subsystems in terms of organization structure and behavioral attributes. The greater these differences, that is, the more differentiated are the three subsystems, the more important is the task of integrating the three subsystems.

---

[38] Lawrence and Lorsch, "Differentiation and Integration in Complex Organizations," pp. 7–8.

Differentiation, Integration, and Effectiveness

The fact that departments within a single organization are differentiated in terms of organization and behavioral attributes is well established in the Lawrence and Lorsch research. Furthermore, the differentiation is in response to the departments' efforts to cope with their relevant subenvironments. The issue which must now be considered is the relationship between differentiation, integration, and effectiveness.

Lawrence and Lorsch propose that the relative effectiveness of an organization is directly related to the extent to which it achieves required differentiation. In other words, given the state of the subenvironment, there exists an optimal degree of differentiation that the organization should seek to achieve. Furthermore, given the attainment of optimal differentiation, the departments must then be integrated to the degree necessitated by the total environment. As

Table 12–3
Differentiation, Integration, and Effectiveness for the Six Organizations

Organization	Differentiation Score	Integration Score	Effectiveness Score
I	High	High	High
II	High	High	High
III	Low	High	Median
IV	High	Low	Median
V	High	Low	Low
VI	Low	Low	Low

Source: Adapted from Paul R. Lawrence and Jay W. Lorsch, "Differentiation and Integration in Complex Organizations," *Administrative Science Quarterly* (June 1967), p. 27, Figure 1.

noted earlier, the techniques employed to achieve the required integration range from rules and procedures to mutual adjustment.

The analysis which Lawrence and Lorsch used to examine these issues will not be elaborated here. Let us simply say that they calculated three scores for each of the six organizations: a score to measure the degree of attainment of required differentiation, a score to measure the degree of attainment of required integration, and a score to measure the effectiveness of the total organization.[39] Since the six firms operated in the same industry, the researchers could assume that required integration and differentiation were the same for all firms. Table 12–3 summarizes these findings. The scores were rank-ordered and placed into high, median, and low categories.

The data in Table 12–3 indicate that effectiveness is related to the degree of required differentiation and integration. Clearly the two high performance organizations, I and II, have achieved high differentiation *and* integration, whereas the median and low performance organizations failed to achieve this relationship. The lowest performance organization, VI, achieved low differ-

---

[39] The effectiveness score was based upon "change in profits over the five years prior to the study, change in sales volume over the same period, and percentage of current sales volume accounted for by products developed within the last five years. . . ." Ibid., p. 25.

entiation *and* integration. Thus the findings are consistent with the researchers' expectations.

An Interpretation of Lawrence and Lorsch's Findings

The differentiation-integration approach is based upon the fundamental viewpoint that there is no one best way to organize. But this approach goes further to show that a number of different types of organizations can exist within a single large organization. As Lawrence and Lorsch have shown, a large firm may find it quite necessary to organize its production department quite differently from its research department. One department may tend toward the bureaucratic design, the other toward the System 4 design. The differences in the organizations are due to the differences in the environments to which the two departments must adapt. The more stable and certain the subenvironment the more bureaucratic should be the departmental organization structure; the more dynamic and uncertain the subenvironment the more System 4 should be the departmental structure.

The process of departmentalizing creates the necessity for integrating the activities of the departments. The integration of separate, yet interdependent, activities is a familiar problem in the management of organizations. The classical writers proposed that the problem could be solved through the creation of rules, procedures, plans, and a hierarchical chain of command which placed managers in the position of integrators or coordinators. The solutions of System 4 proponents, however, differ in that they espouse teams, integrators, and group-centered decision making. Lawrence and Lorsch observe that either the bureaucratic or the System 4 approach is appropriate depending upon the situation. The techniques of the classical writers are appropriate in those organizations which confront relatively homogeneous and certain environments. Thus, organizations which confront stable and certain—market, technical-economic, and scientific—subenvironments can use classical integrative techniques.

Organizations which confront relatively diverse and uncertain environments, such as the chemical and foods industry, must rely upon integrative techniques espoused by System 4 proponents. Group-centered decision making, mutual adjustment through network communications, and integrative teams are necessary to integrate highly differentiated departments. The relatively more successful firms are those which recognize and adopt the appropriate organization designs for their departments, and the appropriate methods to integrate their departments.

ENVIRONMENTAL UNCERTAINTY, INFORMATION PROCESSING, AND ADAPTIVE DESIGN STRATEGIES

The relationships among environment, technology, and organization structure can be synthesized. The key concept is *information* and the key idea is that organizations must effectively receive, process, and act on information to achieve performance. Information flows into the organization from the subenvironments. The information enables the organization to respond to market, technological, and resource changes. The more rapid the changes, the greater the necessity for, and availability of, information.[40]

As Lawrence and Lorsch observed, organizations existing in relatively certain and unchanging environments rely upon hierarchical control, rules and procedures, and planning to integrate the behavior of subunits. These integrative methods are fundamental features of classical organization designs and are effective as long as the environment remains stable and predictable. The information-processing requirements are relatively modest in such environments. For example firms manufacturing and selling paper containers can plan production schedules with relative assurance that sudden shifts in demand, resource supply, or technology will not disrupt the schedule. Information requirements consist almost solely of projections from historical sales, cost, and engineering data.

Organizations existing in dynamic and complex environments, however, are unable to rely upon traditional information-processing and control techniques. Changes in market demand, resource supplies, and technology disrupt plans and require adjustments *during* task performance. On-the-spot adjustments to production schedules and task performance disrupt the organization. Coordination is made more difficult because it is impossible to preplan operations and to devise rules and procedures. It is imperative to acquire information which reflects environmental changes; "the greater the uncertainty, the greater the amount of information that must be processed among decision makers during task completion in order to achieve a given level of performance."[41]

From a managerial perspective, the effect of environmental uncertainty and increased flow of information is to overload the organization with exceptional cases. As a greater number of nonroutine, consequential events occur in the organization's environment, managers are more and more drawn into day-to-day operating matters. Problems develop as plans become obsolete and as the various functions' coordinative efforts break down. Some organizations are designed from their inception to deal with information-processing demands; most, however, must confront the problem at a point in time subsequent to their creation. For these organizations which discover that their present design is incapable of dealing with the demands of changing environments, the problem becomes one of selecting an appropriate adaptive strategy. The two general approaches are (1) reduce the need for information and (2) increase capacity to process information.

---

[40] The development of theory relating information-process and organization structure has been discussed in various sources. The more recent and most publicized sources are Jay Galbraith, *Designing Complex Organizations* (Reading, Mass.: Addison-Wesley Publishing Co., 1973); and Jay Galbraith, *Organization Design* (Reading, Mass.: Addison-Wesley Publishing Co., 1977).

[41] Jay Galbraith, "Organization Design: An Information Processing View," *Interfaces* (May 1974), p. 28.

Strategies to Reduce the Need for Information

Managers can reduce the need for information by reducing the (1) number of exceptions that occur and (2) number of factors to be considered when the exceptions do occur. These two ends can be achieved by creating slack resources or by creating self-contained units.[42]

Creating Slack Resources.   Slack resources include stockpiles of materials, manpower, and other capabilities which enable the organization to respond to uncertainty. Other examples include lengthening planning periods, production schedules, and lead times. These practices limit the number of exceptional cases by increasing the time span within which a response is necessary. For example, job-order manufacturers can intentionally overestimate the time required to complete a customized product, thus allowing time to deal with any difficulties that arise.

An additional effect of slack resources is to reduce the interdependence between units within the organization. If inventory is available to meet unexpected sales, no interaction is required between production and sales units. If inventory is not available, production and sales units must necessarily interact and coordinate their activities.

It is obvious that creating slack resources has cost implications. Excess inventory (safety stocks, buffer stocks) represents money that can be invested; thus carrying costs will increase. Extended planning, budgeting, and scheduling time horizons lower expected performance. Whether the strategy of creating slack resources is optimal depends upon careful balancing of the relevant costs and benefits.

Creating Self-Contained Units.   Creating slack resources can be undertaken within the present organization structure. Creating self-contained units involves a complete reorganization away from functional, toward product, customer or territorial bases. Each unit is provided its own resources—manufacturing, personnel, marketing, and engineering. Ordinarily accounting, finance, and legal functions would remain centralized and made available to the new units on an "as needed" basis. Reorganization around products, customers, or territories enables the organization to achieve desired flexibility and adaptability, but at the cost of lost efficiency.

In terms of information processing, self-contained units inherently face less environmental uncertainty than the larger whole. They deal with a complementary grouping of products or customers and do not have to coordinate activities with other units. With reduced required coordination, the units do not have to process as much information as before the reorganization.

Strategies to Increase Capacity to Process Information

Instead of reducing the amount of information needed, managers may choose to increase the organization's capacity to process it. Two strategies accomplish this objective, (1) invest in vertical information systems or (2) create lateral relationships.

---

[42] Based upon J. Galbraith, "Organization Design: An Information Processing View."

Investing in Vertical Information Systems. The result of increased environmental uncertainty is information overload. Managers are simply inundated with information which requires action of some kind. A strategic response to the problem is to invest in information-processing systems, such as computers, clerks, and executive assistants. These resources process information more quickly, and format the data in more efficient language.

Creating Lateral Relationships. As the necessity for increased coordination among functional units intensifies, decisions must be made which cross authority lines. In Chapter 10, we discussed the process by which management can move in successive steps from cross-functional task forces to matrix organization structure. The effect of introducing lateral relationships is to facilitate joint decision making among the functional units, but without the loss of efficiency due to specialization. The cost of the strategy is an increase in the number of managers who deal with the environment. The roles of managers in *boundary spanning* positions are particularly demanding; the success of this strategy depends upon how effectively the role occupants perform. The following section reviews some of the issues associated with these key jobs.

Boundary-Spanning Roles

Boundary-spanning roles perform two functions: (1) to gather information and (2) to represent the organization.[43] Sales personnel, purchasing agents, sales persons, lobbyists, public relations personnel, market researchers, and personnel recruiters are a few of the job titles which gather information and represent the organization. Roles of this type exist at the interface between the organization and its environments; they can be termed *external boundary roles*.

Internal boundary roles, in contrast, exist within the organization at the interface between subunits such as functional and product departments. Product managers, expediters, integrators, and liaison personnel are examples of roles which exist between subunits. As we have seen, organizations cope with environmental uncertainty and increase information by establishing these types of roles. They perform tasks that are similar to those performed by external boundary roles, except that they gather information which facilitates joint decision making.

The demands on those who perform boundary spanning positions are qualitatively different from others in the organization. These unique demands result from the fact that the role occupant must deal with often conflicting expectations, but without the authority to settle the disagreement.[44]

Role Conflict. Boundary spanners are often caught between people who expect different, and often incompatible, behaviors. Product managers

---

[43] Howard Aldrich and Diane Herker, "Boundary Spanning Roles and Organization Structure," *Academy of Management Review* (April 1977), p. 218.

[44] The following discussion is based upon Dennis W. Organ, "Linking Pins Between Organizations and Environment," in Dennis W. Organ, ed., *The Applied Psychology of Work Behavior* (Dallas, Tex.: Business Publications, Inc., 1978), pp. 509–19.

in matrix organizations for example, must balance the interests of marketing personnel who want high quality products and production personnel who desire manufacturing efficiency. The product manager has authority over neither group; and consequently must balance these interests and reach effective decisions through informal influence based upon deference and expertise. The company negotiator must deal simultaneously with the demands of fellow managers as well as union spokespersons. Each segment of the environment or the organization has its own set of goals, beliefs, and values. To the extent that there are great differences among these sets, the boundary spanning role is made more difficult. People having high tolerance for ambiguity and desire for relative freedom from close supervision, i.e., autonomy, would have the greatest chance of performing effectively because they would be able to cope with the conflict.

Lack of Authority. Boundary spanners do not have position power; that is, authority is not delegated to them. They must achieve their performance levels through other means. An industrial salesperson, for example, can attempt to influence customer demand by becoming extremely knowledgeable about the customers' technical and production methods. By doing so, he or she is able to influence the customers' decisions with respect to purchasing the organizations' products.

Agents of Change. Some boundary spanning positions are created to facilitate change and innovation. For example, key roles in research and development labs are those which link the lab to the various informational sources in the environment.[45] We have already noted the manner in which organizations respond to the necessity for new product innovation by creating product task forces, teams, and managers. Indeed the need to innovate arises coincidentally with environmental and technological pressures and demands. Yet the fact that boundary spanners are advocates for change places them in conflict with organizational subunits which desire stable operations, such as manufacturing, data processing, and personnel departments.

Thus we see that the adaptation of organizations to increasing uncertainty, and need for information involves changes in organization structure at the micro and macro levels. Managers can choose to cope with information processing demands by either reducing the need or by increasing the organization's capability to process it. If managers choose to cope with informational needs by creating lateral relationships, the cost of the strategy must be calculated to include the behavioral demands of employees in boundary-spanning roles.

The ability to obtain information and the effectiveness of boundary spanning are consequences of matching organization design with environmental demands. Placid, unchanging environments pose no serious problem for gathering information. Past conditions are adequate predictions of future conditions. Yet as Lawrence and Lorsch point out, it is necessary to view the environment as consisting of several parts. One part can be constant—requiring a bureau-

---

[45] Michael L. Tushman, "Special Boundary Roles in The Innovation Process," *Administrative Science Quarterly* (December 1977), pp. 587–605.

cratic structure to deal with it; whereas another part can be dynamic—requiring a System 4 type organization and appropriate boundary-spanning roles. Any general model of organization design must consider the information processing and boundary-spanning requirements of the organization in its environments.

AN ENVIRONMENTAL-CONTINGENT MODEL OF ORGANIZATION DESIGN

The state of knowledge regarding the managerial function of organizing is sufficient to outline a general model of organization design. Such a model would propose guidelines for the design of an organization in any institutional setting—business firms, universities, hospitals, governmental agencies, or any other setting in which people join together to accomplish a task. These guidelines must necessarily be stated in relatively broad terms since we are discussing the general problem of organization design as confronted in any institution. The starting point in the general model of organization design is systems theory.

As was first discussed in Chapter 3 where we considered the problem of organization effectiveness, systems theory suggests that we should conceptualize an organization as one element of a larger set of elements; the total set of interacting and interdependent elements is termed a system. We can combine systems theory and the analyses of Woodward and Lawrence and Lorsch to arrive at an understanding of the relationship between an organization and the larger system, or *environment,* in which it exists. Figure 12–4

Figure 12–4
The Four Subenvironments of an Organization

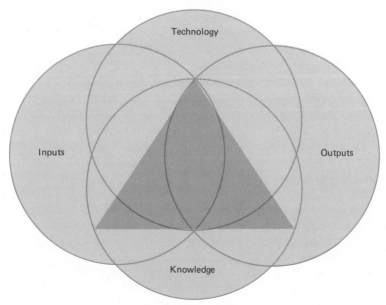

illustrates this conceptualization in which the organization is viewed as inter-acting within a total environment which consists of four subenvironments: input, technology, knowledge, and output.

The organization takes inputs from the environment and processes them through the application of technology into an output which is returned to the larger environment. A business firm takes raw materials from the environment and processes them into goods and services; a school takes people and processes them into graduates who contribute to other organizations; a hospital takes sick people and returns well people; a government agency takes and solves problems which confront society. This input-process-output cycle is carried on in the context of knowledge related to the current and projected state of the input, technological, and output subenvironments.

The most effective organization design is one which is consistent with the demands of each of these subenvironments; but the relationship between and among the subenvironments and the organization is very complex. Some concepts exist which facilitate an understanding of these complexities.

The Output Subenvironment

The most critical managerial decision is the selection of the output market which the organization will serve. This decision determines in large measure the nature and type of input, technology, and knowledge subenvironments which will, in turn, serve the organization. The decision to supply packing cartons rather than petrochemicals involves a simultaneous decision to utilize a certain kind of input, technology, and knowledge. Similarly, the decisions to train physicians, rather than accountants; to treat critically—rather than chronically—ill people; and to solve water pollution rather than solid waste problems involve simultaneous decisions to use certain inputs and technolo-gies in the context of a prevailing state of knowledge.

These interrelationships among the four parts of the subenvironment are implied in Figure 12–4 by the overlapped sets. Some interrelationships can be noted. For example, the decision to enter into certain output markets is constrained by the technological requirement. A decision to enter the automo-bile, petroleum, and chemical industries involves a decision to make costly investments in the machines and processes required to produce these out-puts. The technological requirement can be so great as to discourage firms from entering these markets.

The output subenvironment for any organization can be characterized in terms of (1) the rate of change in the requirements for new and different outputs, (2) the degree to which the organization can know with certainty the current and future demand for its output, (3) the length of time between a decision to supply or not to supply an output, and (4) the response (feed-back) from the market, or output subenvironment. The relative certainty of market information and the time span of feedback are related in the sense that lengthy feedback time is associated with relative uncertainty. At the same time the two should be separated to account for the possibility of rapid feedback of uncertain results. For example, the manufacturer of a fad item may know as soon as the product is introduced that the customers reject it, yet still not know what they would buy. It is also possible to have certain information coupled with long-term feedback. For example, a governmental agency which is charged with the task of controlling air pollution may know with considerable certainty the current demand for its output (the solution to the problem of air pollution), but not know for some period of time whether it has solved the problem.

The relative importance of these three attributes is not fully known. Lawrence and Lorsch weighted them equally in their scale. In a general sense flexible technology and System 4 organization are required to the extent that the output subenvironment is subject to rapid change, uncertain information, and long-term feedback; whereas, routine technology and bureaucratic organization are required in stable markets with certain information and short-run feedback.

The Input Subenvironment

Inputs can consist of raw materials, people, and problems. As identified above, business firms process raw materials; schools and hospitals process people; and governmental agencies process problems. If the inputs are stable and unchanging over time, we would expect the organization and its subunits to tend toward the bureaucratic design. For example, a firm which processes corrugated paper into packing cartons, a school which has a selective admissions policy, a hospital which treats only selected patients, or a government agency which deals with a single problem, say unemployment compensation, would all share the common characteristic of dealing with an unchanging input. On the other hand many organizations seek to take on larger tasks involving more diverse and changeable inputs. Examples of such organizations include chemical and plastic manufacturers, land-grant universities with open admissions policies, municipal hospitals, and multiproblem government agencies, such as the Department of Health, Education, and Welfare. These organizations confront a more diverse and uncertain input subenvironment than those which restrict their range of activities to the completion of one task.

The intrinsic characteristics of all inputs regardless of setting is the extent to which they are homogeneous, that is, uniform from unit to unit. In a sense, the homogeneity of inputs is related to the output. But there are instances in which homogeneous inputs are transformed into several different outputs; the textile, petroleum, and chemical industries reflect this situation. The interaction of inputs and outputs is critical for the technological decision.

The Technology Subenvironment

Technology can be defined generally as "the actions that an individual performs upon an object with or without the aid of tools or mechanical devices, in order to make some change in that object.''[46] As noted above, the technology of business firms consists primarily of man-machine operations. Furthermore, a range of technology is available to business firms from single job-order to process manufacturing. The choice of technology is related not only to the type of input which the firm processes, but also to the output which is to be returned to the environment. Constant, unchanging inputs which are to be processed into fairly homogeneous outputs require mass production techniques; varied and changeable inputs which are to be processed into many different outputs demand job-order production; constant and unchanging inputs which are to be processed into many different outputs require process production techniques. Thus the relationship between the output required, the nature of technology, and inputs is straightforward.

Nonbusiness organizations can be analyzed in a similar manner keeping in mind that the concept of technology in these settings refers to the application of analytical techniques, mainly knowledge, rather than the application of machines and tools. A school which permits the enrollment of many different kinds of students, undergraduate and graduate, and which seeks to process these students into a variety of specialties, must use a technology very similar to the job-order printer: each student is more or less under direct supervision of the faculty who teach the specialty the student pursues. The curriculum will be quite flexible with courses tailor-made to the student's needs. A school which enrolls a homogeneous student body which pursues a single specialty, say engineering or accounting, will use "assembly line technology." That is, the curriculum is specified and there is little deviation from the prescribed norms. We can also see how the "assembly line technology" would be appropriate for hospitals which specialize in the treatment of tuberculosis and for governmental agencies which specialize in tax collection.

The general characteristic of technology which is relevant for the organization design decision is the extent to which it is routine. That is, routine technology involves the same actions to be performed each time the person acts on the object, on input. Nonroutine technology occurs when the same action cannot be performed each time the person acts on the object, or input. The more routine the actions, the more bureaucratic is the appropriate organization since the actions of each person can be prescribed in detail by staff specialists. The techniques of scientific management (motion and time study, work simplification, and time standards) are most applicable in routine technology. But if one must use nonroutine technology, the organization must be oriented toward System 4 since all actions cannot be prescribed prior to performance.

The Knowledge Subenvironment

The knowledge subenvironment pervades the input, technology, and output environments. Each of these subenvironments is subject to considerable

---

[46] Charles Perrow, "A Framework for the Comparative Analysis of Organizations," *American Sociological Review* (April 1967), p. 195.

change. Knowledge about inputs may be quite stable, yet be dynamic in the technology and output subenvironments. For example, the scientific knowledge in the petroleum industry is very dynamic in the technology and output subenvironments. New products and new processes are constantly being developed in the research laboratories of oil companies. The reverse is true for the textile industry in which the input subenvironment is constantly providing new fabrics, such as polyester knits. In other industries the technology subenvironment may be more dynamic than either the input or output subenvironments. For example, the printing, railroad, and mining industries have introduced new technology over time, with little change in inputs and outputs.

The knowledge subenvironments in nonbusiness organizations can also be identified. The technology in hospitals is the treatment process and in universities it is the teaching process. A comparison of these two examples suggest considerable difference in the rate of change in the two technologies. Medical research is continuously devising new treatment technologies, and the success of a hospital depends upon the adoption of these new approaches as they appear; the inputs and outputs remain constant. The university is quite different in that it is experiencing considerable change in inputs and outputs but little change in the technology. Certainly new knowledge is being produced by the research faculty, yet the traditional classroom approach remains the basic technology for passing on that new knowledge to the students. Consequently, universities create departments which attempt to learn more about the student body, present and prospective, and about what society is demanding in the form of new careers; yet comparatively little effort is expended to identify new technologies of teaching.

The two aspects of the knowledge subenvironment which the manager must identify are its rate of change and its focus. As seen above, the rate of change can vary both within and among the subenvironments. The focus of the knowledge may be toward the development of new outputs, inputs, or technology. As first observed by Woodward, and more recently by Lawrence and Lorsch, the success of an organization depends upon its response to the key subenvironment, that is, the "dominant competitive strategy." The relationship between research and development and production and marketing depends upon the focus of new knowledge. For example, if new knowledge is created in the output subenvironment, but less so in the technology subenvironment, the research and development department must be integrated to a greater extent with marketing than with production. If however, new technological innovations develop rapidly, the integration must occur to a greater extent between research and development and production than between research and development and marketing.

AN INTEGRATIVE FRAMEWORK

Managers must consider many complex factors and variables to design an optimal organization structure. The most important of these considerations are shown in Figure 12–5. The material presented in Chapters 10, 11, and

Figure 12-5
An Integrative Framework for Organization Design

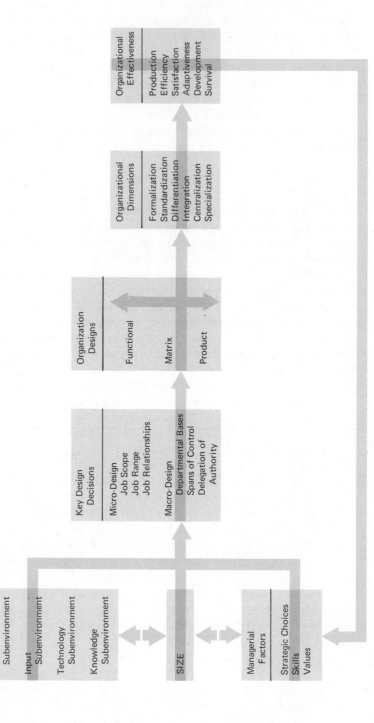

12 reflects the current state of knowledge regarding the micro and macro issues of organization design. As we have seen, the *key design decisions* are division of labor, departmentalization, spans of control, and delegation of authority. These decisions reflect *environmental* and *managerial factors* as well as the actual and contemplated *size* of the organization. The interactions of these factors and the key decisions are complex; managers do not have the luxury of designing a "one-best way" structure. Instead the optimal design depends upon the situation as determined by the interaction of size, environmental, and managerial factors. Matching the appropriate structure to these factors is the essence of *contingency design* theory and practice.

The overall structure of tasks and authority which results from the key decisions is a specific *organization design.* The alternative designs range along a continuum with functional organizations at one extreme and product at the other. The matrix design, at the midpoint, represents a balance between the two extremes.

Organization structures differ on many dimensions, the more important being shown in Figure 12–5. In general, functional organizations are more formalized, standardized, centralized, and specialized than product organizations. They are also less differentiated and achieve integration through hierarchy, rules and procedures, and planning. Product organizations, however, must achieve integration through lateral relationship and mutual adjustment. The effect of these dimensions is to channel behavior of individuals and groups into patterns which contribute to effective organization performance.

MAJOR ISSUES FOR THE MANAGER TO CONSIDER

A. The task and authority relationships among jobs and groups of jobs must be defined and structured according to rational bases. Historically, practitioners and theorists have recommended two specific, yet contradictory, theories for designing organization structures.

B. One theory, termed "classical design," is based upon the assumption that the more effective organization structure is characterized by highly specialized jobs, homogeneous departments, narrow spans of control, and relatively centralized authority. The bases for these assumptions are to be found in the historical circumstances within which this theory developed. It was a time of fairly rapid industrialization which encouraged public and private organizations to emphasize the production and efficiency criteria of effectiveness. To achieve these ends, classical design theory proposes a single "one best" way to structure an organization.

C. In recent years, beginning with the human relations era of the 1930s and sustained by the growing interest of behavioral scientists in the study of management and organization, an alternative to classical design theory has been developed. This theory, termed "System 4 design" proposes that the more effective organization has relatively despecialized jobs, heterogeneous departments, wide spans of control, and decentralized authority. Such organization

structures, it is argued, not only achieve high levels of production and efficiency, but also satisfaction, adaptiveness, and development.

D. The design of effective organizational structure cannot be guided by a single
    "one best way" theory. Rather, the manager must adopt the point of view
    that either the bureaucratic or System 4 design is more effective for the total
    organization or for subunits within the organization.

E. The manager must identify and describe the relevant subenvironments of the
    organization in terms of outputs, inputs, technology, and knowledge. These
    subenvironments determine the relationships within units, among units, and
    between units and their subenvironments.

F. The relationships among the subenvironments must be analyzed in terms of
    required linkages. Of particular concern is the determination of the dominant
    subenvironment.

G. The manager must evaluate each subenvironment in terms of its rate of change,
    relative certainty, and time span of feedback. These conditions are the key
    variables for determining the formal structure of tasks and authority.

H. Each subunit structure is designed along the bureaucratic–System 4 continuum
    in a consistent manner with the state of environmental conditions. Specifically,
    slower rates of change, greater certainty, and shorter time spans of feedback
    are compatible with the bureaucratic design; the converse is true for the System
    4 design.

I. Concurrently with the design of subunit structures is the design of integrative
    techniques. The appropriate techniques, whether rules, plans, or mutual adjust-
    ment, depend upon the degree of subunit differentiation. The greater the differ-
    entiation the greater the need for mutual adjustment techniques. At the other
    extreme, the greater the need for rules and plans.

DISCUSSION AND REVIEW QUESTIONS

1. Explain the rationale for the argument that there is "one best way" to design
    an organization.

2. "Any time a group forms to accomplish a task, a hierarchy of authority *must*
    be created." Comment.

3. All organizations have elements of bureaucracy. Can you think of any instance
    for which this statement is not true?

4. What is the basis of the argument that bureaucracies tend to become conserva-
    tive in their actions?

5. What is the basis of the argument that System 4 organization is the one best
    way to organize? Do you agree?

6. Do you believe it would be easier to change an organization from a bureaucracy
    to a System 4, or from a System 4 to a bureaucracy? Explain.

7. Do you believe that any real-world organizations can be termed System 4?
    Do you believe there are any "ideal type" bureaucracies? If not, of what use
    are these theories?

8. What are the basic flaws in the arguments of those who propose that there is
    "one best way" to organize?

9. Use the characteristics of bueaucratic and System 4 organization to describe two different organizations which you know about. After you have determined the organizational differences, see if you can relate the differences to technological and environmental differences.

10. What are the counterparts to the market, technical-economic, and scientific subenvironments of a university? A hospital? A professional football team?

11. What criteria of effectiveness were used in the Woodward research? Compare these with the criteria used in the Lawrence and Lorsch research.

12. Discuss the manner in which technology and environmental certainty interact to determine the most effective organization.

13. Although not the main focus of this chapter, we have suggested ways in which the structure of an organization is related to such processes as communications, interactions, and time orientations. As a general rule, are you prepared to accept the argument that the structure does, in fact, determine important aspects of these processes? Discuss your reasoning.

14. Based upon whatever information is at your disposal, rank from high to low the environmental uncertainty of a college of arts and sciences, a college of engineering, a college of business, and a college of education. What does your ranking suggest about the integration techniques which would be appropriate in each college?

ADDITIONAL REFERENCES

Blau, P. M. "A Formal Theory of Differentiation in Organizations." *American Sociological Review* (1970), pp. 201–18.

———, and Scott, W. R. *Formal Organizations.* San Francisco: Chandler Publishing Co., 1962.

Burack, E. H. "Industrial Management in Advanced Production Systems." *Administrative Science Quarterly* (1967), pp. 479–500.

Burns, T., and Stalker, G. W. *The Management of Innovation.* London: Tavistock Publications, 1961.

Chandler, A. *Strategy and Structure.* Cambridge, Mass.: The M.I.T. Press, 1962.

Corey, E. R., and Star, S. H. *Organization Strategy: A Marketing Approach.* Boston: Division of Research, Harvard Business School, 1971.

Davis, K. "Evolving Models of Organizational Behavior." *Academy of Management Journal* (1968) pp. 27–38.

Gordon, L. V. "Correlates of Bureaucratic Orientation." *Manpower and Applied Psychology* (1969), pp. 54–59.

Harvey, E. "Technology and Structure in Organizations," *American Sociological Review* (1968), pp. 247–49.

Hunt, R. G. "Technology and Structure in Organizations," *American Sociological Review* (1968), pp. 247–49.

Jurkovich, R. "A Core Typology of Organization Environments." *Administrative Science Quarterly* (September 1974), pp. 380–94.

Lynch, B. P. "An Empirical Assessment of Perrow's Technology Construct." *Administrative Science Quarterly* (September 1974), pp. 338–56.

Miewald, R. D.   "The Greatly Exaggerated Death of Bureaucracy." *California Management Review* (1970), pp. 65–69.

Mohr, L. B. "Organizational Technology and Organizational Structure." *Administrative Science Quarterly* (1970), pp. 444–59.

Osborn, R. N., and Hunt, J. G.   "Environment and Organizational Effectiveness." *Administrative Science Quarterly* (June 1974), pp. 231–46.

Pennings, J. M.   "The Relevance of the Structural-Contingency Model for Organizational Effectiveness." *Administrative Science Quarterly* (1975), pp. 393–410.

Perrow, C.   *Organizational Analysis: A Sociological View.* Belmont, Calif,: Wadsworth Publishing Co., 1970.

Pheysey, D. C.; Payne, R. L.; and Pugh, D. S.   "Influence of Structure on Organizational and Group Levels." *Administrative Science Quarterly* (1971), pp. 61–73.

Reimann, B. D.   "Dimensions of Structure in Effective Organizations." *Academy of Management Journal* (December 1974), pp. 693–708.

Segal, M.   "Organization and Environment: A Typology of Adaptability and Structure." *Public Administration Review* (May–June 1974), pp. 212–20.

Sherman, H.   *It All Depends: A Pragmatic Approach to Organization.* Tuscaloosa: University of Alabama Press, 1966.

Stevenson, T. E.   "The Longevity of Classical Theory." *Management International Review* (1968), pp. 77–94.

Tannenbaum, A. S.; Mozina, S.; Jerorsek, J.; and Likert, R.   "Testing a Management Style." *European Business* (1970), pp. 60–68.

Thompson, J. D., ed. *Approaches to Organizational Design.* Pittsburgh: University of Pittsburgh Press, 1966.

Urwick, L.   *Notes on the Theory of Organization.* New York: American Management Association, 1952.

CASE FOR ANALYSIS

DEFINING THE ROLE OF A LIAISON OFFICER

Recently the governor of a southeastern state created the Department for Human Resources. It was in fact a combination of many formerly distinct state agencies which carried out health and welfare programs. The organization chart of the department is shown in Exhibit 1. The functions of each of the bureaus as noted in the governor's press release are as follows:

The Bureau for Social Insurance will operate all income maintenance and all income supplementation programs of the Department for Human Resources. That is, it will issue financial support to the poor, unemployed, and needy, and will issue food stamps and pay for medical assistance.

The Bureau for Social Services will provide child welfare services, foster care, adoptions, family services, and all other general counseling in support of families and individuals who require assistance for successful and adequate human development.

The Bureau for Health Services will operate all programs of the Department that provide health service including all physical and mental health programs. This bureau will take over the functions of the Department of Health, the Department of Mental Health, and the Commission for Handicapped Children.

The Bureau for Manpower Services will operate all manpower development and job placement programs of the Department, including all job recruitment

Exhibit 1
Department for Human Resources

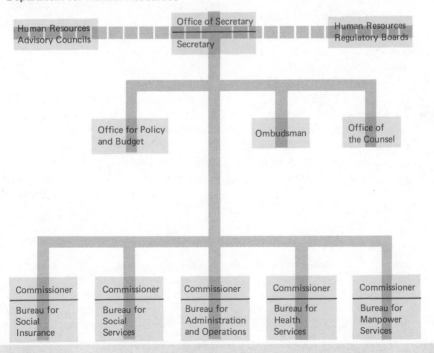

and business liason functions, job training, and worker readiness functions and job counseling and placement.

The Bureau for Administration and Operations will consolidate numerous support services now furnished by 19 separate units such as preaudits, accounting, data processing, purchasing, duplicating, for all the Department.

Very soon after the department began to operate in its reorganized form, it became apparent that major problems were traceable to the Bureau of Administration and Operations (BAO). Prior to reorganization each department had had its own support staffs—data processing, accounting, personnel, and budgeting. Those staffs and equipment had all been relocated and brought under the direction of the BAO Commissioner. Employees who had once specialized in the work of one area, such as mental health, were now expected to perform work for all the bureaus. In addition, it was necessary to revise forms, procedures, computer programs, accounts, and records to conform to the new department's policies.

Consequently the department began to experience administrative problems. Payrolls were late and inaccurate, payments to vendors and clients were delayed, and personnel actions got lost in the paper work. Eventually the integrity of the department service programs was in jeopardy.

The executive staff of the department, consisting of the secretary, commissioner, and administrator of the Office for Policy and Budget, soon found itself spending more time dealing with these administrative problems then with policy formulation. It was apparent that the department's effectiveness would depend upon its ability to integrate the functions of BAO with the needs of the program bureaus. It was also apparent that the executive staff was not the appropriate body to deal with these issues. Aside from the inordinate amount of time being spent on the administrative problems, a great deal of interpersonal conflict was generated among the commissioners.

The BAO Commissioner was instructed by the Secretary to give his full-time attention to devising a means for integrating the administrative functions. After consultation with his staff, the idea of an Administrative Liaison Officer was formulated. The staff paper which described this new job is shown in Exhibit 2. The BAO Commissioner presented the paper to the executive staff for discussion and adoption. According to the BAO Commissioner, there was simply no procedural or planning means for integrating the administrative functions. Rather, it would continue to be a conflict-laden process which would require the undivided attention of an individual assigned to each of the four bureaus.

Exhibit 2
Description of Responsibilities, Administrative Liaison Officer

Introduction

Executive Order 78–777 abolished the former Human Resources agencies and merged their functions into a new single department. A prime element in the organizational concept of the new department is the centralization of administrative and support activities into a Bureau for Administration and Operations which supports the four program bureaus of the Department. While the centralization of these administrative and support activities only included those functions that were located in centralized administrative units in the former Human Resources agencies, the size of the Department for Human Resources dictates that extra levels of effort be applied to insure close coordination and cooperation between the four program bureaus and the Bureau for Administration and Operations.

As one element in the comprehensive range of efforts now being applied to insure a high level of responsiveness and cooperation between the Bureau for Administration and Operations and each program bureau, there will be created within the Office of the Commissioner for Administration and Operations four positions for Administrative Liaison Officers, one of which will be assigned responsibility for liaison with each program bureau.

Responsibilities

1. Each Administrative Liaison Officer will provide assistance to the program bureau commissioner and other officials of the program bureau to which assigned in the:
   a. Identification and definition of the administrative and operational support needs of that program bureau;
   b. Determination of the relative priorities of those needs for services;
   c. Identification of programmatic and operational requirements of the program bureau that may be assisted by the enforcement of administrative regulations by the Bureau for Administration and Operations;
   d. Identification of resources available within the Bureau for Administration and Operations that may be of value to the program bureau;
   e. Coordination of the delivery of services by the various divisions of the Bureau for Administration and Operations to the program bureau;
   f. Interpretation of data and information provided by the Bureau for Administration and Operations; and
   g. Interpretation and distribution of administrative regulations and procedures issued by the Bureau for Administration and Operations with respect to its responsibilities under policies delineated by the Secretary and the commissioners of the Department for Human Resources
2. Each Administrative Liaison Officer will provide assistance to the Commissioner for Administration and Operations and other officials of the Bureau for Administration and Operations in the:
   a. Development of strategies for providing the maximum possible quality and quantity of support services that can be made available to the officer's particular program bureau within budgetary and policy constraints;
   b. Understanding of special needs and problems of respective program bureaus;
   c. Identification of new procedures and systems whereby services rendered to the program bureau can result in improved coordination between all organizational units of the Department for Human Resources;
   d. Identification of inadequacies or gaps in presently available services provided by the Bureau for Administration and Operations:
   e. Direction and/or coordination of task forces and other temporary organizational units created within the Bureau for Administration and Operations assigned to provide resources specific to the program bureau; and

    f. Supervision of all personnel of the Bureau for Administration and Operations that may be on a temporary duty assignment to the program bureau to which the officer is assigned.

Operational Arrangement

1. The Administrative Liaison Officer will be appointed to a position within the Office of the Commissioner for Administration and Operations.
2. The assignment of an Administrative Liaison Officer to a program bureau will require the concurrence of the commissioner of that program bureau.
3. The Office of the Administrative Liaison Officer will be physically located within the suite of offices of the program bureau commissioner to whom the officer is assigned.
4. The Administrative Liaison Officer will attend all staff meetings of the commissioner of the program bureau to which assigned and all staff meetings of the Commissioner for Administration and Operations.

Questions for Consideration

1. Evaluate the concept of "Administrative Liaison Officer" as a strategy for achieving integration. Is this an example of the mutual adjustment strategy?
2. How will the officers achieve integration when they will have no authority over either the administrative functions or the programs which are to be integrated?
3. What would be the most important personal characteristics to look for in an applicant for these positions?

EXPERIENTIAL EXERCISE

ORGANIZING A NEW BUSINESS

Objectives

To increase the readers' understanding of the organizational design problem in the context of a new business.

Related Topics

Chapters 10, 11, and 12 provide the reader sufficient information.

Starting the Exercise

Form groups of five to eight individuals toward the end of a class meeting. Each group will meet for 5–10 minutes and identify a specific type of business that will be the focus of their exercise. For convenience the groups can be encouraged to select one of the fast-food franchise restaurants. Most readers are familiar with these businesses and have sufficient knowledge of their operations to complete the exercise.

In the interim, before the next meeting, each group member will complete the six steps of the exercise. The groups will meet during class time to share answers and to prepare a group report. The reports will be presented at the second class meeting.

Instructions for the Exercise

1. State the primary mission of your business. What functions must be performed to accomplish the mission.
2. Describe the environment in which your business must operate in terms of the relevant technological, competitive, resource subenvironments. Identify the relative certainty with which information about these subenvironments will be received.
3. Write job descriptions for each class of jobs for each function, including managerial and nonmanagerial jobs.
4. Draw an organization chart and describe how the roles and functions will be integrated.
5. What important knowledge and skills will be required for each of the key roles in the organization?
6. What crucial decisions are to be made which will determine the success of the business?
7. Meet in assigned groups and share your work. Prepare a group plan which embodies the best ideas generated by the group members. Compare your plan with those of other groups and modify if you think necessary.

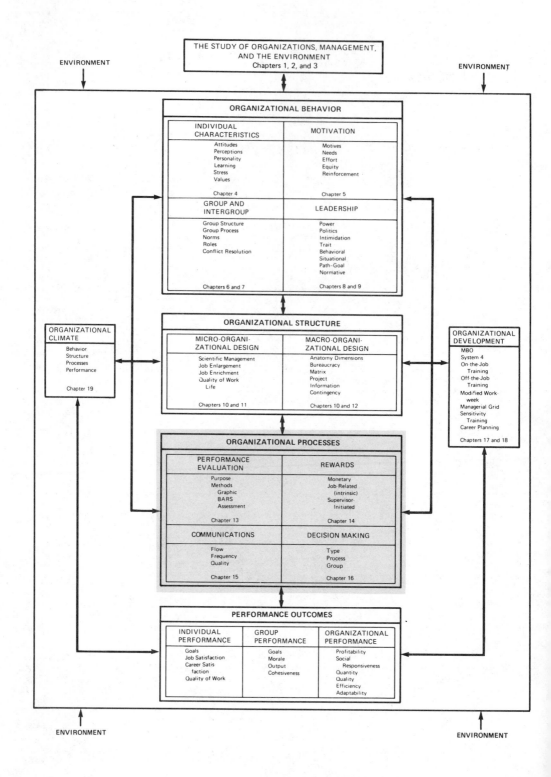

Part Four
Processes of Organizations

Chapter 13

Performance Evaluation

AN ORGANIZATIONAL ISSUE FOR DEBATE
Using a Trait-Oriented Performance Evaluation*

ARGUMENT FOR

An important decision that managers make is to determine how a performance evaluation will be used. Performance evaluation programs have been used to assess an employee's traits, behavior, and output. Many organizations make evaluation decisions using systems that evaluate personality traits. A trait is an enduring behavioral response expressed by individuals facing various stimuli. Popularly used traits in performance evaluation programs include: dependability, technical competence, commitment, and initiative.

The assumption made by some individuals using personality traits is that there is a relationship between these selected traits and individual job performance. The trait-oriented evaluation system is assumed by some users to be relatively inexpensive to implement, informative, and as accurate as behavioral- or results-oriented program. Since subjectivity cannot be completely eliminated from any performance evaluation system, there is sufficient reason to employ the least expensive program.

Another argument supporting a trait-oriented system focuses on the overemphasis on results. Excessive emphasis on results is associated with excessive job-related stress, excessive paperwork, and a tighter control system. The negative consequences of overemphasizing results are dysfunctional and not conducive to the actual development of employees. It can be reasoned that if quality of work-life improvements are to occur, there must be less emphasis on bottom-line results.

ARGUMENT AGAINST

Opponents of trait-oriented performance evaluation programs believe that results-oriented evaluations are needed. They agree that certain personality traits are important in performing some jobs. However, their argument is that traits are so ingrained and difficult to determine that few managers can successfully evaluate or alter them significantly. Traits are also considered less helpful for use in coaching and feedback sessions involving a rater and ratee. The rater is not able to cite examples of specific job behaviors that can be corrected or modified to improve performance.

To serve judgmental and developmental purposes, performance evaluation must emphasize both behavior and results. The program must examine those job-related behaviors and results over which the individual employee has control. Individualized goal setting evaluations between a superior and subordinate with feedback of results and behaviorally anchored rating scales (BARS) are two programs that can, if used correctly, provide some information on job-related behaviors and results. Of course, these two evaluation methods also have limitations and problems. These weaknesses of goal setting and BARS programs are more tolerable than those of a trait program.

---

* The issues of performance evaluation are discussed in W. J. Kearney, "Performance Appraisal: Which Way to Go?" *MSU Business Topics* (Winter 1977), pp. 58–64.

INTRODUCTION

No organization has a choice as to whether or not it should formally or informally evaluate its employees and their job performance. Just as people must be paid a fair wage or salary for working, it is inevitable that the performance of all employees will be evaluated by someone at some time. A survey of approximately one thousand firms indicated that 80 percent have some type of formal evaluation system, the majority of which were started since the 1960s.[1]

Under a formalized evaluation system, supervisors and managers are encouraged to observe the behavior of subordinates. This chapter focuses on the problems, contributions, and types of formal performance evaluation systems. The challenge facing managers involves finding an evaluation approach that provides an equitable and informative basis for evaluating the performance of employees. This is not a small challenge because every system has strengths, weaknesses, and costs that need to be evaluated carefully. In some organizations there may be a need to use more than one evaluation approach. The important theme of the chapter is not whether formal evaluation programs should be used, but what programs should be used and how they should be used.

PERFORMANCE EVALUATION: INEVITABLE

All of us are involved in evaluating people, places, and objects. The sales person attempting to sell a suit is evaluated, the meal at an exquisite restaurant or even a fast food emporium such as McDonald's is evaluated, and the vacation in the Colorado mountains is evaluated. The lawyers, doctors, and dentists that are chosen to solve problems and diagnose pains are evaluated. Many of these evaluations are informal, rather nonsystematic, and often incomplete.

Systematic and formal performance evaluations within organizations became popular after World War II. Walter Dill Scott convinced the United States Army to use a rating system for evaluating officers.[2] However, not until the early 1950s did business organizations begin evaluating technical, professional, and managerial employees. This emphasis was tied closely with a new wave of interest in management development programs. It was suggested that formal evaluation, on a regular basis, was a necessary part of any systematic and effective management development program.

At about the same time that technical, professional, and managerial employees were beginning to be formally evaluated, interest in rating the job performance of hourly paid or operating employees began to decline. A major

---

[1] Glen H. Varney, "Performance Appraisal: Inside and Out," *The Personnel Administrator* (November-December 1972), p. 16.

[2] W. D. Scott and R. C. Clothier, *Personnel Management* (New York: McGraw-Hill, 1941), pp. 217–18.

reason for this decline in evaluation was that at the operating level, promotion and other rewards were so often regulated by seniority or job tenure.

Accompanying this change in emphasis has been a shift in terminology. An older term, *merit rating,* was restricted to the formal rating of hourly paid employees. It was usually used in developing pay, transfer, and promotion programs. The newer terms *performance evaluation* or *appraisal* place a special emphasis upon the development of employees. They also use an evaluation interview between the rater and ratee. Consequently, *performance evaluation* will be defined as the systematic, formal evaluation of an employee with respect to his/her job performance and potential for future development.

Evaluating or appraising anything involves setting a value on it. Generally, there is no such thing as a universally accepted value. The values placed on an antique automobile, for example, will vary depending on whether it is appraised for insurance purposes, an auction sale, or for tax purposes. Even if the factors evaluated are agreed upon, the value set for the car will still vary with the person making the appraisal. Each appraiser will rate various characteristics differently than any other appraiser.

Compared to an individual employee, an antique car is easy to appraise. What makes an individual exert effort to perform the job and how valuable the resulting performance is, are subjects of interest for organizational researchers and managers. Early in a manager's career it becomes apparent that evaluations of subordinates' job performance are subject to controversy and disagreement. In addition, managers understand that subjectivity is a realistic part of evaluation programs. Subjectivity can be minimized, but to assume that it can be totally eliminated is unrealistic when undertaking performance evaluation programs.

Since performance evaluation is inevitable and is to some degree subjective, managers need to gather information that is relevant, accurate, and sufficiently complete. Managers that gather this type of information eventually will have to address the following questions: (1) What is the purpose of the evaluation; (2) What criteria should be evaluated; (3) What are some of the pitfalls of evaluation to avoid; (4) What method(s) of performance evaluation is best suited to accomplish the purpose?; and (5) How can performance evaluation become a development experience for subordinates?

PURPOSES OF PERFORMANCE EVALUATION

Many varieties of performance evaluation programs are now being used in organizations. In most organizations the evaluation program is designed to provide both the individual and organization (manager) with information about job performance. However, before any performance evaluation program is selected there should be a clear understanding among raters and ratees about the objectives of the system. Two broadly stated purposes of performance evaluation are to reach an *evaluative* or *judgmental* conclusion about job performance and to *develop* employees through the program.[3] These two broadly stated purposes are compared in Table 13–1. Notice the differences in time orientation, objectives, and roles of the ratee and rater.

Organizations are becoming increasingly aware that managers must clearly identify the purpose of the performance evaluation program. The judgmental and developmental purposes are certainly not mutually exclusive. In fact, surveys of performance evaluation practices indicate that many organizations have both a judgmental and developmental purpose.[4]

Table 13–1
Two Major Purposes of Performance Evaluation: A Comparison

Points of Comparison	Broad Evaluation Purposes	
	Judgmental	*Developmental*
Time orientation	Past performance	Preparation for future performance
Objective	Improving performance by changing behavior through reward system	Improving performance through self-learning and personal growth
Method	Use of rating scales, comparisons, and distributions	Counseling, mutual trust, goal setting, and career planning
Supervisor's role . . . . (rater)	A judge who appraises	A supportive counseling and encouraging person who listens, helps, and guides
Subordinate's role . . . . (ratee)	Listener, reacts and attempts to defend past performance	Actively involved in charting out future job performance plans

Source: Adapted from L. L. Cummings and Donald P. Schwab, *Performance In Organizations* (Glenview, Ill.: Scott, Foresman & Co., 1973), p. 5, Table 1–1.

Specific Purposes

Managers are continually faced with making judgments concerning the job performance of subordinates. For example, judgments are made about promotions and pay raises. Most experts recommend that evaluation sessions that address salary or promotion should be kept separate from those dealing with personal and career development. The rationale for the separation is based on the differences in the judgmental and developmental purposes of performance evaluation illustrated in Table 13–1.

A well-designed and implemented performance evaluation program can have a motivational impact upon ratees. It can encourage improvement, de-

---

[3] L. L. Cummings and Donald P. Schwab, *Performance in Organizations* (Glenview, Ill.: Scott, Foresman & Co., 1973). p. 5.

[4] Varney, "Performance Appraisal."

velop a sense of responsibility, and increase organizational commitment. Performance evaluation can also be motivational if it can provide ratees with some understanding of what is expected of them.

Another specific purpose of performance evaluation is the improvement of managerial understanding. A formal program encourages managers to observe the behavior of subordinates. Through increased and more thorough observations, improved mutual understanding between supervisors and subordinates can result.

Performance evaluation information also provides a basis for planning, training, and development. Such areas of weakness in technical competence, communication skills, and problem-solving techniques can be identified and analyzed.

A research purpose can also be accomplished through performance evaluation. The accuracy of selection decisions can be determined by comparing performance evaluations with such selection devices as test scores and interviewers' ratings.

Although the two broad purposes of performance evaluation are judgmental and developmental, the specific reasons for using it transcend the organization. Some of these more *specific* purposes are summarized in Table 13–2.

Table 13–2
Specific Purposes of Performance Evaluation

Motivation
Promotion
Dismissal
Salary increases
Wage increases
Improved managerial awareness of
  subordinate job tasks and problems
Improved subordinate understanding of
  management's view of his/her performance
Identifying training and development needs
Evaluating effectiveness of selection and
  placement decisions

One other important and often forgotten purpose of performance evaluation is to reduce favoritism in making important managerial decisions. This reason is not shown in Table 13–2, but it is extremely important to many employees. It is not shown in Table 13–2 because it is a subjective factor, while the other purposes cited are specific and related to the broad judgmental and developmental categories. The negative effects of perceived favoritism include strained supervisor-subordinate relationships, low morale, and dissatisfaction with company policies.[5]

---

[5] P. Pigors and C. A. Myers, *Personnel Administration* (New York: McGraw-Hill Book Co., 1977), p. 270.

JOB PERFORMANCE: CONCEPTUALLY

The importance of good job performance to the success of any organization is an accepted fact. Without good job performance at all levels of an organization, goal attainment becomes extremely difficult and uncertain. If an organization is not meeting its goals, the probability that individual employees are meeting their personal job-related goals significantly decreases—especially over the long run.[6]

Employee job performance is considered to be directly a consequence of (1) the abilities, traits, and interests of the employee; and (2) the motivational level of the employee. There is some debate about how these two and other variables combine to influence performance.[7] Expectancy motivation theory discussed in Chapter 5, proposes that ability, traits, interests, and motivation interact to determine performance. That is, performance can be predicted by assessing ability, traits, interests, and motivation level. Of course, accurately assessing a person's motivation level is easier to discuss or theorize about than to actually measure.

Organizational research has also indicated that the relationship between an employee's achieving good performance and his or her ability, traits, interests, and motivation to perform is influenced by other variables. Some of the often mentioned intervening or mediating variables discussed in earlier chapters include job design, organizational design, leadership, rewards, and role clarity.[8] Therefore, a thorough analysis of how good performance occurs attempts to account for at least the most significant mediating variables.

The notion of *good* performance has been an issue of concern among managers. What is considered to be good performance is an important question. Good performance for one manager may be producing more units. Another manager may want better quality of output or a more responsible attitude. What is considered good depends upon managerial judgments and values as well as organizational values. There are also some who propose that making decisions about whether performance is good or bad depends upon societal values.[9] Therefore, it seems reasonable to assume that before one can answer whether performance is good—the individual, the manager, the organization, and society must be considered. In addition, each of these four perspectives needs to be considered from a short- and long-run perspective.

Typically, a manager ignores the individual employee's assessment of what is good performance. Likewise, the individual employee ignores the manager's appraisal of what is good performance. This suggests one potential contribution of performance evaluation, namely being able to integrate differ-

---

[6] R. M. Steers, *Organizational Effectiveness: A Behavioral View* (Santa Monica: Goodyear Publishing Co., 1977), p. 124.

[7] Cummings and Schwab, *Performance in Organizations,* p. 46.

[8] Reexamine Chapters 3–10 for discussions of the impact of other variables on performance.

[9] A. K. Korman, *Organizational Behavior* (Englewood Cliffs, N.J.: Prentice-Hall, Inc., 1977), p. 350.

ent perspectives of what constitutes good job performance. There are presently some performance evaluation programs that at least consider three perspectives—the individual employee (ratee), the manager (rater), and the organization. To date, most performance evaluation programs are so individually oriented that the societal perspective is not a main focal point. However, when evaluating the effectiveness of an organization on a factor such as social responsibility, the societal perspective becomes another important benchmark.

THE PERFORMANCE CRITERION ISSUE OF EVALUATION

The performance evaluation program at any level within the organization hierarchy must at some point focus on the criterion issue. A *criterion* is a variable that has dimensionality.[10] It may be a physiological variable, such as an increase in blood pressure when being asked to speed up production. It may be an economic variable, such as cost per unit, or a psychological variable such as commitment toward an organization. In performance evaluation the *criterion* is the dependent or predicted measure for appraising the effectiveness of an individual employee. This definition applies to the individual level of analysis. At the organizational level of analysis, the point of discussion centers on evaluating organizational effectiveness. The majority of our discussion of performance evaluation will concentrate on the individual level which, of course, is a contributor to organizational effectiveness.

Requirements of a Performance Criterion

There are a number of requirements that should be met before a variable qualifies as a performance criterion. First, a criterion should be *relevant* to the individual and the organization. Determining what is relevant is itself controversial. Some person or group must make a judgment about what constitutes relevance. Once the relevant criterion has been selected, there must be an effort to develop a sound and valid measure of the variable.

Second, the criterion must be *stable* or reliable. This involves agreement between different evaluations, at different points in time. If the results from the two different evaluations show little agreement, there would be some uncertainty about whether the criterion was stable.

Third, a performance criterion may be relevant and reliable and still be useless in evaluating employees. A criterion is useful only if it can *discriminate* between good performers and poor performers. If all employees are good performers then there is no need to discriminate. If, however, there are good, average, and poor performers in a plant, office, or laboratory then the evaluation criterion must discriminate.

Finally, the criterion must be *practical.* The criterion must mean something to the rater and ratee. If the criterion serves no useful or practical function, then it becomes something that is evaluated but offers no meaning.

---

[10] Robert M. Guion, *Personnel Testing* (New York: McGraw-Hill Book Co., 1965), p. 90.

Meeting these four requirements does not provide the answer to two questions: (1) Should one criterion be used to measure job performance? and (2) Should the criterion be an economic, physiological, or some abstract variable?

Criterion or Criteria?

The use of the term criterion, a single noun, has resulted from the search for years to find the "ultimate criterion." Thorndike stated:

> . . . The ultimate criterion for a production line worker might be that he perform his task, maintaining the tempo of the line, with the minimum of defective products requiring rejection upon inspection, that he be personally satisfied with the task. . .[11]

This statement adequately represents the view of those who believe that a single criterion exists for every job.

There have been arguments against using a single ultimate criterion to evaluate performance. The arguments against the use of a single criterion center on logic and empiricism. Logically, it is argued that combining such variables as quantity and quality of production, satisfaction, and turnover is like adding apples, automobiles, and basketballs.[12] It is further argued that good performance is not unitary for different jobs for the same person, for different persons on the same job, or for different aspects of the same job for the same person.

The second reason for opposing the ultimate criterion concerns research results. The overwhelming majority of studies within organizations indicates that a single criterion cannot explain the variance among employee performances.[13]

In general, there is ample evidence to support either the ultimate criterion or multiple criteria arguments. In some situations, especially at the policy-making level, a single criterion is needed to reach a managerial decision. In other cases, involving promotion, salary and wage decisions, transfer, and counseling, multiple criteria can be useful in illustrating why a particular decision is made or a specific development program recommended. It would be extremely difficult to explain a promotion decision on the basis of a Thorndike-type statement using a single criterion. Of course, if the employee receives the promotion, he or she may not mind the use of an ultimate criterion for reaching the decision.

---

[11] R. L. Thorndike, *Personnel Selection* (New York: John Wiley, 1949), p. 11.

[12] D. E. Roach and R. J. Wherry, "Performance Dimensions of Multi-Line Insurance Agents," *Personnel Psychology* (Summer 1970), p. 239–50.

[13] W. K. Kirchner, "Relationships between Supervisory and Subordinate Ratings of Technical Personnel," *Journal of Industrial Psychology* (1966), pp. 56–60; and F. L. Schmidt and L. B. Kaplan, "Composite vs. Multiple Criteria: A Review and Resolution of The Controversy," *Personnel Psychology* (Autumn 1971), pp. 419–34.

Some Other Issues Involving Criteria

Selecting appropriate criteria to use in performance evaluation is further complicated by the fact that they are often dynamic. That is, criteria that are valid, reliable, and practical at one point in an employee's career may become inappropriate over a period of time. For example, during the first year or so on the job various criteria may be applied and have meaning to the rater and ratee. However, as the employee acquires experience, confidence, and career goals, these original criteria may not be appropriate.

Another controversial issue concerning criteria involves the activities versus results debate. The job performance of any person can be viewed in terms of the activities performed and the effort made by the individual.[14] A professional boxer does road work, exercises, works on the light and heavy punching bags, and spars in preparing for a fight. These are *activities* that hopefully will accomplish the desired result, a victory. Performance evaluation programs can focus either on activities or results or both. The boxer focuses first on activities and then results.

Any performance evaluation program that concentrates on either activities or results to the exclusion of the other, often produces problems because employees learn what is important and work at this aspect of the job. For example, if production output is a major criterion for assessing performance, assembly-line workers may produce as many units as possible so that they receive a good evaluation. The production quantity orientation may result in poor quality products being manufactured at high costs because of the excessive amount of rejects.

On the other hand, a program of performance evaluation which appraises only activities has some limitations. First, it would encourage only activities and disregard accomplishments. For example, if our assembly line worker is only evaluated on whether safety rules were followed and his or her work area was properly prepared for production, there may be too few units made for eventual sale.

It seems appropriate to suggest that whenever possible, performance evaluation criteria should be established for both activities and results. If any performance evaluation program addresses either activities or results criteria at the exclusion of the other, there may be little attention paid to organizational and personal goal accomplishment. Organizations often focus on results, while activities seem to be important to groups and individuals. Therefore, so that all parties can benefit as much as possible from the performance evaluation program, results and activities criteria should be developed when possible.[15]

---

[14] Lyman W. Porter, Edward E. Lawler III, and J. Richard Hackman, *Behavior In Organizations* (New York: McGraw-Hill Book Co., 1975), pp. 324–25 has an excellent discussion of the activities versus results controversy.

[15] Ibid, p. 326.

JOB ANALYSIS AND PERFORMANCE EVALUATION

The point has been made that criteria development is an extremely important part of performance evaluation. One needs to specifically examine jobs and how the organization divides its tasks into individual jobs before criteria that are reliable, valid, and practical emerge. The description of how one job differs from another in terms of demands, activities, and skills required is *job analysis.*

Broadly stated, job analysis is devoted to the gathering and analysis of job-specific information. The job analyst is interested in specifying the unique characteristics or structure of characteristics which differentiates one job from another. By careful analysis of the job's characteristics, a summary statement of what an employee on the job actually does is developed. This is called a *job description.* Furthermore, a dollar value is attached to the job, enabling the organization to relate the dollar value of the job to the value of other jobs. The assignment of dollar values is called *job evaluation.* As stated earlier, performance evaluation distinguishes the performance and potential among employees on the basis of various criteria. Figure 13–1 presents the relationships between job analysis and performance evaluation.

The work of job analysis involves collecting information about the job. Different methods such as a questionnaire to ask employees about the job, interviewing employees, observing employees, or using a panel of job knowledgeable experts are often used to identify job demands, activities, and needed skills. The more observations and information gathered, the better

Figure 13–1
Job Analysis and Performance Evaluation: A Relationship

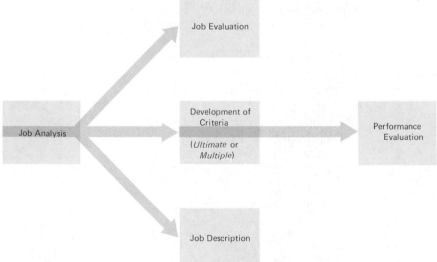

Source: Adapted from Frank J. Landy and Don A. Trumbo, *Psychology of Work Behavior* (Homewood, Ill.: The Dorsey Press, 1976), p. 97.

the job analysis. However, time, cost, and other constraints play a role in determining which information gathering procedures to use.

An excellent example of how to involve employees in the job analysis is offered by McCormick et al.[16] These researchers have developed over a number of years a questionnaire called the Position Analysis Questionnaire (PAQ). This questionnaire asks employees about six major categories of work activity. These are information input, mediation processes, work output, interpersonal activities, work situation and job context, and miscellaneous (e.g., job demands and responsibilities). Responses to the PAQ statements can provide guidance for developing the job analysis and job performance criteria.

Through the job analysis a manager is provided with clues about which criteria can be used to evaluate successful performance of the job. There are several kinds of criteria commonly used in organizations. The type of criteria used depends on such factors as the type of job, the time period covered by the evaluation, and the purposes to be served by the evaluation program. The criteria used for the research and development scientist working in an organizational laboratory are different than criteria used to evaluate the first-line supervisor or the sales person. Guion identified three categories of performance criteria: *objective* data, or production oriented measures; *personnel* data; and *judgmental* data.[17] For some jobs more than one of these criteria sets are used, while for others only one set is appropriate.

Objective Criteria for Evaluation

Objective criteria may be used for some jobs, such as assembly-line production, clerical, and sales jobs. The manager can count the number of generators manufactured, the number of accident claims filed per day, or the volume of used cars sold. These are certainly worthwhile indicators of job performance for some jobs.

Even when objective measures such as quantity and quality of output seem appropriate, there may be some problems. Objective results often are not stable from day to day or month to month. A high performer this week may be an average performer next week. If the supervisor bases the evaluation on the poor performance-time data sample, the employee would be rated low. Thus, it is important to use a representative sample of performance data collected over a normal time period in reaching performance evaluation conclusions.

Another potential problem with using objective measures is that often employees cannot control factors that influence the criteria. The equipment may be obsolete, receipt of resources needed to do the job may be erratic, or the employee may be asked to train an understudy during the work day.

---

[16] E. J. McCormick, P. Jeanneret, and R. C. Mecham, "A Study of Job Characteristics and Job Dimensions As Based on the Position Analysis Questionnaires," *Journal of Applied Psychology* (August, 1972), Monograph, pp. 347–68.

[17] Guion, *Personnel Testing,* pp. 91–96.

Personnel Criteria for Evaluation

A second set of criteria that can and is often used for various jobs is personnel measures. These kinds of employee behaviors include absences, tardiness, accident frequency, and rate of wage or salary advancement. Each of these measures must be treated with caution. For example, it is necessary to examine "excused" and "unexcused" absenteeism. These two types of absence indicate different behaviors on the part of employees. Also, rate of wage or salary advancement can be influenced by market position, organizational plans, union demands, and the financial posture of the organization.

Again, it should be noted that many jobs are just not suited for either objective or personnel criteria for performance evaluation. This means that the performance on some jobs must, in many cases, be evaluated on the basis of judgmental criteria.

Judgmental Criteria for Evaluation

Since objective and personnel criteria are not available, valid, or practical for evaluating employee performance for some jobs, there is a need to rely on rater judgments. These judgments may take the form of rating scales, comparisons, checklists, or critical incidents. The majority of performance evaluations of managerial, technical, and professional employees use judgmental criteria. When using such criteria, it is important to minimize rater subjectivity.

PERFORMANCE EVALUATION METHODS: TRADITIONAL

If pressed for an answer most managers could offer a general description of the job performance of subordinates. However, a more formal and systematic procedure than asking for managerial or supervisor opinions is usually used. Managers usually attempt to select a performance evaluation procedure that will minimize conflict with ratees, provide relevant feedback to ratees, and contribute to the achievement of organizational goals. Basically, the manager attempts to find, develop, and implement a performance evaluation program that can benefit the employee, other managers, the work group, and the organization.

As is the case with most managerial procedures and applied organizational behavior practices, there are no universally accepted methods of performance evaluation that fit every purpose, person, or organization. What is effective in IBM will not necessarily work in General Mills. In fact what is effective within one department or for one group in a particular organization will not necessarily be right for another unit or group within the same company. The only important point agreed upon by managers and organizational researchers is that some type of measuring device or procedure be used to record data on a number of performance criteria so that subjectivity in reward, development, and other managerial decisions is minimized.

Graphic Rating Scales

The oldest and most widely used performance evaluation procedure, the scaling technique, appears in many forms. Generally, the rater is supplied with a printed form, one for each subordinate to be rated. The form contains a number of job performance qualities and characteristics to be rated. The rating scales are distinguished by (1) how exactly the categories are defined; (2) the degree to which the person interpreting the ratings can tell what response was intended by the rater, and (3) how carefully the performance dimension is defined for the rater.

Figure 13–2 presents samples of some of the common rating scale formats. The first distinguishing feature between rating scales, the meaning of the possible response categories, is usually handled by the use of anchors. Anchor statements or words are placed at points along a scale. Rating scales (a), (b), (c), and (h) use anchors.

The second distinguishing feature among rating scales is the degree to which the person interpreting the ratings can tell what response was intended. The clarity of response intention is exemplified in scales (e), (f), and (g).

Quality of work can be interpreted differently by various raters. Therefore, a performance dimension needs to be defined for each rater. Scales (a), (b), (e), and (g) give the rater little dimension definition. Scales (c) and (h) provide the rater with a fairly good idea of performance dimension definition.

Ranking Methods

Some managers use a rank order procedure to evaluate all subordinates. The subordinates are ranked according to their relative worth to the company or unit on one or more performance dimensions. The procedure followed usually involves identifying the best performer and the worst performer. They are ranked in the first and last positions on the ranking list. The next best and next poorest performers are then filled in on the list. This rank ordering continues until all subordinates are placed on the list. The rater is forced to discriminate by the rank ordering performance evaluation method.

There are some problems with the ranking method. It is likely that ratees in the central portion of the list will not be much different from each other on the performance rankings. Another problem involves the size of the group of subordinates being evaluated. It becomes more difficult to validly rank large groups of subordinates.

There are other forms of performance evaluation ranking programs that are used. For example, in the *paired comparison* method, every subordinate is compared with every other. The supervisor is asked to identify the best performer from each pair. If a supervisor had eight subordinates he or she would have:

$$\text{Pairs} = \frac{N(N-1)}{2}$$

Figure 13–2
Some Samples of Rating Scale Formats

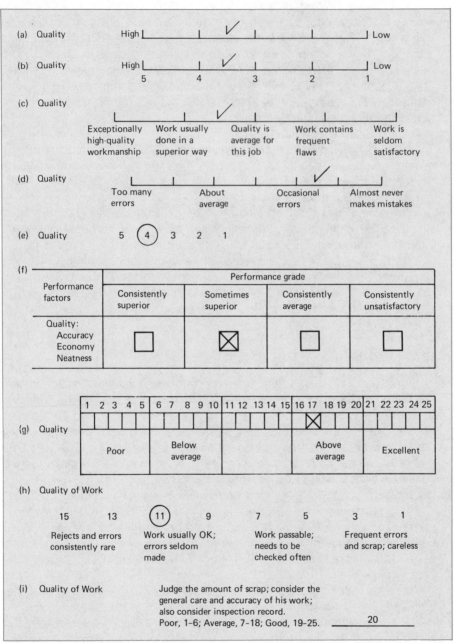

Variations on a graphic rating scale; each line represents one way in which a judgment of the quality of a person's work may be given. (From *Personnel Testing*, p. 98, by Guion. Copyright 1965, McGraw-Hill Book Company.)

or

$$\frac{8(8-1)}{2} = 28 \text{ lists to make comparisons on.}$$

If the supervisor has many more than 8 to 15 subordinates to be rated, the number of pairs becomes tiring and difficult to judge.

Weighted Checklists

The weighted-checklist rating consists of a number of statements that describe various types and levels of behavior for a particular job or group of jobs. Each statement has a weight or value attached to it. The rater evaluates each subordinate by checking those statements that describe the behavior of the individual. The check marks and the corresponding weights are summated for each subordinate.

The weighted checklist makes the rater think in terms of specific job behavior. However, this procedure is difficult to develop and very costly. Separate checklists are usually established for each different job or group of jobs.

Descriptive Essays

The essay method of performance evaluation requires the rater to describe each ratee's strong and weak points. Some organizations require every rater to discuss specific points in the evaluation, while others allow the rater to discuss whatever he or she believes is appropriate. One problem of the unstructured essay evaluation is that it provides little opportunity to compare ratees on specific performance dimensions. Another limitation is the writing skills of raters. Some individuals are effective writers, while others are not very good at writing descriptive analyses of subordinates' strengths and weaknesses with regard to job performance.

RATING ERRORS

The descriptions of just four of the numerous types of performance evaluation judgments point out problems and potential errors of each. The major problems and errors can be *technical* in the form of poor reliability, validity, and practicality or rater misuse. In some situations raters are extremely harsh or easy in their evaluations. These are referred to as *strictness or leniency* rater errors. The harsh rater gives ratings which are lower than the average ratings usually given to subordinates. The lenient rater tends to give higher ratings than the average level given to subordinates. Figure 13–3 illustrates the distribution of lenient and harsh ratings. These kinds of rating errors typically result because the rater is applying personal standards to the particular performance evaluation system being used. For example, the words outstanding or average may mean different things to various raters.

Figure 13–3
Example of Leniency and Harshness in Performance Ratings

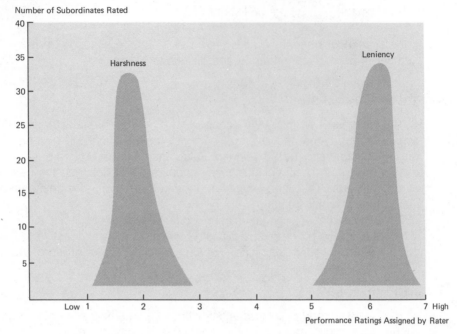

Number of Subordinates Rated

Performance Ratings Assigned by Rater

Another problem is called the *halo error*. The term "halo" suggests that there is a positive or negative aura around an individual employee. This aura influences the raters evaluation in about the same way for all performance dimensions considered. Halo error is due to the rater's inability to discriminate between the different dimensions being rated. It is also caused by the rater assuming that a particular dimension is extremely important. The rating on this dimension influences all of the other dimension evaluations.

Central tendency error occurs when a rater fails to assign either extremely high or extremely low ratings. That is, the rater tends to rate almost all ratees around the average. A graphic illustration of the central tendency error is shown in Figure 13–4. This type of evaluation error provides little information for making promotion, compensation, training, career planning, and development decisions. Everyone is about the same—average. Playing it safe by rating everyone average does not enable the manager to integrate performance evaluation with reward or employee development programs.

In many performance evaluation programs the most recent behaviors of ratees tend to color ratings. Using only the most recent behaviors to make evaluations can result in what is called the *recency of events* error. Forgetting to include important past behaviors can introduce a strong bias into the evaluation. Ratees usually are aware of this tendency and become visible, interested, productive, and cooperative just before the formal evaluation occurs.

Figure 13–4
Example of Central Tendency Error in Performance Ratings

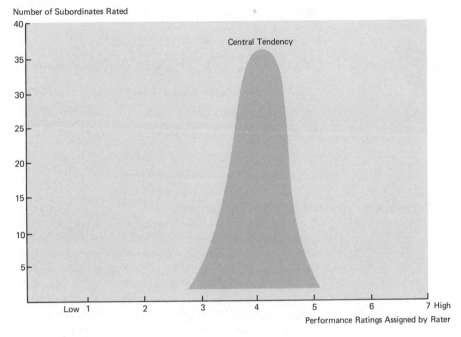

According to research findings,[18] various rating errors such as leniency, harshness, halo, central tendency, and recency of events are likely to be minimized if

1. Each dimension addresses a single job activity rather than a group of activities.
2. The rater on a regular basis can observe the behavior of the ratee while the job is being accomplished.
3. Terms like "average" are not used on a rating scale, since different raters have various reactions to such a term.
4. The rater does not have to evaluate large groups of subordinates. Fatigue and difficulty in discriminating between ratees become major problems when large groups of subordinates are evaluated.
5. Raters are trained to avoid such errors as leniency, harshness, halo, central tendency, and recency of events.
6. The dimensions being evaluated are meaningful, clearly stated, and important.

---

[18] For discussions of minimizing rating errors see H. J. Bernardin and C. S. Walter, "The Effects of Rater Training and Diary Keeping On Psychometric Error in Ratings," *Journal of Applied Psychology* (February 1977) pp. 64–69; and R. G. Burnaska and T. D. Hollman, "An Empirical Comparison of the Relative Effects of Rater Response Bias on Three Rating Scale Formats," *Journal of Applied Psychology,* (June 1974), pp. 307–12.

In addition to these guidelines there are other forms of performance evaluation that attempt to minimize rating errors. Two of the more recently developed approaches are the use of behaviorally anchored rating scales (BARS) and management by objectives (MBO).

PERFORMANCE EVALUATION METHODS: BARS AND MBO

In an effort to improve on the reliability, validity, and practicality of traditional performance evaluations, some organizations have used various behaviorally-based and goal-setting programs. The behaviorally based programs attempt to examine what the employee does in performing the job. The objective or goal oriented programs typically examine the results or accomplishments of the employee.

Behaviorally Anchored Rating Scales

Smith and Kendall developed a procedure which is referred to as behaviorally anchored rating scales (BARS) or behavioral expectation scales (BES).[19] The BARS approach relies on the use of "critical incidents" to construct the rating scale. Critical incidents are examples of specific job behaviors which appear in determining various levels of performance. Once the important areas of performance are identified and defined by employees who know the job, critical incident statements are used as anchors to discriminate between high, moderate, and low performance. The BARS rating form usually covers 6 to 10 specifically defined performance dimensions each with various descriptive anchors. Each dimension is based on observable behaviors and is meaningful to employees being evaluated.

An example of a BARS rating scale for the engineering competence performance dimension for engineers is presented in Figure 13–5. The dimension is defined for the rater, the anchors define the particular response categories for the rater, and the response made by the rater is specific and easy to interpret. The feedback provided by the BARS is specific and meaningful. If the ratee is given a 1.5 on this dimension, he or she is provided with the specific performance incident that the rater used to make such a rating.

Developing a BARS

The originally suggested steps to develop a BARS have been applied as recommended or varied slightly to fit a particular situation.[20] The following

[19] P. C. Smith and L. M. Kendall, "Retranslation of Expectations: An Approach to the Construction of Unambiguous Anchors for Rating Scales," *Journal of Applied Psychology* (April 1963), pp. 149–55.

[20] H. J. Bernadin, M. B. LaShells, P. C. Smith, and K. M. Alvares, "Behavioral Expectation Scales: Effects of Developmental Procedures and Formats," *Journal of Applied Psychology* (February 1976), pp. 75–79.

Figure 13–5
A BARS Performance Dimension

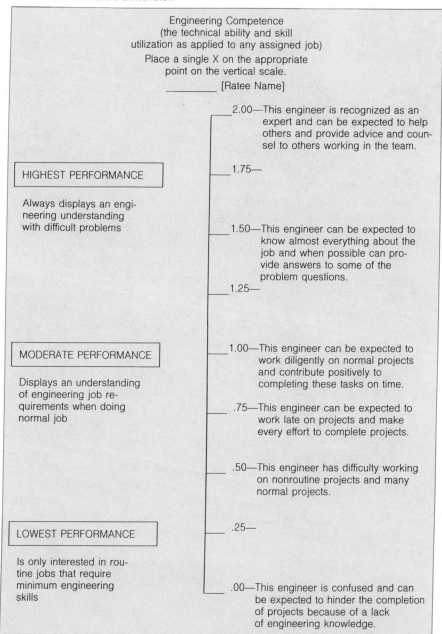

Engineering Competence
(the technical ability and skill
utilization as applied to any assigned job)
Place a single X on the appropriate
point on the vertical scale.
_____ [Ratee Name]

2.00—This engineer is recognized as an
expert and can be expected to help
others and provide advice and counsel to others working in the team.

HIGHEST PERFORMANCE

1.75—

Always displays an engi-
neering understanding
with difficult problems

1.50—This engineer can be expected to
know almost everything about the
job and when possible can provide answers to some of the
problem questions.

1.25—

MODERATE PERFORMANCE

1.00—This engineer can be expected to
work diligently on normal projects
and contribute positively to
completing these tasks on time.

Displays an understanding
of engineering job re-
quirements when doing
normal job

.75—This engineer can be expected to
work late on projects and make
every effort to complete projects.

.50—This engineer has difficulty working
on nonroutine projects and many
normal projects.

LOWEST PERFORMANCE

.25—

Is only interested in routine jobs that require
minimum engineering
skills

.00—This engineer is confused and can
be expected to hinder the completion
of projects because of a lack
of engineering knowledge.

steps or some that are quite similar are found in most discussions of the development of a BARS.

Step I. The jobs to which the final BARS will be applied need to be identified. The jobs selected should allow the rater to observe ratee behaviors on a fairly regular basis.

Step II. A group of subordinates and/or supervisors who are knowledgeable about the job meet to indentify and define all of the important characteristics that contribute to successful performance. In most cases, at least 20 employees make up this group.

Step III. A second group (if possible) is asked to take the important characteristics identified in Step II and select the most important performance dimensions from the list. They then define high, moderate, and low performance in these areas. The dimensions selected should be observable, associated with individual and not group performance, and meaningful. It is not uncommon for the 20 to 40 dimensions selected in Step 2 to be reduced. Through elimination and consolidation, there are usually 6 to 10 performance dimensions that are defined and finally generated in Step III.

Step IV. The group is then asked to write critical behaviorial incidents which apply to the 6 to 10 performance dimensions. They write incidents that describe high, moderate, and low performance. It is common for a group of 20 employees developing a BARS to prepare over 500 behavioral incidents.

Step V. The behavioral incidents are listed in random order in a questionnaire. The group (or another new group if possible) is asked to place each incident in the performance dimension category that it best fits. This is called "retranslation," since it is similar to a quality control check used to determine whether a translation from one language to another is accurate. If an item is assigned to a performance dimension by 70 percent or more of the group, it is kept for final consideration. This requirement indicates that the performance dimension and behavioral incidents are being interpreted similarly by different job knowledgeable employees.

Step VI. The group is next asked to consider each of the dimensions and incidents surviving Step V and place a scale value on the incidents. The range of the scale values in Figure 13–5 is 0 to 2.00 with intervals of .25. A value of 2.00 indicates high performance and a .00, low performance. The means and standard deviations are computed for the assigned behavioral incidents. The standard deviation indicates the amount of agreement between the participants. The items retained should have low standard deviation values. In Figure 13–5, six behavioral incidents were eventually retained for the engineering competence dimension.

Step VII. The final BARS is then pilot tested using raters who did not participate in the development steps. This pilot testing can identify any problems of interpretation or presentation that were overlooked by the development group(s).

The development steps generally take from two to five days. The result is a BARS that is job-related and uses specific behavioral incidents as anchors on the rating scale. In some cases a number of groups are used to develop the BARS. Consequently, it may require time and resources to develop the final form.

Proposed Advantages of BARS

There have been a number of proposed advantages associated with the use of a BARS. It is assumed that since job knowledgeable employees participate in the actual development steps, the final form will be reliable, valid, and meaningful. It should also cover the full domain of the job. A common problem of traditional performance evaluation programs is that they do not tap the full domain of the job.[21]

The use of BARS is also valuable for providing insights when developing training programs. The skills to be developed are specified in terms of actual behavioral incidents rather than abstract or general skills. Trainees in a BARS based program could learn expected behaviors and how job performance is evaluated.[22]

The pro-BARS literature also implies that through the use of a behaviorally anchored system—leniency, halo, and central tendency errors will be reduced. These errors are assumed to be minimized because of the independence between dimensions rated and the reliability of the BARS.[23] There are, however, some critics of the BARS who present results that indicate that this approach is not always the most reliable, valid, and practical. They also suggest that more research is needed comparing BARS with other traditional evaluation methods on such factors as leniency, central tendency, halo error, and dimension independence.[24]

Despite the amount of time, cost, and the procedural problems of developing and implementing a BARS, there seems to be some specific advantages of such a system. Specifically, a BARS program could minimize subordinate or ratee defensiveness toward evaluation. By being involved in the development of a BARS, subordinates can make their inputs known. These inputs can be incorporated in the final BARS. As McGregor pointed out, many superiors are uncomfortable about judging someone and acting out the role of an evaluator.[25] The BARS development steps could include both superiors and subordinates. In a sense then, all parties involved can contribute to

---

[21] J. P. Campbell, M. D. Dunnette, R. D. Arvey, and L. W. Hellervik, "The Development and Evaluation of Behaviorally Based Rating Scales," *Journal of Applied Psychology* (February 1973), pp. 15–22.

[22] M. R. Blood, "Spin-offs from Behavioral Expectation Scale Procedures," *Journal of Applied Psychology* (August 1974), pp. 513–15.

[23] S. Zedeck and H. T. Baker, "Nursing Performance As Measured By Behavioral Expectation Scales: A Multitrait-Multirater Analysis," *Organizational Behavior and Human Performance* (June 1972), pp. 457–66.

[24] D. P. Schwab, H. G. Henneman III., and T. A. DeCotiis, "Behaviorally Anchored Rating Scales: A Review of The Literature," *Personnel Psychology* (Winter 1975), pp. 549–62.

[25] D. McGregor, "An Uneasy Look at Performance Appraisal," *Harvard Business Review* (May–June 1957), pp. 89–94.

the creation of the evaluation criteria (dimensions) and the behavioral incidents used as anchors.

Another specific advantage of using BARS that should not be overlooked is that the evaluation program concentrates on job-specific and relevant behaviors. Many performance evaluation programs are abstract and not meaningful to either ratees or raters. Thus, when providing feedback to ratees, the raters must convert the ratings to examples of actual job behavior. There is in many cases variance in raters' abilities to make these conversions from the rating scale to meaningful job behaviors. The BARS already contains the behaviors for the superior to use in developing the evaluation counseling interview.

Objectives or Goal Performance Evaluations

In the traditional and BARS evaluation programs, the rater is making judgments about the performance of subordinates. There are behavioral scientists, organizational researchers, and managers who believe that a results-based program is more efficient and informative. One popular results-based program is called management by objectives (MBO). An MBO program typically involves the establishment of objectives (also referred to as goals) by the supervisor alone or jointly by the supervisor and a subordinate.

MBO is far more than just an evaluation approach. It is usually a part of an overall motivational program, planning technique, or organizational change and development program. More details on MBO will be presented later in Chapter 18.

An MBO performance evaluation program focuses on what an employee achieves. The key features of a typical MBO program are as follows:

1. Superior and subordinate meet to discuss and jointly set goals for subordinates for a specified period of time (e.g., six months or one year).
2. Both the superior and subordinate attempt to establish goals that are realistic, challenging, clear, and comprehensive. The goals also should be related to organizational and personal (the subordinate) needs.
3. The criteria for measuring and evaluating the goals are agreed upon.
4. The superior and subordinate establish some intermediate review dates when the goals will be reexamined.
5. The superior plays more of a coaching, counseling, and supportive role and less the role of a judge and jury.
6. The entire process focuses upon results accomplished and counseling subordinates, and not upon activities, mistakes, and organizational requirements.

MBO-type programs have been used in organizations throughout the world.[26] Approximately 40 percent (200) of Fortune's 500 largest industrial

---

[26] G. P. Latham and G. A. Yukl, "A Review of Research on the Application of Goal Setting in Organizations," *Academy of Management Journal* (December 1975), pp. 824–43.

firms report using MBO-type programs.[27] Like each of the performance evaluation programs already discussed, there are both benefits and potential costs associated with using MBO. The assumed benefits include better planning, improved motivation because of knowledge of results, basing evaluation decisions on results instead of on personality or personal traits, improving commitment through participation, and improving supervisory skills in such areas as listening, counseling, and evaluating. These are certainly significant benefits, but they are not always accomplished in MBO programs. Using MBO is no sure way to improve upon the problems associated with performance evaluation programs. It too, has some potential and real problems. The fact that MBO stresses results is a benefit that can also be a problem. Focusing only on results may take attention away from how to accomplish the goals. A subordinate receiving feedback about what has been achieved may still not be certain about how to make performance corrections. A manager may tell a subordinate that the quality control goal was missed by 3.5 percent, but this type of feedback is incomplete. The subordinate missing his or her goals needs feedback or guidance on how to accomplish the quality control goal in the future.

Other problems that have been linked to MBO programs include: improper implementation, lack of top management involvement, too much emphasis on paper work, failing to use an MBO system that best fits the needs of the organization and employees, and inadequate training preparation for employees who are asked to establish goals.[28]

A final limitation or cost of MBO is that comparisons of subordinates are difficult. In traditional performance evaluation programs, all subordinates are rated on common dimensions. In MBO, each individual usually has a different set of goals that is difficult to compare across a group of subordinates. The superior must make reward decisions not only on the basis of goals achieved, but also on his or her conception of the kind of goals that were accomplished. The feeling of achieving goals will generally wear thin among subordinates if the accomplishment is not accompained by meaningful rewards.

PERFORMANCE EVALUATION: THE ASSESSMENT CENTER

The assessment center technique was pioneered by Douglas Bray and his associates at American Telephone and Telegraph Company in the mid-1950s. In the 1970s, it has become a popular evaluation technique used in organizations of all sizes. The foundation of this technique is a series of situational exercises in which candidates for promotion, training, or other managerial programs take part over a 2- to 3-day period while being observed and rated. The exercises are simulated management tasks and include such

---

[27] J. Singular, "Has MBO Failed?" *MBA* (October 1975), pp. 47–50.

[28] J. M. Ivancevich, "Different Goal Setting Treatments and Their Effects on Performance and Job Satisfaction," *Academy of Management Journal* (September 1977), pp. 406–19; and J. M. Ivancevich, J. H. Donnelly, Jr. and J. L. Gibson, "Evaluating MBO: The Challenges Ahead," *Management by Objectives* (Winter 1976), pp. 15–24.

techniques as role playing, in-basket, and case analysis. In some assessment centers, personal interviews and psychological tests are also used to make evaluations.[29]

Purposes of Assessment Centers

Since individual ratees are observed in a controlled setting (the center), raters can compare the performances of candidates or employees on a first-hand basis. Organizations using assessment centers include the Bell Telephone Companies, Sears Roebuck, J. C. Penney, IBM, General Motors, Tenneco, General Electric, Exxon, Ford Motor Company, Universal Oil Products, Internal Revenue Service, and the Department of Agriculture. These and other centers are used:

1. To identify individuals who are suited for a particular type or level of management job.
2. To determine individual and group training and development needs.
3. To identify individuals for promotion to positions that are quite different from their current positions; for example, sales people, technicians, or engineers being considered for managerial positions. Because the new managerial jobs would require such different skills and abilities than a sales or engineering job, it is difficult to determine a candidate's ability before the promotion. The assessment center attempts to identify some indicators of managerial ability before the decision is made.

Dimensions Measured by Assessment Centers

There are different dimensions measured in assessment centers depending upon the purpose of the evaluation. Such dimensions as interpersonal skills, communication ability, creativity, quality of problem-solving skills, tolerance for stress and ambiguity, and planning ability are some of the commonly assessed dimensions. Several studies have shown that different raters derive similar ratings on these types of dimensions.[30]

IBM has conducted studies of its assessment center programs. All show a positive relationship between center ratings and various criteria of success.[31] Such variables as energy level, communication skills, aggressiveness, and self-confidence were rated in the IBM program.

Chevrolet sales divisions select candidates for assessment centers by using nine dimensions for measuring managerial potential. Some of these are: judgment, use of time, job knowledge, and interpersonal communications. The candidates that are rated the highest on these nine dimensions

[29] R. B. Finkle, "Managerial Assessment Centers," in *Handbook of Industrial and Organizational Psychology*, M. D. Dunnette, ed. (Chicago: Rand McNally, 1976), pp. 861–88.

[30] D. W. MacKinnon, "An Overview of Assessment Centers," Technical Report No. 1, Center for Creative Leadership, Greensboro, N.C. (May 1975).

[31] W. E. Dodd, "Summary of IBM Assessment Validations," Paper presented as part of the symposium: "Validity of Assessment Centers," at the 79th Annual Convention of the American Psychological Assn., 1971.

are selected for the assessment center evaluation. In the center, potential for higher-level position responsibility is rated.[32]

A Typical Program

There is no universally used set of exercises applied in assessment centers. Most programs, however, do use management simulated games, in-basket exercises, and leaderless group discussions. An example of an assessment center schedule is presented in Figure 13–6.

Figure 13–6
Format for a Typical 2½-Day Assessment Center

Day 1	Day 2	Day 3
A. Orientation of Approximately 12 Ratees.	A. Individual Decision-Making Exercise—Ratees are asked to make a decision about some problem that must be solved. (*Raters* observe fact finding skills, understanding of problem-solving procedures, and risk-taking propensity.)	A. Individual Case Analysis and Presentation. (*Raters* observe problem-solving ability, method of preparation, ability to handle questions, and communication skills.)
B. Break-up into Groups of Six or Four to Play Management Simulated Game. (*Raters* observe: planning ability, problem-solving skill, interaction skills, communication ability.)		B. Evaluation of Other Ratees. (Peer evaluations.)
C. Psychological Testing—Measure verbal and numerical skills.	B. In-Basket Exercise. (*Raters* observe decision making under stress, organizing ability, memory, and ability to delegate.)	
D. Interview with Raters. (*Raters* discuss goals, motivation, and career plans.)	C. Role-Play of Performance Evaluation Interview. (*Raters* observe empathy, ability to react, counseling skills, and how information is used.)	
E. Small Group Discussion of Case Incidents. (*Raters* observe confidence, persuasiveness, decision-making flexibility.)	D. Group Problem Solving. (*Raters* observe leadership ability and ability to work in a group.)	

After the assessment program, the raters meet to discuss and evaluate all candidates. The assessment center raters are usually managers two or more levels above the ratees. They are used because they are familiar with the jobs for which ratees are being considered and because by participating they can improve their evaluation skills and techniques.

Problems of Concern

Again it must be stated that evaluating employee performance in any setting is extremely difficult. One of the potential problems of the assessment center evaluation procedure is that it is so pressure packed. Outstanding employees

---

[32] F. M. McIntyre, "Unique Program Developed By Chevrolet Sales," *Assessment and Development* (January 1975).

who have contributed to the organization may simply not perform well in the center. Raters may be embarrassed by not being able to justify ratings or because of their limited ability to identify key behaviors.

Another dangerous problem involves the feelings of individuals who receive mediocre or poor evaluations. Employees who receive a poor evaluation may leave the organization or be demoralized for an extended period of time. It is natural for the highly-rated participants in centers to be identified as "comers" or individuals to develop. The poorly-rated participants may be viewed as "losers."

Basing promotion decisions or identifying individuals with high potential on the results of a single assessment center experience is questionable. The research evidence on the reliability and validity of assessment centers is still somewhat mixed.[33] Until more evidence is available, the assessment center may be useful for only some situations and some evaluation decisions. It is another evaluation procedure that has both potential benefits and problems.

A Review of Potential Performance Evaluation Programs

Table 13–3 summarizes the main points of the various approaches discussed. The usefulness of each method is debatable. In some organizations one system is more useful because of the type of individuals doing the rating or the criteria being used. Every program discussed thus far has both costs and benefits. Since performance evaluation is such an integral part of managing within organizations, recognizing the strengths, weaknesses, and best uses for a particular program is an important job for managers.

THE PERFORMANCE EVALUATION PROGRAM IN PRACTICE

Although developing a systematic program for performance evaluation is extremely important, there are other managerial practices which are just as significant. It is extremely important to decide who will do the rating, who will be rated, when rating should take place, and how to integrate performance evaluation into the work cycle. These decisions set the general tone for the overall administration of the performance evaluation program.

Who Should Rate?

Five possible parties can serve as raters: (1) supervisor(s) of the ratee; (2) organizational peers; (3) the ratee; (4) subordinates of the ratee; and (5) individuals outside the work environment.[34] In the majority of situations,

---

[33] R. J. Klimoski and W. J. Strickland, "Assessment Centers—Valid or Merely Prescient," *Personnel Psychology* (Autumn 1977), pp. 353–61.

[34] Cummings and Schwab, *Performance in Organizations*, pp. 101–2.

Table 13–3
Managerial Points of Interest When Selecting a Performance Evaluation Program

Point of Interest	Programs						
	Graphic Rating Scales	Ranking	Checklists	Essay	BARS	MBO	Assessment Centers
Acceptability to subordinates	Fair	Fair/poor	Fair	Poor	Good	Generally good	—
Acceptability to management	Fair	Fair/poor	Fair	Poor	Good	Generally good	—
Useful in reward allocations	Poor	Poor	Fair	Fair	Good	Good	Fair/good
Useful in counseling and developing subordinates	Poor	Poor	Poor	Fair	Good	Good	Good
Meaningful dimensions	Rarely	Rarely	Sometimes	Rarely	Often	Often	Often
Ease of developing actual program	Yes	Yes	Yes	No	No	No	No
Development costs	Low	Low	Low	Moderately high	High	High	High

the rater is the immediate supervisor of the person rated. Because of frequent contact, he or she is assumed to be most familiar with the employee's performance. In addition, many organizations consider performance evaluation as an integral part of the immediate supervisor's job. The supervisor's evaluations are often reviewed by higher management, thereby maintaining managerial control over the evaluation program.

Various surveys show that a number of business organizations use group ratings to evaluate managerial personnel.[35] Members of the group could include superiors, subordinates, and peers. In some companies, peer evaluation systems are used. One study of agents in three life insurance companies indicated the higher the peer scores, the higher the rate of success in performing the job.[36] In programs using peer evaluations, it appears that superiors emphasize work initiative, while peers considered getting along with others to be extremely important.

There is some interest in using self-evaluations. The major claims supporting this approach include improving the employee's understanding of job performance, increased personal commitment because of participation in the performance evaluation process, and reduced hostility between superiors and subordinates over ratings. Some employers fear that self-ratings will be unusually high. In one study of technical employees, subordinates rated themselves higher than did their supervisors.[37] Another study of subordinates in General Electric resulted in some interesting conclusions. Forty subordinates completed self-evaluations, while 41 were rated in the usual manner by their managers. More defensiveness about the ratings was noted among the individuals rated by their supervisors. In a three-month follow-up after the evaluation interviews, supervisors reported that 16 of the 41 manager-appraised subordinates were not performing well, as compared to only 8 of the 40 self-rated employees.[38]

There is some support for increased use of multiple evaluations. The major advantage of using superior, peer, and self-ratings is that it provides a great deal of information about the ratee.[39] In making decisions about promotion, training and development, and career planning as much information as possible is needed to suggest the best alternative courses of action for the employee.

[35] M. Novit, "Performance Appraisal and Dual Authority: A Look at Group Appraisal," *Management of Personnel Quarterly* (Spring 1969), p. 3.

[36] E. C. Mayfield, "Peer Nominations: A Neglected Tool," *Personnel* (July–August 1971), p. 40.

[37] W. K. Kirchner, "Relationships between Supervisory and Subordinate Ratings," pp. 57–60.

[38] G. A. Bassett and H. H. Meyer, "Performance Appraisal Based On Self-Review," *Personnel Psychology* (Winter 1968), pp. 421–30.

[39] J. B. Miner, "Management Appraisal: A Review of Procedures and Practices," in H. L. Tosi, R. J. House, and M. D. Dunnette, eds., *Managerial Motivation and Compensation: A Selection of Readings* (E. Lansing, Michigan: Division of Research Graduate School of Business, 1972), pp. 412–28.

When to Rate?

There is no specific schedule for rating employees. Informal performance evaluations occur continuously. In general, one evaluation a year is provided for older or more tenured employees. Newer employees are usually evaluated more frequently than older employees. The time to rate will depend on the situation and the intent of the evaluation. If performance evaluations are too far apart or occur too infrequently, the feedback received by the ratee may not be able to be used to make improvements.

An evaluation program solely for the sake of rating employees will soon lose any potential value or motivational impact unless it becomes integrated with the main emphasis of the organization. The judgment and development purposes will show through when both the ratees and raters understand each others roles in the process. The rater must clarify, coach, counsel, and provide feedback. On the other hand, the ratee must understand rater expectations, his or her own strengths and weaknesses, and the goals that need to be accomplished. These various roles can become clear if the performance evaluation program is considered a continual process that focuses both on task accomplishment and personal development.

THE FORMAL EVALUATION INTERVIEW

Regardless of how individual job performance information is collected—whether by a BARS, an assessment center, or a rating scale—the rater must provide formal feedback to the ratee. Without formal feedback, the ratee will have difficulty making necessary modifications to improve performance, matching individual job performance expectations with the rater, and assessing progress being made toward the accomplishment of career goals.

The performance evaluation feedback interview should be a part of any program from the beginning. It should focus on the job performance of the ratee. Generally, raters feel uncomfortable about discussing ratee weaknesses or problems. On the other hand, ratees often become defensive when personal weaknesses or failures are pointed out by a rater. Kay, Meyer, and French reviewed the relationship between comments focusing on subordinate weaknesses in a feedback interview and defensive comments made by the ratees.[40] They found that as critical comments increased, subordinate defensiveness increased. Furthermore, they concluded that praise in the feedback sessions was ineffective. They assumed that since most raters first praise then criticize and finally praise to end the feedback session, ratees become conditioned to this sequence. In essence, praise becomes a conditioned stimulus preceeding the arrival of criticism.

If the performance evaluation program is acceptable to the rater and ratee, there is a higher probability that the feedback interview can be more than

---

[40] E. Kay, H. Meyer, and J. R. P. French, "Effects of Threat in a Performance Appraisal Interview," *Journal of Applied Psychology* (October 1965), pp. 311–17.

a praise-criticism-praise sequence. The acceptability of any program depends upon such factors as: (1) how the evaluation will be used; (2) who developed the program; (3) whether the criteria are fair; (4) how good the rater is in evaluating performance; and (5) whether the rater has sufficient time to spend planning for, implementing, and providing feedback in the program? It should be noted that providing effective feedback information requires skill, time, and patience. Feedback has both positive and negative consequences. Poorly presented performance evaluation feedback can result in distrust, hostility, dissatisfaction, and turnover. Effective evaluation feedback can be motivational and encourage the development of ratees.

Too often performance evaluation interviews focus on the past year or on plans for the short run. Rarely do a manager and subordinate discuss careers.[41] It is important for managers to have knowledge about the various career tracks and requirements available within the organization. The manager should be able to view the job performance of subordinates and be able to help create tasks that are challenging but not unattainable. This also means that the creation of challenging tasks will help prepare subordinates for future jobs which require the use of more skills and abilities. Basically, it seems worthwhile for managers to consider and be prepared to discuss the lifelong sequence of job experiences and jobs of subordinates, as part of the evaluation interview. Only through managerial consideration of career goals can the evaluation process in reality become a development experience as well as a judgmental analysis of job performance.

MAJOR ISSUES FOR THE MANAGER TO CONSIDER

A. Performance evaluation occurs in most organizations. It is a formal process that systematically involves the evaluation of subordinates' job performance and potential for future development.

B. Performance evaluation is used in a broad sense to make judgments and to develop subordinates. In a more specific sense it has motivational, improved knowledge, research, promotion, and training and development purposes.

C. An important step in developing any performance evaluation program involves the establishment of criteria. A criterion is a dependent or predicted measure for appraising the effectiveness of employees. A good criterion must be relevant, stable, able to discriminate between ratees, and practical. Three broad areas of criteria used are production, personnel, and judgment.

D. A few of the widely used performance evaluation programs are graphic rating scales, ranking procedures, weighted checklists, and descriptive essays. These procedures often result in raters making rating errors. The most common errors are harshness and leniency, halo effect, central tendency, and recency of events. Some methods available for reducing these errors include eliminat-

---

[41] G. W. Dalton, P. H. Thompson, and R. L. Price, "A New Look at Performance By Professionals," *Organizational Dynamics* (Summer 1977), pp. 19–42.

ing terms such as *average* on the scales, having raters rate a small number of individuals instead of many people, and training raters to recognize the most common error tendencies.

E. The behaviorally anchored rating scale (BARS) is a form of evaluation that uses critical incidents or examples of specific job behaviors to determine various levels of performance. The development of the BARS is time consuming and costly, but can involve the joint participation of raters and ratees. This joint effort can result in more acceptance of the evaluation program by raters and ratees.

F. A results-based performance evaluation program is called management by objectives (MBO) or goal setting. The program typically involves a superior/ subordinate meeting to discuss and jointly set goals for subordinates for a specified period of time. The superior plays more of a coaching and supportive role in this results-based program.

G. The assessment center technique has become a popular evaluation technique in the past two decades. The foundation of this program is a set of exercises in which candidates for promotion, training, or other managerial programs take part—over a 2- to 3-day period—while being observed and rated. One major problem with this program involves the participants who are rated low. They can become extremely demoralized about their future careers in the organization.

H. An important factor to consider in appraising performance is the integration of the program into overall organizational procedures. The integration effort requires that the roles and practices of the rater and ratee must focus on task and personal development.

I. The performance evaluation feedback interview(s) is an essential part of any program. Feedback provides information about how others view the ratee's job performance. Without feedback, knowledge about progress, development, and clarity about expectations is difficult to attain. Another important part of feedback involves relating performance and progress to career development. Feedback of recent results and activities plus events for the near future should be combined with discussions about organizational career tracks and requirements for the long-run.

DISCUSSION AND REVIEW QUESTIONS

1. How can common rating errors result in problems in a performance evaluation program?

2. What are the main differences between a behaviorally-anchored rating scale (BARS) and a graphic rating scale?

3. What role can subordinates play in developing the evaluation system that will be used by their superiors?

4. Why is it important for the rater to be able to observe behavior in most performance evaluation programs?

5. Is management by objectives a program that could be used to evaluate goal accomplishment? Explain.

6. It is often stated that any performance evaluation program contains some degree of subjectivity. Do you agree?

7. Why is development considered an important purpose of performance evaluation?

8. Some claim that the assessment center is a pressure packed experience or a "fishbowl" exercise. Why are these statements made?

9. Why is job analysis an important antecedent to the development of criteria and the actual performance evaluation program used?

10. Why is the performance evaluation interview such an important part of the process of appraisal?

ADDITIONAL REFERENCES

Anthony, W. P., and Nicholson, E. A. *Management of Human Resources: A Systems Approach to Personnel Management*. Columbus, Ohio: Grid, Inc., 1977.

Beatty, R. W., and Schneier, C. E. *Personnel Administration: An Experiential Skill-Building Approach*. Reading, Mass.: Addison-Wesley Publishing Co., 1977.

Burack, E. H. "Career Path—Why All The Confusion?" *Human Resource Management* (Summer 1977), pp. 21–27.

———, and Smith, R. D. *Personnel Management: A Human Resource Systems Approach*. St. Paul: West Publishing Co., 1977.

Buzzotta, V. R.; Lefton, R. E.; and Sherberg, M. "Coaching and Counseling: How You Can Improve the Way It's Done," *Training and Development Journal* (December 1977), pp. 50–60.

Ciminero, A. R.; Calhoun, K. S.; and Adams, H. E., eds. *Handbook of Behavioral Assessment*. New York: John Wiley & Sons, Inc., 1977.

Haynes, M. G. "Developing An Appraisal Program" Parts I and II. *Personnel Journal* (January 1978 and February 1978), pp. 14–19 and pp. 66–67, 104, 107.

Jacobs, A. A. "What's Wrong with Performance Evaluation Programs?" *Supervisory Management* (July 1977), pp. 10–15.

Jaffee, C. O.; Frank, F. D.; and Rollins, J. B. "Assessment Centers: The New Method for Selecting Managers," *Human Resource Management* (Summer 1976), pp. 5–11.

Locher, A. H., and Teel, K. S. "Performance Appraisal—A Survey of Current Practices," *Personnel Journal* (May 1977), pp. 245–47, 254.

McAfee, F. and Green, B. "Selecting A Performance Appraisal Method," *Personnel Administrator* (June 1977), pp. 61–64.

Maier, N. R. F. *The Appraisal Interview: Three Basic Approaches*. La Jolla, Calif.: University Associates, 1976.

Mollenhoff, D. V. "How to Measure Work by Professionals," *Management Review* (November 1977), pp. 39–43.

Salton, G. J. "The Focused Web-Goal Setting in the MBO Process," *Management Review* (January 1978), pp. 46–50.

Steers, R. M., and Spencer, D. G. "Achievement Needs and MBO Goal-Setting," *Personnel Journal* (January 1978), pp. 26–28.

CASE FOR ANALYSIS

THE EVALUATION OF A PERFORMANCE EVALUATION PROGRAM

Mike Pecaro, the project manager for the new power plant being constructed for the Atlanta, Georgia area by Brady Engineering Construction, was called into the vice president's office to discuss some complaints about the company's performance evaluation program. In order to determine whether the complaints of engineers, technicians, and machinists were justified, Mike was asked to critique the present evaluation system. The system used eight dimensions that were assumed to be associated with good performance. The rating scale being used ranged from 1 to 7, with 7 being a rating given for the highest level of performance. The three highest rated engineers in Mike's group were used as reference points for purposes of discussion. The ratings are presented in Exhibit 1.

Exhibit 1
Ratings for Three Best Performers in Mike Pecaro's Group

Performance Dimension	Bob Lowry	Tony Nelson	Randy Anderson
Quality of work	6	6	7
Dependability	6	7	7
Cooperation	7	6	7
Customer image	7	7	7
Meeting budget requirements	6	7	7
Development of subordinates	7	6	6
Problem-solving skill	6	7	6
Technical competence	7	7	7
Total Score	52	53	54

Don Baker, the vice president, wanted Mike to critique the soundness of the overall performance evaluation program. He was interested in whether the performance dimensions were meaningful to the engineers, technicians, and machinists. The same dimensions were being used for each group. One of the major and loudest complaints had to do with the relevance of some of the dimensions. Listed below are some of the complaints received from employees:

Machinist: The evaluation dimensions mean nothing since I have no control over some of them. I never interact with customers. Why am I rated on this dimension?

Technician: Everyone is rated about average so the rating system is really a failure.

Technician: The performance dimensions are a mystery to all of us. What does dependability mean? What is an example of problem solving skill?

Engineer: My supervisor never provides me with any feedback on progress. I have to guess at how I am doing. I have no idea of where I am going in the company.

Engineer: The performance evaluation never covers the long run. It only focuses on the short run or yesterday's results. I do not like this emphasis.

Engineer: My supervisor really doesn't know how to use the evaluation program. He uses it just to exercise tighter control of my activities. Shouldn't it be used to help me make improvements?

Mike was not surprised to hear these kind of complaints since he also felt uneasy about the performance evaluation program. He told Don that most of the comments were on target. He rated the present system unreliable, inaccurate, and uninformative. The present rating system had some flaws that could be eliminated. Based on the seemingly endless list of complaints, Mike recommended that the present system be reevaluated by a committee of supervisors and subordinates. Don wanted some time to think about the possible solutions to the growing negative reactions to the present system.

Questions for Discussion

1. What type of system is presently being used to evaluate performance at Brady?
2. What problems and errors with the present system of evaluation are displayed in the list of complaints?
3. What are some of the possible solutions available for correcting the shortcomings of the present program?

EXPERIENTIAL EXERCISE

THE FACTS OF ORGANIZATIONAL LIFE

Objectives

1. To illustrate how difficult it is to use performance evaluation when making promotion choices.
2. To emphasize the impact of outside forces on performance evaluation programs.
3. To consider how a performance evaluation decision may become complex.

Related Topics

The government's role in performance evaluation will be illustrated in this exercise. The difficulty of informing individuals that they will not be promoted is considered.

Starting the Exercise

Set up groups of five to eight students for the 40 to 60 minute first phase of the exercise. If possible include men and women in all groups. The groups should be separated from each other and asked to reach a decision within the group. Before the groups are established, each person should read the facts of the situation.

The Facts

The Sebring Electronics Corporation is located in Baton Rouge, Louisiana. The company has, over the past five years, incorporated a performance evaluation program for operating employees that is generally viewed as a fair system. The company has maintained a steady rate of growth and has reached a point where two new supervisors are needed. Since the company motto is to "hire, develop, promote, and reward from within," it is now the job of a management committee to locate the best two new supervisors.

The performance evaluation program was designed to provide needed information to make promotion, wage and salary, training and development, and career planning decisions. Recently, there has been pressure applied by the federal government to play down the role of performance evaluation in making various decisions. The government wants Sebring to initiate affirmative action to promote more females, blacks, and chicanos. Presently, of the 96 managerial personnel in the Baton Rouge facility, only 6 were female, 3 were black, and 2 were chicano.

The six employees being considered for the two supervisory vacancies are considered the best within the company for the promotions. They are:

Tony Santos: Chicano; age 37; married; 4 children; 2 years college; 9 years with Sebring.

Barbara Golding: White, age 32; married; 1 child; 3 years college; 6 years with Sebring.

Mark Petro: White; age 38; married; 2 children; 1 year college; 7 years with Sebring.

Denny Slago: White; age 39; single; high school graduate; 10 years with Sebring.

Bobby Green: Black; age 38; married; 2 years college; 8 years with Sebring.

George Nelson: White; age 40; single; 3 years college; 7 years with Sebring.

The performance records of these six individuals have been carefully scrutinized. Average performance over a two-year period is presented in Exhibit A. These data are being weighed heavily by the committee to make the final choices.

Exercise Procedures

Phase I: 40 to 60 minutes

1. Each group is to select two employees for the promotions. A group consensus should be the final step in reaching agreement. The group should also develop a statement supporting their decision.

2. The group decisions should be placed on a board or chart in front of all class members and discussed.

Phase II: 40 minutes

1. Assume that Barbara Golding and Bobby Green were selected for the promotion.

Exhibit A
Two-Year Performance Evaluation of Six Top Candidates for Promotion

| Candidate for Promotion | Objective Performance Dimensions* | | | | Subjective Performance Dimensions | | | |
	Quantity†	Quality‡ %	Cost§	Absences‖ (unexcused %)	Develops Assistants	Potential for Promotion	Cooperative Attitude	Communication Skills
Tony Santos	138.7	87.4	1.61	5.1	Good	Good	Fair	Good
Barbara Golding	106.4	85.8	1.74	8.1	Good	Good	Good	Fair
Mark Petro	110.8	89.6	1.39	6.2	Good	Good	Good	Excellent
Denny Slago	165.7	94.6	1.02	3.0	Excellent	Excellent	Good	Good
Bobby Green	120.8	86.8	1.41	5.9	Excellent	Good	Fair	Good
George Nelson	169.7	95.1	1.00	2.1	Good	Good	Excellent	Good

* The quantity, quality, and cost measures are weekly averages. The absence indicator is the average of four six-month periods of review.
† Higher mean score indicates more quantity.
‡ Higher mean score indicates better quality.
§ Lower mean score indicates better cost control.
‖ Lower mean score indicates better absence record.

2. Select two people from the class to role play an interview between the chairperson of the promotion committee and Denny Slago.

3. Denny is concerned about the decision and is very upset about not being selected. The committee chairperson's role is to explain to Denny why he was not selected.

4. If possible, use two different role-play groups. Have one group wait outside of the room during the first role play. In one role play have a women play the role of the chairperson. In the second role play, have a woman act out the role of Denny.

5. As a class, consider the impact of any promotion decision at Sebring on the four employees who were not selected. Also consider whether any performance evaluation program would make the Sebring decision any easier.

Chapter 14

Reward Processes

AN ORGANIZATIONAL ISSUE FOR DEBATE

The Pay for Performance Controversy

ARGUMENT FOR

Merit pay or "pay for job performance" as a basis for rewarding employees is a widely accepted management practice. Although some argue about the relative importance of pay compared with other extrinsic and intrinsic rewards, there is general agreement in management circles that pay is an important reward for most employees. If two employees are hired to perform the same job and one is a better performer, surely the high performer should be paid more for his or her superior performance.

Almost all managerial employees and many non-managers are paid using a merit pay system. One alternative is to set a minimum level of pay for each job and then provide incremental increases until an upper level of compensation is reached. This approach is criticized because it has little motivational power. Under such a plan an employee is rewarded with pay increases simply for attending and staying on the job. Under a pay for performance plan, the highest performers receive the largest increases and the poorest performers receive the smallest or no increases at all. Thus, management has available a "carrot" or a "stick" to motivate better performance. The "carrot" is used for high performers and the "stick" is applied to low performers.

ARGUMENT AGAINST

Despite the logical attractiveness of the pay for performance plan, experience shows clearly that it is a pipedream. Typically, managers do not discriminate and give small rewards to individuals in the same job, regardless of performance differences. An example of this behavior is seen in a pay increase range for a large petrochemical company for middle managers being from 4.8 percent to 6.2 percent. Everyone gets about the same pay raise.

A major problem with merit pay plans is the fact that an employee's increases are based primarily on supervisory judgments. It is assumed that a supervisor can make objective, reliable, and valid distinctions between individual job performances. Who actually accepts the judgments of others about personal matters such as job performance? Are the judgments really objective, reliable, and valid?

The supervisor's role in the process creates another problem. It reminds the employee that the "boss" controls the limited rewards available. In this respect the pay reward is a little demeaning to many people. They have to virtually perform for a few "crumbs."

Another problem with the pay for performance approach is that it forces employees to compete for rewards. Since pay dollars are limited, a system of paying for performance forces employees to think in win-lose terms. "If I win a raise, someone else loses a raise." Unfortunately, this mentality is usually detrimental to organizational effectiveness.

Do the problems of a pay for performance plan make it necessary to totally revamp current organizational compensation packages? Even before this is done, it may be necessary to reeducate managers about the fallacies of "carrot" and "stick" strategies with 1980s employees. The worker of the 1980s is not the same as employees of earlier times.

INTRODUCTION

After either a formal or informal performance evaluation occurs, managers distribute various rewards to employees. The manner and timing of distributing rewards are important issues that managers must address almost daily. Managers distribute such rewards as pay, transfers, promotions, praise, and recognition. They can also help create the climate that results in more challenging and satisfying jobs. Because these rewards are considered important by employees, they have significant effects on behavior and performance. In this chapter we are concerned with how intrinsic and extrinsic rewards are distributed by managers. The reactions of people to rewards are also discussed. We also examine the response of employees to rewards received in organizational settings. Administering rewards is another topic reviewed. The role of rewards in organizational membership, absenteeism, turnover, and commitment is presented.

Objectives of the Reward Process

To attract people to join the organization, to keep coming to work, and to motivate them to perform at high levels, managers reward employees. Employees exchange their time, ability, skills, and effort for valued rewards that managers have available for distribution. This relationship between the organization and its employees has been called the "psychological contract." Schein states the psychological contract as follows.

> The individual has a variety of expectations of the organization and the organization a variety of expectations of him or her. These expectations not only cover how much work is to be performed for how much pay, but also involves the whole pattern of rights, privileges, and obligations between the worker and the organization.[1]

There are, of course, stories of broken psychological contracts. An example of a broken psychological contract took place in the office of a manager in a chemical company:

> Don was considered to be an excellent laboratory design engineer by his boss, Jim. He always finished his assignments efficiently and on time. Don was upset about not receiving a promotion. He felt that Jim had promised him the next promotion opportunity. It was Jim's understanding that he would recommend someone for the promotion, but the executive selection committee had the final say. Don asked Jim, "Why did you promise me something you couldn't deliver?" Jim's response was, "I'm sorry that my recommendation of you was not accepted, but you know from past examples that the executive selection

---

[1] Edgar H. Schein, *Organizational Psychology* (Englewood Cliffs, N.J.: Prentice-Hall, 1970), p. 12.

committee has a mind of its own. You are just going to have to be patient and your time will come.''

This example shows that Don believes a psychological contract was broken. The promotion reward process in this chemical company was such that Don's boss did not totally control the distribution of the promotion reward. Of course, other contributors to the breaking of this psychological contract exist, such as miscommunications of expections, misunderstandings, and faulty perceptions.

A Model of Individual Rewards

A model that illustrates how rewards fit into the overall policies and programs of an organization could prove useful to managers. As stated above the main objectives of reward programs are (1) to attract qualified people to *join* the organization; (2) to keep employees coming to work; and (3) to motivate employees to achieve high levels of performance. Figure 14–1 pre-

Figure 14–1
The Reward Process: Individual Level Only

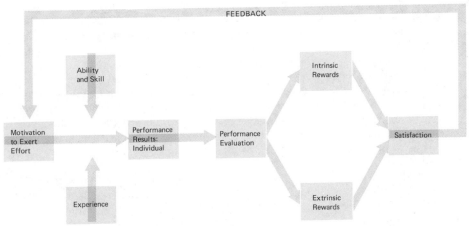

sents a model that attempts to integrate satisfaction, motivation, performance, and rewards. Reading the model from left to right suggests that the motivation to exert effort is not enough to cause acceptable performance. Performance results from a combination of effort and the level of ability, skill, and experience of an individual. The performance results of the individual are evaluated either formally or informally by management. As a result of the evaluation, two types of rewards can be distributed, intrinsic or extrinsic. The rewards are evaluated by the individual. To the extent that the rewards are satisfactory and equitable, the individual achieves a level of satisfaction.

REWARDS AND SATISFACTION

A significant amount of research has been done on what determines whether individuals will be satisfied with rewards. Lawler has concisely summarized five conclusions based on the behavioral science research literature. They are:

1. *Satisfaction with a reward is a function of both how much is received and how much the individual feels should be received.* This conclusion has as its basis the comparisons that people make. When individuals receive less than they feel they should there is some dissatisfaction.
2. *An individual's feelings of satisfaction are influenced by comparisons with what happens to others.* People tend to compare their efforts, skills, seniority, and job performance with those of others. They then attempt to compare rewards. That is, they examine inputs (their own) with inputs of others relative to the rewards received.
3. *Satisfaction is influenced by how satisfied employees are with both intrinsic and extrinsic rewards.* There is some debate among researchers whether intrinsic or extrinsic rewards are more important in determining job satisfaction. The debate has not been settled because most studies suggest that both types of rewards are important. One clear message from the research is that extrinsic and intrinsic rewards satisfy different needs.
4. *People differ in the rewards they desire and in how important different rewards are to them.* Individuals differ on what rewards they prefer. In fact, at different points in a person's career, at different ages, and in various situations rewards preferred vary.
5. *Some extrinsic rewards are satisfying because they lead to other rewards.* There are some extrinsic rewards that lead to other more preferred rewards. For example, the size of a person's office or whether the office has carpet or drapes often is considered a reward because it indicates the individual's status and power. Money is a reward that leads to other things such as prestige, autonomy and independence, security, and shelter.[2]

The relationship between rewards and satisfaction is not perfectly understood, nor is it static in nature. It changes because people and the environment change. There are, however, some important considerations that managers could use to develop and distribute rewards. First, there must be enough rewards available so that basic human needs are satisfied. Federal legislation, union contracts, and managerial fairness have provided at least minimal rewards in most work settings. Second, individuals tend to compare their rewards with others. If inequities are perceived, dissatisfaction will occur. Regardless of the quantity of rewards individuals receive, people make comparisons. Finally, managers distributing rewards must recognize large individual differences. Unless individual differences are considered, it is likely that the reward process will invariably be less effective than desired. Any reward package should be sufficient to (1) satisfy basic needs (e.g., food,

---

[2] Edward E. Lawler III. "Reward Systems," in J. Richard Hackman and J. Lloyd Suttle, eds., *Improving Life at Work* (Santa Monica: Goodyear Publishing Co., 1977), pp. 163–226.

shelter, clothing); (2) be considered equitable; and (3) be individually oriented.[3]

INTRINSIC AND EXTRINSIC REWARDS

The rewards shown in Figure 14–1 are classified into two broad categories, *extrinsic* and *intrinsic*. Whether we are discussing extrinsic or intrinsic rewards it is important to first consider the rewards *valued* by the person. An individual will put forth little effort unless the reward has *value*. Both extrinsic and intrinsic rewards can have value.

Extrinsic rewards are those external to the job. Included in this category are promotions, improved work equipment and facilities, opportunity to socialize with co-workers, financial rewards such as pay and fringe benefits, and receiving recognition from the superior. On the other hand, *intrinsic rewards* are associated directly with "doing the job." They are rewards that can satisfy such needs as being responsible, autonomous, challenged, and accomplishing worthwhile job duties. The intrinsic rewards flow from the person's performance of the job, and are sometimes considered self-rewards. For example, a person must decide whether a particular level of performance is really challenging and worthy of feeling that something meaningful has been accomplished. On the other hand, extrinsic rewards are distributed by a manager.

Extrinsic Rewards

Financial Rewards: Salary and Wages. Money is a major extrinsic reward. It has been said that "although it is generally agreed that money is the major mechanism for rewarding and modifying behavior in industry . . . very little is known about how it works."[4] To really understand how money modifies behavior, the perceptions and preferences of a person being rewarded financially must be understood. Of course, this is a challenging task for a manager to complete successfully. It requires careful attention and observation of the person. In addition, the manager must be trusted so that the person will communicate his or her feelings about financial rewards.

Money plays many roles in influencing people in organizations. First, money could be a *conditioned reinforcer* because it is usually associated with such reinforcers as food, housing, clothing, and recreation. As a conditioned reinforcer, pay could be thought of as a first-level outcome that leads to food and other second-level outcomes. Second, money can be viewed as an incentive or goal which is capable of reducing need deficiencies. Money acts as an incentive *before* the employee acts or performs and a reward *after* the act is performed. Third, money can serve as an *anxiety-reducer;*

---

[3] Ibid., p. 168.

[4] R. L. Opsahl and M. D. Dunnette, "The Role of Financial Compensation in Industrial Motivation," *Psychological Bulletin* (August 1966), p. 114.

that is, a common characteristic of man is to be anxious about financial obligations. Thus, money can reduce anxiety.

Many organizations utilize some type of incentive pay plan to motivate employees. Lawler presents the most comprehensive summary of various pay plans and their effectiveness as motivators.[5] Each plan is evaluated on the basis of the following questions:

1. How effective is it in creating the perception that pay is related to performance?
2. How well does it minimize the perceived negative consequences of good performance?
3. How well does it contribute to the perception that important rewards other than pay (e.g., praise and interest shown in the employee by a respected superior) result in good performance? A summary of Lawler's ideas is presented in Table 14–1.

Table 14–1
Evaluation of Pay-Incentive Plans in Organizations

Type of Pay Plan	Performance Measure	Perceived Pay Performance Linkage	Minimization of Negative Consequences	Perceived Relationship between Other Rewards and Performance
Salary plan				
For individuals	Productivity	Good	Neutral	Neutral
	Cost effectiveness	Fair	Neutral	Neutral
	Superiors' rating	Fair	Neutral	Fair
For group	Productivity	Fair	Neutral	Fair
	Cost effectiveness	Fair	Neutral	Fair
	Superiors' rating	Fair	Neutral	Fair
For total organization	Productivity	Fair	Neutral	Fair
	Cost effectiveness	Fair	Neutral	Fair
	Profits	Neutral	Neutral	Fair
Bonus plan				
For individuals	Productivity	Excellent	Poor	Neutral
	Cost effectiveness	Good	Poor	Neutral
	Superiors' rating	Good	Poor	Fair
For group	Productivity	Good	Neutral	Fair
	Cost effectiveness	Good	Neutral	Fair
	Superiors' rating	Good	Neutral	Fair
For total organization	Productivity	Good	Neutral	Fair
	Cost effectiveness	Good	Neutral	Fair
	Profits	Fair	Neutral	Fair

Source: Adapted from Edward E. Lawler III, *Pay and Organizational Effectiveness* (New York: McGraw-Hill, 1971), Table 9–3, p. 165.

---

[5] Edward L. Lawler III, *Pay and Organizational Effectiveness* (New York: McGraw-Hill, 1971), pp. 164–70.

By looking at each criteria separately, some interesting patterns evolve. The individual salary and bonus plans seem to be best if management is attempting to link pay and performance. The least effective way of accomplishing this is to implement a total organizational salary plan. This makes sense if you think the individual does not perceive his or her impact on a total organizational plan.

The bonus plans are generally more effective than the salary plans. This is especially noticeable for the first criterion of linking pay and performance. Bonus plans typically are related to the current performance of employees. Salary plans, on the other hand, are often related to past performance. Neither pay plan minimizes the potential negative consequences of linking pay and performance. Perhaps it is futile to think about developing a perfect pay plan.

If management is attempting to relate nonpay rewards to performance, the group and total organization plans seem better suited than individual plans. In essence, if people believe that other rewards stem from performance, they would tend to encourage improved performance among peers throughout the organization.

This discussion should clearly illustrate that no one plan can accomplish every desirable objective. The evidence indicates that bonus plans, where they can be used, are generally the best type of salary or wage plan. Individually based plans also seem to be superior to group and organizational plans.

Pay plans, when linked to performance, have a number of parts. First, the more challenging and responsible jobs require special pay considerations. Second, the seniority of a worker must be considered. Third, the inflationary cost-of-living factors must also be considered. Fourth, the individual's actual performance must be evaluated in the most objective manner and a pay amount assigned to this rating.

Financial Rewards: Fringe Benefits. In most cases fringe benefits are primarily financial. There are some cases, however, such as IBM's recreation program for employees and General Mill's picnic grounds that are not entirely financial. The major financial fringe benefit in most organizations is the pension plan. For most employees, the opportunity to participate in the pension plan is a valued reward. The current work period of an employee and when a plan would begin to pay off are factors to consider when examining the pension plan's influence on behavior. Fringe benefits such as pension plans, hospitalization, and vacations are not usually contingent on the performance accomplishments of employees. In most cases fringe benefit plans are based on seniority or attendance.

Interpersonal Rewards. The manager has some power to distribute such interpersonal rewards as status and recognition. By assigning individuals to prestigious jobs, the manager can attempt to improve or remove the status a person possesses. However, if co-workers do not believe a person merits a particular job, it is likely that status will not be enhanced. Managers by reviewing performance can grant what they consider to be improved status job changes in some situations. The manager and co-workers both play a role in granting job status.

Much of what was just stated about status applies also to recognition. In a reward context *recognition* refers to acknowledging employee achievement that could result in improved status. Recognition from a manager could include public praise, expressions of a job well done, or receiving special attention. The extent to which recognition is motivating depends, as do most rewards, on its perceived value and on the connection the individual sees between it and behavior.[6]

Promotions.   For many employees, promotion does not happen often; some never experience it in their job careers. The manager making a promotion reward decision attempts to match the right person with the job. The criteria that are often used to reach promotion decisions are performance or seniority. Performance, if it can be accurately assessed, is often given significant weight in promotion reward allocations.

Intrinsic Rewards

Completion.   The ability to start and finish a project or job is important to some individuals. These people value what is called task completion. The completion of a task and its effect on a person is a form of self-reward. An example of such a self-reward would be a situation in which an employee takes on a project or job such as designing the plans for a power plant and does each part of the design task. This employee would start and complete the entire task. Some people have a need to complete tasks. Opportunities that allow such people to complete tasks can have a powerful motivating effect. In some job situations managers can create the climate, job layout, and assignments so that an individual with a need for task completion can experience a sense of completing the job.

Achievement.   Achievement is a self-administered reward that is derived when a person reaches a challenging goal. McClelland has found that there are individual differences in striving for achievement.[7] Some individuals seek challenging goals, while others tend to accomplish moderate or low goals. In goal setting programs it has been proposed that difficult goals result in a higher level of individual performance than do moderate goals. However, even in such programs individual differences must be considered before reaching conclusions about the importance of achievement rewards.

Autonomy.   There are some people who want jobs that provide them with the right and privilege to make decisions and operate without being closely supervised. A feeling of autonomy could result from the freedom to

---

[6] Lyman W. Porter, "Turning Work into Nonwork: The Rewarding Environment," in M. D. Dunnette, *Work and Nonwork in the Year 2001* (Belmont, Calif.: Wadsworth Publishing Co., 1973), p. 113.

[7] David C. McClelland, *The Achieving Society* (Princeton, N.J.: D. Van Nostrand, 1961).

do what the employee considers best in a particular situation. In jobs that are highly structured and controlled by management, it is difficult to create tasks that employees would consider as leading to a feeling of autonomy. The case of a steelworker describes such a job:

> Mike worked long and hard in the blast furnace area of a steel company. He explained his job in the following way: "I can not move or go to the restroom without some supervisor checking me out. This place gets on my nerves because I'm treated like a horse. Work, work, work. I know the job better than any of those stiffs from Pittsburgh, but I am told when, how, and what to do. If I could only show somebody that I have pride in my work, they might change their tune. I'll probably die without ever being allowed to be a real person who thinks and acts for himself."

The plight of Mike centers on the issue of autonomy. He clearly expresses a need to operate for himself without being closely supervised. Interestingly, Mike's supervisor informed one of the authors that Mike had to be watched and closely supervised because he was lazy and had a bad attitude. Working out these differences in Mike's need and the supervisor's opinions is required before anything positive happens in this particular situation.

Personal Growth. The personal growth of any individual is a unique experience. A person who is personally growing senses his or her development and can see how capabilities are being expanded. By expanding capabilities a person is able to maximize or at least satisfy skill potential. For example, a young management trainee who is given difficult and varied tasks during the first years of employment would be able to develop skills. This early testing and development would hopefully lead to more growth in the trainee's skill potential. If some people are not allowed or encouraged to develop their skills they often become dissatisfied with their jobs and organizations.

In this section some of the numerous extrinsic and intrinsic rewards available on jobs are presented. Some of the other popular rewards include feedback about performance, personal time off, job rotation, stock options, offices with windows, and educational opportunities. Managers would probably need to familiarize themselves with what rewards are available or can be created in their particular situation.

Those rewards included in this section are distributed or created by managers, work groups, or the individual. Table 14–2 summarizes the rewards we have discussed. As the table indicates the manager plays either or both a direct and an indirect role in developing and administering the rewards.

REWARDS AND JOB PERFORMANCE

There is agreement among behavioralists and managers that extrinsic and intrinsic rewards can be used to motivate job performance. It is also clear that certain conditions must exist if rewards are to motivate good job perfor-

Table 14–2
Types and Sources of Some Popular Extrinsic and Intrinsic Rewards

	Source of Reward		
Type	Manager	Group	Individual
I. Extrinsic			
A. Financial			
1. Salary and wages	D		
2. Fringe benefits	D		
B. Interpersonal	D	D	
C. Promotion	D		
II. Intrinsic			
A. Completion	I		D
B. Achievement	I		D
C. Autonomy	I		D
D. Personal growth	I		D

D = The direct source of the reward.
I = The indirect source of the reward.

mance: they must be *valued* by the person and they must be related to the level of job performance that is to be motivated.[8]

The Value of Rewards

In Chapter 5 expectancy motivation theory was presented. It was stated that according to the theory, every behavior has associated with it (in a person's mind), certain outcomes or rewards or punishments. In other words, an assembly-line worker believes that if he or she behaves in a certain way, he or she will get certain things. This is a description of the *performance-outcome expectancy.* The worker may expect that a steady performance of 10 units a day will eventually result in a transfer to a more challenging job. On the other hand, a worker may expect that the steady 10 units a day performance will result in being considered a "rate buster" by co-workers.

Each outcome has a *valence* or value to the person. Outcomes such as pay, promotion, a reprimand, or a better job have different values for different people. This occurs because each person has different needs and perceptions. Thus, in considering which rewards to use, a manager has to be astute at considering individual differences. Using rewards that have little motivational value would be like throwing away time, personal energy, and resources. On the other hand, if valued rewards are used to motivate they can result in the exertion of effort to achieve high levels of performance.

The Performance Evaluation Connection

In most cases a performance evaluation occurs before extrinsic rewards are distributed. If such rewards are to be motivators, they must be tied to

---

[8] Lyman W. Porter, Edward E. Lawler III., and J. Richard Hackman, *Behavior in Organizations* (New York: McGraw-Hill, 1975), p. 352.

measured performance. The criteria of sound performance evaluation was discussed in the previous chapter. It was stated that the performance criteria used must be relevant, reliable, and practical as well as able to discriminate between good performers and poor performers. Unless these criteria are met, employees will have a difficult time determining the connection between performance and extrinsic rewards.

The difficulties of developing good measures of performance have been discussed in Chapter 13. However, if extrinsic rewards are to motivate positive behavior, some type of performance evaluation is necessary. Even though performance evaluation is used there still will be concern expressed by employees about reward equity, amount, and timeliness. Managers are faced with a continual struggle because employees, like the managers themselves, want more rewards. The manager must also select a system for properly administering rewards.

ADMINISTERING REWARDS

Managers are faced with the decision of how to administer rewards. Three major theoretical approaches to reward administration are: (1) positive reinforcement, (2) modeling and social imitation, and (3) expectancy.[9]

Positive Reinforcement

As discussed in Chapter 5, in administering a positive reinforcement program, the emphasis is on the desired behavior that leads to job performance, rather than performance alone. The basic foundation of administering rewards through positive reinforcement is the relationship between behavior and its consequences. Consequences are viewed as outcomes in an employee's environment related to the demonstration of certain behaviors. If the consequence increases the occurrence of a behavior it is called a reinforcer. For example, being recognized by a respected supervisor may increase the number of units being produced by a person. It is assumed that positive reinforcers such as pay, praise, or recognition can be effective in shaping desired job behaviors if they are closely linked to the performance they are meant to influence. If a manager can identify behavior that leads to high levels of performance, select the most effective positive reinforcers that shape the behavior, and distribute the reinforcers on some form of effective schedule, job performance can be improved.

The application of positive reinforcement is used in many organizations.[10] However, in many cases the program of administering positive reinforcement is done poorly. A glaring example of a poorly designed reinforcement effort took place in an engineering organization.

---

[9] Porter, "Turning Work into Nonwork," p. 122 suggests three approaches. He introduces operant conditioning. We believe that when rewards are being discussed positive reinforcement should be used.

[10] W. Clay Hammer and Ellen P. Hamner, "Behavior Modification on the Bottom Line," *Organizational Dynamics* (Spring 1976), pp. 2–21.

The company recently implemented a bonus system that was designed to improve the completion time on construction projects and subprojects. If the projects were completed before scheduled deadlines, the entire project team would be given two days off from work with pay. The program was initiated ten months ago and approximately 12 construction projects were brought in under the scheduled deadline. To date, not a single project team member has received any time off for this exceptional performance. The director of all construction projects has stated that the company has been too busy with backlogged contracts to give anyone time off. He promised that all the time owed the employees would be granted when a slack in contracts occurred.

Obviously, this engineering company example points out the problem of a lengthy time lag between the behavior and receiving the positive reinforcer. The reward, receiving time off, has already probably lost its ability to shape behavior such as finishing projects before deadlines. In addition, by not delivering the promised rewards, management may have alienated workers so that any future attempts to shape behavior through positive reinforcers are doomed to fail. It probably would have been better for management not to have started the so-called time off bonus program.

While positive reinforcement can be a useful method to shape desired behavior, other considerations concerning the type of reward schedule to use are also important. We have already discussed schedules of positive reinforcement in both Chapters 4 and 5. Suffice it to say that managers should explore the possible consequences of different types of reward schedules for individuals. It is important to know how employees respond to continuous, fixed interval, and fixed ratio schedules. In addition, managers could benefit from understanding how individuals respond to different forms of monetary and nonmonetary positive reinforcers.

Modeling and Social Imitation[11]

There is little doubt that many human skills and behaviors are learned by what Bandura calls observational learning, or simply, imitation.[12] Observational learning equips a person to duplicate a response, but whether it is actually imitated depends on whether the model person was rewarded or punished for particular behaviors. If a person is to be motivated he or she must observe models receiving reinforcements that are valued. For example, if a respected informal leader is praised for doing an excellent job by her manager, other members of the group would observe this application of a positive reinforcer. If praise is a valued reward the other members may attempt to imitate the behavior which resulted in receiving praise. Through modeling, employees can learn attitudes, emotions, and styles, as well as anxieties,

---

[11] The discussion of Porter, "Turning Work into Non-work," stimulated the development of this section.

[12] A. Bandura and R. H. Walters, *Social Learning and Personality Development* (New York: Holt, Rinehart & Winston, 1963).

frustrations, and bad work habits like goldbricking, resisting management initiated programs, and not attending work.

In order to use modeling to administer rewards, managers would need to determine who responds to this approach. In addition, selecting appropriate models would be a necessary step. Finally, the context in which modeling occurs needs to be considered. That is, if high performance is the goal and it is almost impossible to achieve because of limited resources, the manager should conclude that modeling is not appropriate. Some managers using modeling have attempted to force it on employees when the situation did not warrant such an approach. Managers must judge the appropriateness of using modeling to administer rewards.

Expectancy Theory

In practice the expectancy-theory approach is incorporated in Figure 14–1. It states that the effort expended by an employee to perform a job is a joint function of both the *value* the person attaches to obtaining rewards (extrinsic and intrinsic) and the expectation (perceived chance or probability) that a specific level of energy will be enough to receive the reward.

The expectancy approach like the other two methods of administering rewards requires managerial action. Managers must determine the kinds of rewards employees desire and do whatever is possible to distribute them or create conditions so that what is available in the form of rewards can be applied. In some situations it is just not possible to provide the rewards that are valued and preferred. Therefore, managers often have to increase the desirability of other available rewards.

A manager can and often will use principles from each of the three methods of administering rewards—positive reinforcement, modeling, and expectancy. Each of these methods indicates that job performance of employees is a result of the application of effort. To generate the effort to perform, managers could use positive reinforcers, modeling, and expectations to get the job done. It should be remembered that performance may never be satisfactorily accomplished if employees are deficient in problem-solving skills, specific abilities, and experience. To get the most from administering rewards a manager needs to have employees that have the ability, skill, and experience to perform.

REWARDS AND ORGANIZATIONAL MEMBERSHIP

As stated earlier a major objective of a reward system is to attract people to join or become members of an organization. This involves people making organizational and job choices. The notion of how an individual moves from outside to inside an organization is called *organizational entry.*[13] There are

---

[13] John P. Wanous, "Organizational Entry: The Individual's Viewpoint," in J. Richard Hackman, Edward E. Lawler III, and Lyman W. Porter, eds., *Perspectives on Behavior in Organizations* (New York: McGraw-Hill, 1977), pp. 126–35.

a number of research studies that examine the organizational entry decisions of employees. Most of these studies indicate that people are attracted to organizations which are rated highest on the individuals' expectations about what the organization will be like and their goals and values. It appears that people will choose the organization which they believe will result in the best set of outcomes or rewards. This behavior seems reasonable because being able to obtain valued rewards leads to high levels of satisfaction.

In an interesting study of job choice, individuals were asked to rate the jobs they were considering in terms of their chances of achieving a number of goals. These individuals were also asked to rank the goals in order of importance. The data showed that these individuals were attracted to those organizations that were seen as being instrumental for the attainment of their preferred goals.[14]

The attraction of members to an organization depends to some extent on how people in the external market view the possible rewards offered by the organization. If the reward image of the company is clear and people value the potential rewards there will be attraction. Just as rewards can be used to attract people to join, they can and are used to motivate individuals to remain with the organization.

REWARDS AND TURNOVER AND ABSENTEEISM

Turnover has been defined as the movement of individuals across the membership boundary of a system such as an organization.[15] Individual movement across membership boundaries typically includes "accessions" and "separations." Separations from organizations are due to "quits," "lay-offs," or "discharges." The main focus in this section will be on "quits." Some research indicates that "quits" are related to job satisfaction.[16] However, when turnover is examined in relation to organizational effectiveness there are some problems.

Some managers assume that low turnover is a mark of an effective organization. This view is somewhat controversial because a high "quit" rate means more expense for an organization. However, some organizations would benefit if disruptive and low performers quit. Thus, the issue of turnover needs to focus on the *frequency* and on *who* is leaving.

Ideally if managers could develop reward systems that retained the best performers and caused poor performers to leave, the overall effectiveness of an organization would improve. To approach this ideal state an equitable and favorably compared reward system must exist. The feeling of *equity* and *favorable comparison* has an external orientation. That is, the equity of

[14] Victor H. Vroom, "Organizational Choice: A Study of Pre- and Post-Decision Processes," *Organizational Behavior and Human Performance* (December 1966), pp. 212–25.

[15] James L. Price, *The Study of Turnover* (Ames, Iowa: The Iowa State University Press, 1977), p. 4.

[16] Lyman Porter and Richard Steers, "Organizational Work and Personal Factors in Employee Turnover and Absenteeism," *Psychological Bulletin* (April 1973), pp. 151–76.

rewards and favorableness involves comparisons to external parties. This orientation is used because "quitting" most often means that a person leaves one organization for an alternative elsewhere. Of course, if an organization had an endless stream of extrinsic and intrinsic rewards and could increase the level of rewards distributed, high performers could usually be retained. This is a very costly reward strategy that most organizations are not able to afford.

There is no perfect means for retaining high performers. It appears that a reward system that is based on *merit* should encourage most of the better performers to remain with an organization. There also has to be some differential in the reward system that discriminates between high and low performers. The point being that the high performers must receive significantly more extrinsic and intrinsic rewards than the low performers. Identifying high performers is a task that was included in our discussion of performance evaluation. As stated by many behaviorists, managing turnover means managing satisfaction. This requires connecting rewards to job performance—a very challenging managerial job.[17]

Absenteeism, no matter for what reason, is a costly and disruptive problem facing managers. It is costly because it reduces output and disruptive because schedules and programs must be modified. Employees attend work because they are motivated to do so. The level of motivation will remain high if an individual feels that attendance will lead to more valued rewards and fewer negative consequences than alternative behaviors.

In most organizations when nonmanagers are absent it means that they will lose some pay, not be given better job opportunities, and will not be able to interact with co-workers. These rewards may not be significant enough for a person to attend work. Unless the rewards of attendance are strong enough, absenteeism will be a problem. In some organizations punishment in the form of threats of dismissal or penalties are used to discourage absenteeism. The use of punishment in controlling absenteeism is minimized because of union contract specifications limiting its use, the unpredictable consequences of such a practice, and the strong possibility of bringing about "quits"—which may be more costly and disruptive than the absenteeism problem.

There has been some research on reward systems and attendance. In an interesting study, researchers used a poker incentive plan to improve attendance. Each day as an employee came to work and was on time, he was allowed to select one card from a regular playing deck. At the end of a five-day week, the employees who attended every day on time would have a regular five-card hand. The highest hand won $20.[18] There were eight winners, one for each department. This plan seemed to result in a decrease of absenteeism of 18.7 percent. This study did not compare the poker incen-

---

[17] Lawler, "Reward Systems," p. 169.

[18] E. Pedalino and V. Gamboa, "Behavior Modification and Absenteeism: Intervention in One Industrial Setting," *Journal of Applied Psychology* (December 1974), pp. 694–98.

tive plan with any other system, so whether it would be better than some other reward system is not known. However, it was better than when no bonus or prize was distributed for attendance.

Another study reported the effects of an employee-developed bonus plan on attendance. Three work groups developed a plan that offered a cash bonus to workers who attended work regularly.[19] The results indicated that job attendance improved significantly. Further data from the study showed what happens when a plan developed by some individuals is imposed on other people. The plan developed by the three groups was applied to two other groups in the organization. The findings indicated that it was not effective in reducing absenteeism. The success of a reward plan involving employee participation was linked to where the plan was developed.

Managers appear to have some influence over attendance behavior. They have the ability to punish, establish bonus systems, and allow employee participation in developing plans. Whether any of these or other approaches will reduce absenteeism is determined by the value of the rewards perceived by employees, the amount of the reward, and whether employees perceive a relationship between attendance and rewards. These same characteristics appear every time we analyze the effects of rewards on organizational behavior.

REWARDS AND ORGANIZATIONAL COMMITMENT

There is little research on the relationship between rewards and organizational commitment. *Commitment* to an organization involves three attitudes: (1) a sense of identification with the organization's goals; (2) a feeling of involvement in organizational duties; and (3) a feeling of loyalty for the organization.[20] There are indications that commitment, or rather its absence, can reduce organizational effectiveness. People who are committed are less likely to quit and accept other jobs. Thus, the costs of high turnover are not incurred. In addition, committed and highly skilled employees require less supervision. A system of close supervision and rigid monitoring control processes is time consuming and costly. Furthermore, a committed employee perceives the value and importance of integrating individual and organizational goals. The employee thinks of his or her goals and the organization's in personal terms.

A study of upper-middle managers in large organizations reported some of the organizational rewards that significantly influence commitment. Some of these factors were:

---

[19] Edward E. Lawler III and J. Richard Hackman, "The Impact of Employee Participation in the Development of Pay Incentive Plans: A Field Experiment," *Journal of Applied Psychology* (December 1969), pp. 467–71.

[20] Bruce Buchanan, "To Walk an Extra Mile: The Whats, Whens, and Whys of Organizational Commitment," *Organizational Dynamics* (Spring 1975), pp. 67–80.

Personal Importance. The experience of being considered a valuable and productive member of an organization.

Realization of Expectations. Those managers who were able to fulfill expectations because the organization fulfilled its promises reported more commitment.

Job Challenge. Challenging, interesting, and self-rewarding job assignments appeared to strengthen commitment. The study also found that the job experience in the first year continued to shape the attitudes of managers into the future.

This study indicated that intrinsic rewards are important for the development of organizational commitment. Organizations able to meet employee needs by providing achievement opportunities and by recognizing achievement when it occurs had a significant impact on commitment in this study. Thus, managers need to develop intrinsic reward systems which focus on personal importance or self-esteem, integrating individual and organizational goals, and building jobs that are challenging.

DIFFERENT MANAGERIALLY INITIATED REWARD SYSTEMS

The typical list of rewards that managers can and do distribute in organizations has been discussed above. We all know that pay, fringe benefits, and opportunities to achieve challenging goals are considered rewards by most people. It is also generally accepted that rewards are administered by managers through such processes as reinforcement, modeling, and expectancies. What are some of the newer, yet largely untested reward programs which some managers are experimenting with? Three different and largely untested approaches to rewards are cafeteria fringe benefits, banking time off, and paying all employees a salary.

Cafeteria-Style Fringe Benefits

A cafeteria-style fringe benefit plan involves management placing an upper limit on how much the organization is willing to spend on the total package. The employee is then asked to decide how he or she would like to receive the total fringe benefit amount. The employee is able to develop a personally attractive fringe benefit package. Some employees take all of the fringes in cash or purchase special medical protection plans. The cafeteria plan provides individuals with the benefits they prefer rather than what someone else establishes for them.

There are some administrative problems associated with cafeteria plans. Because of the different preferences of employees, records become more complicated. For a large organization with a cafeteria plan, a computer system is almost essential to do the record keeping. Another problem involves receiving group insurance premium rates. Most life and medical insurance premiums are based on the number of employees participating. It is difficult to determine what the participation level will be under a cafeteria plan.

TRW Corporation has placed approximately 12,000 employees on a cafeteria plan. It allows employees to rearrange and redistribute their fringe benefit packages every year. Over 80 percent of the TRW participants changed their benefit packages since the plan was initiated.[21]

Banking Time Off

A *time-off* feature is attractive to most people. The example above of the engineering company highlighted such a time-off program when it was not operating efficiently. In essence, most companies have a time-off system built into their vacation programs. Employees receive different amounts of time off based on the number of years worked for the organization. An extension of such a time-off reward could be granted for certain levels of performance. That is, a bank of time-off credits could be built up contingent on performance achievements. Some organizations today are selecting their best performers to attend educational and training programs.

One company in Houston selects the best performers and provides them with an opportunity to attend an executive educational program. Being eligible is largely contingent on the performance record of the individual. Those finally selected are given two Fridays off a month to attend classes.

Another organization in Chicago selects an employee each week as the outstanding contributor to organizational performance. There are 50 selections made each year. In January of the subsequent year the selectees receive 2 days off for each time they were selected as the best performer. In this organization the *time-off* reward is considered very important. There are only 130 employees eligible for the time-off reward and 24 earned it this past year.

The All-Salaried Team

In most organizations managers are paid salaries and nonmanagers receive wages. The practice of paying all employees a salary is supposed to improve loyalty, commitment, and self-esteem. The notion of being a part of a team is projected by the salary-for-everyone practice. One benefit of the all-salary practice considered important by nonmanagers is the elimination of punching a time clock. Some consider a time clock a degrading piece of equipment. To date rigorous investigations of the influence, if any, of an all-salary practice are not available. It does seem to have promise when applied to some employees.

The link between the performance evaluation system and reward distribution was shown in Figure 14–1. The discussion of this and other linkages in the reward process suggest the complexity of using rewards to motivate

---

[21] Lawler, "Reward Systems," p. 182.

better performance. Managers need to use judgment, diagnosis, and the resources available to reward their subordinates. As shown, administering rewards is perhaps one of the most challenging and frustrating tasks that managers must perform.

MAJOR ISSUES FOR THE MANAGER TO CONSIDER

A. The major objectives of the reward processes are to attract people to join the organization, to keep them coming to work, and to motivate them to perform at high levels.

B. It is general knowledge that there are certain reward process issues that should be addressed if any objectives are to be accomplished. Namely, there must be enough rewards to satisfy basic needs, people make comparisons between what rewards they receive and what others receive, and individual differences in reward preferences are important issues for consideration.

C. Management can and must distribute both extrinsic and intrinsic rewards. *Extrinsic* rewards are those that are external to the job such as promotions, fringe benefits, and pay. *Intrinsic* rewards are associated with doing the job. They include responsibility, challenge, and meaningful work.

D. If extrinsic and/or intrinsic rewards are to motivate good job performance, they must be *valued* by the employee and linked to the level of performance that is expected.

E. Managers have many means available for administering extrinsic and intrinsic rewards. Three of the most popular methods include positive reinforcement, modeling, and applying expectancy theory principles.

F. Rewards, if used effectively, can affect such organizational behaviors as membership, turnover, absenteeism, and commitment. The research evidence showing how rewards influence these behaviors is still rather limited.

G. Some newer and different reward strategies used by managers include cafeteria style fringe benefits, banking time off, and an all-salaried work force.

H. The reward process is complex but extremely important in encouraging, sustaining, and developing organizational effectiveness and individual job performance.

DISCUSSION AND REVIEW QUESTIONS

1. Most managers use an array of rewards and punishment to accomplish desired outcomes. However, most systems are designed around a number of features such as merit, seniority, or attendance. Why is it almost impossible to distribute rewards on the basis of merit?

2. Develop a list of extrinsic and intrinsic rewards that are important to you. What kind of organization and job would be able to provide you with these rewards?

3. Have you ever been rewarded by modeling? Present a personal experience that shows how modeling influenced you.

4. The timing of receiving a reward is especially important when implementing positive reinforcement? Why?

5. Herzberg contends that pay is basically an extrinsic reward. Do you now agree with this premise? Why?

6. What managerial skills and abilities are needed to derive the most benefit from administering rewards?

7. It has been said that distributing rewards carefully and equitably is an investment in the most important organizational resource, people. Do you agree?

8. Some of the newer reward plans like cafeteria fringe benefits and banking time off have not really met the test of science. What type of research is needed to determine whether these kinds of plans are organizationally successful?

9. There are some who believe that no matter how attractive an organization's extrinsic and intrinsic rewards, there will be some employees who remain dissatisfied. What could account for this?

10. If equity and favorable comparisons are so important in reward systems, how can an organization develop a program that is generally viewed as equitable and favorable?

ADDITIONAL REFERENCES

Broedling, L. A. "The Uses of the Intrinsic-Extrinsic Distinction In Explaining Motivation and Organizational Behavior." *Academy of Management Review* (1977), pp. 267–76.

Hammer, T. H., and Bacharach, S. D., eds. *Reward Systems and Power Distribution in Organizations: Searching for Solutions.* New York: Cornell University, 1977.

Kerr, S. "On the Folly of Rewarding A, While Hoping for B." *Academy of Management Journal* (1975), pp. 769–83.

Macy, B. A., and Mirvis, P. H. "Measuring Quality of Work and Organizational Effectiveness in Behavioral Economic Terms," *Administrative Science Quarterly* (1976), pp. 212–26.

Mirvis, P. H., and Lawler, E. E., III. "Measuring the Financial Impact of Employee Attitudes." *Journal of Applied Psychology* (1977), pp. 1–8.

Porter, L. W.; Crampon, W. J.; and Smith, F. J. "Organizational Commitment and Managerial Turnover: A Longitudinal Study." *Organizational Behavior and Human Performance* (1976), pp. 87–98.

Pritchard, R. D.; Campbell, K. M.; and Campbell, D. J. "Effects of Extrinsic Financial Rewards on Intrinsic Motivation." *Journal of Applied Psychology* (1977), pp. 9–15.

Salancik, G. R. "Commitment Is Too Easy!" *Organizational Dynamics* (1977), pp. 62–80.

CASE FOR ANALYSIS

THE EFFORT, PERFORMANCE, PAY DILEMMA AT JUSTIS CORPORATION

John Hankla is a generator assembler working for the Justis Manufacturing Corporation. The company employs approximately 4,200 nonunionized workers and 495 managerial personnel. Justis manufacturers repair parts and generators which are used for construction equipment.

The assemblers in what has become known as the Arco unit work the day shift and have worked for the company an average of 15 years. Each of the assemblers has worked for the company for at least eight years and is paid an hourly wage. The wage program for assemblers is related primarily to seniority and performance. The new plant manager, Paul Slanker, wants to continue integrating the performance of assemblers with the wage increases that are granted every 12 to 15 months.

The performance of assemblers in the Arco unit is evaluated by the shift foremen, Randy Jones and Paul. They use an evaluation form that focuses on quantity of output, quality control, promptness of completing task assignments, and intragroup aid provided by idle assemblers. The intragroup factor is concerned with the steps taken by assemblers who have completed their work on the generator to help others on the line who have fallen behind for some reason.

The line is a straight flow processing arrangement with six work stations. These stations are arranged as shown in Exhibit 1.

The wages of the 12 assemblers range from $3.98 to $6.25 an hour.

Exhibit 1

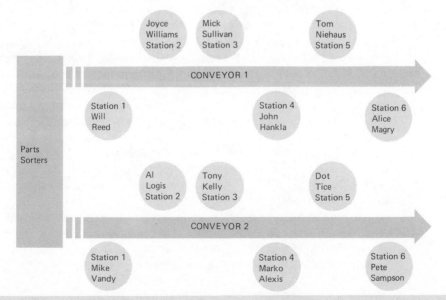

Each assembler is trained and able to work at any of the six work stations. They typically work at one station for periods of up to four months and then rotate to another station on the line. Randy and Paul believe that John is without doubt the best performer. He has continually helped others on conveyor 1 and 2 to reduce the backlogs that often occur.

Paul and Randy believe that with current inflationary conditions an increase in pay would be a desirable reward for any of the assemblers. They further believe that competition is a force which needs to be examined carefully, especially with regard to productivity per person. Although Justis has much the same equipment as its two competitors, it is top management's opinion that the performance and the effort expended by Justis's employees are not up to the level of the competition. They want supervisors to improve the effort and performance of their subordinates.

The plan for improving performance focuses on wages. Paul and Randy have decided to raise John's merit increase by 10 percent above any of the other assemblers. They believe that Joyce, Marko, and Tom have the same ability and skill as John, but do not exert the effort needed to perform as well. Pete, Alice, Al, and Mick are just slightly less skilled than the high-skill group but do not seem to be motivated to improve their skill levels. Tony, Mike, Dot, and Will just do not have the same level of skills as the others.

The assemblers, because of their close proximity to each other, often exchange thoughts about the job, the company, the management, and the pay-performance-ability linkage in the organization. This has led to comparisons and in some instances arguments about who is the best worker, the best company person, and the most likely to be promoted to the supervisory level of management. In the past eight years, four people have been promoted to management positions from the Arco unit.

The first person notified about this year's merit increase was Joyce Williams. She received a raise of 4.8 percent. Next, was Tom Niehaus who received a raise of 5.0 percent. The third person was Al Logis who received a raise of 4.4 percent. John was the fourth person notified of the merit increase plus his supplemental increase for superior performance which resulted in a total merit increase of 16.4 percent. The other raises ranged from 4.0 to 6.4 percent.

The notification of merit increases took five weeks to complete. The assembly line gossip immediately identified a difference between most of the increases and John's. Almost immediately the Arco unit's productivity decreased and its backlogs increased. Its monthly production over the past two years is shown in Exhibit 2; current production is shown by the darker line, last year production is shown by the lighter line.

Although Paul knew he was no statistician the decrease in productivity and the sustained lower level of output between June and October worried him. He called Randy in to discuss the problems in the Arco unit. Paul wanted to work out a motivation plan that would get the unit "pointed in the right direction" again.

Exhibit 2

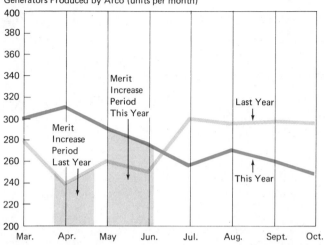

Generators Produced by Arco (units per month)

Questions for Consideration

1. Do you believe that it is possible to think about the problems identified in this situation in terms of a need satisfaction model? Explain.

2. Should the decrease in productivity have been expected by Paul and Randy? Why?

3. It the type of work performed by the Arco unit suited for the type of performance evaluation and pay plan used by management? Explain.

EXPERIENTIAL EXERCISE

MAKING CHOICES ABOUT REWARDS

Objectives

1. To illustrate individual differences in reward preferences.

2. To emphasize how both extrinsic and intrinsic rewards are considered important.

3. To enable people to explore the reasons for reward preferences of others.

Related Topics

Since rewards are so pervasive in organizational settings, they tend to be linked to merit, seniority, and attendance. In fact, they are so related to organizational behavior that few issues of work life can be discussed without mentioning rewards.

Starting the Exercise

Initially individuals will work alone establishing their own list of reward preferences after reviewing Exhibit A. Then the instructor will set up groups of four to six students to examine individual preferences and complete the exercise.

The Facts

It is possible to develop an endless list of on-the-job rewards. Presented in a random fashion in Exhibit A are some of the rewards that could be available to employees.

Exhibit A
Some Possible Rewards for Employees

Company picnics	Recognition	Participation in decisions
Watches	Smile from manager	Stock options
Trophies	Feedback on performance	Vacation trips for performance
Piped-in music	Feedback on career progress	Manager asking for advice
Job challenge	Larger office	Informal leader asking for advice
Achievement opportunity	Club privileges	Office with a window
Time off for performance	More prestigious job	The privilege to complete a job:
Vacation	More job involvement	Start to finish
Autonomy	Use of company recreation	
Pay increase	facilities	

Exercise Procedures

Phase I: 25 minutes

1. Each individual should set up from the Exhibit a list of extrinsic and intrinsic rewards.

2. Each person should then rank order from most important to least important the two lists.

3. From the two lists rank the *eight* most important rewards. How many are extrinsic and how many are intrinsic?

Phase II: 30 minutes

1. The instructor will set up groups of four to six individuals.

2. The two lists in which the extrinsic and intrinsic categories are developed should be discussed.

3. The final rank orders of the eight most important rewards should be placed on a board or chart at the front of the room.

4. The rankings should be discussed within the groups. What are the major differences displayed?

Chapter 15

The Process of Communication

AN ORGANIZATIONAL ISSUE FOR DEBATE
*The Value of Upward Communication**

ARGUMENT FOR

While the classical organization structure formally provides for downward and upward communication, the downward system seems to dominate the upward system in most organizations. As a result, most organizational communication is one way, from higher to lower levels without obtaining any reactions and/or questions from subordinates. In addition, traditional systems—grievance procedures, suggestion systems, employee publications, and "open-door" policies—instituted in many organizations have not worked.

As a result, managers must encourage the free flow of upward communication and encourage subordinates to express their opinions and offer suggestions for improvement. They must seek to develop an atmosphere of trust between themselves and subordinates. Research has indicated that two-way communication is more accurate than one-way communication. However, how accurate it is depends a great deal on the amount of trust the subordinate has in the superior. Under the right conditions communication could take the form of summaries, proposals, and recommendations from subordinates. This will not only improve decision making and organizational performance, but also the attitudes and satisfaction of subordinates.

ARGUMENT AGAINST

The studies indicating that two-way communication is more effective have always involved complex problems requiring two-way communication for solution. They have also been conducted mostly in laboratory situations and involved problems which have nothing to do with those faced by individuals in most organizations.

In the majority of situations, understanding is easy to achieve and two-way communication is not critical. Besides, it takes time and that is a cost most organizations cannot afford. Time is a valuable resource in most organizations. In highly-structured organizations, where the problems are routine, one-way communication is more than adequate if care is taken. This is not to say that the situation might be different in a scientific laboratory than in a police or fire department.

We must also remember the realities of organizational life. Subordinates often purposely withhold information which they think is unpleasant or would displease their superior. Also, distortions and cover-ups occur because a subordinate wants to avoid looking incompetent to a superior.

---

* For research and discussion on this issue see H. J. Leavitt and R. A. H. Mueller, "Some Effects of Feedback on Communications," *Human Relations* (1951), pp. 401–10; W. V. Haney, "A Comparative Study of Unilateral and Bilateral Communication," *Academy of Management Journal* (June 1964), pp. 128–36; W. V. Haney, *Communication in Organizational Behavior* (Homewood, Ill.: Richard D. Irwin, Inc., 1973); and K. H. Roberts and C. A. O'Reilly III, "Failures in Upward Communication in Organizations: Three Possible Culprits," *Academy of Management Journal* (June 1974), pp. 205–15.

INTRODUCTION

One of the important purposes of an organization *structure* is to facilitate the *processes* of *communication* and *decision making*. The remainder of this section of the book discusses these two fundamental processes.

This chapter will focus on communication, while the process of decision making will be the subject of the next chapter. However, both processes are similar in that they pervade everything managers do. The managerial functions of planning, organizing, and controlling all involve managers in specific decisions and communication. In fact, the management functions of planning, organizing, and controlling become operationalized only through communicative activity. When making decisions, managers must both acquire and disseminate information. Thus, communication is critical since managers rarely work with "things" but rather with "information about things."

The Importance of Communication

"You said to get to it as soon as I could, how did I know you meant now!" "How did I know she was really serious about resigning!" In these and similar situations, someone usually ends up saying "What we have here is a failure to communicate." This statement has meaning to everyone because each of us has faced situations in which the basic problem was communication. Whether on a person-to-person basis, nation-to-nation, in organizations, or in small groups, breakdowns in communication are pervasive.

It would be extremely difficult to find an aspect of a manager's job that does not involve communication. Serious problems arise when directives are misunderstood, casual kidding in a work group leads to anger, or when informal remarks by a top-level manager are distorted. Each of these is a result of a breakdown somewhere in the process of communication.

Accordingly, the pertinent question is not whether managers engage in communication or not, because communication is inherent to the functioning of an organization. Rather, the pertinent question is whether managers will communicate well or poorly. In other words, communication itself is unavoidable to an organization's functioning; only *effective* communication is avoidable. *Every manager must be a communicator.* In fact, everything a manager does communicates something in some way to somebody or some group. The only question is, "with what effect?" While this may appear an overstatement at this point, it will become apparent as you proceed through the chapter. Despite the tremendous advances in communication and information technology, communication between people in organizations leaves much to be desired. Communication between people does not depend on technology but rather on forces in people and their surroundings. It is a "process" that occurs "within" people.

THE COMMUNICATION PROCESS

The general process of communication is presented in Figure 15–1. The process contains five elements—the communicator, the message, the me-

Figure 15–1
The Communication Process

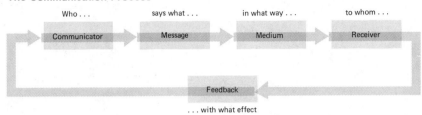

dium, the receiver, and feedback. It can be simply summarized as: Who . . . says what . . . in what way . . . to whom . . . with what effect?[1] To appreciate each element in the process we must examine how communication works.

How Communication Works

Communication experts tell us that effective communication is the result of a common understanding between the communicator and the receiver. In fact, the word communication is derived from the Latin *(communis)*, meaning common. The communicator seeks to establish a "commoness" with a receiver(s). Hence we can define communication as the *transmission of information and understanding through the use of common symbols*. The common symbols may be verbal or nonverbal. We shall see later that in the context of an organization structure information can flow up and down (vertical), across (horizontal), and down and across (diagonal).

The most widely used contemporary model of the process of communication has evolved mainly from the work of Shannon and Weaver, and Schramm.[2] These researchers were concerned with describing the general process of communication which could be useful in all situations. Despite its technical jargon, the model which evolved from their work is useful for understanding communication. The basic elements include a communicator, an encoder, a message, a medium, a decoder, a receiver, feedback, and noise. The model is presented in Figure 15–2. Each element in the model can be examined in the context of an organization.

The Elements of Communication

Communicator.   In an organizational framework, the communicator is an employee with ideas, intentions, information, and a purpose for communicating.

---

[1] These five questions were first suggested by H. D. Lasswell, *Power and Personality* (New York: W. W. Norton, 1948), pp. 37–51.

[2] Claude Shannon and Warren Weaver, *The Mathematical Theory of Communication* (Urbana: University of Illinois Press, 1948); and Wilbur Schramm, "How Communication Works," in Wilbur Schramm, ed., *The Process and Effects of Mass Communication* (Urbana: University of Illinois Press, 1953), pp. 3–26.

Figure 15–2
A Communication Model

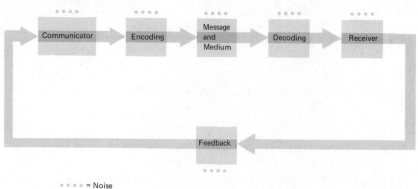

● ● ● ● = Noise

Encoding. Given the communicator, an encoding process must take place which translates the communicator's ideas into a systematic set of symbols—into a language expressing the communicator's purpose. The major form of encoding is language. For example, accounting information, sales reports, and computer data are translated into a message. The function of encoding then is to provide a form in which ideas and purposes can be expressed as a message.

Message. The result of the encoding process is the message. The purpose of the communicator is expressed in the form of the message—either verbal or nonverbal. Managers have numerous purposes for communicating such as to have others understand their ideas, to understand the ideas of others, to gain acceptance of themselves or their ideas, or to produce action. The message then is what the individual hopes to communicate to the intended receiver, and the exact form it takes depends to a great extent on the medium used to carry the message. Decisions relating to the two are inseparable.

Medium. The medium is the carrier of the message. Organizations provide information to members in a variety of ways, including face-to-face, telephone, group meetings, computers, memos, policy statements, reward systems, production schedules, and sales forecasts.

Not as obvious, however, are *unintended messages* that can be sent by silence or inaction on a particular issue as well as decisions of which goals and objectives *not* to be pursued and which methods *not* to utilize. Finally, such nonverbal message senders as facial expressions, tone of voice, and body movements also communicate. For example, a decision to utilize one type of performance evaluation rather than another, or a smile from a superior, are types of information. This is what was meant earlier by the statement that everything a manager does communicates.[3]

Decoding-Receiver. In order for the process of communication to be completed, the message must be decoded in terms of relevance to the re-

---

[3] See George W. Porters, "Non-verbal Communications," *Training and Development Journal* (June 1969), pp. 3–8.

ceiver. Decoding is a technical term for the receiver's thought processes. Decoding then involves interpretation. Receivers interpret (decode) the message in light of their own previous experiences and frames of reference. The closer the decoded message is to the intent desired by the communicator, the more effective is the communication. This underscores the importance of the communicator being "receiver-oriented."

Feedback. The provision for feedback in the communication process is desirable.[4] *One-way* communication processes are those which do not allow receiver-to-communicator feedback. This may increase the potential for distortion between the intended message and the received message.[5] A feedback loop provides a channel for receiver response which enables the communicator to determine whether the message has been received and has produced the intended response. *Two-way* communication processes provide for this important receiver-to-communicator feedback. For the manager, communication feedback may come in many ways. In face-to-face situations *direct* feedback through verbal exchanges is possible as well as such subtle means as facial expressions of discontent or misunderstanding. In addition, *indirect* means (such as declines in productivity, poor quality of production, increased absenteeism or turnover, and a lack of coordination and/or conflict between units) may indicate communication breakdowns.

Noise. In the framework of human communication, noise can be thought of as those factors that distort the intended message. They may occur in each of the elements of communication. For example, a manager may be under a severe time constraint and may be forced to act without communicating or may communicate hastily with incomplete information. A subordinate may attach a different meaning to a word or phrase than intended by the manager.

The elements discussed in this section are essential for communication to occur. They should not, however, be viewed as separate. They are, rather, descriptive of the acts which have to be performed for any type of communication to occur. The communication may be vertical (superior-subordinate, subordinate-superior) horizontal (peer-peer), or involve one individual and a group, but the elements discussed here must be present.

COMMUNICATING WITHIN ORGANIZATIONS

The design of an organization should provide for communication in four distinct directions: downward, upward, horizontal, and diagonal. Since they establish the framework within which communication in an organization takes

---

[4] For a theoretical discussion of feedback see D. M. Herold and M. M. Greller, "Feedback: The Definition of a Construct," *Academy of Management Journal* (March 1977), pp. 142–47.

[5] For the classic experimental study comparing one-way and two-way communications see Harold J. Leavitt and R. A. H. Mueller, "Some Effects of Feedback on Communications," *Human Relations* (1951), pp. 401–10. Also see H. J. Leavitt, *Managerial Psychology* (Chicago: University of Chicago Press, 1978).

place, let us briefly examine each one. This will enable us to better appreciate the barriers to effective organizational communication and means to overcome these barriers.[6]

Downward Communication. Downward communication flows from individuals in higher levels to those in lower levels of the hierarchy. The most common forms are job instructions, official memos, policy statements, procedures, manuals, and company publications. In many organizations downward communication is often both inadequate and inaccurate. This is seen in the often-heard statement among organization members that "We have absolutely no idea what's happening." Such complaints are indicative of inadequate downward communication and the need of individuals for information relevant to their jobs. The absence of job-related information can create unnecessary stress among organization members.[7]

Upward Communication. An effective organization needs upward communication as much as it needs downward communication. In such situations, the communicator is at a lower level in the organization than the receiver. We shall see later that effective upward communication is difficult to achieve, especially in larger organizations. However, successful upward communication is often necessary for sound decision making. Some of the most common upward communication flows are suggestion boxes, group meetings, and appeal or grievance procedures. In the absence of these, people somehow find ways to adapt to nonexistent or inadequate upward communication channels. This has been evidenced by the emergence of "underground" employee publications in many large organizations.[8]

Horizontal Communication. Often overlooked in the design of most organizations is the provision for horizontal flow of communication. When the chair of the accounting department communicates with the chair of the marketing department concerning course offerings in a College of Business Administration, the flow of communication is horizontal. Although vertical (upward and downward) communication flows are the primary considerations in organizational design, effective organizations also need horizontal communication. Horizontal communication is necessary for the coordination and integration of diverse organizational functions—for example, between production and sales in a business organization and different departments or colleges within a university.

Since mechanisms for assuring horizontal communication ordinarily do not exist in an organization's design, its facilitation is left to individual managers. Peer to peer communication is often necessary for coordination and can also provide social need satisfaction.

---

[6] For a recent general discussion see S. B. Bacharach and M. Aiken, "Communication in Administrative Bureaucracies," *Academy of Management Journal* (September 1977), pp. 365–77.

[7] J. M. Ivancevich and J. H. Donnelly, Jr., "A Study of Role Clarity and Need for Clarity in Three Occupational Groups," *Academy of Management Journal* (March 1974), pp. 28–36.

[8] See J. S. Lublin, "Underground Papers in Corporations Tell It Like It Isn't," *The Wall Street Journal,* S.W.ed. (November 3, 1971), p. 9.

Diagonal Communication.   While probably the least used channel of communication in organizations, diagonal communication is important in those situations where members cannot communicate effectively through other channels. For example, a comptroller of a large organization may wish to conduct a distribution cost analysis. One part may involve the sales force sending a special report directly to the comptroller rather than going through the traditional channels in the marketing department. Thus, the flow of communication would be diagonal as opposed to vertical (upward) and horizontal. In this case a diagonal channel would be the most efficient in terms of time and effort for the organization.

BARRIERS TO EFFECTIVE ORGANIZATIONAL COMMUNICATION

A good question at this point is "Why does communication break down?" The answer on the surface is relatively easy. The necessary elements for communication have been identified as the communicator, encoding, the message, the medium, decoding, the receiver, and feedback. If *any one* of these elements is defective *in any way,* clarity of meaning and understanding will not occur. Many barriers can impede the process of communication, resulting in "noise" and an eventual communication breakdown. The barriers identified are by no means the only ones that exist. They are, however, common barriers which are prevalent in both face-to-face communication and in nonverbal communication within organization structures. Let us examine some of these major barriers.

Frame of Reference

Different individuals can interpret the same communication differently depending on their previous experience. This results in variations in the encoding and decoding processes. Communication specialists agree that this is the most important factor that breaks down the "commonness" in communications. When the encoding and decoding processes are alike, communication is most effective. When they become different, communication tends to break down. Thus, while the communicator is actually speaking the "same language" as the receiver, the message conflicts with the way the receiver "catalogs" the world. This problem is depicted in Figure 15–3. The interior areas in this diagram represent the accumulated experiences of the participants in the communication process. If a large area is shared in common, effective communication is facilitated. If a large area is not shared in common—if there has been no common experience—then communication becomes impossible, or at best highly distorted. The important point is that communicators can encode and receivers can decode, only in terms of their experiences.

As a result, distortion often occurs because of differing frames of reference. Teenagers perceive things differently than their parents, and college deans

Figure 15–3
Overlapping Fields of Experience

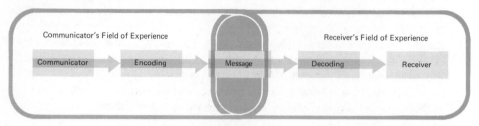

perceive problems differently than faculty members. People in various organizational *functions* interpret the same situation differently. A business problem will be viewed differently by the marketing manager than the plant manager. An efficiency problem in a hospital will be viewed by the nursing staff from their frame of reference and experiences which may result in different interpretations than those of the physician staff. Different *levels* in the organization will also have different frames of reference. First-line supervisors have frames of reference that differ in many respects from those of vice presidents. They are in different positions in the organizations structure and this influences their frames of reference. As a result, their needs, values, attitudes, and expectations will differ and often result in unintentional distortion of communication. This is not to say that either group is wrong or right. All it means is that, in any situation, individuals will choose a part of their own past experiences that relates to the current experience and that is helpful in forming conclusions and judgments. Unfortunately, these incongruencies in encoding and decoding result in barriers to effective communication. We shall see that many of the other barriers examined in this section are also the result of variations in encoding and decoding.

Selective Listening

This is a form of selective perception in which we tend to "block out" new information, especially if it conflicts with what we believe. Thus, when we receive a directive from management we are apt to notice only those things that reaffirm our beliefs. Those things that conflict with our preconceived notions we either do not note at all or we distort to confirm our preconceptions.

For example, a notice may be sent to all operating departments that costs must be reduced if the organization is to earn a profit. Such communication may not achieve its desired effect because it conflicts with the "reality" of the receivers. Thus, operating employees may ignore or be amused by such information in light of the large salaries, travel allowances, and expense accounts of some executives. Whether or not they are justified is irrelevant; what is important is that such preconceptions result in breakdowns in communication. In other words, if we only hear what we want to hear, we cannot be disappointed.

Value Judgments

In every communication situation, value judgments are made by the receiver. This basically involves assigning an overall worth to a message prior to receiving the entire communication. Value judgments may be based upon the receiver's evaluation of the communicator, previous experiences with the communicator, or the message's anticipated meaning. Thus, a hospital administrator may pay little attention to a memorandum from a nursing team leader because "she's always complaining about something." A college professor may consider a merit evaluation meeting with the department chair as "going through the motions" because the faculty member perceives the chair as having little or no power in the administration of the college. A cohesive work group may form negative value judgments concerning all actions by management.

Source Credibility

Source credibility is the trust, confidence, and faith the receiver has in the words and actions of the communicator. The level of credibility that the receiver assigns to the communicator in turn directly effects how the receiver views and reacts to words, ideas, and actions of the communicator.

Thus, how subordinates view a communication from their manager is affected by their evaluation of the manager. This of course is heavily influenced by previous experiences with the manager. Again we see that everything a manager does, communicates. A group of hospital medical staff who view the hospital administrator as less then honest, manipulative, and not to be trusted are apt to assign nonexistent motives to any communication from the administrator. Union leaders who view management as exploiters and managers who view union leaders as political animals are likely to engage in little real communication.

Semantic Problems

Communication has been defined as the transmission of *information* and *understanding* through the use of *common symbols*. Actually, we cannot transmit understanding. We can only transmit information in the form of words, which are the common symbols. Unfortunately, the same words may mean entirely different things to different people. The understanding is in the receiver, not in the words.

When a college dean announces that a "budget increase" is necessary for the growth of the college, the dean may have in mind the necessity for new classroom facilities, an expanded library, and new faculty. To some faculty members, however, growth may be perceived as excess funds that can be used for faculty research and salary increases.

Again, because different groups use words differently, communication can often be impeded. This is especially true with abstract or technical terms or phrases. A "cost-benefit study" would have meaning to those involved in the administration of the hospital but probably mean very little to the staff physicians. In fact, it may even carry a negative meaning. Concepts like "trusts," "profits," and "Treasury bills" may have concrete meaning to bank executives but little or no meaning to bank tellers. Thus, because words mean different things to different people, it is possible for a communicator to speak the same language as a receiver but still not transmit *understanding*.

Filtering

Filtering is a common occurrence in upward communication in organizations. It amounts to the "manipulation" of information so that it is perceived as positive by the receiver. Subordinates "cover up" unfavorable information in messages to their superiors. The reason for such "filtering" should be clear; this is the direction (upward) which carries control information to management. Management makes merit evaluations, grants salary increases, and promotes individuals based on what it receives by way of the upward channel. The temptation to "filter" is likely to be strong at every level in the organization.

In-Group Language

Each of us has undoubtedly had associations with experts and been subjected to highly technical jargon, only to learn that the words or phrases describe very simple procedures or very familiar objects. Many students are asked by researchers to "complete an instrument as part of an experimental treatment." The student soon learns that this involves nothing more than filling out a pencil-and-paper questionnaire.

Often, occupational, professional, and social groups develop their own words or phrases which have meaning only to members. Such special language can serve many useful purposes. It can provide members with feelings of belongingness, cohesiveness, and, in many cases, self-esteem. It can also facilitate effective communication *within* the group. The use of in-group language can, however, result in severe communication breakdowns when outsiders or other groups are involved. This is especially the case when groups use such language in an organization, not for the purpose of transmitting information and understanding, but rather to communicate a "mystique" about the group or its function.

Status Differences

Organizations often express hierarchical rank through a variety of symbols—titles, offices, carpets, secretaries, etc. Such status differences can result in the perception of a threat on the part of someone lower in the hierarchy which can prevent or distort communication. Rather than look incompetent, a nurse may prefer to remain quiet instead of expressing an opinion or asking a question of the nursing team leader.

Many times, superiors in their quest to utilize their time efficiently enhance this barrier. The governmental administrator or bank vice president may only be accessible by advanced appointment or by passing the careful quizzing of a secretary. This widens the communication gap between superiors and subordinates.

Time Pressures

The pressure of time is an important barrier to communication. An obvious problem is that managers do not have the time to communicate frequently with every subordinate. However, time pressures can often lead to far more serious problems than this. *Short circuiting* is a failure of the formally pre-scribed communication system which often is the result of time pressures. What it means simply is that someone has been left out of the formal channel of communication who normally would be included.

For example, suppose a salesperson needs a rush order for a very impor-tant customer and goes directly to the production manager with the request since the production manager owes the salesperson a favor. Other members of the sales force get word of this and become upset over this preferential treatment and report it to the sales manager. Obviously, the sales manager would know nothing of the "deal" since the sales manager has been short circuited. However, in some cases the necessity to go through formal channels is extremely costly or impossible from a practical standpoint. Consider the impact on a hospital patient if a nurse had to report a malfunction in some critical life support equipment in an intensive care unit to the nursing team leader who in turn reported it to the hospital engineer who instructed a staff engineer to make the repair.

Communication Overload

One of the vital tasks performed by a manager is decision making. One of the necessary conditions for effective decisions is *information*. Because of the advances in communication technology, the difficulty is not in generating information. In fact, the last decade has often been described as the "Informa-tion Era" or the "Age of Information." Managers often feel "buried" by the deluge of information and data they are exposed to. As a result, people cannot absorb or adequately respond to all of the messages directed to them. They "screen out" the majority of messages, which in effect means they are never decoded. Thus, the area of organizational communication is one in which "more" is not always "better."

The barriers to communication discussed here, while common, are by no means the only ones which exist. Figure 15–4 illustrates the impact of these barriers on the process of communication. Examining each barrier indicates that they are either *within individuals* (e.g., frame of reference, value

Figure 15–4
Barriers to Effective Communication

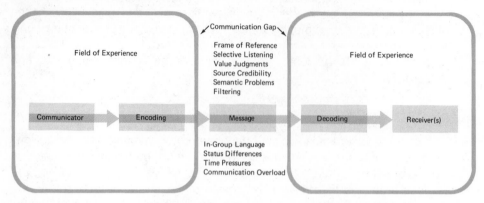

judgments), or *within organizations* (e.g., in-group language, filtering). This point is important because attempts to improve communication must by necessity focus on changing people and/or changing the organization structure.[9]

IMPROVING COMMUNICATION IN ORGANIZATIONS

Managers striving to become better communicators have two separate tasks they must accomplish.[10] First, they must improve their *messages*— the information they wish to transmit. Second, they must seek to improve their own *understanding* of what other people are trying to communicate to them. What this means is becoming better encoders and decoders. *They must strive not only to be understood but also to understand.* The techniques discussed here will contribute to accomplishing these two important tasks.

Following Up

This involves assuming you are misunderstood and, whenever possible, attempting to determine if the intended meaning was actually received. As we have seen, meaning is often in the mind of the receiver. An accounting unit leader in a government office passes on notices to the accounting staff members of openings in other agencies. While this may be understood among long-time employees as a friendly gesture on the part of the department head, a new employee might interpret it as an evaluation of poor performance and a suggestion to leave.

---

[9] See P. M. Muchinsky, "Organizational Communication: Relationships to Organizational Climate and Job Satisfaction," *Academy of Management Journal* (December 1977), pp. 592–607, for a recent study on the importance of communication.

[10] For a different discussion that is based on similar ideas, see Leonard R. Sayles and George Strauss, *Human Behavior in Organizations* (Englewood Cliffs, N.J.: Prentice-Hall, Inc., 1966), p. 246.

Regulating Information Flow

This involves the regulation of communication to ensure an optimum flow of information to managers, thereby eliminating the barrier of "communication overload."[11] Communication is regulated in terms of both quality and quantity. The idea is based on the *exception principle* of management which states that only significant deviations from policies and procedures should be brought to the attention of superiors. In terms of formal communication, then, superiors should be communicated with only on matters of exception and not for the sake of communication.

As we saw in the section on the structure of organizations, certain types of organization structures would be more amenable to this principle than others. Certainly, in Likert's System 4 organization with its emphasis on free flowing communication, this principle would not apply. However, those organizations more toward the bureaucratic end of the "bureaucratic-system 4 continuum" would find this principle useful.

Utilizing Feedback

Earlier in the chapter, feedback was identified as an important element in effective two-way communication. It provides a channel for receiver response which enables the communicator to determine whether the message has been received and produced the intended response.

In face-to-face communication, direct feedback is possible. However, in downward communication, inaccuracies often occur because of insufficient opportunity for feedback from receivers. Thus, a memorandum addressing an important policy statement may be distributed to all employees but this does not guarantee that communication has occurred. One might expect that feedback in the form of upward communication would be encouraged more in System 4 organizations but the mechanisms discussed earlier which can be utilized to encourage upward communication are found in many different organizational designs. A healthy organization needs effective upward communication if its downward communication is to have any chance of being effective. The point is that developing and supporting mechanisms for feedback involves far more than following up on communications.

Empathy

This involves being receiver-oriented rather than communicator-oriented. The form of the communication should depend largely on what is known about the receiver(s). Empathy requires communicators to figuratively place themselves in the receivers' shoes for the purpose of anticipating how the message is likely to be decoded.

---

[11] This is described as the principle of "sufficiency" by William G. Scott and Terence R. Mitchell, *Organizational Theory: A Structural and Behavioral Analysis* (Homewood, Ill.: Richard D. Irwin, Inc., 1972), p. 161.

It is vital that a manager understands and appreciates the process of decoding. Decoding involves perceptions, and the message will be "filtered" through the person. Empathy is the ability to put oneself in the other person's role and to assume the viewpoints and emotions of that individual. For vice presidents to communicate effectively with supervisors, for faculty to communicate effectively with students, and for government administrators to communicate effectively with minority groups, empathy is often an important ingredient. Many of the barriers to effective communication discussed can be reduced with empathy. Remember that the greater the gap between the experiences and background of the communicator and receiver, the greater the effort which must be made to find a common ground of understanding— where there are overlapping fields of experience.[12]

Repetition

Repetition is an accepted principle of learning. Introducing repetition or redundancy into communication (especially that of a technical nature) insures that if one part of the message is not understood, there are other parts which carry the same message. New employees are often provided the same basic information in several different forms when first joining an organization. Likewise, students receive much redundant information when first entering a university. This is to insure that registration procedures, course requirements, and such new terms as matriculation and quality points are communicated.

Encouraging Mutual Trust

We know that time pressures often negate the possibility that managers can follow up communication and encourage feedback or upward communication every time they communicate. Under such circumstances, an atmosphere of mutual confidence and trust between managers and their subordinates can facilitate communication.[13] Subordinates judge for themselves the quality of the relationship they perceive with their superior. Managers who develop a climate of trust will find following up on each communication less critical and without a loss in understanding among subordinates. This is because they have fostered high "source credibility" among subordinates.

---

[12] A technique known as *sensitivity training* has been utilized for many purposes in organizations, one of which is to improve the ability of managers to empathize. It will be discussed in Chapter 17.

[13] See Karlene H. Roberts and Charles A. O'Reilly III, "Failures in Upward Communication in Organizations: Three Possible Culprits," *Academy of Management Journal* (June 1974), pp. 205–15; and Leland P. Bradford, Jack R. Gibb, and Kenneth D. Benne, eds., *T-Group Theory and Laboratory Method: Innovation in Re-Education* (New York: John Wiley & Sons, Inc., 1965), pp. 285–86.

Effective Timing

Individuals are bombarded with literally thousands of messages daily. Many are never decoded and received because of the impossibility of taking them all in. It is important for managers to note that while they are attempting to communicate with a receiver, other messages are being received simultaneously. The message sent may not be "heard." Messages are more likely to be understood when they are not competing with other messages.

Many organizations use "retreats" when important policies or changes are taking place. A group of executives may be sent to a resort to undertake an important corporate policy issue, or a group of college faculty may "retreat" to an off-campus site to design a new curriculum. On an everyday basis, effective communication can be facilitated with the proper timing of major announcements. Many of the barriers discussed earlier are often the result of poor timing which results in distortions and value judgments.

Simplifying Language

Complex language has been identified as a major barrier to effective communication. Students often suffer when their teachers use technical jargon that transforms simple concepts into complex puzzles.

Universities are not the only place, however, where this occurs. Government agencies are also known for their often incomprehensible communications. We have already noted instances where professional people attempt to communicate with individuals outside of their group using the in-group language. Managers must remember that effective communication involves transmitting *understanding* as well as information. If the receiver does not understand, then there has been no communication. In fact, many of the techniques discussed in this section have as their sole purpose the promotion of understanding. Managers must encode messages in words, appeals, and symbols that are meaningful to the receiver.

Effective Listening

It has been said that to improve communication, managers must seek to be understood, but also to *understand*. This involves listening. One method of encouraging someone to express true feelings, desires, and emotions is to listen. Just listening is not enough; one must listen with understanding. Can managers develop listening skills? There are numerous pointers for effective listening that have been found to be effective in organizational settings. For example, one writer cites "Ten Commandments for Good Listening": stop talking, put the speaker at ease, show the speaker you want to listen, remove distractions, empathize with the speaker, be patient, hold your temper, go easy on argument and criticism, ask questions, and stop talking.[14] Note

---

[14] Keith Davis, *Human Behavior at Work* (New York: McGraw-Hill Book Co., 1972), p. 394.

that to stop talking is both the first and the last commandment. Another writer lists five "Guides for Listening": avoid making value judgments, listen to the full story, recognize feelings and emotions, restate the other's position, and question with care.[15]

Such lists of guidelines can be potentially useful for managers. However, more important than these lists is the *decision to listen.* The above guidelines are useless unless the manager makes the conscious decision to listen. The realization that effective communication involves being understood as well as understanding is probably far more important than lists of guidelines. Then and only then can such guidelines become useful.

Using the Grapevine

The grapevine is an important informal communication channel that exists in all organizations. It basically serves as a bypassing mechanism, and in many cases is faster than the formal system it bypasses. It has been aptly described in the following manner: "With the rapidity of a burning train, it filters out of the woodwork, past the manager's office, through the locker room and along the corridors."[16] Because it is flexible and usually involves face-to-face communication, the grapevine transmits information rapidly. The resignation of an executive may be common knowledge long before it is officially announced.

For management, the grapevine may frequently be an effective means of communication. It is likely to have a stronger impact on receivers because it is face-to-face and allows for feedback. Because it satisfies many psychological needs, the grapevine will always exist. No manager can do away with it. Research indicates that over 75 percent of the information in the grapevine is accurate.[17] Of course, the 25 percent which is distorted can be devastating. The point, however, is that if the grapevine is inevitable, managers should seek to utilize it or at least attempt to increase its accuracy. One way to minimize the undesirable aspects of the grapevine is to improve other forms of communication. If information exists on issues relevant to subordinates, then damaging rumors are less likely to develop.

In conclusion, it would be hard to find an aspect of a manager's job that does not involve communication. If everyone in the organization had common points of view, communicating would be easy. Unfortunately this is not the case. Each member comes to the organization with a distinct personality, background, experience, and frame of reference. The structure of the organization itself influences status relationships and the distance (levels) between individuals, which in turn influence the ability of individuals to communicate.

---

[15] Henry L. Sisk, *Organization and Management* (Cincinnati: South-Western Publishing Co., 1977), pp. 350–74.

[16] Davis, *Human Behavior at Work,* p. 267.

[17] Ibid.

In this chapter, we have tried to convey the basic elements in the process of communication and what it takes to communicate effectively. These elements are necessary whether the communication is face-to-face or written and communicated vertically, horizontally, or diagonally within an organization structure. Several common communication barriers were discussed as well as several means to improve communication. Figure 15–5 illustrates the

Figure 15–5
Improving Communication in Organizations (narrowing the communication gap)

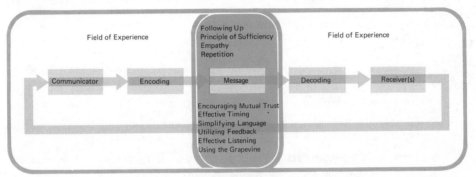

means that can be used to facilitate more effective communication. We realize that often there is not time to utilize many of the techniques for improving communication, and that skills such as empathy and effective listening are not easy to develop. The figure does, however, illustrate the challenge of communicating effectively and suggests what is required. It shows that communicating is a matter of transmitting and receiving. Managers must be effective at both. They must understand as well as be understood.

MAJOR ISSUES FOR THE MANAGER TO CONSIDER

A. Communication is one of the vital processes which breathe life into an organization structure. Communication is unavoidable in an organization's work; only *effective* communication is avoidable.

B. The quality of managerial decisions depends in large part on the quality of information available. Communication is the transmission of information and understanding through the use of common symbols.

C. Everything a manager does communicates. The only question is, with what effect? Every manager is a communicator.

D. The process of communication consists of several basic elements which must always be present if effective communication is to result.

E. Organization design and the communication process are inseparable. The design of an organization must provide for communication in three distinct directions: vertical, horizontal, and diagonal.

F. When the encoding and decoding processes are homogeneous, communication is most effective. When they become heterogeneous, communication tends to break down. Numerous barriers exist which contribute to communication breakdowns. Managers must be aware of those barriers which are relevant to their situations.

G. Numerous techniques exist which aid in improving communication and can be utilized by managers. However, a prerequisite to their use is the conscious realization by the individual manager that communication involves understanding as well as being understood. An effective communicator must also be an effective receiver.

DISCUSSION AND REVIEW QUESTIONS

1. What do we really mean when we say that everything a manager does communicates?

2. Discuss why organizational design and communication flow are so closely related.

3. Discuss how communication flow and the contingency view of organization design are related.

4. Think of a classroom situation in terms of the basic elements of communication: communicator, encoding, message, medium, decoding, receiver, and feedback. Identify each element and discuss the activities involved. For example, who is the communicator, what is the message, who is the receiver, etc. Is effective communication occurring? Why? Identify where, if at all, breakdowns are occurring and why.

5. Think of a situation from your own life in which communication between yourself and another individual or group was not possible. Identify the barriers. What might you have done to overcome these barriers?

6. Discuss what the following statement means to you. "To communicate effectively, one must be understood but also must understand."

7. Think of a situation in which you have been the receiver in a one-way communication process. Describe it. Can you think of some reasons why certain individuals might not like it? Think of reasons why some people might prefer it.

8. Choose a technique discussed in the chapter that you believe can help you become a more effective communicator. Why have you chosen it? How do you plan to implement it?

ADDITIONAL REFERENCES

Beckett, J. A. *Management Dynamics: The New Synthesis.* New York: McGraw-Hill Book Company, 1971.

Dewherst, H. D. "Influence of Perceived Information-Sharing Utilization." *Academy of Management Journal* (1971), pp. 305–15

Ellis, D. S. *Management and Administrative Communication.* New York: Macmillan Publishing Co., 1978.

Ericson, R. F. "Organizational Cybernetics and Human Values." *Academy of Management Journal* (1970), pp. 49–66.

Gibb, J. R. "Communication and Productivity." *Personnel Administration* (1964), pp. 485–87.

Greenbaum, H. H. "The Audit of Organizational Communication." *Academy of Management Journal* (1974), pp. 139–54.

———, "Management's Role in Organizational Communication Analysis." *Journal of Business Communication* (1972), pp. 39–52.

Lewis, G. H. "Organization in Communication Networks." *Comparative Group Studies* (1971), pp. 149–60.

Mears, P. "Structuring Communication in a Working Group." *Journal of Communication* (1974), pp. 71–79.

Rockey, E. H. *Communicating in Organizations.* Cambridge, Mass: Winthrop Publishers, Inc., 1977.

Rodgers, C. *On Becoming a Person.* Boston: Houghton Mifflin Company, 1961.

Schemerhorn, J. R. "Information Sharing as an Interorganizational Activity." *Academy of Management Journal* (1977), pp. 148–53.

Wiener, N. *Cybernetics: or, Control and Communication in the Animal and the Machine.* New york: John Wiley and Sons, 1948.

———, *The Human Use of Human Beings.* Garden City, N.Y.: Doubleday and Co., Anchor Books, 1954.

CASE FOR ANALYSIS

LEIGH RANDELL

Leigh Randell is Supervisor of In-Flight Services at the Atlanta base of Omega Airlines. Omega Airlines is a very successful regional air carrier with routes throughout the south and southwest. In addition to Atlanta, it has bases in six other major cities.

Ms. Randell's job involves supervision of all in-flight services and personnel at the Atlanta base. She has been with the airline for seven years and in her present job for two years. For five years she was a flight attendant and was asked by management to assume her present management position. While actually preferring flying to a permanent ground position, she decided to try the management position. In her job, she reports directly to Kent Davis, Vice President of In-Flight Services.

During the last year, Leigh has observed what she believes is a great deal of duplication of effort between flight attendants and passenger-service personnel (in-terminal personnel) with respect to the paperwork procedures for boarding passengers. This she believes has often resulted in unnecessary delays in departures of many flights. This especially appears to be the case with through flights, those which do not originate or terminate in Atlanta. Since the majority of Omega's flights are of this type in Atlanta, she believes that it is probably not a major problem at Omega's other bases or at smaller airports. Thus, she has decided to try to develop a more efficient procedure for coordinating the efforts of flight attendants and passenger-service personnel which would simplify the boarding procedures, thereby reducing ground time and increasing passenger satisfaction through closer adherence to departure times.

In this respect she has, on three occasions during the last two months, written memos to Tom Ballard, Passenger Services Representative for Omega at the Atlanta base. Tom's job involves supervision of all passenger service personnel. He has been with Omega for five years, having joined their management training program immediately after graduating from college. He reports directly to Alan Brock, Vice President of Passenger Services at the Atlanta base. Exhibit 1 presents the organization structure for the Atlanta base. Each time, Leigh has requested information regarding specific procedures, time, and costs for the boarding of passengers on through flights. She has received no reply from Tom Ballard.

Last week Leigh wrote a memo to Kent Davis in which she stated:

> For several months I have been trying to develop a new method for facilitating the boarding of passengers on through flights by more closely coordinating the efforts of In-Flight Services and Passenger Services. The results would be a reduction in clerical work, costs, ground time, and closer adherence to departure times for through flights. Unfortunately, I have received no cooperation at all in my efforts from the Passenger Services Representative. I have made three written requests for information each of which has been ignored. Needless

Exhibit 1

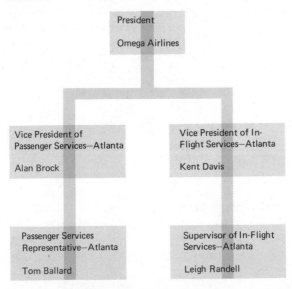

to say this has been very frustrating to me. While I realize that my beliefs may not always be correct, in this instance I am only trying to initiate something that will be beneficial to everyone involved: Passenger Services, In-Flight Services, and most important, Omega Airlines. I would like to meet with you to discuss this matter and the possibility of my transferring back to flight duty.

A telephone call by Kent Davis to Alan Brock and then to Tom Ballard summoned them all to a hastily called conference. Tom Ballard was mildly asked why he had not furnished the information to Leigh that she had requested.

"Too busy," he said. "Her questions were out of sight. There was no time for me to answer this sort of request. I've got a job to do. Besides, I don't report to her."

"But Tom, you don't understand," Kent Davis said. "All Ms. Randell is trying to do is improve the present system of boarding passengers on through flights. She has taken the initiative to work on something that might benefit everyone."

Tom Ballard thought for a moment. "No," he replied, "it didn't look like that to me. You know I've also had ideas on how to improve the system for quite some time. Anyway, she's going about it all wrong."

Questions for Consideration

1. What barriers to effective communication do you detect in this case?
2. Is anyone "wrong" in this situation? By what other means could Leigh have requested the information from Tom Ballard? What do you think of Tom Ballard's reaction? Why?

3. While communicating information vertically up or down the organization does not present a major problem, why is it that horizontal and diagonal communication are more difficult to attain? What would you recommend to the management of Omega Airlines to remedy this situation? Why do you believe your recommendations would improve communication in the organization?

EXPERIENTIAL EXERCISE

FRUSTRATION, CLARITY, ACCURACY

Objectives

1. To display the features of the communication process.
2. To identify the differences between one-way and two-way communications.
3. To examine the reactions of individuals to one- and two-way communications.

Related Topics

The communication process is pervasive in any organization. Therefore, communication is related to any topic discussed in organizational behavior, organizational theory, or management.

Starting the Exercise

The instructor will give the same message to two separate groups. These groups will receive the private message only one time. They are not permitted to ask the instructor any questions about the message.

The Facts

The instructor will serve as the initiator of a message to two separate groups of 3 or 4 students. The groups will attempt to develop a clear understanding of what the instructor said. They will then return to the main classroom where other students will serve as communication chains for the message. Both a one-way and two-way chain will be used. To complete both the one- and two-way communication versions of this exercise, a minimum of 22 students will be needed. If a class does not have 22 students, the instructor will need to make some modifications.

Exercise Procedure

Phase I: Group Communication: 10 minutes

1. Group 1 and Group 2, consisting of three or four students will be selected. The groups should be isolated from each other to receive the message. The instructor will read *one time* the same message to the two groups in their separate rooms or isolated areas. Each group will discuss the message for no more than *5* minutes.

Phase II: One-Way Communication: 10 minutes

1. Four students who are not in Groups 1 or 2 will serve as the *chain* for one of the groups and four other students will serve as the chain for the other group. A representative of Group 1 will whisper the message to the first person in the four-person chain, who, in turn, will pass on the private message to the second member and so on. Talking between members in the chain is not permitted. Only *one* person, the transmitter, is permitted to speak. The last person in the chain will write the message down and hand it to the instructor. The same one-way communication process will be followed in Group 2.

Phase III: Two-Way Communication: 20 minutes

1. Four new students who have not participated in either Phases 1 or 2 will serve as the Group 1 chain. A representative of Group 1 will discuss the message with the first person in the chain. The representative and the first person can discuss the message privately from other members in the chain. When the discussants are ready and within the allocated time limit, the first person in the chain will then discuss privately the message with the second person in the chain. These private two-way discussions will continue until time has expired or the last person in the chain hears the message and writes it for the instructor. The same two-way communication process will be followed in Group 2.

Phase IV: Analysis of the Exercise: 20 minutes

1. Each participant should evaluate the exercise. Some of the issues to consider are

    a. One-way versus two-way communication accuracy.

    b. Attitudes of the different participants—Were any participants frustrated? About what?

    c. What were some of the barriers to effective communication?

Chapter 16

The Process of Decision Making

AN ORGANIZATIONAL ISSUE FOR DEBATE

The Decision Participation Controversy*

ARGUMENT FOR

Many researchers and managers believe that most organization members desire opportunities to participate in the process of decision making. They believe that increased decision participation increases commitment to the organization, job satisfaction, personal growth and development, and acceptance of change. Thus, rather than authority, the manager's mode of influence is based more on reciprocity and collaboration.

Besides leading to greater satisfaction, and as a result, greater effort, performance, and effectiveness, the supporters of this viewpoint have an additional rationale for decision participation. They point out that many problems faced by organizations are becoming increasingly complex, requiring knowledge in sophisticated areas, and are of the type that the organization has not faced in the past. These problems may be technological, human or societal. As a result knowledge and expertise in many different areas are needed to solve these problems. Since knowledge and expertise are widely distributed throughout the organization, wider participation will likely increase the quality of managerial decisions.

ARGUMENT AGAINST

Many practicing managers and researchers believe that in organizational settings people prefer a great amount of clarity in what is expected of them. This need for security in knowing what behavior is expected results in a great deal more respect for the manager who acts decisively. These individuals believe that trying to achieve consensus in a group is upsetting to the group and a waste of organizational resources and time. Since managers are a dominant mode of influence in the organization, they must recognize this and act upon it. The world of a decision maker may be a lonely one but managers must accept the responsibility that the "buck stops" with them. Nothing is more dysfunctional than the "participation ritual" which many managers engage in. Here managers go through the process of participation for the purpose of selling decisions which have already been made, by making them look like group decisions. If managers fail to take charge of group activities, they abdicate their role as manager and performance will be negatively effected.

---

* Much research and opinion exists on this issue. For comprehensive reviews see V. H. Vroom and P. W. Yetton, *Leadership and Decision-making* (Pittsburgh: University of Pittsburgh Press, 1973); and P. Blumberg, *Industrial Democracy: The Sociology of Participation* (New York: Schocken Books, 1974). For a recent study see J. W. Driscoll, "Trust and Participation in Organizational Decision Making as Predictors of Satisfaction," *Academy of Management Journal* (March 1978), pp. 44–56.

INTRODUCTION

The focus of this chapter is decision making. It is the last of those which establishes a framework for understanding the behavior of people in organizations. However, this in no way reflects a lack of importance. If anything, being last points up just how important decision making is. In fact, the quality of the decisions managers reach is the yardstick of their effectiveness. Thus, the flow of the preceding material leads logically to a discussion of decision making: that is, people behave *as individuals* and as members *of groups, within* an *organization structure* and *communicate* for many reasons, the important one of which is to *make decisions.* This chapter, therefore, will describe and analyze decision making in terms which reflect the way in which people decide as a consequence of the information they receive both through the organization *structure* and also through the *behavior* of important other persons and groups.

In the last three decades, the systematic analysis of decision making has become known as "decision theory." Decision theory is firmly rooted in the fields of statistics and the behavioral sciences and has as its goal to make decision making less of an art and more of a science. Since World War II operations researchers, statisticians, computer scientists, and behavioral scientists have sought to identify those elements in decision making which are common to all decisions and thus provide a framework for decision makers to enable them to more effectively analyze a complex situation containing numerous alternatives and possible consequences. We shall see in this chapter that much progress has been made in analyzing and describing certain important aspects of decision making. In other equally important aspects, however, much progress remains to be made.

TYPES OF DECISIONS

While managers in various kinds of organizations may be separated by background, lifestyle, and distance, they all sooner or later must make decisions. That is, they face a situation involving several alternatives and their decision involves a comparison between the alternatives and an evaluation of the outcome. In this section our purpose is to move away from a general definition of a decision and present a classification system into which various kinds of decisions can be placed.

Specialists in the field of decision theory have developed several ways of classifying different types of decisions. For the most part these classification systems are similar, differing mainly in terminology. We shall use the widely adopted distinction suggested by Herbert Simon.[1] Simon distinguishes between two types of decisions:

1. Programmed Decisions. If a particular situation occurs often, a routine procedure will usually be worked out for solving it. Thus, decisions are pro-

---

[1] Herbert Simon, *The New Science of Management Decision* (New York: Harper & Row, 1960), pp. 5–6.

grammed to the extent that they are repetitive and routine and a definite procedure has been developed for handling them.

2. Nonprogrammed Decisions. Decisions are nonprogrammed when they are novel and unstructured. As such there is no established procedure for handling the problem, either because it has not arisen in exactly the same manner before or because it is complex or extremely important. Such decisions deserve special treatment.

While the two classifications are broad, they point out the importance of differentiating between programmed and nonprogrammed decisions. The managements of most organizations face great numbers of programmed

Table 16–1
Types of Decisions

	Programmed Decisions	*Nonprogrammed Decisions*
Type of problem	Frequent, repetitive, routine, much certainty regarding cause and effect relationships	Novel, unstructured, much uncertainty regarding cause and effect relationships
Procedure	Dependence upon policies, rules, and definite procedures	Necessity for creativity, intuition, tolerance for ambiguity, creative problem solving
Examples	*Business firm:* Periodic reorders of inventory	*Business firm:* Diversification into new products and markets
	University: Necessary grade-point average for good academic standing	*University:* Construction of new classroom facilities
	Health care: Procedure for admitting patients	*Health care:* Purchase of new experimental equipment
	Government: Merit system for promotion of state employees	*Government:* Reorganization of state government agencies

decisions in their daily operations. Such decisions should be treated without expending unnecessary organizational resources on them. On the other hand, the nonprogrammed decision must be properly identified as such since it is this type of decision making that forms the basis for allocating billions of dollars worth of resources in our economy every year. Unfortunately, it is this type of human decision process that we know the least about.[2] Table 16–1 presents a breakdown of the different types of decisions with examples of each type in different kinds of organizations. It indicates that programmed and nonprogrammed decisions require different kinds of procedures and apply to distinctly different types of problems.

---

[2] See Peer Soelberg, "Unprogrammed Decision Making," *Proceedings, 26th Annual Meeting, The Academy of Management 1966,* pp. 3–16.

Traditionally, programmed decisions have been handled through rules, standard operating procedures, and the structure of the organization which develops specific procedures for handling them. More recently, operations researchers through the development of mathematical models have facilitated the handling of these types of decisions.

On the other hand, nonprogrammed decisions have traditionally been handled by general problem-solving processes, judgment, intuition, and creativity. Unfortunately, modern management techniques have not made nearly the advances in improving nonprogrammed decision making as they have with programmed decision making.[3]

Ideally, the main concern of top management should be nonprogrammed decisions, while first-level management should be concerned with programmed decisions. Middle managers in most organizations concentrate mostly on programmed decisions, although in some cases they will participate in nonprogrammed decisions. In other words, the nature, frequency, and degree of certainty surrounding a problem should dictate at what level of management the decision should be made.

Obviously, problems arise in those organizations where top management expends much time and effort on programmed decisions. One unfortunate result of this practice is a neglect of long-range planning. In such cases, long-range thinking is subordinated to other activities whether the organization is successful or is having problems. If the organization is successful, this justifies continuing the policies and practices that achieved it. If the organization experiences difficulty, these current problems enjoy first priority and occupy the time of top management.[4]

Finally, the neglect of long-range planning usually results in an overemphasis on short-run control. This results in a lack of delegation of authority to lower levels of management which often has adverse effects on motivation and satisfaction.

THE DECISION-MAKING PROCESS

Decisions should be thought of as *means* rather than ends. They are the *organizational mechanisms* through which an attempt is made to achieve a desired state. They are, in effect, an *organizational response* to a problem. Every decision is the outcome of a dynamic process which is influenced by a multitude of forces. This process is presented diagramatically in Figure 16–1. The reader should not, however, interpret this to mean that decision making is a fixed procedure. Instead, it is presented here as a sequential process rather than a series of steps. This enables us to examine each element in the normal progression that leads to a decision.

---

[3] See Herbert A. Simon, *The Shape of Automation* (New York: Harper & Row, Inc., 1965).

[4] See A. D. H. Kaplan, *Big Enterprise in a Competitive System* (Washington, D.C.: The Brookings Institution, 1954), for the classic study on the importance of long-range strategic planning. For example, it notes that of the 100 largest business organizations in 1909, only 36 remained in 1948.

Figure 16–1
The Decision-Making Process

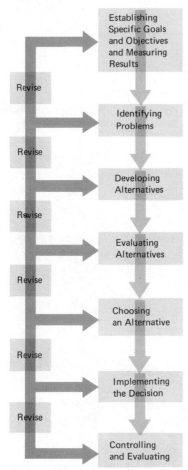

Examination of Figure 16–1 reveals that it is more applicable to nonprogrammed decisions than to programmed decisons. Problems that occur infrequently with a great deal of uncertainty surrounding the outcome require that the manager utilize the entire process. For those problems which occur frequently it is not necessary to consider the entire process. If a policy is established to handle such problems it will not be necessary to develop and evaluate alternatives each time the problem arises.

Establishing Specific Goals and Objectives and Measuring Results

Organizations need goals and objectives in each area where performance influences the effectiveness of the organization. If goals and objectives are adequately established they will dictate what results must be achieved and what measures will indicate whether or not they have been achieved.

Identifying Problems

A necessary condition for a decision is a problem. That is, if problems did not exist, then there would be no need for decisions.[5] This underscores the importance of establishing goals and measurable objectives. How critical a problem is for the organization is measured by the difference between levels of performance specified in the organization's goals and objectives and the levels of performance attained. Of course, if performance does not meet a predetermined objective, the problem may be with the objective. In order for objectives to be useful, they must permit the establishment of meaningful standards for effective control. For example, assume that, based on valid indicators, a university projects its enrollment in five years to be 15,000 students. If at the end of five years its enrollment is 11,500 students the school has a problem if the original objective was realistic. Assuming the objective was realistic, then the next phase is the development of alternatives to solve the problem. Otherwise the original objective must be revised. This is indicated by the darker lines in Figure 16–1.

Developing Alternatives

Before making a decision, feasible alternatives should be developed (actually these are potential solutions to the problem) and the potential consequences of each considered. This is really a search process where the relevant internal and external environments of the organization are investigated to provide information that can be developed into possible alternatives. Obviously, this search is conducted within certain time and cost constraints since only so much effort can be devoted to developing alternatives. Thus in the example above the university president would examine such factors as educational programs offered, faculty performance, the economic environment in the state, and competition from other learning institutions. Based upon this, various alternatives would be developed to solve the problem.

Evaluating Alternatives

Once alternatives are developed they must be evaluated and compared. In every decision situation the objective in making a decision is to select the alternative that will produce the most favorable outcomes and the least unfavorable outcomes. This once again points up the necessity of objectives and goals, since in selecting from among alternatives the decision maker

---

[5] Two excellent references on this and related problems are W. E. Pounds, "The Process of Problem Finding," *Industrial Management Review* (Fall 1969), pp. 1–19; and C. E. Watson, "The Problems of Problem Solving," *Business Horizons* (August 1976), pp. 88–94.

should be guided by the previously established goals and objectives. The alternative-outcome relationship is based on three possible conditions:

1. *Certainty*—the decision maker has complete knowledge of the probability of the outcomes of each alternative.
2. *Uncertainty*—the decision maker has absolutely no knowledge of the probability of the outcomes of each alternative.
3. *Risk*—the decision maker has some probabilistic estimate of the outcomes of each alternative.

Decision making under conditions of risk is probably the most common situation. It is in evaluating alternatives under these conditions that statisticians and operations researchers have made important contributions to decision theory.[6] Their methods have proved especially useful in the analysis and ranking of alternatives.

Choosing an Alternative

The purpose in selecting an alternative is to solve a problem in order to achieve predetermined goals and objectives. This point is an important one. It means that a decision is not an end in itself but only a means to an end. While the decision maker chooses the alternative that hopefully will result in the achievement of the objective, the actual selection should not be viewed as an isolated act. If this occurs, it is likely that the factors that led to and lead from the decision will be excluded. Specifically, those following the decision include implementation, control, and evaluation. The critical point is that decision making is *more* than an act of choosing, it is a dynamic process.[7]

Unfortunately for most managers, situations rarely exist in which one alternative singularly achieves the objective without having some impact either positively or negatively on some other objective. Often situations exist where two objectives cannot be optimized simultaneously. If one is *optimized,* the other is *suboptimized.* For example, in a business organization, if production is optimized, employee morale may be suboptimized or vice versa. Another example would be where a hospital superintendent optimizes a short-run objective such as maintenance costs at the expense of a long-run objective such as high-quality patient care. Thus, the multiplicity of organizational objectives complicates the real world of the decision maker.[8]

A situation could also exist where attainment of an organizational objective would be at the expense of a societal objective. The reality of this situation

---

[6] For a study see F. Luthans and R. Koester, "The Impact of Computer-Generated Information on the Choice Activity of Decision Makers," *Academy of Management Journal* (June 1976), pp. 328–32.

[7] This important point is discussed in detail in E. F. Harrison, *The Managerial Decision-Making Process* (Boston: Houghton Mifflin Co., 1975). This is an excellent comprehensive work on the subject of managerial decision making.

[8] See R. L. Daft, "System Influence on Organizational Decision Making: The Case of Resource Allocation," *Academy of Management Journal* (March 1978), pp. 6–22.

is clearly seen in the rise of ecology groups, environmentalists, and the consumerism movement. Apparently these groups question the priorities (organizational as against societal) of certain organizational decision makers. In any case, whether an organizational objective conflicts with another organizational objective or a societal objective, the values of the decision maker will influence strongly the alternative chosen. Individual values were discussed earlier and their influence on the decision-making process should be clear.

Thus, in most managerial decision making, *optimal* solutions are often impossible. This is because the decision maker cannot possibly know all available alternatives, the consequences of each, and their probability of occurrence. Thus, rather than being an *optimizer,* the decision maker is a *satisficer,* selecting the alternative that meets an acceptable standard of acceptance.

Implementing the Decision

Any decision is little more than an abstraction if it is not implemented. In other words, the choice must be effectively implemented in order to achieve the objective for which it was made. It is entirely possible that a "good" decision may be hurt by poor implementation. Thus, in this sense, implementation may be more important than the actual activity of choosing the alternative.

Since in most situations implementing decisions involves people, the actual test of the soundness of a decision is their behavior relative to the decision. While a decision may be technically sound, it can easily be undermined by dissatisfied subordinates. Subordinates cannot be manipulated in the same manner as other resources. Thus, a manager's job is not limited to skill in choosing good solutions, but also includes the knowledge and skill necessary to transform the solution into behavior in the organization.[9] This is done by effectively communicating through individuals and groups.

Control and Evaluation

Effective managment involves periodic measurements of actual results. Actual results are compared to planned results (the objective) and if deviations exist, changes must be made. Here again, we see the importance of measurable objectives. If they do not exist then there is no way to judge performance. If actual results do not match planned results then changes must be made in the solution chosen, its implementation, or in the original objective if it is deemed unattainable. Let us return again to the college president referred to earlier whose school is facing declining enrollments. Assume the president decides to hire professional recruiters to recruit new freshmen from all states in the union. The president's objective is a 10 percent increase in enrollment over a two-year period. If at the end of the period enrollment has increased only 3 percent, either the original objective was overstated, the use of profes-

---

[9] Alvar O. Elbing, *Behavioral Decisions in Organizations* (Glenview, Ill.: Scott, Foresman, 1970), p. 322.

sional recruiters (the chosen alternative) to achieve the objective was not wise, or the wrong recruiters were chosen (implementation of the chosen alternative). If the original objective must be revised, then the entire decision-making process will be reactivated. The important point is that once a decision is implemented, a manager cannot assume that the outcome will meet the original objective. Some system of control and evaluation is necessary to make sure the *actual results* are consistent with the *planned-for results* when the decision was made.

From the discussion of the decision-making process, the reader should see why there are some people who argue that *what managers do is make decisions*. There is some truth in this argument because the steps in the decision-making process are much like the *functions and activities of managers* presented in Chapter 3.

BEHAVIORAL INFLUENCES ON INDIVIDUAL DECISION MAKING

Several behavioral factors influence the decision-making process. Some influence only certain aspects of the process while others influence the entire process. The important point, however, is that each may have an impact and, therefore, must be understood in order to fully appreciate decision making as a process in organizations. Four individual behavioral factors—values, personality, propensity for risk, and potential for dissonance—will be discussed in this section. Each has been shown to have a significant impact on the decision-making process.

Values

The reader has already been introduced to the role of values in Chapter 3. In the context of decision making they can be thought of as guidelines a person uses when confronted with a choice situation. They are acquired early in life and are a basic (often taken for granted) part of an individual's thoughts. The influence of values on the decision-making process is profound:

In *establishing objectives,* value judgments are necessary regarding the selection of opportunities and the assignment of priorities.

In *developing alternatives,* it is necessary to make value judgments about the various possibilities.

When *choosing an alternative,* the values of the decision maker influence which alternative is chosen.

When *implementing* the decision, value judgments are necessary in choosing the means for implementation.

In the *evaluation and control* phase, value judgments cannot be avoided when taking corrective action.[10]

---

[10] Harrison, *The Management Decision-Making Process,* p. 42.

It is clear that values pervade the decision-making process. They are reflected in the decision maker's behavior prior to making the decision, making the actual choice, and putting it into effect.

Personality

Decision makers are influenced by many psychological forces both conscious and subconscious. One of the most important is their personality, which is strongly reflected in the choices they make. One study has attempted to determine the effect of selected personality variables on the process of decision making.[11] The study did not focus solely on a set of personality variables but included three sets of variables.

1. *Personality variables.* These include the attitudes, beliefs, and needs of the individual.
2. *Situational variables.* These pertain to the external, observable situations in which individuals find themselves.
3. *Interactional variables.* These pertain to the momentary state of the individual as a result of the interaction of a specific situation with characteristics of the individual's personality.

The study's conclusions concerning the influence of personality on the decision-making process were as follows:

It is unlikely that one person can be equally proficient in all aspects of the decision-making process. Results suggested that some people will do well in one part of the process, while others will do better in another part.

Different characteristics such as intelligence are associated with different phases of the decision-making process.

The relation of personality to the decision-making process may vary for different groups on the basis of such factors as sex and social status.[12]

An important contribution of this study was that it determined that the personality traits of the decision maker combine with certain situational and interactional variables to influence the decision-making process.

Propensity for Risk

From personal experience the reader is undoubtedly aware that decision makers vary greatly in their propensity to take risks. This one specific aspect of personality strongly influences the decision-making process. A decision

---

[11] Orville C. Brun, Jr. et al., *Personality and Decision Processes* (Stanford, Calif.: Stanford University Press, 1962).

[12] For a recent study on the effects of sex on decision making see P. A. Renwick and H. Tosi, "The Effects of Sex, Marital Status, and Educational Background on Selected Decisions," *Academy of Management Journal* (March 1978), pp. 93–103.

maker with a low aversion to risk will establish different objectives, evaluate alternatives differently, and select different alternatives than another decision maker in the same situation who has a high aversion to risk. The latter will attempt to make choices where the risk or uncertainty is low or where the certainty of the outcome is high. We shall see later in the chapter that in many cases, individuals are more bold, innovative, and advocate greater risk-taking following participation in a group than they display individually. Apparently, individuals are more willing to accept risk as members of a group.

Potential for Dissonance

While much attention has been focused on the forces and influences on the decision maker prior to making a decision, and on the actual decision, only recently has attention been given to what happens after a decision has been made. Specifically, behavioral scientists have focused attention on the occurrence of postdecision anxiety.

The occurrence of postdecision anxiety is related to what Festinger calls "cognitive dissonance."[13] His theory states that there is often a lack of consistency or harmony among an individual's various cognitions (for example, attitudes, beliefs, and so on) after a decision has been made. That is, there will be a conflict between what the decision maker knows and believes and what was done, and as a result the decision maker will have doubts and second thoughts about the choice that was made. In addition, there is a likelihood that the intensity of the anxiety will be greater when any of the following conditions exist:

1. The decision is an important one psychologically and/or financially.
2. There are a number of foregone alternatives.
3. The foregone alternatives have many favorable features.[14]

Each of these conditions is present in many decisions in all types of organizations. We can expect, therefore, that postdecision dissonance will be present among many decision makers, especially those at higher levels in the organization.

When dissonance occurs, it can, of course, be reduced by admitting that a mistake had been made. Unfortunately, it has been found that many individuals are reluctant to admit they have made a wrong decision. These individuals will more likely use one or more of the following methods to reduce their dissonance:

1. Seek information that supports the wisdom of their decision.
2. Selectively perceive (distort) information in a way to support their decision.
3. Change their attitudes to a less favorable view of the foregone alternatives.

---

[13] Leon Festinger, *A Theory of Cognitive Dissonance* (New York: Harper & Row, 1957), Chapter 1.

[14] Ibid.

4. Avoid the importance of the negative aspects and enhance the positive elements.[15]

While each of us may resort to some of this behavior in our personal decision making, it is easy to see how a great deal of it could be extremely harmful in terms of organizational effectiveness. The potential for dissonance is influenced heavily by one's personality, specifically one's self-confidence and persuasibility. In fact, all of the behavioral influences are closely interrelated and are only isolated here for purposes of discussion. For example, what kind of a risk-taker you are and your potential for anxiety following a decision are very closely related, and both are strongly influenced by your personality, perceptions, and value system. Before managers can fully understand the dynamics of the decision-making process, they must appreciate the behavioral influences upon themselves and other decision makers in the organization when they make decisions.

GROUP DECISION MAKING

The first parts of this chapter focused on individuals making decisions. However, a great deal of decision making in most organizations is acheived through committees, teams, task forces, and other forms of groups. This is because managers frequently face situations where they must seek and combine judgments in group meetings. This is especially true for nonprogrammed problems which are novel with much uncertainty regarding the outcome. In most organizations it is unusual to find decisions of this type made by one individual on a regular basis. This is because the increased complexity of many organizational problems requires specialized knowledge in numerous fields usually not possessed by one person. This, coupled with the reality that the decision must eventually be accepted and implemented by many units throughout the organization, has increased the use of the collective approach to the decision-making process. The result for many managers has been an endless amount of time spent in committee and other group meetings. It has been found that as much as 80 percent of many managers' working time is spent in committee meetings.[16]

Individual versus Group Decision Making

There is considerable debate over the relative effectiveness of individual versus group decision making. For example, groups usually take more time

---

[15] W. J. McGuire, "Cognitive Consistency and Attitude Change," *Journal of Abnormal and Social Psychology* (1960), pp. 345–53. Also see J. S. Adams, "Reduction of Cognitive Dissonance by Seeking Consonant Information," *Journal of Abnormal and Social Psychology* (1961), pp. 74–78; J. Mills, E. Aronsen, and H. Robinson, "Selectivity in Exposure to Information." *Journal of Abnormal Psychology* (1959), pp. 250–53; and D. S. Holmes and B. K. Houston, "Effectiveness of Situation Redefinition and Affective Isolation in Coping with Stress," *Journal of Personality and Social Psychology* (1974), pp. 212–18.

[16] A. H. VandeVen, *An Applied Experimental Test of Alternative Decision-Making Processes* (Kent, Ohio: Center for Business and Economic Research Press, Kent State University, 1973).

to reach a decision than individuals do, but the bringing together of individual specialists and experts also has its benefits since the mutually reinforcing impact of their interaction results in a better decision being made. In fact, a great deal of research has shown that consensus decisions with five or more participants are superior to individual decision making, majority vote, and leader decision.[17] Unfortunately, open discussion has been found to be negatively influenced by such behavioral factors as the pressure to conform, the influence of a dominant personality type(s) in the group, "status incongruity" where lower status participants are inhibited by higher status participants and "go along" even though they believe their ideas are superior, and finally, when certain participants attempt to influence others because they are perceived to be expert in the problem area.[18]

Certain decisions appear to be better made by groups while others appear better suited for individual decision making. Nonprogrammed decisions appear to be better suited for group decision making. The nature of such problems usually calls for pooled talent in arriving at a solution; decisions are of such importance that they are usually made by top managers and to a somewhat lesser extent by middle managers.

In terms of the decision-making process itself, the following points concerning group processes for nonprogrammed decisions can be made:

1. In *establishing objectives* groups are probably superior to individuals because of the greater amount of knowledge available.
2. In *identifying alternatives,* individual efforts of group members are necessary to ensure a broad search in the various functional areas of the organization.
3. In *evaluating alternatives,* the collective judgment of the group, with its wider range of viewpoints, seems superior to that of the individual decision maker.
4. In *choosing an alternative* it has been shown that group interaction and achievement of consensus usually results in groups accepting more risk than an individual decision maker. In any event, the decision is more likely to be accepted as a result of the participation of those affected by its consequences.

---

[17] For examples, see Charles Holloman and Harold Henrick, "Adequacy of Group Decisions as a Function of Decision-Making Process," *Academy of Management Journal* (June 1972), pp. 175–84; and Andrew H. VandeVen and Andre Delbecq, "Nominal versus Interacting Group Processes for Committee Decision-Making Effectiveness," *Academy of Management Journal* (June 1972), pp. 203–12.

[18] For examples, see Solomon Asch, "Studies of Independence and Conformity," *Psychological Monographs* (1956), pp. 68–70; Norman Dalkey and Olaf Helmer, "An Experimental Application of Delphi Method to Use of Experts," *Management Science* (April 1963), pp. 458–67; E. M. Bridges, W. J. Doyle, and D. J. Mahan, "Effects of Hierarchical Differentiation on Group Productivity, Efficiency, and Risk-Taking," *Administrative Science Quarterly* (Fall 1968), pp. 305–39; Victor Vroom, Lester Grant, and Timothy Cotten, "The Consequences of Social Interaction in Group Problem-Solving," *Organizational Behavior and Human Performance* (February 1969), pp. 77–95; and P. A. Collaras and L. R. Anderson, "Effect of Perceived Expertise upon Creativity of Members of Brainstorming Groups," *Journal of Applied Psychology* (April 1969), pp. 159–63.

5. *Implementation* of a decision, whether or not it is made by a group, usually is accomplished by individual managers. Thus, since a group cannot be held responsible, responsibility necessarily rests with the individual manager.[19]

Figure 16–2 summarizes the research on group decision making. It presents the relationship between the probable quality of the decision and the method utilized to reach the decision. It indicates that as we move from "individual" to "consensus," the quality of the decision increases. Note also that each successive method involves a higher level of mutual influence by group members. Thus, for a complex problem requiring pooled knowledge, the quality of the decision is likely to be higher as the group moves toward achieving consensus.

Figure 16–2
Relationship between Probable Quality of Group Decision and Method Utilized

Probable Quality of Decision

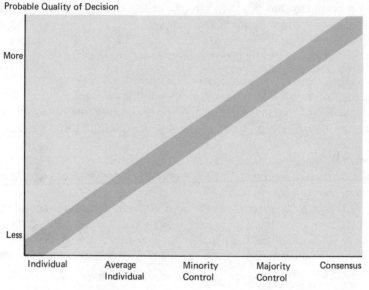

Method of Utilization of Group Resources

Source: Adapted from J. Hall and V. O'Leary, "The Utilization of Group Resources in Decision Making," National Training Laboratories, PSOTD, 1967, p. 4.

Managing Group Decisions

If groups are better suited for nonprogrammed decisions then it is important that an atmosphere which fosters creativity be created. In this respect group decision making might be similar to brainstorming in that discussion must be freeflowing and spontaneous. All group members must participate and the evaluation of individual ideas suspended in the beginning to encourage

---

[19] Based on Harrison, *The Management Decision-Making Process,* p. 211.

Figure 16–3
Creative Group Decision Making

Group Structure

The group is composed of heterogeneous, generally competent personnel who bring to bear on the problem diverse frames of reference, representing channels to each relevant body of knowledge (including contact with outside resource personnel who offer expertise not encompassed by the organization), with a leader who facilitates creative process.

Group Roles

Behavior is characterized by each individual exploring with the entire group all ideas (no matter how intuitively and roughly formed) that bear on the problem.

Group Processes

The problem-solving process is characterized by:
—Spontaneous communication between members (not focused on the leader).
—Full participation from each member.
—Separation of idea generation from idea evaluation.
—Separation of problem definition from generation of solution strategies.
—Shifting of roles, so that interaction which mediates problem solving (particularly search activities and clarification by means of constant questioning directed both to individual members and the whole group) is not the sole responsibility of the leader.
—Suspension of judgment and avoidance of early concern with solutions, so that emphasis is on analysis and exploration, rather than on early solution commitment.

Group Style

The social-emotional tone of the group if characterized by:
—A relaxed, nonstressful environment.
—Ego-supportive interaction, where open give-and-take between members is at the same time courteous.
—Behavior that is motivated by interest in the problem, rather than concern with short-run payoff.
—Absence of penalties attached to any espoused idea or position.

Group Norms

—Are supportive of originality and unusual ideas, and allow for eccentricity.
—Seek behavior that separates source from content in evaluating information and ideas.
—Stress a nonauthoritarian view, with a realistic view of life and independence of judgment.
—Support humor and undisciplined exploration of viewpoints.
—Seek openness in communication, where mature, self-confident individuals offer "crude" ideas to the group for mutual exploration without threat to the individual for "exposing" himself.
—Deliberately avoid credence to short-run results, or short-run decisiveness.
—Seek consensus, but accept majority rule when consensus is unobtainable.

Source: Andre L. Delbecq, "The Management of Decision Making within the Firm: Three Strategies for Three Types of Decision Making," *Academy of Management Journal* (December 1967), pp. 334–35.

participation. However, a decision must be reached and this is where it differs from brainstorming. Figure 16–3 presents guidelines for developing the permissive atmosphere so important for creative group decision making.

Improving Group Decisions

It seems safe to say that in many instances group decision making is preferable to individual decision making. But we have all heard the statement, "A camel is a racehorse designed by a committee." Thus, while the necessity of group decision making and its benefits are recognized there are also numerous problems associated with it, some of which have already been noted. Practicing managers are in need of specific techniques which will enable them to increase the benefits from group decision making while reducing the problems associated with it.

We shall examine two techniques which, when properly utilized, have been found to be extremely useful in increasing the creative capability of a group in generating ideas and understanding problems in order to arrive at better group decisions. Such a situation is necessary when individuals from diverse groups in the organization must pool their judgments in order to create a satisfactory course of action for the organization. The two techniques are known as the Delphi Technique and the Nominal Group Technique.

The Delphi Technique. This technique involves the solicitation and comparison of anonymous judgments on the topic of interest through a set of sequential questionnaires interspersed with summarized information and feedback of opinions from earlier responses.[20]

The Delphi process retains the advantage of several judges while removing the biasing effects which might occur during face-to-face interaction. The basic approach has been to collect anonymous judgments by mail questionnaire. For example, the members independently generate their ideas to answer the first questionnaire and return it. The staff members summarize the responses as the group consensus, and feed this summary back along with a second questionnaire for reassessment. Based on this feedback, the respondents independently evaluate their earlier responses. The underlying belief is that the consensus estimate will result in a better decision after several rounds of anonymous group judgment. While it is possible to continue the procedure for several rounds, studies have shown essentially no significant change after the second round of estimation.[21]

The Nominal Group Technique (NGT). NGT has gained increasing recognition in health, social service, education, industry, and government organizations.[22] The term "nominal" was adopted by earlier researchers

[20] Norman Dalkey, *The Delphi Method: An Experimental Study of Group Opinion* (Santa Monica: The Rand Corporation, 1969).

[21] Norman Dalkey, *Experiments in Group Prediction* (Santa Monica: The Rand Corporation, 1968).

[22] See Andre L. Delbecq, Andrew H. VandeVen, and David H. Gustafson, *Group Techniques for Program Planning* (Glenview, Ill.: Scott, Foresman and Company, 1975). The discussion here is based on this work.

to refer to processes which bring people together but do not allow them to communicate verbally. Thus, the collection of people is a group "nominally," or "in name only." We shall see, however, that NGT in its present form actually combines both verbal and nonverbal stages.

Basically, NGT is a structured group meeting that proceeds as follows: A group of individuals (seven to ten) sit around a table but do not speak to each other. Rather, each person writes ideas on a pad of paper. After five minutes, a structured sharing of ideas takes place. Each person around the table presents one idea. A person designated as recorder writes the ideas on a flip chart in full view of the entire group. This continues until all participants indicate they have no further ideas to share. There is still no discussion.

The output of this phase is a list of ideas (usually between 18 and 25). The next phase involves structured discussion in which each idea receives attention before voting. This is achieved by asking for clarification, or stating the degree of support for each idea listed on the flip chart. The next stage involves independent voting in which each participant, in private, selects priorities by ranking or voting. The group decision is the mathematically pooled outcome of the individual votes.

Both the Delphi technique and NGT are relatively new, but each has had an excellent record of successes. Basic differences between them are:

1. Delphi participants are typically anonymous to each other, while NGT participants become acquainted.
2. NGT participants meet face to face around a table, while Delphi participants are physically distant and never meet face to face.
3. In the Delphi process, all communications between participants is by way of written questionnaires and feedback from the monitoring staff. In NGT, communication is direct between participants.[23]

Practical considerations, of course, often influence which technique is used. For example, such factors as the number of working hours available, costs, and the physical proximity of participants will influence which technique is selected.

Our discussion here is not designed to make the reader an expert in the Delphi process or NGT.[24] Our purpose throughout this section has been to indicate the frequency and importance of group decision making in every type of organization. The two techniques discussed are practical devices with the purpose of improving the *effectiveness* of group decisions.

Decision making is a common responsibility shared by all executives, regardless of functional area or management level. Managers are required, every day, to make decisions that shape the future of their organization as well as their own futures. The quality of these decisions is the yardstick of their effectiveness. Some of these decisions may have strong impact on the organization's success, while others will be important but less crucial.

---

[23] Ibid., p. 18.

[24] The reader desiring to learn more about each of these techniques is encouraged to consult Delbecq, VandeVen, and Gustafson, *Group Techniques for Program Planning*.

The important point, however, is that *all* will have some effect (positive or negative, large or small) on the organization.

MAJOR ISSUES FOR THE MANAGER TO CONSIDER

A. Decision making is a fundemental process in organizations. Managers make decisions as a consequence of the information (communication) they receive through the organization structure and the behavior of individuals and groups within it.

B. Decision making distinguishes managers from nonmanagers. The quality of decisions managers make determines their effectiveness as managers.

C. Decisions may be classified as programmed or nonprogrammed depending on the type of problem. Most programmed decisions should be made at the first level in the organization while nonprogrammed decisions should be made mostly by top managment.

D. Decision making should not be thought of as an end but as a *means* to achieve organizational goals and objectives. They are organizational responses to problems.

E. Decision making should be viewed as a multiphased *process* of which the actual choice is only one phase.

F. The decision-making process is influenced by numerous environmental and behavioral factors. Different decision makers may select different alternatives in the same situation because of different values, perceptions, and personalities.

G. A great deal of nonprogrammed decision making is carried on in group situations. Much evidence exists to support the claim that in most instances, though problems do exist, group decisions are superior to individual decisions. Two relatively new techniques (the Delphi Technique and the Nominal Group Technique) exist which have the purpose of improving the effectiveness of group decisions. The management of collective decision making must be a vital concern for future managers.

DISCUSSION AND REVIEW QUESTIONS

1. In terms that are satisfactory to you, define a decision.

2. Describe two situations you faced which called for programmed decisions on your part and two which called for nonprogrammed decisions. What were some of the differences between them? Did this influence your decision-making approach? In what way(s)?

3. Think of a decision you made recently in response to a problem you faced. Describe it in terms of the decision-making process presented in Figure 16–1.

4. For decision-making purposes, why are goals and objectives so important?

5. Think of a major decision you made recently. It may have involved your personal life, a major purchase, etc. Do you believe there were any behavioral influences upon your decision? Discuss them.

6. What is your attitude toward risk? Has it ever influenced a decision you made? Discuss it. What are the implications of this discussion?

7. Have you ever been a member of a committee, task force, etc. which was charged with making some type of decision? Describe it in terms of your satisfactions, dissatisfactions, problems, etc.

ADDITIONAL REFERENCES

Alutto, J., and Vredenburgh, D. "Characteristics of Decisional Participation by Nurses." *Academy of Management Journal* (1977), pp. 341–47.

Collins, B. E., and Guetzhow, H. *A Social Psychology of Group Processes for Decision Making.* New York: John Wiley & Sons, 1964.

Dalkey, N. C. *The Delphi Method: An Experimental Study of Group Opinion.* Rand Corporation, June 1969.

Delbecq, A. L. "The Management of Decision Making within the Firm: Three Strategies for Three Types of Decision Making." *Academy of Management Journal* (1967), pp. 329–39.

Drucker, P. *The Effective Executive.* New York: Harper & Row, 1967.

Duncan, W. J. *Decision Making and Social Issues.* Hinsdale, Ill.: Dryden Press, 1973.

Eells, R., and Walton, C. *Conceptual Foundations of Business.* Homewood, Ill.: Richard D. Irwin, 1974.

Gustafson, D. H.; Shukla, R. M.; Delbecq, A.; and Walster, G. W. "A Comparative Study of Differences in Subjective Likelihood Estimates Made by Individuals, Interacting Groups, Delphi Groups, and Nominal Groups." *Organizational Behavior and Human Performance* (1973), pp. 280–91.

Hall, E. J.; Mouton, J.; and Blake, R. R. "Group Problem-Solving Effectiveness under Conditions of Pooling versus Interaction." *Journal of Social Psychology* (1963), pp. 147–57.

Halter, A. N., and Dean, G. W. *Decisions under Uncertainty with Research Applications.* Cincinnati: South-Western Publishing Co., 1971.

Huber, G., and Delbecq, A. L. "Guidelines for Combining the Judgment of Individual Members in Decision Conferences." *Academy of Management Journal* (1972), pp. 161–74.

Kahn, H., and Weiner, A. H. *The Year 2000: a Framework for Speculation on the Next Thirty-Five Years.* New York: Macmillan, 1967.

Kogan, N., and Wallach, M. A. *Risk-Taking: A Study in Cognition and Personality.* New York: Holt, Rinehart and Winston, 1964.

Lindley, D. V. *Making Decisions.* New York: John Wiley & Sons, 1971.

Miller, D. W., and Starr, M. K. *The Structure of Human Decisions.* Englewood Cliffs, N.J.: Prentice-Hall, Inc., 1967.

Schmidt, W. H. *Organizational Frontiers and Human Values.* Belmont, Calif.: Wadsworth Publishing Co., 1970.

Sharkansky, I. *Public Administration: Policy Making in Government Agencies.* Chicago: Markham Publishing Co., 1972.

Shull, F. A.; Delbecq, A. L.; and Cummings, L. L. *Organizational Decision Making.* New York: McGraw Hill Book Co., 1970.

Simon, H. A. *Models of Man.* New York: John Wiley and Sons, 1957.

————. *Sciences of the Artificial.* Cambridge, Mass.: The M.I.T. Press, 1969.

Tersine, R. J., and Riggs, W. E. "The Delphi Technique: A Long-Range Planning Tool." *Business Horizons* (1976), pp. 51–56.

White, J. K. "Generalizability of Individual Difference Moderators of the Participation in Decision Making—Employee Response Relationship." *Academy of Management Journal* (1978), pp. 36–43.

CASE FOR ANALYSIS

THE FACULTY DECISION

Tom Madden slipped into his seat at the meeting of the faculty of the College of Business Administration of Longley University. He was 10 minutes late because he had come completely across campus from another meeting which had lasted 1½ hours. "Boy!" he thought, "if all of these meetings and committee assignments keep up, I won't have time to do anything else."

"The next item of importance," said the Dean, "is consideration of the feasibility report prepared by the Assistant Dean, Dr. Jackson, for the establishment of our Latin American MBA Program."

"What's that?" Tom whispered to his friend Jim Lyon sitting next to him.

"Ah, Professor Madden," winked Lyon, "evidently you've not bothered to read this impressive document," passing Tom the 86-page report, "otherwise you'd know."

"Heck, Jim, I've been out of town for two weeks on a research project and have just come from another meeting."

"Well, Tom," chuckled Jim, "the report was circulated only three days ago to, as the Dean put it, 'insure we have faculty input into where the college is going.' Actually, Tom, I was hoping you'd read it because then you could have told me what was in it."

"Dr. Jackson," said the Dean, "why don't you present a summary of your excellent report on what I believe is an outstanding opportunity for our college, the establishment of an MBA program in Latin America."

"Hey, Jim," said Tom, "they've got to be kidding, we're not doing what we should be doing with the MBA we've got here on campus. Why on earth are we thinking about doing another one 3,000 miles away?"

Jim shrugged. "Some friend of the Dean's or Jackson's from down there must have asked them, I guess."

While the summary was being given, Tom thumbed through the report. He noted that they were planning to offer the same program they offered in the United States. "Certainly," he thought, "their students' needs are different from ours." He also noted that faculty were going to be sent from the United States on one- to three-year appointments. "You would think that whenever possible they would seek local instructors who were familiar with the needs of local industry," Tom thought. He concluded in his own mind, "Actually, why are we even getting involved in this thing in the first place? We don't have the resources."

When Jackson finished the summary, the Dean asked, "Are there any questions?"

"I wonder how many people have had the time to read this report in three days and think about it," Tom thought to himself.

"Has anybody thought through this entire concept?" Tom spoke up. "I mean. . . ."

"Absolutely, Professor Madden," the Dean answered. "Dr. Jackson and I have spent a great deal of time on this project."

"Well, I was just thinking that. . . ."

"Now, Professor Madden, surely you don't question the efforts of Dr. Jackson and myself. Had you been here when this meeting started, you would know all about our efforts. Besides, it's getting late and we've got another agenda item to consider today, the safety and security of final examinations prior to their being given."

"No further questions," Tom said.

"Wonderful," said the Dean. "Then I will report to the President that the faculty of the College of Business Administration unanimously approves the Latin American MBA program. I might add, by the way, the president is extremely pleased with our method of shared decision making. We have made it work in this college while other colleges are having trouble arriving at mutually agreed-upon decisions.

"This is a great day for our college. Today we have become a multinational university. We can all be proud."

After the meeting, as Tom headed for the parking lot, he thought, "What a way to make an important decision. I guess I shouldn't complain though, I didn't even read the report. I'd better check my calendar to see what committee meetings I've got the rest of the week. If I've got any more I'll. . . ."

Questions for Consideration

1. Analyze this exercise and outline as many factors as possible which influenced the faculty decision in this case—either positively or negatively.

2. Does this exercise indicate that shared decision making cannot be worthwhile and effective? How could it be made more effective in the College of Business Administration?

3. Do you believe decision making of this type may be more worthwhile and effective in some types of organizations than in others? Discuss.

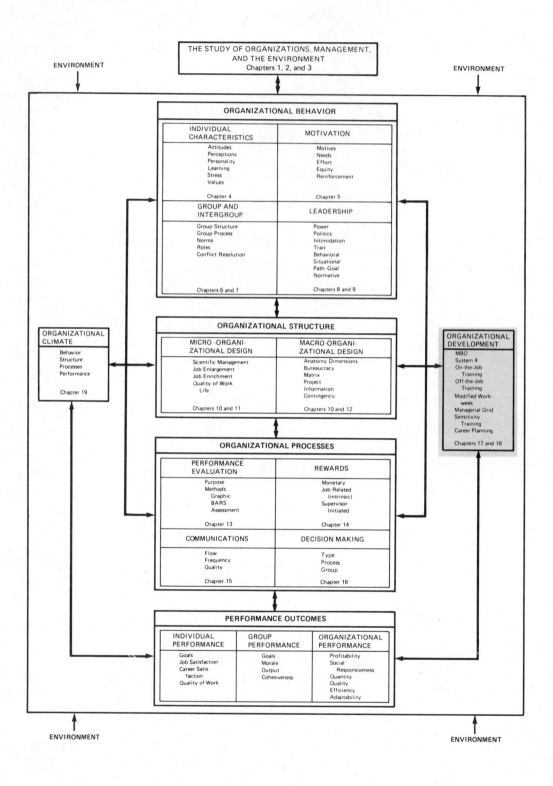

ENVIRONMENT

ENVIRONMENT

THE STUDY OF ORGANIZATIONS, MANAGEMENT,
AND THE ENVIRONMENT
Chapters 1, 2, and 3

ORGANIZATIONAL BEHAVIOR

INDIVIDUAL CHARACTERISTICS	MOTIVATION
Attitudes	Motives
Perceptions	Needs
Personality	Effort
Learning	Equity
Stress	Reinforcement
Values	
Chapter 4	Chapter 5

GROUP AND INTERGROUP	LEADERSHIP
Group Structure	Power
Group Process	Politics
Norms	Intimidation
Roles	Trait
Conflict Resolution	Behavioral
	Situational
	Path-Goal
	Normative
Chapters 6 and 7	Chapters 8 and 9

ORGANIZATIONAL STRUCTURE

MICRO-ORGANIZATIONAL DESIGN	MACRO-ORGANIZATIONAL DESIGN
Scientific Management	Anatomy Dimensions
Job Enlargement	Bureaucracy
Job Enrichment	Matrix
Quality of Work	Project
Life	Information
	Contingency
Chapters 10 and 11	Chapters 10 and 12

ORGANIZATIONAL CLIMATE

Behavior
Structure
Processes
Performance

Chapter 19

ORGANIZATIONAL DEVELOPMENT

MBO
System 4
On-the-Job
  Training
Off-the-Job
  Training
Modified Work-
  week
Managerial Grid
Sensitivity
  Training
Career Planning

Chapters 17 and 18

ORGANIZATIONAL PROCESSES

PERFORMANCE EVALUATION	REWARDS
Purpose	Monetary
Methods	Job-Related
Graphic	(intrinsic)
BARS	Supervisor-
Assessment	Initiated
Chapter 13	Chapter 14

COMMUNICATIONS	DECISION MAKING
Flow	Type
Frequency	Process
Quality	Group
Chapter 15	Chapter 16

PERFORMANCE OUTCOMES

INDIVIDUAL PERFORMANCE	GROUP PERFORMANCE	ORGANIZATIONAL PERFORMANCE
Goals	Goals	Profitability
Job Satisfaction	Morale	Social
Career Satis-	Output	Responsiveness
faction	Cohesiveness	Quantity
Quality of Work		Quality
		Efficiency
		Adaptability

ENVIRONMENT

ENVIRONMENT

Part Five

Developing Organizational Effectiveness

Chapter 17

Organizational Development: Improving Performance

AN ORGANIZATIONAL ISSUE FOR DEBATE

External Change Agents Are Necessary for Successful OD

ARGUMENT FOR

Successful instances of organization development (OD) are always (or at least usually) the result of intervention by a person or group external to the organization itself. The rationale for this position is that external persons are not caught up in the day-to-day operations of the organization and are able to see problems and causes of problems more clearly than those who must work within it. The change agent is able to see the issues because he or she is neutral and impartial, having no vested interest or personal stake in the organization. Managers and staff personnel already in the organization are unable to see clearly the problems, and indeed, may be part of them.

Moreover, so the argument goes, external change agents are solely able to undertake the necessary steps which bring about development. They alone are able to present unbiased information which indicates the necessity to change attitudes and behaviors. Through attitude defreezing and refreezing, successful organizational development occurs. But managers whose attitudes require change cannot themselves be the catalyst for changing the attitudes of others.

Support for the position is to be found in research studies and case histories. One researcher documented the differences to be found in the strategies associated with successful versus unsuccessful OD efforts. He concluded that successful OD strategy invariably was associated with the use of an external change agent.

ARGUMENT AGAINST

The argument against is based on the idea that organization development efforts vary from company to company. In some instances the developmental effort may involve nothing more than changes in job descriptions and departmental bases. In other instances the OD effort may involve fundamental changes in personal and interpersonal variables. Thus the necessity for an external change agent rests in part on the depth of intervention.

Alternatives to the exclusive use of external change agents include establishing a corporate-level Organization-Development Department, hiring an OD specialist, training a member of the personnel department, and assigning OD responsibility to the management-development department. Each of these alternatives has advantages and disadvantages. Although the existence of internal change agents does not preclude the use of external change agents their existence provides reasonable alternatives to the exclusive use of external parties.

INTRODUCTION

The process by which managers sense and respond to the necessity for change has been the focus of much research and practical attention in recent years. If managers were able to design perfect sociotechnical organizations and if the scientific, market, and technical environments were stable and predictable, there would be no pressure for change. But such is not the case. The statement that "we live in the midst of constant change" has become a well-worn but relevant cliché. Of course, the need for change affects organizations differently; those which operate in relatively certain environments need to be less concerned with change than those which operate in less certain environments. But, even managers in certain environments must continually combat the problems of complacency.[1]

The literature and practice which deal with the process of organizational change cannot be conveniently classified because of the yet unsettled nature of this aspect of organizational behavior. Various conceptualizations and theories and their meanings and interpretations are subject to considerable disagreement. The current trend is to use the term Organizational Development (OD) to refer to the process of preparing for and managing change. Since we will use the term in this and the next chapter, it is important that we clarify our meaning and interpretation.

In its most restrictive usage, OD refers to *sensitivity training*.[2] In this context, OD stresses the process by which people in organizations become more aware of themselves and others. The emphasis is on the psychological states of employees which inhibit their ability to communicate and interact with other organizational members. The assumption is that organizational effectiveness can be increased if people can engage in honest and open discussion of issues. We will have more to say about sensitivity training in the following chapter.

A slightly more encompassing definition of OD states:

> Using knowledge and techniques from the behavioral sciences, organizational development is a *process* which attempts to increase organizational effectiveness by integrating individual desires for growth and development with organizational goals. Typically, this process is a planned change effort which involves a total system over a period of time, and these change efforts are related to the organization's mission.[3]

This definition acknowledges the existence of methods other than sensitivity training. For example, participative management, job enrichment, management by objectives, and the managerial grid are some alternative methods

---

[1] Chris Argyris, *Management and Organizational Development* (New York: McGraw-Hill Book Co., 1971), p. 20.

[2] See Stanley M. Herman, "What Is This Thing Called Organizational Development?" *Personnel Journal* (August 1971), pp. 595–603.

[3] W. Warren Burke and Warren H. Schmidt, "Management and Organizational Development," *Personnel Administration* (March 1971), p. 45.

for integrating individual and organizational objectives.[4] This definition also acknowledges the fact that OD is a planned process over time which must be justified in terms of organizational effectiveness. The definition, however, is still incomplete for our purposes.

The concept of OD must be broad enough to include not only the behavioral approach, but others as well. The following definition identifies all the significant aspects of OD:

> The term "Organization development". . . implies a normative, re-education strategy intended to affect systems of beliefs, values, and attitudes within the organization so that it can adapt better to the accelerated rate of change in technology, in our industrial environment and society in general. It also includes formal organizational restructuring which is frequently initiated, facilitated and reinforced by the normative and behavioral changes.[5]

The three subobjectives of OD are "changing attitudes or values, modifying behavior, and inducing change in structure and policy."[6] However, it is conceivable that the strategy might well emphasize one or another of these subobjectives. For example, if the structure of an organization is optimal in management's view, the OD process might attempt to educate personnel to adopt behaviors consistent with the structure. Such would be the case of leadership training in participative management in an organization which already has a System 4 structure.

Moreover the concept of OD must include the possibility of programs aimed at providing personnel with technical skills. It is entirely possible that effective change is not forthcoming simply because people in the organization do not have technical skills to cope with it. Management may determine that attitudes, behavior, and structure are appropriate yet the organization cannot respond to change because key personnel simply do not have the skills to respond. The skill training programs of industry and government are as important a part of OD as are the more fashionable programs such as sensitivity training.

Organizational development as the term is used in contemporary management practice has certain distinguishing characteristics:

1. *It Is Planned.* OD is a data-based approach to change which involves all of the ingredients that go into managerial planning. It involves goal setting, action planning, implementation, monitoring, and taking corrective action when necessary.
2. *It Is Problem-Oriented.* OD attempts to apply theory and research from a number of disciplines, including behavioral science, to the solution of organization problems.

---

[4] William B. Eddy, "Beyond Behavioralism? Organization Development in Public Management," *Public Personnel Review* (July 1970), p. 171.

[5] Alexander Winn, "The Laboratory Approach to Organizational Development: A Tentative Model of Planned Change," paper read at the Annual Conference, British Psychological Society, Oxford, September 1968, p. 1, and cited in Robert T. Golembiewski, "Organizational Development in Public Agencies: Perspectives on Theory and Practice," *Public Administration Review* (July/August 1969), p. 367.

[6] Ibid., p. 367.

3. *It Reflects a Systems Approach.* OD is both systemic and systematic. It is a way of more closely linking the human resources and potential of an organization to its technology, structure, and management processes.
4. *It Is an Integral Part of the Management Process.* OD is not something that is done to the organization by outsiders. It becomes a way of managing organizational change processes.
5. *It Is Not a "Fix-It" Strategy.* OD reflects a continuous and ongoing process. It is not a series of ad hoc activities designed to implement a specific change. It takes time for it to become a way of life in the organization.
6. *It Focuses on Improvement.* The emphasis of OD is on improvement. It is not just for "sick" organizations or for "wealthy" ones. It is something that can benefit almost any organization.
7. *It Is Action-Oriented.* The focus of OD is on accomplishments and results. Unlike some other approaches to change which tend to describe how organizational change takes place, the emphasis is on getting things done.
8. *It Is Based upon Sound Theory and Practice.* OD is not a gimmick or a fad. It is solidly based upon the theory and research of a number of disciplines.[7]

These characteristics of contemporary organizational development indicate that managers who implement OD programs are committed to making fundamental changes in organizational behavior. In doing so, they must recognize the necessity to view the OD program as a learning exercise which embodies certain well-established principles. These learning principles are presented in the next section.

LEARNING PRINCIPLES IN THE CONTEXT OF OD PROGRAMS

To better understand how changes are brought about in individuals it is essential to comprehend the various principles of learning discussed in Chapter 4. Managers can design a theoretically sound OD program and not achieve any of the anticipated results because they overlooked the importance of providing reinforcement or continuous feedback to employees. These are principles of learning, and they should be tailored to the needs of the group that is affected by the program.

Expectations and Motivations

People must want to learn. They may want more skill in a particular job or more understanding of the problems of other units of the firm. Some people recognize this need and are receptive to experiences which will aid them in developing new skills or new empathy. Others reject the need or play it down, because learning is to them an admission that they are not

---

[7] Newton Margulies and Anthony P. Raia, *Conceptual Foundations of Organizational Development* (New York: McGraw-Hill Book Co., 1978), p. 25.

completely competent in their jobs. These kinds of people face the prospect of change with different expectations and motivations. Determining the expectations and motivations of people is not an easy task. It is, however, a task which must be undertaken. The point to remember is that not everyone wants to participate in a change program and it is management's responsibility to show employees why they should want to change.

Reinforcement and Feedback

An important principle of learning is that of reinforcement. This principle suggests that when people receive positive rewards, information, or feelings for doing something, it becomes more likely that they will do the same thing in the same or similar situation.[8] The other side of the coin involves the impact of punishment for a particular response. It is assumed that punishment will decrease the probability of doing the same or similar thing at another time. The principle then implies that it would be easier to achieve successful change through the use of positive rewards. It can also be said that reinforcement can occur when the knowledge or skill acquired in a training program is reinforced through a refresher course.

A major problem associated with reinforcement is the determination of reinforcers. That is, what will serve as the appropriate reinforcer of desired behavior? For some people, money or praise is an effective reinforcer, while others respond more to a refresher type of training experience. Once again situations and individuals determine effective reinforcement. The feedback concept is similar to the principle of reinforcement. Employees generally desire knowledge on how they are doing. This is especially true after a change program has been implemented. Providing information about the progress of a unit or group of employees lets the employees take corrective action. A number of studies indicate that employees perform more effectively on a variety of tasks when they have feedback than when it is absent.[9]

The timing of feedback is a factor that should be considered. Most college students want to know their course grade as soon as possible after the final examination. The same need to know exists for managers who have set objectives for the next year. They want to know immediately if their objectives are acceptable. Thus the immediacy of feedback is an issue to consider. Feedback provided a long time after a personal action has occurred will probably not be as effective as providing feedback immediately after the action. As one might anticipate, individuals differ in their receptivity to feedback concerning their actions. In general, it is more favorably received by employees who have motivation to improve themselves and/or their unit.[10]

---

[8] For the most recent statement by the most widely recognized spokesman for the principle of reinforcement, see B. F. Skinner, *About Behaviorism* (New York: Alfred A. Knopf, 1974).

[9] Victor Vroom, *Work and Motivation* (New York: John Wiley & Sons, 1964), pp. 242–43.

[10] For an experiment concerning feedback, see Larry L. Cummings, Donald P. Schwab, and Marc Rosen, "Performance and Knowledge of Results as Determinants of Goal Setting," *Journal of Applied Psychology* (December 1971), pp. 526–30.

Transfer of Learning

Management must guard against the possibility that what was learned at a training site is lost when transferring a person to the actual work site. If things have gone well, only a minimum amount will be lost in this necessary transfer. A possible strategy for keeping the loss to a minimum is to make the training situation similar to the actual workplace environment. Another procedure is to reward the newly learned behavior. If the colleagues and superiors approve new ideas or new skills, newly trained people will be encouraged to continue to behave in the new way. If they behave negatively they will be discouraged from persisting with attempts to use what has been learned. This is one of the reasons that it has been suggested that superiors be trained before subordinates. The superior, if trained and motivated, can serve as a reinforcer and feedback source for the subordinate who has left the training confines and is now back on the job.

There are numerous other principles of learning that will prove invaluable when attempting to manage OD programs. Those noted above, however, are current issues discussed in the OD literature. The manager who fails to consider them when introducing an OD program will have a difficult time improving organizational effectiveness.

An OD program must be designed systematically. This argues for an analytical approach which breaks down the process into constituent steps, logically sequenced. For this purpose a model is proposed which identifies the key elements and decison points which managers can follow. This model is described in the next section and the remainder of this chapter elaborates on each of the steps in the model.

A MODEL FOR MANAGING
ORGANIZATIONAL DEVELOPMENT

The model which we propose is described in Figure 17–1 and consists of eight steps which are linked in a logical sequence. A manager considers each of them, either explicitly or implicitly, to undertake an OD program. The prospects of initiating successful change can be enhanced when the manager explicitly and formally goes through each successive step.

The model presumes that forces for change continually act upon the organization; this assumption reflects the dynamic character of the modern world. At the same time it is the manager's responsibility to sort out the information that he receives from the organization's information system and other sources which reflect the magnitude of change forces. The information is the basis for recognizing the need for change; it is equally desirable to recognize when change is *not* needed. But, once the manager recognizes that something is malfunctioning he must then diagnose the problem and identify relevant alternative techniques. The selected technique must be appropriate to the problem, as constrained by limiting conditions. One example of a limiting condition which we have discussed in an earlier chapter is the prevailing character of group norms. The informal groups may support some change

Figure 17–1
A Model for the Management of Organization Development

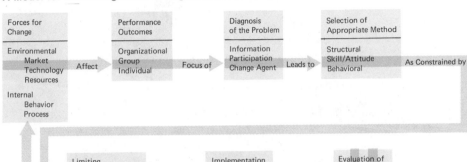

techniques but may sabotage others. Other limiting conditions include leadership behavior, legal requirements, and economic conditions.

Finally, the manager must implement the change and monitor the change process and change results. The model includes feedback to the implementation step and to the forces for change step. These feedback loops suggest that the change process itself must be monitored and evaluated. The mode of implementation may be faulty and lead to poor results, but responsive action could correct the situation. Moreover, the feedback loop to the initial step recognizes that *no* change is final. A new situation is created within which problems and issues will emerge; a new setting is created which will itself become subject to change. The model suggests no "final solution," rather it emphasizes that the modern manager operates in a dynamic setting wherein the only certainty is change itself.

The process by which the solution to one problem creates new problems is widely recognized. Blau and Scott refer to it as the "dialectic processes of change"[11] and they illustrate the dilemma through a number of examples. They observe that assembly line techniques increase production but, at the same time, employee absenteeism and turnover increase. Assembly line work is often monotonous and routine; it alienates workers and creates discontent; morale declines and personnel problems emerge. A whole new set of problems is created by the solution itself. This phenomenon must be taken into account as a manager considers changes.

---

[11] Peter M. Blau and W. Richard Scott, *Formal Organizations* (San Francisco: Chandler Publishing Co., 1962), pp. 250–53.

FORCES FOR CHANGE

The forces for change can be classified conveniently into two groups. They are: (1) environmental forces and (2) internal forces. Environmental forces are beyond the control of the manager. Internal forces operate inside the firm and are generally within the control of management.

Environmental Forces

The manager of a business firm has historically been concerned with reacting to changes in the *marketplace*. Competitors introduce new products, increase their advertising, reduce their prices, or increase their customer service. In each case, a response is required unless the manager is content to permit the erosion of profit and market share. At the same time changes occur in customer tastes and incomes. The firm's products may no longer have customer appeal; customers may be able to purchase more expensive, higher quality forms of the same product.

The enterprise system generally eliminates from the economic scene those firms which do not adjust to market conditions. The isolated-from-reality manager who ignores the signals from the market will soon confront the more vocal (and louder) signals of discontented stockholders. But, by that time, the appropriate change may well be dissolution of the firm—the final solution.

A second source of market forces are those which supply the firm with its resources. A change in the quality and quantity of human resources can dictate changes in the firm. For example, the adoption of automated processes can be stimulated by a decline in the supply of labor. The techniques of coal mining and tobacco farming have greatly changed during recent years due to labor shortages. We can also understand how changes in the materials supply can cause the firm to substitute one material for another. Rayon stockings and synthetic rubber tires are direct outgrowths of war-induced shortages in raw materials. We need not catalog the whole range of possible changes in the resource markets which stimulate organizational change. The potential is great, however, and must be recognized.

The second source of environmental change forces is *technology*. The knowledge explosion since World War II has introduced new technology for nearly every business function. Computers have made possible high-speed data processing and the solution to complex production problems. New machines and new processes have revolutionized the way many products are manufactured and distributed. Computer technology and automation have affected not only the technical conditions of work, but the social conditions as well. New occupations have been created and others have been eliminated. The slowness to adopt new technology which reduces costs and improves quality will show itself in the financial statements sooner or later. Technological advance is a permanent fixture in the business world and, as a force for change, it will continue to demand attention.[12]

---

[12] Thomas J. Watson, Jr., "Technological Change," in Arthur O. Lewis, Jr., ed., *Of Men and Machines* (New York: E. P. Dutton & Co., 1963), pp. 295–309.

Finally the third environmental force is *social and political* change. Business managers must be "tuned in" to the great movements over which they have no control but which, in time, influence their firm's fate. Sophisticated mass communications and international markets create great potential for business, but also pose great threat to those managers unable to understand what is going on. Concurrently, the drive for social equality poses new issues for managers which had not been previously confronted. Finally, to add to the scene, the relationship between government and business becomes much closer as new regulations are imposed. These pressures for change reflect the increasing complexity and interdependence of modern living. The traditional functions of organizations are being questioned and new objectives are being advanced. No doubt, the events of the future will intensify external environmental forces for change.

Internal Forces

The forces for change which occur within the organization can be traced to *process* and to *behavioral* causes. Process forces include breakdowns in decision making and communications. Decisions are either not being made, are made too late, or are of poor quality. Communications are short-circuited, redundant, or simply inadequate. Tasks are not undertaken or not completed because the person responsible did not "get the word." A customer order is not filled, a grievance is not processed, or an invoice is not filed and the supplier is not paid because of inadequate or nonexistent communications. Interpersonal and interdepartmental conflicts reflect breakdowns in organizational processes.

Low levels of morale and high levels of absenteeism and turnover are symptoms of behavioral problems that must be diagnosed. A wildcat strike or a walkout may be the most tangible sign of a problem, yet such tactics are usually employed because they arouse the management to action. In most organizations a certain level of employee discontent exists and a great danger is to ignore their complaints and suggestions. But the process of change includes the *recognition* phase and it is at this point that management must decide to act or not to act.

No doubt in many organizations, the need for change goes unrecognized until some major catastrophe occurs. The employees strike or seek the recognition of a union before the management finally recognizes the need for action. Whether it takes a whisper or a shout, by some means the need for change must be recognized; and once recognized, the exact nature of the problem must be diagnosed.

DIAGNOSIS OF A PROBLEM

Appropriate action is necessarily preceded by diagnosis of the symptoms of the problem. Experience and judgment are critical to this phase unless the problem is readily apparent to all observers. Ordinarily, however, managers can disagree on the nature of the problem. There is no formula for accurate diagnosis, but the following three questions point the manager in the right direction:

1. What is the problem as distinct from the symptoms of the problem?
2. What must be changed to resolve the problem?
3. What outcomes (objectives) are expected from the change and how will such objectives be measured?

The answers to these questions can come from information ordinarily found in the organization's information system. Or it may be necessary to generate ad hoc information through the creation of committees or task forces. Meetings between managers and employees provide a variety of points of view which can be sifted through by a smaller group. Technical operational problems may be easily diagnosed, but more subtle behavioral problems usually entail extensive analysis. One approach for diagnosing the problem is the attitude survey.

Attitude surveys can be administered to the entire work force or to a representative sample. The survey permits the respondents to evaluate and rate—management, pay and pay-related items, working conditions, equipment, and other job-related factors. The appropriate use of such surveys requires that the questionnaire be completed anonymously so that employees can express their views freely and without threat, whether real or imagined. The objective of the survey is to pinpoint the problem or problems as perceived by the members of the organization. Subsequent discussions of the survey results, at all levels of the organization, can add additional insights into the nature of the problem.

The survey is a useful diagnostic approach if the potential focus of change is the total organization. If smaller units or entities are the focus, the survey technique may not be a reliable source of information. For example, if the focus is a relatively small work group, diagnosis of the problem is better accomplished through individual interviews followed by group discussion of the interview data. In this approach the group becomes actively involved in sharing and interpreting perception of problems.

Problem identification of individual employees comes about through interviews and personnel department information. Consistently low performance evaluations are indicators that problems exist, but it is often necessary to go into greater detail. Identification of individuals' problems is far more difficult than identification of organizational problems. Thus the diagnostic process must stress the use of precise and reliable information.

Managers must make two key decisions prior to undertaking the diagnostic phase. They must determine the degree to which subordinates will participate in the process and they must decide whether a change agent will be used. These two decisions have implications not only for the diagnostic process but also for the eventual success of the entire program.

The Degree of Subordinate Participation

The degree to which subordinates participate in decisions which affect their activities has been the subject of much practical and theoretical discussion. Fayol, for example, spoke of the principle of centralization in terms of the extent to which subordinates contribute to decision making. The researchers at the Hawthorne plant discovered the positive impact of supervisory styles which permit employees some say in the way they do their work. In fact, the Hawthorne studies produced the first scientific evidence of the relationship between employee participation and production Other studies followed, including the influential Coch and French[13] and Lewin[14] research which provided evidence that participation by subordinates could lead to higher levels of production, satisfaction, and efficiency.

Despite the considerable research, many unanswered questions remain regarding the relationships between subordinate participation, production, and acceptance of change. Moreover, whether actual participation or perceived participation is the more important factor bearing on organizational effectiveness, is not completely settled. It may be that all subordinates do not aspire to participate, but do desire the *opportunity* to do so when the occasion arises.[15] Nevertheless, the tendency in much of the current literature on development methods and strategies is to take the position that active participation is a cardinal requirement for successful OD programs. This position is much more a matter of espousing a set of values than a matter of scientific evidence.

Changing Values.   The values which are held by those who espouse participative management are an expanded version of McGregor's Theory Y assumptions. As observed by two influential writers whose ideas are reflected in Table 17–1, these values are in transition and though not completely accepted in managerial practice, they are being adopted by ever-increasing numbers of managers. These values reflect the growing importance of the humanistic point of view. One can see that if the new set of values is adopted, that is, if one accepts the idea that subordinates are basically good with untapped abilities which can be used in active problem solving for the organization's benefit, important implications follow. For example, subordinates will be actively involved in the development program from its very inception. Not only will they participate in the identification of jobs to be enlarged, but they will also participate in determining whether, for example, job enrichment is the proper method to use.

The *degree* to which subordinates are actively involved in the development program can be constrained by situational factors. But the strategic decision regarding subordinate participation is not simply an either-or decision. A continuum more aptly describes the decision, as shown in Figure 17–2. The figure identifies two extreme positions (unilateral and delegated) and a middle-of-the-road approach (shared) to change.[16]

[13] Lester Coch and John R. P. French, Jr., "Overcoming Resistance to Change," *Human Relations* (August 1948), pp. 512–32.

[14] Kurt Lewin, "Frontiers in Group Dynamics," *Human Relations* (June 1947), pp. 5–41.

[15] See T. O. Jacobs, *Leadership and Exchange in Formal Organizations* (Alexandria, Va.: Human Resources Research Organization, 1971), pp. 204–9, for a review of research bearing on this issue.

[16] Larry E. Greiner, "Patterns of Organization Change," *Harvard Business Review* (May–June 1967), pp. 119–30.

Table 17-1
The Transition of Values Underlying OD Strategy

Away from:	*Toward:*
1. A view of man as essentially bad.	1. A view of man as basically good.
2. Avoidance or negative evaluation of individuals.	2. Confirming them as human beings.
3. A view of individuals as fixed.	3. Seeing them as being in process.
4. Resisting and fearing individual differences.	4. Accepting and utilizing them.
5. Utilizing an individual primarily with reference to his job description.	5. Viewing him as a whole person.
6. Walling off the expression of feelings.	6. Making possible both appropriate expression and effective use.
7. Maskmanship and game-playing.	7. Authentic behavior.
8. Use of status for maintaining power and personal prestige.	8. Use of status for organizationally relevant purposes.
9. Distrusting people.	9. Trusting them.
10. Avoiding facing others with relevant data.	10. Making appropriate confrontation.
11. Avoidance of risk taking.	11. Willingness to risk.
12. A view of process work as being unproductive effort.	12. Seeing it as essential to effective task accomplishment.
13. A primary emphasis on competition.	13. Much greater emphasis on collaboration.

Source: Robert Tannenbaum and Sheldon A. Davis, "Values, Man, and Organizations," *Industrial Management Review* (Winter 1969), pp. 67–86.

Unilateral Approach. At one extreme, subordinates make no contribution to the development, or change, program. The definition and solution to the problem are proposed by management. The use of unilateral authority can appear in three forms:

1. *By Decree.* This is simply a situation in which the superior dictates a program. There is little upward communication and subordinates are expected to accept the program without asking questions. This form assumes that subordinates will accept the program because it is being stated by authority figure that they deal with—the "boss."

2. *By Replacement.* This form involves the replacement of personnel and it is based upon the premise that key personnel are the crucial factors in developing the organization. The replacement decision is a top-down decision since top-level executives develop the plan for replacing personnel.

Figure 17-2
Strategies for Introducing Major and/or Minor Changes

Unilateral	Shared	Delegated
(emphasis on management reaching decisions)	(emphasis on interaction and sharing of authority between manager and subordinates)	(emphasis on subordinates reaching decisions)

3. *By Structure.* This form attempts to alter the organizational structure by administrative fiat. An example is when a manager's span of control is increased or decreased.

Delegated Approach.   At the other extreme from the unilateral approach is the delegated approach. In this approach the subordinates actively participate in the development program, in one of two forms.[17]

1. *The Discussion Group.*   Managers and their subordinates meet, discuss the problem, and identify the appropriate development method. The managers refrain from imposing their own solution upon the group. The assumption of this approach is that two-way discussion and problem solving among subordinates and managers results in more motivated groups.
2. *The T-Group.*   The emphasis of the T-group is on increasing an individual's self-awareness. The T-group is less structured than the discussion approach, but in this context the T-group is designed to initiate the development program and it is not the central focus. For example, the T-group could identify MBO as the development method to be implemented.

The delegated approach focuses on having the subordinates interact with the superior and eventually work out a development approach. It is a major step, if used correctly, in creating a climate of full subordinate participation.

Shared Approach.   This approach is built upon the assumption that authority is present in the organization and must be exercised after, and only after, giving careful consideration to such matters as the magnitude of the development effort, the people involved, and the time available for introducing the method. This approach also focuses upon the sharing of authority to make decisions. This approach is employed in two slightly different formats:

1. *Group Decision Making.*   The problem is defined by management and communicated to the subordinates. The subordinates are then free to develop alternative solutions and to select what they believe is the best method to be implemented. It is assumed that the subordinates will feel a greater commitment to the solution because they participated in selecting a course of action.
2. *Group Problem Solving.*   This form stresses both the definition of the problem and the selection of a possible solution. Here authority is shared throughout the process from problem identification to problem solution. It is assumed that the group, because it is involved in the entire decision process, will have increased insight into understanding the development program that is finally implemented.

A report which surveyed published cases of organizational change notes that the shared approach was relatively more successful than the unilateral or delegated approaches.[18] The two extreme positions result in less than full utilization of the human resources of the organization: The unilateral ap-

---

[17] Ibid., pp. 121–22.
[18] Ibid., pp. 119–30.

proach ignores the contribution of employees, and the delegated approach ignores the contribution of managers; the shared approach represents a "balance between maximized feelings of independence and the need for enforcing policy and authority."[19]

The Shared Approach: Some Preconditions.   Before the shared strategy can be successful, certain preconditions with respect to employees must exist. They are:

1. An intuitively obvious factor is that employees must want to become involved. They may for any number of reasons reject the invitation. They may have other needs, such as getting on with their own work, for example. Or they may view the invitation to participate as a subtle (but not too subtle) attempt by managers to manipulate them toward an already predetermined solution. If the organizational climate includes perceptions of mistrust and insincerity, any attempt to involve workers will be viewed by them in cynical terms.

2. The employees must be willing and able to voice their ideas. Even if they are willing and able, they must have some expertise in some aspect of the analysis. Certainly the technical problems associated with computer installation or automated processes are beyond the training of typical employees, yet they may have valuable insights into the impact of the machinery on their jobs. But even if they have knowledge, they must be able to articulate their ideas.

3. Managers must feel secure in positions. If insecure, then they will perceive any participation by employees as a threat to their authority. They may view employee participation as a sign of weakness or as undermining their status. They must be able to give credit to good ideas and to give explanations for ideas of questionable merit. As is evident, managers' personalities and leadership styles must be compatible with the shared authority approach if it is to be a successful strategy.

4. Finally, managers must be open-minded to employees' suggestions. If they have predetermined the solution, the participation by employees will soon be recognized for what it is. Certainly managers have final responsibility for the outcome, but they can control the situation by specifying beforehand the latitude of the employees. They may define objectives, establish constraints, or whatever, so long as the participants know what is expected of them.[20]

Successful organizational development strategies emphasize sharing authority among managers and employees. The shared approach involves the personnel in a process which not only minimizes resistance to change, but which also maximizes acceptance through the application of basic learning principles.

---

[19] Paul C. Agnew and Francis L. K. Hsu, "Introducing Change in a Mental Hospital," *Human Organization* (Winter 1960), p. 198.

[20] Arnold S. Judson, *A Manager's Guide to Making Changes* (New York: John Wiley & Sons, 1966), pp. 109–13.

The Role of Change Agents

Because there is a tendency to seek answers in traditional solutions, the intervention of an outsider is usually necessary. The intervener, or change agent, brings a different perspective to the situation and serves as a challenge to the status quo.

The success of any change program rests heavily on the quality and workability of the relationship between the change agent and the key decision makers within the organization. Thus, the form of intervention is a crucial phase.

To intervene is to enter into an ongoing organization, or among persons, or between departments for the purpose of helping them improve their effectiveness.[21] There are a number of forms of intervention that are used in organizations. First, there is the *external* change agent who is asked to intervene and provide recommendations for bringing about change. Second, there is the *internal* change agent. This is the individual who is working for the organization and knows something about its problems. Finally, a number of organizations have used a combination *external-internal* change team to intervene and develop programs. This approach attempts to use the resources and knowledge base of the external and internal change agents.

Each of the three forms of intervention has advantages and disadvantages. The external change agent is often viewed as an outsider. This belief when held by employees inside the company results in the need to establish rapport between the change agent and decision makers. The change agent's views on the problems faced by the organization are often different from the decision maker's views and this leads to problems in establishing rapport. The differences in viewpoints often result in the mistrust of the outsider (external change agent) by the policy makers or a segment of the policy makers.

The internal change agent is often viewed as being more closely associated with one unit or group of individuals than any other. This perceived favoritism leads to resistance to change on the part of others not included in the circle of close friends. The internal interventionist, however, is familiar with the organization and its personnel and this knowledge can be valuable in preparing for and implementing change.

The third type of intervention, the combination external-internal team, is the rarest but seems to have an excellent chance for success. In this type of intervention the outsider's objectivity and professional knowledge are blended with the insider's knowledge of the organization and its human resources. This blending of knowledge often results in increased trust and confidence among the parties involved. The ability to communicate and develop a more positive rapport is communicated throughout the organization and can reduce the resistance to any change which is forthcoming.

---

[21] See Chris Argyris, *Intervention Theory and Method* (Reading, Mass.: Addison-Wesley Publishing Co., 1970); and Fritz Steele, *Consulting for Organizational Change* (Amherst: University of Massachusetts Press, 1975).

The change agent, whether internal or external to the organization can relate to the organization according to one or more models.[22]

The Medical Model. Perhaps the most basic of all models, the medical model places the change agent in the role of advisor. The organization requests the change agent to assist in clarifying the problems, diagnosing the causes, and recommending courses of action. The organization retains the responsibility for accepting or rejecting the change-agents' recommendations. The relationship is analogous to the physican-consultant arrangement; that is, the physician may seek opinions from other experts, but the choice of therapy remains with the physician.

The Doctor-Patient Model. The application of this model places the organization in the position of a "patient" who suspects that something is wrong. The change agent—the "doctor"—diagnoses and prescribes a solution which, of course, can be rejected by the patient. Yet by virtue of the relationship, the organization will usually adopt the change-agent's recommendations. The change agent engages in diagnostic and problem-identification activities jointly with the organization. To the extent that the organization is totally involved in the process, the more likely will management accept the recommended solution.

The Engineering Model. This model is used when the organization has performed the diagnostic work and has decided upon a specific solution. For example, management desires to implement a MBO or job enrichment program and it seeks the services of experts to aid in the implementation. An alternative form of the model is when the organization has defined the problem-excessive turnover, inter-group competition, or ineffective leadership behavior, for example—and requests the change agent to specify a solution. The general characteristic of the model, however, is that the diagnostic phase is undertaken by management.

The Process Model. The process model is widely used by OD consultants. It involves the action *collaboration* of the change agent and the organization through which the management is encouraged to see and understand organizational problems. Through joint efforts managers and change agents try to comprehend the factors in the situation which must be changed to improve performance. The change agent avoids taking sole responsibility for either diagnosis or prescription; rather, the emphasis is placed upon enabling management to comprehend the problems. The change-agents' emphasis is teaching management *how* to diagnose, rather than doing it for management.

The choice of appropriate model depends upon characteristics of the change agent, the organization, and the situation. It is not a matter of one model being superior in all instances, rather for any given circumstance an appropriate model exists.

Change agents facilitate the diagnostic phase by gathering, interpreting,

---

[22] Based upon Newton Margulies and Anthony P. Raia, *Conceptual Foundations of Organizational Development*, pp. 108–14.

and presenting data. Although the accuracy of data is extremely important, of equal importance is the way in which the data are interpreted and presented. There are generally two ways in which this is accomplished. First, the data are discussed with a group of top managers, who are asked to make their own diagnosis of the information; or, second, change agents may present their own diagnoses without making explicit their frameworks for analyzing the data. A problem with the first approach is that top management tends to see each problem separately. Each manager views his or her problem(s) as being the most important and fails to recognize other problem areas. The second approach has inherent problems of communication. External change agents often have difficulty in the second approach because they become immersed in theory and various conceptual frameworks which are less realistic than the managers would like.[23]

A more general difficulty with either of these approaches derives from the close relationship between diagnosis and action.[24] One important guideline for managers of OD programs is that the method should not be separated from the diagnosis. In many OD programs the emphasis appears to be on the implementation of a particular method with little concern for whether it is appropriate. For example, Blake and Mouton concentrate on implementing the managerial grid across different companies,[25] and Seashore and Bowers designed an action program for the Banner organization based on participative management prior to the diagnosis of specific problem areas.[26] Instead of a "canned" approach in which the diagnosis and method are the same for different companies, a more "tailored" approach to change is needed. That is, interventions which fit the particular problems of an organization are needed. This belief is supported by Mann when he states, "Change processes organized around objective new social facts about one's own organizational situation have more force for change than those organized around general principles about human behavior."[27]

ALTERNATIVE DEVELOPMENT TECHNIQUES

The choice of the particular technique depends upon the nature of the problem which management has diagnosed. Management must determine which alternative is most likely to produce the desired outcome, whether it be improvement in the skills, attitudes, behavior, or structure. As we have noted, diagnosis of the problem includes specification of the outcome which

---

[23] Stanley Seashore and David Bowers, *Changing the Structure* and *Functioning of an Organization: Report of a Field Experiment* (Ann Arbor: Survey Research Center, University of Michigan, 1963).

[24] Jay W. Lorsch and Paul Lawrence, "The Diagnosis of Organizational Problems," in Margulies and Raia, eds., *Organizational Development,* p. 219.

[25] Robert R. Blake and Jane S. Mouton, *The Managerial Grid* (Houston, Texas Gulf Publishing Co., 1964).

[26] Seashore and Bowers, *Changing the Structure and Functioning of an Organization.*

[27] Floyd Mann, "Studying and Creating Change," in W. Bennis, K. Benne, and R. Chin, eds., *The Planning of Change* (New York: Holt, Rinehart, and Winston, 1961), pp. 605–13.

management desires from the change. In the following chapter we will describe a number of change methods, some of which have been discussed in previous chapters. They will be classified according to whether the major focus of the technique is to change skills and attitudes, behavior, or structure. This classification of approaches to organizational change in no way implies a distinct division among the types. On the contrary, the interrelationships among knowledge, skills, attitudes, behavior, and structure must be acknowledged and anticipated.

An important contribution of behavioral research is the documentation of the impact of structure on attitudes and behavior. Over-specialization and narrow spans of control can lead to low levels of morale and low production.[28] At the same time, the technology of production, distribution, and information processing can affect the structural characteristics of the firm,[29] as well as attitudes and sentiments.[30] The fact that these interrelationships are so pronounced might suggest a weakness in our classification scheme; but, in defense of it, the techniques can be distinguished on the basis of their major thrust or focus—whether skills, attitudes, behavior, or structural.

RECOGNITION OF LIMITING CONDITIONS

The selection of any developmental technique should be based upon diagnosis of the problem, but the choice is tempered by certain conditions that exist at the time. Scholars identify three sources of influence on the outcome of management development programs which can be generalized to cover the entire range of organizational development efforts, whether attitudinal, behavioral, or structural. They are leadership climate, formal organization, and organizational culture.

Leadership climate refers to the nature of the work environment which results from "the leadership style and administrative practices" of superiors. Any OD program which does not have the support and commitment of management has a slim chance of success. At least managers must be neutral toward the change. We can also understand that the style of leadership may itself be the subject of change; for example, the managerial grid and System 4 are direct attempts to move managers toward a certain style— open, supportive, and group-centered. But, it must be recognized that the participants may be unable to adopt such styles if they are not compatible with their own superior's style.

The formal organization must also be compatible with the proposed change. The formal organization includes the effects on the environment resulting from the philosophy and policies of top management, as well as "legal

---

[28] Rensis Likert, *The Human Organization* (New York: McGraw-Hill Book Co., 1967).

[29] Joan Woodward, *Industrial Organization* (New York: Oxford University Press, 1967); and Frank J. Jasinski, "Adapting Organization to New Technology," *Harvard Business Review,* vol. 37 (January–February 1959), pp. 79–86.

[30] Harriet O. Ronken and Paul R. Lawrence, *Administering Changes: A Case Study of Human Relations in a Factory* (Boston: Division of Research, Harvard Business School, 1952).

precedent, organizational structure, and the systems of control." Of course, each of these sources of impact may itself be the focus of a change effort; the important point is that a change in one must be compatible with all others. For example, a change in structure which will eliminate employees contradicts a policy of guaranteed employment.

The organizational culture refers to the impact on the environment resulting from "group norms, values, and informal activities." The impact of traditional behavior which is sanctioned by group norms, but not formally acknowledged, was first documented in the Hawthorne studies. A proposed change in work methods or the installation of an automated device can run counter to the expectations and attitudes of the work group and, if such is the case, the OD strategy must anticipate the resulting resistance.

The implementation of OD, which does not consider the constraints imposed by prevailing conditions within the present organization, may of course amplify the problem that initiated the process. Even if implemented, the groundwork for subsequent problems is made more fertile than what could ordinarily be expected. Taken together, these conditions constitute the climate for change and they can be positive or negative.

IMPLEMENTING THE METHOD

The implementation of the OD method has two dimensions—*timing* and *scope.* Timing refers to the selection of the appropriate point in time to initiate the method and scope refers to the selection of the appropriate scale. The matter of timing is strategic and depends upon a number of factors, particularly the organization's operating cycle and the groundwork which has preceded the program. Certainly if a program is of considerable magnitude, it is desirable that it not compete with day-to-day operations, thus, the change might well be implemented during a slack period. On the other hand, if the program is critical to the survival of the organization, then immediate implementation is in order. The scope of the program depends upon the strategy. The program may be implemented throughout the organization; overnight it becomes a *fait accompli.* Or, it may be phased into the organization level by level, department by department. The shared strategy makes use of a phased approach, which limits the scope but provides feedback for each subsequent implementation.

The method which is finally selected is not implemented on a grand scale; rather it is implemented on a small scale in various units throughout the organization. For example, an MBO program can be implemented in one unit or at one level at a time. The objective is to experiment with the method, that is, to test the validity of the diagnosed solution. As the management learns from each successive implementation, the total program is strengthened. Not even the most detailed planning can anticipate all the consequences of implementing a particular method. Thus it is necessary to experiment and to search for new information that can bear on the program.

As the experimental attempts provide positive signals that the program is proceeding as planned, there is a reinforcement effect. The personnel will be encouraged to accept the change required of them and to enlarge the scope of their own efforts. The acceptance of the change is facilitated by the positive results.

EVALUATING THE PROGRAM

An OD program represents an expenditure of organizational resources in exchange for some desired end result. The resources take the form of money and time which have alternative uses. The end result is in the form of increased organizational effectiveness—production, efficiency, and satisfaction in the short run; adaptiveness and development in the intermediate run; survival in the long run. Accordingly, some provision must be made to evaluate the program in terms of expenditures and results. The evaluation phase has two problems to overcome: the acquisition of data which measure the desired objectives, and the determination of the expected trend of improvement over time.

The acquisition of information which measures the sought-after objective is the relatively easier problem to solve, although it certainly does not lend itself to naive solutions. As we have come to understand, the stimulus for change is the deterioration of performance criteria which management traces to structural and behavioral causes. The criteria may be any number of effectiveness indicators, including profit, sales volume, absenteeism, turnover, scrappage, or costs. The major source of feedback for those variables is the organization's information system. But if the change includes the expectation that employee satisfaction must be improved, the usual sources of information are limited, if not invalid. It is quite possible for a change to induce increased production at the expense of declining employee satisfaction. Thus, if the manager relies on the naive assumption that production and satisfaction are directly related, the change may be incorrectly judged successful when cost and profit improve.

To avoid the danger of overreliance on production data, the manager can generate ad hoc information which measures employee satisfaction. The benchmark for evaluation would be available if an attitude survey had been used in the diagnosis phase, as was the case in the MBO program of the state department of health. The definition of acceptable improvement is difficult when evaluating attitudinal data, since the matter of "how much more" positive the attitude of employees should be is quite different than the matter of "how much more" productive they should be. Nevertheless, if a complete analysis of results is to be undertaken, attitudinal measurements must be combined with production and other effectiveness measurements.

The second evaluation problem is the determination of the trend of improvement over time. The trend itself has three dimensions: (1) the first indication of improvement, (2) the magnitude of improvement, and (3) the duration of the improvement. In Figure 17–3 three different patterns of change for a particular effectiveness criterion are illustrated.

Figure 17–3
Three Patterns of Change in Results through Time

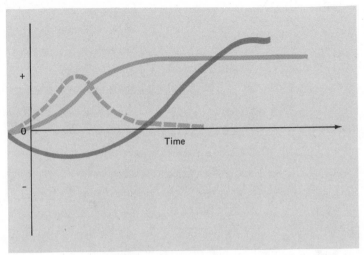

In the change illustrated by the lighter solid line, improvement is slight during the early periods of time, but rises and maintains itself at a positive level. The dashed line illustrates a marked increase, but followed by deterioration and a return to the original position. The darker solid line describes a situation in which the early signs indicate a decrease, but followed by a sharp rise toward substantial improvement. The patterns demonstrate only three of a number of possible relationships. A well-devised OD program would include an analysis of what pattern can be expected. The actual pattern can then be compared to the expected.

Ideally, the pattern would consist of an index which measures both the attitudinal and performance variables. Figure 17–4 illustrates a model which describes the necessary information for such an index. The solid line is the expected pattern through time. It shows a movement into acceptable behavior prior to a movement into acceptable performance. The expected pattern may, of course, assume any configuration. The dashed line is the plot of actual change through time. It reflects not only what is happening, but also the impact of corrective action which management takes to keep the change on course. If the expected pattern is valid as originally conceived, then management's objective is to minimize the oscillations around the planned results.

In a practical sense, the effectiveness of an OD program cannot be evaluated if objectives have not been established before it was implemented. A program which was undertaken to make the organization "a better place to work," or to develop the "full potential of the employees," cannot be evaluated. If on the other hand measurable criteria which are valid indicators of "better places to work" and "full potential" are collected during the diagnostic phase and subsequently tracked as the program is undertaken, bases

Figure 17–4
Expected and Actual Pattern of Results

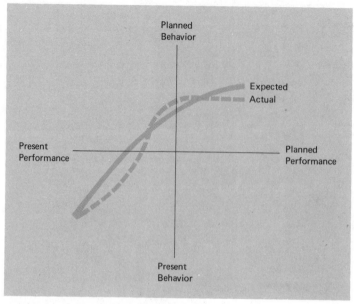

Source: Jeremiah J. O'Connell, *Managing Organizational Innovation* (Homewood, Ill.: Richard D. Irwin, Inc., 1968), p. 156.

for evaluation exist. A considerable body of literature exists which describes methods of evaluation, and managers of OD programs should consult it for guidance in program evaluation.[31]

Generally, an evaluation model would follow the steps of evaluative research. The steps include:

1. Determining program objectives.
2. Describing the activities undertaken to achieve the objectives.
3. Measuring effects of the program.
4. Establishing baseline points against which changes can be compared.
5. Controlling extraneous factors, preferably through the use of a control group.
6. Detecting unanticipated consequences.

The application of this model will not always be possible. For example, managers do not always specify objectives in precise terms and control groups are difficult to establish in some instances. Nevertheless, the difficulties of evaluation should not discourage attempts to evaluate.[32]

---

[31] Achilles A. Armenakis, Hubert S. Feild, and Don C. Mosely, "Evaluation Guidelines for the OD Practitioner," *Personnel Journal* (Spring 1975), pp. 39–44; and William M. Evan, ed., *Organizational Experiments* (New York: Harper & Row, Publishers, 1971).

[32] Henry W. Reicken, "Memorandum on Program Evaluation," in Wendell L. French, Cecil H. Bell, Jr., and Robert A. Zawacki, eds., *Organization Development* (Dallas: Business Publications, Inc., 1978), pp. 416–20.

This chapter has discussed the steps in the organizational development model. The reader should recognize that each step is important not only in its own right, but also as it affects each subsequent step. For example, an incorrect diagnosis of the problem could result in the selection of an inappropriate technique. Actual experience documents the fact that no amount of organizational restructuring will resolve problems which are rooted in attitude and skill deficiencies. Similarly, the development of attitudes and behaviors cannot have long-lasting effects if the structure of tasks and authority relationships are hostile to the newly learned attitudes and behaviors.

There are no guarantees that correct managerial decisions are forthcoming from the use of any model. Much is left to managerial judgment. Nevertheless, the model presented in this chapter does introduce the appropriate questions and issues.

MAJOR ISSUES FOR THE MANAGER TO CONSIDER

A. The necessity to consider organizational development arises from changes in the inter- and extra-organizational environment. Changes in input, output, technological, and scientific subenvironments may indicate the need to consider the feasibility of a long-term, systematically managed program for changing the structure, process, and behavior of the organization. Even in the absence of environmental changes, organizational processes and behavior may become dysfunctional for achieving organizational effectiveness.

B. The diagnosis of present and potential problems involves the collection of information which reflects the level of organizational effectiveness. Data which measure the current states of production, efficiency, satisfaction, adaptiveness, and development must be gathered and analyzed. The purpose of diagnosis is to trace the causes of the problem to one or more formal and informal components.

C. In addition to serving as the bases for problem identification, the diagnostic data also establish the basis for subsequent evaluation of the organizational development effort.

D. The problem must be diagnosed and managers can undertake the analysis by considering three questions:

1. What is the problem as distinct from its symptoms?
2. What must be changed to resolve the problem?
3. What outcomes are expected and how will these outcomes be measured?

The managerial response to these questions should be stated in terms of criteria which reflect organizational effectiveness. Measurable outcomes such as production, efficiency, satisfaction, adaptiveness, and development must be linked to skill, attitudinal, behavioral, and structural changes which are necessitated by the problem identification.

E. Managers must evaluate the impact of limiting conditions. For example, if the organizational climate is conducive to the shared strategy, the employees would have been brought into the diagnostic process and participated with management from that point on. Through shared authority, the problem would be associated with skill, attitude, behavioral, and structural causes and the appropriate method selected. If employee participation is inappropriate because the necessary preconditions do not exist, management must unilaterally define the problem and select the appropriate method. Whether the problem is related to skill, attitude, behavioral, or structural causes, the strategy must include provision for the learning principles of feedback, reinforcement, and transfer. Without these principles none of the development methods whether sensitivity training, managerial grid, management by objectives, job enrichment, or System 4 organization has a maximum chance of success.

F. The logical last step of the OD process is the decision to provide for an evaluation procedure. The ideal situation would be to structure the procedure in the manner of an experimental design. That is, the end results should be operationally defined and measurements should be taken, before and after, in both the organization undergoing development and in a second organization (the "control group"). Or, if the scope of the program is limited to a subunit, a second subunit could serve as a control group. The purpose of an evaluation is not only necessitated by management's responsibility to account for its use of resources, but also to provide feedback. Corrections can be taken in the implementation phase based upon this feedback.

DISCUSSION AND REVIEW QUESTIONS

1. Is it correct to argue that if either Maslow's or Herzberg's theory of motivation is valid then management should expect employees to have a need to participate in decision making? Explain your answer.

2. Is it correct to argue that if employees desire to participate they should be permitted to do so? Explain your answer.

3. Critique your instructor's teaching approach in terms of his or her utilization of learning principles.

4. Under what circumstances would the unilateral strategy be appropriate for implementing an OD method? Use the concept of organizational climate in your answer.

5. Assume that you are responsible for implementing a MBO system in an organization and that a unilateral strategy has been used. What problems of employee commitment can you anticipate, and how would you overcome these problems?

6. "The benefits derived from traditional training programs are so intangible that it makes little sense to measure them." Comment on this statement made by the training officer of a large corporation.

7. Identify the learning principles that are implemented in the shared strategy.

8. What OD strategy would likely be used in an organization that tends toward a bureaucracy? Explain your answer in terms of alternative strategies that are available.

9. Explain the difficulties you would encounter in attempting to obtain diagnostic information from the members of two groups who believe that they compete for scarce resources.

10. Describe the factors which would sustain the process model of change-agent behavior.

ADDITIONAL REFERENCES

Armenakis, A. A., and Feild, H. S. "Evaluation of Organizational Change Using Non-Independent Criterion Measures." *Personnel Psychology* (1975), pp. 39–44.

Bennis, W. G. *Changing Organizations.* New York: McGraw-Hill, 1966.

Burke, W., ed. *Contemporary Organizational Development.* Washington, D.C.: NTL Institute for Applied Behavioral Science, 1972.

Friedlander, F., and Brown, L. "Organizational Development." *Annual Review of Psychology* (1974), pp. 219–341.

Greiner, L. E. "Evolution and Revolution as Organizations Grow." *Harvard Business Review* (1972), pp. 37–46.

Halal, W. "Organizational Development in the Future." *California Management Review* (1974), pp. 35–41.

Havelock, R. G., and Havelock, M. G. *Training for Change Agents.* Ann Arbor, Mich.: Center for Research on Utilization of Scientific Knowledge, 1973.

Herman, S. M., and Korenich, M. *Authentic Management: A Gestalt Orientation to Organizations and Their Management.* Reading, Mass.: Addison-Wesley Publishing Co., 1977.

House, R. J. *Management Development: Design, Evaluation, and Implementation.* Ann Arbor: University of Michigan, 1967.

Kilmann, R. H., and Herden, R. P. "Toward a Systemic Methodology for Evaluating the Impact of OD Interventions on Organization Effectiveness." *Academy of Management Review* (1976), pp. 87–98.

King, A. S. "Expectation Effects in Organizational Change." *Administrative Science Quarterly* (1974), pp. 221–30.

Lippitt, G. L. *Organization Renewal.* New York: Appleton-Century-Crofts, 1969.

Lippitt, R.; Watson, J.; and Westely, B. *The Dynamics of Planned Change.* New York: Harcourt, Brace & World, 1958.

Miles, R. E., and Ritchie, J. B. "Participative Management: Quality vs. Quantity." *California Management Review* (1971), pp. 48–56.

O'Connell, J. J. *Managing Organizational Innovation.* Homewood, Ill.: Richard D. Irwin, Inc., 1968.

Partain, J., ed. *Current Perspectives on Organizational Development.* Reading, Mass.: Addison-Wesley, 1973.

Patten, T. H., and Dorey, L. E. "Long-Range Results of a Team Building OD Effort." *Public Personnel Journal* (1977) pp. 31–50.

Schein, V. E. "Political Strategies for Implementing Change." *Group and Organizational Studies* (1977), pp. 42–48.

Sirota, D., and Wolfson, A. D. "Pragmatic Approach to People Problems." *Harvard Business Review* (1973), pp. 120–28.

Sofer, C. *The Organization from Within.* London: Quadrangle Books, 1962.

Tichy, N. M. "How Different Types of Change Agents Diagnose Organizations." *Human Relations* (1975), pp. 771–79.

Varney, G. *An Organization Development Approach to Management Development.* Reading, Mass.: Addison-Wesley Publishing Co., 1976.

CASE FOR ANALYSIS

EVALUATION OF AN MBO PROGRAM

The attitude survey data which the State Health Department collected as a part of its OD program served as a basis for evaluating the program. The program was based upon the MBO method and it was designed to develop the managerial capabilities of program directors, among other objectives. The initial diagnosis had indicated that program directors were by and large not involved in decision making because division directors, their immediate supervisors, preferred the directive style of management. One of the consequences of this style was the relatively short supply of program directors who were promotable to more responsible positions.

The OD program was designed to develop, through training and experience, the division directors' ability to work with their program directors in less directive, more participative ways. It was also anticipated that program directors would need training in how to accept and implement the increased authority. The external change agent also believed, and the top management agreed with him, that the program must build in the opportunities for division and program directors to meet and make decisions.

Accordingly, the program provided for the division directors and the commissioner's office to meet as a group on a regular basis. During these meetings they studied the literature on participative management and MBO. Equally important, they also learned the commissioner's philosophy and attitudes toward management. Training materials containing journal articles and case studies were provided and discussed during the sessions. And to focus the discussion of the group on real, rather than hypothetical problems, the attitude survey data were analyzed and evaluated by the division directors.

During this period division directors were expected to train the program directors of their respective divisions. They were to meet the first or second day after each of their sessions with their program directors and discuss, interpret, and elaborate the materials which they themselves had been studying. In this manner the division directors not only assumed the roles of coaches, but the program directors were also made aware of the commissioner's intent to develop a climate which encouraged and supported participative management and increased delegation of authority.

The training period preceded by six months the development of goal statements for each division. These statements would serve as the bases for allocating the department's budget among the divisions. It was expected that the division directors would develop these statements jointly with program directors and that this experience would reinforce the learning presumed to have occurred during the training sessions.

Two months after the completion of the training sessions and funding decisions, a second attitude survey was undertaken. The questionnaire was completed by all employees. The respondents remained anonymous except for the designation of certain demographic and job information, including level in the managerial hierarchy. Thus it was possible to combine the responses of program and division directors to obtain group means. The change agent presented the data from the second attitude survey to the division directors. He noted one result that he believed they should discuss and analyze. That result seemed to indicate that one of the objectives of the program had not been attained, that being the intended downward delegation of authority to program directors.

A number of questions on the questionnaire measured the perceived amount of authority. Generally, the program directors indicated that their authority had declined since the first attitude survey. One particularly interesting question to which all the directors responded on both occasions was stated as follows:

How much "say" do you think each of the following people usually has in deciding work objectives of the departmental program? *Circle one in each line across.*

	Usually Has a Great Deal of Say	Quite a Bit of Say	Some Say	Just a Little Say	Usually Has no Say at All
Program directors	1	2	3	4	5
Division heads	1	2	3	4	5
The commissioner's office	1	2	3	4	5

Exhibits 1 and 2 present the group means to this question for the division directors (solid line) and program directors (dashed line). Plainly the program directors' perceptions of what had happened during the prevous year were

Exhibit 1
**Group Means for Response of Division and Program Directors,
1971, prior to OD Program**

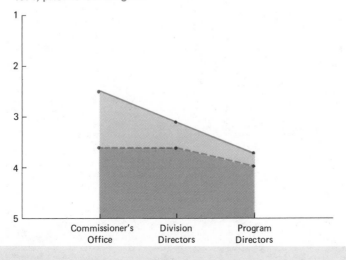

Exhibit 2
Group Means for Responses of Division and Program Directors,
1972, after OD Program

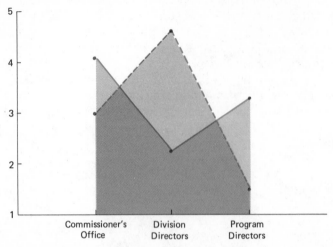

contrary to what was supposed to happen. They believed, as indicated by
their responses, that not only did they have less say in their programs, but
that division directors had considerably more than before. And the division
directors reported that they had considerably less and that program directors
had more "say" in deciding work objectives.

The division directors were confused by the questionnaire results. How
could it be, they asked the change agent, that despite our efforts they believe
that we have more and they have less authority? Are the data reliable? Is
there any other evidence to indicate that the program has backfired, at least
as it was to affect program directors? What do we do now? Scrap it and
start all over?

Questions for Consideration

1. What would be your answers to the division directors if you were the change
   agent?
2. What other kinds and sources of information would be useful in determining
   the validity of the attitude survey data?
3. How likely is it that efforts which managers undertake to delegate authority will
   be perceived by subordinates as efforts to centralize authority?

Methods and Applications of Organizational Development

AN ORGANIZATIONAL ISSUE FOR DEBATE

Sensitivity Training as an Effective OD Technique

ARGUMENT FOR*

Sensitivity training is a learning experience which emphasizes human relations skills. "The training is designed to help good managers become better managers." The proponents of sensitivity training believe that the inability to deal with others—subordinates, superiors, peers, and clients—is a major cause of organizational problems. The learning that occurs in sensitivity training sessions provides managers with greater awareness of their own values, motives, and assumptions.

The evidence for the effectiveness of sensitivity training is testimonial in nature. That is, participants state that they have learned to cope with frustrations, anxieties, and stress in their jobs as a consequence of their training. As one participant stated: "Through becoming more aware of others' problems, I found that my problems were not unique. As a result, I achieved more inner peace and ability to face some of the problems of our team."

Wives of executives often participate with their husbands. As one executive's wife stated: "I gained a deeper understanding of the tremendous stress and strain my husband is constantly under. I had not understood his problems before and tended to blame him for poor communication. Now we both realize our joint responsibility for communication, and more importantly, how we can go about it." This wife's reaction to the training is shared by many others who have gone through it.

_____
* Based upon Leland P. Bradford, "How Sensitivity Training Works" in Alfred J. Marrow, *The Failure of Success* (New York: AMACOM, 1972) pp. 241–56.

ARGUMENT AGAINST†

The arguments which support those who believe that the claims of sensitivity training are overstated rest upon research findings. The research efforts attempt to evaluate the impact of sensitivity training on participants. The conclusion of the research is that there is little evidence to indicate changes in participants' "standings on objective measures of attitudes, values, outlooks, interpersonal perceptions, self-awareness, or interpersonal sensitivity." Thus even though participants often report that they believe that these changes have occurred as a consequence of sensitivity training, there are no objective facts to support their beliefs.

Another claim of sensitivity training is that participants are better able to analyze problems, synthesize information, face and resolve interpersonal conflict, and implement solutions. At present no research evidence exists to support these claims, largely because researchers have spent their efforts to evaluate the human relations effects of sensitivity training. Thus even though much personal testimonial evidence supports sensitivity training, empirical research data support the counter argument.

_____
† Based upon Marvin D. Dunnette and John P. Campbell, "Laboratory Education: Impact on People and Organizations" in Walter Nord, ed., *Concepts and Controversy* in *Organizational Behavior* (Pacific Palisades, Calif.: Goodyear Publishing Company Inc., 1972), pp. 455–82.

INTRODUCTION

The management of organizational development requires the designation of an end result, the selection of a method to achieve that end result, and the implementation of the method. The desired end result can be stated in terms of improved production, efficiency, satisfaction, adaptiveness, and development, separately or in some combination. Furthermore, a variety of methods are available to assist the manager in achieving the end results. These range from changing structure to changing behavior. This chapter continues the discussion by elaborating upon the issues and problems associated *with alternative development methods.*

DEPTH OF INTENDED CHANGE

The diagnostic process is critical to the eventual success of the OD program, yet there are no easily mastered approaches which guarantee accurate diagnosis. Managers can, however, undertake diagnosis in a systematic manner by recognizing that the problem may be rooted in either the formal or informal components of the organization. In Figure 18–1 the organization is depicted as an iceberg. The formal components of an organization are analogous to that part of an iceberg which is above water; the informal components lie "below water." As indicated in Figure 18–1, the formal components are observable, rational, and oriented to structural factors. The informal components are, on the other hand, not observable to all people, affective, and oriented to process and behavioral factors.

The problems of the organization as indicated by ineffective levels of production, efficiency, satisfaction, adaptiveness, and development can be traced to one or more formal and informal components. And even though the diagnostic information may indicate that the source of the problem is a formal component, the manager must recognize the potential impact of a change in an informal component if the formal component is changed.

Generally speaking, the greater the scope and magnitude of the problem, the more likely it is that the problem will be found in the informal components. At the same time, the greater the problem, the greater the magnitude and extent of intended change. That is, as the "target" of the OD program lies deeper in the "organizational iceberg," the more fundamental is the intended change. At one extreme are problems which lie with the *structure* of the organization. Job definitions, departmentalization bases, spans of control, and delegated authority can be manipulated. At the other extreme are problems which lie with the *behavior* of groups and individuals. These problems are related to personal views, value orientations, feelings, and sentiments as well as activities, sentiments, and roles within and among groups. And while these behaviors can certainly be affected by changes in structure, they are ordinarily deep-seated and must be directly confronted.

Figure 18–1
The Organizational Iceberg

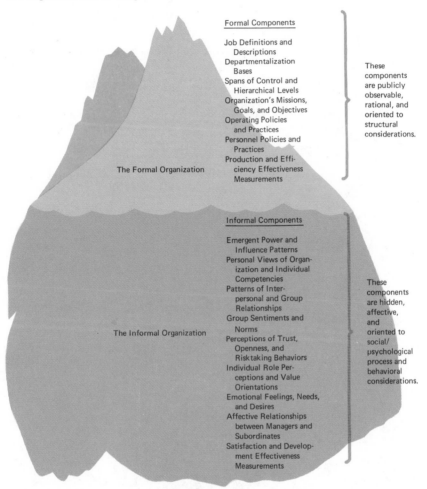

Formal Components

Job Definitions and
    Descriptions
Departmentalization
    Bases
Spans of Control and
    Hierarchical Levels
Organization's Missions,
    Goals, and Objectives
Operating Policies
    and Practices
Personnel Policies and
    Practices
Production and Effi-
    ciency Effectiveness
    Measurements

These components are publicly observable, rational, and oriented to structural considerations.

The Formal Organization

Informal Components

Emergent Power and
    Influence Patterns
Personal Views of Organ-
    ization and Individual
    Competencies
Patterns of Inter-
    personal and Group
    Relationships
Group Sentiments and
    Norms
Perceptions of Trust,
    Openness, and
    Risktaking Behaviors
Individual Role Per-
    ceptions and Value
    Orientations
Emotional Feelings, Needs,
    and Desires
Affective Relationships
    between Managers and
    Subordinates
Satisfaction and Develop-
    ment Effectiveness
    Measurements

These components are hidden, affective, and oriented to social/psychological process and behavioral considerations.

The Informal Organization

Source: Adapted from Richard J. Selfridge and Stanley L. Sokolik, "A Comprehensive View of Organizational Development," *M.S.U. Business Topics* (Winter 1975), p. 47.

The relationship between source of problem and degree of intended change is illustrated in Figure 18–2; it suggests that there are 10 levels, or targets, of an OD program.[1] As we noted above, as the target moves from left to right and, consequently, deeper into the organization the OD program can be expected to be more person- and group-centered. It will rely more

[1] The relationship between depth of organization and intended change is more popularly termed "depth of intervention." We have chosen to term it "degree of intended change" to highlight the issues associated with change, rather than those related to intervention. See Roger Harrison, "Choosing the Depth of Organizational Intervention," *Journal of Applied Behavioral Science* (April–May 1970), pp. 181–202, for an original discussion of the concept.

Figure 18–2
Model of Organizational Development Targets

STRUCTURAL TARGETS					BEHAVIORAL TARGETS				
Level I	*Level II*	*Level III*	*Level IV*	*Level V*	*Level VI*	*Level VII*	*Level VIII*	*Level IX*	*Level X*
Organizational Structure	Operating Policies and Practices	Personnel Policies and Practices	Job Performance Appraisal and Improvement	Management Attitudes and Skills	Non-management Attitudes and Skills	Intergroup Behavior	Intragroup Behavior	Individual Behavior	Individual-Group Behavior

Depth of intended change

LOW ←——————————————————→ HIGH

Adapted from Richard J. Selfridge and Stanley L. Sokolik, "A Comprehensive View of Organizational Development," *MSU Business Topics* (Winter 1975), p. 49.

upon socio-psychological and less upon technical-economic knowledge. Levels I through IV involve the formal structure, policies, and practices of the organization; levels V and VI involve skills and attitudes of managerial and nonmanagerial personnel; and levels VII through X involve the behavior of groups and individuals. For each of these levels, one or more OD *methods* exist as possible solutions. Only after the problem and its level are diagnosed should the method be selected. The remainder of this chapter will review a sample of the growing number of OD methods.

STRUCTURAL DEVELOPMENT METHODS

Structural development in the context of organizational change refers to managerial action which attempts to improve effectiveness through a change in the formal structure of task and authority relationships. At the same time we must recognize that the structure creates human and social relationships which over time can become ends for the members of the organization. These relationships, once defined and made legitimate by management, introduce an element of stability.[2] Members of the organization may resist efforts to disrupt these relationships.

Structural changes affect some aspect of the formal task and authority definitions. As we have seen, the design of an organization involves the definition and specification of job range and depth, the grouping of jobs in departments, the determination of the size of groups reporting to a single manager, and the delegation of authority. Within this framework, the communication and decision-making processes occur. Three methods designed to change all or some aspect of the organization structure are discussed in this section. They are management by objectives (MBO), flexitime and System 4. These methods are appropriate for consideration when the problem is diagnosed as being in levels I through IV.

Management by Objectives

Management by objectives (MBO) has been widely discussed during the last two decades. One of the early proponents of MBO, Peter Drucker, proposed a process which would allow managers to participate in the establishment of goals and objectives for their units. The process can also include the participation of nonmanagers in the determination of their specific objectives. According to Drucker the only conditions which must be satisfied are that the objectives must be defined in terms of their contribution to the total organization and that the person who establishes them must have sufficient control to accomplish them.

---

[2] R. K. Ready, *The Administrator's Job* (New York: McGraw-Hill Book Co., 1967), pp. 24–30.

The original work of Drucker and subsequent writings by others[3] provide the basis for three guidelines for implementing MBO:

1. Superiors and subordinates meet and discuss objectives which if met would contribute to overall goals.
2. Superiors and subordinates jointly establish attainable objectives for the subordinates.
3. Superiors and subordinates meet at a predetermined later date to evaluate the subordinates' progress toward the objectives.

The exact procedures employed in implementing MBO vary from organization to organization and from unit to unit. However, the basic elements of objective setting, participation of subordinates in objective setting, and feedback and evaluation are usually parts of any MBO program. The intended consequences of MBO include improved contribution to the organization, improved attitudes and satisfaction of participants, and greater role clarity. MBO is highly developed and widely used in business organizations, but its applicability in health-care and governmental organizations has not been completely tested. In this section we will describe an OD project which was undertaken in a state department of health and which resulted in the implementation of an MBO system.

The project began with the administration of an attitude questionnaire to all employees in the department. The purpose of the attitude survey was twofold: To provide information for pinpointing attitudinal problems and to provide base-line measurements for follow-up studies. The same attitude questionnaire was administered to the state department of mental health employees, the "control group." The two departments are quite similar in mission and employee characteristics such as age, educational level, and length of service. Subsequent comparisons of the attitude data would indicate problems as they arose in the department as related to the OD program.

The attitude data became the focus of discussion in training sessions attended by the division directors and the commissioner of health. The discussions focused on the problems identified in the attitude survey. It was found, for example, that there was considerable ambiguity in the minds of employees about the goals and means for achieving goals. This finding substantiated the judgment of management that MBO should be implemented in the health department.

The group identified their own training needs as the discussions continued through the months and the trainer, a university professor, supplied the appropriate literature and materials. The division directors read the technical litera-

---

[3] Peter Drucker, *The Practice of Management* (New York: Harper and Brothers, 1954); George Odiorne, *Management by Objectives* (New York: Pitman Publishing Co., 1965); and W. J. Reddin, *Effective Management by Objectives* (New York: McGraw-Hill Book Co., 1970). For two recent reviews, see Henry Tosi, "Effective and Ineffective MBO," *Management by Objectives*. vol. 4, no. 3 (1975), pp. 7–14 and John M. Ivancevich, James H. Donnelly, Jr., and James L. Gibson, "Evaluating MBO: The Challenge Ahead," *Management by Objectives,* vol. 4, no. 3 (1975), pp. 15–23. For specific discussions and case studies of applications of MBO in health-care and governmental organizations, see *First Tango in Boston: A Seminar on Organizational Change and Development* (Washington, D.C.: National Training and Development Services, 1973); and "Management by Objectives in the Federal Government," *The Bureaucrat* (Winter 1974).

ture on MBO and participative management. They also held periodic informal discussions with the program directors of their own divisions. In this manner the entire management cadre was involved in the OD program.

Subsequent to the training sessions the division directors, in consultation with their own subordinates, prepared goal statements which became the basis for subsequent discussions with the commissioner and his staff. The goal statements listed in order of priority the major objectives of each division. The number of objectives depended upon the scope of each division's activities and ranged from 5 to 15. In addition, the resource requirement for each objective was estimated and indicated in the statements. The outcome of the discussion between each division director and the commissioner was mutually agreed-upon sets of objectives and resource allocations.

The management group met periodically to discuss the problems that they had experienced in the first phase of the MBO cycle. Among the problems it identified was the difficulty of obtaining accounting data pertaining to their objectives. The typical governmental accounting procedures as used in the health department emphasized the determination of program cost and included allocations of administrative cost on rather arbitrary bases. These cost data were not compatible with or pertinent to divisional goals. A second problem was more fundamental to the MBO method and not so easily resolved as the accounting problem: the identification of effectiveness criteria for divisional objectives. The discussions indicated that the management group tended to overemphasize production criteria at the expense of efficiency and satisfaction criteria. Some attention was given to development and adaptiveness criteria, but it was relatively little. These issues were confronted and the discussion shifted to the matter of reporting progress at the six-month review date.

The six-month review discussions between the commissioner and each of the division directors indicated the necessity for revisions in light of revised priorities and planning premises. The revised objectives prevailed during the next six months and the cycle began anew.

The program undertaken in the health department reflected the main features of OD as we have defined it here:

1. The program was long-term and systematically planned.
2. The managerial personnel at all levels confronted organizational problems as revealed by diagnostic data.
3. The training sessions were designed to facilitate the discussion of mutual problems with technical literature serving as a source of help in the resolution of these problems.
4. The MBO method was integrated into the organization only after careful experimentation and consideration.

System 4 Organization

According to Likert an organization can be described in terms of eight operating characteristics. They are: (1) leadership, (2) motivation, (3) communication, (4) interaction, (5) decision making, (6) goal setting, (7) control, and (8) performance. Furthermore, the nature of each of these characteristics can be located on a continuum through the use of a questionnaire which members of the firm (usually managers) complete. The means of each response category are calculated and plotted to produce an organizational profile as shown in Figure 18–3.

To diagnose the extent to which a particular organization approximates the System 4 structure, Likert has devised a measurement device. The instrument is a 51-item questionnaire which is completed by the employees of an organization. The employees indicate their perceptions of the extent to which the processes which define the System 4 organization are present in their own organization. The means of the responses are calculated and plotted along the continua which describe the eight processes. Figure 18–3 illustrates the profiles of two manufacturing firms.

The profiles illustrate the differences which can occur in organizational processes. In Likert's terms, the organization described by the lighter line clearly tends toward the classical design, whereas the organization defined by the darker line tends toward a System 4 organization. If the theory of System 4 is valid, we should expect the organization on the right to be more effective than the one to the left. Furthermore, both organizations could be improved by a developmental plan that would move each organization closer to the right, or closer to System 4. This result would be predicted on the basis of the universalistic nature of System 4 theory, which is to say that the theory predicts that System 4 is the most effective organization design.

The change toward System 4 involves measuring the present state of the firm through the use of the questionnaire. Subsequent training programs emphasize the concepts of System 4 and the application of the concepts to the present organization. Through the use of supportive, group-oriented leadership and the equalization of authority to set goals, implement control, and make decisions, higher earnings and efficiency should ordinarily result (according to Likert).[4] These results derive from positive changes in employee attitudes which are induced by the structural changes.[5] As the point has been made by others, "To obtain lasting change, one does not try to change people, but rather to change the organizational constraints that operate upon them."[6]

Various OD programs utilizing System 4 concepts have been reported in the literature.[7] Here we will describe a program which combined manage-

[4] Rensis Likert, *The Human Organization* (New York: McGraw-Hill Book Co., 1967).

[5] Ibid., p. 47.

[6] Eliot D. Chapple and Leonard R. Sayles, *The Measure of Management* (New York: Macmillan, 1961), p. 202.

[7] An important illustration is reported in Alfred J. Marrow, David G. Bowers, and Stanley E. Seashore, *Management by Participation* (New York: Harper & Row, 1967). This report documents the effort of the Harwood company management to transform the Weldon company, which it purchased in 1961, into a System 4 organization. A follow-up study of the Harwood experience is reported in Stanley E. Seashore and David G. Bowers, "Durability of Organizational Change," *American Psychologist,* vol. 25 (March 1970), pp. 227–33. Also see W. F. Dowling, "At General Motors: System 4 Builds Performance and Profits," *Organizational Dynamics* (Winter 1975) pp. 23–38.

Figure 18–3
Organizational Profiles for Two Manufacturing Firms

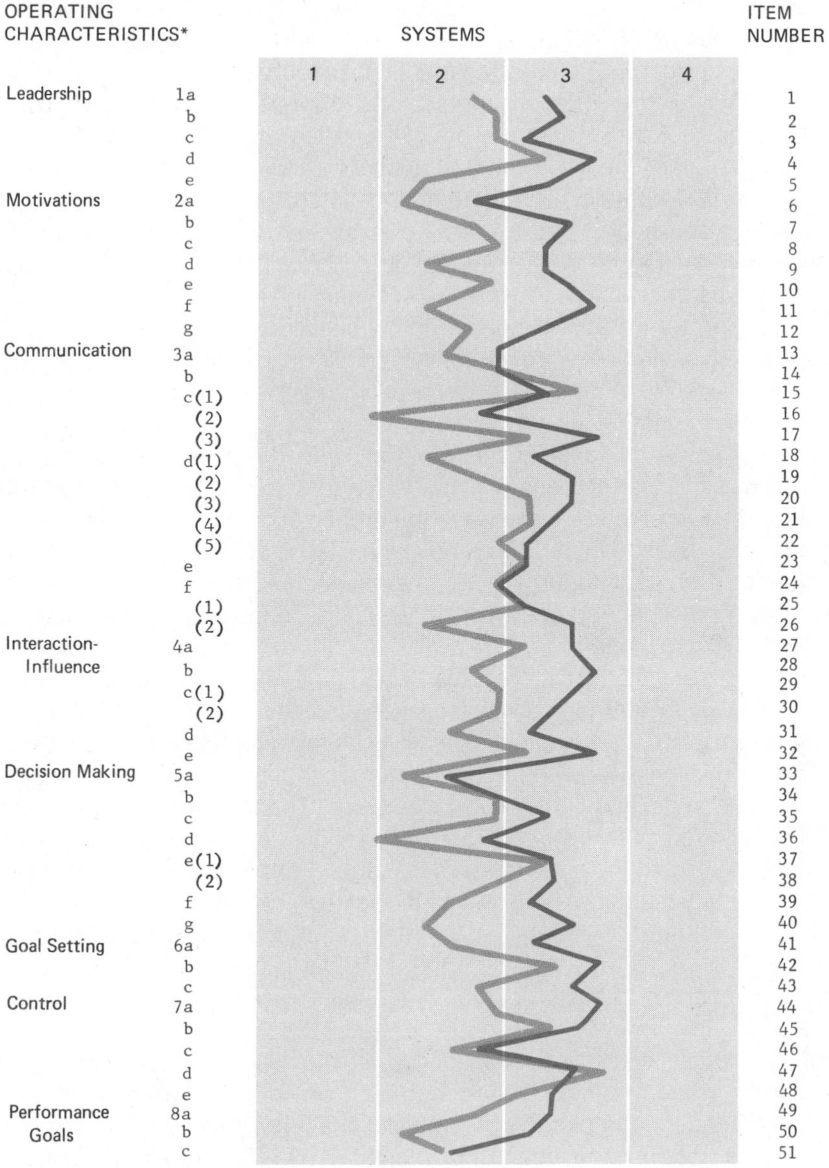

OPERATING
CHARACTERISTICS*

SYSTEMS

ITEM
NUMBER

OPERATING CHARACTERISTICS*		SYSTEMS				ITEM NUMBER
		1	2	3	4	
Leadership	1a					1
	b					2
	c					3
	d					4
	e					5
Motivations	2a					6
	b					7
	c					8
	d					9
	e					10
	f					11
	g					12
Communication	3a					13
	b					14
	c(1)					15
	(2)					16
	(3)					17
	d(1)					18
	(2)					19
	(3)					20
	(4)					21
	(5)					22
	e					23
	f					24
	(1)					25
	(2)					26
Interaction- Influence	4a					27
	b					28
	c(1)					29
	(2)					30
	d					31
	e					32
Decision Making	5a					33
	b					34
	c					35
	d					36
	e(1)					37
	(2)					38
	f					39
	g					40
Goal Setting	6a					41
	b					42
	c					43
Control	7a					44
	b					45
	c					46
	d					47
	e					48
Performance Goals	8a					49
	b					50
	c					51

* Each of the eight characteristics is measured by a number of items. Leadership, for example, is measured by five questionnaire items (1a–e).

ment training (Level V) and structural change (Level I). Essentially, the program was designed to develop attitudes and behaviors which would be compatible with a System 4 organization.[8]

The target of the development effort was the sales unit of a business firm, specifically 16 sales managers. The group consisted of a national sales manager, 2 divisional managers, and 13 regional managers. The short-run goals of the program were (1) to integrate the 16 managers into an effective team following the appointment of a new national sales manager, a divisional manager, and three regional managers, (2) to facilitate the development and acceptance of new roles for the regional managers who, with the introduction of a new product line, would have to spend 90 percent of their time in managerial work, rather than the present 40 percent, and (3) to confront and resolve certain communication and interpersonal problems which remained as a result of the personnel changes. The main difficulty was the regional managers' perception that the new national head was so aggressive that he would dominate the divisional managers.

The long-run goals of the program were (1) to make more congruent actual and preferred behaviors (the managers feared that mistrust and secrecy would be required to succeed in the organization, but they preferred trusting and open relationships), (2) to move the organization more toward the System 4 end of the continuum, and (3) to experiment with a "bottom-up" approach to OD (the usual approach is "topdown," as in the case of the health department OD program).

To get at these objectives, the sales managers engaged in training during which they experimented with the kinds of behaviors appropriate for a System 4 organization. Learning exercises which emphasized interpersonal and intergroup relations were an important part since these are the key relationships involved in building integrated work teams. The training sessions culminated in a confrontation between regional and divisional managers and between the division and the national sales manager. These confrontations encouraged the managers to share and to test the value of openness and problem solving in the organization. However, the real test of openness and problem solving would come in the context of the everyday work of the organization; that is, whether the behavior learned in the training sessions could be transferred back to the workplace.

To obtain some indication of the lasting effects of the training session and to gauge progress toward the development of a System 4 organization, the managers completed the organizational profile questionnaire prior to the training session and again four months later. There was no control group available. Obviously the absence of a control group limits the analysis and the results must be validated by other means such as observation of actual workplace behavior. Given these limitations, the differences between the before and after measures indicated that movement had been made toward

---

[8] This OD program is reported in Robert T. Golembiewski and Stokes B. Carrigan, "Planned Change in Organization Style Based on the Laboratory Approach," *Administrative Science Quarterly* (March 1970), pp. 79–93.

the System 4 organization and that this movement had been facilitated by the training methodology. Thus the behavior learned in the training sessions appears to have been made a part of the organization structure.

Flexible Working Hours

Structural techniques vary widely in the scope of change produced. One technique which is relatively narrow but which may have far-reaching implications is flexible working hours. This technique provides employees the opportunity to select (within limits) the hours each day during which they work. For example, they are permitted to report to work from 7:00 to 9:00 A.M. and leave anytime between 4:00 and 6:00 P.M. Employees may choose the number of hours per day they will work, but must work a specified number during a specified period, such as a week or month. In a very real sense the technique is a form of participative management and includes aspects of job enrichment.

The essential feature of flexible working hours is that it results in a major change in employees' job range. They, rather than management, decide when they will come to work; their control over their own work and leisure time is increased significantly. The technique directly applies the assumption that self-control is a more effective motivator of high performance than external, i.e., managerial, control.[9]

Flexible working hours, or flexitime, are relatively widespread. A recent survey indicated that 12.8 percent of all nongovernment organizations with two or more employees used flexitime and that 5.8 percent of all employees were on flexitime. The effects of flexitime are generally favorable; it raises morale and satisfaction, reduces tardiness, absenteeism, and turnover, and increases productivity.[10] At the same time, the job of management is made more difficult because of the necessity to schedule work coverage. Generally, the results of flexitime programs have met the expectations of management.

The success of flexible working hours can be accounted for by various motivational theories. Maslow and Herzberg's theories both explain the manner in which autonomy leads to satisfaction. Thus the technique can be viewed as one of a family of techniques designed to change job content. Job enrichment and job enlargement are designed to accomplish aims similar to those of flexible working hours. In some instances job enrichment may involve too great a cost to appeal to management. In such instances flexible working hours may be an appropriate alternative.

SKILL AND ATTITUDE DEVELOPMENT METHODS

The development of skills and attitudes requires training programs of a periodic or continuing nature. These programs are designed to improve partic-

---

[9] Alvar O. Elbing, Herman Gadon, and John R. M. Gordon, "Flexible Working Hours: The Missing Link," *California Management Review* (Spring 1975) pp. 50–57.

[10] Stanley D. Nollen and Virginia H. Martin, *Alternative Work Schedules: Flexitime* (New York: AMACOM, 1978.)

ipants' knowledge, skills, and attitudes toward their jobs and the organization. The training may be part of a larger effort such as MBO, job enrichment, or System 4 programs, or it may be directed toward the development of specific objectives. In the usual case, managerial training is directed toward the development of communication and decision-making skills, thus developing the organization's fundamental processes.

Because of the multiplicity of training programs we will only describe some of the more representative and widely publicized types in this section. Some of the advantages and disadvantages associated with each program will be described. The attainment of desired objectives such as knowledge acquisition or improvement in job performance will also be examined.

On-the-Job Training

A popular philosophy over the years has been to train employees on the job. It is assumed that if training occurs off the job there will be a loss in performance when trainees are transferred back to the job. It is also proposed that from an economic standpoint the on-the-job training is best since employees are producing while they undergo training. There are, however, a number of shortcomings in on-the-job training. First, employees may be placed in a stress-laden situation even before learning the job. This may result in accidents or poor initial attitudes about the job. Second, the area in which a person is being trained is often congested. Finally, if a number of trainees are learning in various job locations, the trainer must move around constantly to monitor their performance.

Job-Instruction Training. Formulated during World War II by the War Manpower Board, this program provides a set of guidelines for undertaking on-the-job training for white- and blue-collar employees. After trainees are introduced to the job, they receive a step-by-step review and demonstration of the job functions. When trainees are sufficiently confident that they understand the job they demonstrate their ability to perform the job. This demonstration continues until the trainees reach a satisfactory level of performance.[11]

The objective of this approach is to bring about a positive change in performance which is reflected in higher production, lower scrap costs, and so on. This type of training is best suited for jobs that have specific content. Variations of this program are used in universities in preparing doctoral candidates for teaching and research careers and in hospitals in preparing nurses for new job duties. A crucial point to recognize is that the trainer must have the technical skill to perform the job which the trainee is performing. Note also that the trainer must understand the importance of repetition, active participation, and immediate constructive feedback.

Junior Executive Boards. This technique, popularized by the McCormick Company, concentrates on providing junior-level (middle- and lower-

---

[11] Bernard M. Bass and James A. Vaughn, *Training in Industry: The Management of Learning* (Belmont, Calif.: Wadsworth Publishing Co., 1966), p. 89.

level managers) with top-level management problem-solving experience. The junior executive may serve on a committee or junior board that is considering some major decision concerning investments or personnel planning. The assumption in this type of training is that the trainee will acquire an appreciation for decisions being made "upstairs" and this can be translated into a better overall view of the organization's direction and difficulties. In addition, the ability of the junior executive to contribute to problem solving can be assessed. In effect management is teaching the trainee and determining the trainee's ability to cope with major problems. The value of such a program depends upon the trainee's readiness to cope with these problems and the feedback received about performance.

Off-the-Job Training

Traditionally organizations have found that it is necessary to provide training that supplements on-the-job efforts. Some of the advantages of off-the-job training were determined in a survey of 147 executives whose firms had used university executive training programs.[12] Some of the advantages cited were:

1. It lets executives get away from the pressures of the job and work in a climate in which "party-line" thinking is discouraged and self-analysis is stimulated.
2. It presents a challenge to executives that, in general, enhances their motivation to develop themselves.
3. It provides resource people and resource material—faculty members, fellow executives, and literature—that contribute suggestions and ideas for the executives to "try on for size" as they attempt to change, develop, and grow.

The theme of the advantages cited above is that trainees by being away from job pressures are more stimulated to learn. This is certainly debatable since it is questionable whether much of what is learned can be transferred back to the job. Attending a case problem-solving program in San Diego is quite different from facing irate customers in Detroit. Despite the difficulty of transferring knowledge from the classroom-type environment to the office, plant, or hospital, these programs are still very popular and widely utilized.

The Lecture Method. This is probably the most widely used method of training because it is a relatively inexpensive way to distribute information to a large audience. The effectiveness of the lecture method is best achieved in programs in which knowledge acquisition by participants is the objective.[13] Thus, if changing attitudes is the primary objective of a training program, it

---

[12] Winston Oberg, "Top Management Assesses University Executive Programs," *Business Topics* (Spring 1963), pp. 7–27.

[13] C. Verner and G. Dickinson, "The Lecture, an Analysis and Review of Research," *Adult Education* (Winter 1967), pp. 85–100.

would seem that the lecture method could not accomplish this objective by itself.

A main attraction of the lecture method is its simplicity and the control it is supposed to give to the trainer. The lecture can be prepared weeks or months ahead of time and the material can be used again. Despite the advantage of preparing the lecture before presentation, the procedure doesn't insure that learning will occur. A critical point often forgotten is that the audience must be motivated to learn. In training programs that participants are required to attend, their presence doesn't insure motivation. The best developed and planned lecture may not achieve any impact if the participants are not ready to learn.

The Discussion or Conference Approach.   This method provides the participants with opportunities to exchange ideas and recollections of experience. Through the interaction in the sessions the participants stimulate each other's thinking, broaden their outlook, and also improve their communicative abilities.[14]

The role of participants is relatively passive in the lecture method, while in the discussion group trainees have many opportunities to participate. The trainer serves as a resource person and provides immediate feedback. Because of the active interaction between trainer and participants the trainer must be highly skilled. If interpersonal skills are to be improved and/or knowledge acquired, the trainer must understand the importance of reinforcing positive behavior and feeding back clearly the contribution of each participant to the group discussion.

The Case Study and Role-Playing Method.   This method provides trainees with a description of some events that actually occurred in an organization. The case may describe the manner in which a nursing supervisor is trying to motivate subordinates or the type of wage and salary program implemented in a retail store. Trainees read the case, identify the problems, and reach solutions.

In role playing, trainees are asked to participate actively in the case study. That is, they act out a case as if it were a play. One participant may be the nurse supervisor and three other participants may play the roles of subordinates. The rationale is that by role playing the participants can actually "feel" what the cases are all about.

A survey study of 117 training directors in the largest United States corporations provides some insight into what these practitioners believe can be accomplished by lecture, case, and role playing.[15] Questions concerning the effectiveness of nine training methods (case, conference, lecture, games, films, programmed instruction, role playing, sensitivity training, and television) were asked the directors. Table 18–1 shows how they ranked the lecture,

---

[14] Cf. Dale Yoder, *Personnel Management and Industrial Relations* (Englewood Cliffs, N.J.: Prentice-Hall, 1962).

[15] Stephen J. Carroll, Frank T. Paine, and John M. Ivancevich, "The Relative Effectiveness of Alternative Training Methods for Various Training Objectives," *Personnel Psychology* (Fall 1972), pp. 495–509.

Table 18–1
Rank Order of Three Training Methods in Accomplishing Training Objectives

Method	Objectives			
	Knowledge Acquisition	Changing Attitudes	Improving Problem-Solving Skills	Improving Interpersonal Skills
Lecture	9	8	9	8
Case	2	4	1	4
Role playing	7	2	3	2

case, and role-playing methods on accomplishing four objectives. The table indicates that in the four training objective areas the lecture method is considered a weak technique. This low rating is reflected by the fact that most training efforts use lectures as a supplement to other methods and not as the primary vehicle for creating the desired changes. The training directors believe that role playing can be effective in changing attitudes. Role playing seems especially effective if the subjects participating in the role playing are asked to take the point of view opposite to their own.

The case method was rated highest in effectiveness for improving problem-solving skills. However, only a number of research studies exist to substantiate this belief. Fox found that about one third of the students exposed to case study improved significantly in their ability to handle case problems, about a third showed moderate improvement, and a third made no improvement.[16]

The training directors' opinions and limited research seem to indicate that the case method is best suited for improving problem-solving skills, while the role-playing method is somewhat effective in improving interpersonal skills. It would seem that determining what each of the training methods can best accomplish is of primary importance to managers. Developing a role-playing training program to improve the knowledge of participants does not seem appropriate in light of the research on the subject and the opinions of expert practitioners.

BEHAVIORAL DEVELOPMENT METHODS

Levels VII through X require methods which delve deeply into group and individual behavior processes. Intergroup, intragroup, individual-group, and individual behavior are often confounded by emotional and perceptual processes which interfere with effective organizational functioning. These development targets have received the greatest amount of attention from OD experts and, consequently, a considerable number of methods have been devised for attacking them. Instead of cataloging these methods, only four will be discussed in detail—the managerial grid, sensitivity training, team

---

[16] W. M. Fox, "A Measure of the Effectiveness of the Case Method in Teaching Human Relations," *Personnel Administration* (July–August 1963), pp. 53–57.

building, and career planning. They are the more readily used methods since they tend to span at least two and potentially three levels of targets.

The Managerial Grid

The managerial grid program is based upon a conceptualization of a particular style of leadership behavior.[17] The two dimensions which the developers of the program, Blake and Mouton, identify are concern for production and concern for people. A balanced concern for production and people is the most effective leadership style according to Blake and Mouton and is termed 9,9. The program requires not only the development of this style, *but also the development of group behavior which supports and sustains it.* The entire program consists of six sequential phases which are undertaken over a three- to five-year period.

The six phases can be separated into two major segments.[18] The first two phases provide the foundation for the latter four phases. The latter four phases build on the beginning foundation.

1. Laboratory-Seminar Training. This is typically a one-week conference designed to introduce the manager to the grid philosophy and objectives. From 12 to 48 managers are assigned as members of problem-solving groups. These seminars are conducted by line managers of the company who have already been through this initial grid training phase.

The seminar begins by determining and reviewing each participant's style of behavior concerning production and people. It continues with 50 hours of problem solving, focusing upon situations involving interpersonal behavior and its influences on task performance. Each group regularly assesses its problem-solving performance. This immediate face-to-face feedback sets the stage for phase 2.

2. Intragroup Development. This begins after phase 1 when superiors and immediate subordinates explore their managerial styles and operating practices as a group. It is anticipated that the climate of openness and candor which was established in phase 1 will carry over into the second phase. Taken together the first two phases provide conditions which are designed to:

> . . . enable managers to learn managerial grid concepts as an organizing framework for thinking about management practices;
>
> . . . build improved relationships between groups, among colleagues at the same level, and between superiors and subordinates;
>
> . . . make managers more critical of outworn practices and precedents while

---

[17] Robert R. Blake and Jane S. Mouton, *The Managerial Grid* (Houston: Gulf Publishing Co., 1964).

[18] The descriptions of the six phases are based primarily upon Robert R. Blake, Jane S. Mouton, Louis B. Barnes, and Larry E. Greiner, "Breakthrough in Organization Development," *Harvard Business Review* (November–December 1964), pp. 133–35; and Robert R. Blake, Jane S. Mouton, Richard L. Sloma, and Barbara P. Loftin, "A Second Breakthrough in Organization Development," *California Management Review* (Winter 1968), pp. 73–78.

extending their problem-solving capacities in interdependent situations. Words like "involvement" and "commitment" become real in terms of day-to-day tasks.[19]

3. Intergroup Development. This phase involves group-to-group working relationships and focuses on building 9,9 group roles and norms beyond the single work group. Situations are established whereby tensions that typically exist between groups are identified and discussed by group members.

The objective of this phase is to move the groups from the usual "we win–you lose" patterns to a joint problem-solving activity. This procedure also helps to link managers who are at the same management level but belong to different work units.

4. Organizational Goal Setting. The immediate objective of the fourth phase is to set up a model of an effective organization for the future. The development of a future organization blueprint involves developing convictions about ideal management practices by testing existing ones and setting practical attainable objectives within a time framework. Through the use of the total organization, planned goals at each level will hopefully be linked.

5. Goal Attainment. This phase uses some of the same group and educational procedures as phase 1 but the major concern is the total organization. Once the special task groups define the problem areas other groups are set up throughout the organization. These groups are given a written "task paragraph" which describes the problem and the goal. Group members are given packets of information on the issue under discussion. The group members study the packets and then are given a test on its content. Once the information is understood and agreement is reached within the group, it begins to work on corrective steps.

6. Stabilization. The final phase is a period of stabilizing the changes brought about in prior phases. A period of time, perhaps as long as a year, is necessary after the first five phases to identify weaknesses and take corrective actions in the goals set and the plans implemented. This phase also enables management to evaluate the total program.

One of many efforts to undertake managerial grid-based development occurred in the Sigma Plant, a part of the Piedmont Corporation. The plant had been facing strained relationships between the operating and engineering departments. Specifically, accusations of "empire building" were a common reference made to various departments. In addition to this problem Piedmont merged with another company. This merger disrupted the long-standing rapport between Sigma Plant and its parent organization. These problems and others led to the intervention of Blake and Mouton.

The managerial grid six-phase program began in November 1962 with 40 managers and the first phase continued until the summer of 1963, by

---

[19] Blake, Mouton, Barnes, and Greiner, "Breakthrough in Organizational Development," p. 137. The development of effective group behavior can be the central focus of an OD program. For example, see John R. Kimberly and Warren R. Nielsen, "Organizational Development and Change in Organizational Performance," *Administrative Science Quarterly* (June 1975), pp. 191–206.

which time 800 managers and technicians had completed it. Since we already know the six phases it would seem appropriate to evaluate the success of the program.

Productivity and profits increased during 1963 when the managerial grid program was in effect. Table 18–2 indicates that total production increased somewhat (with fewer employees), and profits more than doubled. These figures although promising, do not provide a complete explanation for the improvement at Sigma. First, Sigma's business involves widely fluctuating market prices and other noncontrollable factors. Possible higher revenues or lower material costs could explain the profit increases. In addition, new automatic equipment might have resulted in the reduced labor force and increased profit picture. Finally, an overall personnel reduction of 600 em-

Table 18–2
Sigma Operating Results (in percentages)

	1960*	1961	1962	1963
Gross revenue	100	101.6	98.2	106.6
Raw material costs	100	98.8	97.2	103.2
Noncontrollable				
operating costs	100	97.5	101.8	104.6
Controllable				
operating costs	100	95.0	94.1	86.2
Net profit before taxes	100	229.0	118.0	266.0
Number of employees	100	95.5	94.1	79.5
Total production units	100	98.5	98.2	102.2

* 1960 is used as a base year, since it was the first year that Sigma's records could be compared with postmerger years.

Source: Adapted from Robert R. Blake, Jane S. Mouton, Louis B. Barnes, and Larry E. Greiner, "Breakthrough in Organization Development," *Harvard Business Review* (November–December 1964), p. 142.

ployees might have been the major reason for the improved profit picture in 1963. As Blake and Mouton caution the reader, it is diffcult to draw simple cause-and-effect conclusions about the grid program.

Behavioral changes were measured but it was difficult to develop an accurate set of indices. The primary difficulty in accurately assessing what, if anything, the grid program was accomplishing was the fact that scientific research of the program began after the grid approach was initiated. However, some of the indicators used to assess behavioral change included:

1. The frequency of meetings among managers.
2. The changes in promotion criteria for management appraisals.
3. The number of transfers within the plant.

Findings indicated that the number of formal meetings increased 31 percent when before-grid and after-grid meeting schedules were compared. Questionnaire data also showed managers reporting an average of 12.4 percent more time in "group problem-solving" meetings.

Promotion criteria changed after the grid program began. Younger managers in line positions appeared to have a better chance to be promoted than their older counterparts in staff positions. These changes suggest a shift in the authority structure of the plant, with line managers becoming more highly rewarded than technical-staff managers.

Manager transfers increased 52 percent after the grid program began. The researchers believe that this increase in internal movement suggests greater flexibility within the plant, and increased transfers to outside company units suggest stronger ties with headquarters and other operating plants.

Attitudinal and value changes were assessed by using a survey question-naire. Managers reported their views of organizational relationships during the fall of 1963 as compared with a year earlier. Perceived improvement was highest in intergroup and interdepartmental relationships although it was impressively high in the other areas too. Improvement was higher in adminis-trative-line areas than in technical-staff areas.

The findings suggest that the Sigma managerial grid program made some contribution to production and profits, practices and behavior, and attitudes and values among managers. The implications of this managerial study sug-gest that this type of change effort can assist organizations under certain conditions. These conditions include:

1. A management that is willing to be patient and understands that striking results from a change effort may not be forthcoming for some time.
2. An organization whose work requires some interdependent effort and common values.
3. An educational-training approach that builds group problem solving around work-related problems.

The longevity of the managerial grid method suggests that it is more than a fad to practicing managers. Thus, it would appear that more rigorous studies of what it can and cannot accomplish are required. Only by properly studying this approach can those interested in implementing it as a developmental method generally understand how it can change employee behavior.

Team Building

The managerial grid attempts to develop a group structure to support and sustain a particular leadership style. It is not necessary, however, to develop group behavior around 9,9 or any other leadership model. Rather group behavior can be developed to perform more effectively through an intervention technique termed team building. Whereas the managerial grid is a comprehensive technique, the focus of team building is the work group.

The purpose of team building is to enable work groups to more effectively get their work done, to improve their performance. The work group may be existing, or relatively new, command and task groups. The specific aims of the intervention include setting goals and priorities, analyzing the ways the group does its work, examining the group's norms and processes for communicating and decision making, and examining the interpersonal relationships within the group. As each of these aims is undertaken, the group is placed in the position of having to recognize explicitly the contributions, positive and negative, of each group member.[20]

The process by which these aims is achieved begins with *diagnostic* meetings. Often lasting an entire day, the meetings enable each group member to share with other members his or her perceptions of problems. If the group is large enough, subgroups engage in discussion and report their ideas to the total group. The purpose of these sessions is to obtain the views of all members and to make these views public. That is, diagnosis, in this context, implies the value of "open confrontation" of issues and problems that previously were talked about in relative secrecy.

Problem identification, and consensus as to their priority, is an initial and important step. However *a plan of action* must be agreed upon. The action plan should call on each group member or members to undertake a specific action to alleviate one or more of the problems. If for example, an executive committee agrees that one of its problems is lack of understanding and commitment to a set of goals, a subgroup can be appointed to recommend goals to the total group at a subsequent meeting. Other group members can work on other problems. For example, if problems are identified in the relationship among the members, a subgroup initiates a process for examining the roles of each member.[21]

Team-building interventions do not always require a complex process of diagnostic and action meetings. For example, the chief executive of a large manufacturing firm recognized that conflict within his executive group was creating defensiveness between the functional departments. He also recognized that his practice of dealing on a one-to-one basis with each of the executive group members, each of whom headed a functional department, contributed to the defensiveness and conflict. Rather than viewing themselves as team members having a stake in the organization, the functional heads viewed each other as competitors. The chief executive's practice of dealing with them individually confirmed their beliefs that they managed relatively independent units.

To counteract the situation, the chief executive adopted the simple expedient of requiring the top group to meet twice weekly. One meeting focuses on operating problems, the other on personnel problems. The ground rule for these meetings is that the group must reach consensus on decisions. After one year of such meetings, company-oriented decisions were being made and the climate of interunit competition was replaced by cooperation.[22]

Team building is also effective when new groups are being formed. Prob-

---

[20] Richard Beckhard, "Optimizing Team-Building Efforts," *Journal of Contemporary Business* (Summer 1972), p. 24.

[21] Wendell L. French and Cecil H. Bell, Jr., *Organization Development* (Englewood Cliffs, N.J.: Prentice-Hall, Inc., 1973), pp. 112–20.

[22] Virginia E. Schein and Larry E. Greiner, "Can Organization Development Be Fine-Tuned to Bureaucracies?" *Organizational Dynamics* (Winter 1977), p. 54.

lems often exist when new organizational units, project teams, or task forces are created. Typically such groups have certain characteristics which must be overcome if they are to perform effectively. For example:

1. Confusion exists as to roles and relationships.
2. Members have a fairly clear understanding of short-term goals.
3. Group members have technical competence which puts them on the team.
4. Members often pay more attention to the tasks of the team than to the relationship among the team members.

The result of these characteristics is that the new group will focus initially on task problems, but ignore the relationship issues. By the time relationship problems begin to surface, the group is unable to deal with them and the performances begin to deteriorate.

To combat these tendencies, the new group should schedule team-building meetings during the first weeks of its life. The meetings should take place away from the work site; one- or two-day meetings are often sufficient. The format of such meetings varies, but essentially the purpose is to provide time for the group to work through its timetable and the roles of members in reaching the groups objectives. An important outcome of the meeting is to establish understanding about each member's contribution to the team and the reward for that contribution.[23]

Career Planning

Problems at the individual level are often diagnosed as the result of mismatches between people and their jobs. People grow and change, they develop skills, attitudes, and beliefs throughout their lives which may be incompatible with the demands of their work. Life situations change away from the workplace as children come and go, as marriages strengthen or decay. The intertwining of work and living creates dynamic forces which effect in strong measure job performance.

Initial career choices reflect a person's interests, personality, self-identity, and social background at the time. But these factors change. Career planning techniques are not only a reflection of an organization's commitment to the aspirations of its employees, but are also valid responses to ineffective individual performance.[24]

Career planning and development involves an intervention process which encourages individuals to focus on their past, present, and future states. Specifically the process enables individuals to consider the following points:[25]

---

[23] Richard Beckhard, *Organization Development* (Reading, Mass.: Addison-Wesley Publishing Co., 1969), pp. 28–29.

[24] Douglas T. Hall, *Careers in Organizations* (Pacific Palisades, Calif.: Goodyear Publishing Company, Inc., 1976), pp. 11–22.

[25] French and Bell, *Organization Development,* pp. 144–46.

1. An assessment of life and career paths to the present time, including important events and choices as well as personal strengths and weaknesses.
2. A formulation of future goals related to desired lifestyle and career path.
3. The establishment of a plan which specifies goals, action steps, and target dates.

These points are considered by each individual after engaging in exercises which require explicit analyses. Although the specific format of the exercise may vary, the following is representative:

First Phase

1. Draw a straight line from left to right to represent your life span. The length represents your total life experience and future expectations.
2. Indicate on the line where you are now.
3. Prepare an inventory of important happenings, including:
    a. Peak experiences you have had.
    b. Things you do well.
    c. Things you do poorly.
    d. Things you would like to stop doing.
    e. Things you would like to learn to do well.
    f. Peak experiences you would like to have.
    g. Values you want to achieve.
    h. Things you would like to start doing now.
4. Discussion of each person's statements in subgroups.

Second Phase

1. Write your own obituary.
2. Form pairs and write a eulogy for your partner.
3. Discussion in subgroups.[26]

The value of providing opportunities for employees to assess their lives and careers depends largely upon the commitment of organizations. The forms of that commitment are money and time, money to sponsor the training and time of employees to participate. But if done properly, benefits can accrue to individuals and organizations. For example, career planning:

> Demonstrates the larger social responsibility of a mature organization.
> Indicates to adult employees that the organization cares about them.
> Prepares individuals to change in society, organizations, and themselves.
> Releases the potential of the individual on behalf of the organization.[27]

Career planning is closely related to management by objectives, but it includes life, as well as job, accomplishments. This technique commits the

---

[26] Ibid., pp. 144–45.

[27] Gordon L. Lippitt, "Developing Life Plans: A New Concept and Design for Training and Development," *Training and Development Journal* (May 1970), p. 3.

organization to a process which recognizes the value of each individual and to an effort to integrate individual and organizational aspirations.

Sensitivity Training

This highly publicized development method focuses on individual and individual-group problems. "Sensitivity" in this context means sensitivity to self and self-other relationships. An assumption of sensitivity training is that the causes of poor task performance are the emotional problems of people who must collectively achieve the goal. If these problems can be removed, a major impediment to task performance is consequently eliminated. Sensitivity training stresses "the *process* rather than the *content* of training and focuses upon *emotional* rather than *conceptual* training."[28] Thus, we can see that this form of training is quite different from traditional forms of training which stress the acquisition of a predetermined set of concepts with immediate application to the workplace.

The process of sensitivity training includes a group (a T-group) which in most cases meets at some place away from the job. The group, under the direction of a trainer, can engage in a group dialogue which has no agenda and no focus. The objective is to provide an environment which produces its own learning experiences.[29] As group members engage in the dialogue they are encouraged to learn about themselves as they deal with others. They explore their needs and their attitudes as revealed through their behavior toward others in the group and through the behavior of others toward them. The T-group may be highly unstructured. As one who participated in sensitivity training points out, "It [sensitivity training] says 'Open your eyes. Look at yourself. See how you look to others. Then decide what changes, if any, you want to make and in which direction you want to go.' "[30]

The role of trainers in the T-group is to facilitate the learning process: according to Kelly, they are "to observe, record, interpret, sometimes to lead, and always to learn."[31] The artistry and style of trainers are critical variables in determining the direction of the T-group's sessions. They must walk the uneasy path of unobtrusive leadership. They must be able to interpret the role of participants and encourage them to analyze their contributions without being perceived as a threat themselves. Unlike the group therapist, the T-group trainers deal with people who are considered normal, but who have come together to learn. The usually described role of trainers is that of "permissive, nonauthoritarian, sometimes almost nonparticipative" leadership.

---

[28] Henry C. Smith, *Sensitivity to People* (New York: McGraw-Hill Book Co., 1966), p. 197. Emphasis added.

[29] L. P. Bradford, J. R. Gibb, and K. D. Benne, *T-Group Theory and Laboratory Method* (New York: John Wiley & Sons, 1964).

[30] Alfred J. Marrow, *Behind the Executive Mask* (New York: American Management Association, 1964), p. 51.

[31] Joe Kelly, *Organizational Behavior,* rev. ed. (Homewood, Ill.: Richard D. Irwin, Inc., and The Dorsey Press, 1974), p. 664.

The critical test of sensitivity training is whether the experience itself is a factor leading to improvement in task performance. It is apparent that even if the training induces positive changes in the participant's sensitivity to self and others, such behavior may be either not possible or not permissible back in the work place. The participant must deal with the same environment and the same people as before the training. The open, supportive, and permissive environment of the training sessions is not likely to be found on the job. Even so, the proponent of sensitivity training would reply that the participants are better able to deal with the environment and to understand their own relationship to it. We would also recognize that sensitivity training may well induce negative changes in some participants' ability to perform their organizational task; the training sessions can be occasions of extreme stress and anxiety. The capacity to deal effectively with stress varies among individuals, and the outcome may be dysfunctional for some participants.

The scientific evidence to date suggests mixed results for the effectiveness of sensitivity training as a change method.[32] Managers must critically examine this technique in terms of the kinds of changes they desire and those which are possible given the existence of conditions which limit the range of possible changes. In this light the manager must determine whether the changes induced by sensitivity training are instrumental for organizational purposes and whether prospective participants are able to tolerate the potential anxiety of the training.

The current thinking of OD specialists is that, while sensitivity training may have a "significant impact on most participants," it is not enough "from the standpoint of organizational improvement." More and more we see the use of sensitivity training as one aspect of a total program. A now-famous application of sensitivity training at TRW Systems is illustrative of the way in which the total organization is the target of change. As Davis has observed:

> The notion very early in the TRW Systems effort was to focus on changes in the on-going culture itself: the norms, rewards, systems, and processes. If all we did was to have a lot of people attend sensitivity training, this might indeed be useful to them as individuals, but its usefulness would be quite limited with respect to the total organization.[33]

The inconclusive results regarding the relationships between sensitivity training and organizational effectiveness have caused managers to become skeptical about its continual use.[34] That skepticism and the concern of OD

---

[32] See Robert J. House, "T-Group Education and Leadership Effectiveness: A Review of the Empirical Literature and a Critical Evaluation," *Personnel Psychology* (Spring 1967) pp. 1–32; and John P. Campbell and Marvin D. Dunnette, "Effectiveness of T-Group Experiences in Managerial Training and Development," *Psychological Bulletin* (August 1968), pp. 73–104.

[33] S. Davis, "An Organic Problem-Solving Method of Organizational Change," *Journal of Applied Behavioral Science* (January–February 1967), pp. 3–21 as quoted in Fred I. Steele, "Can T-Group Training Change the Power Structure?" *Personnel Administration* (November 1970), p. 50.

[34] William J. Kearney and Desmond D. Martin, "Sensitivity Training: An Established Management Development Tool?" *Academy of Management Journal* (December 1974), pp. 755–60.

experts to improve their methods have led to a number of variations on the basic sensitivity approach. These variations tend to delve less deeply into the non-work-related feelings and sentiments of the participants and instead focus only on task-relevant behavior. These variants have not been fully evaluated in terms of organizational effectiveness, yet their existence suggests a continuing place for sensitivity training-type methods in organizational development literature and practice.

AN OVERVIEW

This and the preceding chapter comprise an integral unit which, for sake of presentation, has been separated. We should now bring the two chapters together by restating the model to emphasize the key decisions which managers must make.

Forces for Change

The forces for change are either external or internal. No management decision is required in this step of the model except to provide for the information system which senses the external and internal environment. Of particular concern is the necessity for continually monitoring the organizational climate. Problems associated with low morale, communication breakdowns, and ineffective leadership are associated with climate variables.

Recognition of the Need for Change

This step is crucial to the entire development process. It is at this point that managers decide to act. If in management's judgment the forces for change are significant, the process moves to the next step, diagnosis.

Diagnosis of the Problem

The key decision in this step is whether the stimulus for change should be acted upon. This decision can be approached by making three related decisions:

1. What is the problem as distinct from its symptoms?
2. What must be changed to resolve the problem?
3. What outcomes are expected and how will these outcomes be measured?

The managerial response to these questions should be stated in terms of criteria which reflect organizational effectiveness. Measurable outcomes such as production, efficiency, satisfaction, adaptiveness, and development must be linked to skill, attitudinal, behavioral, and structural changes which are necessitated by the problem identification.

If the organizational climate is conducive to the shared strategy, the employees would have been brought into the process at the recognition of need step and participated with management from that point on. Through shared authority, the problem would be associated with skill, attitude, behavioral, and structural causes and the appropriate technique selected.

If the climate is not conducive to employee participation because the necessary preconditions do not exist, management must unilaterally define the problem and select the appropriate method. Whether the problem is related to skill, attitude, behavioral, or structural causes, the strategy must include provision for the learning principles of feedback, reinforcement, and transfer. Without these principles none of the development methods, whether sensitivity training, managerial grid, management by objectives, job enrichment, or System 4 organization has a maximum chance of success.

The model, therefore, emphasizes that the OD program be specifically tailored to the problems and personnel of the organization. It recommends against the implementation of "canned" approaches which are the current rage in the literature. Throughout our discussions of organizational design, motivation, and leadership, we have stressed the situational approach. This point of view is fundamental to the process of organizational development and change.

Recognition of Limiting Conditions

Inherent in the situational approach is the understanding that each organization must adapt in unique ways to its environment. Accordingly, conditions are created which limit the range of development methods and strategies available to management. The leadership style, the formal organization, and group norms all come together and are reflected by the organizational climate. A development method such as sensitivity training or System 4 organization will fail if the climate does not support the behavioral changes induced by the OD program. The learning cannot be transferred to the workplace.

Selection of Method

The analysis of the problem, identification of alternatives, and recognition of constraints lead to the selection of the most promising method. The selection is based upon the principle of maximizing expected returns to the organization if the decision is characterized by risk or by one of the principles of uncertainty. The latter include the maximin, maximax, and minimax principles and the selection depends primarily upon the style of the manager.

Implementation of the Method

The implementation decision involves scope and timing. The shared approach prescribes a limited scope accompanied by feedback to participants. Timing relates to when the method will be implemented and there are no specific guidelines except that the method should be initiated when it is least disruptive to the day-to-day routine.

Evaluating the Method

The logical last step of the OD process is the decision to provide for an evaluation procedure. The ideal situation would be to structure the procedure in the manner of an experimental design. That is, the end results should be operationally defined and measurements should be taken before and after in both the organization undergoing development and an organization not undergoing development. Or if the scope of the program is limited to a subunit, a second subunit could serve as a control group.

The purpose of the evaluation is not only necessitated by management's responsibility to account for its use of resources, but also to provide feedback. Corrections can be taken in the implementation phase based upon this feedback. Subsequent implementations can benefit from the feedback.

We have now concluded the section which deals with organizational development. Much of the discussion in previous chapters has been mentioned in our elaboration of the development model. Concepts such as organizational design, structure, decision making, communications, motivation, groups, and leadership are apparent and important for the management of development and change.

MAJOR ISSUES FOR THE MANAGER TO CONSIDER

A. After diagnosing the problem and identifying the target for change, management must select the most promising development method. The philosophy of OD emphasizes that the correct order of analysis is problem to method, not method to problem.

B. Management must tailor the OD program to the problems and personnel of the organization. Throughout our discussions of organizational design, motivation, and leadership, we have stressed the contingency approach. This point of view is fundamental to the process of organizational development and change.

C. Inherent in the contingency approach is the understanding that each organization must adapt in unique ways to its environment. Accordingly, conditions are created which limit the range of development methods and strategies available to management. A development method such as sensitivity training or System 4 will fail if management does not support the behavioral changes induced by the OD program.

D. The analysis of the problem, identification of alternatives, and recognition of constraints lead to the selection of the most promising method and strategy. The selection is based upon the principle of maximizing expected returns to the organization.

E. Although there is by nature considerable overlap among the levels for which a particular method is appropriate, each has a primary focus. One should not expect, for example, that MBO will be effective in changing behaviors at level X, although it may affect to a degree the behavior at levels VII and VIII.

F. The number of OD methods is considerable and ever-increasing. Only a few of the more widely used ones have been discussed. Managers considering the possibility of OD should consult a more detailed description of them. Several such descriptions appear in the citations and additional references to this chapter.

DISCUSSION AND REVIEW QUESTIONS

1. Do you believe that changes are required in processes, behaviors, or structure in the college you attend?

2. Which organizational development method described in the chapter would you recommend to your university's president for implementation? Why?

3. What are the implicit value judgments of the organizational development techniques described in this chapter? Do you agree with them?

4. Could professors use the approaches of MBO and job enrichment in the management of their classrooms; that is, could they, for example, "enrich" the roles of students? What difficulties might they encounter?

5. Describe how you would go about designing a managerial grid training program for a group of campus student leaders.

6. What are the differences between job enrichment and System 4 organization? Are the differences simply matters of emphasis, or are there fundamental differences?

7. What would be the most serious limiting condition for each of the development methods discussed in this chapter?

8. What specific motivation theories explain the apparent success of flexitime? Develop fully your answer.

9. Explain how team-building exercises apply group-development theory as explained in Chapter 6.

10. Can a person engage in career path development exercises if that person has no career goals? Explain. Do you believe that career goals are essential for career success? Explain.

ADDITIONAL REFERENCES

Beckhard, R. *Organizational Development: Strategies and Models*. Reading, Mass.: Addison-Wesley, 1969.

Bennis, W. G. *Organizational Development: Its Nature, Origins, and Prospects*. Reading, Mass.: Addison-Wesley, 1969.

Burke, W. W. "Management and Organizational Development: What Is the Target of the Change?" *Personnel Administration* (1971), pp. 44–56.

Connor, P. E. "A Critical Inquiry into Some Assumptions and Values Characterizing OD." *Academy of Management Review* (1977), pp. 635–44.

Corprew, J., and Davis, H. "An Organization Development Effort to Improve Instruction at a University." *Educational Technology* (1975), pp. 44.

Crockett, W. J. "Team Building: One Approach to Organizational Development." *Journal of Applied Behavioral Science* (1970), pp. 291–306.

Cummings, G.; Molloy, E. S.; and Glen, R. H. "Intervention Strategies for Improving Productivity and the Quality of Work Life." *Organizational Dynamics* (1975), pp. 52–68.

Davis, H. J., and Weaver, K. M. *Alternate Workweek Patterns: An Annotated Bibliography of Selected Literature.* Washington, D.C.: National Council for Alternative Work Patterns, 1978.

Eddy, W. B. "From Training to Organization Change." *Personnel Administration* (1971), pp. 37–43.

Filley, A. C. *Interpersonal Conflict Resolution.* Glenview, Ill.: Scott, Foresman and Company, 1975.

Fink, S. L.; Beak, J.; and Taddeo, K. "Organizational Crisis and Change." *Journal of Applied Behavioral Science* (1971), pp. 15–37.

French, W. L., and Bell, C. H., Jr. *Organization Development.* Englewood Cliffs, N.J.: Prentice-Hall, 1973.

Golembiewski, R. T.; Hilles, R.; and Kagno, M. S. "A Longitudinal Study of Flexi-Time Effects: Some Consequences of an OD Structural Intervention." *Journal of Applied Behavioral Science* (1974), pp. 503–32.

Heller, F. A. "Group Feed-Back Analysis as a Change Agent." *Human Relations* (1970), pp. 319–33.

Herman, S. M. "What Is This Thing Called Organizational Development?" *Personnel Journal* (1971), pp. 595–603.

Hornstein, H. A., and Tichy, N. M. "Developing Organization Development for Multinational Organizations." *Columbia Journal of World Business* (1976), pp. 124–37.

Kaufman, R. "Organizational Improvement: A Review of Models and an Attempted Synthesis." *Group and Organizational Studies* (1976), pp. 474–95.

Lawrence, P. R. and Lorsch, J. W. *Developing Organizations: Diagnosis and Action.* Reading, Mass.: Addison-Wesley, 1969.

Lippitt, R.; Watson, J.; and Westley, B. *The Dynamics of Planned Change.* New York: Harcourt, Brace & World, 1958.

Luthans, F., and Kreitner, R. *Organizational Behavior Modification.* Glenview, Ill.: Scott, Foresman and Company, 1975.

McClelland, D. C. "Toward a Theory of Motive Acquisition." *American Psychologist* (1965), pp. 321–33.

Margulies, N., and Wallace, J. *Organizational Change: Techniques and Applications.* Glenview, Ill.: Scott, Foresman and Company, 1973.

Nadler, D. A. "The Use of Feedback for Organizational Change." *Group and Organizational Studies* (1976), pp. 177–86.

Plovnick, M., and Fry, R. "New Developments in OD Technology." *Training and Development Journal* (1975), pp. 19–25.

Schein, V. E.; Maurer, E. H.; and Novak, J. F. "Impact of Flexible Working Hours on Productivity." *Journal of Applied Psychology* (1977), pp. 463–65.

Schneier, C. E. "Behavior Modification in Management: A Review and Critique." *Academy of Management Journal* (1974), pp. 528–48.

Scott, D. "Productive Partnership Coupling MBO and TA." *Management Review* (1976), pp. 12–19.

Seashore, S. E., and Bowers, D. G. *Changing the Structure and Functioning of an Organization.* Ann Arbor: University of Michigan Survey Research Center, 1963.

Stephenson, T. E. "Organization Development—A Critique." *Journal of Management Studies* (1975), pp. 249–65.

Taylor, J. C. "Some Effects of Technology in Organization Change." *Human Relations* (1971), pp. 105–23.

Warrick, D. D. "Applying OD to the Public Sector." *Public Personnel Management* (1976), pp. 186–90.

White, S. E., and Mitchell, T. R. "Organization Development: A Review of Research Content and Design." *Academy of Management Review* (1976), pp. 57–73.

Winn, A. "Social Change in Industry: From Insight to Implementation." *Journal of Applied Behavioral Science* (1966), pp. 170–84.

CASE FOR ANALYSIS

DEVELOPING EFFECTIVE WORKTEAMS*

The Saga Administrative Corporation was created in the 1940s to provide food service to universities and other institutions. The company was so successful that its revenues increased nearly 13 times during the 1960s to a figure of $147 million in 1970. At that time the company was providing food service to some 450 universities across the country. The organization of the company was along territorial lines; the food service managers at institutions reported to district managers who in turn reported to regional managers. The Vice President for Food Service, located in Menlo Park, California, had responsibility for food service operations and was the ultimate source of authority for all decisions regarding food service.

The rapid expansion of the company during the 1960s had caused considerable upheaval in the way Saga had typically functioned. The philosophy of the Chairman of the Board reflected that of the company's founders; it stated, essentially, that the "Saga way" was to prosper by promoting within the company a sense of respect for the dignity of each individual employee and by encouraging a spirit of entrepreneurism. Employees throughout the organization should be made to feel that they had contributions to make and that they should exercise initiative and independent action. The company's top management knew from experience that the food service manager at a particular institution faced unique problems and must be willing and able to make decisions. But apparently this philosophy had been lost during the expansion period. More and more, it seemed to top management, managers all down the line looked to headquarters for decisions. Attitude surveys were undertaken in 1964 and 1967 and they indicated that managers viewed headquarters as a "Big Daddy," which always knew best.

In response to their own views of the situation and the results of the attitude surveys, Saga's executives met with two OD experts from the UCLA faculty. That meeting, held in April 1968, was the initial step in the development of an OD program in Saga. But at that time there was no commonly held view as to exactly what was wrong or what was required to correct it. The executives simply felt that a more effective organization was needed and that they wanted to do whatever was required to develop it.

As a first step the executive group appointed one of their own members to direct the program. His first task was to diagnose the problems and then select a method or set of methods which would be appropriate for Saga. During May 1968, he held meetings throughout the country with managers from all levels of the hierarchy. The focus of the meetings was the data from the attitude surveys. The managers were encouraged to express their interpretations of the meanings of the attitudes reflected in the data. The

---

* This case is based upon William J. Crockett, Robert E. Gaernter, and Sam Farry, "Humanistic Management in a Fast-Growing Company," in Alfred J. Marrow, ed., *The Failure of Success* (New York: AMACOM, 1972), pp. 275–85.

issues which continually emerged from these meetings centered on feelings of isolation and aloneness. The food service managers at institutions simply felt that they no longer were parts of the organization. Resentment and frustration were prevalent emotions. The institutional food service managers were particularly vocal and stated that if they bucked decisions up the line it was because headquarters wanted it that way.

The director of the OD effort listened carefully to the discussions at these meetings. It was apparent that the OD method must focus on building mechanisms which would restore the philosophy of Saga and make it real in the company's operations. A concept was needed and it seemed that Likert's idea of interlocking work teams would fit Saga's situation. The geographical dispersion of the company made it possible to think of teams of food service managers and their district managers which would function as decision-making groups. But to build these teams required more than simply stating that they existed and defining their authority. It was necessary to restore the confidence of managers in the good intentions of top management.

The team-building program was thus defined as a method for developing individual, group, and individual-group behavior. The mechanics of the program were as follows:

1. The Vice President for Food Services and his four area managers met in June 1968. This group met first and confronted the issues and problems which kept it from functioning effectively.
2. Area managers met with their district managers throughout the fall of 1968. Like the initial meetings held with the vice presidents, these meetings created a renewed sense of trust and confidence. The group confronted its problems, and communication was more frank and open than in previous meetings.
3. District managers and institutional food service managers met throughout the first six months of 1970. The meetings were based upon materials and experience obtained from earlier sessions between upper-level management.

The process of team-building began at the top and moved successively down into the organization. Information was shared at every level; expectations, attitudes, and feelings were confronted and discussed. The underlying assumption was that these teams could function effectively only if they were able to communicate authentically. As one manager observed: "What's changed is not that problems go away, but that we can now find out about them for ourselves, we can discuss them openly, and we don't have to conduct an attitude survey to know how we feel."

Questions for Consideration

1. What were the fundamental problems which the Saga OD program sought to resolve?

2. Must any rapidly expanding company experience problems similar to those of Saga?
3. What value orientation underlies the "Saga way" philosophy?

EXPERIENTIAL EXERCISE

REORIENTING AN EXCELLENT PERFORMER

Objectives

1. To examine the process of reviewing career planning decisions.
2. To illustrate some of the major problems facing individuals involved in the career planning process.

Related Topics

Career planning is related to organizational change and development topics such as goal setting, individual growth, and group development.

Starting the Exercise

Each student should first consider his or her own career and plans for the future. This will set the theme for participating in the exercise.

The Facts

Roger Belhurst is a 50-year-old district sales manager for Rockhurst Corporation. He has been in his present position for ten years. His superior rates Roger as outstanding in every area in the performance evaluation program. Unfortunately, order cutbacks and the lack of promotion opportunities have kept Roger in his current position. In addition, Roger's superior has stated that, "Roger is in a position that uses his skills and abilities optimally." Roger disagrees and believes that he is being put on the shelf and will not be promoted. His present attitudes about the company, his job, and the future are poor.

Exercise Procedures

Phase I: Group Analysis: 15 minutes

1. The instructor will select two groups of five to seven people. Each group will analyze the Roger Belhurst case. The groups should develop a career plan which would result in an improvement in Roger's overall attitudes. Each group will make five-minute presentations to the class.

Phase II: Evaluation: 15 minutes

1. A third group of three to five people will serve as evaluators of the analysis presented by the two groups. The evaluators should develop a set of criteria and apply these to the two *five*-minute presentations. They should then decide

which presentation is better. When one group is presenting the solution to Roger's career plan, the second group should not be present in the room.

Phase III: Critique: 20–30 minutes

1. The entire class should reflect and critique the presentations and the evaluations. During the critique the following questions should be answered:

    a.   Why was one group's analysis and career plan better than the other group's?

    b.   What criteria were used by the evaluators to rate the two group presentations?

    c.   What would be Roger's reaction to the career plan?

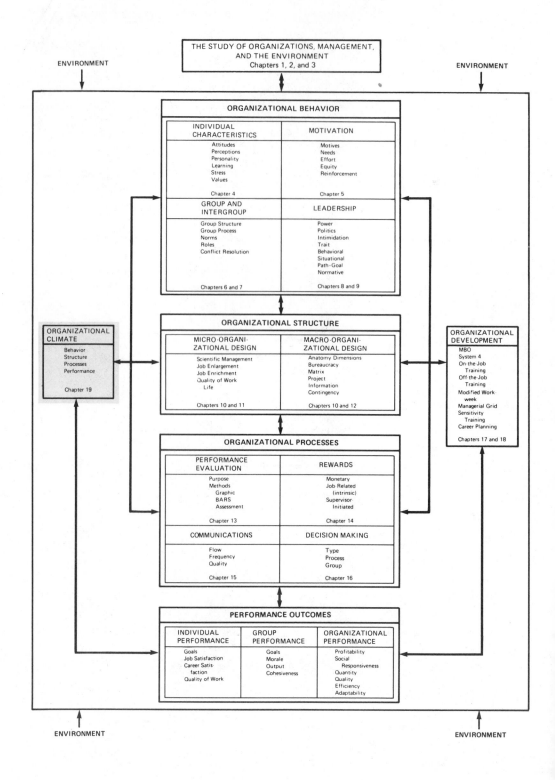

ENVIRONMENT   ENVIRONMENT

THE STUDY OF ORGANIZATIONS, MANAGEMENT,
AND THE ENVIRONMENT
Chapters 1, 2, and 3

ORGANIZATIONAL BEHAVIOR

INDIVIDUAL CHARACTERISTICS	MOTIVATION
Attitudes	Motives
Perceptions	Needs
Personality	Effort
Learning	Equity
Stress	Reinforcement
Values	
Chapter 4	Chapter 5

GROUP AND INTERGROUP	LEADERSHIP
Group Structure	Power
Group Process	Politics
Norms	Intimidation
Roles	Trait
Conflict Resolution	Behavioral
	Situational
	Path-Goal
	Normative
Chapters 6 and 7	Chapters 8 and 9

ORGANIZATIONAL STRUCTURE

MICRO-ORGANI-ZATIONAL DESIGN	MACRO-ORGANI-ZATIONAL DESIGN
Scientific Management	Anatomy Dimensions
Job Enlargement	Bureaucracy
Job Enrichment	Matrix
Quality of Work	Project
Life	Information
	Contingency
Chapters 10 and 11	Chapters 10 and 12

ORGANIZATIONAL PROCESSES

PERFORMANCE EVALUATION	REWARDS
Purpose	Monetary
Methods	Job-Related
Graphic	(intrinsic)
BARS	Supervisor-
Assessment	Initiated
Chapter 13	Chapter 14

COMMUNICATIONS	DECISION MAKING
Flow	Type
Frequency	Process
Quality	Group
Chapter 15	Chapter 16

ORGANIZATIONAL CLIMATE

Behavior
Structure
Processes
Performance

Chapter 19

ORGANIZATIONAL DEVELOPMENT

MBO
System 4
On-the-Job
  Training
Off-the-Job
  Training
Modified Work-
  week
Managerial Grid
Sensitivity
  Training
Career Planning

Chapters 17 and 18

PERFORMANCE OUTCOMES

INDIVIDUAL PERFORMANCE	GROUP PERFORMANCE	ORGANIZATIONAL PERFORMANCE
Goals	Goals	Profitability
Job Satisfaction	Morale	Social
Career Satis-	Output	Responsiveness
faction	Cohesiveness	Quantity
Quality of Work		Quality
		Efficiency
		Adaptability

ENVIRONMENT   ENVIRONMENT

Part Six

An Integrating Concept

Chapter 19
Organizational
Climate

Chapter 19

Organizational Climate

INTRODUCTION

We have stated repeatedly that managing organizational behavior necessitates understanding the *behavior* of people, the organization *structure* within which they interact, and the organizational *processes* of communication, decision making, rewards, and performance evaluation. A logical question at this point is "What is the result of the interaction of these phenomena?" As indicated in our framework presented throughout the book, one result of the interaction of individual and group behavior, conflict, leadership styles, organization structure, communication, and so forth, is *organizational climate*.

What is organizational climate? Before defining it in a formal way we shall try to relate it to something the reader is probably personally familiar with. How many times have you or someone you know said something like "That's a good organization to work for"; "They are much more demanding and stricter in that school than others"; or "This division of the company is much more informal than the one I used to work in"?

What is really being expressed is that organizations and in many cases subunits of organizations seem to have their own personalities or characteristics. Think for a moment about organizations with which you interact. If you have different attitudes toward them along lines like the ones above, you already have an intuitive grasp of the concept of organizational climate. Consider the following statement:

> Every organization has properties or characteristics possessed by many other organizations; however, each organization has its own unique constellation of characteristics and properties. *Organizational climate* is the term used to describe this psychological structure of organizations. Climate is thus the "feel," "personality," or "character" of the organization's environment.[1]

This internal environment or "climate" could be one of trust, progressiveness, fear, confidence, security, etc. Whatever that climate, your psychological feel-

---

[1] Andrew J. DuBrin, *Fundamentals of Organizational Behavior* (New York: Pergamon Press, 1974), p. 331.

ings would probably mirror the internal functioning of that organization or subunit.[2] In summary, organizations have personalities—and organizational climate is a measure of that personality. Thus, organizational climate is a very appropriate topic for our concluding chapter since it is heavily influenced by the *behavior* of the individuals in the organization, the *structure* of the organization and the organizational *processes.*

ORGANIZATIONAL CLIMATE, BEHAVIOR, STRUCTURE, PROCESSES, AND PERFORMANCE

Throughout this chapter we shall be discussing organizational climate from the point of view of a member of the organization. In other words, while customers have perceptions of business firms, and students of their schools, our concern here is with how employees experience the organization.

Finally, the topic of organizational climate is perhaps one of the most controversial in the current organizational behavior research literature. There are serious disagreements among theorists and researchers concerning such critical issues as (1) whether the concept of organizational climate even exists, in other words if there is such a thing as organizational climate; (2) what the concept encompasses, that is, what are its components; (3) whether organizational climate and job satisfaction are, in reality, the same; and (4) the appropriate means to measure organizational climate.[3] These are serious issues which need to be resolved. However, it is not appropriate in this chapter to review theoretical arguments and problems of measurement. Rather, our purpose is to present a discussion of organizational climate which is relevant for those concerned with managing organizational behavior. We do believe that organizational climate is a concept that managers must be aware of when managing organizational behavior. While our discussion at times may appear definitive, it is not and its tentative nature should be underscored. Being tentative, however, only means that much more theoretical and measurement research must be done on what we call organizational climate.

There is no shortage of definitions of organizational climate. We believe the following definition is useful:

---

[2] See Benjamin Schneider, "Organizational Climates: An Essay," *Personnel Psychology* (Winter 1975), p. 447–80. He notes that researchers studying the internal functioning of systems have used the term organizational climate in place of internal environment.

[3] For representative examples, see L. R. James and A. P. Jones, "Organizational Climate: A Review of Theory and Research," *Psychological Bulletin* (December 1974), pp. 1096–1112; L. K. Waters, D. Roach, and N. Batlis, "Organizational Climate Dimensions and Job-Related Attitudes," *Personnel Psychology* (Autumn 1974), pp. 465–76; W. LaFollette, and H. P. Sims, Jr., "Is Satisfaction Redundant with Organizational Climate?" *Organizational Behavior and Human Performance* (April 1975), pp. 257–78; P. M. Muchinsky, "An Assessment of the Litwin and Stringer Organization Climate Questionnaire: An Empirical and Theoretical Extension of the Sims and LaFollette Study," *Personnel Psychology* (Autumn 1976), pp. 371–92; and R. L. Payne, S. Fineman, and T. D. Wall, "Organizational Climate and Job Satisfaction: A Conceptual Synthesis," *Organizational Behavior and Human Performance* (June 1976), pp. 45–62.

Figure 19–1
Organizational Climate, Behavior, Structure, Processes, and Performance

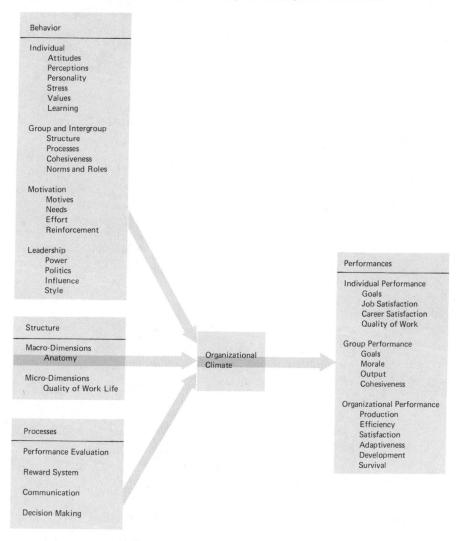

the set of characteristics that describe an organization and that *(a)* distinguish the organization from other organizations, *(b)* are relatively enduring over time, and *(c)* influence the behavior of people in the organization.[4]

For the individual employee, the climate helps shape attitudes and expectancies about the organization. It also has a link with the behavior, structure, and processes of the organization. This link is illustrated in our performance model (Figure 3–3) and is isolated in summary form in Figure 19–1.

---

[4] G. A. Forehand and B. V. H. Gilmer, "Environmental Variation in Studies of Organizational Behavior," *Psychological Bulletin* (December 1964), pp. 361–82.

The reader should be able to see that the concept of organizational climate can serve as a useful integrative device for this book. Figure 19–1 indicates that the three major topics of discussion throughout the book: human behavior, organizational structure, and organizational process are not isolated phenomena. In fact, they are very closely related and interact to influence what we are describing as the work environment or climate of an organization. Organizational climate transcends individual and group dimensions and is experienced across many diverse structural units within the organization with a resulting impact on organizational performance. This relationship is shown in Figure 19–1. For the manager it would seem that the concept of organizational climate has value for several specific reasons.[5]

There is some evidence that one type of climate may be effective in one situation but not in another. For example, we may find one type of climate when an organization or subunit faces a high degree of task uncertainty, unstructured problems, and a rapidly changing environment. Such a situation may confront an advertising agency or the research and development department of a chemical manufacturer. The opposite type of climate may exist when an organization faces low task uncertainty, structured problems, and a static environment. Such a situation may confront a governmental agency or an assembly line department in a manufacturing plant.

The congruence between the individual employee (e.g., personality) and the climate of the organization has been shown to influence the individual's performance and satisfaction.

When behavior, structure, or process variables are changed, the climate of the organization may be positively or negatively influenced. Practicing business executives have understood this intuitively for years. They can often be heard observing "The organization takes on the personality of the one at the top," and "For any change to be effective it must start at the top." The point is that climate of an organization can be influenced by its managers. When a new governor reorganizes the structure of the state government agencies, this structural change may result in a change in climate resulting in positive or negative changes in performance.

Societal Influences on Organizational Climate

In the past many managers were able to create climates that resulted in adequate levels of performance and creativity by using well-developed approaches to job design and reward systems. However, such is usually not

---

[5] For representative and related research see M. J. Brookes and A. Kaplan, "The Office Environment: Space Planning and Affective Behavior," *Human Factors* 14 (1972), pp. 373–91; R. D. Pritchard and B. W. Karasick, "The Effects of Organizational Climate on Managerial Job Performance and Job Satisfaction," *Organizational Behavior and Human Performance* (February 1973), pp. 126–47; F. E. Kast and J. W. Rosenzweig, eds., *Contingency Views of Organization and Management* (Chicago: Science Research Associates, 1973); D. Robey, "Computers and Organization Structure: A Review and Appraisal of Empirical Studies," *Proceedings of the National Academy of Management* (August 1974); and H. K. Downey, D. Hellriegal, and J. Slocum, Jr., "Congruence between Individual Needs, Organizational Climate, Job Satisfaction and Performance," *Academy of Management Journal* (March 1975), pp. 149–55.

the case today nor is it likely to be in the future. Trends shaping our society in the present will almost certainly influence the climates of organizations of the future. This also underscores the necessity of future managers understanding the concept of organizational climate. Let us briefly examine some of these important societal trends and their implications.[6]

Educational Levels.   As a result of modern education it is reasonable to assume that employees now tend to be more aware of the world around them. They will be seeking jobs that more fully utilize their skills and abilities.

Diversity of the Workforce.   The last two decades have seen a dramatic increase in the number of women and minority group workers. With such diversity the creation of a motivating and creative organizational work environment will become more difficult.

Technological Advances.   Many organizations now operate with equipment completely different from what they used 20 years ago or less. Many contemplate even greater changes in the future.

Union Contracts.   Union contracts directly affect what organizations can do in two important areas which influence organizational climate—job design and reward systems.

Government Regulations.   Although many of the great number of government regulations have no direct impact on areas which affect organizational climate, they all tend to decrease the organization's options. It will become increasingly difficult for organizations to operate in an individualized nonstandardized manner that fits the needs of a diverse workforce.

Organizational Growth.   Our society's work environment is increasingly dominated by large organizations. It is difficult to create motivating, creative work environments in large organizations where employees are less able to see a clear connection between their own behavior and the overall performance of the organization.

Attractiveness of Nonwork.   With leisure a major growth industry in our society, nonwork is becoming more attractive. The point is that with increasing recreational and educational opportunities available, work will have to offer something to the employee that cannot be obtained off the job.

These societal trends will mean that profit-making organizations will be dealing with a different kind of customer, and government with a different kind of citizen. More important for our purposes are the implications for managers attempting to foster organizational climates which result in high degrees of motivation and creativity. This will be increasingly more difficult because they will be facing a different kind of subordinate. At the same time, however, it will become increasingly more important if adequate levels of organizational performance are to be maintained.

Some Properties of Organizational Climate

Our discussion has suggested that a set of properties interacts to form an organizational climate. Exactly what this set is comprised of has certainly

---

[6] From Edward E. Lawler III, "Developing a Motivating Work Climate," *Management Review* (July 1977), pp. 25–28, 37–38.

not been uncovered. Much research has, however, been conducted with the purpose of identifying these properties. It would be useful at this point to review some selected studies and the properties of organizational climate they have identified.

Halpin and Crofts' Study. An important study of organizational climate was conducted in a public school organization.[7] The researchers identified eight properties of organizational climate:

1. Esprit—a perception by the employees that their social needs are being satisfied, and at the same time, they are enjoying a sense of task accomplishment.
2. Consideration—a perception by employees of a supportive atmosphere where management treats them as human beings.
3. Production—a perception that superiors are highly directive.
4. Aloofness—the emotional distance perceived between the manager and subordinate.
5. Disengagement—perceiving that you are merely "going through the motions" to complete a task.
6. Hindrance—feeling that you are being burdened with "busy work."
7. Intimacy—enjoyment of friendly relationships found in the total organization.
8. Thrust—demonstration by management of task-oriented behavior which shows a desire to motivate the work force, to "get the organization moving."

Litwin and Stringer's Study. This study identified several properties of organizational climate:[8]

1. Structure—the organization's rules, regulations, red tape, and constraints.
2. Challenge and responsibility—the feeling of "being one's own boss."
3. Rewards—the feeling of being adequately and equitably rewarded by the organization.
4. Warmth and support—the feeling of helpfulness, supportiveness, and good fellowship in the work environment.
5. Risk and risk taking—the amount of challenge and risk in the work environment.
6. Tolerance for conflict—the degree to which the work environment can tolerate different opinions.
7. Organizational identity—the degree of group loyalty perceived by members.
8. Performance standards and expectations—the perceived importance of performance and the clarity of the expectations concerning performance.

---

[7] A. W. Halpin and D. B. Crofts, *The Organizational Climate of Schools* (Chicago: The University of Chicago Press, 1963).

[8] See G. H. Litwin and R. Stringer, "The Influence of Organizational Climate on Human Motivation" (Paper presented at a conference on organizational climates, Foundation for Research on Human Behavior, Ann Arbor, Mich., March 1966); and *Motivation and Organizational Climate* (Boston: Division of Research, Harvard Graduate School of Business Administration, 1968), pp. 45–65.

Schneider and Bartlett's Study. The final study reviewed here involved sales agencies in two different insurance companies.[9] The results revealed the following properties of organizational climate:

1. Managerial support—the interest of the manager in the development and progress of subordinates.
2. Managerial structure—the manager's practice of requiring agents to comply with stated procedures.
3. Concern for new employees—management's degree of interest in the training of new agents.
4. Intra-agency conflict—the amount of conflict between groups in the agency, the presence of "in groups," and the undercutting of managerial authority.
5. Independence—the amount of autonomy perceived by the agents.
6. Overall satisfaction—the general contentment of agents with various management and the agency practices and activities.

These researchers believe that within the agencies studied the six properties identified are possible predictors of how an insurance agent will perform.

Why have we reviewed these three studies? Examination of the properties identified in the three studies indicates that, as is the case with so many other organizational behavior concepts, similar factors are often discussed but different descriptive labels are utilized. Since the early development of any field is rarely a consciously planned effort, this situation is likely to exist. There does, however, appear to be some commonalities in these and other lists of climate properties. Most of the lists include about the same number of properties and usually include structure, conflict, rewards, warmth, autonomy or very similar properties. However, we believe that it is too early in the study of organizational climate to attempt a definitive synthesis of the numerous properties identified in the research literature.

Measuring Organizational Climate

Trying to measure organizational climate is an attempt to capture the essence, environment, order, and pattern of an organization or a subunit. This must involve, therefore, soliciting perceptions of organizational members about the various attributes and elements of the organization or subunit.

The diagnosis of organizational climate is usually undertaken through the use of a structured survey questionnaire. In Chapter 2 we discussed the necessity of constructing reliable and valid research instruments. We noted that it is a difficult and time consuming task best left to the qualified technical expert. Figure 19–2 presents four items from an early version of a questionnaire designed to measure organizational climate developed by Litwin and Stringer. The items presented—designed to measure the property of risk—were part of a much larger number of items designed to measure all of the

---

[9] B. Schneider and C. J. Bartlett, "Individual Differences and Organizational Climate, I, The Research Plan and Questionnaire Development," *Personnel Psychology* (Autumn 1968), pp. 323–34.

Figure 19–2
Example of Four Questionnaire Items Designed to Measure the "Risk" Property of Organizational Climate

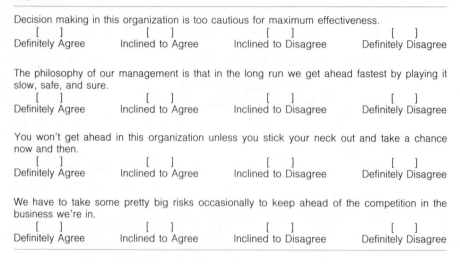

Decision making in this organization is too cautious for maximum effectiveness.

[   ]   [   ]   [   ]   [   ]
Definitely Agree   Inclined to Agree   Inclined to Disagree   Definitely Disagree

The philosophy of our management is that in the long run we get ahead fastest by playing it slow, safe, and sure.

[   ]   [   ]   [   ]   [   ]
Definitely Agree   Inclined to Agree   Inclined to Disagree   Definitely Disagree

You won't get ahead in this organization unless you stick your neck out and take a chance now and then.

[   ]   [   ]   [   ]   [   ]
Definitely Agree   Inclined to Agree   Inclined to Disagree   Definitely Disagree

We have to take some pretty big risks occasionally to keep ahead of the competition in the business we're in.

[   ]   [   ]   [   ]   [   ]
Definitely Agree   Inclined to Agree   Inclined to Disagree   Definitely Disagree

properties of organizational climate identified by Litwin and Stringer.[10] Recall that the risk property of climate concerns the challenges and riskiness in the job and in the organization: Is there an emphasis on taking calculated risks, or is playing it safe the best way to operate? The items illustrate how the properties of organizational climate are usually assessed.

Earlier we noted that there were methodological as well as theoretical issues surrounding organizational climate as yet unresolved. There is considerable controversy as to whether it is possible to meaningfully measure and diagnose organizational climate by obtaining perceptions of members that are truly descriptive of the climate. Many believe that the perceptions are really evaluations and are influenced by the personal attributes of the members and how satisfied or dissatisfied they are with the organization.[11]

Most researchers, writers, and many practicing managers seem to be in

---

[10] See Litwin and Stringer, *Motivation and Organizational Climate,* pp. 66–92, for a complete discussion of the complexity involved, and detail and time required to develop a reliable research instrument. Their discussion outlines each stage of testing and revision. The sample items in Figure 19–2 are from an initial version of the instrument and are used here only for illustrative purposes.

[11] For discussions of the measurement problems associated with organizational climate see R. E. Johanesson, "Some Problems in the Measurement of Organizational Climate," *Organizational Behavior and Human Performance* (August 1973), pp. 118–44; S. Lirtzman, R. House, and J. Rizzo, "An Alternative to Organization Climate: The Measurement of Organization Practices," *Proceedings of the National Academy of Management* (August 1973); H. P. Sims, Jr. and W. LaFollette, "An Assessment of the Litwin and Stringer Organization Climate Questionnaire," *Personnel Psychology* (Spring 1975), pp. 19–38; and P. M. Muchinsky, "An Assessment of the Litwin and Stringer Organization Climate Questionnaire: An Empirical and Theoretical Extension of the Sims and LaFollette Study"; R. W. Woodman and D. C. King, "Organizational Climate: Science or Folklore?" *Academy of Management Review* (October 1978), pp. 816–26.

agreement that the concept of organizational climate offers great promise. When the problems associated with its measurement can be adequately understood, its promise will be much closer to being realized.

Some Specific Determinants of Organizational Climate

In the performance model utilized throughout the book and in Figure 19–1 we have indicated the relationship between performance, organizational climate and the behavior, structure, and processes of the organization. In this section we shall examine more specifically some of the possible determinants of organizational climate.[12]

Economic Conditions.   Many of the proposed properties could be influenced by the condition of the economy. Perceptions of risk, rewards, and conflict might vary depending on how the organization is affected by upswings and downswings in the economy.

Leadership Style.   The type of leadership style which permeates from the top of the organization is likely to have a major impact on organizational climate. It is likely to influence the styles adopted by managers at all levels in· the organization.

Organizational Policies.   Specific policies (for example, "promotion from within") can influence organizational climate. We saw in the chapter on intergroup conflict that the environment for competition and conflict is affected by managerial policies.

Managerial Values.   These were discussed earlier in the text. The values of top managers are almost certain to affect the organizational climate. As a result, some organizations may be perceived by members as being paternalistic, impersonal, formal or informal, aggressive, passive, trustworthy or not trustworthy.[13]

Organizational Structure.   An organization structured according to traditional bureaucratic principles is likely to have a different climate than one organized according to Likert's System 4 organization design.

Member Characteristics.   The age, dress, and behavior of organizational members or even the number of male versus female managers could have an impact on certain properties of organizational climate.

Type of Activity.   The activity the organization engages in will probably affect its climate. An airline, a space technology firm, a government agency, a bank, and an exclusive retail store are likely to differ in organizational climate. This climate may influence the type of individuals attracted as possible employees and how they behave if they become employees.

TWO FIELD STUDIES OF ORGANIZATIONAL CLIMATE

A useful means to illustrate the potential of the concept of organizational climate is to review some field research in which it was the major focus. A

---

[12] Adapted from DuBrin, *Fundamentals of Organizational Behavior,* pp. 334–40.

[13] For a very interesting discussion of organizational climate along these lines see S. W. Gellerman, *People, Problems, and Profits* (New York: McGraw-Hill Book Co., 1960).

Figure 19–3
Organizational Climate in Public Utility Office

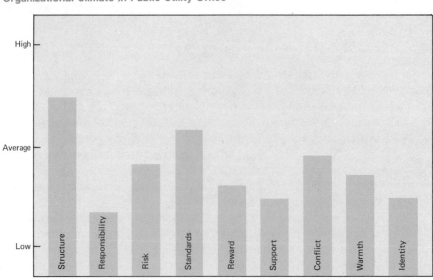

number of field studies have been conducted which investigate organizational climate. We have selected two because they touch upon many of the concepts discussed in this chapter and throughout the book.

Organizational Climate in the Office of a Public Utility

This study conducted by Litwin and Stringer involved women who worked in the service department of a large public utility.[14] Most of the 30 women who worked in the office were college graduates in their early twenties. They serviced customer complaints, took orders for new equipment, and answered questions concerning billings and the numerous services offered by the utility.

The company had a policy to hire female college graduates for these positions because they believed that these women possessed the sound judgment and tact needed for dealing with irate customers. Often in the past, many of the employees of this department worked only one or two years before resigning.

The climate in the office was determined by personal interviews and by a structured questionnaire (previously discussed). The following responses are typical of the personal interview responses:

The climate in this office is one of frustration even though the personnel at your own level are friendly.

The pressures are great—not just because the standards are nothing less than perfection—but there are miles of red tape, constant attention to petty details, and constant criticism. There is a certain satisfaction in doing a job well which helps balance this out, but there is not as much

---

[14] From Litwin and Stringer, *Motivation and Organizational Climate*, pp. 147–52.

Figure 19–4
Need Patterns in Public Utility Office

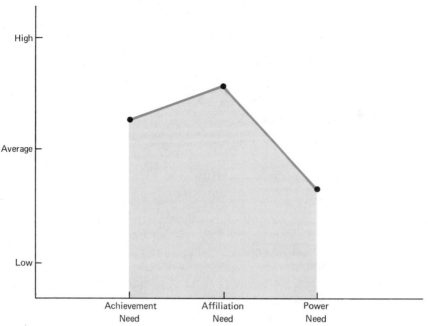

pride in one's work as there could be. However, the people in the office get along well together, and this helps to relieve the tension somewhat. . . .

. . . to excel is equated with pleasing high management, not self-satisfaction. Since management is not respected, antagonism exists and a desire not to excel exists.

The responses to personal interviews and the survey questionnaire provided researchers with some knowledge of the climate in the office. A profile is presented in Figure 19–3.[15] It indicates that the women perceived a relatively high degree of structure. Responsibility and risk were relatively low, but standards were high. This was stressed in the second personal interview response above.

Finally, the data indicated that the women perceived relatively low amounts of reward, support, and identity. They perceived the climate to be cold and unfriendly, allowing little opportunity for the development of group loyalty and identity.

In addition to measuring the perceived organizational climate, the researchers also assessed the women's need strengths. This was also done with a structured questionnaire. The average responses from the women are shown in Figure 19–4.[16] The responses indicate that the women were about average

---

[15] Adapted from Ibid., p. 150.
[16] Ibid., p. 151.

in the need for achievement and the need for affiliation, and below average in the need for power.

When the organizational-climate results and the need results were studied, it became apparent that the hiring policies of the organization were not compatible with the needs of the people hired. There was little congruence between the needs of the women hired and the climate in which they were expected to perform. Turnover and absenteeism were serious problems. This particular office continually ranked in the lowest third of all company offices on these two measures. In addition, detailed measures of service and sales performance of the group indicated they were average or below average on these performance measures.

Organizational Climate in a Hospital

This field study examined organizational climate in a 450-bed teaching-referral hospital.[17] One of the objectives of the study was to examine the employees' perceptions of both the organizational climate and their job satisfaction. Hospitals are complex organizations for several reasons, one being the numerous and diverse groups that work within them: physicians, medical technicians, nurses, diagnostic personnel, clerical personnel, and administrators. This complicates managerial performance. For example, several researchers have described the nursing profession as having a "blurred image."[18] That is, nurses may not know exactly what their role in the hospital is, and this could affect performance.

Organizational climate in this study was measured using a questionnaire which included the eight properties of organizational climate identified by Halpin and Crofts.[19] These were defined earlier in the chapter and include:

1. Aloofness
2. Consideration
3. Disengagement
4. Esprit
5. Hindrance
6. Intimacy
7. Production
8. Thrust

Nurses, hospital administrators, and diagnostic personnel were asked to respond to the questionnaire. In addition, the job satisfaction of each group was measured by another structured questionnaire designed to measure how their jobs satisfied three specific needs: self actualization, autonomy, and esteem.

One important step in analyzing the data obtained from 35 nurses, 99 administrators, and 28 diagnosticians was to relate the influence of the various properties of organizational climate on the satisfaction levels of the three

---

[17] J. M. Ivancevich and H. L. Lyon, *Organizational Climate, Job Satisfaction, Role Clarity, and Selected Emotional Reaction Variables in a Hospital Milieu* (Lexington, Kentucky: Office of Developmental Services, University of Kentucky, May 1972).

[18] W. Bennis, "Leadership Theory and Administrative Behavior: The Problem of Authority," *Administrative Science Quarterly* (December 1959), pp. 259–301; and J. E. Haas, *Role Conception and Group Consensus* (Columbus: Ohio State University, 1964).

[19] Halpin and Crofts, *The Organizational Climate of Schools*.

needs for each group. The impact of the various climate properties upon need satisfaction was different for each group. Table 19–1 summarizes the major influences of the various climate properties upon need satisfaction for each group.

Table 19–1 indicates that the satisfaction of the self-actualization needs of the nursing groups is influenced most by a climate that is low in hindrance and disengagement and higher in esprit. Administrators in this hospital derive self-actualization need satisfaction in a climate that is high in thrust and consideration. The different combinations of the properties of the hospital's climate certainly can be of use to policymakers in this hospital.

Table 19–1
Major Influences of Organizational Climate Properties on Need Satisfaction for Three Hospital Groups

Group	Need		
	Self-Actualization	Autonomy	Esteem
Nurses	—Hindrance —Disengagement +Esprit	—Hindrance	—Disengagement +Espirit
Administrators	+Thrust +Consideration	+Esprit +Thrust	+Esprit +Thrust
Diagnosticians	+Thrust +Consideration	+Thrust +Consideration	+Consideration

CHANGING ORGANIZATIONAL CLIMATE

An appropriate question at his point is "Can organizational climate be changed?" While fundamental changes in organizational climate are not easily or quickly made, research evidence does indicate that change is possible and has occurred.[20]

One study found that by making managers aware of the organizational climate they have created as well as the aspects of their own behavior that have created the climates, significant changes in climate can be accomplished at the work group level. The researchers collected data from groups of salesmen before and after their managers were trained to change the climate. The researchers found considerable changes in sense of responsibility, rewards received, role clarity, and team spirit.[21]

[20] This section is based on George G. Gordon and Bonnie E. Goldberg, "Is There a Climate for Success?" *Management Review* (May 1977), pp. 37–44.

[21] David C. McClelland and David H. Burnhan, "Power Is the Great Motivator," *Harvard Business Review* (March–April 1976), pp. 100–110.

A recent study examined changing the organizational climate of a large corporation.[22] For the period 1967–71, International Harvester experienced serious problems. A new chairman of the board was appointed with a mandate to improve performance. One of his first actions was to have an organizational climate study conducted among senior management. Four distinct perceptions were uncovered: (1) a lack of a sense of direction, (2) insufficient delegation of authority and discouragement of individual initiative, (3) an emphasis on short-term decision making, and (4) highly strained communications.[23]

As a result of this and other studies, the chairman instituted a program to alter the basic way the organization was managed. This included changes in organizational structure, planning system, management development, and reward systems. The changes were implemented over a three-year period and a follow-up study indicated definite improvements in some areas with problems remaining in some others.

Both of these studies indicated that changing organizational climate is possible. Obviously the magnitude of the desired changes (that is, the dimensions being changed) and the size of the organization will influence the complexity and length of time needed to complete the change.

A POSTSCRIPT

In Part I of this book, we indicated that our goal was to communicate knowledge to the reader. Specifically, knowledge of the *behavior* of individuals in organizations, the ways in which organizations are *structured,* and the *processes* which take place within organizations. The ultimate purpose was to achieve more *effective management of organizational behavior.* We believe that this knowledge, in addition to your on-the-job experiences, will increase the probability of your becoming an effective manager in a shorter period of time. This is because it will enable you to "make sense" of your experience and thereby make it more meaningful, more quickly. While there are undoubtedly other ways to present the current knowledge in organizational behavior, we have found the behavior-structure-process format to be extremely useful.

We also noted at the outset of the book that the chances are very good that educated persons will sooner or later find themselves in some type of managerial position whether or not they ever took formal courses or specific training in the field. If this is true, the question therefore, is not whether you will ever be a manager, but rather *when* you are, how effective or ineffective a manager you will be. We firmly believe that the knowledge gained from studying this book will increase your chances of becoming an effective manager. This has been our theme throughout, the achievement of organizational effectiveness through enlightened management. Thus, although the chal-

---

[22] Robert Rock, *The Chief Executive Officer Managing the Human Resources of a Large Diversified Industrial Company* (Doctoral dissertation, Harvard University, 1976).

[23] See Gordon and Goldberg, "Is There a Climate for Success?"

lenges of the future may appear frightening in many respects, the opportunities available for the manager with proper training are unlimited.

MAJOR ISSUES FOR THE MANAGER TO CONSIDER

A. Organizational climate is a term used to describe the unique constellation of characteristics and properties associated with an organization or subunit and shared by its members. Many writers believe it has much promise as an integrative concept in organizational behavior.

B. Each work organization creates a number of different types of climate. Thus, the type of climate found will depend on the unit of analysis. The type of climate found in one department might differ from another and both might differ from that of the total organization.

C. At this writing, most assessments of organizational climate have not been sufficiently descriptive or valid to enable the development of a definitive synthesis of its properties.

D. Leadership patterns, organization structure, individual and group behavior, and decision making and communication processes can all affect organizational climate.

E. Organizational climate can influence such performance factors as the quality of work and job satisfaction.

F. It is unlikely that a unique set of organizational climate properties will be developed for every type of organization. Consistent with the contingency view we may find that different types of climate will be more effective based on the type of task, problems, and environment faced by the organization or subunit.

G. An understanding and appreciation of the concept of organizational climate should aid a manager in understanding how organizational practices, policies, and procedures are reflected in human behavior.

H. Both theoretical and methodological problems related to the concept of organizational climate exist. Serious measurement issues must be resolved before any organizational climate questionnaire can be used with complete confidence.

DISCUSSION AND REVIEW QUESTIONS

1. Select any organization, group, or other unit of analysis of which you are a member. Describe it in detail using one of the sets of organizational climate properties discussed in the chapter. What are your conclusions? Be specific.

2. Can the concept of organizational climate ever be really useful for practicing managers? Should an organization measure its various climates periodically? Discuss.

3. If you were a manager could you make effective use of information on your employees' perceived organizational climate? How?

4. What do you believe is the climate in the class in which you use this textbook?

5. Compare the climate in this class with that of another you are presently taking. Are they different? In what ways? Have these differences affected your performance? In what ways? With what results?

6. Do you believe that a change in the structure of an organization can influence the climate? Discuss.

7. Would it benefit an organization to measure its various climates on a longitudinal basis? Discuss.

8. Could organizational climate influence an individual's response to a motivation technique such as job enrichment? In what ways?

ADDITIONAL REFERENCES

Campbell, J. P.; Dunnette, M. D.; Lawler, E. E., III; and Weick, K. E., Jr. *Managerial Behavior, Performance and Effectiveness.* New York: McGraw-Hill, 1970.

Downey, H. K.; Hellriegel, D.; Phelps, M.; and Slocum, J. W., Jr. "Organizational Climate and Job Satisfaction: A Comparative Analysis." *Journal of Business Research* (1974), pp. 233–48.

Friedlander, F., and Margulies, N. "Multiple Impacts of Organizational Climate and Individual Systems Upon Job Satisfaction." *Personnel Psychology* (1969), pp. 171–83.

Guion, R. M. "A Note on Organizational Climate." *Organizational Behavior and Human Performance* (1973), pp. 120–25.

Muchinsky, P. M. "Organizational Communication: Relationship to Organizational Climate and Job Satisfaction." *Academy of Management Journal* (1977), pp. 592–607.

Newman, J. E. "Development of a Measure of Perceived Work Environment (PWE)." *Academy of Management Journal* (1977), pp. 520–34.

Payne, R. L., and Pheysey, D. G. "Stern's Organizational Climate Index: A Reconceptualization and Application To Business Organizations." *Organizational Behavior and Human Performance* (1971), pp. 77–98.

Payne, R. L., and Pugh, D. S. "Organizational Structure and Climate." In M. Dunnette, ed. *Handbook of Industrial and Organizational Psychology.* Chicago: Rand McNally, 1976.

Prien, E. P., and Ronan, W. W. "An Analysis of Organizational Characteristics." *Organizational Behavior and Human Performance* (1971), pp. 215–34.

Schneider, B. "Organizational Climate: Individual Preferences and Organizational Realities." *Journal of Applied Psychology* (1972), pp. 211–17.

———. "The Perception of Organizational Climate: The Customers View." *Journal of Applied Psychology* (1973), pp. 248–56.

Taguiri, R., and Litwin, G., eds. *Organizational Climate: Explorations of a Concept.* Boston: Division of Research, Graduate School of Business Administration, Harvard University, 1968.

Wallace, M. J.; Ivancevich, J. M.; and Lyon, H. L. "Measurement Modifications For Assessing Organizational Climate." *Academy of Management Journal* (1975), pp. 82–97.

Appendix A

Experimentation in the Behavioral Sciences

INTRODUCTION

In Chapter 2 we noted that the experimental method is the prototype of the scientific approach. It is the ideal toward which we strive but unfortunately do not always achieve. In this appendix we shall examine a number of different approaches which can be used in designing experiments. To illustrate the various approaches we shall use an example of a training program being offered to a group of first-line supervisors. The task of the researcher is to design an experiment which will permit the assessment of the degree to which the program influenced the performance of the supervisors. We will use the following symbols in our discussion:

$S =$ the subjects, the supervisors participating in the experiment.
$O =$ the observation and measurement devices used by the researcher (that is, ratings of supervisors' performance by superiors).
$X =$ the experimental treatment, the manipulated variable (that is, the training program).
$R =$ the randomization process.[1]

We shall examine six different designs which vary in degree of sophistication and point out the problems associated with each one. In each design the training program (X) is the independent variable, and performance is the dependent variable.

One-Shot Design

If we assume that all supervisors go through the training program it will be difficult for the researchers to evaluate it. This is because the researchers

---

[1] R. H. Helmstader, *Research Concepts in Human Behavior* (New York: Appleton-Century-Crofts, 1970); and William G. Scott and Terence R. Mitchell, *Organization Theory: A Structural and Behavioral Analysis* (Homewood, Ill.: Richard D. Irwin, Inc., and The Dorsey Press, 1976).

cannot compare performance scores with earlier scores before the training program. In addition they cannot compare the group with another group which did not undergo the training program. Thus, this design is called a *one-shot* design and is diagrammed as follows:

$$X \quad O$$

The letter X stands for the experimental treatment (that is, the training program) and O for the observation. This is the measure of performance on the job and would probably be presented in the form of an average score based on ratings of superiors. However, the researchers can in no way determine whether performance was influenced at all by the training program. This experimental design is rarely used because of its weaknesses.

One-Group Pretest-Posttest Design

The previous design can be improved upon by first gathering performance data on the supervisors, instituting the training program, and then remeasuring their performance. This is diagrammed as follows:

$$O_1 \quad X \quad O_2$$

Thus, a pretest is given in time period one, the program is administered, and a posttest is administered in time period two. If $O_2 > O_1$, the differences can be attributed to the training program.

There are numerous factors which can confound the results obtained with this design. For example, suppose new equipment has been installed between O_1 and O_2. This could explain the differences in the performance scores. Thus, a *history* factor may have influenced our results. There are numerous other factors which also could influence our results. The most occurring ones are listed along with the definition of each one in Table 1.[2] Examination of Table 1 indicates that results achieved in this design may also be confounded by *maturation* (supervisors may learn to do a better job between O_1 and O_2 which would increase their performance regardless of training), *testing* (the measure of performance in O_1 may have made the supervisors aware that they were being evaluated which may make them work harder and increase their performance), and *instrumentation* (if the performance observations were made at different times of the day when fatigue could pay a role, the results could be influenced). Each of these factors offers other explanations for changes in performance than the training program. Obviously, this design can be improved upon.

Static-Group Comparison Design

In this design, half of the supervisors would be allowed to sign up for the training. Once the enrollment reached 50 percent of the supervisors, the training program would begin. After some period of time the group of

---

[2] Ibid.

Table 1
Some Sources of Error in Experimental Studies

Factor	Definition
1. History	Events other than the experimental treatment (X) which occurred between premeasurement and postmeasurement.
2. Maturation	Changes in the subject group with the passage of time which are not associated with the experimental treatment (X).
3. Testing	Changes in the performance of the subjects because previous measurement of their performance made them aware they were part of an experiment (that is, measures often alter what is being measured).
4. Instrumentation	Changes in the measures of participants' performance that are the result of changes in the measurement instruments or conditions under which the measuring is done (for example, wear on machinery, boredom, fatigue on the part of observers).
5. Selection	When participants are assigned to experimental and control groups on any basis other than random assignment. Any other selection method will result in systematic biases which will result in differences between groups which are unrelated to the effects of the experimental treatment (X).
6. Mortality	If some participants drop out of the experiment before it is completed, the experimental and control groups may not be comparable.
7. Interaction effects	Any of the above factors may interact with the experimental treatment, resulting in confounding effects on the results. For example, the types of individuals withdrawing from a study (mortality) may differ for the experimental group and the control group.

supervisors who enrolled in the program would be compared with those who did not enroll. This design is diagrammed as follows:

Since the supervisors were not randomly assigned to each group it is highly possible that the group that enrolled are the more highly motivated or more intelligent supervisors. Thus, *selection* is a major problem with this design. However, note that the addition of a *control group* (comparison group) has eliminated many of the error factors associated with the first two designs. The problem here is that the subjects were not randomly assigned to the experimental group (undergoing training) and the control group (no training). Therefore, it is possible that differences may exist between the two groups that are not related to the training.

The three designs discussed thus far (one-shot, one-group pretest-posttest, static-group comparisons) have been described as "pseudo-experimental" or "quasi-experimental" designs. When true experimentation cannot be achieved, these designs (especially the last two) are preferred over no research at all or over relying on personal opinion. The following three designs can be considered "true" experimental designs because the researcher has complete control over the situation in the sense of determining precisely who will participate in the experiment and which subjects will or will not receive the experimental treatment.

Pretest-Posttest Control Group Design

This design is one of the simplest forms of true experimentation used in the study of human behavior. It is diagrammed as follows:

$$R \quad O_1 \quad X \quad O_2$$
$$R \quad O_1 \quad \quad O_2$$

Note that this design is similar to the one-group pretest-posttest design except that a control group has been added and the participants have been randomly assigned to both groups. Which group is to receive the training (experimental group) and which will not (control group) is also randomly determined. The two groups may be said to be equivalent at the time of the initial observations, and when the final observations are made, and different only in that one group has received training while the other has not. In other words if the change from O_1 to O_2 is greater in the experimental than from O_1 to O_2 in the control group we can attribute it to the training program rather than selection, testing, maturation, and so forth.

The major weakness of the pretest-posttest control group design is one of *interaction* (selection and treatment), where individuals are aware they are participating in an experiment. In other words, being observed the first time makes all participants work more diligently, both those who are in the training program and those who are in the control group. Here the participants in the training program will be more receptive to training because of the pretest. This problem of interaction can be overcome by using a posttest-only control group design.

Posttest-Only Control Group Design

In this design, participants are randomly assigned to two groups, the training is administered to one group, and scores on posttests are compared (performance evaluated). It is diagrammed as follows:

$$R \quad X \quad O$$
$$R \quad \quad O$$

This eliminates the problem of the previous design by not administering a pretest. However, the dependent variable (performance) is an ultimate rather than a relative measure of achievement. The researcher also does not have a group which was pretested and posttested without receiving the experimental treatment (training program). Such a group can provide valuable information on the effects of history, maturation, instrumentation, and so on. However, where a pretest is difficult to obtain or where its use is likely to make the participants aware that an experiment is being carried on, this approach may be much preferred to the pretest-posttest control group design.

Solomon Four-Group Design

This design is a combination of the previous two designs and is diagrammed as follows:

Group 1	R	O_1	X	O_2
Group 2	R	O_1		O_2
Group 3	R		X	O_2
Group 4	R			O_2

Where gain or change in behavior is the desired dependent variable, this design should be used. This design is the most desirable of all of the designs examined here. While it does not control any more sources of invalid results, this does permit the estimation of the extent of the effects of some of the sources of error. In our example here, the supervisors are randomly assigned to four groups two of which will receive the training, one with a pretest and one without. Therefore, the researcher can examine among other things the effects of history (Group 2), testing (Group 2 to Group 4), and testing-treatment interaction (Group 1 to Group 3). Clearly, this design is the most complex, utilizing more participants, and will be more costly. The added value of the additional information will have to be compared to the additional costs.

This appendix has examined a number of different approaches to designing experiments. While there are other approaches, these are widely used. Our purpose has been to familiarize the reader with experimentation in the behavioral sciences. A complete treatment of the subject is beyond the scope of this text.[3]

---

[3] For a complete coverage of this area see Fred N. Kerlinger, *Foundations of Behavioral Research* (New York: Holt, Rinehart, & Winston, 1973), pp. 300–376; and Helmstader, *Research Concepts in Human Behavior,* pp. 91–121.

Glenn Taylor

Dick Spencer

Excelsior Bakeries, Inc.

A Case of Misunderstanding: Mr. Hart and Mr. Bing

GLENN TAYLOR*

Glenn Taylor, age 50, held the position of vice president for finance and controller of the Sage Electronics Company.

Sage was a large and profitable electronics company which manufactured and marketed its products on a worldwide basis; its stock was listed on a major stock exchange. Mr. Taylor had joined the company ten years earlier as an assistant treasurer. Prior to joining Sage he had had a very successful career in the field of public accounting. Sage in fact used to be one of his clients when he worked for a large public accounting firm.

Taylor's work at Sage was impressive, and James Johnson, Sage's president, considered him one of the ablest men in top management. On several occasions James Johnson had credited Taylor for playing a valuable role in the rapid growth and success of the company. In recent years Sage had made a number of acquisitions, and Taylor had played a key role in negotiating the purchase terms. In addition, and almost single-handedly, Taylor had introduced most of the planning and control systems which guided the company. These systems included a management-by-objectives program and both long- and short-term profit planning systems involving budgeting of sales and expenses which were used for control purposes. They had been introduced as part of a major reorganization of Sage which took place several years ago. Taylor had designed the systems for use by line managers at the request of James Johnson, who had hired him originally.

Glenn Taylor was born and raised in the Presbyterian faith. He considered himself a religious person, and tried to practice his religious principles in business. Business associates respected his high moral and ethical standards and his sense of fair play. Discussing his job, Glenn stated: "Central to the idea of controllership, it seems to me, are the ideas of responsibility, controls, and defining the rules of the game. The rules have to be administered fairly."

In the spring of 1970, Mr. Taylor hired Philip Hawkins as a special staff assistant. Hawkins started work on July 1, just three weeks after he had received his M.B.A. degree from a well-known eastern school of business administration. Hawkins had been in the top third of his graduating class; and although he had concentrated in finance and accounting, he had taken several courses in the organizational behavior area as part of his second-year program. During his second year Hawkins had written a research report on the behavioral aspects of control systems which Taylor considered "quite interesting." Though Hawkins viewed his staff assignment with excitement, he considered it as a stepping stone to a line position within 12 to 15 months in one of Sage's divisions. When Hawkins accepted the job in early May, Taylor said that he would have a real problem for him when he started work, and he would appreciate hearing his views on it then. "In fact," Taylor said, "I'll write it out in case form on a confidential basis and give it to you on your first day of work." Without inquiring about the nature of the problem,

Hawkins replied that he would look forward to tackling Taylor's case problem when he returned to Sage.

Glenn Taylor had been thinking long and hard about the problem he would write out for Philip Hawkins, for it had been bothering him for a considerable length of time. While he had talked about the problem with his wife and with Kenneth Johnson, who was both vice president for domestic operations of Sage and a close friend, he had never talked about it to anyone else inside or outside of the company. He did say, however, that he had informed the president, James Johnson, "in general" about the situation. James Johnson and Kenneth Johnson were brothers and major stockholders of the company. (See Exhibit 1 for an abbreviated organization chart.)

Exhibit 1

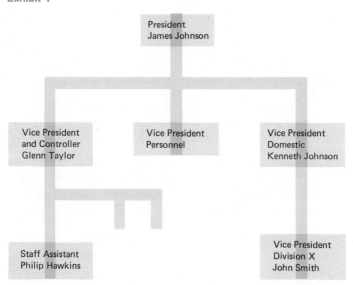

President
James Johnson

Vice President
and Controller
Glenn Taylor

Vice President
Personnel

Vice President
Domestic
Kenneth Johnson

Staff Assistant
Philip Hawkins

Vice President
Division X
John Smith

Before giving his written case to Philip after they had lunched together on July 1, Glenn emphasized the confidential nature of this problem. "Confidentially," said Glenn, "the biggest damn problem I have is John Smith. Sometimes I think I should say the hell with it and forget it, but I'm afraid if I do that it will hurt the company too much." He suggested that Philip read the case that evening and that they get together to discuss it the following day. Philip thought this approach made sense and was flattered that Taylor was willing to confide in him. Before departing for a meeting Glenn said, "John Smith is the problem, and if you can solve this problem you will go a long way in Sage." The written case which Glenn gave to Philip appears below:

John Smith is one of the key executives in charge of operations for a significant geographical area of my company. He has been an employee for over

15 years, first in the role of a production supervisor, then division production manager. There were other position changes until his present position as a divisional domestic vice president.

He has enjoyed a succession of promotions and is highly regarded by all those who have worked for him. In part, this is a reflection of his personality, as the other side of the coin is being reflected in difficulties I am encountering with him.

First, John is a law unto himself and gives favorite treatment to those working for him. He freely disregards company personnel practices and procedures and administers to his people as he chooses. His secretary gets the highest salary of any secretary in the company, works on a time schedule ignoring regular office hours, etc. This situation is widely recognized and resented by many others, but he has always gotten away with it and as a result he considers this his prerogative.

As he has progressed, this disregard for policy has become more noticeable on a higher level, even to the point of disregarding presidential requests or responding to them in such a way that they have been disregarded for all practical purposes. For example, he has never chosen to completely comply with annual profit-plan requests. He will present location plans without review and personal commitment, or at times he will submit data sufficiently different from standard forms to make collation and comparison difficult.

This has been accompanied by attempts to impose an iron curtain over the flow of information. This occurs with him personally and with operations under his supervision. When I request a meeting to discuss mutual problems, it rarely takes place unless forced by me.

Communications with others working under him become most troublesome, and strong measures are sometimes required to keep avenues of communication open to operations. Relationships with an operating location become noticeably different when he is in charge of it or when his responsibility no longer covers it.

This can be very unfortunate since many of our mutual areas of responsibility frequently overlap into areas with which he has no knowledge. To date we have been fortunate in preventing any serious losses, but solely by accident.

He works hard—long hours—travels a large part of his time—is unstinting as to his time on company affairs. He has a keen, analytical mind, but tends to let small things prevent his deciding on major things.

Personally, away from the office we get along fine. He is affable, good company, and there is a free, open conversation without strain.

These relationships also appear to apply to others at his level and above.

When Philip entered Glenn's office late in the afternoon on July 2, Glenn offered him a seat and then closed his office door. He told his secretary they were not to be disturbed.

Taylor *(laughing):* Well, Phil, I bet you didn't run into any cases like my case in your business school studies. Believe me, Phil, this guy is getting away with *murder* over there. I sure would like to know what to do about it next. . . .

Hawkins: Glenn, I don't know whether I can be of any help, but I would like to try. I wonder, though, if. . . .

Taylor *(excitedly):* The whole trouble is this guy thinks he's a law unto himself . . .

he runs his damned division the way *he* wants to and says to *hell* with everybody else! I don't know, maybe the best thing for me to do is. . . .

Hawkins: Excuse me, Glenn, but frankly I'm still not clear just on some of the facts here. For example, just what is the background history on this problem?

Taylor: Ever since John was promoted to the vice presidency several years ago the relations between our people have become more and more difficult. It's gotten to the point now where my people come to me and say they can't get any information out of that division, and they're supposed to get reports as a matter of course. . . . They're spending so much time trying to pry things loose there that other divisions and problems are suffering. When we finally do get stuff from him it's likely to be scratched on the back of an envelop or something—absolutely no thought has gone into it, obviously. I tell you, he has no regard for the problems we're trying to deal with here.

Hawkins: Glenn, do you think a part of this problem may be explained by the image of your office? We had a lot of case studies about that at the B School, and I found that to be the case in my research report.

Taylor: You have put your finger on something there. There can be no doubt about it. We're known as the checkers, the probers, and the spies. The office of the controller does not have a good image, and it is part of the problem. But we have a job to do, too, and I am responsible for developing full reports that go to the board of directors.

Hawkins: I wonder what it's like working for a guy like Smith. . . .

Taylor: Oh, I can tell you he gets tremendous loyalty—his people just love him. He goes to bat for them, too . . . his secretary is the highest paid in the entire company. And this is pretty well true of many of his people—they get more pay and benefits and sometimes even faster promotions than any other division—I tell you, after John's been in a slot for a while it begins to close up to any kind of corporate-wide control. . . . The guy is really getting away with murder. . . .

Hawkins: What do you think Smith himself thinks about all this?

Taylor: Well, he's convinced he's doing what he should. He's a real seat-of-the-pants manager—he just doesn't take any time for the systems we've introduced. He's been around a long time—he's 46 now—and he knows this business inside out. It's like pulling eye teeth to get any information out of him. He doesn't pay any attention to routine requests of mine for meetings—and he certainly never takes the initiative to arrange one or ever try to find out what our procedures are. The only time we get together is when I *force* a meeting.

Hawkins: He must be difficult to deal with.

Taylor: That's for sure. But it's funny, you know, he's not an angry type. Off the job, as I wrote in the case, we get together occasionally at a party at Jim or Ken Johnson's club and everything's fine—we get along fine. . . . I've only seen him mad about something once. That was when he was trying to protect another secretary of his after she had caused all kinds of trouble over in another division getting information she had no business getting—those people wanted Smith's head! Well, the personnel director and I put our foot down. Smith got mad, I got mad and I held firm. I said, "That girl has to go, and that's the way it's going to be!" He backed down at that point.

Hawkins: What does Smith's boss—Kenneth Johnson—know about all this?

Taylor: Oh, Ken is very aware of all this. He knows the whole story, but he says he has the same trouble with John as I do. He can't get any information either. He's wringing his hands over this guy running his division like it was his own company.

Hawkins: Well, what about the president? Does he know about it? Can't he get action?

Taylor: Yeah, he knows about it too . . . we've *had* to tell him why there are gaps in our reports or where the unlikely estimates come from.

Hawkins: Why doesn't he crack down?

Taylor: Well, the trouble is, Smith does turn in the results—he gets the profits. Last year he turned in the most profits of any division in the company. It's been like that just about every job he has. He's always gotten the promotions, all along the line since he came to Sage 15 years ago.

Hawkins: Oh, I see. . . .

Taylor: I'll tell you, though, something has got to be done. I think Jim is beginning to see more and more the problems Smith is causing—and *could* cause. He told me last week he was going to look into this whole thing again.

Hawkins: You mentioned there were problems he *could* cause. What kinds of things?

Taylor: Why, my God, he's writing contracts with suppliers and making sales agreements all the time with nobody around here knowing about it! A year ago he was about to sign a licensing agreement with another manufacturer that would have put us smack into a lot of trouble because of a new product being developed by another division! He just charges ahead, thinking only for himself. The key point is that Smith could hurt the long-run profitability of the company in the area of trademarks, patents, and taxes. He almost gave away the company's patents in one horror case, and if he changed one licensing agreement the way he wanted to it would have cost the company $25,000 in taxes. There is a need for close cooperation between Smith and me, otherwise there will be lost profits.

Hawkins: Who runs his division while he's away? You say he travels a great deal and he's away now on a long business trip.

Taylor: Ken Johnson is trying to run it, and he's asked me for help. As a matter of fact, I have a meeting with him tomorrow to see what we can do. Apparently, Smith's people are tighter than ever since he's been away—Ken says they won't tell him any more now than they ever did.

Hawkins: What kinds of things have you thought of doing?

Taylor: I've beat my head on this one so much with so little results to show for it that I've just about decided to say "to hell with it." I don't know. . . . I suppose if I didn't care what happened to the company I would just sit back and do my job and let the chips fall where they may, but I'm not like that; I couldn't do that after all the effort that's gone into building up the new organization.

Continuing, Taylor stated:

Smith and I have never competed. He always gets promoted, yet he is a complete nonconformist who gets away with murder. He causes serious morale problems with his peers who try to follow our team management concepts. Here is a good question for you: What do you do when a guy rejects management concepts (management by objectives, long-range planning, and budgets, for example) and still makes better than average profits? Top management has worked hard to develop what it considers the best available management and control techniques. To be honest, Phil, it may be that the best thing for me to do is to say "the hell with it," but I find it hard to accept defeat and admit that "seat-of-the-pants" management is best after all.

As Taylor talked about his case, Philip noted that he got red in the face on several occasions and appeared quite nervous. Philip knew that this was a serious matter for Glenn Taylor, and he truly wanted to help him with his problem.

DICK SPENCER*

After the usual banter when old friends meet for cocktails, the conversation between a couple of University professors and Dick Spencer, a former student who was now a successful businessman, turned to Dick's life as a vice president of a large manufacturing firm.

"I've made a lot of mistakes, most of which I could live with, but this one series of incidents was so frustrating that I could have cried at the time," Dick said in response to a question. "I really have to laugh at how ridiculous it is now, but at the time I blew my cork."

Spencer was plant manager of Modrow Company, a Canadian branch of the Tri-American Corporation. Tri-American was a major producer of primary aluminum with integrated operations ranging from the mining of bauxite through the processing to fabrication of aluminum into a variety of products. The company also made and sold refractories and industrial chemicals. The parent company had wholly owned subsidiaries in five separate U.S. locations and had foreign affiliates in 15 different countries.

Tri-American mined bauxite in the Jamaican West Indies and shipped the raw material by commercial vessels to two plants in Louisiana where it was processed into alumina. The alumina was then shipped to reduction plants in one of three locations for conversion into primary aluminum. Most of the primary aluminum was then moved to the companies' fabricating plants for further processing. Fabricated aluminum items included sheet, flat, coil, and corrugated products; siding; and roofing.

Tri-American employed approximately 22,000 employees in the total organization. The company was governed by a board of directors which included the chairman, vice chairman, president, and twelve vice presidents. However, each of the subsidiaries and branches functioned as independent units. The board set general policy, which was then interpreted and applied by the various plant managers. In a sense, the various plants competed with one another as though they were independent companies. This decentralization in organizational structure increased the freedom and authority of the plant managers, but increased the pressure for profitability.

---

* This case was developed and prepared by Dr. Margaret Fenn, Graduate School of Business Administration, University of Washington. Reprinted by permission.

The Modrow branch was located in a border town in Canada. The total work force in Modrow was 1,000. This Canadian subsidiary was primarily a fabricating unit. Its main products were foil and building products such as roofing and siding. Aluminum products were gaining in importance in architectural plans, and increased sales were predicted for this branch. Its location and its stable work force were the most important advantages it possessed.

In anticipation of estimated increases in building product sales, Modrow had recently completed a modernization and expansion project. At the same time, their research and art departments combined talents in developing a series of twelve new patterns of siding which were being introduced to the market. Modernization and pattern development had been costly undertakings, but the expected return on investment made the project feasible. However, the plant manager, who was a Tri-American vice president, had instituted a campaign to cut expenses wherever possible. In his introductory notice of the campaign, he emphasized that cost reduction would be the personal aim of every employee at Modrow.

Salesman.   The plant manager of Modrow, Dick Spencer, was an American who had been transferred to this Canadian branch two years previously, after the start of the modernization plan. Dick had been with the Tri-American Company for 14 years, and his progress within the organization was considered spectacular by those who knew him well. Dick had received a Master's degree in Business Administration from a well-known university at the age of 22. Upon graduation he had accepted a job as salesman for Tri-American. During his first year as a salesman, he succeeded in landing a single, large contract which put him near the top of the sales-volume leaders. In discussing his phenomenal rise in the sales volume, several of his fellow salesmen concluded that his looks, charm, and ability on the golf course contributed as much to his success as his knowledge of the business or his ability to sell the products.

The second year of his sales career, he continued to set a fast pace. Although his record set difficult goals for the other salesmen, he was considered a "regular guy" by them, and both he and they seemed to enjoy the few occasions when they socialized. However, by the end of the second year of constant travelling and selling, Dick began to experience some doubt about his future.

His constant involvement in business matters disrupted his marital life, and his wife divorced him during the second year with Tri-American. Dick resented her action at first, but gradually seemed to recognize that his career at present depended on his freedom to travel unencumbered. During that second year, he ranged far and wide in his sales territory, and successfully closed several large contracts. None of them was as large as his first year's major sale, but in total volume he again was well up near the top of salesmen for the year. Dick's name became well known in the corporate headquarters, and he was spoken of as "the boy to watch."

Dick had met the president of Tri-American during his first year as a salesman at a company conference. After three days of golfing and socializing they developed a relaxed camaraderie considered unusual by those who observed the developing friendship. Although their contacts were infrequent after the conference, their easy relationship seemed to blossom the few times they did meet. Dick's friends kidded him about his ability to make use of his new friendship to promote himself in the company, but Dick brushed aside their jibes and insisted that he'd make it on his own abilities, not someone's coattail.

By the time he was 25, Dick began to suspect that he did not look forward to a life as a salesman for the rest of his career. He talked about his unrest with his friends, and they suggested that he groom himself for sales manager. "You won't make the kind of money you're making from commissions," he was told, "but you will have a foot in the door from an administrative standpoint, and you won't have to travel quite as much as you do now." Dick took their suggestions lightly, and continued to sell the product, but was aware that he felt dissatisfied and did not seem to get the satisfaction our of his job that he had once enjoyed.

By the end of his third year with the company Dick was convinced that he wanted a change in direction. As usual, he and the president spent quite a bit of time on the golf course during the annual company sales conference. After their match one day, the president kidded Dick about his game. The conversation drifted back to business, and the president, who seemed to be in a jovial mood, started to kid Dick about his sales ability. In a joking way, he implied that anyone could sell a product as good as Tri-American's, but that it took real "guts and know-how" to make the products. The conversation drifted to other things, but this remark stuck with Dick.

Sometime later, Dick approached the president formally with a request for a transfer out of the sales division. The president was surprised and hesitant about this change in career direction for Dick. He recognized the superior sales ability that Dick seemed to possess, but was unsure that Dick was willing or able to assume responsibilities in any other division of the organization. Dick sensed the hesitancy, but continued to push his request. He later remarked that it seemed that the initial hesitancy of the president convinced Dick that he needed an opportunity to prove himself in a field other than sales.

Troubleshooter.   Dick was finally transferred back to the home office of the organization and indoctrinated into productive and administrative roles in the company as a special assistant to the senior vice president of production. As a special assistant, Dick was assigned several troubleshooting jobs. He acquitted himself well in this role, but in the process succeeded in gaining a reputation as a ruthless headhunter among the branches where he had performed a series of amputations. His reputation as an amiable, genial, easy-going guy from the sales department was the antithesis of the reputation of a cold, calculating headhunter which he earned in his troubleshooting role. The vice president, who was Dick's boss, was aware of the reputation which Dick had earned but was pleased with the results that were obtained. The faltering departments that Dick had worked in seemed to bloom with new life and energy after Dick's recommended amputations. As a result, the vice president began to sing Dick's praises, and the president began to accept Dick in his new role in the company.

Management Responsibility.   About three years after Dick's switch from sales, he was given an assignment as assistant plant manager of an English branch of the company. Dick, who had remarried, moved his wife and family to London, and they attempted to adapt to their new routine. The plant manager was English, as were most of the other employees. Dick and his family were accepted with reservations into the community life as well as into the plant life. The difference between British and American philosophy and performance within the plant was marked for Dick who was imbued with modern managerial concepts and methods. Dick's directives from headquarters were to update and upgrade performance in this branch. However, his power and authority were less than those of his superior, so he constantly found himself in the position of having to soft pedal or withhold suggestions that he would have liked to make, or innovations that he would have liked to introduce. After a frustrating year and a half, Dick was suddenly made plant manager of an old British company which had just been purchased by Tri-American. He left his first English assignment with mixed feelings and moved from London to Birmingham.

As the new plant manager, Dick operated much as he had in his trouble-shooting job for the first couple of years of his change from sales to administration. Training and reeducation programs were instituted for all supervisors and managers who survived the initial purge. Methods were studied and simplified or redesigned whenever possible, and new attention was directed toward production which better met the needs of the sales organization. A strong controller helped to straighten out the profit picture through stringent cost control; and, by the end of the third year, the company showed a small profit for the first time in many years. Because he felt that this battle was won, Dick requested transfer back to the United States. This request was partially granted when nine months later he was awarded a junior vice president title, and was made manager of a subsidiary Canadian plant, Modrow.

Modrow Manager.   Prior to Dick's appointment as plant manager at Modrow, extensive plans for plant expansion and improvement had been approved and started. Although he had not been in on the original discussions and plans, he inherited all the problems that accompany large-scale changes in any organization. Construction was slower in completion than originally planned, equipment arrived before the building was finished, employees were upset about the extent of change expected in their work routines with the installation of additional machinery and, in general, morale was at a low ebb.

Various versions of Dick's former activities had preceded him, and on his arrival he was viewed with dubious eyes. The first few months after his arrival were spent in a frenzy of catching up. This entailed constant conferences and meetings, volumes of reading of past reports, becoming acquainted with the civic leaders of the area, and a plethora of dispatches to and from the home office. Costs continued to climb unabated.

By the end of his first year at Modrow, the building program had been completed, although behind schedule, the new equipment had been installed, and some revamping of cost procedures had been incorporated. The financial picture at this time showed a substantial loss, but since it had been budgeted as a loss, this was not surprising. All managers of the various divisions had worked closely with their supervisors and accountants in planning the budget for the following year, and Dick began to emphasize his personal interest in cost reduction.

As he worked through his first year as plant manager, Dick developed the habit of strolling around the organization. He was apt to leave his office and appear anywhere on the plant floor, in the design offices, at the desk of a purchasing agent or accountant, in the plant cafeteria rather than the executive dining room, or wherever there was activity concerned with Modrow. During his strolls he looked, listened, and became acquainted. If he observed activities which he wanted to talk about, or heard remarks that gave him clues to future action, he did not reveal these at the time. Rather he had a nod, a wave, a smile, for the people near him, but a mental note to talk to his supervisors, managers, and foremen in the future. At first his presence disturbed those who noted him coming and going, but after several exposures to him without any noticeable effect, the workers came to accept his presence and continue their usual activities. Supervisors, managers, and foremen, however, did not feel as comfortable when they saw him in the area.

Their feelings were aptly expressed by the manager of the siding department one day when he was talking to one of his foremen: "I wish to hell he'd stay up in the front office where he belongs. Whoever heard of a plant manager who had time to wander around the plant all the time. Why doesn't he tend to his paper work and let us tend to our business?"

"Don't let him get you down," joked the foreman. "Nothing ever comes of his visits. Maybe he's just lonesome and looking for a friend. You know how these Americans are."

"Well, you may feel that nothing ever comes of his visits, but I don't. I've been called into his office three separate times within the last two months. The heat must really be on from the head office. You know these conferences we have every month where he reviews our financial progress, our building progress, our design progress, etc.? Well, we're not really progressing as fast as we should be. If you ask me we're in for continuing trouble."

In recalling his first year at Modrow, Dick had felt constantly pressured and badgered. He always sensed that the Canadians he worked with resented his presence since he was brought in over the heads of the operating staff. At the same time he felt this subtle resistance from his Canadian work force, he believed that the president and his friends in the home office were constantly on the alert, waiting for Dick to prove himself or fall flat on his face. Because of the constant pressures and demands of the work, he had literally dumped his family into a new community and had withdrawn into the plant. In the process, he built up a wall of resistance toward the demands of his wife and children who, in turn, felt as though he was abandoning them.

During the course of the conversation with his University friends, be began to recall a series of incidents that probably had resulted from the conflicting pressures. When describing some of these incidents, he continued to emphasize the fact that his attempt to be relaxed and casual had backfired. Laughingly, Dick said, "As you know, both human relations and accounting were my weakest subjects during the Master's program, and yet they are two fields I felt I needed the most at Modrow at this time." He described some of the cost procedures that he would have liked to incorporate. However, without the support and knowledge furnished by his former controller, he busied himself with details that were unnecessary. One day, as he describes it, he overheard a conversation between two of the accounting staff members with whom he had been working very closely. One of them commented to the other, "For a guy who's a vice president, he sure spends a lot of time breathing down our necks. Why doesn't he simply tell us the kind of systems he would like to try, and let us do the experimenting and work out the budget?" Without commenting on the conversation he overheard, Dick then described himself as attempting to spend less time and be less directive in the accounting department.

Another incident he described which apparently had real meaning for him was one in which he had called a staff conference with his top-level managers. They had been going "hammer and tongs" for better than an hour in his private office, and in the process of heated conversation had loosened ties, taken off coats, and really rolled up their sleeves. Dick himself had slipped out of his shoes. In the midst of this, his secretary reminded him of an appointment with public officials. Dick had rapidly finished up his conference with his managers, straightened his tie, donned his coat, and had wandered out into the main office in his stocking feet.

Dick fully described several incidents when he had disappointed, frustrated, or confused his wife and family by forgetting birthdays, appointments, dinner engagements, etc. He seemed to be describing a pattern of behavior which resulted from continuing pressure and frustration. He was setting the scene to describe his baffling and humiliating position in the siding department. In looking back and recalling his activities during this first year, Dick commented on the fact that his frequent wanderings throughout the plant had resulted in a nodding acquaintance with the workers, but probably had also resulted in foremen and supervisors spending more time getting ready for his visits and reading meaning into them afterwards than attending to their specific duties. His attempts to know in detail the accounting procedures being used required long hours of concentration and detailed conversations with the accounting staff, which were time-consuming and very frustrating for him, as well as for them. His lack of attention to his family life resulted in continued pressure from both wife and family.

The Siding Department Incident. Siding was the product which had been budgeted as a large profit item of Modrow. Aluminum siding was gaining in popularity among both architects and builders, because of its possibilities in both decorative and practical uses. Panel sheets of siding were shipped in standard sizes on order; large sheets of the coated siding were cut to specifications in the trim department, packed, and shipped. The trim shop was located near the loading platforms, and Dick often cut through the trim shop on his wanderings through the plant. On one of his frequent trips through the area, he suddenly became aware of the fact that several workers responsible for the disposal function were spending countless hours at high-speed saws cutting scraps into specified lengths to fit into scrap barrels. The narrow bands of scrap which resulted from the trim process varied in length from 7 to 27 feet and had to be reduced in size to fit into the disposal barrels. Dick, in his concentration on cost reduction, picked up one of the thin strips, bent it several times and filled it into the barrel. He tried this with another piece, and it bent very easily. After assuring himself that bending was possible, he walked over to a worker at the saw and asked why he was using the saw when material could easily be bent and fitted into the barrels, resulting in saving time and equipment. The worker's response was, "We've never done it that way, sir. We've always cut it."

Following his plan of not commenting or discussing matters on the floor, but distressed by the reply, Dick returned to his office and asked the manager of the siding department if he could speak to the foreman of the scrap division. The manager said, "Of course, I'll send him up to you in just a minute."

After a short time, the foreman, very agitated at being called to the plant manager's office, appeared. Dick began questioning him about the scrap disposal process and received the standard answer: "We've always done it that way." Dick then proceeded to review cost-cutting objectives. He talked about the pliability of the strips of scrap. He called for a few pieces of scrap to demonstrate the ease with which it could be bent, and ended what he thought was a satisfactory conversation by requesting the foreman to order heavy-duty gloves for his workers and use the bending process for a trial period of two weeks to check the cost saving possible.

The foreman listened throughout most of this hour's conference, offered several reasons why it wouldn't work, raised some questions about the record-keeping process for cost purposes, and finally left the office with the forced agreement to try the suggested new method of bending, rather than cutting, for disposal. Although he was immersed in many other problems, his request was forcibly brought home one day as he cut through the scrap area. The workers were using power saws to cut scraps. He called the manager of the siding department and questioned him about the process. The manager explained that each foreman was responsible for his own processes, and since Dick had already talked to the foreman, perhaps he had better talk to him again. When the foreman arrived, Dick began to question him. He received a series of excuses, and some explanations of the kinds of problems they were meeting by attempting to bend the scrap material. "I don't care what the problems are," Dick nearly shouted, "when I request a cost-reduction program instituted, I want to see it carried through."

Dick was furious. When the foreman left, he phoned the maintenance department and ordered the removal of the power saws from the scrap area immediately. A short time later the foreman of the scrap department knocked on Dick's door reporting his astonishment at having maintenance men step into his area and physically remove the saws. Dick reminded the foreman of his request for a trial at cost reduction to no avail, and ended the conversation by saying that the power saws were gone and would not be returned, and the foreman had damned well better learn to get along without them. After a stormy exit by the foreman, Dick congratulated himself on having solved a problem and turned his attention to other matters.

A few days later Dick cut through the trim department and literally stopped to stare. As he described it, he was completely nonplussed to discover gloved workmen using hand shears to cut each piece of scrap.

EXCELSIOR BAKERIES, INC.*

Upon completing my junior year in college in early June, I returned to my hometown, Pottersville, New York. The next day I went to see Roger Farnum, the plant superintendent of the local branch of Excelsior Bakeries, Inc., to find out when I should report for work. I had worked at the Excelsior plant the previous summer as a general helper on the slicing and wrapping crew for hamburger and hot dog rolls. Since I was a union member and had spoken to Farnum during spring vacation about a job for this summer, I was positive of being rehired.

When I walked into the office, Farnum said jokingly: "Hi, George! Ready to go to work for a change after all that book learning?" I was rather surprised to see Farnum so jovial and cordial. I remembered him as always having a long face and never saying more than two words at a time. I finally answered: "Yes, sir, any time you say and as soon as possible."

"Well, on the recommendation of Murphy, you're going to run the hamburger and hot dog machine this summer. Murphy wants to work on the ovens; and since we don't want to change a regular worker over to the wrapper just for a couple of months, we figured you would accept the added responsibility and could handle the job."

Phil Murphy, a regular employee of the plant, had run the wrapping machine last summer and had been leader of a crew of three other summer workers and me. I had visited Murphy at the plant during spring vacation, and he had told me he was going to work on the ovens this year because it was

---

During the winter following the events described in this case, the writer submitted it as a report for a course in administration he was taking in a graduate school of business.

daywork and paid more. I had casually mentioned to him at that time to try to get me the wrapping machine job, but I hadn't thought of it again, since it had always been assigned to a regular worker.

I was extremely pleased to accept the job, for I knew it meant 6 cents more an hour, and it would entail some leadership responsibility. I thought to myself: "Now I will be part of management and not just another worker."

Farnum told me to report for work that following Sunday, a week earlier than I had expected, so I could familiarize myself with the machine before the "rush season" started.

Excelsior Bakeries, Inc., was a large firm with many plants spread across the entire United States. The Pottersville branch produced mainly white, rye, whole wheat, and French bread, but supplemented these major lines with hamburger and hot dog rolls, dinner rolls, doughnuts, and other bakery products. It also distributed, in its area of operation, pies, cakes, crackers, and other specialities produced in the Boston plant.

Pottersville was located in a region noted for its many summer resorts, camps, and hotels, which are open from June until September. During the summer season, production and sales of the local Excelsior plant increased tremendously as the summer population swelled the normal demand. This seasonal rise was especially significant in hot dog and hamburger rolls, whose sales increased over the winter months by approximately 100–150 percent in June, 150–250 percent in July, and 250–300 percent in August. Because of this great seasonal increase, the company had to hire about 15 employees just for the 3 summer months. Five of the "extra help" were needed on the wrapping crew for hot dog and hamburger rolls. These workers were usually drawn from college students on vacation, employment agencies, and transients. In the past several years the extra help had been predominantly college students, because they were more dependable and willing to remain on the job right up to Labor Day.

After I reported to work, I spent the first week with the regular employees. Ed Dugan, a past operator of the wrapping machine, worked with me, teaching me all the techniques of operating the machine efficiently. The machine was rather old and had to be tended carefully at all times so that the cellophane wrapping paper would not jump off the rollers. The wrapping paper was expensive, and Joe McGuire, the night foreman, "blew his top" whenever a lot of paper was wasted.

Exhibit 1 shows the working area and the positions of each operator on the slicing and wrapping crew. Worker No. 1 took the pans of rolls from the racks and fed the rolls out on a conveyor, which carried them into the slicing machine. Worker No. 2 stacked the sliced rolls into two rows, one on top of the other, making groups of eight or one dozen. Worker No. 3 slid the groups of rolls down the table to worker No. 4, who fed them into the wrapping machine. Worker No. 5, the wrapping machine operator and crew leader, placed the wrapped packages in a box, keeping count of the actual number packaged. The work was rather routine and extremely monotonous and boring. Workers No. 1 through No. 4 continually exchanged positions in order to break the monotony.

Exhibit 1
Wrapping Machine Layout

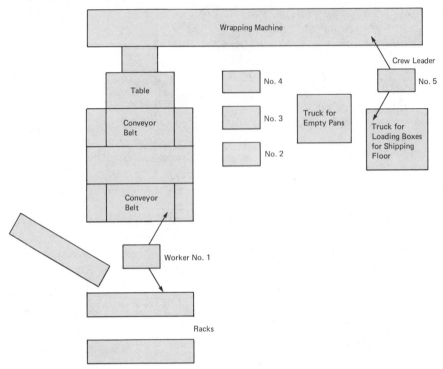

The plant employees worked on a five-day week—working on Sunday and Monday; off on Tuesday; working Wednesday, Thursday, and Friday; and off again on Saturday. Production was on daily orders from the various sales routes. The salesmen left the plant early in the morning with their loaded trucks and, after making their deliveries, returned in the afternoon with the orders for the next day. The volume varied from day to day, and the rolls were ready for wrapping at varying times. Therefore, the wrappers generally reported for work at a different time each day, being notified by the plant superintendent. Usually, the crew began about 6:00 to 8:00 P.M. and worked until all the orders were filled for that night. The number of hours worked ranged from 7 to 15 or even more. All time over eight hours was overtime and paid for as time and a half. If a worker was a union member, the company had to guarantee him seven hours' pay for any night on which it called him in. If there were not seven hours of slicing and wrapping, the foreman found something else for the men to do, such as thoroughly cleaning the machines, greasing the pans, or doing other odd jobs. If a man wished, though, he could ask to punch out before seven hours were up, thereby forfeiting the guaranteed seven hours' pay for that night and receiving pay only for the hours he had worked.

Four different types of packages were wrapped on the machine: hamburger and hot dog dozen-roll packages, and hamburger and hot dog packages of eight rolls. A different size and type of paper was used for each package. Different-sized plates had to be used in the machine also. On an average night a complete changeover of the machine had to be made about six times, each alteration taking about ten minutes. In addition, it took about five minutes to replace a roll of paper when it ran out, and two to three minutes to replace the labels and seals. During these changeovers and replacements, which were made by the machine operator, the rest of the crew smoked cigarettes out on the shipping dock or else folded boxes for the operator if he needed them. I never asked anyone to make boxes if he wanted to have a cigarette or wanted to get a drink of water. But if a man was just sitting around or "goofing off," I would ask him to fold boxes, as the crew is supposed to do during these breaks. McGuire hated to see anyone sit around, but he never begrudged anyone a cigarette.

With the start of my second week, orders rose, and the rest of the summer help was called in. I was very pleased when three of my close friends were assigned to my crew. Art Dunn, a student at Williams, had worked on the wrapping crew with me the previous summer, as had Jack Dorsey, a student at the University of Vermont. Bill Regan, a Fordham student, had not worked for Excelsior the previous summer; but he had lived next door to me, and we had grown up together. The four of us had been close friends during high school days and since graduation, even though we went to different colleges. Harry Hart, the fourth man, was also new to the wrapping crew. Hart had graduated from high school a year before the rest of us and was attending the University of Massachusetts. We old-timers were already union members. The new men joined soon after they began work.

With the help of Dunn and Dorsey, I was able to train Regan and Hart quickly; and within a couple of nights, they were thoroughly proficient in all four positions. During these first two nights, Dunn and Dorsey thoroughly indoctrinated Regan and Hart into the "code" of the wrapping crew.

Excelsior Bakeries offered college students an excellent opportunity to make a considerable amount of money during the summer, paying an hourly rate of $1.63 and providing plenty of overtime. The code of the wrapping crew was a concerted group action to set the number of hours to be worked on a certain night. At the beginning of the night's work, the crew could fairly well estimate from the production orders just how long it should take to put the work out. If it was estimated to take about eight hours, the crew would purposely slow down to stretch it to nine or nine and a half hours, so they could get overtime pay. On almost any night the work could be stretched out by an hour or so. Only on big nights of 12 or more hours did the crew work at normal speed. As an indication of the effectiveness of this slowdown, there were several occasions when a seven- or eight-hour night was estimated, but the crew "pushed the stuff through" and finished in six hours in order to have a few beers before the local bar closed at 3:00 A.M.

As a member of this crew the previous summer, I was one of the strong advocates of this code. If a new worker or a temporary replacement from somewhere else in the plant appeared on the crew, he had to conform, or the group gave him much verbal abuse or the even worse "silent treatment." These were unbearable conditions, and the new man always accepted the code.

Murphy, the previous year's leader, although a regular employee of the plant, had cooperated with the group and never complained. He used to say: "After all, I want the overtime, too!"

After the first few nights of work, I noticed the code had begun to operate. I had never stopped to think of the effects this slowdown had on management and the operations of the plant. It raised labor production costs, delayed the salesmen in leaving for their routes, and raised other problems as well. At first, I was rather confused as to whether I should allow this practice to continue or, as "part of management," put my foot down and take action to stop it. Because I could not think of any satisfactory course of action which would satisfy everyone, I allowed the code to operate. I rationalized myself into believing: "Well, if management isn't going to do anything about it, why the hell should I worry about it?"

The first couple of weeks went smoothly. The only problems I had to face were minor arguments among the crew and the usual horseplay and "goofing off" in the middle hours of the morning.

McGuire, the night foreman, occasionally would say to me, smiling: "Took you guys a pretty long time to get those rolls out tonight, didn't it?" or, on a really short night: "You can really shove those rolls through when you feel like having a few brews!" McGuire could not see us working from his office, as the line of racks blocked his view, but he regularly walked over to check on us. When he appeared, the man feeding the slicing machine would place the rolls on the conveyor belt "back to back" with no space in between, the maximum rate at which the crew could operate. When he was in his office or "up front," a space of about 6 to 12 inches was allowed between rolls, thereby reducing the speed of production by 10 to 15 percent.

Occasionally, a "little war" would break out between the wrapping crew and two doughnut men across the aisle from the wrapping machine. The members of each group would throw doughnuts or hot dog and hamburger rolls at the others. One night, one of these battles was beginning to get out of hand to the point where the boys had stopped work. I reprimanded them and told them to "knock it off" and get back to work. Regan called me a "company man," and Dunn said something about the "lieutenant with the gold-plated bars."

I was trying to ignore the comments when suddenly I heard the paper snap. I stopped the machine and adjusted it; but even after the machine had been adjusted, package after package kept coming through unwrapped or "crippled." I tried everything I knew to find the cause of the trouble; but just when I thought I had the machine running properly, something else would go wrong. By this time, I was ready to give up and call McGuire for his advice.

Then I noticed the four crewmen having a good laugh for themselves. I had been so concerned about trying to change the adjustments on the machine that I had not noticed Regan tinkering with the machine at the other end. He was also feeding the hot dog rolls improperly, breaking them before putting them in the machine so they would slide off and get caught, thereby drawing unevenly on the paper. I lost my temper completely and was in the process of a real argument with Regan and the rest of the crew when McGuire came down to see why the machine was shut down. When he asked, I stuttered: "Hell, Joe, these—ah—this damn machine isn't drawing right. I've tried everything, but I think I've finally found the real reason. Let's try it now, fellas!"

That night, when I was making my final count with McGuire and the shipping foreman, I was considerably short on hot dog rolls, because of the many losses caused by Regan's tampering with the machine. McGuire gave me quite a reprimand and said I'd better "watch it."

The next night, when I came to work, Farnum stopped me and asked why I had lost so much paper the night before. I told him it was a breakdown in the machine. He gave me orders to weigh each roll of paper before we started wrapping each night and to weigh it again when we finished. I was to record the weights on tabulation control sheets kept in his office.

That night, before starting work, I told the crew what had happened and what McGuire and Farnum had said to me. I told them that I was being held responsible for paper and production control, and that I would tolerate no more "horsing around," especially tampering with the machine. I emphasized that I would not go "on the carpet" again for *anyone*.

Relations between me and the crew, with the exception of Hart, were rather strained for a couple of nights. None of them said very much to me. Also, I did not go swimming or play golf with them for a couple of days, as we usually did every afternoon. However, I had no more incidents of this sort, and the crew continued to meet the output schedule as they had previously. Gradually, the incident was forgotten, and relations among us became what they had been before.

During the latter part of August, the annual Excelsior clambake was held. In the late afternoon, McGuire called me over to the bar to have a drink. Mr. Farnum and Mr. Sommers, the plant general manager, were with him. McGuire threw his arm around me and said to Farnum: "George did a great job this summer on the wrapper, didn't he, Rog?"

"Best season we've had so far, Joe."

A CASE OF MISUNDERSTANDING:

MR. HART AND MR. BING*

In a department of a large industrial organization there were seven workers (four men and three women) engaged in testing and inspecting panels of electronic equipment. In this department one of the workers, Bing, was having trouble with his immediate supervisor, Hart, who had formerly been a worker in the department. Had we been observers in this department we would have seen Bing carrying two or three panels at a time from the racks where they were stored to the bench where he inspected them together. For this activity we would have seen him charging double or triple set-up time. We would have heard him occasionally singing at work. Also we would have seen him usually leaving his work position a few minutes early to go to lunch, and noticed that other employees sometimes accompanied him. And had we been present at one specific occasion, we would have heard Hart telling Bing that he disapproved of these activities and that he wanted Bing to stop doing them. However, not being present to hear the actual verbal exchange that took place in this interaction, let us note what Bing and Hart each said to a personnel representative.

What Bing Said

In talking about his practice of charging double or triple setup time for panels which he inspected all at one time, Bing said:

This is a perfectly legal thing to do. We've always been doing it. Mr. Hart, the supervisor, has other ideas about it, though; he claims it's cheating the company. He came over to the bench a day or two ago and let me know just how he felt about the matter. Boy, did we go at it! It wasn't so much the fact that he called me down on it, but more the way in which he did it. He's a sarcastic bastard. I've never seen anyone like him. He's not content just to say in a manlike way what's on his mind, but he prefers to do it in a way that makes you want to crawl inside a crack in the floor. What a guy! I don't mind being called down by a supervisor, but I like to be treated like a man, and not humiliated like a school teacher does a naughty kid. He's been pulling this stuff ever since he's been promoted. He's lost his friendly way and seems to be having some difficulty in knowing how to manage us employees. He's a changed man over what he used to be like when he was a worker on the bench with us several years ago.

When he pulled this kind of stuff on me the other day, I got so damn mad I called in the union representative. I knew that the thing I was doing was permitted by the contract, but I was intent on making some trouble for Mr. Hart, just because he persists in this sarcastic way of handling me. I am about fed up with the whole damn situation. I'm trying every means I can to get myself transferred out of this group. If I don't succeed and I'm forced to stay on here, I'm going to screw him in every way I can. He's not going to pull this kind of kid stuff any longer on me. When the union representative questioned him on the case, he finally had to back down, because according to the contract an employee can use any time-saving method or device in order to speed up the process as long as the quality standards of the job are met.

You see, he knows that I do professional singing on the outside. He hears the people talking about my career in music. I guess he figures I can be so cocky because I have another means of earning some money. Actually, the employees here enjoy having me sing while we work, but he thinks I'm disturbing them and causing them to "goof-off" from their work. Occasionally, I leave the job a few minutes early and go down to the washroom to wash up before lunch. Sometimes several others in the group will accompany me, and so Mr. Hart automatically thinks I'm the leader and usually bawls me out for the whole thing.

So, you can see, I'm a marked man around here. He keeps watching me like a hawk. Naturally, this makes me very uncomfortable. That's why I'm sure a transfer would be the best thing. I've asked him for it, but he didn't give me any satisfaction at the time. While I remain here, I'm going to keep my nose clean, but whenever I get the chance, I'm going to slip it to him, but good.

What Hart Said

Here, on the other hand, is what Hart told the personnel representative:

Say, I think you should be in on this. My dear little friend Bing is heading himself into a show-down with me. Recently it was brought to my attention that Bing has been taking double and triple set-up time for panels which he is actually inspecting at one time. In effect, that's cheating, and I've called him down on it several times before. A few days ago it was brought to my attention again, and so this time I really let him have it in no uncertain terms. He's been getting away with this for too long and I'm going to put an end to it once and for all. I know he didn't like me calling him on it because a few hours later he had the union representative breathing down my back. Well, anyway, I let them both know I'll not tolerate the practice any longer, and I let Bing know that if he continues to do this kind of thing, I'm inclined to think the guy's mentally deficient, because talking to him has actually no meaning to him whatsoever. I've tried just about every approach to jar some sense into that guy's head, and I've just about given it up as a bad deal.

I don't know what it is about the guy, but I think he's harboring some deep feelings against me. For what, I don't know, because I've tried to handle that bird with kid gloves. But his whole attitude around here on the job is one of indifference, and he certainly isn't a good influence on the rest of my group. Franklin, I think he purposely tried to agitate them against me at times, too. It seems to me he may be suffering from illusions of grandeur, because all he does all day long is sit over there and croon his fool head off. Thinks he's a Frank Sinatra! No kidding! I understand he takes singing lessons and he's working with some of the local bands in the city. All of which is OK by me; but when his outside interests start interfering with his efficiency on the job, then I've got to start paying closer attention to the situation. For this reason I've been keeping my eye on that bird and if he steps out of line any more, he and I are going to part ways.

You know there's an old saying, "You can't make a silk purse out of a sow's ear." The guy is simply unscrupulous. He feels no obligation to do a real day's work. Yet I know the guy can do a good job, because for a long time he did. But in recent months he's slipped, for some reason, and his whole attitude on the job has changed. Why, it's even getting to the point now where I think he's inducing other employees to "goof off" a few mintues before the lunch whistle and go down to the washroom and clean up on company time.

I've called him on it several times, but words just don't seem to make any lasting impression on him. Well, if he keeps it up much longer, he's going to find himself on the way out. He's asked me for a transfer, so I know he wants to go. But I didn't give him an answer when he asked me, because I was storming mad at the time, and I may have told him to go somewhere else."

Glossary of Terms

Adaptiveness. A criterion of effectiveness which refers to the ability of the organization to respond to change which is induced by either internal or external stimuli. An equivalent term is flexibility, although adaptiveness connotes an intermediate time frame whereas flexibility is ordinarily used in a short-run sense.

Affect. Refers to the feelings of a person with emphasis on the emotional content.

Assembly-Line Technology. A form of manufacturing in which component parts are brought together and combined into a single unit of output. It is used to produce relatively standard products which have a mass market.

Assessment Centers. An evaluation technique that uses situational exercises to identify promotable, trainable, and high potential employees.

Attitudes. Mental states of readiness for need arousal.

Authority. Authority resides in the relationship between positions and in the role expectations of the position occupants. Thus, an influence attempt based on authority is generally not resisted because when joining an organization individuals become aware that the exercise of authority is required of supervisors and compliance is required of subordinates. The recognition of authority is necessary for organizational effectiveness and is a cost of organizational membership.

Banking Time Off. A reward practice of allowing employees to build up time off credits for such things as good performance or attendance. The employee would then receive the time off in addition to the regular vacation time granted by the organization because of seniority.

Behavior Modification. An approach to motivation that uses the principles of operant conditioning.

Behaviorally Anchored Rating Scales (BARS). A rating scale developed by raters and/or ratees that uses critical behavorial incidents as interval anchors on each scale. Approximately 6 to 10 scales with behavioral incidents are used to derive the evaluation.

Boundary Spanning Role. The role of an individual who must relate to two different systems, usually an organization and some part of its environment.

Bureaucratic Theory. The theory developed by Max Weber that defined the characteristics of an organization which maximizes stability and controllability of its members. The ideal-type bureaucracy is an organization which contains all the elements to a high degree.

Cafeteria Fringe Benefits. The employee is allowed to develop and allocate a personally attractive fringe benefit package. The employee is instructed what the total fringe benefits allowed will be and then distributes the benefits according to his or her preferences.

Case Study. Examination of numerous characteristics of one person or group, usually over an extended time period.

Central Tendency Error. The tendency to rate all ratees around an average score.

Classical Design Theory. A body of literature which evolved from scientific manage-

567

ment, classical organization, and bureaucratic theory. The theory emphasizes the design of a preplanned structure for doing work. It minimizes the importance of the social system.

Classical Organization Theory. A body of literature which developed from the writings of managers who proposed principles of organization. These principles were intended to serve as guidelines for other managers.

Coercive Power. An influence over others based upon fear. A subordinate perceives that failure to comply with the wishes of a superior would lead to punishment or some other negative outcomes.

Cognition. This is basically what individuals know about themselves and their environment. Cognition implies a conscious process of acquiring knowledge.

Cognitive Dissonance. A mental state which occurs when there is a lack of consistency or harmony among an individual's various cognitions (for example, attitudes, beliefs, and so on) after a decision has been made.

Command Group. The command group is specified by the formal organization chart. The group of subordinates who report to one particular manager constitutes the command group.

Commitment. A sense of identification, involvement, and loyalty expressed by an employee toward the company.

Communication. The transmission of information and understanding through the use of common symbols.

Confrontation Conflict Resolution. A strategy which focuses on the conflict and attempts to resolve it through such procedures as rotation of key group personnel, the establishment of superordinate goals, improving communications, and similar approaches.

Conscious Goals. The main goal a person is striving toward and is aware of when directing behavior.

Consideration. Leader acts which imply showing supportive concern for the followers in a group.

Content Motivation Theories. Theories which focus on the factors within the person that energize, direct, sustain, and stop behavior.

Contingency Design Theory. An approach to designing organizations which states that the effective structure depends upon factors in the situation.

Continuous Reinforcement. A schedule that is designed to reinforce behavior every time the exhibited behavior is correct.

Counterpower. Leaders exert power on subordinates and subordinates exert power on leaders. Power is a two-way flow.

Criterion. The dependent or predicted measure for appraising the effectiveness of an individual employee.

Decentralization. Basically this entails pushing the decision-making point to the lowest managerial level possible. It involves the delegation of decision-making authority.

Decision Acceptance. Important criterion in Vroom-Yetton model that refers to the degree of subordinate commitment to the decision.

Decision Quality. Important criterion in Vroom-Yetton model that refers to the objective aspects of a decision that influence subordinates' performance aside from any direct impact on motivation.

Decisions. Decisions are the organizational mechanisms through which an attempt is made to achieve a desired state. They are organizational responses to a problem.

Decoding. This is the mental procedure which a receiver of a message goes through to decipher a message.

Defensive Behavior. When an employee is blocked in attempts to satisfy needs to achieve goals, one or more defense mechanisms may be evoked. They include withdrawal, aggression, substitution, compensation, repression, and rationalization.

Delegated Strategy. An OD strategy which precludes participation by management. The employees through case discussion or sensitivity training determine the OD program.

Delegation. The process by which authority is distributed downward in an organization.

Delphi Technique. A technique for improving group decisions. It involves the solicitation and comparison of anonymous judgments on the topic of interest through a set of sequential questionnaires interspersed with summarized information and feedback of opinions from earlier responses.

Departmentalization. The manner in which an organization is structurally divided. Some of the more publicized divisions are by function, territory, product, customer, and project.

Development. A criterion of effectiveness which refers to the ability of the organization to increase its capacity to respond to current and future environmental demands. Equivalent or similar terms include institutionalization, stability, and integration.

Differential Piece-rate System. An incentive wage system that pays a fixed rate for all production up to standard, but a higher rate for all pieces once the standard is met.

Differentiation. An important concept in the Lawrence and Lorsch research which refers to the process by which subunits in an organization develop particular attributes in response to the requirements imposed by their particular subenvironments. The greater the differences among the subunits' attributes, the greater the differentiation.

Dominant Competitive Strategy. A concept defined in the Lawrence and Lorsch research to refer to the subenvironment which is crucial to the organization's success. The dominant strategy may be production, marketing, or product development depending upon the industry.

Downward Communication. Downward communication flows from individuals in higher levels of organization structure to those in lower levels. The most common type is job instructions and related information from superior to subordinate.

Dysfunctional Intergroup Conflict. Any confrontation or interaction between groups that hinders the achievement of organizational goals.

Effectiveness. In the context of organizational behavior effectiveness refers to the optimal relationship among five components: production, efficiency, satisfaction, adaptiveness, and development.

Efficiency. A short-run criterion of effectiveness which refers to the ability of the organization to produce outputs with minimum use of inputs. The measures of efficiency are always in ratio terms, such as benefit/cost, cost/output, and cost/time.

Encoding. This is the converting of an idea into an understandable message by a communicator.

End-Result Principles. The principles which classicists defined as the desirable results or organizing efforts, namely, order, stability, initiative, and esprit de corps.

Environmental Certainty. A concept in the Lawrence and Lorsch research which refers to three characteristics of a subenvironment that determine the subunit's requisite differentiation. The three characteristics are rate of change, certainty of information, and time-span of feedback or results.

Environmental Diversity. A concept in the Lawrence and Lorsch research which refers to the differences among the three subenvironments in terms of certainty.

Equity Theory of Motivation. A theory which examines discrepancies within a person after the individual has compared his or her input/output ratio to a reference person.

ERG Theory of Motivation. A theory developed and tested by Alderfer which categorizes needs as existence, relatedness, and growth.

Expectancy. The perceived likelihood that a particular act will be followed by a particular outcome.

Expectancy Theory. In this theory the employee is viewed as faced with a set of first-level outcomes. The employee will select an outcome based upon how this choice is related to second-level outcomes. The preferences of the individual are based upon the strength (valence) of desire to achieve a second-level state and the perception of the relationship between first- and second-level outcomes.

Experiment. An investigation to be considered an experiment must contain two elements—manipulation of some variable (independent variable) and observation of the results (dependent variable).

Expert Power. Capacity to influence related to some expertise, special skill, or knowledge. It is a function of the judgment of the less powerful individual that the other person has ability or knowledge that exceeds his own.

Extinction. The decline in response rate because of nonreinforcement.

Extrinsic Rewards. Those rewards such as pay, promotion, or fringe benefits which are external to the job.

Field Experiment. In this type of experiment the investigator attempts to manipulate and control variables in the natural setting rather than in a laboratory.

Fixed Interval Reinforcement. A situation in which a reinforcer is applied only after the passage of a certain period of time since the last reinforcer was applied.

Formal Groups. The demands and processes of the formal organization lead to the formation of different types of groups. Specifically, two types of groups specified by the formal organization are: the command group and the task group.

Friendship Group. An informal group that is established in the workplace because of some common characteristic and may extend the interaction of members to include activities outside the workplace.

Functional Intergroup Conflict. A confrontation between groups that enhances and benefits the achievement of organizational goals.

Goal Orientation. A concept which refers to the focus of attention and decision making among members of a subunit.

Goal Participation. The amount of involvement a person has in setting task and personal development goals.

Graicunas' Model. Proposition that an arithmetic increase in the number of subordinates results in a geometric increase in the number of relationships under the jurisdiction of the superior. Graicunas set this up in a mathematical model

$$C = N\left(\frac{2^N}{2} + N - 1\right)$$

where

$N=$ number of employees reporting to a superior.
$C=$ number of potential relationships.

Grapevine. An informal communication network that exists in organizations and short-circuits the formal channels.

Grid Training. A leadership development method proposed by Blake and Mouton which emphasizes the necessary balance between production and person-orientation.

Group. Two or more employees who interact with each other in such a manner that the behavior and/or performance of a member is influenced by the behavior and/or performance of other members.

Group Cohesiveness. The attraction of members to the group in terms of the desirability of group membership to the members. In a straightforward manner, this is the "stick-togetherness" quality of a group.

Halo Error. A positive or negative aura around a ratee that influences a rater's evaluation.

Hawthorne Studies. A series of studies undertaken at the Chicago Hawthorne Plant of Western Electric from 1924 to 1933. The studies made major contributions to the knowledge of the importance of the social system of an organization. They provided the impetus for the human relations approach to organizations.

History. One of the sources of error in experimental results. It consists of events other than the experimental treatment which occur between pre- and post-measurement.

Horizontal Communication. Horizontal communication occurs when the communicator and the receiver are at the same level in the organization.

Incentive Plan Criteria. To be effective in motivating employees incentive plans should (1) be related to specific behavioral patterns (for example, better performance), (2) be immediately received after displaying the behavior, and (3) reward the employee for consistently displaying the desired behavior.

Informal Groups. Informal groups are natural groupings of people in the work situation since they appear in response to man's social need to associate with others. Two specific types are interest groups and friendship groups.

Information Flow Requirements. The amount of information which must be processed by an organization, group or individual to perform effectively.

Initiating Structure. Leadership acts which imply structuring job tasks and responsibilities for followers.

Instrumentality. The relationship between first- and second-level outcomes.

Instrumentation.   One of the sources of error in experimental results. It is changes in the measure of participants' performance that are the result of changes in the measurement instruments or conditions under which the measuring is done (for example, wear on machinery, fatigue on the part of observers).

Integration.   A concept in the Lawrence and Lorsch research which refers to the process of achieving unity of effort among the organization's various subsystems. Techniques for achieving integration range from rules and procedures and plans to mutual adjustment.

Interaction.   Refers to any interpersonal contact in which one individual can be observed acting and one or more other individuals responding to the action.

Interaction Effects.   When any of the sources of errors in experimental results interact with the experimental treatment resulting in confounding results. For example, the types of individuals withdrawing from any experiment (mortality) may differ for the experimental group and the control group.

Interest Group.   A group that forms because of some special topic of interest. Generally, when the interest declines or a goal has been achieved, the group disbands.

Intergroup Conflict.   The conflict between groups which can be functional or dysfunctional.

Interpersonal Orientation.   A concept which refers to whether a person is more concerned with achieving good social relations as opposed to achieving a task.

Interpersonal Rewards.   Extrinsic rewards such as receiving recognition or being able to socially interact on the job.

Interrole Conflict.   This type of conflict is the result of facing multiple roles. It occurs because individuals simultaneously perform many roles, some of which have conflicting expectations.

Intervention.   The process by which either outsiders or insiders assume the role of a change agent in the OD program.

Intrapersonal Conflict.   The conflict which a person faces internally, as when an individual experiences personal frustration, anxiety, and stress.

Intrarole Conflict.   This type of conflict is more likely to occur when a given role has a complex role set. It occurs when different individuals define a role according to different sets of expectations, making it impossible for the person occupying the role to satisfy all.

Intrinsic Rewards.   Those rewards which are part of the job itself. The responsibility, challenge, and feedback characteristics of the job are examples.

Job Analysis.   The description of how one job differs from another in terms of demands, activities, and skills required.

Job Content.   The perception of factors which define the general nature of a job.

Job Definition.   The first subproblem of the organizing decision. It involves the determination of the task requirements of each job in the organization.

Job Depth.   This refers to the amount of control which an individual has to alter or influence the job and the surrounding environment.

Job Description.   A summary statement of what an employee actually does on the job.

Job Enlargement.   An administrative action that involves increasing the range of a job. Supposedly this action results in better performance and a more satisfied work force.

Job Enrichment. An approach developed by Herzberg that seeks to improve task efficiency and human satisfaction by means of building into people's jobs greater scope for personal achievement and recognition, more challenging and responsible work, and more opportunity for individual advancement and growth.

Job Evaluation. The assignment of dollar values to a job.

Job-Order Technology. A form of production in which products are tailor-made to customer specifications.

Job Range. This designates the number of operations a job occupant performs to complete a task.

Job Relationships. The interpersonal relationships required of or made possible by a job.

Job Rotation. A form of training which involves moving an employee from one to another work station. In addition to the training objective, this procedure is also designed to reduce boredom.

Laboratory Experiment. The key characteristic of laboratory experiments is that the environment in which the subject works is created by the researcher. The laboratory setting permits the researcher to control closely the experimental conditions.

Leader-Member Relations. A factor in the Fiedler contingency model which refers to the degree of confidence, trust, and respect followers have in the leader.

Learning. The process by which a relatively enduring change in behavior occurs as a result of practice.

Learning Transfer. An important learning principle which emphasizes the carryover of learning into the workplace.

Legitimate Power. Capacity to influence derived from the position of a manager in the organizational hierarchy. Subordinates believe they "ought" to comply.

Linking-Pin Function. An element of System 4 organization which views the major role of managers to be that of representative of the group they manage to higher-level groups in the organization.

Lockheed Model. A span of control model that identifies relevant variables for establishing spans of control. Some of the variables included are the complexity of functions, the coordination of subordinates required, and the direction and control required by subordinates.

Locus of Control. A personality characteristic that specifies people who see the control of their lives as coming from inside themselves as *internalizers.* People who believe that their lives are controlled by external factors are *externalizers.*

Maturation. One of the sources of error in experimental studies. It results from changes in the subject group with the passage of time which are not associated with the experimental treatment.

Maturity. An important life cycle leadership concept which includes achievement motivation, the willingness and ability to take responsibility, task relevant education, and experience of an individual or a group.

MBO. A process that specifies that superiors and subordinates will jointly set goals for a specified time period and then meet again to evaluate the subordinates' performance in terms of the previously established goals.

Merit Rating. A formal rating system that is applied to hourly paid employees.

Modeling. A method of administering rewards that relies on observational learning.

An employee learns the behaviors that are desirable by observing how others are rewarded. It is assumed that behaviors will be imitated if the observer views a distinct link between performance and rewards.

Modified Workweek. A procedure that involves reducing the number of days an employee works in a week. Instead of working five days, an employee may work four days, 10 hours per day.

Mortality. One of the sources of error in experimental studies. It occurs when participants drop out of the experiment before it is completed, resulting in the experimental and control groups not being comparable.

Motion Study. The process of analyzing work to determine the preferred motions to be used in the completion of a task.

Motivator-Hygiene Theory. The Herzberg approach that identifies conditions of the job which operate primarily to dissatisfy employees when they are not present (hygiene factors—salary, job security, work conditions, and so on). There are also job conditions that when present lead to high levels of motivation and job satisfaction. However, if these conditions are not present, they do not prove highly dissatisfying. They include achievement, growth, and advancement opportunities.

Multiple Roles. This concept describes the notion that most individuals play many roles simultaneously because they occupy many different positions in a variety of institutions and organizations.

Need Hierarchy Model. Maslow assumed that man is a wanting animal whose needs depend on what he already has. This in a sense means that a satisfied need is not a motivator. Man's needs are organized in a hierarchy of importance. The five need classifications are—physiological, safety, belongingness, esteem, and self-actualization.

Needs. The deficiencies that an individual experiences at a particular point in time.

Noise. Interference in the flow of a message from a sender to a receiver.

Nominal Group Technique. A recent technique for improving group decisions. It is a structured group meeting that includes both verbal and nonverbal stages.

Nonprogrammed Decisions. Decisions are nonprogrammed when they are novel and unstructured. As such there is no definite procedure for handling the problem either because it has not arisen in exactly the same manner before or because it is complex or extremely important.

Operant. Behaviors amenable to control by altering consequences (rewards and punishments) which follow them.

Optimal Balance. The most desirable relationship among the criteria of effectiveness. Optimal, rather than maximum, balance must be achieved in any case of more than one criterion.

Organizational Climate. A set of properties of the work environment, perceived directly or indirectly by the employees, assumed to be a major force in influencing employee behavior.

Organizational Development. A planned process of reeducation and training designed to facilitate organizational adaptation to changing environmental demands.

Organizational Profile. A diagram which shows the responses of members of an organization to the questionnaires which Likert devised to measure certain characteristics of an organization.

Organizations. Organizations are differentiated from other collections of people by their goal-directed behavior. That is, they pursue goals and objectives that can be more effectively achieved by the concerted action of individuals. They possess three important characteristics: behavior, structure, and processes.

Path-Goal Leadership Model. A theory which suggests that it is necessary for a leader to influence the followers' perception of work goals, self-development goals, and paths to goal attainment. The foundation for the model is the expectancy motivation theory.

Perception. The process by which an individual gives meaning to the environment. It involves organizing and interpreting various stimuli into a psychological experience.

Performance Evaluation. The systematic, formal evaluation of an employee's job performance and potential for future development.

Person-Role Conflict. This type of conflict occurs when role requirements violate the basic values, attitudes, and needs of the individual occupying the position.

Personal-Behavioral Leadership Theories. A group of leadership theories that are based primarily on the personal and behavioral characteristics of leaders. They focus on *what* leaders do and/or *how* they behave in carrying out the leadership function.

Personality. A stable set of characteristics and tendencies that determine commonalities and differences in the behavior of people.

Personality Test. Instruments used to measure emotional, motivational, interpersonal, and attitude characteristics that make up a person's personality.

Pooled Interdependence. This type of work interdependence occurs when it is not necessary for the groups to interact except through the total organization which supports them.

Position Power. A factor in the Fiedler contingency model which refers to the power inherent in the leadership position.

Power. The ability to influence another person's behavior.

Process. In systems theory, the process element consists of technical and administrative activities which are brought to bear on inputs in order to transform them into outputs.

Process Motivation Theories. Theories which provide a description and analysis of the process of how behavior is energized, directed, sustained, and stopped.

Process Principles. The organization principles as defined by Fayol which define the desirable behavior of managers as they deal with subordinates.

Process Technology. An advanced form of manufacturing in which a homogeneous input is converted into a relatively standardized output having a mass market.

Production. A criterion of effectiveness which refers to the organization's ability to provide the outputs which the environment demands of it.

Programmed Decisions. Decisions are programmed to the extent that they are repetitive and routine and a definite procedure has been developed for handling them.

Punishment. Presenting an uncomfortable consequence for a particular behavior response or removing a desirable reinforcer because of a behavior response. Managers can punish by application or punish by removal.

Ranking Methods. The ranking of ratees on the basis of relevant performance dimensions.

Recency of Events Error. The tendency to be biased in ratings by recent events.

Reciprocal Interdependence. In this type of work interdependence the output of each group serves as input to other groups in the organization.

Referent Power. Power based on a subordinate's identification with a superior. The more powerful individual is admired because of certain traits, and the subordinate is influenced because of this admiration.

Reward Power. An influence over others based on hope of reward; the opposite of coercive power. A subordinate perceives that compliance with the wishes of a superior will lead to positive rewards, either monetary or psychological.

Role. Role relates to the expected behavior patterns attributed to a particular status position.

Role Conflict. Because of the multiplicity of roles and role sets, it is possible for an individual to face a situation of the simultaneous occurrence of two or more role requirements for which the performance of one precludes the performance of the other. This situation is described as role conflict.

Role of Money. The potential roles of money are: (1) a conditioned reinforcer, (2) an incentive which is capable of satisfying needs, (3) an anxiety-reducer, and (4) serves to erase feelings of dissatisfaction.

Role Set. This refers to those individuals who have expectations for the behavior of the individual in the particular role. The more expectations the more complex the role set.

Satisfaction. A criterion of effectiveness which refers to the organization's ability to gratify the needs of its participants. Equivalent terms include morale and voluntarism.

Scalar Chain. The graded chain of authority which is created through the delegation process.

Scientific Management. A body of literature which emerged during the period 1890–1930 and which reports the ideas and theories of engineers concerned with such problems as job definition, incentive systems, and selection and training.

Selection. One of the sources of error in experimental studies. It occurs when participants are assigned to experimental and control groups on any basis other than random assignment. Any other selection method will result in systematic biases which will result in differences between groups which are unrelated to the effects of the experimental treatment.

Sensitivity Training. A form of educational experience which stresses the process and emotional aspects of training.

Sequential Interdependence. This type of work interdependence occurs when one group must complete some task before another group can complete its task.

Shared Approach. An OD strategy which involves managers and employees in the determination of the OD program.

Situational Theory of Leadership. This approach to leadership advocates that leaders understand their own behavior, the behavior of their subordinates, and the situation before utilizing a particular leadership style. It requires diagnostic skills in human behavior on the part of the leader.

Span of Control. This is the number of subordinates reporting to a superior. The span is a factor that affects the shape and height of an organization structure.

Status. In an organizational setting it relates to positions in the formal or informal structure. In the formal organization it is designated while in informal groups it is determined by the group.

Status Consensus. The agreement of group members about the relative status of members of the group.

Strictness or Leniency Rater Errors. The harsh rater gives ratings that are lower than the average ratings usually given. The lenient rater is just the opposite. He or she tends to give higher ratings than the average level.

Structural Principles. The principles which can guide the manager in designing the formal task and authority relationships in an organization.

Structure. The established patterns of interacting and coordinating the technology and human assets of an organization.

Structure (in group context). The term structure used in the context of groups refers to the standards of conduct applied by the total group, the communication system, and the reward and sanction mechanisms of the group.

Survey. A survey usually attempts to measure one or more characteristics in many people, usually at one point in time. Basically they are used to investigate current problems and events.

System 4 Organization. The universalistic theory of organization design which is proposed by Likert. The theory is defined in terms of overlapping groups, "linking pin" management, and the principle of "supportiveness."

Systems Theory. An approach to the analysis of organizational behavior which emphasizes the necessity for maintaining the basic elements of input-process-output and for adapting to the larger environment which sustains the organization.

Task Goal. A performance-based goal that serves as a benchmark.

Task Group. A group of individuals working as a unit to complete a project or job task.

Task Structure. A factor in the Fiedler contingency model which refers to how structured a job is with regard to requirements, problem-solving alternatives, and feedback on the correctness of accomplishing the job.

Technology. An important concept which can have many definitions in specific instances but which refers generally to actions, physical and mental, which an individual performs upon some object, person, or problem in order to change it in some way.

Testing. One of the sources of error in experimental studies. It occurs when changes in the performance of the subject occur because previous measurement of his performance made him aware he was part of an experiment.

Therbligs. The term used to identify fundamental hand motions.

Time Orientation. A concept which refers to the time horizon of decisions. Employees may have relatively short- or long-term orientations depending upon the nature of their tasks.

Time Study. The process of determining the appropriate elapsed time for the completion of a task.

Tolerance of Ambiguity. The tendency to perceive ambiguous situations or events as desirable. On the other hand, intolerance of ambiguity is the tendency to perceive ambiguous situations or events as sources of threat.

Trait Theory of Leadership.   An attempt to identify specific characteristics (physical, mental, personality) which are associated with leadership success. It relies on research which relates various traits to certain success criteria.

Type A Personality.   Associated with research conducted on coronary heart disease. The Type A person is an aggressive driver who is ambitious, competitive, task oriented, and always on the move. Rosenman and Friedman, two medical researchers, suggest that Type A's have more heart attacks than Type B's.

Unilateral Strategy.   An OD strategy which precludes participation by employees. The management hierarchy exercises authority to determine the OD program.

Universal Design Theory.   A point of view which states that there is "one best way" to design an organization.

Upward Communication.   Upward communication flows from individuals in lower levels of organization structure to those in higher levels. Some of the most common upward communication flows are suggestion boxes, group meetings, and appeal or grievance procedures.

Valence.   The strength of a person's preference for a particular outcome.

Vroom-Yetton Model.   A leadership model that specifies which leadership decision making procedures will be most effective in each of several different situations. Two leadership styles proposed are autocratic (AI, and AII), two are consultative (CI and CII), and one is joint decision oriented (leader and the group, GII).

Weighted Checklist.   A rating system consisting of statements that describe various types and levels of behavior for a particular job. Each of the statements is weighted according to importance.

Woodward Research.   A path-breaking research project which documented the association between technology and organization structure and stimulated a wide range of subsequent studies which contribute to the contingency design point of view.

Name Index

Subject Index

A

Ability, defined, 101–2
Absenteeism, 396–98
Academy of Management Review, 22
Acceptance priority rule, 219
Achievement, 111, 390
Achievement-oriented leader, 224
Adaptiveness, defined, 31
Affiliation, 111
Agents of change, 326–27
Aggression, 106
Alternatives, 436–38, 443
Ambiguity, tolerance of, 77–78
American Cyanamid Co., 258
American Sociological Review, 22
Anthropology, 15
Anxiety, 67
Arapahoe Chemical Co., 295
Assessment center technique, 367–70
AT&T (American Telephone and Telegraph
    Company), 41, 287, 295, 367
Attitudes, 71–74
    formation, 72–73
    questionnaire, 490
    surveys, 466
Authoritative command, 173–74
Authority, 43, 186–87
    delegation of, 255–58
    lack of, 326
    responsibility principle, 306
Autonomy, job, 390–91
Avco, 258
Avoidance, 173
    learning of, 84

B

Banking time off, 400
Behavior
    of groups, 135–60
    modification, 121–26
    personality and, 77–79
Behavioral causes of change, 465
Behavioral development methods, 499–509
Behavioral sciences, 13–22
    experimentation in, 539
    methods of inquiry, 17–32
    research in, 15–16
    view of people, 64
Behaviorally Anchored Rating Scales, 362–
    66
Behaviorism, decision making and, 439–42
Bell Telephone System, 41
Bethlehem Steel, 284
Boundary-spanning roles, 325–27

B (continued, right column)

Bureaucratic
    design, mass production and, 316–17
    organization theory, 307–8

C

Cafeteria-style fringe benefits, 399–400
Carborundum, 258–59
Career planning, 505–7
Case study, 17–18, 498–99
Cases for analysis, 54–57, 92–93, 131–33,
    159–60, 180–81, 203–4, 231–32, 267–70,
    299–300, 337–39, 377–78, 403–4, 426–
    27, 451–52, 482–84, 515–16, 546–66
Caterpillar Tractor, 259
Central tendency error, 360
Centralization, principle of, 306
Change(s)
    agents
        external, 457
        role of, 471–73
    depth of, 486–89
    and development, 38
    forces for, 464–65
    innovation, 326–27
    process, 462–63
Chevrolet sales division, 368–69
Chrysler Corporation, 5
Classical
    conditioning, 79–81
    organization theory, 305–6
Classical School of Management, 39–40
Climate, 38–39
Coercive power, 187
Cohesiveness, group, 148–50
Cognitive dissonance, 441
College students, values of, 49–50
Command group, 138
Commitment/motivation, 260
Communication, 176
    barriers to, 413–18
    decreased, 171–72
    defined, 409
    elements of, 409–11
    improving, 418–23
    overload, 417–18
    process, 37–38, 408–27
    types, 411–13
Communications Satellite Consortium, 26
Competition, 177
Completion, job, 390
Compromise, 173
Conflict, 67
    intergroup, 161–77
    rule, 219